Acknowledgments

ISAK DINESEN, excerpt from *Out of Africa* by Isak Dinesen, published by Random House, Inc. Copyright © 1938 by Random House, Inc.

RICHARD CONNELL, "The Most Dangerous Game," from *O. Henry Memorial Award Prize Stories of 1924.* Copyright 1924 by Richard Connell. Copyright renewed, 1952 by Louise Fox Connell. Reprinted by permission of Brandt & Brandt Literary Agents, Inc.

H. H. MUNRO, "The Open Window," from *The Short Stories of Saki,* by H. H. Munro. Copyright 1930 by The Viking Press, Inc. Reprinted by permission of The Viking Press, Inc.

JAMES THURBER, "The Secret Life of Walter Mitty," from *My World—And Welcome to It,* by James Thurber. Copyright © 1943 by James Thurber. Copyright © 1970 by Helen W. Thurber. Published by Harcourt Brace Jovanovich, Inc. Reprinted by permission of Mrs. James Thurber. Originally appeared in *The New Yorker.*

IRWIN SHAW, "The Dry Rock," from *Mixed Company: Collected Short Stories of Irwin Shaw,* by Irwin Shaw. Copyright by Irwin Shaw. Reprinted by permission of Irwin Shaw.

MORLEY CALLAGHAN, "A Sick Call," excerpt from *Morley Callaghan Stories,* by Morley Callaghan. Reprinted by permission of The Macmillan Company of Canada Limited.

RUDYARD KIPLING, "The Gardener," copyright 1926 by Rudyard Kipling from *Debits and Credits* by Rudyard Kipling. Reprinted by permission of The Executors of the Estate of Mrs. George Bambridge and Doubleday & Company, Inc. and by permission of the National Trust of Great Britain and Macmillan London Limited.

JOHN GALSWORTHY, "The Japanese Quince," used by permission of Charles Scribner's Sons from *A Motley and Caravan* by John Galsworthy. Copyright 1910 Charles Scribner's Sons; renewal copyright 1938 Ada Galsworthy. Distributed in Canada by permission of William Heineman Ltd Publishers.

RALPH ELLISON, "Flying Home," from *The Best Short Stories by Negro Writers.* Reprinted by permission of William Morris Agency, Inc. on behalf of the author. Copyright © 1944 (renewed) by Ralph Ellison.

TRUMAN CAPOTE, "A Tree of Night," from *A Tree of Night and Other Stories,* by Truman Capote. Copyright 1945 and renewed 1973 by Truman Capote. Reprinted by permission of Random House, Inc.

CARSON McCULLERS, "A Tree, A Rock, A Cloud," from *Collected Short Stories & the Novel, The Ballad of the Sad Cafe,* by Carson McCullers. Copyright 1955 by Carson McCullers. Reprinted by permission of Houghton Mifflin Co.

JOHN UPDIKE, "A & P," from *Pigeon Feathers and Other Stories,* by John Updike. Copyright © 1962 by John Updike. Reprinted by permission of Alfred A. Knopf, Inc. This story originally appeared in *The New Yorker.*

FLORENCE ENGEL RANDALL, "The Watchers," from *Harper's Magazine.* Reprinted by permission of the author and her agent, Raines & Raines. Copyright © 1965 by Harper's Magazine, Inc.

DOROTHY PARKER, "But the One on the Right," by Dorothy Parker. Copyright © 1929 by Dorothy Parker. Reprinted by permission of Viking Penguin Inc. Originally appeared in *The New Yorker.*

KATHERINE MANSFIELD, "The Lady's Maid," from *The Short Stories of Katherine Mansfield, by Katherine Mansfield,* published by Alfred A. Knopf, Inc. Copyright 1922 by Alfred A. Knopf, Inc. and renewed 1950 by John Middleton Murry. Reprinted by permission of Alfred A. Knopf, Inc.

FRANK O'CONNOR, "First Confession," from *The Stories of Frank O'Connor,* by Frank O'Connor. Reprinted by permission of Alfred A. Knopf, Inc. and AD Peters & Co. Ltd.

DORIS LESSING, "The Nuisance," from *African Stories,* by Doris Lessing. Copyright © 1951, 1953, 1954, 1957, 1958, 1962, 1963, 1964, 1965 by Doris Lessing. Reprinted by permission of Simon & Schuster, a Division of Gulf & Western Corporation, and Curtis Brown, Ltd.

RING LARDNER, "Haircut" by Ring Lardner from *The Love Nest and Other Stories.* Reprinted by permission of Charles Scribner's Sons. Copyright 1925, 1953 by Ellis A. Larnner.

DANIEL KEYES, "Flowers for Algernon," from *Science Fiction Hall of Fame.* Copyright © 1959 by Mercury Press, Inc. Reprinted by permission of the author.

GINA BERRIAULT, "The Stone Boy," by Gina Berriault. Copyright 1957 by Gina Berriault. First published in *Mademoiselle.* By permission of Toni Strassman, Agent.

D. H. LAWRENCE, "The Shadow in the Rose Garden," from *The Complete Short Stories of D. H. Lawrence.* Copyright 1934 by Frieda Lawrence. © renewed 1962 by Angelo Ravagli and C. Montague Weekly, Executors of the Estate of Frieda Lawrence Ravagli. Reprinted by permission of Viking Penguin Inc.

THOMAS MANN, "The Infant Prodigy," from *Stories of Three Decades* by Thomas Mann. Translated by H. T. Lowe-Porter. Copyright 1936 and renewed 1964 by Alfred A. Knopf, Inc. By permission of Alfred A. Knopf, Inc.

JOHN STEINBECK, "The Chrysanthemums," from *The Long Valley,* by John Steinbeck. Copyright 1938, copyright © renewed 1966 by John Steinbeck. All rights reserved. Reprinted by permission of Viking Penguin Inc.

JAMES JOYCE, "A Little Cloud," from *Dubliners* by James Joyce. Copyright © 1967 by the Estate of James Joyce. Originally published by B. W. Huebsch, Inc. in 1916. Reprinted by permission of Viking Penguin Inc.

D. H. LAWRENCE, "The Shades of Spring," from *The Complete Short Stories of D. H. Lawrence*. Copyright 1934 by Frieda Lawrence, © renewed 1962 by Angelo Ravagli and C. Montague Weekly, Executors of the Estate of Frieda Lawrence Ravagli. Reprinted by permission of Viking Penguin Inc.

SHERWOOD ANDERSON, "Unlighted Lamps." Reprinted by permission of Harold Ober Associates Incorporated. Copyright © 1921 by B. W. Huebsch, Inc. Renewed 1948 by Eleanor Copenhaver Anderson.

VIRGINIA WOOLF, "The String Quartet," from *A Haunted House and Other Stories*, by Virginia Woolf, copyright 1944, 1972 by Harcourt Brace Jovanovich, Inc. Reprinted by permission of the publisher. Distribution in Canada by permission of the Author's Literary Estate and The Hogarth Press.

KATHERINE BRUSH, "Night Club," from Harper's Magazine. Reprinted by permission of Harold Ober Associates Incorporated. Copyright 1927 by Katherine Brush, renewed.

ERNEST HEMINGWAY, "The Killers," from *Men Without Women*, by Ernest Hemingway. "The Killers" by Ernest Hemingway from *Men Without Women* is used by permission of Charles Scribner's Sons. Copyright 1927, © 1955 by Charles Scribner's Sons.

WILLIAM FAULKNER, "That Evening Sun," from *Collected Short Stories by William Faulkner*. Copyright 1931 and renewed 1959 by William Faulkner. Reprinted by permission of Random House, Inc.

ALBERT MALTZ, "The Happiest Man on Earth," from *Afternoon in the Jungle: The Selected Short Stories of Albert Maltz*, by Albert Maltz. By permission of Liveright Publishing Corporation. Copyright 1935, 1938, 1940, 1941, 1950, 1960, 1968, 1970 by Albert Maltz.

JEAN-PAUL SARTRE, "The Wall," translated by Maria Jolas, from *The Bedside Book of Famous French Stories*, edited by Belle Becker and Robert N. Linscott. Copyright 1945 and renewed 1973 by Random House, Inc. Reprinted by permission of Random House, Inc.

FRANZ KAFKA, "A Hunger Artist." Reprinted by permission of Schocken Books Inc. from *The Penal Colony* by Franz Kafka. Copyright © 1948 by Schocken Books Inc. Copyright renewed © 1975 by Schocken Books Inc.

EUDORA WELTY, "A Visit of Charity," from *A Curtain of Green and Other Stories*. Copyright 1941, 1969 by Eudora Welty. Reprinted by permission of Harcourt Brace Jovanovich, Inc.

JESSAMYN WEST, "Love, Death, and the Ladies' Drill Team," from *Love, Death, and the Ladies' Drill Team*," by Jessamyn West. Copyright 1951 by Jessamyn West. Reprinted from her volume *Love, Death, and the Ladies' Drill Team* by permission of Harcourt Brace Jovanovich, Inc.

FLANNERY O'CONNOR, "Everything That Rises Must Converge," from *Everything That Rises Must Converge* by Flannery O'Connor. Copyright © 1961, 1965 by the Estate of Mary Flannery O'Connor. Reprinted with permission of Farrar, Straus and Giroux, Inc.

MORDECAI RICHLER, "Some Grist for Mervyn's Mill," from *The Street* by Mordecai Richler. Reprinted by permission of The Canadian Publishers, McClelland and Stewart Limited, Toronto, and by permission of Monica McCall, International Creative Management. Copyright © 1969, Mordecai Richler.

GABRIEL GARCÍA MÁRQUEZ, "The Handsomest Drowned Man in the World," from *Leaf Storm and Other Stories*, by Gabriel García Márquez. Copyright © 1971 by Gabriel García Márquez. Reprinted by permission of Harper & Row, Publishers, Inc.

JOHN UPDIKE, "The Music School," from *The Music School* by John Updike. Copyright © 1964 by John Updike. Reprinted by permission of Alfred A. Knopf, Inc. This story originally appeared in *The New Yorker*.

JOHN CHEEVER, "The Swimmer," from *The Stories of John Cheever*, by John Cheever. Copyright © 1964 by John Cheever. Reprinted by permission of Alfred A. Knopf., Inc.

YUKIO MISHIMA, "Three Million Yen," from *Death in Midsummer and Other Stories*, by Yukio Mishima. Copyright © 1966 by New Directions Publishing Corporation. Reprinted by permission of New Directions Publishing Corporation. Translated by Edward G. Seidensticker.

TONI C. BAMBARA, "The Lesson," from *Gorilla, My Love*, by Toni C. Bambara. Copyright © 1972 by Toni C. Bambara. Reprinted by permission of Random House, Inc.

RENATA ADLER, "Brownstone," from *Speedboat*, by Renata Adler. Copyright © 1973 by Renata Adler. Reprinted by permission of Random House, Inc.

DONALD BARTHELME, "The School" from *Amateurs* by Donald Barthelme. Copyright © 1974, 1976 by Donald Barthelme. "The School" originally appeared in *The New Yorker*.

MARK STRAND, "Mr. and Mrs. Baby," from *The New Yorker*. Reprinted by permission; © 1979 The New Yorker Magazine, Inc.

This book is dedicated to
Henry S. Wolf
and
Russel B. Nye

. . . now we come to the passage. You can just see a little *peep*
of the passage in Looking-glass House, if you leave the door
of our drawing-room wide open: and it's very like our passage
as far as you can see, only you know it may be quite different
on beyond.

LEWIS CARROLL

OF THE MILLENIUM

At the time when the near return of Christ to the earth had become
a certainty, a Committee was formed to decide upon the arrangements
for His reception. After some discussion, it sent out a circular which
prohibited all waving and throwing about of palm-branches as well as
all cries of "Hosanna."

When the Millennium had been going on for some time, and joy was
universal, Christ one evening said to Peter that He wanted, when
everything was quiet, to go out for a short walk with him alone.

"Where do you want to go, my Lord?" Peter asked.

"I should like," answered the Lord, "just to walk from the Praeto-
rium, along that long road, up to the Hill of Calvary."

ISAK DINESEN

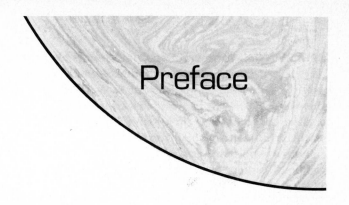

Preface

  The Short Story: A Contemporary Looking Glass contains a substantial collection of short stories and a considerable amount of material about short stories. We hope that students and instructors alike will find the selections enjoyable and the various introductory sections and individual discussions both interesting and helpful. Since we enjoy short stories ourselves, the last thing we want to do is discourage anyone from cultivating a personal interest in this important literary form.

  At the outset, we have included a brief historical review of the forerunners of the modern short story. We have done this because we think the review will put the genre into perspective and help students to understand, and thus to enjoy, the stories in the book.

  Part I, "Structural Elements of the Modern Short Story," discusses five basic elements: plot, character, emotion, symbolism, and theme. The section includes a general introduction as well as a detailed discussion of each element. Each detailed discussion is accompanied by two or three illustrative stories. Part II, "Points of View in the Modern Short Story," explains the various vantage points from which an author can present the action of a story. This section includes a detailed introduction and eleven illustrative stories. Part III, "Historical Evolution of the Modern Short Story," details the development of the genre in the nineteenth century and its subsequent growth to a more varied and experimental form in the twentieth century. In addition, the section summarizes the literary beliefs and practices of each of the thirty-seven authors who are represented.

  Part IV, "Writing About Short Stories," tells how to write papers that analyze the various story elements, as well as those that discuss historical influences or compare and contrast two or more works.

  Each story in Parts I and II is accompanied by an analysis—entitled "By Way of Discussion"—that focuses primarily on either structure or point of view. In Part III each story is followed by a set of questions—entitled "For Study, Discussion, and Writing"—rather than an analysis. Experience has taught us that students are likely to do a better job of handling discussion questions if they have had the opportunity to study and discuss a number of short story analyses. However, for instructors who would prefer to use the introductions to Parts I and II with stories not accompanied by analyses, the "For Additional Reading" lists in each of the individual sections of the two parts provide appropriate stories found in other sections of the book.

The Short Story: A Contemporary Looking-Glass lends itself to many teaching approaches. For instructors who wish to adopt a topical approach, we have included a carefully worked out table of contents that groups the stories into ten currently relevant categories, more than can be found in most books with topical arrangements. Another table of contents arranges all of the stories in chronological order. This should prove attractive to instructors who prefer a purely historical approach. Instructors who wish to organize an entire course around structural elements and point of view will find the "For Additional Reading" listings that we have supplied in Parts I and II a big help.

Our story selections have three things in common: each is interesting to read, has literary merit, and offers a clear example of what it is intended to illustrate. Furthermore, the authors represent a variety of nationalities, races, and ethnic groups, and include a substantial number of first-rate women writers. The stories span a wide range of reading levels and are arranged in a general progression from easy to more challenging. We have used all of the stories in our own classrooms, and we fancy that we have used them successfully.

In preparing our introductions, "By Way of Discussion" analyses, and "For Study, Discussion, and Writing" listings, we have aimed for an easy, informal style that would help make both learning and teaching a little less austere but no less sound. To stimulate interest and discussion, we have, in a few instances, provided story interpretations that we hope students and instructors will enjoy taking issue with. Since none of our discussions is either definitive or comprehensive, instructors who wish to challenge them will find ample opportunity to lead their students far beyond our introductory remarks. Our wish has been to stimulate discussion, not to freeze interpretation.

The instructor's manual accompanying *The Short Story: A Contemporary Looking-Glass* is a substantial work in itself. It expands upon and illuminates the book's introductions, story analyses, and lists of discussion questions. A detailed analysis is included for each of the stories of Part III, for which the book provides only discussion questions; and these analyses are keyed to the book's discussion questions. Similarly, sets of discussion questions keyed to the stories and story analyses in Parts I and II are provided. In short, we have done everything we could to make the manual a legitimate teaching tool.

Finally, we would like to acknowledge the capable assistance of the following very nice people, without whose help and professional guidance *The Short Story: A Contemporary Looking-Glass* might never have seen the light of day: Marilyn M. Brandt of North Carolina State University; John Cooke of the University of New Orleans; Robert T. Self of Northern Illinois University; Deborah Connor, Richard Garretson, and Christine Pellicano at Random House; and our own colleagues Joseph Dugas, Donald Hanzek, Fern Kay Harris, Monica Klever, Cindy Roberts, Wanda Smith, David Vinopal, and Lucy Wright.

ELLIOTT L. SMITH
ANDREW W. HART

Contents

part 3
Historical Evolution of the Modern Short Story 281

NINETEENTH-CENTURY ORIGIN AND DEVELOPMENT 282

part **4**

Writing Papers About Short Stories   661

Topical Listing
of Stories

III. THE EXPERIENCES OF YOUTH

IV. SOCIAL ALIENATION

V. GOD AND RELIGION

VI. PSYCHOLOGICAL IMPAIRMENT

VII. MEN AND WOMEN

VIII. WIT AND HUMOR

IX. FEAR AND HORROR

X. STORIES WITH SURPRISES

Chronological Listing of Stories

Forerunners of the Modern Short Story

F or as long as we human creatures have possessed the power of speech, we have been spinning tales. Sometimes we have spun them in an effort to describe our experiences or to make our experiences more palatable or understandable, but almost as often our motive has been to enlarge upon the truth as we have perceived it. As a matter of fact, according to one theory of the origin of language, our crafty old troglodyte ancestors developed speech so that they could tell one another something *besides* the truth once in a while. And when humans finally developed written language— only a few thousand years ago—our ability to record and embellish the truth took a quantum leap forward. Suddenly the tale outlived the teller, and what had been an oral tradition became a piece of literature.

Myths, folk tales, and legends were the stuff of our ancestors' seemingly innate impulse to tell tales. The word "mythology," derived from the Greek words *mythos*, meaning "story" or "legend," and *logia*, meaning "sayings" or "discourse," literally means "the telling of stories." Animism, a belief that all living things have souls, played an important part in the formation of early myths. The word "animism" is derived from the Latin word *anima*, meaning "breath," "spirit," or "soul." When early men and women pondered the differences between living people and dead people, they concluded that the primary difference was the presence of breath in the living. From this observation came the notion that the breath, or soul, of the dead had passed into the bodies of animals, trees, and other objects found in nature. As a result of this notion, many early tales tell about animals who possess human intelligence and sensibilities. Owls become wise, foxes clever and cunning, lions brave, and lambs gentle. Similarly, we have stories in which a grief-stricken tree sheds tears of blood, stars guide lost travelers, boats sail without a crew, and horses warn their masters of impending danger. In fact, the whole of nature is often presented as though it were operating with an awareness of itself.

Arising from one impulse or another, short stories have always been with us. For example, an Egyptian collection entitled *The Tales of the Magicians* may have been composed as early as five thousand years ago. *The Epic of Gilgamesh*, a Babylonian verse tale recounting the legend of the warlike king of Erech as he searches for, obtains, and then loses the magic plant that gives eternal life, was written almost four thousand years ago. From the fourth through the second centuries B.C., the Hebrews recorded many of the stories that make up the Old Testament and the Apocrypha. These tales include narratives about the Creation, the conflict between Cain and Abel, the Flood, Jonah and the whale, and the trials of Job. Later on, Jesus Himself, in the literary tradition of the Hebrew people, used the parable, a type of short story, in His teachings.

The ancient Greeks were involved with various forms of short fiction. Eight centuries before Christ, at the dawn of Hellenic civilization, Homer, the half-legendary author of the *Iliad* and the *Odyssey*, was spinning amazing tales. The still-popular fables of Aesop, a blind Greek slave, date from the sixth century B.C.

The Greek historians Xenophon and Herodotus often included stories in their works. In fact, Herodotus, called the "father of history" by the Roman orator Cicero, thought of himself as a creator and reciter of *logoi*, "things for telling," or tales. Writing in a simple, natural style not unlike that of many modern short-story writers, he filled his *History* with brief fictionalized episodes in an effort to make the work more interesting. "Polycrates and His Emerald Ring" and "Arion and the Dolphin" are two outstanding examples of the short fiction of Herodotus.

In ancient India, too, written short fiction was well known among the literate. About 480 B.C. a collection called *The Jataka*, or "birth stories," appeared and circulated widely. Although the tales of *The Jataka*, being stories of the former lives of the Buddha, are supposed to have a serious ethical or religious intent, their actual concerns seem to be with everyday or practical wisdom. In fact, there is much humor in many of the stories.

Another Indian collection, entitled *The Panchatantra*, has for centuries been one of the world's most popular books. Dating from the third or fourth century A.D., it was written as a manual for the instruction of the sons of the upper classes. *The Panchatantra* includes many little fables that few people fail to find amusing. One begins with two men riding a donkey. When they are criticized for so mistreating this beast of burden, one gets down and walks alongside. When they are again criticized for mistreating the beast, the second man climbs down and both walk alongside, leading the animal. When another group of people, also feeling sorry for the donkey because of the way it has been treated, again criticizes the two men, the fellows begin carrying the animal. Soon thereafter, the men meet another group of people, who label them fools for carrying a donkey. Appropriately, one of the men concludes that you can't please everybody.

Although Roman literature is in large measure imitative of earlier

Greek works, the short story was aptly developed among a good many Roman writers. For example, Livy (Titus Livius, 59 B.C.–A.D. 17), the Roman historian, in Book II of his *History of Rome* presents the story of "Horatius at the Bridge" with such clarity and matter-of-factness that it is compelling even to the modern reader. In another place Livy skillfully tells the story of "Romulus and Remus." According to legend, the twin brothers, who were born to Rhea Silvia and the god Mars, founded the city of Rome in 753 B.C.

In the opening years of the first century A.D., the Roman poet Ovid (Publius Ovidius Naso, 43 B.C.–A.D. 17?) wrote the *Metamorphoses*. In this collection of carefully linked myths people are miraculously transformed into animals and various other things. Julius Caesar, for example, is transformed into a star. Also active in the first century A.D. was Petronius (Gaius Petronius Arbiter, died A.D. 66?), a pleasure-loving satirist at Nero's court. At least two of Petronius' stories have stood the test of time, coming down to us in what remains of his ribald romance *Satyricon*: "Matron of Ephesus" and "Trimalchio's Dinner." The latter tale presents a savagely humorous episode of vulgarity involving a freedman who has recently become quite wealthy—a subject for satire and ridicule throughout Western literature.

Lucius Apuleius, a second-century Roman writer (born A.D. 125?), is the author of *The Golden Ass*, the only Latin romance to survive in its entirety. The work is narrated in the first person by Lucius of Corinth, a licentious fellow with an exuberant desire to learn about life and people. While he is visiting a sorceress in Thessaly, he persuades a young woman to steal a magic potion that has the power to transform a person into an owl. As luck would have it, however, he takes the wrong potion and is turned into an ass. In this unfortunate condition Lucius wanders about Greece, passing in and out of the hands of a series of owners who mistreat him. Sprinkled throughout the narrative are many lively short stories of mystery, intrigue, witchcraft, and love. "The Dream" and "Cupid and Psyche" are two such stories.

During the Middle Ages several types of short narrative flourished. The Roman Church made extensive use of the *exemplum*, a brief didactic story intended to teach proper Christian behavior. Collections of *exempla*, arranged according to subject, were prepared for preachers to use in their sermons. An example of such a collection, produced in the early thirteenth century, is Jacques de Vitry's *Exempla*. These tales became very popular among medieval congregations, a fact that motivated many a good priest to allow his sermons to become little more than a series of humorous anecdotes.

The *fabliau*, on the other hand, was a bawdy little versified tale that made no pretense of improving anyone's character. Immensely popular among ordinary people, these ribald stories poked fun at everyday human weaknesses, especially those growing out of vanity and gullibility. Women, priests, scholars, and husbands of unfaithful wives were often the butts of the buffoonery detailed in *fabliaux*. The product of an oral folk tradition, these bawdy tales were told and retold for many years before finally being written down. "The Miller's Tale," from Geoffrey

Chaucer's *Canterbury Tales*, is an example of the *fabliau* form in the hands of a consummate storyteller and literary artist.

Among the upper classes during the Middle Ages, the most popular type of short fiction was the romance. The peasants could neither read these fanciful tales nor understand their extravagances. The subjects of the medieval romances were courtly love, chivalry, and high adventure. One group of romances deals with the life of King Arthur and the Knights of the Round Table. Another recounts the life and adventures of Charlemagne and his paladin Roland, and a third details the exploits of Alexander the Great.

A typical medieval romance describes a quest. The protagonist, a knight, sets out on a journey to obey some sworn command, rescue a maiden, or seek the Holy Grail (the cup used by Jesus at the Last Supper). Along the way he has a variety of adventures, many of which are unrelated to the original goal of the journey. It is the retelling of these episodic adventures that comprises the stuff of medieval romantic short stories.

Toward the end of the medieval period, the novella, a type of short story originating in Italy, became popular. Novellas dealt with scandalous love affairs, exaggerated acts of chivalry, and twisted mythology. The form reached its high point in 1352 with the publication of the *Decameron*, by Giovanni Boccaccio. The *Decameron* is a collection of one hundred tales supposedly told over a period of ten days by a group of seven young women and three young men who have fled the plague in Florence and are staying in a country villa. For almost three hundred years after Boccaccio, Italian writers continued to supply Western literature with volumes of short narratives of varying quality.

During the Renaissance and for a time afterward, the popularity and influence of short fiction spread throughout Europe. The trend was consistently toward the realistic treatment of material. During the seventeenth and eighteenth centuries, however, the short story went into a serious decline and almost disappeared in England and Spain.

There are many reasons for the decline, but the mix of them all probably explains why the eclipse was so nearly total. First, readers of the period were more interested in nonfiction, especially the essay, the newly emerging journalism, and writing dealing with social and political realities in a world that was suddenly becoming urbanized. Second, there was also the impact of a new literary form, the novel. With greater numbers of people possessing not only the ability to read but also the free time to enjoy reading, the longer work of fiction became enormously popular. And, finally, there was a growing interest in travel and travel literature and, closely related to both, in strange and unusual biographies.

The short story did not cease to exist in the eighteenth century; it was only comatose, waiting to be revived as a more mature and sophisticated type of fiction. Even during its hibernation there were signs of its subsequent rebirth, especially in the essays of such Britishers as Joseph Addison, Richard Steele, Daniel Defoe, and Samuel Johnson, as well as in the lively fictional works that the Frenchman Voltaire used as vehicles to present his philosophical ideas during the Enlightenment. The revival came in the nineteenth century, occurring more or less simultaneously in Germany, the United States, France, and Russia.

The specific details of the revival and what followed it are presented in Part III of this text, "Historical Evolution of the Modern Short Story." Suffice it to say here that the modern short story has been, since the first moments of its existence, an incarnation of imaginative writing able to deal with the social, political, and psychological elements that help make up the "stew" of the modern age. The modern short story is the literary genre that is the most reflective of and, more often than not, the most critical of our peripatetic, industrialized, urbanized, homogenized, and sometimes tranquilized society. For this reason our study is entitled *The Short Story: A Contemporary Looking-Glass.*

Structural Elements of the Modern Short Story

1

Before beginning to investigate the structure of the modern short story, we must first try to define what the genre is. This exercise might not be necessary if, over the years, the short story had not been considered a poor relative of the novel and given so little serious critical attention, or if the short story were not so lively and vital a form used by so many writers with different notions about what they are doing.

It is amazing how often one comes across comments suggesting that the short story is merely a short novel or even an unfinished novel. Short stories, such a view implies, are little pieces that novelists whip off when they do not feel up to doing really serious work. The logic here is as false as calling a watercolor an unfinished oil painting or a ballad an unfinished epic. The truth is that the novel and the short story are two different literary forms. The novel deals primarily with histories or long strings of events, the short story with situation and impression. The novel is a season, perhaps a whole year; the short story is a single storm, a cold front or a warm front quickly passing through, although not necessarily quickly forgotten. Many fine novelists have been merely "competent" at the short story. Likewise, many consummate short-story writers have been less than outstanding at the longer genre. Guy de Maupassant, a giant of the nineteenth-century short story, was unable to handle the novel with anywhere near the same facility. In the twentieth century, Sherwood Anderson and Eudora Welty, both acclaimed for their short stories, have received little attention for their longer works. And there are virtually legions of competent, even revered, novelists who have had no success at all with the short story.

So, what is a modern short story? Answers to this question often run to opposite poles. At one extreme we may be told that a short story can be anything the author wants it to be. At the other we may be confronted with such an elaborate array of rules and prescriptions that half of the current practitioners of the genre could not be considered short-story writers. Neither extreme will bear close scrutiny. It is nonsense to say that a short story can be anything. An essay relating a personal experience may not sensibly be called a short story, even at the insistence of the author; nor is a newspaper article a short story—in spite of what some of the so-called new journalists might proclaim. On the other hand, we cannot list a dozen or so features and demand that a piece of short fiction include a specific number of them in order to be labeled a modern short story. Because the genre is alive and constantly evolving, almost any rigid definition is likely to need revision after the passage of a little time. Thus we propose to define the modern short story with a minimum of prescriptions.

We will begin our definition by saying that the modern short story is a distinct literary genre having certain characteristics:

1. It is always fictional.

2. It is seldom more than thirty printed pages in length, and it often is less than ten.
3. It is written in prose, although it may include verse.
4. It deals with a single unified consideration, either a dramatized incident or something remembered or imagined.
5. It places strong emphasis on character and human values against a backdrop of contemporary society.
6. It contains conflict, crisis, climax, and resolution, either acted out or implied.
7. It seeks, like a lyric poem, to make a single point or impression and then subside.

Not every short piece of fiction, then, is a modern short story. A tale is not a short story, nor is a sketch or a novella. Tales—such as many early works by E. T. A. Hoffmann and the pieces in Washington Irving's *Tales of a Traveller*—are usually long on action and short on characterization, theme, and other literary subtleties. The tale is often thought of as the immediate forerunner of the modern short story.

The term "sketch" has been borrowed from art, where it refers to a preliminary drawing made as a first step toward a fully developed work. Historically, the literary sketch has been a very brief composition, simply constructed and often showing little interest in the intricacies of plot, detailed characterization, or narrative dramatization. Examples include the sketches in Mark Twain's *The Innocents Abroad*, Charles Dickens' *Sketches by 'Boz'*, and Washington Irving's *The Sketch Book*.

The novella, or short novel, is generally longer than the short story and shorter than the full novel. Most often it treats a series of incidents, although it may focus on a single major one. The novella includes more complete characterization than a short story and usually includes an undertow of emphasis on the passage of time. Examples include Ernest Hemingway's *The Old Man and the Sea*, John Steinbeck's *Of Mice and Men*, and Katherine Ann Porter's *Noon Wine*.

The modern short story, in its continuing development, has made extensive use of the devices of other types of writing. Imagine the modern short story as the disk within the octagon in the following diagram.

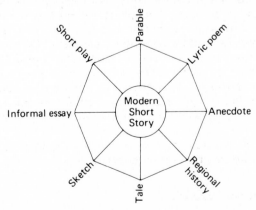

The octagon, we may further imagine, is made of a strong material such as steel: the short-story disk, on the other hand, is molded from something pliable and ductile. The disk is connected to the octagon at eight points. Each connection links the modern short story to a type of writing that has important similarities to it. Connections are made with parables, lyric poems, anecdotes, regional history, tales, sketches, informal essays, and short plays. The connecting bands are rubber cords strong enough to pull the disk out of round yet not strong enough either to distort the octagon or to destroy the disk.

Although the modern short story may contain qualities of all eight types of writing, in the hands of one author or another it may be pulled and stretched into a form resembling one or two more closely than any of the rest. Regional writers, for example, make extensive use of regional history. Writers of propaganda with a particular viewpoint to set forth may create stories that come very close to being thinly disguised essays. Some authors may use so much dialogue that their stories are like one-act plays and can be easily adapted to the stage or screen. Stories intended to point up some moral often approximate the form of the Biblical parable.

Within this relatively flexible framework there are restraints. Short stories are fictional, and like lyric poems they strive for a single impact. They present one major incident, either dramatized or reflected upon, and they deal with human feelings and motivations against the backdrop of contemporary society.

Having made our preliminary pass at defining the modern short story, we now turn to a consideration of the short story's structure. Like any sophisticated piece of literature, the short story is made up of several interacting elements. The five structural components of the modern short story are *plot, character, emotion, symbolism,* and *theme.* Whether you are reading a short story or writing one, you are likely to perform your task with greater understanding if you are aware of the artistic devices that can shape each element.

Plot is the basic structural element of the modern short story. Plot may be defined simply as "what happens"; it is a series of interrelated actions. In traditionally structured stories, plot is revealed overtly—that is, we are told incident by incident what takes place. In other stories, however, the plot may be considered covert—that is, we are required to try to make sense of incidents presented by implication or indirection. A variation of the covert plot involves actions that are remembered, recalled, or imagined, usually by a narrator who is one of the characters in the story. All stories have plot, although the overt plot of a fast-moving action story may seem more obvious to many readers.

The element of *character* embraces the creation and portrayal of the individual characters who appear in the story. In the modern short story virtually all character development is dramatized. The characters reveal themselves through their words, thoughts, and actions. Only in the weakest stories does the author tell us directly what kind of person someone is. Since most of us are interested in human personalities, fictional or

otherwise, few people complain about having to make their own judgments about character.

Emotion involves the emotions experienced by the characters in the
story and the emotions the author wishes the reader to experience. Frequently, these will not be the same emotions. For example, a reader who
strongly dislikes a particular character may experience disappointment
or even anger when the character experiences joy. Like character, emotion is usually revealed indirectly; it is dramatized or acted out. Few of us
would be convinced by an author who interrupted a story to tell us—in a
footnote, for example—when we should be pleased or when we should
be angry.

Symbolism is an element in almost all imaginative writing, and the
modern short story is no exception. Authors seldom tell us overtly that
something is a symbol. Symbolism too is dramatic rather than expository—that is, it is employed to *show* rather than *tell*. The simplest use of
symbolism consists of little more than associating a concrete object with
an idea. A small plastic crucifix, for example, may be used to symbolize
Christianity or some aspect of Christian behavior. A softly curved stone
may be used to symbolize traditional femininity, or a river may become a
symbol of time, the passage of time, or fate.

When groups or patterns of symbols are employed in a story, symbolism can become complex, for the author might be using symbols for
more than one purpose. They may be intended to reinforce what the
other structural elements of the story are suggesting, or they may dramatize deeper, opposing, or ironic meanings. Since the ability to appreciate literary symbolism requires some understanding of both human
psychology and the traditional uses of symbolism in literature, a little
time spent with heavily symbolic stories may be necessary before you
are able to spot a symbol and say what it represents.

Finally, we come to *theme*. The theme of a story is simply what the
story is about, what the author is trying to say or suggest without scrawl-
ing the message on the side of a building. The best stories seldom contain a single theme; most are open to many interpretations. Themes can
seldom be summed up in simple little statements like "Your sins will find
you out" or "There is no such thing as a free lunch," and they will be
dramatized or implied, not spelled out in a "see there" paragraph at the
story's conclusion. Often, theme may do no more than persuade the
reader to think about a subject or situation in a new way.

Having taken a brief glance at the five structural elements of the modern short story, we will now examine each one in detail.

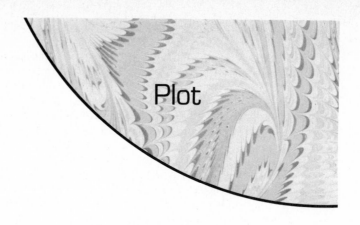

Plot

P lot is what happens; it is a series of interrelated actions carefully selected by the author. We will begin our discussion of plot with another drawing.

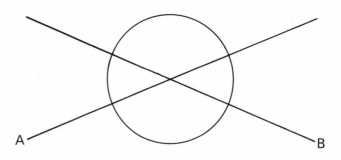

The diagram shows our original short-story disk, but with two intersecting lines running through it.

Line A represents the complete life, from birth to death, of the main character in the story. Generally, although not always, this character tries to accomplish something worthwhile during the course of the story. This something may be as substantial as winning the Olympic decathlon, but it may be as subtle as trying to sort out why one small child mistreats another. We do not call this character a hero because the modern age is militantly antiheroic. In fact, it almost seems that we moderns possess an innate dislike for people who, we suspect, have abilities that place them above the common herd. We take great relish in telling demeaning tales about them, and sometimes we even assassinate them. So, instead of calling the main character a hero, we use the term *protagonist*.

Line B represents the complete life, from birth to death, of the person or persons, force or forces, opposed to the protagonist. Even when this character is evil and vicious, we no longer call him or her a villain because modern psychology has made us aware of the fine line separating good and evil. So, we call this character an *antagonist*. In all fairness, we must point out that the antagonist is not always a bad person. In fact, the modern short story being what it is—a contemporary looking-glass—the protagonist isn't always such a pleasant chap either. In any case, the clash of actions or ideas between the protagonist and antagonist creates the *conflict*, which will be resolved in the course of the story.

The story itself takes place inside the disk. The parts of lines A and B that extend beyond the disk represent events in the protagonist's and antagonist's lives that occurred before the story begins or will occur after the story ends—assuming that both or either survives the story. At the point where the lives of the protagonist and antagonist enter the disk, the story begins, generally with the presentation of some seemingly minor occurrence that gets things moving. Frequently, this occurrence will be a miniature version of the conflict that is to follow. A man who is later to kill his brother might do something to call his brother's reputation into question, thus placing the two men in a position of conflict. This part of the plot is the *precipitating incident*.

Everything that occurs in the story from the precipitating incident to the point on the drawing at which Line A intersects Line B comes under the general term *rising action*. Once the nature of the conflict—between the protagonist and the antagonist—is established, the plot moves along and the intensity of the conflict heightens. When it becomes impossible for the protagonist to carry on in the same manner as heretofore—conditions are simply too oppressive—we have reached the point of *crisis*. The crisis is a situation so unacceptable to the protagonist that he or she resolves to take some action to change things in a major way. When this action is taken, the traditional plot reaches the moment of highest intensity and greatest change, the point at which Line A and Line B intersect. Some action is done that can never be undone: the trigger is pulled, launching the fatal bullet on its path. We call this element of plot the *climax*.

Before moving beyond the climax, we should back up and examine a few more elements of plot that occur within the area of rising action. Many times, just before the climax, the protagonist of a traditional action story will be in a position where all plans of action seem to promise equally bad results. For example, the only choice may seem to be how the protagonist will be executed or which unfaithful colleague she or he will be forced to trust; ultimate success seems out of the question. This element of the plot is the *dilemma*.

Often closely associated with the dilemma are two other elements. The first involves the telling of brief episodes, or frame-stories, that took place before the story began. The protagonist, wondering how he ever got into a particular mess, thinks back. The author then relates an incident from the past that explains, perhaps by implication, the beginnings of the protagonist's current predicament. We call this plot device a *flashback*.

The protagonist, still facing a dilemma, may also try to look forward, hoping to discover some avenue of escape by imagining various alternate futures. These brief imagined episodes are *narrative projections*. On the basis of some system of logic, the protagonist is likely to select one of these imaginings as offering the best chance for success, however slim. Both the flashback and the narrative projection offer the author opportunities for avoiding the mechanical and sometimes monotonous presentation of plot in chronological order. In motion pictures both effects are achieved through the cinematographic lap dissolve, in which one scene fades out while another simultaneously fades in.

In the well-structured action story, the protagonist will not be so conspicuously superior or inferior to the antagonistic forces that the outcome of the story is inevitable. Sensible plot dictates that the protagonist and the antagonist have at least the appearance of equality. The creation of this appearance of equality is known as the *balancing of forces*. The balance is frequently attained, especially in a story with a strong central character, by having the protagonist struggle against not only an external adversary (antagonist) but also against contradictory personal impulses.

For example, when a pacifistic protagonist is opposed by an antagonist who is determined not only to thwart him but also to kill him, the protagonist struggles not only with the antagonist and his own instinct to live but also with his belief that it is wrong to kill another human being under any circumstances, even to survive. This device is called a *multiple struggle*, and it must include both external and internal antagonistic forces. When a protagonist is confronted by two or three human antagonists, a situation of multiple struggle is not created; the protagonist simply has several antagonists.

Everything following the climax of the story comes under the general heading of *falling action*. A particularly important element of falling action is the *denouement*, or *resolution*. The denouement consists of a cluster of incidents—usually solutions, explanations, or hints about the future beyond the short story. It comes at the very end of the story. Frequently the denouement will involve a reestablishment of some kind of relationship between the protagonist and antagonist, if they have survived the earlier conflict. For example, we might have a story in which two aging gunfighters have their last shoot-out, and they have it shooting at each other. Neither is killed, however; and after the smoke clears and the wounds heal, they hang up their guns, sit side by side in comfortable rocking chairs on the front porch of the local saloon, and swap yarns about the old days when they were two very bad hombres. Generally, the denouement was used more effectively in early modern short stories than it is in stories written more recently.

Irony, which involves some discrepancy between what is said, imagined, or anticipated and the actual facts, is also an important element of plot. There are several types of irony, and later on we shall be considering verbal irony and dramatic irony as well as ironic symbols. When we refer to irony of plot, however, we are referring to *irony of situation*. This type of irony involves a discrepancy between the expected outcome of the story and what actually occurs.

Consider, for example, an elaborately plotted story about a child of mixed racial parentage who is born to a diseased mother and an alcoholic father. In spite of his background, the boy has ambition. He believes in the American Dream and works hard to become a rich man. He never takes a day off, never gets drunk, never marries, never does anything to endanger his goal of becoming rich. When he is sixty years old, his broker calls him on the phone and tells him that he is worth a million dollars in cold, hard cash.

For once in his rigorous life, our protagonist decides to celebrate. He stops off at a neighborhood bar and has a few drinks. He also buys everyone in the place a couple of rounds. Being unaccustomed to such carryings-on, when he comes out of the bar and a gust of cold wind slaps him in the face, he stumbles off the curb and falls in the street. A Greyhound bus comes along and mashes him into the pavement. Thus, we have irony of plot; everything seems to suggest one outcome, but the actual result is quite the opposite. Irony of situation can be savage.

Surprise or ironic endings do not always produce the most effective stories. In fact, authors often lay precise hints about what is to follow so that the careful reader will not be surprised or confused by the story's outcome. This device of hinting at or suggesting subsequent developments is called *foreshadowing*.

Although the general intent of foreshadowing is to direct the reader forward toward the conclusion of the plot, the techniques of foreshadowing are not limited to plot. For example, foreshadowing may be achieved by elaborate descriptions, suggestive settings, direct statements made by the narrator, the general atmosphere of the story or tone of the narrator, the recurrent use of a particular image or symbol, and dialogue. In Richard Connell's "The Most Dangerous Game," we get a nice bit of foreshadowing when Rainsford, the protagonist, sitting alone on the deck of the ship in the dark of the night, hears three shots ring out from Ship-Trap Island. The shots foreshadow the three days that Rainsford later spends as a hunted animal on the island.

Stories take place within a specific physical environment, occupy a given span of time, and usually reflect an observable spiritual condition. These three qualities make up the *setting* of the story. Setting involves place, time, and state of mind. It would be inaccurate to call setting simply an element of plot. Although setting is important to the presentation of plot, it is also important to the presentation of the other structural elements. Indeed, setting is important to all aspects of the short story, and the reader should pay careful attention to the way in which shifts in setting may be employed to suggest subtle changes in the story as a whole.

In addition to using setting as the environment for plot, writers often employ setting to reveal character. Thus, a sinister individual may be associated with a gloomy old house or a dismal swamp, a good individual with sunshine and open meadows. Setting can also be used to evoke a particular reaction in the reader. A floral garden may be used to create a romantic or melancholy mood, a dark street to call up feelings of fear or suspicion. Virtually any setting that a reader can relate to because of past experiences or prejudices can be used by clever writers to shape readers' responses.

Before concluding this introduction to plot and moving on to a pair of illustrative stories, we would like to pause and make a couple of additional points. First, it is difficult, perhaps logically impossible, to discuss one structural element of the modern short story without discussing the others, for as a story progresses, all elements develop simultaneously. Nevertheless, one must begin somewhere, and the elements we have chosen to discuss are indispensable to a basic understanding of plot.

Second, the type of plot we have just discussed is most likely to be found in the strongly plotted action story. We realize that many fine modern short stories seem to have no plot at all. We are also familiar with the contention that plot is often only a vehicle for the revelation of character. We do not argue with any of these notions, and later we will have several things to say about them. Nevertheless, students who are getting their first critical look at the short story need fundamental information. The nuances can come later.

Now, keeping in mind that not every story will include all the plot elements we have mentioned, let's see how what we have described applies to Richard Connell's ''The Most Dangerous Game'' and Saki's ''The Open Window.''

RICHARD CONNELL

The Most Dangerous Game

"Off there to the right—somewhere—is a large island," said Whitney. "It's rather a mystery—"

"What island is it?" Rainsford asked.

"The old charts call it 'Ship-Trap Island,' " Whitney replied. "A suggestive name, isn't it? Sailors have a curious dread of the place. I don't know why. Some superstition—"

"Can't see it," remarked Rainsford, trying to peer through the dank tropical night that was palpable as it pressed its thick warm blackness in upon the yacht.

"You've good eyes," said Whitney, with a laugh, "and I've seen you pick off a moose moving in the brown fall bush at four hundred yards, but even you can't see four miles or so through a moonless Caribbean night."

"Nor four yards," admitted Rainsford. "Ugh! It's like moist black velvet."

"It will be light in Rio," promised Whitney. "We should make it in a few days. I hope the jaguar guns have come from Purdey's. We should have some good hunting up the Amazon. Great sport, hunting."

"The best sport in the world," agreed Rainsford.

"For the hunter," amended Whitney. "Not for the jaguar."

"Don't talk rot, Whitney," said Rainsford. "You're a big-game hunter, not a philosopher. Who cares how a jaguar feels?"

"Perhaps the jaguar does," observed Whitney.

"Bah! They've no understanding."

"Even so, I rather think they understand one thing—fear. The fear of pain and the fear of death."

"Nonsense," laughed Rainsford. "This hot weather is making you soft, Whitney. Be a realist. The world is made up of two classes—the hunters and the huntees. Luckily, you and I are the hunters. Do you think we've passed that island yet?"

"I can't tell in the dark. I hope so."

"Why?" asked Rainsford.

"The place has a reputation—a bad one."

"Cannibals?" suggested Rainsford.

"Hardly. Even cannibals wouldn't live in such a God-forsaken place. But it's gotten into sailor lore, somehow. Didn't you notice that the crew's nerves seemed a bit jumpy to-day?"

"They were a bit strange, now you mention it. Even Captain Nielsen—"

"Yes, even that tough-minded old Swede, who'd go up to the devil himself and ask him for a light. Those fishy blue eyes held a look I never saw there before. All I could get out of him was: 'This place has an evil name among sea-faring men, sir.' Then he said to me, very gravely: 'Don't you feel anything?'—as if the air about us was actually poisonous. Now, you mustn't laugh when I tell you this—I did feel something like a sudden chill.

"There was no breeze. The sea was as flat as a plate-glass window. We were drawing near the island then. What I felt was a—a mental chill; a sort of sudden dread."

"Pure imagination," said Rainsford. "One superstitious sailor can taint the whole ship's company with his fear."

"Maybe. But sometimes I think sailors have an extra sense that tells them when they are in danger. Sometimes I think evil is a tangible thing—with wave lengths, just as sound and light have. An evil place can, so to speak, broadcast vibrations of evil. Anyhow, I'm glad we're getting out of this zone. Well, I think I'll turn in now, Rainsford."

"I'm not sleepy," said Rainsford. "I'm going to smoke another pipe on the after deck."

"Good night, then, Rainsford. See you at breakfast."

"Right. Good night, Whitney."

There was no sound in the night as Rainsford sat there, but the muffled throb of the engine that drove the yacht swiftly through the darkness, and the swish and ripple of the wash of the propeller.

Rainsford, reclining in a steamer chair, indolently puffed on his favorite brier. The sensuous drowsiness of the night was on him. "It's so dark," he thought, "that I could sleep without closing my eyes; the night would be my eyelids—"

An abrupt sound startled him. Off to the right he heard it, and his ears, expert in such matters, could not be mistaken. Again he heard the sound, and again. Somewhere, off in the blackness, some one had fired a gun three times.

Rainsford sprang up and moved quickly to the rail, mystified. He strained his eyes in the direction from which the reports had come, but it was like trying to see through a blanket. He leaped upon the rail and balanced himself there, to get greater elevation; his pipe, striking a rope, was knocked from his mouth. He lunged for it; a short, hoarse cry came from his lips as he realized he had reached too far and had lost his balance. The cry was pinched off short as the blood-warm waters of the Caribbean Sea closed over his head.

He struggled up to the surface and tried to cry out, but the wash from the speeding yacht slapped him in the face and the salt water in his open mouth made him gag and strangle. Desperately he struck out with strong strokes after the receding lights of the yacht, but he stopped before he had swum fifty feet. A certain cool-headedness had come to him; it was not the first time he had been in a tight place. There was a chance that his cries could be heard by some one aboard the yacht, but that chance was slender, and grew more slender as the yacht raced on. He wrestled himself out of his clothes, and shouted with all his power. The lights of the yacht became faint and ever-vanishing fireflies; then they were blotted out entirely by the night.

Rainsford remembered the shots. They had come from the right, and doggedly he swam in that direction, swimming with slow, deliberate strokes, conserving his strength. For a seemingly endless time he fought the sea. He began to count his strokes; he could do possibly a hundred more and then—

Rainsford heard a sound. It came out of the darkness, a high screaming sound, the sound of an animal in an extremity of anguish and terror.

He did not recognize the animal that made the sound; he did not try to; with fresh vitality he swam toward the sound. He heard it again; then it was cut short by another noise, crisp, staccato.

"Pistol shot," muttered Rainsford, swimming on.

Ten minutes of determined effort brought another sound to his ears—the most welcome he had ever heard—the muttering and growling of the sea breaking on a rocky shore. He was almost on the rocks before he saw them;

on a night less calm he would have been shattered against them. With his remaining strength he dragged himself from the swirling waters. Jagged crags appeared to jut into the opaqueness, he forced himself upward, hand over hand. Gasping, his hands raw, he reached a flat place at the top. Dense jungle came down to the very edge of the cliffs. What perils that tangle of trees and underbrush might hold for him did not concern Rainsford just then. All he knew was that he was safe from his enemy, the sea, and that utter weariness was on him. He flung himself down at the jungle edge and tumbled headlong into the deepest sleep of his life.

When he opened his eyes he knew from the position of the sun that it was late in the afternoon. Sleep had given him new vigor; a sharp hunger was picking at him. He looked about him, almost cheerfully.

"Where there are pistol shots, there are men. Where there are men, there is food," he thought. But what kind of men, he wondered, in so forbidding a place? An unbroken front of snarled and ragged jungle fringed the shore.

He saw no sign of a trail through the closely knit web of weeds and trees; it was easier to go along the shore, and Rainsford floundered along by the water. Not far from where he had landed, he stopped.

Some wounded thing, by the evidence a large animal, had thrashed about in the underbrush; the jungle weeds were crushed down and the moss was lacerated; one patch of weeds was stained crimson. A small, glittering object not far away caught Rainsford's eye and he picked it up. It was an empty cartridge.

"A twenty-two," he remarked. "That's odd. It must have been a fairly large animal too. The hunter had his nerve with him to tackle it with a light gun. It's clear that the brute put up a fight. I suppose the first three shots I heard was when the hunter flushed his quarry and wounded it. The last shot was when he trailed it here and finished it."

He examined the ground closely and found what he had hoped to find—the print of hunting boots. They pointed along the cliff in the direction he had been going. Eagerly he hurried along, now slipping on a rotten log or a loose stone, but making headway; night was beginning to settle down on the island.

Bleak darkness was blacking out the sea and jungle when Rainsford sighted the lights. He came upon them as he turned a crook in the coast line, and his first thought was that he had come upon a village, for there were many lights. But as he forged along he saw to his great astonishment that all the lights were in one enormous building—a lofty structure with pointed towers plunging upward into the gloom. His eyes made out the shadowy outlines of a palatial château; it was set on a high bluff, and on three sides of it cliffs dived down to where the sea licked greedy lips in the shadows.

"Mirage," thought Rainsford. But it was no mirage, he found, when he opened the tall spiked iron gate. The stone steps were real enough; the massive door with a leering gargoyle for a knocker was real enough; yet about it all hung an air of unreality.

He lifted the knocker, and it creaked up stiffly, as if it had never before been used. He let it fall, and it startled him with its booming loudness. He thought he heard steps within; the door remained closed. Again Rainsford lifted the heavy knocker, and let it fall. The door opened then, opened as suddenly as if it were on a spring, and Rainsford stood blinking in the river of glaring gold light that poured out. The first thing Rainsford's eyes discerned was the largest man Rainsford had ever seen—a gigantic creature, solidly made and black-bearded to the waist. In his hand the man held a long-barreled revolver, and he was pointing it straight at Rainsford's heart.

Out of the snarl of beard two small eyes regarded Rainsford.

"Don't be alarmed," said Rainsford, with a smile which he hoped was disarming. "I'm no robber. I fell off a yacht. My name is Sanger Rainsford of New York City."

The menacing look in the eyes did not change. The revolver pointed as rigidly as if the giant were a statue. He gave no sign that he understood Rainsford's words, or that he had even heard them. He was dressed in uniform, a black uniform trimmed with gray astrakhan.

"I'm Sanger Rainsford of New York," Rainsford began again. "I fell off a yacht. I am hungry."

The man's only answer was to raise with his thumb the hammer of his revolver. Then Rainsford saw the man's free hand go to his forehead in a military salute, and he saw him click his heels together and stand at attention. Another man was coming down the broad marble steps, an erect, slender man in evening clothes. He advanced to Rainsford and held out his hand.

In a cultivated voice marked by a slight accent that gave it added precision and deliberateness, he said: "It is a very great pleasure and honor to welcome Mr. Sanger Rainsford, the celebrated hunter, to my home."

Automatically Rainsford shook the man's hand.

"I've read your book about hunting snow leopards in Tibet, you see," explained the man. "I am General Zaroff."

Rainsford's first impression was that the man was singularly handsome; his second was that there was an original, almost bizarre quality about the general's face. He was a tall man past middle age, for his hair was a vivid white; but his thick eyebrows and pointed military mustache were as black as the night from which Rainsford had come. His eyes, too, were black and very bright. He had high cheek bones, a sharp-cut nose, a spare, dark face, the face of a man used to giving orders, the face of an aristocrat. Turning to the giant in uniform, the general made a sign. The giant put away his pistol, saluted, withdrew.

"Ivan is an incredibly strong fellow," remarked the general, "but he has the misfortune to be deaf and dumb. A simple fellow, but, I'm afraid, like all his race, a bit of a savage."

"Is he Russian?"

"He is a Cossack," said the general, and his smile showed red lips and pointed teeth. "So am I."

"Come," he said, "we shouldn't be chatting here. We can talk later. Now you want clothes, food, rest. You shall have them. This is a most restful spot."

Ivan had reappeared, and the general spoke to him with lips that moved but gave forth no sound.

"Follow Ivan, if you please, Mr. Rainsford," said the general. "I was about to have my dinner when you came. I'll wait for you. You'll find that my clothes will fit you, I think."

It was to a huge, beam-ceilinged bedroom with a canopied bed big enough for six men that Rainsford followed the silent giant. Ivan laid out an evening suit, and Rainsford, as he put it on, noticed that it came from a London tailor who ordinarily cut and sewed for none below the rank of duke.

The dining room to which Ivan conducted him was in many ways remarkable. There was a medieval magnificence about it; it suggested a baronial hall of feudal times with its oaken panels, its high ceiling, its vast refectory table where twoscore men could sit down to eat. About the hall were the mounted heads of many animals—lions, tigers, elephants, moose, bears; larger or more perfect specimens Rainsford had never seen. At the great table the general was sitting, alone.

"You'll have a cocktail, Mr. Rainsford," he suggested. The cocktail was surpassingly good; and, Rainsford noted, the table appointments were of the finest—the linen, the crystal, the silver, the china.

They were eating *borsch*, the rich, red soup with whipped cream so dear to Russian palates. Half apologetically General Zaroff said: "We do our best to preserve the amenities of civilization here. Please forgive any lapses. We are well off the beaten track, you know. Do you think the champagne has suffered from its long ocean trip?"

"Not in the least," declared Rainsford. He was finding the general a most thoughtful and affable host, a true cosmopolite. But there was one small trait of the general's that made Rainsford uncomfortable. Whenever he looked up from his plate he found the general studying him, appraising him narrowly.

"Perhaps," said General Zaroff, "you were surprised that I recognized your name. You see, I read all books on hunting published in English, French, and Russian. I have but one passion in my life, Mr. Rainsford, and it is the hunt."

"You have some wonderful heads here," said Rainsford as he ate a particularly well cooked filet mignon. "That Cape buffalo is the largest I ever saw."

"Oh, that fellow. Yes, he was a monster."

"Did he charge you?"

"Hurled me against a tree," said the general. "Fractured my skull. But I got the brute."

"I've always thought," said Rainsford, "that the Cape buffalo is the most dangerous of all big game."

For a moment the general did not reply; he was smiling his curious red-lipped smile. Then he said slowly: "No. You are wrong, sir. The Cape buffalo is not the most dangerous big game." He sipped his wine. "Here in my preserve on this island," he said in the same slow tone, "I hunt more dangerous game."

Rainsford expressed his surprise. "Is there big game on this island?"

The general nodded. "The biggest."

"Really?"

"Oh, it isn't here naturally, of course. I have to stock the island."

"What have you imported, general?" Rainsford asked. "Tigers?"

The general smiled. "No," he said. "Hunting tigers ceased to interest me some years ago. I exhausted their possibilities, you see. No thrill left in tigers, no real danger. I live for danger, Mr. Rainsford."

The general took from his pocket a gold cigaret case and offered his guest a long black cigaret with a silver tip; it was perfumed and gave off a smell like incense.

"We will have some capital hunting, you and I," said the general. "I shall be most glad to have your society."

"But what game—" began Rainsford.

"I'll tell you," said the general. "You will be amused, I know. I think I may say, in all modesty, that I have done a rare thing. I have invented a new sensation. May I pour you another glass of port, Mr. Rainsford?"

"Thank you, general."

The general filled both glasses, and said: "God makes some men poets. Some He makes kings, some beggars. Me He made a hunter. My hand was made for the trigger, my father said. He was a very rich man with a quarter of a million acres in the Crimea, and he was an ardent sportsman. When I was only five years old he gave me a little gun, specially made in Moscow for me, to shoot sparrows with. When I shot some of his prize turkeys with it, he did not punish me; he complimented me on my marksmanship. I killed my first bear in the Caucasus when I was ten. My whole life has been one prolonged hunt. I went into the army—it was expected of noblemen's sons—and for a time commanded a division of Cossack cavalry, but my real interest was always the hunt. I have hunted every kind of game in every land. It would be impossible for me to tell you how many animals I have killed."

The general puffed at his cigaret.

"After the debacle in Russia I left the country, for it was imprudent for an officer of the Czar to stay there. Many noble Russians lost everything. I, luckily, had invested heavily in American securities, so I shall never have to open a tea room in Monte Carlo or drive a taxi in Paris. Naturally, I continued to hunt—grizzlies in your Rockies, crocodiles in the Ganges, rhinoceroses in East Africa. It was in Africa that the Cape buffalo hit me and laid me up for six months. As soon as I recovered I started for the Amazon to hunt jaguars, for I had heard they were unusually cunning. They weren't." The Cossack sighed. "They were no match at all for a hunter with his wits about him, and a high-powered rifle. I was bitterly disappointed. I was lying in my tent with a splitting headache one night when a terrible thought pushed its way into my mind. Hunting was beginning to bore me! And hunting, remember, had been my life. I have heard that in America business men often go to pieces when they give up the business that has been their life."

"Yes, that's so," said Rainsford.

The general smiled. "I had no wish to go to pieces," he said. "I must do something. Now, mine is an analytical mind, Mr. Rainsford. Doubtless that is why I enjoy the problems of the chase."

"No doubt, General Zaroff."

"So," continued the general, "I asked myself why the hunt no longer fascinated me. You are much younger than I am, Mr. Rainsford, and have not hunted as much, but you perhaps can guess the answer."

"What was it?"

"Simply this: hunting had ceased to be what you call 'a sporting proposition.' It had become too easy. I always got my quarry. Always. There is no greater bore than perfection."

The general lit a fresh cigaret.

"No animal had a chance with me any more. That is no boast; it is a mathematical certainty. The animal had nothing but his legs and his instinct. Instinct is no match for reason. When I thought of this it was a tragic moment for me, I can tell you."

Rainsford leaned across the table, absorbed in what his host was saying.

"It came to me as an inspiration what I must do," the general went on.

"And that was?"

The general smiled the quiet smile of one who has faced an obstacle and surmounted it with success. "I had to invent a new animal to hunt," he said.

"A new animal? You're joking."

"Not at all," said the general. "I never joke about hunting. I needed a new animal. I found one. So I bought this island, built this house, and here I do my hunting. The island is perfect for my purposes—there are jungles with a maze of trails in them, hills, swamps—"

"But the animal, General Zaroff?"

"Oh," said the general, "it supplies me with the most exciting hunting in the world. No other hunting compares with it for an instant. Every day I hunt, and I never grow bored now, for I have a quarry with which I can match my wits."

Rainsford's bewilderment showed in his face.

"I wanted the ideal animal to hunt," explained the general. "So I said: 'What are the attributes of an ideal quarry?' And the answer was, of course: 'It must have courage, cunning, and, above all, it must be able to reason.'"

"But no animal can reason," objected Rainsford.

"My dear fellow," said the general, "there is one that can."

"But you can't mean—" gasped Rainsford.

"And why not?"

"I can't believe you are serious, General Zaroff. This is a grisly joke."

"Why should I not be serious? I am speaking of hunting."

"Hunting? Good God, General Zaroff, what you speak of is murder."

The general laughed with entire good nature. He regarded Rainsford quizzically. "I refuse to believe that so modern and civilized a young man as you seem to be harbors romantic ideas about the value of human life. Surely your experiences in the war—"

"Did not make me condone cold-blooded murder," finished Rainsford stiffly.

Laughter shook the general. "How extraordinarily droll you are!" he said. "One does not expect nowadays to find a young man of the educated class, even in America, with such a naive, and, if I may say so, mid-Victorian point of view. It's like finding a snuff-box in a limousine. Ah, well, doubtless you had Puritan ancestors. So many Americans appear to have had. I'll wager you'll forget your notions when you go hunting with me. You've a genuine new thrill in store for you, Mr. Rainsford."

"Thank you, I'm a hunter, not a murderer."

"Dear me," said the general, quite unruffled, "again that unpleasant word. But I think I can show you that your scruples are quite ill founded."

"Yes?"

"Life is for the strong, to be lived by the strong, and, if need be, taken by the strong. The weak of the world were put here to give the strong pleasure. I am strong. Why should I not use my gift? If I wish to hunt, why should I not? I hunt the scum of the earth—sailors from tramp ships—lascars, blacks, Chinese, whites, mongrels—a thorobred horse or hound is worth more than a score of them."

"But they are men," said Rainsford hotly.

"Precisely," said the general. "That is why I use them. It gives me pleasure. They can reason, after a fashion. So they are dangerous."

"But where do you get them?"

The general's left eyelid fluttered down in a wink. "This island is called Ship-Trap," he answered. "Sometimes an angry god of the high seas sends them to me. Sometimes, when Providence is not so kind, I help Providence a bit. Come to the window with me."

Rainsford went to the window and looked out toward the sea.

"Watch! Out there!" exclaimed the general, pointing into the night. Rainsford's eyes saw only blackness, and then, as the general pressed a button, far out to sea Rainsford saw the flash of lights.

The general chuckled. "They indicate a channel," he said, "where there's none: giant rocks with razor edges crouch like a sea monster with wide-open jaws. They can crush a ship as easily as I crush this nut." He dropped a walnut on the hardwood floor and brought his heel grinding down on it. "Oh, yes," he said, casually, as if in answer to a question, "I have electricity. We try to be civilized here."

"Civilized? And you shoot down men?"

A trace of anger was in the general's black eyes, but it was there for but a second, and he said, in his most pleasant manner: "Dear me, what a righteous young man you are! I assure you I do not do the thing you suggest. That would be barbarous. I treat these visitors with every consideration. They get plenty of good food and exercise. They get into splendid physical condition. You shall see for yourself to-morrow."

"What do you mean?"

"We'll visit my training school," smiled the general. "It's in the cellar. I have about a dozen pupils down there now. They're from the Spanish bark San Lucar that had the bad luck to go on the rocks out there. A very inferior lot, I regret to say. Poor specimens and more accustomed to the deck than to the jungle."

He raised his hand, and Ivan, who served as waiter, brought thick Turkish coffee. Rainsford, with an effort, held his tongue in check.

"It's a game, you see," pursued the general blandly. "I suggest to one of them that we go hunting. I give him a supply of food and an excellent hunting knife. I give him three hours' start. I am to follow, armed only with a pistol of the smallest caliber and range. If my quarry eludes me for three whole days, he wins the game. If I find him"—the general smiled—"he loses."

"Suppose he refuses to be hunted?"

"Oh," said the general, "I give him his option, of course. He need not play that game if he doesn't wish to. If he does not wish to hunt, I turn him over to Ivan. Ivan once had the honor of serving as official knouter to the Great White Czar, and he has his own ideas of sport. Invariably, Mr. Rainsford, invariably they choose the hunt."

"And if they win?"

The smile on the general's face widened. "To date I have not lost," he said.

Then he added, hastily: "I don't wish you to think me a braggart, Mr. Rainsford. Many of them afford only the most elementary sort of problem. Occasionally I strike a tartar. One almost did win. I eventually had to use the dogs."

"The dogs?"

"This way, please. I'll show you."

The general steered Rainsford to a window. The lights from the windows sent a flickering illumination that made grotesque patterns on the courtyard below, and Rainsford could see moving about there a dozen or so huge black shapes; as they turned toward him, their eyes glittered greenly.

"A rather good lot, I think," observed the general. "They are let out at seven every night. If anyone should try to get into my house—or out of it— something extremely regrettable would occur to him." He hummed a snatch of song from the Folies Bergère.

"And now," said the general, "I want to show you my new collection of heads. Will you come with me to the library?"

"I hope," said Rainsford, "that you will excuse me to-night, General Zaroff. I'm really not feeling at all well."

"Ah, indeed?" the general inquired solicitously. "Well, I suppose that's only natural, after your long swim. You need a good, restful night's sleep. To-morrow you'll feel like a new man, I'll wager. Then we'll hunt, eh? I've one rather promising prospect—"

Rainsford was hurrying from the room.

"Sorry you can't go with me to-night," called the general. "I expect rather fair sport—a big, strong black. He looks resourceful—Well, good night, Mr. Rainsford; I hope you have a good night's rest."

The bed was good, and the pajamas of the softest silk, and he was tired in every fiber of his being, but nevertheless Rainsford could not quiet his brain with the opiate of sleep. He lay, eyes wide open. Once he thought he heard stealthy steps in the corridor outside his room. He sought to throw open the door; it would not open. He went to the window and looked out. His room was high up in one of the towers. The lights of the château were out now, and it was dark and silent, but there was a fragment of sallow moon, and by its wan light he could see, dimly, the courtyard; there, weaving in and out in the pattern of shadow, were black, noiseless forms; the hounds heard him at the window and looked up, expectantly, with their green eyes. Rainsford went back to the bed and lay down. By many methods he tried to put himself to sleep. He had achieved a doze when, just as morning began to come, he heard, far off in the jungle, the faint report of a pistol.

General Zaroff did not appear until luncheon. He was dressed faultlessly in the tweeds of a country squire. He was solicitous about the state of Rainsford's health.

"As for me," sighed the general, "I do not feel so well. I am worried, Mr. Rainsford. Last night I detected traces of my old complaint."

To Rainsford's questioning glance the general said: "Ennui. Boredom."

Then, taking a second helping of Crêpes Suzette, the general explained: "The hunting was not good last night. The fellow lost his head. He made a straight trail that offered no problems at all. That's the trouble with these sailors: they have dull brains to begin with, and they do not know how to get about in the woods. They do excessively stupid and obvious things. It's most annoying. Will you have another glass of Chablis, Mr. Rainsford?"

"General," said Rainsford firmly, "I wish to leave this island at once."

The general raised his thickets of eyebrows; he seemed hurt. "But, my dear fellow," the general protested, "you've only just come. You've had no hunting—"

"I wish to go to-day," said Rainsford. He saw the dead black eyes of the general on him, studying him. General Zaroff's face suddenly brightened.

He filled Rainsford's glass with venerable Chablis from a dusty bottle.

"To-night," said the general, "we will hunt—you and I."

Rainsford shook his head. "No, general," he said. "I will not hunt."

The general shrugged his shoulders and delicately ate a hothouse grape. "As you wish, my friend," he said. "The choice rests entirely with you. But may I not venture to suggest that you will find my idea of sport more diverting than Ivan's?"

He nodded toward the corner to where the giant stood, scowling, his thick arms crossed on his hogshead of chest.

"You don't mean—" cried Rainsford.

"My dear fellow," said the general, "have I not told you I always mean what

I say about hunting? This is really an inspiration. I drink to a foeman worthy of my steel—at last."

The general raised his glass, but Rainsford sat staring at him.

"You'll find this game worth playing," the general said enthusiastically. "Your brain against mine. Your woodcraft against mine. Your strength and stamina against mine. Outdoor chess! And the stake is not without value, eh?"

"And if I win—" began Rainsford huskily.

"I'll cheerfully acknowledge myself defeated if I do not find you by midnight of the third day," said General Zaroff. "My sloop will place you on the mainland near a town."

The general read what Rainsford was thinking.

"Oh, you can trust me," said the Cossack. "I will give you my word as a gentleman and a sportsman. Of course you, in turn, must agree to say nothing of your visit here."

"I'll agree to nothing of the kind," said Rainsford.

"Oh," said the general, "in that case—But why discuss that now? Three days hence we can discuss it over a bottle of Veuve Cliquot, unless—"

The general sipped his wine.

Then a businesslike air animated him. "Ivan," he said to Rainsford, "will supply you with hunting clothes, food, a knife. I suggest you wear moccasins; they leave a poorer trail. I suggest too that you avoid the big swamp in the southeast corner of the island. We call it Death Swamp. There's quicksand there. One foolish fellow tried it. The deplorable part of it was that Lazarus followed him. You can imagine my feelings, Mr. Rainsford. I loved Lazarus; he was the finest hound in my pack. Well, I must beg you to excuse me now. I always take a siesta after lunch. You'll hardly have time for a nap, I fear. You'll want to start, no doubt. I shall not follow till dusk. Hunting at night is so much more exciting than by day, don't you think? Au revoir, Mr. Rainsford, au revoir."

General Zaroff, with a deep, courtly bow, strolled from the room.

From another door came Ivan. Under one arm he carried khaki hunting clothes, a haversack of food, a leather sheath containing a long-bladed hunting knife; his right hand rested on a cocked revolver thrust in the crimson sash about his waist. . . .

Rainsford had fought his way through the bush for two hours. "I must keep my nerve. I must keep my nerve," he said through tight teeth.

He had not been entirely clear-headed when the château gates snapped shut behind him. His whole idea at first was to put distance between himself and General Zaroff, and, to this end, he had plunged along, spurred on by the sharp rowels of something very like panic. Now he had got a grip on himself, had stopped, and was taking stock of himself and the situation.

He saw that straight flight was futile; inevitably it would bring him face to face with the sea. He was in a picture with a frame of water, and his operations, clearly, must take place within that frame.

"I'll give him a trail to follow," muttered Rainsford, and he struck off from the rude paths he had been following into the trackless wilderness. He executed a series of intricate loops; he doubled on his trail again and again, recalling all the lore of the fox hunt, and all the dodges of the fox. Night found him leg-weary, with hands and face lashed by the branches, on a thickly wooded ridge. He knew it would be insane to blunder on through the dark, even if he had the strength. His need for rest was imperative and he thought: "I have played the fox, now I must play the cat of the fable." A big tree with a thick trunk and outspread branches was nearby, and, taking care to leave not the slightest mark, he climbed up into the crotch, and stretching out on one of the broad limbs, after a fashion, rested. Rest brought him new confidence and almost a feeling of security. Even so zealous a hunter as General Zaroff could not trace him there, he told himself; only the devil himself could follow that complicated trail through the jungle after dark. But, perhaps, the general was a devil—

An apprehensive night crawled slowly by like a wounded snake, and sleep did not visit Rainsford, altho the silence of a dead world was on the jungle. Toward morning when a dingy gray was varnishing the sky, the cry of some startled bird focused Rainsford's attention in that direction. Something was coming through the bush, coming slowly, carefully, coming by the same winding way Rainsford had come. He flattened himself down on the limb, and through a screen of leaves almost as thick as tapestry, he watched. The thing that was approaching was a man.

It was General Zaroff. He made his way along with his eyes fixed in utmost concentration on the ground before him. He paused, almost beneath the tree, dropped to his knees and studied the ground. Rainsford's impulse was to hurl himself down like a panther, but he saw the general's right hand held something metallic—a small automatic pistol.

The hunter shook his head several times, as if he were puzzled. Then he straightened up and took from his case one of his black cigarets; its pungent incense-like smoke floated up to Rainsford's nostrils.

Rainsford held his breath. The general's eyes had left the ground and were traveling inch by inch up the tree. Rainsford froze there, every muscle tensed for a spring. But the sharp eyes of the hunter stopped before they reached the limb where Rainsford lay; a smile spread over his brown face. Very deliberately he blew a smoke ring into the air; then he turned his back on the tree and walked carelessly away, back along the trail he had come. The swish of the underbrush against his hunting boots grew fainter and fainter.

The pent-up air burst hotly from Rainsford's lungs. His first thought made him feel sick and numb. The general could follow a trail through the woods at night; he could follow an extremely difficult trail; he must have uncanny powers; only by the merest chance had the Cossack failed to see his quarry.

Rainsford's second thought was even more terrible. It sent a shudder of cold horror through his whole being. Why had the general smiled? Why had he turned back?

Rainsford did not want to believe what his reason told him was true, but the truth was as evident as the sun that had by now pushed through the morning mists. The general was playing with him! The general was saving him for another day's sport! The Cossack was the cat; he was the mouse. Then it was that Rainsford knew the full meaning of terror.

"I will not lose my nerve. I will not."

He slid down from the tree, and struck off again into the woods. His face was set and he forced the machinery of his mind to function. Three hundred yards from his hiding place he stopped where a huge dead tree leaned precariously on a smaller, living one. Throwing off his sack of food, Rainsford took his knife from its sheath and began to work with all his energy.

The job was finished at last, and he threw himself down behind a fallen log a hundred feet away. He did not have to wait long. The cat was coming again to play with the mouse.

Following the trail with the sureness of a bloodhound, came General Zaroff. Nothing escaped those searching black eyes, no crushed blade of grass, no bent twig, no mark, no matter how faint, in the moss. So intent was the Cossack on his stalking that he was upon the thing Rainsford had made before he saw it. His foot touched the protruding bough that was the trigger. Even as he touched it, the general sensed his danger and leaped back with the agility of an ape. But he was not quite quick enough; the dead tree, delicately adjusted to rest on the cut living one, crashed down and struck the general a glancing blow on the shoulder as it fell; but for his alertness, he must have been smashed beneath it. He staggered, but he did not fall; nor did he drop his revolver. He stood there, rubbing his injured shoulder, and Rainsford, with fear again gripping his heart, heard the general's mocking laugh ring through the jungle.

"Rainsford," called the general, "if you are within the sound of my voice, as I suppose you are, let me congratulate you. Not many men know how to make a Malay man-catcher. Luckily, for me, I too have hunted in Malacca. You are proving interesting, Mr. Rainsford. I am going now to have my wound dressed; it's only a slight one. But I shall be back. I shall be back."

When the general, nursing his bruised shoulder, had gone, Rainsford took up his flight again. It was flight now, a desperate, hopeless flight, that carried him on for some hours. Dusk came, then darkness, and still he pressed on. The ground grew softer under his moccasins; the vegetation grew ranker, denser; insects bit him savagely. Then, as he stepped forward, his foot sank into the ooze. He tried to wrench it back, but the muck sucked viciously at his foot as if it were a giant leech. With a violent effort, he tore his foot loose. He knew where he was now. Death Swamp and its quicksand.

His hands were tight closed as if his nerve were something tangible that some one in the darkness was trying to tear from his grip. The softness of the earth had given him an idea. He stepped back from the quicksand a dozen feet or so, and, like some huge prehistoric beaver, he began to dig.

Rainsford had dug himself in in France when a second's delay meant death. That had been a placid pastime compared to his digging now. The pit grew deeper; when it was above his shoulders, he climbed out and from some hard saplings cut stakes and sharpened them to a fine point. These stakes he planted in the bottom of the pit with the points sticking up. With flying fingers he wove a rough carpet of weeds and branches and with it he covered the mouth of the pit. Then, wet with sweat and aching with tiredness, he crouched behind the stump of a lightning-charred tree.

He knew his pursuer was coming; he heard the padding sound of feet on the soft earth, and the night breeze brought him the perfume of the general's cigaret. It seemed to Rainsford that the general was coming with unusual swiftness; he was not feeling his way along, foot by foot. Rainsford, crouching there, could not see the general, nor could he see the pit. He lived a year in a minute. Then he felt an impulse to cry aloud with joy, for he heard the sharp crackle of the breaking branches as the cover of the pit gave way; he heard the sharp scream of pain as the pointed stakes found their mark. He leaped up from his place of concealment. Then he cowered back. Three feet from the pit a man was standing, with an electric torch in his hand.

"You've done well, Rainsford," the voice of the general called. "Your Burmese tiger pit has claimed one of my best dogs. Again you score. I think, Mr. Rainsford, I'll see what you can do against my whole pack. I'm going home for a rest now. Thank you for a most amusing evening."

At daybreak Rainsford, lying near the swamp, was awakened by a sound that made him know that he had new things to learn about fear. It was a distant sound, faint and wavering, but he knew it. It was the baying of a pack of hounds.

Rainsford knew he could do one of two things. He could stay where he was and wait. That was suicide. He could flee. That was postponing the inevitable. For a moment he stood there, thinking. An idea that held a wild chance came to him, and, tightening his belt, he headed away from the swamp.

The baying of the hounds drew nearer, then still nearer, nearer, ever nearer. On a ridge Rainsford climbed a tree. Down a watercourse, not a quarter of a mile away, he could see the bush moving. Straining his eyes, he saw the lean figure of General Zaroff; just ahead of him Rainsford made out another figure whose wide shoulders surged through the tall jungle weeds; it was the giant Ivan, and he seemed pulled forward by some unseen force; Rainsford knew that Ivan must be holding the pack in leash.

They would be on him any minute now. His mind worked frantically. He thought of a native trick he had learned in Uganda. He slid down the tree. He caught hold of a springy young sapling and to it he fastened his hunting knife, with the blade pointing down the trail; with a bit of wild grapevine he tied back the sapling. Then he ran for his life. The hounds raised their voices as they hit the fresh scent. Rainsford knew now how an animal at bay feels.

He had to stop to get his breath. The baying of the hounds stopped abruptly, and Rainsford's heart stopped too. They must have reached the knife.

He shinnied excitedly up a tree and looked back. His pursuers had stopped. But the hope that was in Rainsford's brain when he climbed died, for he saw in the shallow valley that General Zaroff was still on his feet. But Ivan was not.

The knife, driven by the recoil of the springing tree, had not wholly failed.

"Nerve, nerve, nerve!" he panted, as he dashed along. A blue gap showed between the trees dead ahead. Ever nearer drew the hounds. Rainsford forced himself on toward that gap. He reached it. It was the shore of the sea. Across a cove he could see the gloomy gray stone of the château. Twenty feet below him the sea rumbled and hissed. Rainsford hesitated. He heard the hounds. Then he leaped far out into the sea. . . .

When the general and his pack reached the place by the sea, the Cossack stopped. For some minutes he stood regarding the blue-green expanse of water. He shrugged his shoulders. Then he sat down, took a drink of brandy from a silver flask, lit a perfumed cigaret, and hummed a bit from "Madame Butterfly."

General Zaroff had an exceedingly good dinner in his great paneled dining-hall that evening. With it he had a bottle of Pol Roger and half a bottle of Chambertin. Two slight annoyances kept him from perfect enjoyment. One was the thought that it would be difficult to replace Ivan; the other was that his quarry had escaped him; of course the American hadn't played the game—so thought the general as he tasted his after-dinner liqueur. In his library he read, to soothe himself, from the works of Marcus Aurelius. At ten he went up to his bedroom. He was deliciously tired, he said to himself, as he locked himself in. There was a little moonlight, so, before turning on his light, he went to the window and looked down at the courtyard. He could see the great hounds, and he called: "Better luck another time," to them. Then he switched on the light.

A man, who had been hiding in the curtains of the bed, was standing there.

"Rainsford!" screamed the general. "How in God's name did you get here?"

"Swam," said Rainsford. "I found it quicker than walking through the jungle."

The general sucked in his breath and smiled. "I congratulate you," he said. "You have won the game."

Rainsford did not smile. "I am still a beast at bay," he said, in a low, hoarse voice. "Get ready, General Zaroff."

The general made one of his deepest bows. "I see," he said. "Splendid! One of us is to furnish a repast for the hounds. The other will sleep in this very excellent bed. On guard, Rainsford. . . ."

He had never slept in a better bed, Rainsford decided.

BY WAY OF DISCUSSION

At the beginning of a story an author will frequently do something to tease the reader's interest. Sometimes this will be related to plot, sometimes not. In "The Most Dangerous Game" Richard Connell uses a bit of dialogue:

> "Off there to the right—somewhere—is a large island," said Whitney. "It's rather a mystery—"
> "What island is it?" Rainsford asked.
> "The old charts call it 'Ship-Trap Island,' " Whitney replied. "A suggestive name, isn't it? Sailors have a curious dread of the place. I don't know why. Some superstition—"

Except for a few jaded souls, most readers will be hooked. We may give this device any number of names: *arousing-of-curiosity, teaser, come-on, hook.* The point is that you should be aware that the author is trying to interest you enough to read fifteen or twenty pages of storytelling.

After delivering the hook, Connell concentrates on painting in the setting, and he uses the setting clearly to suggest that mysterious and evil things are likely to occur. The setting of "The Most Dangerous Game" tends to foreshadow events. Notice such lines as "the dank tropical night . . . was palpable as it pressed its thick warm blackness in upon the yacht." The island, which is part of the setting from the beginning, has a reputation: "Even cannibals wouldn't live in such a God-forsaken place." Whitney points out to Rainsford that the crew is "a bit jumpy" when the yacht is in the neighborhood of Ship-Trap Island. Even Captain Nielsen, a "tough-minded old Swede," has become a little squeamish. Without question, then, the author has made it clear that this is not Coney Island the yacht is sailing by.

After establishing the setting, Connell moves quickly to the precipitating incident. Whitney goes off to bed, and Rainsford is left alone on the deck of the yacht:

> An abrupt sound startled him. Off to the right he heard it, and his ears, expert in such matters, could not be mistaken. Again he heard the sound, and again. Somewhere, off in the blackness, some one had fired a gun three times.
> Rainsford sprang up and moved quickly to the rail, mystified. He strained his eyes in the direction from which the reports had come, but it was like trying to see through a blanket. He leaped upon the rail and balanced himself there, to get greater elevation; his pipe, striking a rope, was knocked from his mouth. He lunged for it; a short, hoarse cry came from his lips as he realized he had reached too far and had lost his balance. The cry was pinched off short as the blood-warm waters of the Caribbean Sea closed over his head.

Then, in a matter of only a few paragraphs, Rainsford, the protagonist, and General Zaroff, the antagonist, face each other. The subsequent conflict is quite intense, with the protagonist coming out the victor, though a somewhat different person. We even have a marvelous little one-line denouement:

> He had never slept in a better bed, Rainsford decided.

Let's back up and take a look at a few other items. We must remember that "The Most Dangerous Game" is a story dominated by plot—action. Any philosophical implications—theme—are minor. Character comes off rather better, however, especially in the case of Rainsford and Zaroff, who are reasonably well drawn although less than totally believable. Notice that Whitney and Ivan occupy similar positions, the former in relation to Rainsford and the latter in relation to Zaroff. What do we learn about Rainsford from the opening episode until he meets Zaroff? He is rich enough to be sailing on a yacht in the Caribbean. He is also a big-game hunter and a fairly narrow-visioned realist with a generally unsentimental view of the world:

> "This hot weather is making you soft, Whitney. Be a realist. The world is made up of two classes—the hunters and the huntees. Luckily, you and I are hunters."

After Rainsford is tossed into the sea, we learn that he can keep his head in a tight spot—even though his own clumsiness got him into the predicament. He is also a strong swimmer, a fact that becomes important later on.

We learn other things about the protagonist after he meets Zaroff. Rainsford is the author of a "book about hunting snow leopards in Tibet." Unlike Zaroff, he has strong moral scruples against hunting humans as if they are some sort of game animal. Most important of all, Rainsford possesses an alert resourcefulness that more than matches Zaroff's own.

General Zaroff, a capable antagonist if there ever was one, is a "civilized" Cossack. Much of the characterization of Zaroff is revealed through externals: London tailor, baronial hall, *borsch*, and filet mignon. Zaroff escaped the Russian Revolution of 1917 and invested his money in American securities. This last fact is probably intended to be ironical in that it is investments in the so-called free world that allow Zaroff to practice his perverse hobby with virtual impunity. In any event, the man is wealthy and sophisticated but cares nothing for traditional human values. Hunting is his only passion, and he owns a most unusual coursing ground—an entire island. We must also not forget his unusual supply of game and his unique collection of trophies.

Then comes the hunt, with Rainsford, through an ironic reversal of fortune—notice the use of irony of situation—cast in the unwilling role of huntee and experiencing the emotions that earlier he would not concede to nonhuman game. The hunt provides the concrete manifestation of the greater conflict between Zaroff and Rainsford. Zaroff has become a monomaniac who cares a great deal more for his own hobby than for the sanctity of human life. As he says of himself, "My whole life has been one prolonged hunt." By contrast, Rainsford is a sportsman. And although he may agree with some of the general's contentions about the strong and the weak of the earth, murder has not been an acceptable form of entertainment for him. The general finds this part of Rainsford's character amusing:

> "One does not expect nowadays to find a young man of the edu-
> cated class, even in America, with such a naive, and, if I may say so,
> mid-Victorian point of view."

Unfortunately, the hunting episode suffers from a serious plot weakness. Why does Zaroff let Rainsford off? Probably he could have killed
Rainsford during any of the first three hunts. After all, the general had
the pistol. Perhaps the old man was weary of life, even life on his own
terms. Perhaps, having at last found a quarry whose cunning matched
his own, he could not forgo the pleasure of prolonging the hunt. Perhaps, like a cat, he enjoyed tormenting his prey. In any event, after the
third encounter, Rainsford faces a mortal dilemma:

> Rainsford knew he could do one of two things. He could stay where
> he was and wait. That was suicide. He could flee. That was postpon-
> ing the inevitable. For a moment he stood there, thinking. An idea
> that held a wild chance came to him, and, tightening his belt, he
> headed away from the swamp.

In the end we learn that Rainsford's idea was a good one. He swims
around to the castle, catches the general completely by surprise in his
own bedroom, and defeats the old man in hand-to-hand combat. At the
close of the story we are given a hint that Rainsford, despite his earlier
horror at Zaroff's sport, might remain on the island and carry on as
Zaroff has in the past. After all, he likes the general's bed. Perhaps he is
not the "righteous young man" his late host thought him to be. But
more likely, the excitement of the hunt involving another human being
may have whetted Rainsford's appetite for "the most dangerous game."

SAKI

The Open Window

"My aunt will be down presently, Mr. Nuttel," said a very self-
possessed young lady of fifteen; "in the meantime you must try and put up
with me."

Framton Nuttel endeavoured to say the correct something which should
duly flatter the niece of the moment without unduly discounting the aunt that
was to come. Privately he doubted more than ever whether these formal visits
on a succession of total strangers would do much towards helping the nerve
cure which he was supposed to be undergoing.

"I know how it will be," his sister had said when he was preparing to migrate to this rural retreat; "you will bury yourself down there and not speak to a living soul, and your nerves will be worse than ever from moping. I shall just give you letters of introduction to all the people I know there. Some of them, as far as I can remember, were quite nice."

Framton wondered whether Mrs. Sappleton, the lady to whom he was presenting one of the letters of introduction, came into the nice division.

"Do you know many of the people round here?" asked the niece, when she judged that they had had sufficient silent communion.

"Hardly a soul," said Framton. "My sister was staying here, at the rectory, you know, some four years ago, and she gave me letters of introduction to some of the people here."

He made the last statement in a tone of distinct regret.

"Then you know practically nothing about my aunt?" pursued the self-possessed young lady.

"Only her name and address," admitted the caller. He was wondering whether Mrs. Sappleton was in the married or widowed state. An undefinable something about the room seemed to suggest masculine habitation.

"Her great tragedy happened just three years ago," said the child; "that would be since your sister's time."

"Her tragedy?" asked Framton; somehow in this restful country spot tragedies seemed out of place.

"You may wonder why we keep that window wide open on an October afternoon," said the niece, indicating a large French window that opened on to a lawn.

"It is quite warm for the time of the year," said Framton; "but has that window got anything to do with the tragedy?"

"Out through that window, three years ago to a day, her husband and her two young brothers went off for their day's shooting. They never came back. In crossing the moor to their favourite snipe-shooting ground they were all three engulfed in a treacherous piece of bog. It had been that dreadful wet summer, you know, and places that were safe in other years gave way suddenly without warning. Their bodies were never recovered. That was the dreadful part of it." Here the child's voice lost its self-possessed note and became falteringly human. "Poor aunt always thinks that they will come back some day, they and the little brown spaniel that was lost with them, and walk in at that window just as they used to do. That is why the window is kept open every evening till it is quite dusk. Poor dear aunt, she has often told me how they went out, her husband with his white waterproof coat over his arm, and Ronnie, her youngest brother, singing, 'Bertie, why do you bound?' as he always did to tease her, because she said it got on her nerves. Do you know, sometimes on still, quiet evenings like this, I almost get a creepy feeling that they will all walk in through that window—"

She broke off with a little shudder. It was a relief to Framton when the aunt bustled into the room with a whirl of apologies for being late in making her appearance.

"I hope Vera has been amusing you?" she said.

"She has been very interesting," said Framton.

"I hope you don't mind the open window," said Mrs. Sappleton briskly; "my husband and brothers will be home directly from shooting, and they always come in this way. They've been out for snipe in the marshes today, so they'll make a fine mess over my poor carpets. So like you men-folk, isn't it?"

She rattled on cheerfully about the shooting and the scarcity of birds, and the prospects for duck in the winter. To Framton it was all purely horrible. He made a desperate but only partially successful effort to turn the talk on to a less ghastly topic; he was conscious that his hostess was giving him only a fragment of her attention, and her eyes were constantly straying past him to the open window and the lawn beyond. It was certainly an unfortunate coincidence that he should have paid his visit on this tragic anniversary.

"The doctors agree in ordering me complete rest, an absence of mental excitement, and avoidance of anything in the nature of violent physical exercise," announced Framton, who laboured under the tolerably wide-spread delusion that total strangers and chance acquaintances are hungry for the least detail of one's ailments and infirmities, their cause and cure. "On the matter of diet they are not so much in agreement," he continued.

"No?" said Mrs. Sappleton, in a voice which only replaced a yawn at the last moment. Then she suddenly brightened into alert attention—but not to what Framton was saying.

"Here they are at last!" she cried. "Just in time for tea, and don't they look as if they were muddy up to the eyes!"

Framton shivered slightly and turned towards the niece with a look intended to convey sympathetic comprehension. The child was staring out through the open window with dazed horror in her eyes. In a chill shock of nameless fear Framton swung round in his seat and looked in the same direction.

In the deepening twilight three figures were walking across the lawn towards the window; they all carried guns under their arms, and one of them was additionally burdened with a white coat hung over his shoulders. A tired brown spaniel kept close at their heels. Noiselessly they neared the house, and then a hoarse young voice chanted out of the dusk: "I said, Bertie, why do you bound?"

Framton grabbed wildly at his stick and hat; the hall-door, the gravel-drive, and the front gate were dimly noted stages in his headlong retreat. A cyclist coming along the road had to run into the hedge to avoid imminent collision.

"Here we are, my dear," said the bearer of the white mackintosh, coming in through the window; "fairly muddy, but most of it's dry. Who was that who bolted out as we came up?"

"A most extraordinary man, a Mr. Nuttel," said Mrs. Sappleton; "could only talk about his illnesses, and dashed off without a word of good-bye or apology when you arrived. One would think he had seen a ghost."

"I expect it was the spaniel," said the niece calmly; "he told me he had a horror of dogs. He was once hunted into a cemetery somewhere on the banks of the Ganges by a pack of pariah dogs, and had to spend the night in a newly dug grave with the creatures snarling and grinning and foaming just above him. Enough to make anyone lose their nerve."

Romance at short notice was her speciality.

BY WAY OF DISCUSSION

In contrast to "The Most Dangerous Game," this story includes little real action. And were it not for the extraordinary character of Vera, "a very self-possessed young lady of fifteen," what action we have would not exist. The plot of "The Open Window" is covert, growing out of the creative imagination of Vera and the morbid and gullible mind of Framton.

Vera's first remark to Framton, "in the meantime you must try and put up with me," is intended to test Framton's social poise by creating a situation that calls for him to say something complimentary. His failure to respond in an appropriate manner stamps him as the bore that he is and prompts Vera to play her trick on him. Of course, Vera needs very little prompting.

Having ascertained by careful questioning that Framton knows nothing about her aunt, Vera then proceeds to concoct her false tale of the hunters' being swallowed up in a bog. This tale, a frame story, is a small masterpiece of design and execution. Its opening line, "Her great tragedy happened just three years ago," doubles as the precipitating incident for the frame story and the hook both for the reader and for Framton. To enhance the story's seeming truthfulness and to increase the shock caused by the hunters' return, Vera embellishes her narrative with an array of specific details: the brown spaniel, the white waterproof carried by the aunt's husband, and the teasing chant of the aunt's younger brother. Realizing that Framton might doubt that such a disaster could occur on familiar terrain, Vera tells him that the unusually wet summer had caused otherwise safe spots to give way without warning. The concluding line of Vera's tale, "Do you know, sometimes on still, quiet evenings like this, I almost get a creepy feeling that they will all walk in through that window," is delivered with a little shudder—Vera is also an adept actress—and it foreshadows the appearance of the hunters, further predisposing Framton to believe that the men are actually ghosts.

Vera's storytelling skill completely deceives Framton, even though an "undefinable something" about the room in which he sits appears to "suggest masculine habitation." As the tale proceeds, Framton's tension steadily mounts, and he silently hails the appearance of the aunt. His relief is short-lived, however. Within moments, the aunt begins discussing the impending return of her menfolk, further unnerving her guest, who is totally convinced that he is dealing with a deranged woman. The climax occurs when the aunt cries, "Here they are at last!" This causes Framton to turn toward the window and then bolt in terror at the sight of the three figures who match exactly Vera's earlier description. The aunt's remark, "One would think he had seen a ghost," adds a neat touch of irony, because poor Framton believes he has indeed seen a ghost, several of them.

The concluding four paragraphs of the story contribute to its denouement. Vera's explanation of Framton's sudden exit is another of her fabrications, but it seems to satisfy her listeners well enough. They are apparently unaware of her penchant for "romance at short notice."

Stories often include one or more flashbacks, brief episodes from the past that throw light on the protagonist's predicament. Such an episode occurs early in this story, when Framton recalls his sister's remarks as he was preparing for his journey:

> "I know how it will be," his sister had said when he was preparing to migrate to this rural retreat; "you will bury yourself down there and not speak to a living soul, and your nerves will be worse than ever from moping."

By pointing up his nervous condition, these remarks lend greater plausibility to Framton's reaction when he sees the "ghosts." This particular flashback has some quality of narrative projection as well, for the sister offers predictions concerning the probable outcome of Framton's journey.

"The Open Window" is a story that provides an example of a protagonist who accomplishes nothing. In fact, the poor fellow, who is just trying to get along on a day-to-day basis, is completely destroyed. Few readers fail to enjoy the clever humor of this story, but most of us feel at least a little sympathy for Framton. All of us can recall times when we have been "had," even if the situation was not quite so dramatic.

FOR ADDITIONAL READING

The following stories, which appear elsewhere in this book, are especially appropriate for an analysis of plot:

1. O. Henry, "The Gift of the Magi" (p. 457)
2. Eudora Welty, "A Visit of Charity" (P. 563)
3. Albert Maltz, "The Happiest Man on Earth" (p. 533)
4. John Cheever, "The Swimmer" (p. 615)

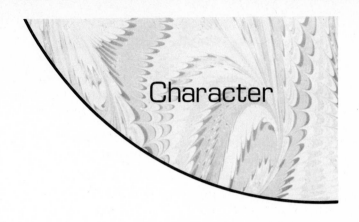

Character

Although plot may be thought of as the skeleton of the short story, the framework that supports the other four structural elements, character is probably the most important element. Why? Because readers are most interested in human personality. Some writers consider plot to be little more than one of several devices for presenting character. In any event, the knowledgeable reader is less intrigued with actions done by characters than with characters doing actions.

For at least two reasons the creation of character is more complex than the devising of plot. We have already mentioned one: to be effective, character must be dramatized, not revealed directly. The second reason has to do with the almost infinite variety of the human personality. No two people are exactly alike. This truth is a constant source of fascination both to writers and to readers. In contrast, the possibilities of plot are severely limited; all plots have long since been discovered and repeated over and over again.

Three ingredients of good characterization are well known to every writer: *consistency, motivation,* and *plausibility. Consistency* means that after a character is introduced as an individual of a certain type, the personality of the character doesn't change drastically without good reason. In "The Most Dangerous Game," for example, General Zaroff is introduced as a villainous yet polite Cossack, and throughout the story he never changes.

Motivation is the reason for a character's action. In the quality story characters do not do things without reason; the motive for their actions is clear to the reader. Although Rainsford is not introduced as a murderer in "The Most Dangerous Game," his ultimate killing of Zaroff is reasonable because of what the general has put him through.

Plausibility means lifelikeness. A plausible character is one who is acceptable as a representative human being, neither too good nor too bad to be true. The point must be made, however, that plausibility requires only the illusion of lifelikeness. A short story cannot present human beings in all their complexity. Many volumes would be required to detail the total personality of even the simplest character. Thus the short-story writer must find the appropriate mix of a few traits that will make the character of a fictional human being believable.

Writers, knowing that through characterization lies their best chance for finding the pearl of originality, sweat blood over their characters. One of the most serious charges you can make against an author's efforts is to say that the characters are inconsistent, unmotivated, or implausible.

How do writers go about delineating character? How do they dramatize the personalities of their characters? An author may simply tell us what a character looks like,—or paint us a word picture. The description of the character might include a description of the character's immediate surroundings (setting) and possessions. The author can, when appropriate, go directly into the mind of the character and tell us what thoughts are there. Character can also be revealed by dialogue. By telling us what a character says, the author implies what sort of person the character is. Remember what Vera's storytelling in ''The Open Window'' revealed about her character.

A recounting of a character's actions may tell even more than do his or her words. For example, in ''The Most Dangerous Game'' it was Rainsford's actions under dire circumstances that revealed his true self. The author may use the opinions of the other characters in the story to reveal some aspect of personality. But here the reader must be cautious, for sometimes these other characters harbor, for a rainbow of reasons, inaccurate opinions. A character's background and personal tastes are also important to the dramatization of personality. Remember how much was suggested about General Zaroff by the simple fact that he was a Cossack who had fled Russia during the revolution of 1917.

So, the devices for dramatizing character are many. Occasionally you may come across a story in which the author tells you outright that the character is heroic, weak, hypocritical, or the like. This method is called *characterization by exposition*. Although it is economical and clear, few sophisticated modern readers find this nondramatic method of characterization convincing. Some modern writers may combine an expository line or two about a character's personality with subsequent dramatized incidents that support the generalizations. Even this approach is relatively rare, however, for readers are likely to view it with suspicion.

Not every character appearing in a story needs to be fully developed. The one or two who are, however—usually the protagonist and the antagonist—are said to be *round*, or *three-dimensional* characters. The others, drawn by the delineation of only two or three dominant traits, are called *flat*, or *one-dimensional* characters. In ''The Most Dangerous Game,'' both Whitney and Ivan are flat characters. An author who uses a mix of round and flat characters must be sure that each is drawn fully enough to justify his or her role in the story.

A one-dimensional character who, under various names, has appeared in so many stories over such a long period of time that readers know exactly what he or she is likely to say, do, feel, and think from the moment of introduction is called a *stock character*. There are dozens of stock characters: the tall, handsome cowboy of few words who rides a white horse, totes a pair of pearl-handled shootin' irons, drinks buttermilk, and cleans up the town while making out with the local schoolmarm; the brilliant but eccentric detective who can solve any crime; the milquetoast husband who is dominated by his wife and ridiculed both by his children and by the community; the anatomically blessed dumb blonde who exudes a kind of tinsel sexuality; the mad scientist or absentminded professor who has no idea of ordinary humanity; the almost imbecilic athlete who remains an imitation child all of his life; the sadistic or fascist cop; the good-hearted ne'er-do-well; the town drunk; the cruel stepmother.

A point to remember is that these were not always stock characters. The very first time that they appeared in a story or novel they were quite original. Unfortunately, readers liked them so well that legions of writers used them over and over until the last glimmer of originality was extinguished. Today the best writers use stock characters mostly for comic or satiric effect.

Similar to the stock character is the literary *caricature*. A literary caricature results when an author takes the already dominant traits of a character and exaggerates them beyond all reasonable bounds. The term has been borrowed from art, where it denotes ludicrously exaggerated sketches or drawings of people.

Generally, caricatures are created deliberately—for the purposes of humor or satire. Sometimes, however, they result because an author has failed to provide a character with a mix of traits that produces the illusion of lifelikeness, or plausibility. In "The Most Dangerous Game" Richard Connell created a caricature in Ivan, the big, strong, dim-witted Cossack. By contrast, it would be a mistake to think of Framton in "The Open Window" as a caricature. Even though the poor fellow is gullible, we know too much about what is going on in his mind to call him a caricature.

Some characters in a story change because of the tensions and drama of the story, and others do not change. A character who changes is often called *dynamic*; one who stays the same is said to be *static*. A character can change and still be consistent, providing the motivation for the change is great enough.

Generally, the protagonist is the story's most dynamic character. Sometimes, however, other characters also change because of what the protagonist does or what is done to the protagonist. Even antagonists may be dynamic, especially if they become sympathetic to or intrigued by the protagonist.

Character change need not be complete or even major to be significant. A simple alteration in attitude, if it is consistent with motivation, can render a character dynamic. Rainsford is the most dynamic character in "The Most Dangerous Game." Clearly he undergoes a significant change, making it possible for him to kill General Zaroff. In "The Open Window" Framton undergoes the greatest change; his condition becomes markedly worse.

An acquaintance with two additional conventions is important to an understanding of the delineation of character in the modern short story—the use of *foils* and the depiction of the *confident(e)*. A *foil* is a person who makes someone else seem better by contrast. One of the best ways to make a brave character appear even braver is to put him next to a coward. A smart woman is even smarter next to a dull one. Although you might automatically think of the antagonist as the foil of the protagonist, this is not always the case. In fact, the protagonist and antagonist may be very much alike. Foils, especially the foils of major characters, are quite often minor characters employed to highlight the major character's most striking traits. Ivan may be considered General Zaroff's foil in "The Most Dangerous Game," and Vera is clearly Framton's foil in "The Open Window."

The use of the confidant is one of the oldest devices in literature. A *confidant* is a close and trusted friend, a sidekick, usually of the protagonist. The protagonist talks to and confides in the confidant, thereby informing the reader about the personality of the protagonist. Examples of the protagonist-confidant relationship are legion. From Cervantes' classic novel *Don Quixote de la Mancha* we have Don Quixote and his confidant Sancho Panza; from Arthur Conan Doyle's detective stories we have Sherlock Holmes and his confidant Dr. Watson; from Shakespeare's play *Romeo and Juliet* we have Juliet and her confidante the nurse. One additional point to be remembered here is that it is not unusual for the protagonist's confidant also to be a foil. Dr. Watson, for example, is both foil to and confidant of Sherlock Holmes.

We will conclude this account of characterization with a brief discussion of *archetypal characters*. For almost as long as we human beings have reflected upon the nature of literature or upon human nature we have assumed the existence of similar themes, plots, and characters in the literature of all peoples advanced enough to have a literature. Time and scholarship have substantiated this assumption. These universal, recurring themes, plots, and characters are known as *archetypes*.

Archetypal characters are characters that have consistently appeared in the literature of all peoples throughout human history. We say that they are true to the human experience. Examples of archetypal characters include the *femme fatale*, the irresistible woman who leads men into difficult or disastrous situations; the earth mother, the all-encompassing woman who is consistently driven to nurture all living things; the Christ figure, or scapegoat, the character who knowingly lays down his life for the benefit of others or is chosen to bear others' guilt; the damned, the individual to whom the gods or fates have decided to be unkind no matter what; the pilgrim, the character who constantly searches for something never to be found; the alter ego, a character who is the double or counterpart of another person in the story. We shall have more to say about archetypes later on.

Taking care not to overlook the plot elements already discussed, let's apply what we have learned about character to an analysis of James Thurber's "The Secret Life of Walter Mitty" and Irwin Shaw's "The Dry Rock."

JAMES THURBER

The Secret Life of Walter Mitty

"We're going through!" The Commander's voice was like thin ice breaking. He wore his full-dress uniform, with the heavily braided white cap pulled down rakishly over one cold gray eye. "We can't make it, sir. It's spoiling for a hurricane, if you ask me." "I'm not asking you, Lieutenant Berg," said the Commander. "Throw on the power lights! Rev her up to 8,500! We're going through!" The pounding of the cylinders increased: ta-pocketa-pocketa-pocketa-*pocketa-pocketa*. The Commander stared at the ice forming on the pilot window. He walked over and twisted a row of complicated dials. "Switch on No. 8 auxiliary!" he shouted. "Switch on No. 8 auxiliary!" repeated Lieutenant Berg. "Full strength in No. 3 turret!" shouted the Commander. "Full strength in No. 3 turret!" The crew, bending to their various tasks in the huge, hurtling eight-engined Navy hydroplane, looked at each other and grinned. "The Old Man'll get us through," they said to one another. "The Old Man ain't afraid of Hell!" . . .

"Not so fast! You're driving too fast!" said Mrs. Mitty. "What are you driving so fast for?"

"Hmm?" said Walter Mitty. He looked at his wife, in the seat beside him, with shocked astonishment. She seemed grossly unfamiliar, like a strange woman who had yelled at him in a crowd. "You were up to fifty-five," she said. "You know I don't like to go more than forty. You were up to fifty-five." Walter Mitty drove on toward Waterbury in silence, the roaring of the SN202 through the worst storm in twenty years of Navy flying fading in the remote, intimate airways of his mind. "You're tensed up again," said Mrs. Mitty. "It's one of your days. I wish you'd let Dr. Renshaw look you over."

Walter Mitty stopped the car in front of the building where his wife went to have her hair done. "Remember to get those overshoes while I'm having my hair done," she said. "I don't need overshoes," said Mitty. She put her mirror back into her bag. "We've been all through that," she said, getting out of the car. "You're not a young man any longer." He raced the engine a little. "Why don't you wear your gloves? Have you lost your gloves?" Walter Mitty reached in a pocket and brought out the gloves. He put them on, but after she had turned and gone into the building and he had driven on to a red light, he took them off again. "Pick it up, brother!" snapped a cop as the light changed, and Mitty hastily pulled on his gloves and lurched ahead. He drove around the streets aimlessly for a time, and then he drove past the hospital on his way to the parking lot.

. . . "It's the millionaire banker, Wellington McMillan," said the pretty nurse. "Yes?" said Walter Mitty, removing his gloves slowly. "Who has the case?" "Dr. Renshaw and Dr. Benbow, but there are two specialists here, Dr. Remington from New York and Mr. Pritchard-Mitford from London. He flew over." A door opened down a long, cool corridor and Dr. Renshaw came out. He looked distraught and haggard. "Hello, Mitty," he said. "We're having the devil's own time with McMillan, the millionaire banker and close personal friend of Roosevelt. Obstreosis of the ductal tract. Tertiary. Wish you'd take a look at him." "Glad to," said Mitty.

In the operating room there were whispered introductions: "Dr. Remington, Dr. Mitty. Mr. Pritchard-Mitford, Dr. Mitty." "I've read your book on strepto-thricosis," said Pritchard-Mitford, shaking hands. "A brilliant performance, sir." "Thank you," said Walter Mitty. "Didn't know you were in the States, Mitty," grumbled Remington. "Coals to Newcastle, bringing Mitford and me up here for a tertiary." "You are very kind," said Mitty. A huge, complicated machine, connected to the operating table, with many tubes and wires, began at this moment to go pocketa-pocketa-pocketa. "The new anesthetizer is giving way!" shouted an interne. "There is no one in the East who knows how to fix it!" "Quiet, man!" said Mitty, in a low, cool voice. He sprang to the machine, which was now going pocketa-pocketa-queep-pocketa-queep. He began fingering delicately a row of glistening dials. "Give me a fountain pen!" he snapped. Someone handed him a fountain pen. He pulled a faulty piston out of the machine and inserted the pen in its place. "That will hold for ten minutes," he said. "Get on with the operation." A nurse hurried over and whispered to Renshaw, and Mitty saw the man turn pale. "Coreopsis has set in," said Renshaw nervously. "If you would take over, Mitty?" Mitty looked at him and at the craven figure of Benbow, who drank, and at the grave, uncertain faces of the two great specialists. "If you wish," he said. They slipped a white gown on him; he adjusted a mask and drew on thin gloves; nurses handed him shining . . .

"Back it up, Mac! Look out for that Buick!" Walter Mitty jammed on the brakes. "Wrong lane, Mac," said the parking-lot attendant, looking at Mitty closely. "Gee. Yeh," muttered Mitty. He began cautiously to back out of the lane marked "Exit Only." "Leave her sit there," said the attendant. "I'll put her away." Mitty got out of the car. "Hey, better leave the key." "Oh," said Mitty, handing the man the ignition key. The attendant vaulted into the car, backed it up with insolent skill, and put it where it belonged.

They're so damn cocky, thought Walter Mitty, walking along Main Street; they think they know everything. Once he had tried to take his chains off, outside New Milford, and he had got them wound around the axles. A man had had to come out in a wrecking car and unwind them, a young, grinning garageman. Since then Mrs. Mitty always made him drive to a garage to have the chains taken off. The next time, he thought, I'll wear my right arm in a sling; they won't grin at me then. I'll have my right arm in a sling and they'll see I couldn't possibly take the chains off myself. He kicked at the slush on the sidewalk. "Overshoes," he said to himself, and he began looking for a shoe store.

When he came out into the street again, with the overshoes in a box under his arm, Walter Mitty began to wonder what the other thing was his wife had told him to get. She had told him, twice, before they set out from their house for Waterbury. In a way he hated these weekly trips to town—he was always getting something wrong. Kleenex, he thought, Squibb's, razor blades? No. Toothpaste, toothbrush, bicarbonate, carborundum, initiative and referendum? He gave it up. But she would remember it. "Where's the what's-its-name?" she would ask. "Don't tell me you forgot the what's-its-name." A newsboy went by shouting something about the Waterbury trial.

. . . "Perhaps this will refresh your memory." The District Attorney suddenly thrust a heavy automatic at the quiet figure on the witness stand. "Have you ever seen this before?" Walter Mitty took the gun and examined it expertly. "This is my Webley-Vickers 50.80," he said calmly. An excited buzz ran around the courtroom. The Judge rapped for order. "You are a crack shot with any sort of firearms, I believe?" said the District Attorney, insinuatingly. "Objection!" shouted Mitty's attorney. "We have shown that the defendant could not have fired the shot. We have shown that he wore his right arm in a sling on the night of the fourteenth of July." Walter Mitty raised his hand briefly and the bickering attorneys were stilled. "With any known make of gun," he said evenly, "I could have killed Gregory Fitzhurst at three hundred feet *with my left hand*." Pandemonium broke loose in the courtroom. A woman's scream rose above the bedlam and suddenly a lovely, dark-haired girl was in Walter Mitty's arms. The District Attorney struck at her savagely. Without rising from his chair, Mitty let the man have it on the point of the chin. "You miserable cur!" . . .

"Puppy biscuit," said Walter Mitty. He stopped walking and the buildings of Waterbury rose up out of the misty courtroom and surrounded him again. A woman who was passing laughed. "He said 'Puppy biscuit,' " she said to her companion. "That man said 'Puppy biscuit' to himself." Walter Mitty hurried on. He went into an A. & P., not the first one he came to but a smaller one farther up the street. "I want some biscuit for small, young dogs," he said to the clerk. "Any special brand, sir?" The greatest pistol shot in the world thought a moment. "It says 'Puppies Bark for It' on the box," said Walter Mitty.

His wife would be through at the hairdresser's in fifteen minutes, Mitty saw in looking at his watch, unless they had trouble drying it; sometimes they had trouble drying it. She didn't like to get to the hotel first; she would want him to be there waiting for her as usual. He found a big leather chair in the lobby, facing a window, and he put the overshoes and the puppy biscuit on the floor beside it. He picked up an old copy of *Liberty* and sank down into the chair. "Can Germany Conquer the World Through the Air?" Walter Mitty looked at the pictures of bombing planes and of ruined streets.

. . . "The cannonading has got the wind up in young Raleigh, sir," said the sergeant. Captain Mitty looked up at him through touseled hair. "Get him to bed," he said wearily. "With the others. I'll fly alone." "But you can't, sir," said the sergeant anxiously. "It takes two men to handle that bomber and the Archies are pounding hell out of the air. Von Richtman's circus is between here and Saulier." "Somebody's got to get that ammunition dump," said Mitty. "I'm going over. Spot of brandy?" He poured a drink for the sergeant and one for himself. War thundered and whined around the dugout and battered at the door. There was a rending of wood and splinters flew through the room. "A bit of a near thing," said Captain Mitty carelessly. "The box barrage is closing in," said the sergeant. "We only live once, Sergeant," said Mitty, with his faint, fleeting smile. "Or do we?" He poured another brandy and tossed it off. "I never see a man could hold his brandy like you, sir," said the sergeant. "Begging your pardon, sir." Captain Mitty stood up and strapped on his huge Webley-Vickers automatic. "It's forty kilometers through hell, sir," said the sergeant. Mitty finished one last brandy. "After all," he said softly, "what isn't?" The pounding of the cannon increased; there was the rat-tat-tatting of machine guns, and from somewhere came the menacing pock-eta-pocketa-pocketa of the new flame-throwers. Walter Mitty walked to the door of the dugout humming "Auprès de Ma Blonde." He turned and waved to the sergeant. "Cheerio!" he said. . . .

Something struck his shoulder. "I've been looking all over this hotel for you," said Mrs. Mitty. "Why do you have to hide in this old chair? How did you expect me to find you?" "Things close in," said Walter Mitty vaguely. "What?" Mrs. Mitty said. "Did you get the what's-its-name? The puppy biscuit? What's in that box?" "Overshoes," said Mitty. "Couldn't you have put them on in the store?" "I was thinking," said Walter Mitty. "Does it ever occur to you that I am sometimes thinking?" She looked at him. "I'm going to take your temperature when I get you home," she said.

They went out through the revolving doors that made a faintly derisive whistling sound when you pushed them. It was two blocks to the parking lot. At the drugstore on the corner she said, "Wait here for me. I forgot something. I won't be a minute." She was more than a minute. Walter Mitty lighted a cigarette. It began to rain, rain with sleet in it. He stood up against the wall of the drugstore, smoking. . . . He put his shoulders back and his heels together. "To hell with the handkerchief," said Walter Mitty scornfully. He took one last drag on his cigarette and snapped it away. Then, with that faint, fleeting smile playing about his lips, he faced the firing squad; erect and motionless, proud and disdainful, Walter Mitty the Undefeated, inscrutable to the last.

BY WAY OF DISCUSSION

"The Secret Life of Walter Mitty" is an excellent example of a story that is completely dominated by a single character. Furthermore, the story gives us an example of a fictional character who has come to epitomize every real-life impractical dreamer. Since 1939, when the story first appeared in *The New Yorker*, millions of readers have taken poor Mitty to their hearts. Today, the term "Walter Mitty" even appears in some dictionaries. For example, *Webster's New Collegiate Dictionary* defines it as "a commonplace unadventurous person who seeks escape from reality through daydreaming."

Despite Mitty's popularity, daydreaming has seldom been regarded as a praiseworthy activity, especially in a no-nonsense society like our own. At best, daydreamers can expect to be dubbed "impractical" or "lazy." At worst, they have been regarded as potential recruits of the Evil One—perhaps on the assumption that "the devil makes work for idle hands." Nonetheless, daydreaming has always been, and continues to be, a universal human activity.

People daydream to compensate for things that are lacking in their lives—romance, respect, the opportunity to play a significant and satisfying role in the world's affairs. Whatever their individual reasons, people daydream, although perhaps not so frequently or flamboyantly as Walter Mitty.

In real life Mitty is not only forgetful and mechanically inept, he is also married to an overbearing henpecker who seems to regard herself more as an exacting mother than as a marriage partner. And that's not all: in his day-to-day activities, Mitty constantly encounters other authority figures—policemen, parking-lot attendants, mechanics—who do their bit to point up his all-too-obvious shortcomings. Small wonder, then, that he constantly seeks escape in daydreams.

Perhaps because daydreamers are after a quick emotional "fix," accuracy often goes by the board in their fantasies. Mitty's daydreams abound in inaccuracies. In his first daydream, Mitty confuses a hydroplane—that is, a motorboat designed to skim along the surface of the water at high speeds—with an airplane. He also imagines himself in a full-dress military uniform, which would actually be worn only on formal or ceremonial occasions. In the second daydream, the stricken banker, Wellington McMillan, develops "coreopsis," in reality a genus of flowering plant. And in the fourth daydream, the Germans are mistakenly called "Archies" rather than "Jerries."

Mitty's daydreams are further characterized by clichés and inept dialogue. Thus, Captain Mitty has a voice like "thin ice breaking," and he wears his cap "pulled down rakishly over one cold gray eye." As he greets Dr. Mitty, Dr. Renshaw whispers, "We're having the devil's own time with McMillan, the millionaire banker and close personal friend of Roosevelt," thereby dragging in factual background information in an incongruous and unbelievable manner. Incidentally, it would appear that Mitty has more than a nodding acquaintance with lurid pulp literature, perhaps the source of many of his own machinations.

Throughout his first three daydreams, Mitty presents himself as a veritable superman. In the first, his superiority stems from physical courage. In the next two, it is based upon special expertise in medicine and guns, combined in the first instance with mechanical genius and in the second with chivalric courage. In each instance, the daydream is both triggered and terminated by some external event—a shouting newsboy, a snapping wife—facts suggesting the ultimate power of the real world to control the fantasy world.

In the German daydream, however, things change, and we see a Walter Mitty who differs sharply from the caricature of the earlier fantasies. Although still heroic, the new Mitty speaks wearily and agrees with the sergeant that life is "forty kilometers through hell"—things the other daydream Mittys would never have done. The real world seems to invade this daydream and Mitty may be about to lose the refuge of his fantasies. At this point in the story Mitty ironically becomes something of a hero, although a hero quite different from the sort he had imagined. Threatened with the possibility of losing his refuge, Mitty bravely accepts the prospect. In what might well be his final heroic fantasy, he says, "To hell with the handkerchief," a line that can be taken to symbolize his acceptance of whatever might come. In today's world, so this ending suggests, there is little or no room for brave deeds. The only heroism possible for most of us consists of enduring with fortitude whatever we must. All of this, it goes without saying, renders Mitty a dynamic character; he is in a process of change. In his own way, he is coming to grips with the real world.

Throughout the course of the story, Thurber never comments directly about Walter Mitty's character. Rather, we are left to make deductions about the character on the basis of Mitty's thoughts and actions and the comments and behavior of the people Mitty encounters. In Mitty's daydreams, however—which very much resemble bad fiction—character is presented directly. We are *told* that Dr. Renshaw is distraught and that Dr. Benbow is craven. Thurber's use of both techniques of characterization demonstrates the superiority of characterization by dramatization. Thurber, it would appear, knows more about the presentation of character than does Mitty.

Although we have not yet discussed symbols in any great detail, we must briefly call attention to two symbols that appear in this story—the gloves and the sling. When worn by Mitty between his daydreams, both are symbols of weakness. The first denotes Mitty's henpecked status, the second his mechanical ineptitude. In the daydreams, however, they are transformed into symbols of strength.

At the start of the second daydream, Mitty removes his gloves slowly—when he *wants* to remove them. At the end of the dream, he draws on thin surgeon's gloves as he prepares to perform the operation that his colleagues cannot handle. This is an instance of ironic symbolism—a subject that we will return to. In any event, it is clear that every element of the daydreams, not just the action, is designed to reinforce the image of Mitty as a self-imagined superman.

IRWIN SHAW

The Dry Rock

"We're late," Helen said, as the cab stopped at a light. "We're twenty minutes late." She looked at her husband accusingly.

"All right," Fitzsimmons said. "I couldn't help it. The work was on the desk and it had to . . ."

"This is the one dinner party of the year I didn't want to be late for," Helen said. "So naturally . . ."

The cab started and was halfway across the street when the Ford sedan roared into it, twisting, with a crashing and scraping of metal, a high mournful scream of brakes, the tinkling of glass. The cab shook a little, then subsided.

The cabby, a little gray man, turned and looked back, worriedly. "Everybody is all right?" he asked nervously.

"Everybody is fine," Helen said bitterly, pulling at her cape to get it straight again after the jolting.

"No damage done," said Fitzsimmons, smiling reassuringly at the cabby, who looked very frightened.

"I am happy to hear that," the cabby said. He got out of his car and stood looking sadly at his fender, now thoroughly crumpled, and his headlight, now without a lens. The door of the Ford opened and its driver sprang out. He was a large young man with a light gray hat. He glanced hurriedly at the cab.

"Why don't yuh watch where the hell yer goin'?" he asked harshly.

"The light was in my favor," said the cabby. He was a small man of fifty, in a cap and a ragged coat, and he spoke with a heavy accent. "It turned green and I started across. I would like your license, Mister."

"What for?" the man in the gray hat shouted. "Yer load's all right. Get on yer way. No harm done." He started back to his car.

The cabby gently put his hand on the young man's arm. "Excuse me, friend," he said. "It is a five-dollar job, at least. I would like to see your license."

The young man pulled his arm away, glared at the cabby. "Aaah," he said and swung. His fist made a loud, surprising noise against the cabby's nose. The old man sat down slowly on the running board of his cab, holding his head wearily in his hands. The young man in the gray hat stood over him, bent over, fists still clenched. "Didn't I tell yuh no harm was done?" he shouted. "Why didn't yuh lissen t' me? I got a good mind to . . ."

"Now, see here," Fitzsimmons said, opening the rear door and stepping out.

"What d'you want?" The young man turned and snarled at Fitzsimmons, his fists held higher. "Who asked for you?"

"I saw the whole thing," Fitzsimmons began, "and I don't think you . . ."

"Aaah," snarled the young man. "Dry up."

"Claude," Helen called. "Claude, keep out of this."

"Claude," the young man repeated balefully. "Dry up, Claude."

"Are you all right?" Fitzsimmons asked, bending over the cabby, who still sat reflectively on the running board, his head down, his old and swollen cap hiding his face, blood trickling down his clothes.

"I'm all right," the cabby said wearily. He stood up, looked wonderingly at the young man. "Now, my friend, you force me to make trouble. Police!" he called, loudly. "*Police!*"

"Say, lissen," the man in the gray hat shouted. "What the hell do yuh need to call the cops for? Hey, cut it out!"

"*Police!*" the old cabby shouted calmly, but with fervor deep in his voice. "Police!"

"I ought to give it to yuh good." The young man shook his fist under the cabby's nose. He jumped around nervously. "This is a small matter," he shouted, "nobody needs the cops!"

"Police!" called the cabby.

"Claude," Helen put her head out the window. "Let's get out of here and let the two gentlemen settle this any way they please."

"I apologize!" The young man held the cabby by his lapels with both large hands, shook him, to emphasize his apology. "Excuse me. I'm sorry. Stop yelling police, for God's sake!"

"I'm going to have you locked up," the cabby said. He stood there, slowly drying the blood off his shabby coat with his cap. His hair was gray, but long and full, like a musician's. He had a big head for his little shoulders, and a sad, lined little face and he looked older than fifty, to Fitzsimmons, and very poor, neglected, badly nourished. "You have committed a crime," the cabby said, "and there is a punishment for it."

"Will yuh talk to him?" The young man turned savagely to Fitzsimmons. "Will yuh tell him I'm sorry?"

"It's entirely up to him," Fitzsimmons said.

"We're a half hour late," Helen announced bitterly. "The perfect dinner guests."

"It is not enough to be sorry," said the cab driver. "*Police . . .*"

"Say, listen, Bud," the young man said, his voice quick and confidential, "what's yer name?"

"Leopold Tarloff," the cabby said. "I have been driving a cab on the streets of New York for twenty years, and everybody thinks just because you're a cab driver they can do whatever they want to you."

"Lissen, Leopold," the young man pushed his light gray hat far back on his head. "Let's be sensible. I hit yer cab. All right. I hit you. All right."

"What's all right about it?" Tarloff asked.

"What I mean is, I admit it, I confess I did it, that's what I mean. All right." The young man grabbed Tarloff's short ragged arms as he spoke, intensely. "Why the fuss? It happens every day. Police are unnecessary. I'll tell yuh what

I'll do with yuh, Leopold. Five dollars, yuh say, for the fender. All right. And for the bloody nose, another pound. What do yuh say? Everybody is satisfied. Yuh've made yerself a fiver on the transaction; these good people go to their party without no more delay."

Tarloff shook his arms free from the huge hands of the man in the gray hat. He put his head back and ran his fingers through his thick hair and spoke coldly. "I don't want to hear another word. I have never been so insulted in my whole life."

The young man stepped back, his arms wide, palms up wonderingly. "I insult him!" He turned to Fitzsimmons. "Did you hear me insult this party?" he asked.

"Claude!" Helen called. "Are we going to sit here all night?"

"A man steps up and hits me in the nose," Tarloff said. "He thinks he makes everything all right with five dollars. He is mistaken. Not with five hundred dollars."

"How much d'yuh think a clap in the puss is worth?" the young man growled. "Who d'yuh think y'are—Joe Louis?"

"Not ten thousand dollars," Tarloff said, on the surface calm, but quivering underneath. "Not for twenty thousand dollars. My dignity."

"His dignity!" the young man whispered. "For Christ's sake!"

"What do you want to do?" Fitzsimmons asked, conscious of Helen glooming in the rear seat of the cab.

"I would like to take him to the station house and make a complaint," Tarloff said. "You would have to come with me, if you'd be so kind. What is your opinion on the matter?"

"Will yuh tell him the cops are not a necessity!" the young man said hoarsely. "Will yuh tell the bastidd?"

"Claude!" called Helen.

"It's up to you," Fitzsimmons said, looking with what he hoped was an impartial, judicious expression at Tarloff, hoping he wouldn't have to waste any more time. "You do what you think you ought to do."

Tarloff smiled, showing three yellow teeth in the front of his small and childlike mouth, curved and red and surprising in the lined and weather-beaten old hackie's face. "Thank you very much," he said. "I am glad to see you agree with me."

Fitzsimmons sighed.

"Yer drivin' me crazy!" the young man shouted at Tarloff. "Yer makin' life impossible!"

"To you," Tarloff said with dignity, "I talk from now on only in a court of law. That's my last word."

The young man stood there, breathing heavily, his fists clenching and un-clenching, his pale gray hat shining in the light of a street lamp. A policeman turned the corner, walking in a leisurely and abstracted manner, his eyes on the legs of a girl across the street.

Fitzsimmons went over to him. "Officer," he said, "there's a little job for you over here." The policeman regretfully took his eyes off the girl's legs and sighed and walked slowly over to where the two cars were still nestling against each other.

"What are yuh?" the young man was asking Tarloff, when Fitzsimmons came up with the policeman. "Yuh don't act like an American citizen. What are yuh?"

"I'm a Russian," Tarloff said. "But I'm in the country twenty-five years now, I know what the rights of an individual are."

"Yeah," said the young man hopelessly. "Yeah . . ."

The Fitzsimmonses drove silently to the police station in the cab, with Tarloff driving slowly and carefully, though with hands that shook on the wheel. The policeman drove with the young man in the young man's Ford. Fitzsimmons saw the Ford stop at a cigar store and the young man jump out and go into the store, into a telephone booth.

"For three months," Helen said, as they drove, "I've been trying to get Adele Lowrie to invite us to dinner. Now we've finally managed it. Perhaps we ought to call her and invite the whole party down to night court."

"It isn't night court," Fitzsimmons said patiently. "It's a police station. And I think you might take it a little better. After all, the poor old man has no one else to speak up for him."

"Leopold Tarloff," Helen said. "It sounds impossible. Leopold Tarloff. Leopold Tarloff."

They sat in silence until Tarloff stopped the cab in front of the police station and opened the door for them. The Ford with the policeman and the young man drove up right behind them and they all went in together.

There were some people up in front of the desk lieutenant, a dejected-looking man with long mustaches and a loud, blonde woman who kept saying that the man had threatened her with a baseball bat three times that evening. Two Negroes with bloody bandages around their heads were waiting, too.

"It will take some time," said the policeman. "There are two cases ahead of you. My name is Kraus."

"Oh, my," said Helen.

"You'd better call Adele," Fitzsimmons said. "Tell her not to hold dinner for us."

Helen held her hand out gloomily for nickels.

"I'm sorry," Tarloff said anxiously, "to interrupt your plans for the evening."

"Perfectly all right," Fitzsimmons said, trying to screen his wife's face from Tarloff by bending over to search for the nickels in his pocket.

Helen went off, disdainfully holding her long formal skirt up with her hand, as she walked down the spit- and butt-marked corridor of the police station toward a pay telephone. Fitzsimmons reflectively watched her elegant back retreat down the hallway.

"I am tired," Tarloff said. "I think I will have to sit down, if you will excuse me." He sat on the floor, looking up with a frail, apologetic smile on his red face worn by wind and rain and traffic-policemen. Fitzsimmons suddenly felt like crying, watching the old man sitting there among the spit and cigarette butts, on the floor against the wall, with his cap off and his great bush of musician's gray hair giving the lie to the tired, weathered face below it.

Four men threw open the outside doors and walked into the police station with certainty and authority. They all wore the same light-gray hats with the huge flat brims. The young man who had hit Tarloff greeted them guardedly. "I'm glad you're here, Pidgear," he said to the man who, by some subtle mixture of stance and clothing, of lift of eyebrow and droop of mouth, announced himself as leader.

They talked swiftly and quietly in a corner.

"A Russian!" Pidgear's voice rang out angrily. "There are 10,000 cab drivers in the metropolitan area, you have to pick a Russian to punch in the nose!"

"I'm excitable!" the young man yelled. "Can I help it if I'm excitable? My father was the same way; it's a family characteristic."

"Go tell that to the Russian," Pidgear said. He went over to one of the three men who had come in with him, a large man who needed a shave and whose collar was open at the throat, as though no collar could be bought large enough to go all the way around that neck. The large man nodded, went over to Tarloff, still sitting patiently against the wall.

"You speak Russian?" the man with the open collar said to Tarloff.

"Yes, sir," Tarloff said.

The large man sat down slowly beside him, gripped Tarloff's knee confidentially in his tremendous hairy hand, spoke excitedly, winningly, in Russian.

Pidgear and the young man who had hit Tarloff came over to Fitzsimmons, leaving the other two men in the gray hats, small, dark men with shining eyes, who just stood at the door and looked hotly on.

"My name is Pidgear," the man said to Fitzsimmons, who by now was impressed with the beautiful efficiency of the system that had been put into motion by the young driver of the Ford—an obviously legal mind like Pidgear, a man who spoke Russian, and two intense men with gray hats standing on call just to see justice done, and all collected in the space of fifteen minutes. "Alton Pidgear," the man said, smiling professionally at Fitzsimmons. "I represent Mr. Rusk."

"Yeah," said the young man.

"My name is Fitzsimmons."

"Frankly, Mr. Fitzsimmons," Pidgear said, "I would like to see you get Mr. Tarloff to call this whole thing off. It's an embarrassing affair for all concerned; nobody stands to gain anything by pressing it."

Helen came back and Fitzsimmons saw by the expression on her face that she wasn't happy. "They're at the soup by now," she said loudly to Fitzsimmons. "Adele said for us to take all the time we want, they're getting along fine."

"Mr. Rusk is willing to make a handsome offer," Pidgear said. "Five dollars for the car, five dollars for the nose . . ."

"Go out to dinner with your husband," Helen muttered, "and you wind up in a telephone booth in a police station. 'Excuse me for being late, darling, but I'm calling from the 8th Precinct, this is our night for street-fighting.' "

"Sssh, Helen, please," Fitzsimmons said. He hadn't eaten since nine that morning and his stomach was growling with hunger.

"It was all a mistake," Pidgear said smoothly. "A natural mistake. Why should the man be stubborn? He is being reimbursed for everything, isn't he? I wish you would talk to him, Mr. Fitzsimmons; we don't want to keep you from your social engagements. Undoubtedly," Pidgear said, eyeing their evening clothes respectfully, "you and the madam were going to an important dinner party. It would be too bad to spoil an important dinner party for a little thing like this. Why, this whole affair is niggling," he said, waving his hand in front of Fitzsimmons' face. "Absolutely niggling."

Fitzsimmons looked over to where Tarloff and the other Russian were sitting on the floor. From Tarloff's face and gestures, even though he was talking in deepest Russian, Fitzsimmons could tell Tarloff was still as firm as ever. Fitzsimmons looked closely at Rusk, who was standing looking at Tarloff through narrow, baleful eyes.

"Why're you so anxious?" Fitzsimmons asked.

Rusk's eyes clouded over and his throat throbbed against his collar with rage. "I don't want to appear in court!" he yelled. "I don't want the whole goddamn business to start all over again, investigation, lawyers, fingerprints . . ."

Pidgear punched him savagely in the ribs, his fist going a short distance, but with great violence.

"Why don't you buy time on the National Broadcasting System?" Pidgear asked. "Make an address, coast to coast!"

Rusk glared murderously for a moment at Pidgear, then leaned over toward Fitzsimmons, pointing a large blunt finger at him. "Do I have to put my finger in your mouth?" he whispered hoarsely.

"What does he mean by that?" Helen asked loudly. "Put his finger in your mouth? Why should he put his finger in your mouth?"

Rusk looked at her with complete hatred, turned, too full for words, and stalked away, with Pidgear after him. The two little men in the gray hats watched the room without moving.

"Claude?" Helen began.

"Obviously," Fitzsimmons said, his voice low, "Mr. Rusk isn't anxious for anyone to look at his fingerprints. He's happier this way."

"You picked a fine night!" Helen shook her head sadly. "Why can't we just pick up and get out of here?"

Rusk, with Pidgear at his side, strode back. He stopped in front of the Fitzsimmonses. "I'm a family man," he said, trying to sound like one. "I ask yuh as a favor. Talk to the Russian."

"I had to go to Bergdorf Goodman," Helen said, too deep in her own troubles to bother with Rusk, "to get a gown to spend the evening in a police station. 'Mrs. Claude Fitzsimmons was lovely last night in blue velvet and silver fox at Officer Kraus's reception at the 8th Precinct. Other guests were the well-known Leopold Tarloff, and the Messrs. Pidgear and Rusk, in gray hats. Other guests included the Russian Ambassador and two leading Italian artillerymen, also in gray hats.' "

Pidgear laughed politely. "Your wife is a very witty woman," he said.

"Yes," said Fitzsimmons, wondering why he'd married her.

"Will yuh for Christ's sake *ask*?" Rusk demanded. "Can it hurt yuh?"

"We're willing to do our part," Pidgear said. "We even brought down a Russian to talk to him and clear up any little points in his own language. No effort is too great."

Fitzsimmons' stomach growled loudly. "Haven't eaten all day," he said, embarrassed.

"That's what happens," Pidgear said. "Naturally."

"Yeah," said Rusk.

"Perhaps I should go out and get you a malted milk," Helen suggested coldly.

Fitzsimmons went over to where Tarloff was sitting with the other Russian. The others followed him.

"Are you sure, Mr. Tarloff," Fitzsimmons said, "that you still want to prosecute?"

"Yes," Tarloff said promptly.

"Ten dollars," Rusk said. "I offer yuh ten dollars. Can a man do more?"

"Money is not the object." With his cap Tarloff patted his nose, which was still bleeding slowly and had swelled enormously, making Tarloff look lopsided and monstrous.

"What's the object?" Rusk asked.

"The object, Mr. Rusk, is principle."

"*You* talk to him," Rusk said to Fitzsimmons.

"All right," Officer Kraus said, "you can go up there now."

They all filed in in front of the lieutenant sitting high at his desk.

Tarloff told his story, the accident, the wanton punch in the nose.

"It's true," Pidgear said, "that there was an accident, that there was a slight scuffle after by mistake. But the man isn't hurt. A little swelling in the region of the nose. No more." He pointed dramatically to Tarloff.

"Physically," Tarloff said, clutching his cap, talking with difficulty because his nose was clogged, "physically that's true. I am not badly hurt. But in a mental sense . . ." He shrugged. "I have suffered an injury."

"Mr. Rusk is offering the amount of ten dollars," Pidgear said. "Also, he apologizes; he's sorry."

The lieutenant looked wearily down at Rusk. "Are you sorry?" he asked.

"I'm sorry," said Rusk, raising his right hand. "On the Bible, I swear I'm sorry."

"Mr. Tarloff," the lieutenant said, "if you wish to press charges, there are certain steps you will have to take. A deposition will have to be taken. Have you got witnesses?"

"Here," Tarloff said with a shy smile at the Fitzsimmonses.

"They will have to be present," the lieutenant said sleepily.

"Oh, God," Helen said.

"A warrant will have to be sworn out, there must be a hearing, at which the witnesses must also be present . . ."

"Oh, God," Helen said.

"Then the trial," said the lieutenant.

"Oh, God!" Helen said loudly.

"The question is, Mr. Tarloff," said the lieutenant, yawning, "are you willing to go through all that trouble?"

"The fact is," Tarloff said unhappily, "he hit me in the head without provocation. He is guilty of a crime on my person. He insulted me. He did me an injustice. The law exists for such things. One individual is not to be hit by another individual in the streets of the city without legal punishment." Tarloff was using his hands to try to get everyone, the Fitzsimmonses, the lieutenant, Pidgear, to understand. "There is a principle. The dignity of the human body. Justice. For a bad act a man suffers. It's an important thing . . ."

"I'm excitable," Rusk shouted. "If yuh want, yuh can hit me in the head."

"That is not the idea," Tarloff said.

"The man is sorry," the lieutenant said, wiping his eyes, "he is offering you the sum of ten dollars; it will be a long, hard job to bring this man to trial; it will cost a lot of the taxpayers' money; you are bothering these good people here who have other things to do. What is the sense in it, Mr. Tarloff?"

Tarloff scraped his feet slowly on the dirty floor, looked sadly, hopefully, at Fitzsimmons. Fitzsimmons looked at his wife, who was glaring at Tarloff, tapping her foot sharply again and again. Fitzsimmons looked back at Tarloff, standing there, before the high desk, small, in his ragged coat and wild gray hair, his little worn face twisted and grotesque with the swollen nose, his eyes lost and appealing. Fitzsimmons shrugged sadly. Tarloff drooped inside his old coat, shook his head wearily, shrugged, deserted once and for all before the lieutenant's desk, on the dry rock of principle.

"O.K.," he said.

"Here," Rusk brought the ten-dollar bill out with magical speed.

Tarloff pushed it away. "Get out of here," he said, without looking up.

No one talked all the way to Adele Lowrie's house. Tarloff opened the door and sat, looking straight ahead, while they got out. Helen went to the door of the house and rang. Silently, Fitzsimmons offered Tarloff the fare. Tarloff shook his head. "You have been very good," he said. "Forget it."

Fitzsimmons put the money away slowly.

"Claude!" Helen called. "The door's open."

Fitzsimmons hated his wife, suddenly, without turning to look at her. He put out his hand and Tarloff shook it wearily.

"I'm awfully sorry," Fitzsimmons said. "I wish I . . ."

Tarloff shrugged. "That's all right," he said. "I understand." His face, in the shabby light of the cab, worn and old and battered by the streets of the city, was a deep well of sorrow. "There is no time. Principle." He laughed, shrugged. "Today there is no time for anything."

He shifted gears and the taxi moved slowly off, its motor grinding noisily.

"Claude!" Helen called.

"Oh, shut up!" Fitzsimmons said as he turned and walked into Adele Lowrie's house.

BY WAY OF DISCUSSION

Irwin Shaw's "The Dry Rock" comes very close to being a brief treatise on the death of principle in modern society. Each point in the thesis is presented as a result of the interactions of a small group of carefully drawn characters. The *dramatis personae* include Claude Fitzsimmons and his sharp-tongued wife Helen; a cabby, Leopold Tarloff; Mr. Rusk, a surly and excitable young man with an apparently shady background; a police officer named Kraus; Alton Pidgear, Rusk's smooth attorney; and four unnamed characters—a large man who speaks Russian, two dark little men in gray hats accompanying Pidgear, and a desk lieutenant. In the distance there is also Adele Lowrie, the hostess of the dinner party to which Helen and Claude have been invited.

In contrast with "The Secret Life of Walter Mitty," this story fairly bulges with characters; but only two of them can be considered dynamic, Tarloff and Fitzsimmons. As a result of all that takes place, only these two men are different at the end of the story from what they were at the beginning. Tarloff realizes that "today there is no time for anything." And Fitzsimmons hates his wife, wondering why he ever married her. All the other characters are static and comparatively flat or one-dimensional, unchanged from the beginning of the story to the end or drawn with only one or two brush strokes.

Actions, dialogue, and appearance are the primary devices used by Irwin Shaw to dramatize character in the story; we are given the thoughts of only one character, Claude Fitzsimmons. Tarloff, the Russian cabby, is intended to be a sympathetic character. After the crash his first concern is for the safety of his passengers. Then he gets slugged in the nose by Rusk, who had driven his Ford through a red light and hit Tarloff's taxi. The police are not particularly interested in Tarloff's injury. Pidgear and the man who speaks Russian try to pressure Tarloff into dropping the charges against Rusk. He has to withstand Helen's sarcasm, and in the end Fitzsimmons, his only ally, deserts him.

Fitzsimmons, through whose eyes we view the story, first has a look at Tarloff:

> He stood there, slowly drying the blood off his shabby coat with his cap. His hair was gray, but long and full, like a musician's. He had a big head for his little shoulders, and a sad, lined little face and he looked older than fifty, . . . and very poor, neglected, badly nourished.

But Tarloff's appearance is misleading. His spirit is not "badly nourished," at least not at the beginning of the story. He is a man of principle. Almost immediately after the crash and the punch, he tells Rusk, "You have committed a crime, . . . and there is a punishment for it." Later, at the police station, he explains his position to the lieutenant. Speaking of Rusk, he says:

> "He is guilty of a crime on my person. He insulted me. He did me an injustice. The law exists for such things. One individual is not to be hit by another individual in the streets of the city without legal punishment. . . . There is a principle. The dignity of the human body. Justice. For a bad act a man suffers. It's an important thing . . ."

Fitzsimmons is sympathetic to Tarloff's predicament, and this sympathy is dramatized in word, deed, and thought. Immediately after Rusk hits Tarloff in the face, Fitzsimmons opens the door of the taxi, steps out into the street, and says to Rusk, "Now, see here." Then he bends over Tarloff, who is sitting on the running board of the cab, and asks, "Are you all right?" When Rusk, wanting to stop Tarloff from calling the police in, asks Fitzsimmons to talk to Tarloff, Fitzsimmons replies flatly, "It's entirely up to him." Not only does Fitzsimmons bring the police officer over to the scene, he also goes along to the police station as a witness on Tarloff's behalf. As Tarloff, weary, sits on the floor at the police station, we are given Fitzsimmons' thoughts about the old immigrant:

> Fitzsimmons suddenly felt like crying, watching the old man sitting there among the spit and cigarette butts, on the floor against the wall, with his cap off and his great bush of musician's gray hair giving the lie to the tired, weathered face below it.

The rest of the characters in the story are there pretty much for the roles they play. Rusk is basically a mindless scoundrel, who seems to have a poor notion about how one should go about staying out of trouble. Pidgear is a stock character—a disreputable attorney trying to keep his shady client out of the hands of the police. Except for Officer Kraus, the other characters at the police station aren't named. Helen is basically a foil to Fitzsimmons, although her sharp tongue helps give her a high profile in the story.

In addition to using sarcasm, Helen is also quite good with *verbal irony*. Verbal irony is the type of irony that occurs when a character says one thing while using words that clearly carry quite a different meaning. The mood and tone of the speaker and words are likely to be totally inappropriate to the intent suggested. Helen is using verbal irony when she expresses her complete displeasure at everything that is happening in the police station in terms of a news item in the society pages:

> "Mrs. Claude Fitzsimmons was lovely last night in blue velvet and silver fox at Officer Kraus's reception at the 8th Precinct. Other guests were the well-known Leopold Tarloff, and the Messrs. Pidgear and Rusk, in gray hats. Other guests included the Russian Ambassador and two leading Italian artillerymen, also in gray hats."

Even Pidgear, who is hardly a connoisseur of wit, cannot let this little soliloquy pass unnoticed. He says to Fitzsimmons, "Your wife is a very witty woman." This Fitzsimmons knows all too well, of course; and he has known it for a long time. Thus, we come to the story within the story of "The Dry Rock."

A careful reading of "The Dry Rock" reveals two plots, one overt and the other covert. The overt plot has to do with Leopold Tarloff, the damage to his cab, the smash he takes in the nose, and the principles he believes in. The covert plot has to do with the conflict that has been simmering in the lives of Claude and Helen Fitzsimmons for years. It is the experience of Tarloff's story that finally brings their relationship to the boiling point.

Fitzsimmons, like Tarloff, believes justice should be served. In the end, though, despite his earlier support of Tarloff, he lacks the strength of character to see that it is served. Thus, when Tarloff, pressed by the lieutenant to drop the charges against Rusk, turns to Fitzsimmons for support, Fitzsimmons merely shrugs sadly, leaving the cabby "deserted once and for all before the lieutenant's desk, on the dry rock of principle." Afterward, Fitzsimmons feels shame and anger, perhaps realizing that this same indecisiveness has contributed to the shambles of his marriage. When Helen calls to him at the door of Adele Lowrie's house, he snaps, "Oh, shut up!" He is ashamed both of the way he has let Tarloff down and of the way he has run his own life.

FOR ADDITIONAL READING

The following stories, which appear elsewhere in this book, are especially appropriate for an analysis of character:

1. Ring Lardner, "Haircut" (p. 185)
2. James Joyce, "A Little Cloud" (p. 461)
3. Toni Cade Bambara, "The Lesson" (p. 634)
4. Anton Chekhov, "Gooseberries" (p. 391)
5. E. T. A. Hoffmann, "The Story of Serapion" (p. 293)

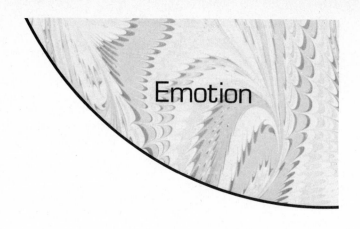

Emotion

I t is often said that the function of nonfiction is to make us understand, the function of fiction to make us understand and feel. Although such a distinction is a little too arbitrary—many times we experience strong emotions as a result of reading nonfiction—it is nevertheless true that fiction derives much of its power and appeal from its emotional impact. Its truths strike our minds all the harder because they are conveyed through our feelings. Most stories, no matter how subtle, arouse some emotion in the reader.

As we said earlier, there are two aspects to the element of emotion. The first relates to the author's dramatization of the emotions experienced by the characters in the story. The second relates to the emotions the author wishes the reader to experience. For the most part, readers of a story key their emotional responses—knowingly or subconsciously—to the actions, observations, experiences, struggles, and emotions of the characters. Effective characterization, then, usually produces in the reader the emotional response the author was hoping to achieve. A story peopled with a parade of static, flat, or stock characters is unlikely to elicit any positive emotion from knowledgeable readers.

Emotion, to be effective, cannot be presented directly. Like plausible character, it must be dramatized. We will begin our discussion of the dramatization of emotion with a consideration of *tone* and *mood*. *Tone* refers to the author's attitude toward the story or the subject of the story. A story's tone may be formal, informal, ironic, somber, serious, playful, patronizing, urbane, sly, condescending, or whatever the author wants it to be.

Mood, on the other hand, refers to the total atmosphere that surrounds and permeates the fictional world in which the story takes place. Mood has to do with the emotional ambience of the story, and it includes the reader's response to that ambience. The reader participates in the story's mood.

The tone of "The Most Dangerous Game" is one of matter-of-fact revelation of the events of the story; the mood becomes progressively more sinister and fearful. The tone of "The Open Window" suggests a sort of clever condescension on the part of the author, but the mood is one of humorous sympathy for poor Framton. Similarly, the tone of "The Secret Life of Walter Mitty" is cleverly ironic and urbane, whereas the mood is one of sympathy for the protagonist Mitty, who is after all just trying to cope with a world over which he has little or no control. Finally, the tone of "The Dry Rock" is almost as detached and objective as that of a newspaper story; but the mood, one of frustration, grows progressively more intense as the futility of Tarloff's faith in legal justice becomes more evident.

Mood and tone are not the only devices a writer has for dramatizing emotion. The careful presentation of a specific single scene can elicit a strong emotional response from readers. So can the precise structuring of a larger situation. The consideration of certain themes may annoy or elate many readers. For example, a story suggesting that homosexuals or blacks possess greater sensitivity than the population at large may offend some readers. In like manner, stories with traditional Jewish or radical feminist themes may displease some readers. But at the same time they may please other readers. Even a single word or phrase of dialogue can bring up all sorts of responses from readers.

The human mind is a tricky and mysterious mechanism, and clever writers have become surprisingly good at bringing up from the subconscious, memories of all sorts of things that we as readers have forgotten. And when such memories are exposed, the reader often reexperiences in his mind emotions and events that happened years before. For example, a precise description of smells can cause a reader's mind to click back to an earlier time. Accounts of the aroma of honeysuckle, rain on the hot ground, a wood fire in autumn, frying chicken, a bakery shop, freshly washed clothes, hot tar, rich pipe tobacco, a musty old book, can be employed by the skillful writer to stir a reader's emotions.

Descriptions of sounds and sensations may also be a useful tool for a writer who wishes to play upon the emotions of readers. Familiar sounds such as a distant piano playing a soft tune, the annoying tapping of a typewriter in the next room, a crying baby, the drone of a high-flying airplane, the report of a high-powered rifle, a cheering crowd of happy spectators, the contented purring of a cat, the howl of the winter wind, or the labored breathing of a dying person may be described to stir the memory of the reader and call forth an emotional response.

In like manner, the description of sensations such as cool water running over one's feet, the gentle stroking of a lover's hair, the wind blowing against one's face, the taste of rich coffee or cold beer, the hot sun burning down upon one's weary body, the pain of a toothache or of a hard blow from a clinched fist, or the elation after being firmly patted on the back for a job well done may produce some emotional response in a reader.

Certain situations can also be counted on to elicit emotional reactions from readers: the mistreatment of a child, the unexpected success of a beleaguered character, the reunion of two lovers after a long separation, a bully getting what he or she deserves, a person returning home after a number of years to find everything horribly changed, almost any situation in which innocent people are harmed or taken advantage of, the recovery of a character from a serious illness. Nostalgia, love, hate, anger, envy, disgust, sympathy, the desire to emulate—these are all emotions that writers try to draw forth from readers.

Irony is another tool for eliciting an emotional response. *Dramatic irony* can be particularly effective. It involves a contrast between what a character believes to be true and what the reader knows to be the facts. For example, if a character gleefully says, "This is going to be the happiest day of my life," and the reader knows that several other characters have carefully planned this to be the day of the unsuspecting character's murder, we have a situation of dramatic irony. Dramatic irony, then, places the reader in God's position of knowing something before the ordinary humans of the story know it. Being in possession of such knowledge can give rise to an intense emotional reaction in the reader, particularly if the reader earnestly wants the misinformed or uninformed character to be told the truth. In fact, it is often from situations involving dramatic irony that the element of suspense arises.

Suspense results when readers are so drawn into the story that they strongly desire a certain outcome but are not at all sure that outcome will occur. Suspense, then, has two aspects: not knowing what will happen *and* desiring a certain thing to happen. When a reader doesn't know what the outcome will be and doesn't care, the element of suspense is not present. Characters in a story do not really experience suspense, nor does the author or the casual reader. Suspense grips involved readers only. They have "bought" the protagonist's dilemma, do not know whether the fictional character will achieve his or her goal, yet desperately want everything to "turn out" all right. Many readers probably experienced a degree of suspense over the outcome of the conflict between Rainsford and General Zaroff in "The Most Dangerous Game." Almost every movie-goer experienced suspense for the fate of McMurphy in the film *One Flew Over the Cuckoo's Nest*.

Sometimes we as readers *sympathize* with a character in a story— that is, we intellectually understand the character and accept what he does as reasonable, even though we ourselves might not have done exactly the same thing under similar circumstances. Most readers probably sympathized with Framton in "The Open Window," with Walter Mitty in "The Secret Life of Walter Mitty," and Tarloff and maybe even with Fitzsimmons in "The Dry Rock."

Sometimes our response may be even greater than ordinary sympathy, but perhaps considerably less reasoned. We may *empathize*—that is, we may share in a character's feelings and emotions almost to the point of vicariously becoming that character, at least for the duration of the story. Empathy is a rare achievement for a short-story writer. It requires not only a very able writer but also a reader willing to be absorbed into the struggles of a fictional character.

One of the most important keys to depicting genuine emotions in the short story—as well as eliciting genuine emotions from the reader—is *restraint*. A little love can be effective; too much love results in melodrama, schmaltz, a tear-jerker. Similarly, the overemphasis of any emotion is self-defeating.

Now let's take a look at how emotion is called forth by Morley Callaghan in "A Sick Call," W. W. Jacobs in "The Monkey's Paw," and Rudyard Kipling in "The Gardener."

MORLEY CALLAGHAN

A Sick Call

Sometimes Father Macdowell mumbled out loud and took a deep wheezy breath as he walked up and down the room and read his office. He was a huge old priest, white-headed except for a shiny baby-pink bald spot on the top of his head, and he was a bit deaf in one ear. His florid face had many fine red interlacing vein lines. For hours he had been hearing confessions and he was tired, for he always had to hear more confessions than any other priest at the cathedral; young girls who were in trouble, and wild but at times repentant young men, always wanted to tell their confessions to Father Macdowell, because nothing seemed to shock or excite him, or make him really angry, and he was even tender with those who thought they were most guilty.

While he was mumbling and reading and trying to keep his glasses on his nose, the house girl knocked on the door and said, "There's a young lady here to see you, father. I think it's about a sick call."

"Did she ask for me especially?" he said in a deep but slightly cracked voice.

"Indeed she did, father. She wanted Father Macdowell and nobody else."

So he went out to the waiting-room, where a girl about thirty years of age, with fine brown eyes, fine cheek-bones, and rather square shoulders, was sitting daubing her eyes with a handkerchief. She was wearing a dark coat with a gray wolf collar. "Good evening, father," she said. "My sister is sick. I wanted you to come and see her. We think she's dying."

"Be easy, child; what's the matter with her? Speak louder. I can hardly hear you."

"My sister's had pneumonia. The doctor's coming back to see her in an hour. I wanted you to anoint her, father."

"I see, I see. But she's not lost yet. I'll not give her extreme unction now. That may not be necessary. I'll go with you and hear her confession."

"Father, I ought to let you know, maybe. Her husband won't want to let you see her. He's not a Catholic, and my sister hasn't been to church in a long time."

"Oh, don't mind that. He'll let me see her," Father Macdowell said, and he left the room to put on his hat and coat.

When he returned, the girl explained that her name was Jane Stanhope, and her sister lived only a few blocks away. "We'll walk and you tell me about your sister," he said. He put his black hat square on the top of his head, and pieces of white hair stuck out awkwardly at the sides. They went to the avenue together.

The night was mild and clear. Miss Stanhope began to walk slowly, because Father Macdowell's rolling gait didn't get him along the street very quickly. He walked as if his feet hurt him, though he wore a pair of large, soft, specially constructed shapeless shoes. "Now, my child, you go ahead and tell me about your sister," he said, breathing with difficulty, yet giving the impression that nothing could have happened to the sister which would make him feel indignant.

There wasn't much to say, Miss Stanhope replied. Her sister had married John Williams two years ago, and he was a good, hard-working fellow, only he was very bigoted and hated all church people. "My family wouldn't have anything to do with Elsa after she married him, though I kept going to see her," she said. She was talking in a loud voice to Father Macdowell so that he could hear her.

"Is she happy with her husband?"

"She's been very happy, father. I must say that."

"Where is he now?"

"He was sitting beside her bed. I ran out because I thought he was going to cry. He said if I brought a priest near the place he'd break the priest's head."

"My goodness. Never mind, though. Does your sister want to see me?"

"She asked me to go and get a priest, but she doesn't want John to know she did it."

Turning into a side street, they stopped at the first apartment house, and the old priest followed Miss Stanhope up the stairs. His breath came with great difficulty. "Oh dear, I'm not getting any younger, not one day younger. It's a caution how a man's legs go back on him," he said. As Miss Stanhope rapped on the door, she looked pleadingly at the old priest, trying to ask him not to be offended at anything that might happen, but he was smiling and looking huge in the narrow hallway. He wiped his head with his handkerchief.

The door was opened by a young man in a white shirt with no collar, with a head of thick, black, wavy hair. At first he looked dazed, then his eyes got bright with excitement when he saw the priest, as though he were glad to see someone he could destroy with pent-up energy. "What do you mean, Jane?" he said. "I told you not to bring a priest around here. My wife doesn't want to see a priest."

"What's that you're saying, young man?"

"No one wants you here."

"Speak up. Don't be afraid. I'm a bit hard of hearing," Father Macdowell smiled rosily. John Williams was confused by the unexpected deafness in the priest, but he stood there, blocking the door with sullen resolution as if waiting for the priest to try to launch a curse at him.

"Speak to him, father," Miss Stanhope said, but the priest didn't seem to hear her; he was still smiling as he pushed past the young man, saying, "I'll go in and sit down, if you don't mind, son. I'm here on God's errand, but I don't mind saying I'm all out of breath from climbing those stairs."

John was dreadfully uneasy to see he had been brushed aside, and he followed the priest into the apartment and said loudly, "I don't want you here."

Father Macdowell said, "Eh, eh?" Then he smiled sadly. "Don't be angry with me, son," he said. "I'm too old to try and be fierce and threatening." Looking around, he said, "Where's your wife?" and he started to walk along the hall, looking for the bedroom.

John followed him and took hold of his arm. "There's no sense in your wasting your time talking to my wife, do you hear?" he said angrily.

Miss Stanhope called out suddenly, "Don't be rude, John."

"It's he that's being rude. You mind your business," John said.

"For the love of God let me sit down a moment with her, anyway. I'm tired," the priest said.

"What do you want to say to her? Say it to me, why don't you?"

Then they both heard someone moan softly in the adjoining room, as if the sick woman had heard them. Father Macdowell, forgetting that the young man had hold of his arm, said, "I'll go in and see her for a moment, if you don't mind," and he began to open the door.

"You're not going to be alone with her, that's all," John said, following him into the bedroom.

Lying on the bed was a white-faced, fair girl, whose skin was so delicate that her cheek bones stood out sharply. She was feverish, but her eyes rolled toward the door, and she watched them coming in. Father Macdowell took off his coat, and as he mumbled to himself he looked around the room, at the mauve-silk bed-light and the light wall-paper with the tiny birds in flight. It looked like a little girl's room. "Good evening, father," Mrs. Williams whispered. She looked scared. She didn't glance at her husband. The notion of dying had made her afraid. She loved her husband and wanted to die loving him, but she was afraid, and she looked up at the priest.

"You're going to get well, child," Father Macdowell said, smiling and patting her hand gently.

John, who was standing stiffly by the door, suddenly moved around the big priest, and he bent down over the bed and took his wife's hand and began to caress her forehead.

"Now, if you don't mind, my son, I'll hear your wife's confession," the priest said.

"No, you won't," John said abruptly. "Her people didn't want her, and they left us together, and they're not going to separate us now. She's satisfied with me." He kept looking down at her face as if he could not bear to turn away.

Father Macdowell nodded his head up and down and sighed. "Poor boy," he said. "God bless you." Then he looked at Mrs. Williams, who had closed her eyes, and he saw a faint tear on her cheek. "Be sensible, my boy," he said. "You'll have to let me hear your wife's confession. Leave us alone a while."

"I'm going to stay right here," John said, and he sat down on the end of the bed. He was working himself up and staring savagely at the priest. All of a sudden he noticed the tears on his wife's cheeks, and he muttered as though bewildered, "What's the matter, Elsa? What's the matter, darling? Are we bothering you? Just open your eyes and we'll go out of the room and leave you alone till the doctor comes." Then he turned and said to the priest, "I'm not going to leave you here with her, can't you see that? Why don't you go?"

"I could revile you, my son. I could threaten you; but I ask you, for the peace of your wife's soul, leave us alone." Father Macdowell spoke with patient tenderness. He looked very big and solid and immovable as he stood by the bed. "I liked your face as soon as I saw you," he said to John. "You're a good fellow."

John still held his wife's wrist, but he rubbed one hand through his thick hair and said angrily, "You don't get the point, sir. My wife and I were always left alone, and we merely want to be left alone now. Nothing is going to separate us. She's been content with me. I'm sorry, sir; you'll have to speak to her with me here, or you'll have to go."

"No; you'll have to go for a while," the priest said patiently.

Then Mrs. Williams moved her head on the pillow and said jerkily, "Pray for me, father."

So the old priest knelt down by the bed, and with a sweet unruffled expression on his florid face he began to pray. At times his breath came with a whistling noise as though a rumbling were inside him, and at other times he sighed and was full of sorrow. He was praying that young Mrs. Williams might get better, and while he prayed he knew that her husband was more afraid of losing her to the Church than losing her to death.

All the time Father Macdowell was on his knees, with his heavy prayer book in his two hands, John kept staring at him. John couldn't understand the old priest's patience and tolerance. He wanted to quarrel with him, but he kept on watching the light from overhead shining on the one baby-pink bald spot on the smooth, white head, and at last he burst out, "You don't understand, sir! We've been very happy together. Neither you nor her people came near her when she was in good health, so why should you bother her now? I don't want anything to separate us now; neither does she. She came with me. You see you'd be separating us, don't you?" He was trying to talk like a reasonable man who had no prejudices.

Father Macdowell got up clumsily. His knees hurt him, for the floor was hard. He said to Mrs. Williams in quite a loud voice, "Did you really intend to give up everything for this young fellow?" and he bent down close to her so he could hear.

"Yes, father," she whispered.

"In Heaven's name, child, you couldn't have known what you were doing."

"We loved each other, father. We've been very happy."

"All right. Supposing you were. What now? What about all eternity, child?"

"Oh, father, I'm very sick and I'm afraid." She looked up to try to show him how scared she was, and how much she wanted him to give her peace.

He sighed and seemed distressed, and at last he said to John, "Were you married in the church?"

"No, we weren't. Look here, we're talking pretty loud and it upsets her."

"Ah, it's a crime that I'm hard of hearing, I know. Never mind, I'll go." Picking up his coat, he put it over his arm; then he sighed as if he were very tired, and he said, "I wonder if you'd just fetch me a glass of water. I'd thank you for it."

John hesitated, glancing at the tired old priest, who looked so pink and white and almost cherubic in his utter lack of guile.

"What's the matter?" Father Macdowell said.

John was ashamed of himself of appearing so sullen, so he said hastily, "Nothing's the matter. Just a moment. I won't be a moment." He hurried out of the room.

The old priest looked down at the floor and shook his head; and then, sighing and feeling uneasy, he bent over Mrs. Williams, with his good ear down to her, and he said, "I'll just ask you a few questions in a hurry, my child. You answer them quickly and I'll give you absolution." He made the sign of the cross over her and asked if she repented for having strayed from the Church, and if she had often been angry, and whether she had always been faithful, and if she had ever lied or stolen—all so casually and quickly as if it hadn't occurred to him that such a young woman could have serious sins. In the same breath he muttered, "Say a good act of contrition to yourself and that will be all, my dear." He had hardly taken a minute.

When John returned to the room with the glass of water in his hand, he saw the old priest making the sign of the cross. Father Macdowell went on praying without even looking up at John. When he had finished, he turned and said, "Oh, there you are. Thanks for the water. I needed it. Well, my boy, I'm sorry if I worried you."

John hardly said anything. He looked at his wife, who had closed her eyes, and he sat down on the end of the bed. He was too disappointed to speak.

Father Macdowell, who was expecting trouble, said, "Don't be harsh, lad."

"I'm not harsh," he said mildly, looking up at the priest. "But you weren't quite fair. And it's as though she turned away from me at the last moment. I didn't think she needed you."

"God bless you, bless the both of you. She'll get better," Father Macdowell said. But he felt ill at ease as he put on his coat, and he couldn't look directly at John.

Going along the hall, he spoke to Miss Stanhope, who wanted to apologize for her brother-in-law's attitude. "I'm sorry if it was unpleasant for you, father," she said.

"It wasn't unpleasant," he said. "I was glad to meet John. He's a fine fellow. It's a great pity he isn't a Catholic. I don't know as I played fair with him."

As he went down the stairs, puffing and sighing, he pondered the question of whether he had played fair with the young man. But by the time he reached the street he was rejoicing amiably to think he had so successfully ministered to one who had strayed from the faith and had called out to him at the last moment. Walking along with the rolling motion as if his feet hurt him, he muttered, "Of course they were happy as they were . . . in a worldly way. I wonder if I did come between them?"

He shuffled along, feeling very tired, but he couldn't help thinking, "What beauty there was to his staunch love for her!" Then he added quickly, "But it was just a pagan beauty, of course."

As he began to wonder about the nature of this beauty, for some reason he felt inexpressibly sad.

BY WAY OF DISCUSSION

In "A Sick Call" there is a clear disparity between the emotions experienced by the characters in the story and those likely to be experienced by many readers. In spite of this difference, however, the story is a very good one.

The author's tone is almost journalistic. Consequently, the mood of the story, even though it includes a near-deathbed scene, is neither grim nor morbid. The tale is told too quickly for the reader to build up any great emotional response. In fact, to the reader the story comes close to being a small essay on the subject of whether a priest has the right to intrude on the privacy of another man's home, even if the man's wife has requested his presence. And at the conclusion of the story, as Father Macdowell leaves the Williams household, he ponders "the question of whether he had played fair with the young man."

The emotions experienced by the four characters in the story are intense. Jane Stanhope, the sister of the sick and perhaps dying woman, desperately fears for her sister's soul. She doesn't want Elsa to die outside the Church, a legitimate wish on the part of a sister and a Roman Catholic. Father Macdowell's emotions center upon his desire to do what he perceives to be his duty. We must believe that he is a good and conscientious priest. We are told:

> he always had to hear more confessions than any other priest at the cathedral; young girls who were in trouble, and wild but at times repentant young men, always wanted to tell their confessions to Father Macdowell, because nothing seemed to shock or excite him, or make him really angry, and he was even tender with those who thought they were the most guilty.

So, although the priest may appear to be a calm and matter-of-fact individual, he must possess great compassion; otherwise, he would not over the years have been so faithful in performing his duties.

The emotions experienced by Elsa and John Williams are even more intense, however. Elsa may be dying, a condition that normally gives rise to strong emotions in any person. She frankly admits to Father Macdowell, "I'm very sick and I'm afraid." Elsa and John have been married outside the Church, a fact that seems to have resulted in Elsa's being cast out by her family. John says to the priest:

> "You don't get the point, sir. My wife and I were always left alone, and we merely want to be left alone now. Nothing is going to separate us. She's been content with me."

So, Elsa's emotions arise from a fear of dying, a fear of dying outside the Church and separated from her family, and from the sorrow of not being able to go on living with her husband, a man she has been content with. Remember, in answer to Father Macdowell's question about Elsa's marriage, Jane tells us, "She's been very happy, father."

Finally, let's look at the emotional state of John Williams, who may be viewed as the story's antagonist, if Father Macdowell is seen as the protagonist. We know that John is an emotional and strong-willed fellow: "he was a good, hard-working fellow, only he was very bigoted and hated all church people." When Father Macdowell first views John through the open door of the apartment, he sees a man distraught:

> At first he looked dazed, then his eyes got bright with excitement when he saw the priest, as though he were glad to see someone he could destroy with pent-up energy.

John loves his wife completely. He doesn't want to lose her. And most of all he doesn't want the Church, in the person of Father Macdowell, to come between him and his wife at this late date, a perfectly understandable wish for a man of his disposition.

It is clear, then, that this is a story of great emotional intensity for the characters involved. For the reader, however, the greatest source of emotion may well be the trick that Father Macdowell plays on John to make possible the administration of the rights of absolution on Elsa. Father Macdowell sends John out of the room for a glass of water so that he can quickly administer absolution. Some readers may be angered by this device; others may be relieved, feeling the act justified. In any event, the good priest does the deed with what he perceives to be the best intentions.

What may distress some readers even more than the trick, however, is the story's conclusion. As the priest is walking down the street thinking about what great beauty there was in John's staunch love for Elsa, suddenly "for some reason he felt inexpressibly sad." Does this mean that Father Macdowell is feeling guilty for having violated the "pagan beauty" of the love John had for Elsa? Does it mean that the priest is saddened by the seemingly innate power of "pagan" love? Or does it mean that

Elsa has just died, with the Church having by trickery come between her and her loving husband forever? We don't know; we can't know for certain. And that ambiguity may be distressing to an involved reader.

W. W. JACOBS

The Monkey's Paw

Without, the night was cold and wet, but in the small parlour of Laburnum Villa the blinds were drawn and the fire burned brightly. Father and son were at chess; the former, who possessed ideas about the game involving radical changes, putting his king into such sharp and unnecessary perils that it even provoked comment from the white-haired old lady knitting placidly by the fire.

"Hark at the wind," said Mr. White, who, having seen a fatal mistake after it was too late, was amiably desirous of preventing his son from seeing it.

"I'm listening," said the latter, grimly surveying the board as he stretched out his hand. "Check."

"I should hardly think that he'd come to-night," said his father, with his hand poised over the board.

"Mate," replied the son.

"That's the worst of living so far out," bawled Mr. White, with sudden and unlooked-for violence; "of all the beastly, slushy, out-of-the-way places to live in, this is the worst. Path's a bog, and the road's a torrent. I don't know what people are thinking about. I suppose because only two houses in the road are let, they think it doesn't matter."

"Never mind, dear," said his wife soothingly; "perhaps you'll win the next one."

Mr. White looked up sharply, just in time to intercept a knowing glance between mother and son. The words died away on his lips, and he hid a guilty grin in his thin grey beard.

"There he is," said Herbert White, as the gate banged to loudly and heavy footsteps came towards the door.

The old man rose with hospitable haste, and opening the door, was heard condoling with the new arrival. The new arrival also condoled with himself, so that Mrs. White said, "Tut, tut!" and coughed gently as her husband entered the room, followed by a tall, burly man, beady of eye and rubicund of visage.

"Sergeant-Major Morris," he said, introducing him.

The sergeant-major shook hands, and taking the proffered seat by the fire, watched contentedly while his host got out whisky and tumblers and stood a small copper kettle on the fire.

At the third glass his eyes got brighter, and he began to talk, the little family circle regarding with eager interest this visitor from distant parts, as he squared his broad shoulders in the chair, and spoke of wild scenes and doughty deeds; of wars and plagues, and strange peoples.

"Twenty-one years of it," said Mr. White, nodding at his wife and son. "When he went away he was a slip of a youth in the warehouse. Now look at him."

"He don't look to have taken much harm," said Mrs. White politely.

"I'd like to go to India myself," said the old man, "just to look round a bit, you know."

"Better where you are," said the sergeant-major, shaking his head. He put down the empty glass, and sighing softly, shook it again.

"I should like to see those old temples and fakirs and jugglers," said the old man. "What was that you started telling me the other day about a monkey's paw or something, Morris?"

"Nothing," said the soldier hastily. "Leastways nothing worth hearing."

"Monkey's paw?" said Mrs. White curiously.

"Well, it's just a bit of what you might call magic, perhaps," said the sergeant-major off-handedly.

His three listeners leaned forward eagerly. The visitor absent-mindedly put his empty glass to his lips and then set it down again. His host filled it for him.

"To look at," said the sergeant-major, fumbling in his pocket, "it's just an ordinary little paw, dried to a mummy."

He took something out of his pocket and proffered it. Mrs. White drew back with a grimace, but her son, taking it, examined it curiously.

"And what is there special about it?" enquired Mr. White as he took it from his son, and having examined it, placed it upon the table.

"It had a spell put on it by an old fakir," said the sergeant-major, "a very holy man. He wanted to show that fate ruled people's lives, and that those who interfered with it did so to their sorrow. He put a spell on it so that three separate men could each have three wishes from it."

His manner was so impressive that his hearers were conscious that their light laughter jarred somewhat.

"Well, why don't you have three, sir?" said Herbert White cleverly.

The soldier regarded him in the way that middle age is wont to regard presumptuous youth. "I have," he said quietly, and his blotchy face whitened.

"And did you really have the three wishes granted?" asked Mrs. White.

"I did," said the sergeant-major, and his glass tapped against his strong teeth.

"And has anybody else wished?" persisted the old lady.

"The first man had his three wishes. Yes," was the reply; "I don't know what the first two were, but the third was for death. That's how I got the paw."

His tones were so grave that a hush fell upon the group.

"If you've had your three wishes, it's no good to you now, then, Morris," said the old man at last. "What do you keep it for?"

The soldier shook his head. "Fancy, I suppose," he said slowly. "I did have some idea of selling it, but I don't think I will. It has caused enough mischief already. Besides, people won't buy. They think it's a fairy tale, some of them; and those who do think anything of it want to try it first and pay me afterward."

"If you could have another three wishes," said the old man, eyeing him keenly, "would you have them?"

"I don't know," said the other. "I don't know."

He took the paw, and dangling it between his forefinger and thumb, suddenly threw it upon the fire. White, with a slight cry, stooped down and snatched it off.

"Better let it burn," said the soldier solemnly.

"If you don't want it, Morris," said the other, "give it to me."

"I won't," said his friend doggedly. "I threw it on the fire. If you keep it, don't blame me for what happens. Pitch it on the fire again, like a sensible man."

The other shook his head and examined his new possession closely. "How do you do it?" he enquired.

"Hold it up in your right hand and wish aloud," said the sergeant-major, "but I warn you of the consequences."

"Sounds like the *Arabian Nights*," said Mrs. White, as she rose and began to set the supper. "Don't you think you might wish for four pairs of hands for me?"

Her husband drew the talisman from his pocket, and then all three burst into laughter as the sergeant-major, with a look of alarm on his face, caught him by the arm.

"If you must wish," he said gruffly, "wish for something sensible."

Mr. White dropped it back in his pocket, and placing chairs, motioned his friend to the table. In the business of supper the talisman was partly forgotten, and afterwards the three sat listening in an enthralled fashion to a second instalment of the soldier's adventures in India.

"If the tale about the monkey's paw is not more truthful than those he has been telling us," said Herbert, as the door closed behind their guest, just in time to catch the last train, "we shan't make much out of it."

"Did you give him anything for it, father?" enquired Mrs. White, regarding her husband closely.

"A trifle," said he, colouring slightly. "He didn't want it, but I made him take it. And he pressed me again to throw it away."

"Likely," said Herbert, with pretended horror. "Why, we're going to be rich, and famous, and happy. Wish to be an emperor, father, to begin with; then you can't be henpecked."

He darted round the table, pursued by the maligned Mrs. White armed with an antimacassar.

Mr. White took the paw from his pocket and eyed it dubiously. "I don't know what to wish for, and that's a fact," he said slowly. "It seems to me I've got all I want."

"If you only cleared the house, you'd be quite happy, wouldn't you!" said Herbert, with his hand on his shoulder. "Well, wish for two hundred pounds, then; that'll just do it."

His father, smiling shamefacedly at his own credulity, held up the talisman, as his son, with a solemn face, somewhat marred by a wink at his mother, sat down at the piano and struck a few impressive chords.

"I wish for two hundred pounds," said the old man distinctly.

A fine crash from the piano greeted the words, interrupted by a shuddering cry from the old man. His wife and son ran toward him.

"It moved," he cried, with a glance of disgust at the object as it lay on the floor. "As I wished, it twisted in my hand like a snake."

"Well, I don't see the money," said his son, as he picked it up and placed it on the table, "and I bet I never shall."

"It must have been your fancy, father," said his wife, regarding him anxiously.

He shook his head. "Never mind, though; there's no harm done, but it gave me a shock all the same."

They sat down by the fire again while the two men finished their pipes. Outside, the wind was higher than ever, and the old man started nervously at the sound of a door banging upstairs. A silence unusual and depressing settled upon all three, which lasted until the old couple arose to retire for the night.

"I expect you'll find the cash tied up in a big bag in the middle of your bed," said Herbert, as he bade them good night, "and something horrible squatting up on top of the wardrobe watching you as you pocket your ill-gotten gains."

He sat alone in the darkness, gazing at the dying fire, and seeing faces in it. The last face was so horrible and so simian that he gazed at it in amazement. It got so vivid that, with a little uneasy laugh, he felt on the table for a glass containing a little water to throw over it. His hand grasped the monkey's paw, and with a little shiver he wiped his hand on his coat and went up to bed.

II

In the brightness of the wintry sun next morning as it streamed over the breakfast table he laughed at his fears. There was an air of prosaic wholesomeness about the room which it had lacked on the previous night, and the dirty, shrivelled little paw was pitched on the side-board with a carelessness which betokened no great belief in its virtues.

"I suppose all old soldiers are the same," said Mrs. White. "The idea of our listening to such nonsense! How could wishes be granted in these days? And if they could, how could two hundred pounds hurt you, father?"

"Might drop on his head from the sky," said the frivolous Herbert.

"Morris said the things happened so naturally," said his father, "that you might if you so wished attribute it to coincidence."

"Well, don't break into the money before I come back," said Herbert as he rose from the table. "I'm afraid it'll turn you into a mean avaricious man, and we shall have to disown you."

His mother laughed, and following him to the door, watched him down the road; and returning to the breakfast table, was very merry at the expense of her husband's credulity. All of which did not prevent her from scurrying to the door at the postman's knock, nor prevent her from referring somewhat shortly to retired sergeant-majors of bibulous habits when she found that the post brought a tailor's bill.

"Herbert will have some more of his funny remarks, I expect, when he comes home," she said, as they sat at dinner.

"I dare say," said Mr. White, pouring himself out some beer; "but for all that, the thing moved in my hand; that I'll swear to."

"You thought it did," said the old lady soothingly.

"I say it did," replied the other. "There was no thought about it; I had just— What's the matter?"

His wife made no reply. She was watching the mysterious movements of a man outside, who, peering in an undecided fashion at the house, appeared to be trying to make up his mind to enter. In mental connection with the two hundred pounds, she noticed that the stranger was well dressed, and wore a silk hat of glossy newness. Three times he paused at the gate, and then walked on again. The fourth time he stood with his hand upon it, and then with sudden resolution flung it open and walked up the path. Mrs. White at the same moment placed her hands behind her, and hurriedly unfastening the strings of her apron, put that useful article of apparel beneath the cushion of her chair.

She brought the stranger, who seemed ill at ease, into the room. He gazed at her furtively, and listened in a preoccupied fashion as the old lady apologized for the appearance of the room, and her husband's coat, a garment which he usually reserved for the garden. She then waited as patiently as her sex would permit, for him to broach his business, but he was at first strangely silent.

"I—was asked to call," he said at last, and stooped and picked a piece of cotton from his trousers. "I come from 'Maw and Meggins'."

The old lady started. "Is anything the matter?" she asked breathlessly. "Has anything happened to Herbert? What is it? What is it?"

Her husband interposed. "There, there, mother," he said hastily. "Sit down, and don't jump to conclusions. You've not brought bad news, I'm sure, sir;" and he eyed the other wistfully.

"I'm sorry—" began the visitor.

"Is he hurt?" demanded the mother wildly.

The visitor bowed in assent. "Badly hurt," he said quietly, "but he is not in any pain."

"Oh, thank God!" said the old woman, clasping her hands "Thank God for that! Thank—"

She broke off suddenly as the sinister meaning of the assurance dawned upon her, and she saw the awful confirmation of her fears in the other's averted face. She caught her breath, and turning to her slower-witted husband, laid a trembling old hand upon his. There was a long silence.

"He was caught in the machinery," said the visitor at length in a low voice.

"Caught in the machinery," repeated Mr. White, in a dazed fashion, "yes."

He sat staring blankly out at the window, and taking his wife's hand between his own, pressed it as he had been wont to do in their old courting days nearly forty years before.

"He was the only one left to us," he said, turning gently to the visitor. "It is hard."

The other coughed, and rising, walked slowly to the window. "The firm wished me to convey their sincere sympathy with you in your great loss," he said, without looking round. "I beg that you will understand I am only their servant and merely obeying orders."

There was no reply; the old woman's face was white, her eyes staring, and her breath inaudible; and on the husband's face was a look such as his friend the sergeant might have carried into his first action.

"I was to say that Maw and Meggins disclaim all responsibility," continued the other. "They admit no liability at all, but in consideration of your son's services, they wish to present you with a certain sum as compensation."

Mr. White dropped his wife's hand, and rising to his feet, gazed with a look of horror at his visitor. His dry lips shaped the words, "How much?"

"Two hundred pounds," was the answer.

Unconscious of his wife's shriek, the old man smiled faintly, put out his hands like a sightless man, and dropped, a senseless heap, to the floor.

III

In the huge new cemetery, some two miles distant, the old people buried their dead, and came back to the house steeped in shadow and silence. It was all over so quickly that at first they could hardly realise it, and remained in a state of expectation as though of something else to happen—something else which was to lighten this load, too heavy for old hearts to bear.

But the days passed, and expectation gave place to resignation—the hopeless resignation of the old, sometimes miscalled apathy. Sometimes they hardly exchanged a word, for now they had nothing to talk about, and their days were long to weariness.

It was about a week after, that the old man, waking suddenly in the night, stretched out his hand and found himself alone. The room was in darkness, and the sound of subdued weeping came from the window. He raised himself in bed and listened.

"Come back," he said tenderly. "You will be cold."

"It is colder for my son," said the old woman, and wept afresh.

The sound of her sobs died away on his ears. The bed was warm, and his eyes heavy with sleep. He dozed fitfully, and then slept until a sudden wild cry from his wife awoke him with a start.

"The paw!" she cried wildly. "The monkey's paw!"

He started up in alarm. "Where? Where is it? What's the matter?"

She came stumbling across the room toward him. "I want it," she said quietly. "You've not destroyed it?"

"It's in the parlour, on the bracket," he replied, marvelling. "Why?"

She cried and laughed together, and bending over, kissed his cheek.

"I only just thought of it," she said hysterically. "Why didn't I think of it before? Why didn't *you* think of it?"

"Think of what?" he questioned.

"The other two wishes," she replied rapidly. "We've only had one."

"Was not that enough?" he demanded fiercely.

"No," she cried triumphantly; "we'll have one more. Go down and get it quickly, and wish our boy alive again."

The man sat up in bed and flung the bedclothes from his quaking limbs. "Good God, you are mad!" he cried, aghast.

"Get it," she panted; "get it quickly, and wish—Oh, my boy, my boy!"

Her husband struck a match and lit the candle. "Get back to bed," he said unsteadily. "You don't know what you are saying."

"We had the first wish granted," said the old woman feverishly; "why not the second?"

"A coincidence," stammered the old man.

"Go and get it and wish," cried his wife, quivering with excitement.

The old man turned and regarded her, and his voice shook. "He has been dead ten days, and besides he—I would not tell you else, but—I could only recognize him by his clothing. If he was too terrible for you to see then, how now?"

"Bring him back," cried the old woman, and dragged him toward the door. "Do you think I fear the child I have nursed?"

He went down in the darkness, and felt his way to the parlour, and then to the mantelpiece. The talisman was in its place, and a horrible fear that the unspoken wish might bring his mutilated son before him ere he could escape from the room seized upon him, and he caught his breath as he found that he had lost the direction of the door. His brow cold with sweat, he felt his way round the table, and groping along the wall until he found himself in the small passage with the unwholesome thing in his hand.

Even his wife's face seemed changed as he entered the room. It was white and expectant, and to his fears seemed to have an unnatural look upon it. He was afraid of her.

"Wish!" she cried, in a strong voice.

"It is foolish and wicked," he faltered.

"Wish!" repeated his wife.

He raised his hand. "I wish my son alive again."

The talisman fell to the floor, and he regarded it fearfully. Then he sank trembling into a chair as the old woman, with burning eyes, walked to the window and raised the blind.

He sat until he was chilled with the cold, glancing occasionally at the figure of the old woman peering through the window. The candle-end, which had burned below the rim of the china candle-stick, was throwing pulsating shadows on the ceiling and walls, until, with a flicker larger than the rest, it expired. The old man, with an unspeakable sense of relief at the failure of the talisman, crept back to his bed, and a minute or two afterwards the old woman came silently and apathetically beside him.

Neither spoke, but lay silently listening to the ticking of the clock. A stair creaked, and a squeaky mouse scurried noisily through the wall. The darkness was oppressive, and after lying for some time screwing up his courage, he took the box of matches, and striking one, went downstairs for a candle.

At the foot of the stairs the match went out, and he paused to strike another; and at the same moment a knock, so quiet and stealthy as to be scarcely audible, sounded on the front door.

The matches fell from his hand and spilled in the passage. He stood motionless, his breath suspended until the knock was repeated. Then he turned and fled swiftly back to his room, and closed the door behind him. A third knock sounded through the house.

"What's that?" cried the old woman, starting up.

"A rat," said the old man in shaking tones—"a rat. It passed me on the stairs."

His wife sat up in bed listening. A loud knock resounded through the house.

"It's Herbert!" she screamed. "It's Herbert!"

She ran to the door, but her husband was before her, and catching her by the arm, held her tightly.

"What are you going to do?" he whispered hoarsely.

"It's my boy; it's Herbert!" she cried, struggling mechanically. "I forgot it was two miles away. What are you holding me for? Let go. I must open the door."

"For God's sake, don't let it in," cried the old man, trembling.

"You're afraid of your own son," she cried, struggling. "Let me go. I'm coming, Herbert; I'm coming."

There was another knock, and another. The old woman with a sudden wrench broke free and ran from the room. Her husband followed to the landing, and called after her appealingly as she hurried downstairs. He heard the chain rattle back and the bottom bolt drawn slowly and stiffly from the socket. Then the old woman's voice, strained and panting.

"The bolt," she cried loudly. "Come down. I can't reach it."

But her husband was on his hands and knees groping wildly on the floor in search of the paw. If he could only find it before the thing outside got in. A perfect fusillade of knocks reverberated through the house, and he heard the scraping of a chair as his wife put it down in the passage against the door. He heard the creaking of the bolt as it came slowly back, and at the same moment he found the monkey's paw, and frantically breathed his third and last wish.

The knocking ceased suddenly, although the echoes of it were still in the house. He heard the chair drawn back, and the door opened. A cold wind rushed up the staircase, and a long loud wail of disappointment and misery from his wife gave him courage to run down to her side, and then to the gate beyond. The street lamp flickering opposite shone on a quiet and deserted road.

BY WAY OF DISCUSSION

W. W. Jacobs' story "The Monkey's Paw" has long been regarded as a classic tale of horror and suspense. Even though its language and quaint little family circle may seem dated to us today, most people will agree that the story is still emotionally powerful. It is probably a mistake, however, to view "The Monkey's Paw" as a tale of the supernatural, as so many readers have done. Internal evidence and the author's restraint indicate that the story may be one of psychological horror rather than of supernaturalism. The primary reason for the story's high level of suspense is that readers are so cleverly drawn into the narrative that they experience almost the same horror as that experienced by Mr. and Mrs. White.

The key issue to determining whether the story includes supernaturalism is whether Herbert, the dead son, really does appear outside the house and bang on the door to gain entry. To resolve this issue, let's reexamine the events leading up to so thunderous a climax.

First, let's consider the credibility of the claims made for the monkey's paw. Sergeant-Major Morris, a "burly man, beady of eye and rubicund of visage," who has for twenty-one years lived the life of a vagabond in faraway places, is the character who brings the supposed talisman into the White household. Is he trustworthy? The evidence suggests that he may not be. He is a drinker and either a romantic or a hustler, and he is into his third glass of whisky—with eyes growing ever brighter—when he begins his tale. And the possibility of additional liquid spirits seems at least part of his motivation for prolonging the telling of it. Even so, we are told next to nothing about the alleged previous episodes involving the paw—the circumstances surrounding the wishes, the nature of the wishes, and their outcomes—and thus are in no position to judge the authenticity of the paw's power.

Evidence likewise suggests that Mr. White has been the target of a carefully orchestrated plan to sell him the paw. Mr White has first learned of the relic several days before the story opens, when Morris mentioned it in passing and then dropped the subject until his visit to the Whites' home. As Morris concludes his grim but intriguing account of how he came to have the talisman, he makes a great show of tossing the paw into the fire but does nothing to stop White from rescuing it from the flames. And, of course, he accepts the "trifle" that Mr. White later proffers. One can't help wondering how much free whisky this tale has brought the major over the years and how many of these paws he has sold. How many of them does he yet have stashed somewhere in a trunk for future evenings?

What of the other listeners at this unusual dinner party? What do they think of the paw? Mrs. White, who later believes in the power of the paw out of grief and desperation, scoffs: "Sounds like the *Arabian Nights*." Herbert comments sarcastically about the paw and about Morris' other adventure stories by saying, "If the tale about the monkey's paw is not more truthful than those he has been telling us, we shan't make much out of it."

Only Mr. White, who has been drinking with Morris, is inclined to believe in the power of the paw, and even he does not fully believe in it until he imagines that the thing moved in his hand after he made a wish for two hundred pounds. Sober the next morning, Mr. White no longer believes that the paw has any power, and the thing is put away on a shelf until ten days after the death of Herbert.

Let's now consider Mr. and Mrs. White's *immediate* response to the news of their son's death and the company's compensation of two hundred pounds:

> Unconscious of his wife's shriek, the old man smiled faintly, put out his hands like a sightless man, and dropped, a senseless heap, to the floor.

This incident is often cited as evidence not only of both parents' belief in the power of the paw but also as evidence of supernaturalism in the story. However, one might argue much more convincingly that both parents were heartbroken and stunned by the grim irony of the situation. They are intelligent, perceptive people—especially Mrs. White. Indeed, this seems to be a convincing explanation of their reactions, especially when one considers how they settle down in the days following their son's death. Neither of them rushes to destroy the monkey's paw, their most likely reaction had they believed it had caused their tragedy. And apparently they accept the money offered by Herbert's employer.

Grief and perhaps the feebleness of age finally weaken Mrs. White. Almost two weeks after her son's death, she remembers the paw and the other two wishes. Mr. White's initial response to her demand that he wish their dead son back from the grave is that she has taken leave of her senses, that the entire episode has been a grisly coincidence, not an instance of malevolent supernaturalism. And except for a moment of emotional and psychological "intoxication," he maintains this position.

Nevertheless, not wanting to defy his wife, Mr. White makes the wish. At first nothing happens. Then, after some time, a knocking at the door begins. Mrs. White remembers that the cemetery is two miles away. If, indeed, the power of the paw was real, it would have taken Herbert a while to make his way home. The story is now at its highest emotional pitch. The knocking becomes progressively louder. Mrs. White tries frantically to get the door open, while Mr. White gropes on his hands and knees to find the paw and make the third wish, returning the boy to his grave.

He locates the paw and makes the wish. Almost simultaneously, the door is thrown open; but nothing is there: "A cold wind rushed up the staircase." Mr. White even rushes out to the front gate and beyond, *but nothing is there*. If we were dealing with a story of the supernatural, if the paw had indeed possessed supernatural power, then something most certainly *would* have been there. At the very least, Mr. White would have overtaken his dead son making his way back to the grave. After all, if we are to assume that wish number two resulted in a long, methodical trip from the grave to the house, then we must likewise assume that wish number three would result in the same type of return trip. But nothing is there! The knocking, like the movement of the paw in Mr. White's hand, has been imagined under conditions that intoxicate the mind.

Jacobs' story is a masterpiece of restraint. Had the author wanted to go all the way down the road of emotional terror and show us the mutilated and partially putrified cadaver of poor Herbert, he could have; but he would have written a story no better than thousands of others of such a genre. But he didn't do this; he stopped short, restrained himself, and moved precariously along the fine line that separates the ordinary piece of hack fiction from a brush stroke of literary art.

RUDYARD KIPLING

The Gardener

One grave to me was given,
  One watch till Judgment Day;
And God looked down from Heaven
  And rolled the stone away.

One day in all the years,
  One hour in that one day,
His Angel saw my tears,
  And rolled the stone away!

Every one in the village knew that Helen Turrell did her duty by all her world, and by none more honourably than by her only brother's unfortunate child. The village knew, too, that George Turrell had tried his family severely since early youth, and were not surprised to be told that, after many fresh starts given and thrown away, he, an Inspector of Indian Police, had entangled himself with the daughter of a retired non-commissioned officer, and had died of a fall from a horse a few weeks before his child was born. Mercifully, George's father and mother were both dead, and though Helen, thirty-five and independent, might well have washed her hands of the whole disgraceful affair, she most nobly took charge, though she was, at the time, under threat of lung trouble which had driven her to the South of France. She arranged for the passage of the child and a nurse from Bombay, met them at Marseilles, nursed the baby through an attack of infantile dysentery due to the carelessness of the nurse, whom she had had to dismiss, and at last, thin and worn but triumphant, brought the boy late in the autumn, wholly restored, to her Hampshire home.

All these details were public property, for Helen was as open as the day, and held that scandals are only increased by hushing them up. She admitted that George had always been rather a black sheep, but things might have been much worse if the mother had insisted on her right to keep the boy. Luckily, it seemed that people of that class would do almost anything for money, and, as George had always turned to her in his scrapes, she felt herself justified— her friends agreed with her—in cutting the whole non-commissioned officer connection, and giving the child every advantage. A christening, by the Rector, under the name of Michael, was the first step. So far as she knew herself, she was not, she said, a child-lover, but, for all his faults, she had been very fond of George, and she pointed out that little Michael had his father's mouth to a line; which made something to build upon.

As a matter of fact, it was the Turrell forehead, broad, low, and well-shaped, with the widely spaced eyes beneath it, that Michael had most faithfully reproduced. His mouth was somewhat better cut than the family type. But Helen, who would concede nothing good to his mother's side, vowed he was a Turrell all over, and, there being no one to contradict, the likeness was established.

In a few years Michael took his place, as accepted as Helen had always been—fearless, philosophical, and fairly good-looking. At six, he wished to know why he could not call her 'Mummy,' as other boys called their mothers. She explained that she was only his auntie, and that aunties were not quite the same as mummies, but that, if it gave him pleasure, he might call her 'Mummy' at bedtime, for a pet-name between themselves.

Michael kept his secret most loyally, but Helen, as usual, explained the fact to her friends; which when Michael heard, he raged.

'Why did you tell? Why did you tell?' came at the end of the storm.

'Because it's always best to tell the truth,' Helen answered, her arm round him as he shook in his cot.

'All right, but when the troof's ugly I don't think it's nice.'

'Don't you, dear?'

'No, I don't, and'—she felt the small body stiffen—'now you've told, I won't call you "Mummy" any more—not even at bedtimes.'

'But isn't that rather unkind?' said Helen softly.

'I don't care! I don't care! You've hurted me in my insides and I'll hurt you back. I'll hurt you as long as I live!'

'Don't, oh, don't talk like that, dear! You don't know what——'

'I will! And when I'm dead I'll hurt you worse!'

'Thank goodness, I shall be dead long before you, darling.'

'Huh! Emma says, " 'Never know your luck." ' (Michael had been talking to Helen's elderly, flat-faced maid.) 'Lots of little boys die quite soon. So'll I. *Then* you'll see!'

Helen caught her breath and moved towards the door, but the wail of 'Mummy! Mummy!' drew her back again, and the two wept together.

At ten years old, after two terms at a prep. school, something or somebody gave him the idea that his civil status was not quite regular. He attacked Helen on the subject, breaking down her stammered defences with the family directness.

' 'Don't believe a word of it,' he said, cheerily, at the end. 'People wouldn't have talked like they did if my people had been married. But don't you bother, Auntie. I've found out all about my sort in English Hist'ry and the Shakespeare bits. There was William the Conqueror to begin with, and—oh, heaps more, and they all got on first-rate. 'Twon't make any difference to you, my being *that*—will it?'

'As if anything could——' she began.

'All right. We won't talk about it any more if it makes you cry.' He never mentioned the thing again of his own will, but when, two years later, he skilfully managed to have measles in the holidays, as his temperature went up to the appointed one hundred and four he muttered of nothing else, till Helen's voice, piercing at last his delirium, reached him with assurance that nothing on earth or beyond could make any difference between them.

The terms at his public school and the wonderful Christmas, Easter, and Summer holidays followed each other, variegated and glorious as jewels on a string; and as jewels Helen treasured them. In due time Michael developed his own interests, which ran their courses and gave way to others; but his interest in Helen was constant and increasing throughout. She repaid it with all that she had of affection or could command of counsel and money; and since Michael was no fool, the War took him just before what was like to have been a most promising career.

He was to have gone up to Oxford, with a scholarship, in October. At the end of August he was on the edge of joining the first holocaust of public-school boys who threw themselves into the Line; but the captain of his O.T.C., where he had been sergeant for nearly a year, headed him off and steered him directly to a commission in a battalion so new that half of it still wore the old Army red, and the other half was breeding meningitis through living over-crowdedly in damp tents. Helen had been shocked at the idea of direct enlistment.

'But it's in the family,' Michael laughed.

'You don't mean to tell me that you believed that old story all this time?' said Helen. (Emma, her maid, had been dead now several years.) 'I gave you my word of honour—and I give it again—that—that it's all right. It is indeed.'

'Oh, *that* doesn't worry me. It never did,' he replied valiantly. 'What I meant was, I should have got into the show earlier if I'd enlisted—like my grandfather.'

'Don't talk like that! Are you afraid of its ending so soon, then?'

'No such luck. You know what K. says.'

'Yes. But my banker told me last Monday it couldn't *possibly* last beyond Christmas—for financial reasons.'

' 'Hope he's right, but our Colonel—and he's a Regular—says it's going to be a long job.'

Michael's battalion was fortunate in that, by some chance which meant several 'leaves,' it was used for coast-defence among shallow trenches on the Norfolk coast; thence sent north to watch the mouth of a Scotch estuary, and, lastly, held for weeks on a baseless rumour of distant service. But, the very day that Michael was to have met Helen for four whole hours at a railway-junction up the line, it was hurled out, to help make good the wastage of Loos, and he had only just time to send her a wire of farewell.

In France luck again helped the battalion. It was put down near the Salient, where it led a meritorious and unexacting life, while the Somme was being manufactured; and enjoyed the peace of the Armentières and Laventie sectors when that battle began. Finding that it had sound views on protecting its own flanks and could dig, a prudent Commander stole it out of its own Division, under pretence of helping to lay telegraphs, and used it round Ypres at large.

A month later, and just after Michael had written Helen that there was nothing special doing and therefore no need to worry, a shell-splinter dropping out of a wet dawn killed him at once. The next shell uprooted and laid down over the body what had been the foundation of a barn wall, so neatly that none but an expert would have guessed that anything unpleasant had happened.

By this time the village was old in experience of war, and, English fashion, had evolved a ritual to meet it. When the postmistress handed her seven-year-old daughter the official telegram to take to Miss Turrell, she observed to the Rector's gardener: 'It's Miss Helen's turn now.' He replied, thinking of his own son: 'Well, he's lasted longer than some.' The child herself came to the front-door weeping aloud, because Master Michael had often given her sweets. Helen, presently, found herself pulling down the house-blinds one after one with great care, and saying earnestly to each: 'Missing *always* means dead.' Then she took her place in the dreary procession that was impelled to go through an inevitable series of unprofitable emotions. The Rector, of course, preached hope and prophesied word, very soon, from a prison camp. Several friends, too, told her perfectly truthful tales, but always about other women, to whom, after months and months of silence, their missing had been miraculously restored. Other people urged her to communicate with infallible Secretaries of organisations who could communicate with benevolent neutrals, who could extract accurate information from the most secretive of Hun prison commandants. Helen did and wrote and signed everything that was suggested or put before her.

Once, on one of Michael's leaves, he had taken her over a munition factory, where she saw the progress of a shell from blank-iron to the all but finished article. It struck her at the time that the wretched thing was never left alone for a single second; and 'I'm being manufactured into a bereaved next of kin,' she told herself, as she prepared her documents.

In due course, when all the organisations had deeply or sincerely regretted their inability to trace, etc., something gave way within her and all sensation—save of thankfulness for the release—came to an end in blessed passivity. Michael had died and her world had stood still and she had been one with the full shock of that arrest. Now she was standing still and the world was going forward, but it did not concern her—in no way or relation did it touch her. She knew this by the ease with which she could slip Michael's name into talk and incline her head to the proper angle, at the proper murmur of sympathy.

In the blessed realisation of that relief, the Armistice with all its bells broke over her and passed unheeded. At the end of another year she had overcome her physical loathing of the living and returned young, so that she could take them by the hand and almost sincerely wish them well. She had no interest in any aftermath, national or personal, of the war, but, moving at an immense distance, she sat on various relief committees and held strong views—she heard herself delivering them—about the site of the proposed village War Memorial.

Then there came to her, as next of kin, an official intimation, backed by a page of a letter to her in indelible pencil, a silver identity-disc, and a watch, to the effect that the body of Lieutenant Michael Turrell had been found, identified, and re-interred in Hagenzeele Third Military Cemetery—the letter of the row and the grave's number in that row duly given.

So Helen found herself moved on to another process of the manufacture—to a world full of exultant or broken relatives, now strong in the certainty that there was an altar upon earth were they might lay their love. These soon told her, and by means of time-tables made clear, how easy it was and how little it interfered with life's affairs to go and see one's grave.

'So different,' as the Rector's wife said, 'if he'd been killed in Mesopotamia, or even Gallipoli.'

The agony of being waked up to some sort of second life drove Helen across the Channel, where, in a new world of abbreviated titles, she learnt that Hagenzeele Third could be comfortably reached by an afternoon train which fitted in with the morning boat, and that there was a comfortable little hotel not three kilometres from Hagenzeele itself, where one could spend quite a comfortable night and see one's grave next morning. All this she had from a

Central Authority who lived in a board and tar-paper shed on the skirts of a razed city full of whirling lime-dust and blown papers.

'By the way,' said he, 'you know your grave, of course?'

'Yes, thank you,' said Helen, and showed its row and number typed on Michael's own little typewriter. The officer would have checked it, out of one of his many books; but a large Lancashire woman thrust between them and bade him tell her where she might find her son, who had been corporal in the A.S.C. His proper name, she sobbed, was Anderson, but, coming of respectable folk, he had of course enlisted under the name of Smith; and had been killed at Dickiebush, in early 'Fifteen. She had not his number nor did she know which of his two Christian names he might have used with his alias; but her Cook's tourist ticket expired at the end of Easter week, and if by then she could not find her child she should go mad. Whereupon she fell forward on Helen's breast; but the officer's wife came out quickly from a little bedroom behind the office, and the three of them lifted the woman on to the cot.

'They are often like this,' said the officer's wife, loosening the tight bonnet-strings. 'Yesterday she said he'd been killed at Hooge. Are you sure you know your grave? It makes such a difference.'

'Yes, thank you,' said Helen, and hurried out before the woman on the bed should begin to lament again.

Tea in a crowded mauve and blue striped wooden structure, with a false front, carried her still further into the nightmare. She paid her bill beside a stolid, plain-featured Englishwoman, who, hearing her inquire about the train to Hagenzeele, volunteered to come with her.

'I'm going to Hagenzeele myself,' she explained. 'Not to Hagenzeele Third; mine is Sugar Factory, but they call it La Rosière now. It's just south of Hagenzeele Three. Have you got your room at the hotel there?'

'Oh yes, thank you. I've wired.'

'That's better. Sometimes the place is quite full, and at others there's hardly a soul. But they've put bathrooms into the old Lion d'Or—that's the hotel on the west side of Sugar Factory—and it draws off a lot of people, luckily.'

'It's all new to me. This is the first time I've been over.'

'Indeed! This is my ninth time since the Armistice. Not on my own account. I haven't lost any one, thank God—but, like every one else, I've a lot of friends at home who have. Coming over as often as I do, I find it helps them to have some one just look at the—the place and tell them about it afterwards. And one can take photos for them, too. I get quite a list of commissions to execute.' She laughed nervously and tapped her slung Kodak. 'There are two or three to see at Sugar Factory this time, and plenty of others in the cemeteries all about. My system is to save them up, and arrange them, you know. And when I've got enough commissions for one area to make it worth while, I pop over and execute them. It *does* comfort people.'

'I suppose so,' Helen answered, shivering as they entered the little train.

'Of course it does. (Isn't it lucky we've got window-seats?) It must do or
they wouldn't ask one to do it, would they? I've a list of quite twelve or fifteen
commissions here'—she tapped the Kodak again—'I must sort them out tonight. Oh, I forgot to ask you. What's yours?'

'My nephew,' said Helen. 'But I was very fond of him.'

'Ah, yes! I sometimes wonder whether *they* know after death? What do you
think?'

'Oh, I don't—I haven't dared to think much about that sort of thing,' said
Helen, almost lifting her hands to keep her off.

'Perhaps that's better,' the woman answered. 'The sense of loss must be
enough, I expect. Well, I won't worry you any more.'

Helen was grateful, but when they reached the hotel Mrs. Scarsworth (they
had exchanged names) insisted on dining at the same table with her, and after
the meal, in the little, hideous salon full of low-voiced relatives, took Helen
through her 'commissions' with biographies of the dead, where she happened
to know them, and sketches of their next of kin. Helen endured till nearly
half-past nine, ere she fled to her room.

Almost at once there was a knock at her door and Mrs. Scarsworth entered;
her hands, holding the dreadful list, clasped before her.

'Yes—yes—I know,' she began. 'You're sick of me, but I want to tell you
something. You—you aren't married, are you? Then perhaps you won't . . .
But it doesn't matter. I've *got* to tell some one. I can't go on any longer like
this.'

'But please——' Mrs. Scarsworth had backed against the shut door, and her
mouth worked dryly.

'In a minute,' she said. 'You—you know about these graves of mine I was
telling you about downstairs, just now? They really *are* commissions. At least
several of them are.' Her eye wandered round the room. 'What extraordinary
wall-papers they have in Belgium, don't you think? . . . Yes. I swear they are
commissions. But there's *one*, d'you see, and—and he was more to me than
anything else in the world. Do you understand?'

Helen nodded.

'More than any one else. And, of course, he oughtn't to have been. He
ought to have been nothing to me. But he *was*. He *is*. That's why I do the
commissions, you see. That's all.'

'But why do you tell me?' Helen asked desperately.

'Because I'm *so* tired of lying. Tired of lying—always lying—year in and
year out. When I don't tell lies I've got to act 'em and I've got to think 'em,
always. *You* don't know what that means. He was everything to me that he
oughtn't to have been—the one real thing—the only thing that ever happened
to me in all my life; and I've had to pretend he wasn't. I've had to watch every
word I said, and think out what lie I'd tell next, for years and years!'

'How many years?' Helen asked.

'Six years and four months before, and two and three-quarters after. I've gone to him eight times, since. To-morrow'll make the ninth, and—and I can't—I *can't* go to him again with nobody in the world knowing. I want to be honest with some one before I go. Do you understand? It doesn't matter about *me*. I was never truthful, even as a girl. But it isn't worthy of *him*. So—so I—I had to tell you. I can't keep it up any longer. Oh, I can't!'

She lifted her joined hands almost to the level of her mouth, and brought them down sharply, still joined, to full arms' length below her waist. Helen reached forward, caught them, bowed her head over them, and murmured: 'Oh, my dear! My dear!' Mrs. Scarsworth stepped back, her face all mottled.

'My God!' said she. 'Is *that* how you take it?'

Helen could not speak, and the woman went out; but it was a long while before Helen was able to sleep.

Next morning Mrs. Scarsworth left early on her round of commissions, and Helen walked alone to Hagenzeele Third. The place was still in the making, and stood some five or six feet above the metalled road, which it flanked for hundreds of yards. Culverts across a deep ditch served for entrances through the unfinished boundary wall. She climbed a few wooden-faced earthen steps and then met the entire crowded level of the thing in one held breath. She did not know that Hagenzeele Third counted twenty-one thousand dead already. All she saw was a merciless sea of black crosses, bearing little strips of stamped tin at all angles across their faces. She could distinguish no order or arrangement in their mass; nothing but a waist-high wilderness as of weeds stricken dead, rushing at her. She went forward, moved to the left and the right hopelessly, wondering by what guidance she should ever come to her own. A great distance away there was a line of whiteness. It proved to be a block of some two or three hundred graves whose headstones had already been set, whose flowers were planted out, and whose new-sown grass showed green. Here she could see clear-cut letters at the ends of the rows, and, referring to her slip, realised that it was not here she must look.

A man knelt behind a line of headstones—evidently a gardener, for he was firming a young plant in the soft earth. She went towards him, her paper in her hand. He rose at her approach and without prelude or salutation asked: 'Who are you looking for?'

'Lieutenant Michael Turrell—my nephew,' said Helen slowly and word for word, as she had many thousands of times in her life.

The man lifted his eyes and looked at her with infinite compassion before he turned from the fresh-sown grass toward the naked black crosses.

'Come with me,' he said, 'and I will show you where your son lies.'

When Helen left the Cemetery she turned for a last look. In the distance she saw the man bending over his young plants; and she went away, supposing him to be the gardener.

BY WAY OF DISCUSSION

Like everybody else, literary critics and English instructors have their preferences and prejudices. Thus, while often perfectly comfortable with ghosts, demons, grotesque characters of every type, and the most uncompromisingly pessimistic view of the human condition, they are likely to react harshly to religious supernaturalism and condemn even a modest amount of tender feeling as gross sentimentality. As a result, "The Gardener," a first-class piece of work, has come in for considerable unjustified criticism. True, emotion is an integral ingredient in the story, but the emotion stems naturally from the subject and, like the supernaturalism, is handled with great economy and restraint. Indeed, it is this very compression that is responsible for the moving impact of the story's climax, when we finally learn the truth about Helen's relationship to Michael.

Actually, a careful between-the-lines reading of the story's opening paragraph provides several hints that Michael is really Helen's son, not the child of her "unfortunate" brother George, as Helen has given out in the village:

> Every one in the village knew that Helen Turrell did her duty by all her world, and by none more honourably than by her only brother's unfortunate child. The village knew, too, that George Turrell had tried his family severely since early youth, and were not surprised to be told that, after many fresh starts given and thrown away, he, an Inspector of Indian Police, had entangled himself with the daughter of a retired non-commissioned officer, and had died of a fall from a horse a few weeks before his child was born. Mercifully, George's father and mother were both dead, and though Helen, thirty-five and independent, might well have washed her hands of the whole disgraceful affair, she most nobly took charge, though she was, at the time, under threat of lung trouble which had driven her to the South of France. She arranged for the passage of the child and a nurse from Bombay, met them at Marseilles, nursed the baby through an attack of infantile dysentery due to the carelessness of the nurse, whom she had had to dismiss, and at last, thin and worn but triumphant, brought the boy late in the autumn, wholly restored, to her Hampshire home.

To conceal her pregnancy, Helen has faked "the threat of lung disease," retreated to the South of France to have her child, and after waiting for him to grow past the newborn stage—a necessary precaution if her scheme is to succeed—brought him back home. In order to quell any possible speculation about her long absence, she explains that she has had to nurse the baby through a siege of dysentery. Helen's deception is completely successful. Ironically, because of her reputation for openness, the village accepts Helen's story without question, even applauding her for doing her duty when she might well have refused to involve herself with the child in any way.

Given the self-righteousness and emotional coldness of the villagers, there is little else that Helen could have done and still continued to live peacefully among them with her child. These are people who have condemned George merely because he has supposedly married outside the officer caste and who regard it as a mercy that his parents are no longer alive to witness his "disgrace." To them, life is a matter of rigid form in which an exaggerated respectability counts for everything, spontaneity and warmth counting for nothing. Thus, when war comes and the casualties start to mount, they quickly evolve a ritual to meet the situation, a ritual completely devoid of human feeling. Of all the villagers, only the postmistress's daughter, who weeps for the man who once gave her sweets, seems as yet uncontaminated by the emotional bankruptcy around her. Had the truth about Helen become known, she could have expected no mercy from these people; they would have made both her life and Michael's a perfect hell.

Ironically, Helen herself has not completely escaped the taint of respectability; nor, of course, is the taint confined to her own particular village. Although her deception does not require her to do so, Helen refers to her brother's entanglement as a "disgrace" and sneers at his wife's social class, saying that the people in it "would do almost anything for money." Later, she is genuinely shocked when Michael admits that he had considered entering the army without a commission. Much the same attitude colors the thinking of the Lancashire woman whose son, to escape the supposed stigma of serving as a common soldier, has enlisted under the name of Smith. Even Mrs. Scarsworth bears the stamp of respectability's baleful influence. When she confesses her real reason for repeated visits to military cemeteries, she says, "He was everything to me that he oughtn't to have been . . . and I've had to pretend he wasn't." In all three instances, false propriety has exacted a heavy price, forcing both Helen Turrell and Mrs. Scarsworth to deny relationships that mean more to them than anything else and depriving the Lancashire woman of the chance to see her son's final resting place.

From the very beginning, the relationship between Helen and Michael is one of strong mutual love. This love is reflected in Michael's deep sense of injury when he learns that Helen has violated a personal confidence, Helen's gentleness in the face of Michael's tirade, and the tearful reconciliation that concludes the episode. Later, when Michael begins to suspect that he might be illegitimate, he feels anxiety, not for himself but for his relationship with his beloved "Auntie." This anxiety is not relieved until Helen assures him, as he lies delirious with the measles, that nothing could possibly make any difference between them. Upon receiving the message that Michael is missing in action, Helen experiences a death of the spirit—a sort of emotional breakdown. Although she goes through the motions of living, she seems always to be moving "at an immense distance" from herself and remains totally untouched by the events around her. This condition lasts until Michael's body has been discovered. Then Helen awakens into "some sort of second life."

Bitter irony pervades Kipling's view of the war and everything connected with it. The fighting itself is likened to some profane species of
factory operation that fabricates battles and "bereaved next-of-kin" with
equal absence of feeling. Then there are the "infallible secretaries" who
nonetheless do fail to find the missing Michael and who couch their
regrets in language reminiscent of a business letter regretting some
company's inability to supply a piece of merchandise. A similar coldness
attends the official notice that Michael's body has been "found, identified, and re-interred in Hagenzeele Third Military Cemetery—the letter
of the row and the grave's number in that row duly given." The entire
journey across the English Channel to "Hagenzeele Third" is, ironically,
made to seem like some sort of vacation trip.

To Helen, however, the journey is no vacation. Rather, it is a waking
nightmare, one in no way helped by her meeting with Mrs. Scarsworth.
Outwardly shallow and chatty, Mrs. Scarsworth seems utterly unlike Hel-
en, though in fact the situations of the two are almost parallel. Like
Helen, Mrs. Scarsworth has posed as a conventional woman. Like Helen,
she harbors a secret that she must conceal from her own "respectable"
villagers in order to protect herself from their moral wrath. In short, both
women are living lives of pretense, a fact symbolically noted when their
first encounter takes place in a tea room with a false front.

Mrs. Scarsworth's agonized confession, made because she can no
longer stand to live a lie, foreshadows the revelation of Michael's true
relationship to Helen. Upon hearing the confession, Helen is overcome
with emotion and can only murmur, "Oh, my dear! My dear!" Mistaking
this response as one of condemnation, Mrs. Scarsworth is angered and
humiliated. She rushes from the room, leaving Helen to endure a troubled night before her walk to the cemetery that holds Michael's remains.

The story reaches its emotional high point when Helen encounters the
supposed gardener—who is actually Jesus Christ—and He tells her,
"Come with me, and I will show you where your son lies." The appearance of Jesus is subtly foreshadowed in a number of ways. For one,
Helen's visit to the grave takes place during the Easter season. For another, it follows immediately after her awakening, or resurrection, to a
second life. Finally, Michael has likewise undergone a sort of resurrection from his temporary grave beneath the farm wall to a permanent
resting place.

The concluding sentence of the story, coupled with the stranger's
awareness of the real relationship between Helen and Michael, makes it
clear that the stranger is Jesus, even if one misses the religious significance of the last six words. These words, as any reader familiar with the
four Gospels would know, are a direct allusion to John 21:11–16, which
tells of Mary Magdalene's visit to Christ's tomb following the crucifixion.
When she arrives, she finds the tomb empty and the area deserted except for one lone individual, the resurrected Jesus. Mary, however, does
not recognize Jesus and, "supposing Him to be the gardener," asks
where the body of her Lord has been taken. This Biblical episode, which
closely parallels the one between Helen and her own "gardener," pro-

vides the most conclusive evidence that the gardener is Christ. For the reader who harbors no prejudice against the possibility of such an appearance, the emotional impact can be substantial.

FOR ADDITIONAL READING

The following stories, which appear elsewhere in this book, are especially appropriate for an analysis of emotion:

1. Gina Berriault, "The Stone Boy" (p. 239)
2. Daniel Keyes, "Flowers for Algernon" (p. 197)
3. Jean-Paul Sartre, "The Wall" (p. 541)
4. D. H. Lawrence, "The Shadow in the Rose Garden" (p. 250)
5. Ivan Turgenev, "The Tryst" (p. 377)

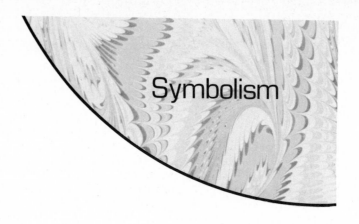

Symbolism

Symbolism has always been an integral part of literature. The writers of classical tales, ancient scriptures, medieval *exempla*, Renaissance plays and novellas, and modern novels, verse, and short stories have all made use of symbols. Modern psychology tells us that it is probably not possible for men and women to deal with the more difficult and sometimes baffling aspects of everyday life without using symbols of one kind or another.

A literary symbol may be an object, a person, a situation, a name, an action, or any other item so employed in a story as to suggest more than its literal meaning. For example, in "The Most Dangerous Game" the name "Zaroff" symbolically suggests the character of the general. Having fled Russia in the revolution that overthrew the czar, he has made himself the veritable czar of Ship-Trap Island. The very blackness that surrounds Ship-Trap Island on the first night of the story symbolizes the evil that is afoot there. The island itself symbolizes and reinforces Zaroff's isolation from the "normal" world of traditional values. Conversely, the lights of the yacht fading like "ever-vanishing fireflies" after Rainsford has fallen into the sea symbolize the world of ordinary civility far removed from the barbarity of Zaroff's island. Another symbol in "The Most Dangerous Game" is the jungle, which represents raw primitiveness. During the course of the hunt there, both Rainsford and Zaroff must draw upon their pure animal cunning to survive. The general's vicious dogs symbolize their master's complete lack of sympathy for anyone who is more than usually successful in eluding his pursuer.

Ironic symbols play an important role in "The Most Dangerous Game." An ironic symbol suggests something or reinforces an idea by the use of an object, situation, action, or the like that would normally be employed to symbolize something quite different. A volume of Shakespeare's plays, for example, might be used to call attention to its owner's illiteracy. Similarly, an elaborate description of a sunrise might be used at the point where an unsympathetic character's spectacularly successful career ends in catastrophe.

Ironic symbols employed in "The Most Dangerous Game" include the bright lights of the chateau visible to Rainsford as he first comes across the structure in the dark of night. Rainsford's "first thought was that he had come upon a village." But these lights are hardly those of a village, and, unlike the fading lights of the yacht, they do not shine forth from a source of domestic civility. The general's evening clothes are also ironic symbols, for such clothing would normally be worn by a person of quite a different temperament from that of the general. In like manner, the cultural symbols that surround the general are ironic: the linen, the crystal, the silver, the china, Rainsford's canopied bed, the fact that the general uses an exclusive London tailor, the tasty cocktails, the *borsch*, the champagne, and the fact that the general can hum a tune from the Folies Bergère. These items could easily be used to dramatize the character of a very refined person, a person who knows something of the lyric qualities of life. They become ironic symbols from their association with an individual who spends his evenings murdering innocent people for sport.

The use of symbols lets authors associate abstract qualities, ideas, or attitudes with specific, concrete objects, actions, and people. To be effective, a symbol must fit naturally into the setting of the story. In "The Monkey's Paw," for example, we can readily believe that someone who had been to India might have brought back a monkey's paw, and we can understand the Whites' fascination with it. The paw as an object of curiosity fits right into the setting of the story, and that is why it becomes an effective symbol of some supposedly malignant force that comes in from the outside to destroy the peaceful domesticity of the White household.

Literary symbols may be *original* or *conventional*. *Original symbols* arise naturally from the total structure of a story. Authors create original symbols as they create entire stories. A *conventional symbol*, on the other hand, while arising naturally from the story, is a symbol that has been used many times by many writers to symbolize a particular idea. The monkey's paw is an original symbol. Conventional symbols include a mirror to symbolize mental reflection, a river to symbolize time or fate, a full beard to symbolize masculine sexuality, a destructive storm to symbolize the indifference of the universe toward human beings.

Elaborate systems of symbols have been present in short stories ever since the genre assumed its modern form in the early nineteenth century. However, the creation of complicated symbolism gained impetus with the rise of psychoanalysis, psychotherapy, and psychiatry. Psychoanalysis originated with Sigmund Freud, who took great delight in trying to substantiate his theories of the human subconscious by citing various classical works of literature.

Modern psychology has been the predominant influence on literary symbolism. Although Freud and subsequent researchers into the human psyche have not always agreed about the make-up of psychological symbols, we can say that they have certain characteristics in common; they

1. frequently occur in dreams;
2. possess greater emotional and psychological power for the person to whom they are a symbol than would any matter-of-fact description of the circumstances they symbolize;
3. bring together various unconscious urges and desires and unite them with conscious elements of a person's life;
4. often arise in the minds of people with greatly dissimilar backgrounds;
5. usually present a picture or situation that calls either for action or for a major decision;
6. may have different meanings at different times for any given person.

To better understand modern literary symbolism, we might draw a parallel between a dream and the short story. A dream is likely to include various symbolic images that are part of the mind's effort to deal with some problem. From the daily activities of an individual's life, various impressions are "piped" into the individual's subconscious. There they are processed, in whatever mysterious ways the mind processes such things, and given back to the individual as the symbolic objects and circumstances of dreams. Thus dreams, with their array of symbols, can provide a sort of answer to the problems of our immediate lives.

Similarly, an author experiences life, creatively "processes" it, and ultimately writes a story about it. Into the story, the author often puts symbols rather than direct statements of the events or situations processed by his or her art. The author does this out of a belief or feeling that symbols have a far greater impact on the reader than will any bald statement of the facts. The reader who experiences the story is in a situation similar to that of the dreamer. The author has become the reader's subconscious. The author's processing of experience has become the dream, and the author's story has become the symbols of the dream. What the reader learns from the story, however, is likely to be something about humanity as a whole rather than simply something personal.

The impact and motivating power of a symbol can be seen in a situation in which a man and wife suspect that their only child has been kidnapped. Several days go by and nothing happens. Then the family receives in the mail not a letter but a faceless ceramic facsimile of a child with a railroad spike through its chest. No letter matter-of-factly detailing the threats of the kidnappers is likely to evoke the horror produced by this symbol.

Generally speaking, psychological symbols, and thus most modern literary symbols, arise from three sources: (1) archetypal images, (2) the personal experiences of individuals, and (3) the cultural experiences of groups. The concept of archetypes was brought to literary criticism by the Swiss psychoanalyst Carl Jung. According to Jung, all peoples share a "collective unconscious"—a blocked-off memory of a common human past. In some instances the collective unconscious predates our experiences as humans and is thus believed to be prelogical, primordial, or instinctual. This shared racial memory is the source of unconscious ideas, patterns of thought, and images that are universally present in individual psyches. Although archetypes can never actually be expressed consciously, authors who wish to employ symbols assumed to be derived from archetypal images are likely to make frequent and elaborate use of such things as descriptions that suggest large breasts or the pregnant belly of a woman; soaring birds, seemingly free of the earth's restraints; dark or moving shadows, foreboding danger; apparently grotesque or animal impulses arising from a will to survive or procreate; and elemental motivation arising from such natural phenomena as heat, cold, noise, and sunlight. In fact, most conventional natural symbols arise from what are supposed to be archetypal images that have acquired symbolic value.

An author who uses personal symbols is probably interested in revealing their meaning only to readers who have had similar experiences. Such symbolism can become inside information to a few kindred souls and thus does not really concern us here. The meaning of cultural symbols, on the other hand, is open to practically any knowledgeable reader who has grown up in the same society as the author. Most Americans, for example, are aware of the symbolic meaning of a bald eagle, a Cadillac, a black cat, or a wedding ring.

Cultural symbols include things that make us what we are. We derive our self-image from an evaluation of cultural symbols. For example, in our society a college diploma is a cultural symbol, and a person who receives this symbol is likely to have a new, heightened sense of self-worth. Not surprisingly, just as we interpret our own lives in terms of cultural symbols, so we also interpret the lives of fictional characters in terms of cultural symbols.

One particular type of symbol may be thought of as archetypal, personal, and cultural. It has become so pervasive in modern literature that it blurs the distinctions among the categories. This is the *Freudian*, or *sexual, symbol*. A Freudian symbol can be any object, image, action, or statement that has sexual implications beyond its literal meaning. Usually it is possible to distinguish between masculine and feminine symbols. Hard, aggressive, penetrating objects may be considered masculine Freudian symbols—sometimes even *phallic symbols*. Soft, rounded, yielding objects may be considered feminine Freudian symbols. According to a Freudian analysis of literature, actions suggestive of sexual activity, such as the riding of a horse, may, when the surrounding circumstances are appropriate, be taken as symbolic of sexual activity or of a suppressed desire for sexual activity.

Modern short stories tend either to be dominated by a single pervasive symbol or to include an elaborate pattern of symbols. "The Dry Rock," "A Sick Call," and "The Monkey's Paw" are dominated by a single symbol. The first is dominated by the symbol of the blow delivered by Rusk to the nose of Tarloff. This belligerent act symbolizes how in the modern, urbanized world people can be humiliated without recourse. In the second story the symbol is Father Macdowell's deaf ear. This symbolizes how the Church, in tending to its own business, may ignore the wishes of other people. The monkey's paw in the third story represents some supposedly malignant external force bent on destroying the peace of the White household. "The Most Dangerous Game" and "The Secret Life of Walter Mitty," on the other hand, are stories with many different symbols, each one contributing to the general unity of its particular story.

Of the three stories that follow, one (John Galsworthy's "The Japanese Quince") is dominated by a single pervasive symbol, another (Ralph Ellison's "Flying Home") includes an elaborate pattern of symbols, and the third (Truman Capote's "A Tree of Night") includes an elaborate pattern of Freudian symbols. Perhaps a gentle warning is in order before we look at these stories, however. Because "symbol-hunting" can be fun, students sometimes carry it too far, seeing symbols everywhere, discovering hidden meanings that authors never dreamed of. Actually, symbols are seldom hidden. They are usually in plain view for any reader to see. The symbols in "The Most Dangerous Game" were not hidden away by the author. To the contrary, the symbolism in Richard Connell's story is straightforward and not at all obscure. The symbolic importance of Walter Mitty's gloves and sling is also clear, as is the symbolic meaning of the punch in "The Dry Rock," Father Macdowell's deaf ear in "The Sick Call," and the false façade on the Belgian café in "The Gardener." The problem is that a reader may believe that such things are too obvious to be symbols.

When you look for symbols, you should look for objects, incidents, actions, descriptions of characters or settings, and so on that generally reinforce the mood of the entire story. Symbols are usually repeated; they are emphasized. Ironic symbols, of course, are another matter. They may be placed in the story to suggest counter or alternate interpretations of events. But most of the time symbols are used to underscore the ideas of the story, to mark in darker brush strokes what the other structural elements are working toward.

Not recognizing a symbol is no crime and is preferable to seeing symbols where none exist. Whether you spot symbols or not, a story will have meaning for you on the literal level. Nevertheless, keep in mind that it is through the use of symbolism that the author hopes to bring to a story a breadth and depth beyond the literal meaning of the words.

JOHN GALSWORTHY

The Japanese Quince

As Mr. Nilson, well known in the City, opened the window of his dressing-room on Campden Hill, he experienced a peculiar sweetish sensation in the back of his throat, and a feeling of emptiness just under his fifth rib. Hooking the window back, he noticed that a little tree in the Square Gardens had come out in blossom, and that the thermometer stood at sixty. "Perfect morning," he thought; "Spring at last!"

Resuming some meditations on the price of Tintos, he took up an ivory-backed hand-glass and scrutinised his face. His firm, well-coloured cheeks, with their neat brown moustaches, and his round, well-opened, clear grey eyes, wore a reassuring appearance of good health. Putting on his black frock coat, he went downstairs.

In the dining-room his morning paper was laid out on the sideboard. Mr. Nilson had scarcely taken it in his hand when he again became aware of that queer feeling. Somewhat concerned, he went to the French window and descended the scrolled iron steps into the fresh air. A cuckoo clock struck eight.

"Half an hour to breakfast," he thought; "I'll take a turn in the Gardens."

He had them to himself, and proceeded to pace the circular path with his morning paper clasped behind him. He had scarcely made two revolutions, however, when it was borne in on him that, instead of going away in the fresh air, the feeling had increased. He drew several deep breaths, having heard deep breathing recommended by his wife's doctor; but they augmented rather than diminished the sensation—as of some sweetish liquor in course within him, together with a faint aching just above his heart. Running over what he had eaten the night before, he could recollect no unusual dish, and it occurred to him that it might possibly be some smell affecting him. But he could detect nothing except a faint sweet lemony scent, rather agreeable than otherwise, which evidently emanated from the bushes budding in the sunshine. He was on the point of resuming his promenade, when a blackbird close by burst into song, and, looking up, Mr. Nilson saw at a distance of perhaps five yards a little tree, in the heart of whose branches the bird was perched. He stood staring curiously at this tree, recognising it for that which he had noticed from his window. It was covered with young blossoms, pink and white, and little bright green leaves both round and spikey; and on all this blossom and these leaves the sunlight glistened. Mr. Nilson smiled; the little tree was so alive and pretty! And instead of passing on, he stayed there smiling at the tree.

"Morning like this!" he thought; "and here I am the only person in the Square who has the—to come out and——!" But he had no sooner conceived this thought, than he saw quite near him a man with his hands behind him, who was also staring up and smiling at the little tree. Rather taken aback, Mr. Nilson ceased to smile, and looked furtively at the stranger. It was his next-door neighbour, Mr. Tandram, well known in the City, who had occupied the adjoining house for some five years. Mr. Nilson perceived at once the awkwardness of his position, for, being married, they had not yet had occasion to speak to one another. Doubtful as to his proper conduct, he decided at last to murmur: "Fine morning!" and was passing on, when Mr. Tandram answered: "Beautiful, for the time of year!" Detecting a slight nervousness in his neighbour's voice, Mr. Nilson was emboldened to regard him openly. He was of about Mr. Nilson's own height, with firm, well-coloured cheeks, neat brown moustaches, and round, well-opened, clear grey eyes; and he was wearing a black frock coat. Mr. Nilson noticed that he had his morning paper clasped behind him as he looked up at the little tree. And, visited somehow by the feeling that he had been caught out, he said abruptly:

"Er—can you give me the name of that tree?"

Mr. Tandram answered:

"I was about to ask you that," and stepped towards it. Mr. Nilson also approached the tree.

"Sure to have its name on, I should think," he said.

Mr. Tandram was the first to see the little label, close to where the black-bird had been sitting. He read it out.

"Japanese quince!"

"Ah!" said Mr. Nilson, "thought so. Early flowerers."

"Very," assented Mr. Tandram, and added: "Quite a feelin' in the air to-day."

Mr. Nilson nodded.

"It was a blackbird singin'," he said.

"Blackbirds," answered Mr. Tandram, "I prefer them to thrushes myself; more body in the note." And he looked at Mr. Nilson in an almost friendly way.

"Quite," murmured Mr. Nilson. "These exotics, they don't bear fruit. Pretty blossom!" and he again glanced up at the blossom, thinking: "Nice fellow, this, I rather like him."

Mr. Tandram also gazed up at the blossom. And the little tree, as if appreciating their attention, quivered and glowed. From a distance, the blackbird gave a loud, clear call. Mr. Nilson dropped his eyes. It struck him suddenly that Mr. Tandram looked a little foolish; and, as if he had seen himself, he said: "I must be going in. Good morning!"

A shade passed over Mr. Tandram's face, as if he, too, had suddenly noticed something about Mr. Nilson.

"Good morning," he replied, and clasping their journals to their backs they separated.

Mr. Nilson retraced his steps towards his garden window, walking slowly so as to avoid arriving at the same time as his neighbour. Having seen Mr. Tandram mount his scrolled iron steps, he ascended his own in turn. On the top step he paused.

With the slanting Spring sunlight darting and quivering into it, the Japanese quince seemed more living than a tree. The blackbird had returned to it, and was chanting out his heart.

Mr. Nilson sighed; again he felt that queer sensation, that chokey feeling in his throat.

The sound of a cough or sigh attracted his attention. There, in the shadow of his French window, stood Mr. Tandram, also looking forth across the Gardens at the little quince tree.

Unaccountably upset, Mr. Nilson turned abruptly into the house, and opened his morning paper.

BY WAY OF DISCUSSION

The quince, which bears a fruit first cultivated in ancient central Asia, is a shrub or small tree botanically related to both the pear and the apple. Quince fruit is shaped somewhat like a pear and is golden yellow. Although the quince blossom has a fragrant aroma, fresh quince is very hard and has such an acid taste that it is never eaten raw. But it can be delightful when cooked, and for this reason it is used to make or flavor marmalades, preserves, and jellies.

When dealing with a story so clearly dominated by a single symbol as this one is, we should take the time to learn something about the symbol. Otherwise, the author's intended meaning is likely to be obscured. Knowing the background of an object used as a literary symbol, however, will not reveal everything about its symbolic meaning. That will come only as we understand how the object is integrated with everything else in the story. So, let's take a look at the total story to see if we can understand what Galsworthy is getting at by using the quince tree as the dominant symbol.

To begin with, we have our protagonist Mr. Nilson, a prominent person in the City. The City, as every English reader would know, is the chief publishing, financial, and business district of central London. But Mr. Nilson does not live in the City. Far from it; he lives on Campden Hill. Campden Hill is a real place, located near Kensington Gardens and the famous Hyde Park. It is a well-heeled residential and cultural area of greater London. Even if you were to visit Campden Hill today—and particularly Holland Park, which may be taken as the area's center—you would scarcely believe that it is a part of the great bustling metropolis of London. It is very quiet, dotted with attractive Georgian houses, and almost swallowed up by carefully maintained trees of every variety.

Nevertheless, Campden Hill is a part of London—as it was in 1910 when Galsworthy wrote "The Japanese Quince"—and the people who live there, people like Mr. Nilson and Mr. Tandram, are the progeny of a complex and regimented urban society. Notice that after Mr. Nilson has first smelled the aroma of the quince blossoms and experienced the unusual internal emptiness, he returns to thoughts of the stock market: he returns to matters that over the years have given his life structure and meaning, items far removed from warm spring days and fragrant blossoms.

But the queer feeling returns, and our protagonist decides, reluctantly, to take a stroll in the Gardens and get some fresh air. Dressed in his black frock coat—notice the symbolic similarity between the appearance and activities of Nilson and Tandram and those of the blackbird—he feels uneasy, almost ill, as he smells the naturally sweet, lemony fragrance of the quince blossom and contemplates the tree itself. As Nilson ruminates on what a pity it is that no one else is out enjoying such a nice morning, he notices Mr. Tandram, also a well-known figure in the City. Symbolically, we have Mr. Nilson, whose name suggests the word "nil," meaning "nothing," "empty," "zero," and we have Mr. Tandram, whose name suggests the word "tandem," meaning "a harnessed team," as of horses or other draft animals. Symbolically, then, we can say that Nilson and Tandram are a pair of dull and insensitive individuals. They are completely controlled by their society and professional positions and possess little or no social grace or understanding of the natural world—that is, the world of nature, as symbolized by the quince tree.

Nilson and Tandram, who are virtual mirror images of each other, talk. And what do they talk about? The morning, the weather, the season, and the quince tree. For five years they have lived next door to each other; but, incredibly, because of convention's rigid dictates they have never spoken to each other: "for, being married, they had not yet had occasion to speak to one another." The quince, then, seems to be responsible for a small miracle on this particular morning. At least the two men have spoken. Neither man knows the name of the tree, however; they have to read the label, which is probably scribbled on a card fastened to the tree by a piece of wire. The British are very thorough about labeling things like trees and flowering bushes, especially when such bushes are located in great metropolitan parks and gardens.

Just as the blossoming quince tree apparently motivates the blackbird to sing, it motivates Nilson and Tandram to talk to each other. Nilson even discovers that he likes Tandram: "Nice fellow, this, I rather like him." But this whole "emotional outpouring" is brought to an abrupt halt when it suddenly strikes Nilson that Tandram, and thus himself as well, "looked a little foolish." Important businessmen from the City, the backbone of British society, can never allow themselves the luxury of looking a little silly. So, the two men quickly part, leaving the quince tree to the blackbird:

> With the slanting Spring sunlight darting and quivering into it, the Japanese quince seemed more living than a tree. The blackbird had returned to it, and was chanting out his heart.

The story seems to be saying that we humans should not only take the time to "stop and smell the roses," in the words of a popular song, but we should also take the time to be civil and to communicate with our fellow creatures. The failure to do these things results in human isolation.

Notice that the use of the blackbird as a symbol for Nilson and Tandram is somewhat ironic. Although the color of the bird is the same as that of the clothing worn by the two men, the bird's eventual surrender to the joy of the tree contrasts sharply with Nilson's and Tandram's refusal to go too far in their sudden impulse toward social intercourse. They are too thoroughly conditioned to allow themselves to surrender to the simple joy of life, symbolically the meaning of the blossoming Japanese quince.

Flying Home

When Todd came to, he saw two faces suspended above him in a sun so hot and blinding that he could not tell if they were black or white. He stirred, feeling a pain that burned as though his whole body had been laid open to the sun which glared into his eyes. For a moment an old fear of being touched by white hands seized him. Then the very sharpness of the pain began slowly to clear his head. Sounds came to him dimly. He done come to. Who are they? he thought. Naw he ain't, I coulda sworn he was white. Then he heard clearly:

"You hurt bad?"

Something within him uncoiled. It was a Negro sound.

"He's still out," he heard.

"Give 'im time. . . . Say, son, you hurt bad?"

Was he? There was that awful pain. He lay rigid, hearing their breathing and trying to weave a meaning between them and his being stretched painfully upon the ground. He watched them warily, his mind traveling back over a painful distance. Jagged scenes, swiftly unfolding as in a movie trailer, reeled through his mind, and he saw himself piloting a tailspinning plane and landing and landing and falling from the cockpit and trying to stand. Then, as in a great silence, he remembered the sound of crunching bone, and now, looking up into the anxious faces of an old Negro man and a boy from where he lay in the same field, the memory sickened him and he wanted to remember no more.

"How you feel, son?"

Todd hesitated, as though to answer would be to admit an inacceptable weakness. Then, "It's my ankle," he said.

"Which one?"

"The left."

With a sense of remoteness he watched the old man bend and remove his boot, feeling the pressure ease.

"That any better?"

"A lot. Thank you."

He had the sensation of discussing someone else, that his concern was with some far more important thing, which for some reason escaped him.

"You done broke it bad," the old man said. "We have to get you to a doctor."

He felt that he had been thrown into a tailspin. He looked at his watch; how long had he been here? He knew there was but one important thing in the world, to get the plane back to the field before his officers were displeased.

"Help me up," he said. "Into the ship."

"But it's broke too bad. . . ."

"Give me your arm!"

"But, son . . ."

Clutching the old man's arm he pulled himself up, keeping his left leg clear, thinking, "I'd never make him understand," as the leather-smooth face came parallel with his own.

"Now, let's see."

He pushed the old man back, hearing a bird's insistent shrill. He swayed giddily. Blackness washed over him, like infinity.

"You best sit down."

"No, I'm O.K."

"But, son. You jus' gonna make it worse. . . ."

It was a fact that everything in him cried out to deny, even against the flaming pain in his ankle. He would have to try again.

"You mess with that ankle they have to cut your foot off," he heard.

Holding his breath, he started up again. It pained so badly that he had to bite his lips to keep from crying out and he allowed them to help him down with a pang of despair.

"It's best you take it easy. We gon' git you a doctor."

Of all the luck, he thought. Of all the rotten luck, now I have done it. The fumes of high-octane gasoline clung in the heat, taunting him.

"We kin ride him into town on old Ned," the boy said.

Ned? He turned, seeing the boy point toward an ox team browsing where the buried blade of a plow marked the end of a furrow. Thoughts of himself riding an ox through the town, past streets full of white faces, down the concrete runways of the airfield made swift images of humiliation in his mind. With a pang he remembered his girl's last letter. "Todd," she had written, "I don't need the papers to tell me you had the intelligence to fly. And I have always known you to be as brave as anyone else. The papers annoy me. Don't you be contented to prove over and over again that you're brave or skillful just because you're black, Todd. I think they keep beating that dead horse because they don't want to say why you boys are not yet fighting. I'm really disappointed, Todd. Anyone with brains can learn to fly, but then what? What about using it, and who will you use it for? I wish, dear, you'd write about this. I sometimes think they're playing a trick on us. It's very humiliating. . . ." He wiped cold sweat from his face, thinking, What does she know of humiliation? She's never been down South. Now the humiliation would come. When you must have them judge you, knowing that they never accept your mistakes as your own, but hold it against your whole race—that was humiliation. Yes, and humiliation was when you could never be simply yourself, when you were always a part of this old black ignorant man. Sure, he's all right. Nice and kind and helpful. But he's not you. Well, there's one humiliation I can spare my-self.

"No," he said, "I have orders not to leave the ship. . . ."

"Aw," the old man said. Then turning to the boy, "Teddy, then you better hustle down to Mister Graves and get him to come. . . ."

"No, wait!" he protested before he was fully aware. Graves might be white. "Just have him get word to the field, please. They'll take care of the rest."

He saw the boy leave, running.

"How far does he have to go?"

"Might' nigh a mile."

He rested back, looking at the dusty face of his watch. But now they know something has happened, he thought. In the ship there was a perfectly good radio, but it was useless. The old fellow would never operate it. That buzzard knocked me back a hundred years, he thought. Irony danced within him like the gnats circling the old man's head. With all I've learned I'm dependent upon this "peasant's" sense of time and space. His leg throbbed. In the plane, instead of time being measured by the rhythms of pain and a kid's legs, the instruments would have told him at a glance. Twisting upon his elbows he saw where dust had powdered the plane's fuselage, feeling the lump form in his throat that was always there when he thought of flight. It's crouched there, he thought, like the abandoned shell of a locust. I'm naked without it. Not a machine, a suit of clothes you wear. And with a sudden embarrassment and wonder he whispered, "It's the only dignity I have. . . ."

He saw the old man watching, his torn overalls clinging limply to him in the heat. He felt a sharp need to tell the old man what he felt. But that would be meaningless. If I tried to explain why I need to fly back, he'd think I was simply afraid of white officers. But it's more than fear . . . a sense of anguish clung to him like the veil of sweat that hugged his face. He watched the old man, hearing him humming snatches of a tune as he admired the plane. He felt a furtive sense of resentment. Such old men often came to the field to watch the pilots with childish eyes. At first it had made him proud; they had been a meaningful part of a new experience. But soon he realized they did not understand his accomplishments and they came to shame and embarrass him, like the distasteful praise of an idiot. A part of the meaning of flying had gone then, and he had not been able to regain it. If I were a prizefighter I would be more human, he thought. Not a monkey doing tricks, but a man. They were pleased simply that he was a Negro who could fly, and that was not enough. He felt cut off from them by age, by understanding, by sensibility, by technol-ogy and by his need to measure himself against the mirror of other men's appreciation. Somehow he felt betrayed, as he had when as a child he grew to discover that his father was dead. Now for him any real appreciation lay with his white officers; and with them he could never be sure. Between ignorant black men and condescending whites, his course of flight seemed mapped by the nature of things away from all needed and natural landmarks. Under some sealed orders, couched in ever more technical and mysterious terms, his path curved swiftly away from both the shame the old man symbolized and the cloudy terrain of white men's regard. Flying blind, he knew but one point of landing and there he would receive his wings. After that the enemy would appreciate his skill and he would assume his deepest meaning, he thought sadly, neither from those who condescended nor from those who praised without understanding, but from the enemy who would recognize his manhood and skill in terms of hate. . . .

He sighed, seeing the oxen making queer, prehistoric shadows against the dry brown earth.

"You just take it easy, son," the old man soothed. "That boy won't take long. Crazy as he is about airplanes."

"I can wait," he said.

"What kinda airplane you call this here'n?"

"An Advanced Trainer," he said, seeing the old man smile. His fingers were like gnarled dark wood against the metal as he touched the low-slung wing.

" 'Bout how fast can she fly?"

"Over two hundred an hour?"

"Lawd! That's so fast I bet it don't seem like you moving!"

Holding himself rigid, Todd opened his flying suit. The shade had gone and he lay in a ball of fire.

"You mind if I take a look inside? I was always curious to see. . . ."

"Help yourself. Just don't touch anything."

He heard him climb upon the metal wing, grunting. Now the questions would start. Well, so you don't have to think to answer. . . .

He saw the old man looking over into the cockpit, his eyes bright as a child's.

"You must have to know a lot to work all these here things."

He was silent, seeing him step down and kneel beside him.

"Son, how come you want to fly way up there in the air?"

Because it's the most meaningful act in the world . . . because it makes me less like you, he thought.

But he said: "Because I like it, I guess. It's as good a way to fight and die as I know."

"Yeah? I guess you right," the old man said. "But how long you think before they gonna let you all fight?"

He tensed. This was the question all Negroes asked, put with the same timid hopefulness and longing that always opened a greater void within him than that he had felt beneath the plane the first time he had flown. He felt light-headed. It came to him suddenly that there was something sinister about the conversation, that he was flying unwillingly into unsafe and uncharted regions. If he could only be insulting and tell this old man who was trying to help him to shut up!

"I bet you one thing . . ."

"Yes?"

"That you was plenty scared coming down."

He did not answer. Like a dog on a trail the old man seemed to smell out his fears and he felt anger bubble within him.

"You sho' scared me. When I seen you coming down in that thing with it a-rollin' and a-jumpin' like a pitchin' hoss, I thought sho' you was a goner. I almost had me a stroke!"

He saw the old man grinning, "Ever'thin's been happening round here this morning, come to think of it".

"Like what?" he asked.

"Well, first thing I know, here come two white fellers looking for Mister Rudolph, that's Mister Graves's cousin. That got me worked up right away. . . ."

"Why?"

"Why? 'Cause he done broke outta the crazy house, that's why. He liable to kill somebody," he said. "They oughta have him by now though. Then here you come. First I think it's one of them white boys. Then doggone if you don't fall outta there. Lawd, I'd done heard about you boys but I haven't never seen one o' you-all. Cain't tell you how it felt to see somebody what look like me in a airplane!"

The old man talked on, the sound streaming around Todd's thoughts like air flowing over the fuselage of a flying plane. You were a fool, he thought, remembering how before the spin the sun had blazed bright against the bill-board signs beyond the town, and how a boy's blue kite had bloomed beneath him, tugging gently in the wind like a strange, odd-shaped flower. He had once flown such kites himself and tried to find the boy at the end of the invisible cord. But he had been flying too high and too fast. He had climbed steeply away in exultation. Too steeply, he thought. And one of the first rules you learn is that if the angle of thrust is too steep the plane goes into a spin. And then, instead of pulling out of it and going into a dive you let a buzzard panic you. A lousy buzzard!

"Son, what made all that blood on the glass?"

"A buzzard," he said, remembering how the blood and feathers had sprayed back against the hatch. It had been as though he had flown into a storm of blood and blackness.

"Well, I declare! They's lots of 'em around here. They after dead things. Don't eat nothing what's alive."

"A little bit more and he would have made a meal out of me," Todd said grimly.

"They bad luck all right. Teddy's got a name for 'em, calls 'em jimcrows," the old man laughed.

"It's a damned good name."

"They the damnedest birds. Once I seen a hoss all stretched out like he was sick, you know. So I hollers, 'Gid up from there, suh!' Just to make sho! An' doggone, son, if I don't see two ole jimcrows come flying right up outa that hoss's insides! Yessuh! The sun was shinin' on 'em and they couldn't a been no greasier if they'd been eating barbecue."

Todd thought he would vomit, his stomach quivered.

"You made that up," he said.

"Nawsuh! Saw him just like I see you."

"Well, I'm glad it was you."

"You see lots a funny things down here, son."

"No, I'll let you see them," he said.

"By the way, the white folks round here don't like to see you boys up there in the sky. They ever bother you?"

"No."

"Well, they'd like to."

"Someone always wants to bother someone else," Todd said. "How do you know?"

"I just know."

"Well," he said defensively, "no one has bothered us."

Blood pounded in his ears as he looked away into space. He tensed, seeing a black spot in the sky, and strained to confirm what he could not clearly see.

"What does that look like to you?" he asked excitedly.

"Just another bad luck, son."

Then he saw the movement of wings with disappointment. It was gliding smoothly down, wings outspread, tail feathers gripping the air, down swiftly—gone behind the green screen of trees. It was like a bird he had imagined there, only the sloping branches of the pines remained, sharp against the pale stretch of sky. He lay barely breathing and stared at the point where it had disappeared, caught in a spell of loathing and admiration. Why did they make them so disgusting and yet teach them to fly so well? It's like when I was up in heaven, he heard, starting.

The old man was chuckling, rubbing his stubbled chin.

"What did you say?"

"Sho', I died and went to heaven . . . maybe by time I tell you about it they be done come after you."

"I hope so," he said wearily.

"You boys ever sit around and swap lies?"

"Not often. Is this going to be one?"

"Well, I ain't so sho', on account of it took place when I was dead."

The old man paused, "That wasn't no lie 'bout the buzzards, though."

"All right," he said.

"Sho' you want to hear 'bout heaven?"

"Please," he answered, resting his head upon his arm.

"Well, I went to heaven and right away started to sproutin' me some wings.

Six good ones, they was. Just like them the white angels had. I couldn't hardly believe it. I was so glad that I went off on some clouds by myself and tried 'em out. You know, 'cause I didn't want to make a fool outta myself the first thing. . . ."

It's an old tale, Todd thought. Told me years ago. Had forgotten. But at least it will keep him from talking about buzzards.

He closed his eyes, listening.

". . . First thing I done was to git up on a low cloud and jump off. And doggone, boy, if them wings didn't work! First I tried the right; then I tried the left; then I tried 'em both together. Then Lawd, I started to move on out among the folks. I let 'em see me. . . ."

He saw the old man gesturing flight with his arms, his face full of mock pride as he indicated an imaginary crowd, thinking, It'll be in the newspapers, as he heard, " . . . so I went and found me some colored angels—somehow I didn't believe I was an angel till I seen a real black one, ha, yes! Then I was sho'—but they tole me I better come down 'cause us colored folks had to wear a special kin' a harness when we flew. That was how come they wasn't flyin'. Oh yes, an' you had to be extra strong for a black man even, to fly with one of them harnesses. . . ."

This is a new turn, Todd thought, what's he driving at?

"So I said to myself, I ain't gonna be bothered with no harness! Oh naw! 'Cause if God let you sprout wings you oughta have sense enough not to let nobody make you wear something what gits in the way of flyin'. So I starts to flyin'. Heck, son," he chuckled, his eyes twinkling, "you know I had to let eve'ybody know that old Jefferson could fly good as anybody else. And I could too, fly smooth as a bird! I could even loop-the-loop—only I had to make sho' to keep my long white robe down roun' my ankles. . . ."

Todd felt uneasy. He wanted to laugh at the joke, but his body refused, as of an independent will. He felt as he had as a child when after he had chewed a sugar-coated pill which his mother had given him, she had laughed at his efforts to remove the terrible taste.

". . . Well," he heard, "I was doing all right 'til I got to speeding. Found out I could fan up a right strong breeze, I could fly so fast. I could do all kin'sa stunts too. I started flying up to the stars and divin' down and zooming roun' the moon. Man, I like to scare the devil outa some ole white angels. I was raisin' hell. Not that I meant any harm, son. But I was just feeling good. It was so good to know I was free at last. I accidentally knocked the tips offa some stars and they tell me I caused a storm and a coupla lynchings down here in Macon County—though I swear I believe them boys what said that was making up lies on me. . . ."

He's mocking me, Todd thought angrily. He thinks it's a joke. Grinning down at me . . . His throat was dry. He looked at his watch; why the hell didn't they come? Since they had to, why? One day I was flying down one of them heavenly streets. You got yourself into it, Todd thought. Like Jonah in the whale.

"Justa throwin' feathers in everybody's face. An' ole Saint Peter called me in. Said, 'Jefferson, tell me two things, what you doin' flyin' without a harness; an' how come you flyin' so fast?' So I tole him I was flyin' without a harness 'cause it got in my way, but I couldn'ta been flyin' so fast, 'cause I wasn't usin' but one wing. Saint Peter said, 'You wasn't flyin' with but one wing?' 'Yessuh,' I says, scared-like. So he says, 'Well, since you got sucha extra fine pair of wings you can leave off yo' harness awhile. But from now on none of that there one-wing flyin', 'cause you gittin' up too damn much speed!' "

And with one mouth full of bad teeth you're making too damned much talk, thought Todd. Why don't I send him after the boy? His body ached from the hard ground and seeking to shift his position he twisted his ankle and hated himself for crying out.

"It gittin' worse?"

"I . . . I twisted it," he groaned.

"Try not to think about it, son. That's what I do."

He bit his lip, fighting pain with counter-pain as the voice resumed its rhythmical droning. Jefferson seemed caught in his own creation.

". . . After all that trouble I just floated roun' heaven in slow motion. But I forgot, like colored folks will do, and got to flyin' with one wing again. This time I was restin' my old broken arm and got to flyin' fast enough to shame the devil. I was comin' so fast, Lawd, I got myself called befo' ole Saint Peter again. He said, 'Jeff, didn't I warn you 'bout that speedin'?' 'Yessuh,' I says, 'but it was an accident.' He looked at me sad-like and shook his head and I knowed I was gone. He said, 'Jeff, you and that speedin' is a danger to the heavenly community. If I was to let you keep on flyin', heaven wouldn't be nothin' but uproar. Jeff, you got to go!' Son, I argued and pleaded with that old white man, but it didn't do a bit of good. They rushed me straight to them pearly gates and gimme a parachute and a map of the state of Alabama . . ."

Todd heard him laughing so that he could hardly speak, making a screen between them upon which his humiliation glowed like fire.

"Maybe you'd better stop awhile," he said, his voice unreal.

"Ain't much more," Jefferson laughed. "When they gimme the parachute ole Saint Peter ask me if I wanted to say a few words before I went. I felt so bad I couldn't hardly look at him, specially with all them white angels standin' around. Then somebody laughed and made me mad. So I tole him, 'Well, you done took my wings. And you puttin' me out. You got charge of things so's I can't do nothin' about it. But you got to admit just this: While I was up here I was the flyinest sonofabitch what ever hit heaven!'"

At the burst of laughter Todd felt such an intense humiliation that only great violence would wash it away. The laughter which shook the old man like a boiling purge set up vibrations of guilt within him which not even the intricate machinery of the plane would have been adequate to transform and he heard himself screaming, "Why do you laugh at me this way?"

He hated himself at that moment, but he had lost control. He saw Jefferson's mouth fall open, "What—?"

"Answer me!"

His blood pounded as though it would surely burst his temples and he tried to reach the old man and fell, screaming, "Can I help it because they won't let us actually fly? Maybe we are a bunch of buzzards feeding on a dead horse, but we can hope to be eagles, can't we? Can't we?"

He fell back, exhausted, his ankle pounding. The saliva was like straw in his mouth. If he had the strength he would strangle this old man. This grinning, gray-headed clown who made him feel as he felt when watched by the white officers at the field. And yet this old man had neither power, prestige, rank nor technique. Nothing that could rid him of this terrible feeling. He watched him, seeing his face struggle to express a turmoil of feeling.

"What you mean, son? What you talking 'bout . . . ?"

"Go away. Go tell your tales to the white folks."

"But I didn't mean nothing like that. . . . I . . . I wasn't tryin' to hurt your feelings. . . ."

"Please. Get the hell away from me!"

"But I didn't, son. I didn't mean all them things a-tall."

Todd shook as with a chill, searching Jefferson's face for a trace of the mockery he had seen there. But now the face was somber and tired and old. He was confused. He could not be sure that there had ever been laughter there, that Jefferson had ever really laughed in his whole life. He saw Jefferson reach out to touch him and shrank away, wondering if anything except the pain, now causing his vision to waver, was real. Perhaps he had imagined it all.

"Don't let it get you down, son," the voice said pensively.

He heard Jefferson sigh wearily, as though he felt more than he could say. His anger ebbed, leaving only the pain.

"I'm sorry," he mumbled.

"You just wore out with pain, was all. . . ."

He saw him through a blur, smiling. And for a second he felt the embarrassed silence of understanding flutter between them.

"What you was doin' flyin' over this section, son? Wasn't you scared they might shoot you for a cow?"

Todd tensed. Was he being laughed at again? But before he could decide, the pain shook him and a part of him was lying calmly behind the screen of pain that had fallen between them, recalling the first time he had ever seen a plane. It was as though an endless series of hangars had been shaken ajar in the air base of his memory and from each, like a young wasp emerging from its cell, arose the memory of a plane.

The first time I ever saw a plane I was very small and planes were new in the world. I was four-and-a-half and the only plane that I had ever seen was a model suspended from the ceiling of the automobile exhibit at the State Fair. But I did not know that it was only a model. I did not know how large a real plane was, nor how expensive. To me it was a fascinating toy, complete in itself, which my mother said could only be owned by rich little white boys. I stood rigid with admiration, my head straining backwards as I watched the gray little plane describing arcs above the gleaming tops of the automobiles. And I vowed that, rich or poor, someday I would own such a toy. My mother had to drag me out of the exhibit and not even the merry-go-round, the Ferris wheel, or the racing horses could hold my attention for the rest of the Fair. I was too busy imitating the tiny drone of the plane with my lips, and imitating with my hands the motion, swift and circling, that it made in flight.

After that I no longer used the pieces of lumber that lay about our back yard to construct wagons and autos . . . now it was used for airplanes. I built biplanes, using pieces of board for wings, a small box for the fuselage, another piece of wood for the rudder. The trip to the Fair had brought something new into my small world. I asked my mother repeatedly when the Fair would come back again. I'd lie in the grass and watch the sky, and each fighting bird became a soaring plane. I would have been good a year just to have seen a plane again. I became a nuisance to everyone with my questions about airplanes. But planes were new to the old folks, too, and there was little that they could tell me. Only my uncle knew some of the answers. And better still, he could carve propellers from pieces of wood that would whirl rapidly in the wind, wobbling noisily upon oiled nails.

I wanted a plane more than I'd wanted anything; more than I wanted the red wagon with rubber tires, more than the train that ran on a track with its train of cars. I asked my mother over and over again:

"Mamma?"

"What do you want, boy?" she'd say.

"Mamma, will you get mad if I ask you?" I'd say.

"What do you want now? I ain't got time to be answering a lot of fool questions. What you want?"

"Mamma, when you gonna get me one . . . ?" I'd ask.

"Get you one what?" she'd say.

"You know, Mamma; what I been asking you. . . ."

"Boy," she'd say, "if you don't want a spanking you better come on an' tell me what you talking about so I can get on with my work."

"Aw, Mamma, you know. . . ."

"What I just tell you?" she'd say.

"I mean when you gonna buy me a airplane."

"Airplane! Boy, is you crazy? How many times I have to tell you to stop that foolishness. I done told you them things cost too much. I bet I'm gon' wham the living daylight out of you if you don't quit worrying me 'bout them things!"

But this did not stop me, and a few days later I'd try all over again.

Then one day a strange thing happened. It was spring and for some reason I had been hot and irritable all morning. It was a beautiful spring. I could feel it as I played barefoot in the backyard. Blossoms hung from the thorny black locust trees like clusters of fragrant white grapes. Butterflies flickered in the sunlight above the short new dew-wet grass. I had gone in the house for bread and butter and coming out I heard a steady unfamiliar drone. It was unlike anything I had ever heard before. I tried to place the sound. It was no use. It was a sensation like that I had when searching for my father's watch, heard ticking unseen in a room. It made me feel as though I had forgotten to perform some task that my mother had ordered . . . then I located it, overhead. In the sky, flying quite low and about a hundred yards off was a plane! It came so slowly that it seemed barely to move. My mouth hung wide; my bread and butter fell into the dirt. I wanted to jump up and down and cheer. And when the idea struck I trembled with excitement: "Some little white boy's plane's done flew away and all I got to do is stretch out my hands and it'll be mine!" It was a little plane like that at the Fair, flying no higher than the eaves of our roof. Seeing it come steadily forward I felt the world grow warm with promise. I opened the screen and climbed over it and clung there, waiting. I would catch the plane as it came over and swing down fast and run into the house before anyone could see me. Then no one could come to claim the plane. It droned nearer. Then when it hung like a silver cross in the blue directly above me I stretched out my hand and grabbed. It was like sticking my finger through a soap bubble. The plane flew on, as though I had simply blown my breath after it. I grabbed again, frantically, trying to catch the tail. My fingers clutched the air and disappointment surged tight and hard in my throat. Giving one last desperate grasp, I strained forward. My fingers ripped from the screen. I was falling. The ground burst hard against me. I drummed the earth with my heels and when my breath returned, I lay there bawling.

My mother rushed through the door.

"What's the matter, chile! What on earth is wrong with you?"

"It's gone! It's gone!"

"What gone?"

"The airplane . . ."

"Airplane?"

"Yessum, jus' like the one at the Fair. . . . I . . . I tried to stop it an' it kep' right on going. . . ."

"When, boy?"

"Just now," I cried, through my tears.

"Where it go, boy, what way?"

"Yonder, there . . ."

She scanned the sky, her arms akimbo and her checkered apron flapping in the wind as I pointed to the fading plane. Finally she looked down at me, slowly shaking her head.

"It's gone! It's gone!" I cried.

"Boy, is you a fool?" she said. "Don't you see that there's a real airplane 'stead of one of them toy ones?"

"Real . . . ?" I forgot to cry. "Real?"

"Yass, real. Don't you know that thing you reaching for is bigger'n a auto? You here trying to reach for it and I bet it's flying 'bout two hundred miles higher'n this roof." She was disgusted with me. "You come on in this house before somebody else sees what a fool you done turned out to be. You must think these here lil ole arms of you'n is mighty long. . . ."

I was carried into the house and undressed for bed and the doctor was called. I cried bitterly, as much from the disappointment of finding the plane so far beyond my reach as from the pain.

When the doctor came I heard my mother telling him about the plane and asking if anything was wrong with my mind. He explained that I had had a fever for several hours. But I was kept in bed for a week and I constantly saw the plane in my sleep, flying just beyond my fingertips, sailing so slowly that it seemed barely to move. And each time I'd reach out to grab it I'd miss and through each dream I'd hear my grandma warning:

> *Young man, young man,*
> *Yo' arms too short*
> *To box with God. . . .*

"Hey, son!"

At first he did not know where he was and looked at the old man pointing, with blurred eyes.

"Ain't that one of you-all's airplanes coming after you?"

As his vision cleared he saw a small black shape above a distant field, soaring through waves of heat. But he could not be sure and with the pain he feared that somehow a horrible recurring fantasy of being split in twain by the whirling blades of a propeller had come true.

"You think he sees us?" he heard.

"See? I hope so."

"He's coming like a bat outa hell!"

Straining, he heard the faint sound of a motor and hoped it would soon be over.

"How you feeling?"

"Like a nightmare," he said.

"Hey, he's done curved back the other way!"

"Maybe he saw us," he said. "Maybe he's gone to send out the ambulance and ground crew." And, he thought with despair, maybe he didn't even see us.

"Where did you send the boy?"

"Down to Mister Graves," Jefferson said. "Man what owns this land."

"Do you think he phoned?"

Jefferson looked at him quickly.

"Aw sho'. Dabney Graves is got a bad name on accounta them killings but he'll call though. . . ."

"What killings?"

"Them five fellers . . . ain't you heard?" he asked with surprise.

"No."

"Everybody knows 'bout Dabney Graves, especially the colored. He done killed enough of us."

Todd had the sensation of being caught in a white neighborhood after dark.

"What did they do?" he asked.

"Thought they was men," Jefferson said. "An' some he owed money, like he do me. . . ."

"But why do you stay here?"

"You black, son."

"I know, but . . ."

"You have to come by the white folks, too."

He turned away from Jefferson's eyes, at once consoled and accused. And I'll have to come by them soon, he thought with despair. Closing his eyes, he heard Jefferson's voice as the sun burned blood-red upon his lips.

"I got nowhere to go," Jefferson said, "an' they'd come after me if I did. But Dabney Graves is a funny fellow. He's all the time making jokes. He can be mean as hell, then he's liable to turn right around and back the colored against the white folks. I seen him do it. But me, I hates him for that more'n anything else. 'Cause just as soon as he gits tired helping a man he don't care what happens to him. He just leaves him stone cold. And then the other white folks is double hard on anybody he done helped. For him it's just a joke. He don't give a hilla beans for nobody—but hisself. . . ."

Todd listened to the thread of detachment in the old man's voice. It was as though he held his words arm's length before him to avoid their destructive meaning.

"He'd just as soon do you a favor and then turn right around and have you strung up. Me, I stays outa his way 'cause down here that's what you gotta do."

If my ankle would only ease for a while, he thought. The closer I spin toward the earth the blacker I become, flashed through his mind. Sweat ran into his eyes and he was sure that he would never see the plane if his head continued whirling. He tried to see Jefferson, what it was that Jefferson held in his hand? It was a little black man, another Jefferson! A little black Jefferson that shook with fits of belly-laughter while the other Jefferson looked on with detachment. Then Jefferson looked up from the thing in his hand and turned to speak, but Todd was far away, searching the sky for a plane in a hot dry land on a day and age he had long forgotten. He was going mysteriously with his mother through empty streets where black faces peered from behind drawn shades and someone was rapping at a window and he was looking back to see a hand and a frightened face frantically beckoning from a cracked door and his mother was looking down the empty perspective of the street and shaking her head and hurrying him along and at first it was only a flash he saw and a motor was droning as through the sun-glare he saw it gleaming silver as it circled and he was seeing a burst like a puff of white smoke and hearing his mother yell, Come along, boy, I got no time for them fool airplanes, I got no time, and he saw it a second time, the plane flying high, and the burst appeared suddenly and fell slowly, billowing out and sparkling like fireworks and he was watching and being hurried along as the air filled with a flurry of white pinwheeling cards that caught in the wind and scattered over the rooftops and into the gutters and a woman was running and snatching a card and reading it and screaming and he darted into the shower, grabbing as in winter he grabbed for snowflakes and bounding away at his mother's, Come on here, boy! Come on, I say! and he was watching as she took the card away, seeing her face grow puzzled and turning taut as her voice quavered, "Niggers Stay From the Polls," and died to a moan of terror as he saw the eyeless sockets of a white hood staring at him from the card and above he saw the plane spiraling gracefully, agleam in the sun like a fiery sword. And seeing it soar he was caught, transfixed between a terrible horror and a horrible fascination.

The sun was not so high now, and Jefferson was calling and gradually he saw three figures moving across the curving roll of the field.

"Look like some doctors, all dressed in white," said Jefferson.

They're coming at last, Todd thought. And he felt such a release of tension within him that he thought he would faint. But no sooner did he close his eyes than he was seized and he was struggling with three white men who were forcing his arms into some kind of coat. It was too much for him, his arms were pinned to his sides and as the pain blazed in his eyes, he realized that it was a straitjacket. What filthy joke was this?

"That oughta hold him, Mister Graves," he heard.

His total energies seemed focused in his eyes as he searched their faces. That was Graves; the other two wore hospital uniforms. He was poised between two poles of fear and hate as he heard the one called Graves saying, "He looks kinda purty in that there suit, boys. I'm glad you dropped by."

"This boy ain't crazy, Mister Graves," one of the others said. "He needs a doctor, not us. Don't see how you led us way out here anyway. It might be a joke to you, but your cousin Rudolph liable to kill somebody. White folks or niggers, don't make no difference. . . ."

Todd saw the man turn red with anger. Graves looked down upon him, chuckling.

"This nigguh belongs in a straitjacket, too, boys. I knowed that the minit Jeff's kid said something 'bout a nigguh flyer. You all know you cain't let the nigguh git up that high without his going crazy. The nigguh brain ain't built right for high altitudes. . . ."

Todd watched the drawling red face, feeling that all the unnamed horror and obscenities that he had ever imagined stood materialized before him.

"Let's git outta here," one of the attendants said.

Todd saw the other reach toward him, realizing for the first time that he lay upon a stretcher as he yelled.

"Don't put your hands on me!"

They drew back, surprised.

"What's that you say, nigguh?" asked Graves.

He did not answer and thought that Graves's foot was aimed at his head. It landed on his chest and he could hardly breathe. He coughed helplessly, seeing Graves's lips stretch taut over his yellow teeth, and tried to shift his head. It was as though a half-dead fly was dragging slowly across his face and a bomb seemed to burst within him. Blasts of hot, hysterical laughter tore from his chest, causing his eyes to pop and he felt that the veins in his neck would surely burst. And then a part of him stood behind it all, watching the surprise in Graves's red face and his own hysteria. He thought he would never stop, he would laugh himself to death. It rang in his ears like Jefferson's laughter and he looked for him, centering his eyes desperately upon his face, as though somehow he had become his sole salvation in an insane world of outrage and humiliation. It brought a certain relief. He was suddenly aware that although his body was still contorted it was an echo that no longer rang in his ears. He heard Jefferson's voice with gratitude.

"Mister Graves, the Army done tole him not to leave his airplane."

"Nigguh, Army or no, you gittin' off my land! That airplane can stay 'cause it was paid for by taxpayers' money. But you gittin' off. An' dead or alive, it don't make no difference to me."

Todd was beyond it now, lost in a world of anguish.

"Jeff," Graves said, "you and Teddy come and grab holt. I want you to take this here black eagle over to that nigguh airfield and leave him."

Jefferson and the boy approached him silently. He looked away, realizing and doubting at once that only they could release him from his overpowering sense of isolation.

They bent for the stretcher. One of the attendants moved toward Teddy.

"Think you can manage it, boy?"

"I think I can, suh," Teddy said.

"Well, you better go behind then, and let yo' pa go ahead so's to keep that leg elevated."

He saw the white men walking ahead as Jefferson and the boy carried him along in silence. Then they were pausing and he felt a hand wiping his face; then he was moving again. And it was as though he had been lifted out of his isolation, back into the world of men. A new current of communication flowed between the man and boy and himself. They moved him gently. Far away he heard a mockingbird liquidly calling. He raised his eyes, seeing a buzzard poised unmoving in space. For a moment the whole afternoon seemed suspended and he waited for the horror to seize him again. Then like a song within his head he heard the boy's soft humming and saw the dark bird glide into the sun and glow like a bird of flaming gold.

BY WAY OF DISCUSSION

"Flying Home" is a story that dramatizes the psychological salvation of a black man by making use of a cluster of symbols. These symbols include an airplane, the act of flying, a number of buzzards, the sun, a dead horse, and a straitjacket. At various points in the story Todd, the protagonist, becomes aware of some of the symbolic value of these items. For example, after old Jefferson has related the fable of his own abortive attempts to fly like the white angels of heaven, Todd screams:

> "Can I help it because they won't let us actually fly? Maybe we are a bunch of buzzards feeding on a dead horse, but we can hope to be eagles, can't we? Can't we?"

To help us understand the story's symbolism, let's look for a moment at the myth of Daedalus. Symbolism frequently makes use of parallels from classical mythology. In Greek mythology Daedalus and his son Icarus were imprisoned for offending the king of Crete. Daedalus, a very clever inventor, fashioned two pairs of wings out of feathers and wax for himself and Icarus. But as the two men made their escape, Icarus flew too near the sun. His wings melted, and he fell into the sea. Daedalus managed to fly on to Sicily. Metaphorically, we may view Todd as an Icarian figure and old Jefferson as a Daedalian one, although the parallels do not exactly match up. An additional characteristic of the use of symbolic parallels in the short story, especially parallels from mythology, is that all the items should not match up too perfectly. When they do, the story often seems unpleasantly artificial.

"Flying Home" has a simple enough plot: Todd, a young black pilot flying a training mission, crashes his plane on an Alabama farm and is rescued from the white racist owner of the land, Dabney Graves, by an old black man named Jefferson. But, of course, the story is much more complex than its plot suggests.

Todd is an estranged young man, a member neither of the world of white people nor of black people. From his youth he has wanted to fly an airplane. Symbolically, this means that he has always wanted to be free to do whatever white people can do. But in the process of trying to realize his dream—both the literal one and the symbolic one—he has cut himself off from his black roots and become a sort of white black man. Thus, at first, he wants no part of the old "peasant" sharecropper, who personifies (symbolizes) everything Todd finds shameful in his race:

> He watched the old man, hearing him humming snatches of a tune as he admired the plane. He felt a furtive sense of resentment. Such old men often came to the field to watch the pilots with childish eyes. At first it had made him proud; they had been a meaningful part of a new experience. But soon he realized they did not understand his accomplishments and they came to shame and embarrass him, like the distasteful praise of an idiot.

But, lying injured and vulnerable, dependent upon Jefferson for his eventual rescue, Todd begins to see the illogic of his own life and attitude. Up until this point, the desire to disprove black inferiority and thereby win white respect has nurtured everything he has done. Now, as he reflects upon his girlfriend's letter and Jefferson's fables, certain things become clear for the first time. Todd realizes that black inferiority is indeed a dead horse, one that he—like the buzzards that Jefferson shooed away—can no longer feed upon. Furthermore, he comes to understand that flying just to gain white approval is not the path to personal fulfillment. To the contrary, it represents the path to psychic suicide, since any such attempt is as foredoomed as Jefferson's angelic efforts.

Like another bird, the mythical Phoenix, Todd has perished symbolically; but he is certain to rise and fly again. And though he is carried ingloriously from the field—notice that this is Graves' field—wearing a straitjacket, Todd is alive, symbolically reborn:

> And it was as though he had been lifted out of his isolation, back into the world of men. A new current of communication flowed between the man and boy and himself. They moved him gently. Far away he heard a mockingbird liquidly calling. He raised his eyes, seeing a buzzard poised unmoving in space. For a moment the whole afternoon seemed suspended and he waited for the horror to seize him again. Then like a song within his head he heard the boy's soft humming and saw the dark bird glide into the sun and glow like a bird of flaming gold.

Symbolically, we see the possibility of Todd's becoming the black eagle that he has dreamed of being, no longer a bloody buzzard ripped apart and smeared across a cockpit windshield. By "black eagle" we mean a complete man, total and autonomous unto himself. Ironically, by crashing, Todd has flown back home to his ethnic roots and is about to begin a more sensible molding of his own manhood, a manhood that will have nothing to do with proving itself to white people—or to black people either, for that matter.

TRUMAN CAPOTE

A Tree of Night

It was winter. A string of naked light bulbs, from which it seemed all warmth had been drained, illuminated the little depot's cold, windy platform. Earlier in the evening it had rained, and now icicles hung along the station-house eaves like some crystal monster's vicious teeth. Except for a girl, young and rather tall, the platform was deserted. The girl wore a gray flannel suit, a raincoat, and a plaid scarf. Her hair, parted in the middle and rolled up neatly on the sides, was rich blondish-brown; and, while her face tended to be too thin and narrow, she was, though not extraordinarily so, attractive. In addition to an assortment of magazines and a gray suede purse on which elaborate brass letters spelled Kay, she carried conspicuously a green Western guitar.

When the train, spouting steam and glaring with light, came out of the darkness and rumbled to a halt, Kay assembled her paraphernalia and climbed up into the last coach.

The coach was a relic with a decaying interior of ancient red-plush seats, bald in spots, and peeling iodine-colored woodwork. An old-time copper lamp, attached to the ceiling, looked romantic and out of place. Gloomy dead smoke sailed the air; and the car's heated closeness accentuated the stale odor of discarded sandwiches, apple cores, and orange hulls: this garbage, including Lily cups, soda-pop bottles, and mangled newspapers, littered the long aisle. From a water cooler, embedded in the wall, a steady stream trickled to the floor. The passengers, who glanced up wearily when Kay entered, were not, it seemed, at all conscious of any discomfort.

Kay resisted a temptation to hold her nose and threaded her way carefully down the aisle, tripping once, without disaster, over a dozing fat man's protruding leg. Two nondescript men turned an interested eye as she passed; and a kid stood up in his seat, squalling, "Hey, Mama, look at de banjo! Hey, lady, lemme play ya banjo!" till a slap from Mama quelled him.

There was only one empty place. She found it at the end of the car in an isolated alcove occupied already by a man and woman who were sitting with their feet settled lazily on the vacant seat opposite. Kay hesitated a second then said, "Would you mind if I sat here?"

The woman's head snapped up as if she had not been asked a simple question, but stabbed with a needle, too. Nevertheless, she managed a smile. "Can't say as I see what's to stop you, honey," she said, taking her feet down and also, with a curious impersonality, removing the feet of the man who was staring out the window, paying no attention whatsoever.

Thanking the woman, Kay took off her coat, sat down, and arranged herself with purse and guitar at her side, magazines in her lap: comfortable enough, though she wished she had a pillow for her back.

The train lurched; a ghost of steam hissed against the window; slowly the dingy lights of the lonesome depot faded past.

"Boy, what a jerkwater dump," said the woman. "No town, no nothin'."

Kay said, "The town's a few miles away."

"That so? Live there?"

No. Kay explained she had been at the funeral of an uncle. An uncle who, though she did not of course mention it, had left her nothing in his will but the green guitar. Where was she going? Oh, back to college.

After mulling this over, the woman concluded, "What'll you ever learn in a place like that? Let me tell you, honey, I'm plenty educated and I never saw the inside of no college."

"You didn't?" murmured Kay politely and dismissed the matter by opening one of her magazines. The light was dim for reading and none of the stories looked in the least compelling. However, not wanting to become involved in a conversational marathon, she continued gazing at it stupidly till she felt a furtive tap on her knee.

"Don't read," said the woman. "I need somebody to talk to. Naturally, it's no fun talking to *him*." She jerked a thumb toward the silent man. "He's afflicted: deaf and dumb, know what I mean?"

Kay closed the magazine and looked at her more or less for the first time. She was short; her feet barely scraped the floor. And like many undersized people she had a freak of structure, in her case an enormous, really huge head. Rouge so brightened her sagging, fleshy-featured face it was difficult even to guess at her age: perhaps fifty, fifty-five. Her big sheep eyes squinted, as if distrustful of what they saw. Her hair was an obviously dyed red, and twisted into parched, fat corkscrew curls. A once-elegant lavender hat of impressive size flopped crazily on the side of her head, and she was kept busy brushing back a drooping cluster of celluloid cherries sewed to the brim. She wore a plain, somewhat shabby blue dress. Her breath had a vividly sweetish gin smell.

"You do wanna talk to me, don't you, honey?"

"Sure," said Kay, moderately amused.

"Course you do. You bet you do. That's what I like about a train. Bus people are a close-mouthed buncha dopes. But a train's the place for putting your cards on the table, that's what I always say." Her voice was cheerful and booming, husky as a man's. "But on accounta *him*, I always try to get us this here seat; it's more private, like a swell compartment, see?"

"It's very pleasant," Kay agreed. "Thanks for letting me join you."

"Only too glad to. We don't have much company; it makes some folks nervous to be around him."

As if to deny it, the man made a queer, furry sound deep in his throat and plucked the woman's sleeve. "Leave me alone, dear-heart," she said, as if she were talking to an inattentive child. "I'm O.K. We're just having us a nice little ol' talk. Now behave yourself or this pretty girl will go away. She's very rich; she goes to college." And winking, she added, "He thinks I'm drunk."

The man slumped in the seat, swung his head sideways, and studied Kay intently from the corners of his eyes. These eyes, like a pair of clouded milky-blue marbles, were thickly lashed and oddly beautiful. Now, except for a certain remoteness, his wide, hairless face had no real expression. It was as if he were incapable of experiencing or reflecting the slightest emotion. His gray hair was clipped close and combed forward into uneven bangs. He looked like a child aged abruptly by some uncanny method. He wore a frayed blue serge suit, and he had anointed himself with a cheap, vile perfume. Around his wrist was strapped a Mickey Mouse watch.

"He thinks I'm drunk," the woman repeated. "And the real funny part is, I am. Oh, shoot—you gotta do something, ain't that right?" She bent closer. "Say, ain't it?"

Kay was still gawking at the man; the way he was looking at her made her squeamish, but she could not take her eyes off him. "I guess so," she said.

"Then let's us have us a drink," suggested the woman. She plunged her hand into an oilcloth satchel and pulled out a partially filled gin bottle. She began to unscrew the cap but, seeming to think better of this, handed the bottle to Kay. "Gee, I forgot about you being company," she said. "I'll go get us some nice paper cups."

So, before Kay could protest that she did not want a drink, the woman had risen and started none too steadily down the aisle toward the water cooler.

Kay yawned and rested her forehead against the windowpane, her fingers idly strumming the guitar: the strings sang a hollow, lulling tune, as monotonously soothing as the Southern landscape, smudged in darkness, flowing past the window. An icy winter moon rolled above the train across the night sky like a thin white wheel.

And then, without warning, a strange thing happened: the man reached out and gently stroked Kay's cheek. Despite the breathtaking delicacy of this movement, it was such a bold gesture Kay was at first too startled to know what to make of it: her thoughts shot in three or four fantastic directions. He leaned forward till his queer eyes were very near her own; the reek of his perfume was sickening. The guitar was silent while they exchanged a searching gaze. Suddenly, from some spring of compassion, she felt for him a keen sense of pity; but also, and this she could not suppress, an overpowering disgust, an absolute loathing: something about him, an elusive quality she could not quite put a finger on, reminded her of—of what?

After a little, he lowered his hand solemnly and sank back in the seat, an asinine grin transfiguring his face, as if he had performed a clever stunt for which he wished applause.

"Giddyup! Giddyup! my little bucker-ROOS . . ." shouted the woman. And she sat down, loudly proclaiming to be, "Dizzy as a witch! Dog tired! Whew!" From a handful of Lily cups she separated two and casually thrust the rest down her blouse. "Keep 'em safe and dry, ha ha ha. . . ." A coughing spasm seized her, but when it was over she appeared calmer. "Has my boy friend been entertaining?" she asked, patting her bosom reverently. "Ah, he's so sweet." She looked as if she might pass out. Kay rather wished she would.

"I don't want a drink," Kay said, returning the bottle. "I never drink: I hate the taste."

"Mustn't be a kill-joy," said the woman firmly. "Here now, hold your cup like a good girl."

"No, please . . ."

"Formercysake, hold it still. Imagine, nerves at your age! Me, I can shake like a leaf, I've got reasons. Oh, Lordy, have I got 'em."

"But . . ."

A dangerous smile tipped the woman's face hideously awry. "What's the matter? Don't you think I'm good enough to drink with?"

"Please, don't misunderstand," said Kay, a tremor in her voice. "It's just that I don't like being forced to do something I don't want to. So look, couldn't I give this to the gentleman?"

"Him? No sirree: he needs what little sense he's got. Come on, honey, down the hatch."

Kay, seeing it was useless, decided to succumb and avoid a possible scene. She sipped and shuddered. It was terrible gin. It burned her throat till her eyes watered. Quickly, when the woman was not watching, she emptied the cup out into the sound hole of the guitar. It happened, however, that the man saw; and Kay, realizing it, recklessly signaled to him with her eyes a plea not to give her away. But she could not tell from his clear-blank expression how much he understood.

"Where you from, kid?" resumed the woman presently.

For a bewildered moment, Kay was unable to provide an answer. The names of several cities came to her all at once. Finally, from this confusion, she extracted: "New Orleans. My home is in New Orleans."

The woman beamed. "N.O.'s where I wanna go when I kick off. One time, oh, say 1923, I ran me a sweet little fortune-telling parlor there. Let's see, that was on St. Peter Street." Pausing, she stooped and set the empty gin bottle on the floor. It rolled into the aisle and rocked back and forth with a drowsy sound. "I was raised in Texas—on a big ranch—my papa was rich. Us kids always had the best; even Paris, France, clothes. I'll bet you've got a big swell house, too. Do you have a garden? Do you grow flowers?"

"Just lilacs."

A conductor entered the coach, preceded by a cold gust of wind that rattled the trash in the aisle and briefly livened the dull air. He lumbered along, stopping now and then to punch a ticket or talk with a passenger. It was after midnight. Someone was expertly playing a harmonica. Someone else was arguing the merits of a certain politician. A child cried out in his sleep.

"Maybe you wouldn't be so snotty if you knew who we was," said the woman, bobbing her tremendous head. "We ain't nobodies, not by a long shot."

Embarrassed, Kay nervously opened a pack of cigarettes and lighted one. She wondered if there might not be a seat in a car up ahead. She could not bear the woman, or, for that matter, the man, another minute. But she had never before been in a remotely comparable situation. "If you'll excuse me now," she said, "I have to be leaving. It's been very pleasant, but I promised to meet a friend on the train. . . ."

With almost invisible swiftness the woman grasped the girl's wrist. "Didn't your mama ever tell you it was sinful to lie?" she stage-whispered. The lavender hat tumbled off her head but she made no effort to retrieve it. Her tongue flicked out and wetted her lips. And, as Kay stood up, she increased the pressure of her grip. "Sit down, dear . . . there ain't any friend . . . Why, we're your only friends and we wouldn't have you leave us for the world."

"Honestly, I wouldn't lie."

"Sit down, dear."

Kay dropped her cigarette and the man picked it up. He slouched in the corner and became absorbed in blowing a chain of lush smoke rings that mounted upward like hollow eyes and expanded into nothing.

"Why, you wouldn't want to hurt his feelings by leaving us, now, would you, dear?" crooned the woman softly. "Sit down—down—now, that's a good girl. My, what a pretty guitar. What a pretty, pretty guitar . . ." Her voice faded before the sudden whooshing, static noise of a second train. And for an instant the lights in the coach went off; in the darkness the passing train's golden windows winked black-yellow-black-yellow-black-yellow. The man's cigarette pulsed like the glow of a firefly, and his smoke rings continued rising tranquilly. Outside, a bell pealed wildly.

When the lights came on again, Kay was massaging her wrist where the woman's strong fingers had left a painful bracelet mark. She was more puzzled than angry. She determined to ask the conductor if he would find her a different seat. But when he arrived to take her ticket, the request stuttered on her lips incoherently.

"Yes, miss?"

"Nothing," she said.

And he was gone.

The trio in the alcove regarded one another in mysterious silence till the woman said, "I've got something here I wanna show you, honey." She rummaged once more in the oilcloth satchel. "You won't be so snotty after you get a gander at this."

What she passed to Kay was a handbill, published on such yellowed, antique paper it looked as if it must be centuries old. In fragile, overly fancy lettering, it read:

LAZARUS

The Man Who Is Buried Alive

A MIRACLE

SEE FOR YOURSELF

Adults, 25¢—Children, 10¢

"I always sing a hymn and read a sermon," said the woman. "It's awful sad: some folks cry, especially the old ones. And I've got me a perfectly elegant costume: a black veil and a black dress, oh, very becoming. *He* wears a gorgeous made-to-order bridegroom suit and a turban and lotsa talcum on his face. See, we try to make it as much like a bona-fide funeral as we can. But shoot, nowadays you're likely to get just a buncha smart alecks come for laughs—so sometimes I'm real glad he's afflicted like he is on accounta otherwise his feelings would be hurt, maybe."

Kay said, "You mean you're with a circus or a sideshow or something like that?"

"Nope, us alone," said the woman as she reclaimed the fallen hat. "We've been doing it for years and years—played every tank town in the South: Singasong, Mississippi—Spunky, Louisiana—Eureka, Alabama . . ." these and other names rolled off her tongue musically, running together like rain. "After the hymn, after the sermon, we bury him."

"In a coffin?"

"Sort of. It's gorgeous, it's got silver stars painted all over the lid."

"I should think he would suffocate," said Kay, amazed. "How long does he stay buried?"

"All told it takes maybe an hour—course that's not counting the lure."

"The lure?"

"Uh huh. It's what we do the night before a show. See, we hunt up a store, any ol' store with a big glass window'll do, and get the owner to let *him* sit inside this window, and, well, hypnotize himself. Stays there all night stiff as a poker and people come and look: scares the livin' hell out of 'em. . . ." While she talked she jiggled a finger in her ear, withdrawing it occasionally to examine her find. "And one time this ol' bindlestiff Mississippi sheriff tried to . . ."

The tale that followed was baffling and pointless: Kay did not bother to listen. Nevertheless, what she had heard already inspired a reverie, a vague recapitulation of her uncle's funeral; an event which, to tell the truth, had not much affected her since she had scarcely known him. And so, while gazing abstractedly at the man, an image of her uncle's face, white next the pale silk casket pillow, appeared in her mind's eye. Observing their faces simultaneously, both the man's and uncle's, as it were, she thought she recognized an odd parallel: there was about the man's face the same kind of shocking, embalmed, secret stillness, as though, in a sense, he were truly an exhibit in a glass cage, complacent to be seen, uninterested in seeing.

"I'm sorry, what did you say?"

"I said: I sure wish they'd lend us the use of a regular cemetery. Like it is now we have to put on the show wherever we can . . . mostly in empty lots that are nine times outa ten smack up against some smelly fillin' station, which ain't exactly a big help. But like I say, we got us a swell act, the best. You oughta come see it if you get a chance."

"Oh, I should love to," Kay said, absently.

"Oh, I should love to," mimicked the woman. "Well, who ask you? Anybody ask you?" She hoisted up her skirt and enthusiastically blew her nose on the ragged hem of a petticoat. "Bu-leeve me, it's a hard way to turn a dollar. Know what our take was last month? Fifty-three bucks! Honey, you try living on that sometime." She sniffed and rearranged her skirt with considerable primness. "Well, one of these days my sweet boy's sure enough going to die down there; and even then somebody'll say it was a gyp."

At this point the man took from his pocket what seemed to be a finely shellacked peach seed and balanced it on the palm of his hand. He looked across at Kay and, certain of her attention, opened his eyelids wide and began to squeeze and caress the seed in an undefinably obscene manner.

Kay frowned. "What does he want?"

"He wants you to buy it."

"But what is it?"

"A charm," said the woman. "A love charm."

Whoever was playing the harmonica stopped. Other sounds, less unique, became at once prominent: someone snoring, the gin bottle seesaw rolling, voices in sleepy argument, the train wheels' distant hum.

"Where could you get love cheaper, honey?"

"It's nice. I mean it's cute. . . ." Kay said, stalling for time. The man rubbed and polished the seed on his trouser leg. His head was lowered at a supplicating, mournful angle, and presently he stuck the seed between his teeth and bit it, as if it were a suspicious piece of silver. "Charms always bring me bad luck. And besides . . . please, can't you make him stop acting that way?"

"Don't look so scared," said the woman, more flat-voiced than ever. "He ain't gonna hurt you."

"Make him stop, damn it!"

"What can I do?" asked the woman, shrugging her shoulders. "You're the one that's got money. You're rich. All he wants is a dollar, one dollar."

Kay tucked her purse under her arm. "I have just enough to get back to school," she lied, quickly rising and stepping out into the aisle. She stood there a moment, expecting trouble. But nothing happened.

The woman, with rather deliberate indifference, heaved a sigh and closed her eyes; gradually the man subsided and stuck the charm back in his pocket. Then his hand crawled across the seat to join the woman's in a lax embrace.

Kay shut the door and moved to the front of the observation platform. It was bitterly cold in the open air, and she had left her raincoat in the alcove. She loosened her scarf and draped it over her head.

Although she had never made this trip before, the train was traveling through an area strangely familiar: tall trees, misty, painted pale by malicious moonshine, towered steep on either side without a break or clearing. Above, the sky was a stark, unexplorable blue thronged with stars that faded here and there. She could see streamers of smoke trailing from the train's engine like long clouds of ectoplasm. In one corner of the platform a red kerosene lantern cast a colorful shadow.

She found a cigarette and tried to light it: the wind snuffed match after match till only one was left. She walked to the corner where the lantern burned and cupped her hands to protect the last match: the flame caught, sputtered, died. Angrily she tossed away the cigarette and empty folder; all the tension in her tightened to an exasperating pitch and she slammed the wall with her fist and began to whimper softly, like an irritable child.

The intense cold made her head ache, and she longed to go back inside the warm coach and fall asleep. But she couldn't, at least not yet; and there was no sense in wondering why, for she knew the answer very well. Aloud, partly to keep her teeth from chattering and partly because she needed the reassurance of her own voice, she said: "We're in Alabama now, I think, and tomorrow we'll be in Atlanta and I'm nineteen and I'll be twenty in August and I'm a sophomore. . . ." She glanced around at the darkness, hoping to see a sign of dawn, and finding the same endless wall of trees, the same frosty moon. "I hate him, he's horrible and I hate him. . . ." She stopped, ashamed of her foolishness and too tired to evade the truth: she was afraid.

Suddenly she felt an eerie compulsion to kneel down and touch the lantern. Its graceful glass funnel was warm, and the red glow seeped through her hands, making them luminous. The heat thawed her fingers and tingled along her arms.

She was so preoccupied she did not hear the door open. The train wheels roaring clickety-clack-clackety-click hushed the sound of the man's footsteps.

It was a subtle zero sensation that warned her finally; but some seconds passed before she dared look behind.

He was standing there with a mute detachment, his head tilted, his arms dangling at his sides. Staring up into his harmless, vapid face, flushed brilliant by the lantern light, Kay knew of what she was afraid: it was a memory, a childish memory of terrors that once, long ago, had hovered above her like haunted limbs on a tree of night. Aunts, cooks, strangers—each eager to spin a tale or teach a rhyme of spooks and death, omens, spirits, demons. And always there had been the unfailing threat of the wizard man: stay close to the house, child, else a wizard man'll snatch and eat you alive! He lived everywhere, the wizard man, and everywhere was danger. At night, in bed, hear him tapping at the window? Listen!

Holding onto the railing, she inched upward till she was standing erect. The man nodded and waved his hand toward the door. Kay took a deep breath and stepped forward. Together they went inside.

The air in the coach was numb with sleep: a solitary light now illuminated the car, creating a kind of artificial dusk. There was no motion but the train's sluggish sway, and the stealthy rattle of discarded newspapers.

The woman alone was wide awake. You could see she was greatly excited: she fidgeted with her curls and celluloid cherries, and her plump little legs, crossed at the ankles, swung agitatedly back and forth. She paid no attention when Kay sat down. The man settled in the seat with one leg tucked beneath him and his arms folded across his chest.

In an effort to be casual, Kay picked up a magazine. She realized the man was watching her, not removing his gaze an instant: she knew this though she was afraid to confirm it, and she wanted to cry out and waken everyone in the coach. But suppose they did not hear? What if they were not really *asleep*? Tears started in her eyes, magnifying and distorting the print on a page till it became a hazy blur. She shut the magazine with fierce abruptness and looked at the woman.

"I'll buy it," she said. "The charm, I mean. I'll buy it, if that's all—just all you want."

The woman made no response. She smiled apathetically as she turned toward the man.

As Kay watched, the man's face seemed to change form and recede before her like a moon-shaped rock sliding downward under a surface of water. A warm laziness relaxed her. She was dimly conscious of it when the woman took away her purse, and when she gently pulled the raincoat like a shroud above her head.

BY WAY OF DISCUSSION

In "A Tree of Night" Truman Capote, who has often characterized himself as a stylistic writer, has created a stylistic story of psychological terror. This terror arises not from supernaturalism but from the repressed childhood memories of the nineteen-year-old protagonist, Kay. The story's many symbols, both Freudian (sexual) and non-Freudian, serve a dual purpose: increased emotional depth and clarification of the meaning of characters and events that might otherwise be difficult to understand.

As we join Kay on the station platform and follow her into her coach, we note an atmosphere (mood) of fear and decadence. The station platform, cold and windswept, is lighted by a string of bulbs that appear to give off no heat. From the station roof hangs a row of icicles resembling the fangs of some strange ice monster, perhaps symbolizing the forgotten but soon-to-resurface terrors that lie buried in Kay's subconscious mind. The coach itself, with its threadbare seats, peeling walls, eddying "dead smoke," and trash-filled aisles, appears the symbolic epitome of decay.

Repression and unassertiveness characterize Kay's features as well as her actions. Her face is thin and narrow, a countenance that may suggest an underlying emotional meagerness. And once she has joined the grotesque couple, she falls quickly under the domination of the woman. At first she is forced into talking with the couple, then into taking a drink, and finally into staying with the couple when she really wishes to leave. She is even unable to ask the conductor to find her another seat.

Kay's repressed nature is dramatized by the way she handles her guitar and by her reaction to the man's behavior with the love charm. The guitar, because of its design and configuration, may be taken as a feminine Freudian symbol. Notice that Kay generally ignores the instrument except when she idly strums its strings and when she disposes of her drink by pouring it into the instrument's sound hole. Thus, symbolically, Kay betrays an indifference toward her own body, perhaps even a contempt for her own sexuality. Her one outburst of anger occurs when the man, who has been fondling the love charm—a feminine Freudian symbol—in an "undefinably obscene" way, puts the charm into his mouth and bites it. "Make him stop, damn it!" Kay shouts at the woman. But when her outburst fails to have any effect, Kay hurries away to the observation platform.

Kay's strange and sinister companions may be viewed as a pair of alter egos who symbolize Kay's buried childhood with all its suppressed memories. Notice that the man looks like an abruptly aged child. He even wears a Mickey Mouse watch, a clever touch. Psychological kinship is further implied by the manner in which he strokes Kay's cheek, as well as by the simultaneous loathing and attraction Kay feels for him. The woman's grossly over-sized head suggests the grotesqueness of the fantasies that once filled Kay's own mind, while the man's muteness and his milky white eyes—like a fortuneteller's clouded crystal ball—reflect Kay's initial inability to see within herself and to articulate her subconscious fears. Finally, there is the parallel between the reawakening of Kay's buried memories and the occupational burial and resurrection of her symbolic counterpart.

This reawakening is foreshadowed when Kay steps onto the observation platform and notices a strange familiarity about the eerie, dreamlike scene that greets her. In truth, Kay has never passed this way before. Symbolically, though, she has entered familiar though forgotten territory—the dreamlike world of her childhood—and within moments will confront once again the undying demons who lie in wait there. Just before this happens, Kay kneels and impulsively touches the globe of the warmly glowing lantern that lights the platform, a gesture suggesting a covert desire to free herself from her sensual inhibitions and an overt desire to find relief from the cold fear that now openly grips her.

Kay's enlightenment, as short-lived as it is, occurs as she gazes into the "harmless vapid" face of her male companion and suddenly recalls the whole host of spooks, spirits, and demons that had once struck terror into her childhood soul. But this experience brings no relief, only an imagined incarnation of the dread wizard man—the worst demon of all and quite likely the ultimate source of her sexual repressions.

As she reenters the coach and takes her old seat, Kay wishes to cry out and awaken the sleeping passengers. But her voice is stopped by the irrational fear that they might all be dead. Nor has awareness allayed her sexual apprehensiveness. Although she expresses a willingness to buy the love charm, the offer arises from fear, not from a willingness to accept her own sexuality. And the offer is met with silence, suggesting that coerced sexuality is psychologically impossible.

As the story ends, Kay succumbs to the terror that besets her, trying to shut it out with her raincoat. In doing this, she also symbolically shuts out life and love, thereby experiencing an emotional death—a result appropriately symbolized when the raincoat is described as a shroud.

FOR ADDITIONAL READING

The following stories, which appear elsewhere in this book, are especially appropriate for an analysis of symbolism:

1. Guy de Maupassant, "The Piece of String" (p. 385)
2. John Steinbeck, "The Chrysanthemums" (p. 269)
3. D. H. Lawrence, "The Shades of Spring" (p. 472)
4. William Faulkner, "That Evening Sun" (p. 519)

Theme

Theme is what a story means, what it says to us; and it results from the interaction of plot, character, emotion, and symbolism. Theme is the sum total of everything that takes place in a story plus the effect all this has on the mind of the reader.

In a tightly constructed story, every element relates directly to the theme. Every incident of plot has been carefully selected, and every character, symbol, instance of irony, and attempt to elicit a particular emotional response has been shaped to advance the theme. It follows, then, that whenever we try to deduce the theme of a story we should consider as many details as possible. Any interpretation that fails to do so is almost certain to be mistaken or incomplete. In arriving at our interpretation, we must also confine ourselves to the facts presented in the story and to inferences that can reasonably be drawn from them. This means that we must not allow our prejudices to muddle our thinking. If we cannot manage our prejudices, our conclusions are likely to be flawed.

Except in stories of the simplest construction, or those that aim openly at preaching or teaching a moral lesson, the theme seldom can be adequately summed up in a short sentence like "Honor is more important than fame" or "It is best to be honest." The theme as it applies to quality fiction is more than just the so-called moral to the story, and any attempt to view it as mere moral will almost certainly harm the richness and subtlety of the story's insights into life.

To illustrate this point, let's consider two possible statements of theme for Rudyard Kipling's "The Gardener":

1. Honesty is the best policy.
2. Under certain circumstances, an individual, to escape society's pressures, may feel compelled to conceal a personal

relationship that means a great deal to him or her. Doing so may indeed preserve that individual from society's wrath. In the end, though, such behavior may exact a much higher price than the individual would have paid by acknowledging the relationship openly.

Clearly, the second statement, inadequate though it may be, reflects the spirit of the story much more faithfully than the moralizing cliché that precedes it. Unlike the first version, the second is not a narrow moral precept for the reader to follow. Instead, it seeks to enlarge the reader's perception of one particular aspect of life.

Stories can often be interpreted in more than one way, depending upon the inferences the reader draws from the facts that are presented. Turning again to "The Gardener," we might take the position that Michael is in truth George's son, not Helen's offspring. Viewed from this perspective, the story is not about the high emotional cost of concealing a deeply felt personal relationship; rather it is about the true nature of motherhood. In that case, the story's theme might be stated like this:

> The essence of motherhood lies not in the mere exercise of giving birth. Rather, it includes a woman's willingness to love and, if need be, to sacrifice for a child once it has been given into her keeping. If she does such things, she is truly entitled to be called the child's mother, even though she may not be its biological parent.

The best, or most effective, themes are those that are long lasting, and long-lasting themes in turn are those that possess universal validity. A universal theme is one that is generally true to human experience everywhere and has been for as long as we have known anything about human nature. Universal themes typically deal with the complexity and variety of love, the pervasiveness of evil, the value of ritual in human society, the young person's initiation into the adult world, an individual's alienation from society, and so on.

As you read the stories in this section, as well as those in the rest of the book, you will notice that theme sometimes arises from one element or pair of elements and sometimes from another element or pair. Theme in Richard Connell's "The Most Dangerous Game" arises almost exclusively from plot. Theme in Irwin Shaw's "The Dry Rock" arises mostly out of the pairing of plot and character. Specific symbols are indispensable to thematic interpretation in John Galsworthy's "The Japanese Quince" and Ralph Ellison's "Flying Home." As a general rule, stories that are disproportionately dominated by plot, character, emotion, or symbolism are weak on theme. A good example of this, as we have already noted, is "The Most Dangerous Game." So much plot leaves little room for meaning—theme.

When you are asked to write papers about the themes of stories, you should keep a number of items in mind. First, a theme says *something* about *something*. A story's theme ought to be expressed in the form of a good, grammatical statement or two, even if those statements include a number of qualifications. A theme cannot be simply "jealousy," "revenge," "nostalgia," "motherhood," or "love." These are vague subjects, not themes.

Next, a story's theme should be a *generalized* statement about life. The theme does not include the particulars of the story. For example, the theme of "The Dry Rock" is not that "In New York City immigrant Russian taxicab drivers are often mistreated by suspected underworld figures." A more generalized statement is necessary for an appropriate formulation of the story's theme:

> In our modern, urbanized society, individuals who are sticklers for principles, even such a fundamental principle as a person's right to protection under the law, are likely to find themselves abandoned by others who have no time to bother with such "troublesome things" as well as by the law itself.

However, in formulating thematic statements, care should also be taken not to *over* generalize. Good stories treat "real-life" fictional characters and situations, and the statement of a story's theme should reflect this fact. For example, the theme of "The Japanese Quince" is not that "The coming of spring can stir up feelings of vague longing in the hearts of human beings." The theme should be more precisely stated:

> The coming of spring can sometimes give rise to the impulse for life, nature, freedom, and beauty even among those monied and conventional people who wield great power in our society. However, this impulse will seldom prevail against the deeply ingrained forces of custom and convention.

A story's theme is its central and unifying consideration and involves virtually every major detail of the story. Thus, stating the theme should not require the use of extensive information from outside the story. Many of the best stories are self-revealing. A story should not give rise to a guessing game in which the reader tries to discover cleverly hidden or disguised messages.

Now, let's examine the themes of Carson McCullers' "A Tree, A Rock, A Cloud," John Updike's "A & P," and Florence Engle Randall's "The Watchers."

CARSON McCULLERS

A Tree, A Rock, A Cloud

It was raining that morning, and still very dark. When the boy reached the streetcar café he had almost finished his route and he went in for a cup of coffee. The place was an all-night café owned by a bitter and stingy man called Leo. After the raw, empty street, the café seemed friendly and bright: along the counter there were a couple of soldiers, three spinners from the cotton mill, and in a corner a man who sat hunched over with his nose and half his face down in a beer mug. The boy wore a helmet such as aviators wear. When he went into the café he unbuckled the chin strap and raised the right flap up over his pink little ear; often as he drank his coffee someone would speak to him in a friendly way. But this morning Leo did not look into his face and none of the men were talking. He paid and was leaving the café when a voice called out to him:

"Son! Hey Son!"

He turned back and the man in the corner was crooking his finger and nodding to him. He had brought his face out of the beer mug and he seemed suddenly very happy. The man was long and pale, with a big nose and faded orange hair.

"Hey Son!"

The boy went toward him. He was an undersized boy of about twelve, with one shoulder drawn higher than the other because of the weight of the paper sack. His face was shallow, freckled, and his eyes were round child eyes.

"Yeah Mister?"

The man laid one hand on the paper boy's shoulders, then grasped the boy's chin and turned his face slowly from one side to the other. The boy shrank back uneasily.

"Say! What's the big idea?"

The boy's voice was shrill; inside the café it was suddenly very quiet.

The man said slowly, "I love you."

All along the counter the men laughed. The boy, who had scowled and sidled away, did not know what to do. He looked over the counter at Leo, and Leo watched him with a weary, brittle jeer. The boy tried to laugh also. But the man was serious and sad.

"I did not mean to tease you, Son," he said. "Sit down and have a beer with me. There is something I have to explain."

Cautiously, out of the corner of his eye, the paper boy questioned the men along the counter to see what he should do. But they had gone back to their beer or their breakfast and did not notice him. Leo put a cup of coffee on the counter and a little jug of cream.

"He is a minor," Leo said.

The paper boy slid himself up onto the stool. His ear beneath the upturned flap of the helmet was very small and red. The man was nodding at him soberly. "It is important," he said. Then he reached in his hip pocket and brought out something which he held up in the palm of his hand for the boy to see.

"Look very carefully," he said.

The boy stared, but there was nothing to look at very carefully. The man held in his big, grimy palm a photograph. It was the face of a woman, but blurred, so that only the hat and the dress she was wearing stood out clearly.

"See?" the man asked.

The boy nodded and the man placed another picture in his palm. The woman was standing on a beach in a bathing suit. The suit made her stomach very big, and that was the main thing you noticed.

"Got a good look?" He leaned over closer and finally asked: "You ever seen her before?"

The boy sat motionless, staring slantwise at the man. "Not so I know of."

"Very well." The man blew on the photographs and put them back into his pocket. "That was my wife."

"Dead?" the boy asked.

Slowly the man shook his head. He pursed his lips as though about to whistle and answered in a long-drawn way: "Nuuu—" he said. "I will explain."

The beer on the counter before the man was in a large brown mug. He did not pick it up to drink. Instead he bent down and, putting his face over the rim, he rested there for a moment. Then with both hands he tilted the mug and sipped.

"Some night you'll go to sleep with your big nose in a mug and drown," said Leo. "Prominent transient drowns in beer. That would be a cute death."

The paper boy tried to signal to Leo. While the man was not looking he screwed up his face and worked his mouth to question soundlessly: "Drunk?" But Leo only raised his eyebrows and turned away to put some pink strips of bacon on the grill. The man pushed the mug away from him, straightened himself, and folded his loose crooked hands on the counter. His face was sad as he looked at the paper boy. He did not blink, but from time to time the lids closed down with delicate gravity over his pale green eyes. It was nearing dawn and the boy shifted the weight of the paper sack.

"I am talking about love," the man said. "With me it is a science."

The boy half slid down from the stool. But the man raised his forefinger, and there was something about him that held the boy and would not let him go away.

"Twelve years ago, I married the woman in the photograph. She was my wife for one year, nine months, three days, and two nights. I loved her. Yes. . . ." He tightened his blurred, rambling voice and said again: "I loved her. I thought also that she loved me. I was a railroad engineer. She had all home comforts and luxuries. It never crept into my brain that she was not satisfied. But do you know what happened?"

"Mgneeow!" said Leo.

The man did not take his eyes from the boy's face. "She left me. I came in one night and the house was empty and she was gone. She left me."

"With a fellow?" the boy asked.

Gently the man placed his palm down on the counter. "Why naturally, Son. A woman does not run off like that alone."

The café was quiet, the soft rain black and endless in the street outside. Leo pressed down the frying bacon with the prongs of his long fork. "So you have been chasing the floozie for eleven years. You frazzled old rascal!"

For the first time the man glanced at Leo. "Please don't be vulgar. Besides, I was not speaking to you." He turned back to the boy and said in a trusting and secretive undertone, "Let's not pay any attention to him, O.K.?"

The paper boy nodded doubtfully.

"It was like this," the man continued. "I am a person who feels many things. All of my life one thing after another has impressed me. Moonlight. The leg of a pretty girl. One thing after another. But the point is that when I had enjoyed anything there was a peculiar sensation as though it was laying around loose in me. Nothing seemed to finish itself up or fit in with the other things. Women? I had my portion of them. The same. Afterwards laying around loose in me. I was a man who had never loved."

Very slowly he closed his eyelids, and the gesture was like a curtain drawn at the end of a scene in a play. When he spoke again his voice was excited and the words came fast—the lobes of his large, loose ears seemed to tremble.

"Then I met this woman. I was fifty-one years old and she always said she was thirty. I met her at a filling station and we were married within three days. And do you know what it was like? I just can't tell you. All I had ever felt was gathered together around this woman. Nothing lay around loose in me any more but was finished up by her."

The man stopped suddenly and stroked his long nose. His voice sank down to a steady and reproachful undertone: "I'm not explaining this right. What happened was this. There were these beautiful feelings and loose little pleasures inside me. And this woman was something like an assembly line for my soul. I run these little pieces of myself through her and I come out complete. Now do you follow me?"

"What was her name?" the boy asked.

"Oh," he said. "I called her Dodo. But that is immaterial."

"Did you try to make her come back?"

The man did not seem to hear. "Under the circumstances you can imagine how I felt when she left me."

Leo took the bacon from the grill and folded two strips of it between a bun. He had a gray face, with slitted eyes, and a pinched nose saddled by faint blue shadows. One of the mill workers signaled for more coffee and Leo poured it. He did not give refills on coffee free. The spinner ate breakfast there every morning, but the better Leo knew his customers the stingier he treated them. He nibbled his own bun as though he grudged it to himself.

"And you never got hold of her again?"

The boy did not know what to think of the man, and his child's face was uncertain with mingled curiosity and doubt. He was new on the paper route; it was still strange to him to be out in the town in the black, queer early morning.

"Yes," the man said. "I took a number of steps to get her back. I went around trying to locate her. I went to Tulsa where she had folks. And to Mobile. I went to every town she had ever mentioned to me, and I hunted down every man she had formerly been connected with. Tulsa, Atlanta, Chicago, Cheehaw, Memphis. . . . For the better part of two years I chased around the country trying to lay hold of her."

"But the pair of them had vanished from the face of the earth!" said Leo.

"Don't listen to him," the man said confidentially. "And also just forget those two years. They are not important. What matters is that around the third year a curious thing began to happen to me."

"What?" the boy asked.

The man leaned down and tilted his mug to take a sip of beer. But as he hovered over the mug his nostrils fluttered slightly; he sniffed the staleness of the beer and did not drink. "Love is a curious thing to begin with. At first I thought only of getting her back. It was a kind of mania. But then as time went on I tried to remember her. But do you know what happened?"

"No," the boy said.

"When I laid myself down on a bed and tried to think about her my mind became a blank. I couldn't see her. I would take out her pictures and look. No good. Nothing doing. A blank. Can you imagine it?"

"Say Mac!" Leo called down the counter. "Can you imagine this bozo's mind a blank!"

Slowly, as though fanning away flies, the man waved his hand. His green eyes were concentrated and fixed on the shallow little face of the paper boy.

"But a sudden piece of glass on a sidewalk. Or a nickel tune in a music box. A shadow on a wall at night. And I would remember. It might happen in a street and I would cry or bang my head against a lamppost. You follow me?"

"A piece of glass . . ." the boy said.

"Anything. I would walk around and I had no power of how and when to remember her. You think you can put up a kind of shield. But remembering don't come to a man face forward—it corners around sideways. I was at the mercy of everything I saw and heard. Suddenly instead of me combing the countryside to find her she begun to chase me around in my very soul. *She* chasing *me*, mind you! and in my soul."

The boy asked finally: "What part of the country were you in then?"

"Ooh," the man groaned. "I was a sick mortal. It was like smallpox. I confess, Son, that I boozed. I fornicated. I committed any sin that suddenly appealed to me. I am loath to confess it but I will do so. When I recall that period it is all curdled in my mind, it was so terrible."

The man leaned his head down and tapped his forehead on the counter. For a few seconds he stayed bowed over in this position, the back of his stringy neck covered with orange furze, his hands with their long warped fingers held palm to palm in an attitude of prayer. Then the man straightened himself; he was smiling and suddenly his face was bright and tremulous and old.

"It was in the fifth year that it happened," he said. "And with it I started my science."

Leo's mouth jerked with a pale, quick grin. "Well none of we boys are getting any younger," he said. Then with sudden anger he balled up a dish-cloth he was holding and threw it down hard on the floor. "You draggle-tailed old Romeo!"

"What happened?" the boy asked.

The old man's voice was high and clear: "Peace," he answered.

"Huh?"

"It is hard to explain scientifically, Son," he said. "I guess the logical expla-nation is that she and I had fleed around from each other for so long that finally we just got tangled up together and lay down and quit. Peace. A queer and beautiful blankness. It was spring in Portland and the rain came every afternoon. All evening I just stayed there on my bed in the dark. And that is how the science come to me."

The windows in the streetcar were pale blue with light. The two soldiers paid for their beers and opened the door—one of the soldiers combed his hair and wiped off his muddy puttees before they went outside. The three mill workers bent silently over their breakfasts. Leo's clock was ticking on the wall.

"It is this. And listen carefully. I meditated on love and reasoned it out. I realized what is wrong with us. Men fall in love for the first time. And what do they fall in love with?"

The boy's soft mouth was partly open and he did not answer.

"A woman," the old man said. "Without science, with nothing to go by, they undertake the most dangerous and sacred experience in God's earth. They fall in love with a woman. Is that correct, Son?"

"Yeah," the boy said faintly.

"They start at the wrong end of love. They begin at the climax. Can you wonder it is so miserable? Do you know how men should love?"

The old man reached over and grasped the boy by the collar of his leather jacket. He gave him a gentle little shake and his green eyes gazed down unblinking and grave.

"Son, do you know how love should be begun?"

The boy sat small and listening and still. Slowly he shook his head. The old man leaned closer and whispered:

"A tree. A rock. A cloud."

It was still raining outside in the street: a mild, gray, endless rain. The mill whistle blew for the six o'clock shift and the three spinners paid and went away. There was no one in the café but Leo, the old man, and the little paper boy.

"The weather was like this in Portland," he said. "At the time my science was begun. I meditated and I started very cautious. I would pick up something from the street and take it home with me. I bought a goldfish and I concen-trated on the goldfish and I loved it. I graduated from one thing to another. Day by day I was getting this technique. On the road from Portland to San Diego——"

"Aw shut up!" screamed Leo suddenly. "Shut up! Shut up!"

The old man still held the collar of the boy's jacket; he was trembling and his face was earnest and bright and wild. "For six years now I have gone around by myself and built up my science. And now I am a master. Son, I can love anything. No longer do I have to think about it even. I see a street full of people and a beautiful light comes in me. I watch a bird in the sky. Or I meet a traveler on the road. Everything, Son. And anybody. All strangers and all loved? Do you realize what a science like mine can mean?"

The boy held himself stiffly, his hands curled tight around the counter edge. Finally he asked: "Did you ever really find that lady?"

"What? What say, Son?"

"I mean," the boy asked timidly. "Have you fallen in love with a woman again?"

The old man loosened his grasp on the boy's collar. He turned away and for the first time his green eyes had a vague and scattered look. He lifted the mug from the counter, drank down the yellow beer. His head was shaking slowly from side to side. Then finally he answered: "No, Son. You see that is the last step in my science. I go cautious. And I am not quite ready yet."

"Well!" said Leo. "Well well well!"

The old man stood in the open doorway. "Remember," he said. Framed there in the gray damp light of the early morning he looked shrunken and seedy and frail. But his smile was bright. "Remember I love you," he said with a last nod. And the door closed quietly behind him.

The boy did not speak for a long time. He pulled down the bangs on his forehead and slid his grimy little forefinger around the rim of his empty cup. Then without looking at Leo he finally asked:

"Was he drunk?"

"No," said Leo shortly.

The boy raised his clear voice higher. "Then was he a dope fiend?"

"No."

The boy looked up at Leo, and his flat little face was desperate, his voice urgent and shrill. "Was he crazy? Do you think he was a lunatic?" The paper boy's voice dropped suddenly with doubt. "Leo? Or not?"

But Leo would not answer him. Leo had run a night café for fourteen years, and he held himself to be a critic of craziness. There were the town characters and also the transients who roamed in from the night. He knew the manias of all of them. But he did not want to satisfy the questions of the waiting child. He tightened his pale face and was silent.

So the boy pulled down the right flap of his helmet and as he turned to leave he made the only comment that seemed safe to him, the only remark that could not be laughed down and despised:

"He sure has done a lot of traveling."

BY WAY OF DISCUSSION

"A Tree, A Rock, A Cloud" describes the spiritual odyssey of a man as he comes by gradual stages to realize the nature of ideal love and to experience its power. Thematically, the story suggests that ideal love is selfless, involving a capacity to love and encompass all nature.

For more than fifty years, until he meets the woman he marries, the man leads a completely selfish and sensual life. Although he enjoys many things, he loves nothing, not even the women with whom he occasionally becomes involved. These he regards as so many pairs of pretty legs. And as a result of this general view, his pleasures bring him no lasting satisfaction, only a sense of disharmony and incompleteness. Once he has married, though, his entire life changes. Everything centers on his new wife, and for the first time he experiences a sense of wholeness. The man imagines himself in love, never stopping to consider the possibility that true love cannot be confined to a single object, cannot be purchased simply by producing "all home comforts and luxuries." When his wife vanishes with another man, his idyll falls to pieces.

After his wife's disappearance, the man's attitude toward love does not at first change. The fact that he consumes more than two years searching for her demonstrates that he still believes love to be a feeling between two particular individuals, that when you have your "one and only" all will be well. But things gradually begin to change when he loses the ability to visualize his wife's appearance except when a piece of glass, a shadow, or some such thing recalls her face for him. (This development foreshadows the old man's later discovery of how love, or the ability to love, develops.) Nevertheless, he continues his debauched way of living. Enlightenment, for lack of a better term, finally occurs when the old man, through thought and meditation, comes to realize that before a man can truly love a woman he must first learn to love nonhuman creatures and even inanimate objects. Love, in fact, may focus on almost anything; and once one has developed the capacity to love nature or whatever, happiness follows, whether or not love is ever returned.

Throughout most of the old man's story, Leo contents himself with delivering sarcastic remarks. However, as the story nears its conclusion, Leo suddenly becomes angry and shouts, "Aw shut up! Shut up! Shut up!" Leo is not angry because he thinks the old man talks too much. Nor does he think the old man a drunk, a dope fiend, or a lunatic. Something far more disturbing has triggered Leo's outburst: the realization that this despised old transient is speaking the truth. Leo has always been "bitter and stingy" without ever stopping to consider what his behavior has cost him in unrealized happiness. Now, forced to contemplate the emptiness of his loveless life, he tightens his face and falls silent before the boy's youthful questions.

And what of the boy's response? Although his questions indicate that he does not understand all that has been said, his desperate looks and shrill, urgent voice suggest a dawning of understanding. Once round-eyed and unthinking, he must now grapple with his own disturbing truth: that love and happiness are not automatic gifts of life. They do not come as part of the package, but must be won—or earned—through a long and difficult process. The insistence with which the boy asks his questions reflects a naïve hope that Leo will denounce the old man as a fraud and thus restore his own imperiled innocence. But Leo is unable to denounce the old man, and the boy's final remark, made flippant in an effort to disguise his true feelings, is magnetized with irony. Although the old man has indeed done a great deal of physical traveling, his spiritual journey has carried him a much greater distance—from the ignorance of selfishness to an enlightened and selfless love of all creation.

JOHN UPDIKE

A & P

In walks these three girls in nothing but bathing suits. I'm in the third checkout slot, with my back to the door, so I don't see them until they're over by the bread. The one that caught my eye first was the one in the plaid green two-piece. She was a chunky kid, with a good tan and a sweet broad soft-looking can with those two crescents of white just under it, where the sun never seems to hit, at the top of the backs of her legs. I stood there with my hand on a box of HiHo crackers trying to remember if I rang it up or not. I ring it up again and the customer starts giving me hell. She's one of these cash-register-watchers, a witch about fifty with rouge on her cheekbones and no eyebrows, and I know it made her day to trip me up. She'd been watching cash registers for fifty years and probably never seen a mistake before.

By the time I got her feathers smoothed and her goodies into a bag—she gives me a little snort in passing, if she'd been born at the right time they would have burned her over in Salem—by the time I get her on her way the girls had circled around the bread and were coming back, without a pushcart, back my way along the counters, in the aisle between the checkouts and the Special bins. They didn't even have shoes on. There was this chunky one, with the two-piece—it was bright green and the seams on the bra were still sharp and her belly was still pretty pale so I guessed she just got it (the suit)—there was this one, with one of those chubby berry-faces, the lips all bunched together under her nose, this one, and a tall one, with black hair that hadn't quite frizzed right, and one of these sunburns right across under the eyes, and a chin that was too long—you know, the kind of girl other girls think is very "striking" and "attractive" but never quite makes it, as they very well know, which is why they like her so much—and then the third one, that wasn't quite so tall. She was the queen. She kind of led them, the other two peeking around and making their shoulders round. She didn't look around, not this queen, she just walked straight on slowly, on these long white prima-donna legs. She came down a little hard on her heels, as if she didn't walk in her bare feet that much, putting down her heels and then letting the weight move along to her toes as if she was testing the floor with every step, putting a little deliberate extra action into it. You never know for sure how girls' minds work (do you really think it's a mind in there or just a little buzz like a bee in a glass jar?) but you got the idea she had talked the other two into coming in here with her, and now she was showing them how to do it, walk slow and hold yourself straight.

She had on a kind of dirty-pink—beige maybe, I don't know—bathing suit with a little nubble all over it and, what got me, the straps were down. They were off her shoulders looped loose around the cool tops of her arms, and I guess as a result the suit had slipped a little on her, so all around the top of the cloth there was this shining rim. If it hadn't been there you wouldn't have known there could have been anything whiter than those shoulders. With the straps pushed off, there was nothing between the top of the suit and the top of her head except just *her*, this clean bare plane of the top of her chest down from the shoulder bones like a dented sheet of metal tilted in the light. I mean, it was more than pretty.

She had sort of oaky hair that the sun and salt had bleached, done up in a bun that was unravelling, and a kind of prim face. Walking into the A & P with your straps down, I suppose it's the only kind of face you *can* have. She held her head so high her neck, coming up out of those white shoulders, looked kind of stretched, but I didn't mind. The longer her neck was, the more of her there was.

She must have felt in the corner of her eye me and over my shoulder Stokesie in the second slot watching, but she didn't tip. Not this queen. She kept her eyes moving across the racks, and stopped, and turned so slow it made my stomach rub the inside of my apron, and buzzed to the other two, who kind of huddled against her for relief, and then they all three of them went up the cat-and-dog-food-breakfast-cereal-macaroni-rice-raisins-season-ings-spreads-spaghetti-soft-drinks-crackers-and-cookies aisle. From the third slot I look straight up this aisle to the meat counter, and I watched them all the way. The fat one with the tan sort of fumbled with the cookies, but on second thought she put the package back. The sheep pushing their carts down the aisle—the girls were walking against the usual traffic (not that we have one-way signs or anything)—were pretty hilarious. You could see them, when Queenie's white shoulders dawned on them, kind of jerk, or hop, or hiccup, but their eyes snapped back to their own baskets and on they pushed. I bet you could set off dynamite in an A & P and the people would by and large keep reaching and checking oatmeal off their lists and muttering "Let me see, there was a third thing, began with A, asparagus, no, ah, yes, applesauce!" or whatever it is they do mutter. But there was no doubt, this jiggled them. A few houseslaves in pin curlers even looked around after pushing their carts past to make sure what they had seen was correct.

You know, it's one thing to have a girl in a bathing suit down on the beach, where what with the glare nobody can look at each other much anyway, and another thing in the cool of the A & P, under the fluorescent lights, against all those stacked packages, with her feet paddling along naked over our checker-board green-and-cream rubber-tile floor.

"Oh Daddy," Stokesie said beside me. "I feel so faint."

"Darling," I said. "Hold me tight." Stokesie's married, with two babies chalked up on his fuselage already, but as far as I can tell that's the only difference. He's twenty-two, and I was nineteen this April.

"Is it done?" he asks, the responsible married man finding his voice. I forgot to say he thinks he's going to be manager some sunny day, maybe in 1990 when it's called the Great Alexandrov and Petrooshki Tea Company or something.

What he meant was, our town is five miles from a beach, with a big summer colony out on the Point, but we're right in the middle of town, and the women generally put on a shirt or shorts or something before they get out of the car into the street. And anyway these are usually women with six children and varicose veins mapping their legs and nobody, including them, could care less. As I say, we're right in the middle of town, and if you stand at our front doors you can see two banks and the Congregational church and the newspaper store and three real-estate offices and about twenty-seven old freeloaders tearing up Central Street because the sewer broke again. It's not as if we're on the Cape; we're north of Boston and there's people in this town haven't seen the ocean for twenty years.

The girls had reached the meat counter and were asking McMahon something. He pointed, they pointed, and they shuffled out of sight behind a pyramid of Diet Delight peaches. All that was left for us to see was old McMahon patting his mouth and looking after them sizing up their joints. Poor kids, I began to feel sorry for them, they couldn't help it.

*   *   *

Now here comes the sad part of the story, at least my family says it's sad, but I don't think it's so sad myself. The store's pretty empty, it being Thursday afternoon, so there was nothing much to do except lean on the register and wait for the girls to show up again. The whole store was like a pinball machine and I didn't know which tunnel they'd come out of. After a while they come around out of the far aisle, around the light bulbs, records at discount of the Caribbean Six or Tony Martin Sings or some such gunk you wonder they waste the wax on, sixpacks of candy bars, and plastic toys done up in cellophane that fall apart when a kid looks at them anyway. Around they come, Queenie still leading the way, and holding a little gray jar in her hand. Slots Three through Seven are unmanned and I could see her wondering between Stokes and me, but Stokesie with his usual luck draws an old party in baggy gray pants who stumbles up with four giant cans of pineapple juice (what do these bums *do* with all that pineapple juice? I've often asked myself) so the girls come to me. Queenie puts down the jar and I take it into my fingers icy cold. Kingfish Fancy Herring Snacks in Pure Sour Cream: 49¢. Now her hands are empty, not a ring or a bracelet, bare as God made them, and I wonder where the money's coming from. Still with that prim look she lifts a folded dollar bill out of the hollow at the center of her nubbled pink top. The jar went heavy in my hand. Really, I thought that was so cute.

Then everybody's luck begins to run out. Lengel comes in from haggling with a truck full of cabbages on the lot and is about to scuttle into that door marked MANAGER behind which he hides all day when the girls touch his eye. Lengel's pretty dreary, teaches Sunday school and the rest, but he doesn't miss that much. He comes over and says, "Girls, this isn't the beach."

Queenie blushes, though maybe it's just a brush of sunburn I was noticing for the first time, now that she was so close. "My mother asked me to pick up a jar of herring snacks." Her voice kind of startled me, the way voices do when you see the people first, coming out so flat and dumb yet kind of tony, too, the way it ticked over "pick up" and "snacks." All of a sudden I slid right down her voice into her living room. Her father and the other men were standing around in ice-cream coats and bow ties and the women were in sandals picking up herring snacks on toothpicks off a big glass plate and they were all holding drinks the color of water with olives and sprigs of mint in them. When my parents have somebody over they get lemonade and if it's a real racy affair Schlitz in tall glasses with "They'll Do It Every Time" cartoons stencilled on.

"That's all right," Lengel said. "But this isn't the beach." His repeating this struck me as funny, as if it had just occurred to him, and he had been thinking all these years the A & P was a great big dune and he was the head lifeguard. He didn't like my smiling—as I say he doesn't miss much—but he concentrates on giving the girls that sad Sunday-school-superintendent stare.

Queenie's blush is no sunburn now, and the plump one in plaid, that I liked better from the back—a really sweet can—pipes up "We weren't doing any shopping. We just came in for the one thing."

"That makes no difference," Lengel tells her, and I could see from the way his eyes went that he hadn't noticed she was wearing a two-piece before. "We want you decently dressed when you come in here."

"We *are* decent," Queenie says suddenly, her lower lip pushing, getting sore now that she remembers her place, a place from which the crowd that runs the A & P must look pretty crummy. Fancy Herring Snacks flashed in her very blue eyes.

"Girls, I don't want to argue with you. After this come in here with your shoulders covered. It's our policy." He turns his back. That's policy for you. Policy is what the kingpins want. What the others want is juvenile delinquency.

All this while, the customers had been showing up with their carts but, you know, sheep, seeing a scene, they had all bunched up on Stokesie, who shook open a paper bag as gently as peeling a peach, not wanting to miss a word. I could feel in the silence everybody getting nervous, most of all Lengel, who asks me, "Sammy, have you rung up their purchase?"

I thought and said "No" but it wasn't about that I was thinking. I go through the punches, 4, 9, GROC, TOT—it's more complicated than you think, and after you do it often enough, it begins to make a little song, that you hear words to, in my case "Hello (*bing*) there, you (*gung*) hap-py *pee*-pul (*splat*)!"—the *splat* being the drawer flying out. I uncrease the bill, tenderly as you may imagine, it just having come from between the two smoothest scoops of vanil-la I had ever known were there, and pass a half and a penny into her narrow pink palm, and nestle the herrings in a bag and twist its neck and hand it over, all the time thinking.

The girls, and who'd blame them, are in a hurry to get out, so I say "I quit" to Lengel quick enough for them to hear, hoping they'll stop and watch me, their unsuspected hero. They keep right on going, into the electric eye; the door flies open and they flicker across the lot to their car, Queenie and Plaid and Big Tall Goony-Goony (not that as raw material she was so bad), leaving me with Lengel and a kink in his eyebrow.

"Did you say something, Sammy?"

"I said I quit."

"I thought you did."

"You didn't have to embarrass them."

"It was they who were embarrassing us."

I started to say something that came out "Fiddle-de-doo." It's a saying of my grandmother's, and I know she would have been pleased.

"I don't think you know what you're saying," Lengel said.

"I know you don't," I said. "But I do." I pull the bow at the back of my apron and start shrugging it off my shoulders. A couple customers that had been heading for my slot begin to knock against each other, like scared pigs in a chute.

Lengel sighs and begins to look very patient and old and gray. He's been a friend of my parents for years. "Sammy, you don't want to do this to your Mom and Dad," he tells me. It's true, I don't. But it seems to me that once you begin a gesture it's fatal not to go through with it. I fold the apron, "Sammy" stitched in red on the pocket, and put it on the counter, and drop the bow tie on top of it. The bow tie is theirs, if you've ever wondered. "You'll feel this for the rest of your life," Lengel says, and I know that's true, too, but remember-ing how he made that pretty girl blush makes me so scrunchy inside I punch the No Sale tab and the machine whirs "pee-pul" and the drawer splats out. One advantage to this scene taking place in summer, I can follow this up with a clean exit, there's no fumbling around getting your coat and galoshes, I just saunter into the electric eye in my white shirt that my mother ironed the night before, and the door heaves itself open, and outside the sunshine is skating around on the asphalt.

I look around for my girls, but they're gone, of course. There wasn't any-body but some young married screaming with her children about some candy they didn't get by the door of a powder-blue Falcon station wagon. Looking back in the big windows, over the bags of peat moss and aluminum lawn furniture stacked on the pavement, I could see Lengel in my place in the slot, checking the sheep through. His face was dark gray and his back stiff, as if he'd just had an injection of iron, and my stomach kind of fell as I felt how hárd the world was going to be to me hereafter.

BY WAY OF DISCUSSION

In Greek mythology, Paris was the son of Priam, king of Troy. When his mother, Hecuba, dreamed that her yet unborn son was a torch that set the whole country on fire, the soothsayer Aesacus was consulted to interpret the dream. Aesacus explained that one day Paris would cause the destruction of Troy. The boy was then given to a slave, along with orders that he should be killed. The slave, however, left young Paris on Mount Ida. A few days later a shepherd found the child and raised him as his own. As he grew to manhood, Paris became very proficient at driving off robbers from the flocks of sheep.

Eris, the evil goddess of Discord, was very unpopular among the Olympian gods and goddesses, and when there was a banquet she was often not invited. She resented such treatment and resolved to make trouble. Her opportunity came at the marriage of King Peleus and the sea nymph Thetis. Eris tossed into the banqueting hall a golden apple on which were written the words "for the fairest." All the goddesses wanted the apple. After the competition had been narrowed down to Hera, Pallas Athena, and Aphrodite, Zeus was asked to judge. But he refused, wanting nothing to do with the matter. Then he suggested that the three goddesses go to Mount Ida, which was near Troy, and let Paris make the judgment. Paris was still there on the mountain, minding his sheep.

Paris was not actually asked to judge which of the goddesses was the most fair, but to consider the bribes each offered him if he selected her as most worthy of the golden apple. Hera promised to make him ruler of all Europe and Asia. Athena promised that as leader of the Trojans he would defeat the Greeks and lay Greece in ruins. But Aphrodite promised him that the most beautiful woman in all the world would be his. Paris gave the apple to Aphrodite, thus incurring the anger of Hera and Athena and not only making his life a very difficult one from that point on but also ultimately causing the Trojan War.

The parallels between "The Judgment of Paris" and the events of "A & P" make it easier to understand what John Updike is getting at in the story. In fact, if we are not aware of the mythical parallels, certain questions about the story are likely to remain a little puzzling. For example, why are there *three* girls in bathing suits? Why would Lengel say to Sammy as Sammy is preparing to leave the store that he is going to feel the results of quitting such an unimportant job for the rest of his life?

Why should Sammy himself feel that from now on the world will be a much harder place for him?

You can, of course, make an entirely literal interpretation of the story and answer those questions solely from the facts presented. But such an effort misses the point. Everything is intended to be seen—by the reader—on two planes simultaneously.

Sammy is no young radical looking for a cause to champion. Nor, for that matter, is he Paris; he is an easygoing, average boy who has even learned to cope with the tedium of a boring job. He enjoys looking at the pretty girls and making harmless wisecracks about things that occur daily in the store. Nevertheless, stirred by Queenie's beauty and angered by the way Lengel has treated her and her companions, Sammy makes a decision that he senses may affect his whole future life—and not pleasantly, at that. But despite this sobering prospect, he never wavers because "it seems to me that once you begin a gesture it's fatal not to go through with it."

What we have here, then, is a clever story that draws upon an incident from classical mythology to reinforce a traditional theme subject: initiation. Sammy, the innocent checkout clerk, suddenly becomes fed up with the whole scene of banal store policy and all that it represents and opts instead for beauty, vitality, youth, and freedom—a decision earlier foreshadowed by his general cheerfulness and mildly irreverent outlook on life. In doing this, Sammy crashes through a sort of moral threshold and assumes a new maturity, although it may be a maturity viewed as suspect by the traditional nine-to-five, workaday world. Sammy has made, as most of us are forced to make at various times as we are growing up, his own little "Judgment of Paris."

FLORENCE ENGLE RANDALL

The Watchers

From the moment Althea awoke that morning, she knew their building had been chosen. She knew it even before she saw the excitement in her husband's eyes as he handed her the official notice that had been put under their door.

"Well," he said, smiling at her while she read it, "what do you think of that?"

"I had a feeling, George," she said, "even before I opened my eyes, I had a feeling that this would happen today."

"We were due to be next," George said. "The setup here is about perfect for it."

"Will you be home early?" She watched him while he sipped his coffee.

"It won't start until late," he said. "It won't start until it gets dark. You know how these things are."

"Just the same," she said, "I couldn't bear it just sitting around and waiting for you. We have so much to do. We have to have dinner first and then change our clothes and find seats. We want to have good seats," she reminded him. "They won't reserve any for us, you know."

"Don't worry about it." He touched her cheek lightly with the back of his hand. "I'll be home in plenty of time."

"Do you have everything? I was never so scared in my life yesterday when I found your gun on the top of the dresser. I just couldn't believe my eyes. I wanted to run after you but I didn't know which route you had taken."

"I always carry a spare," he said. "You know that. I always keep a spare in my coat pocket. Why don't you trust me?"

"I know I'm being foolish," Althea said, kissing him good-bye. "Just be careful, that's all. I don't want you to be so sure of yourself that you'll get careless."

"You be careful," he said. "Do you have to go out today?"

She frowned. "I have to go marketing, and then I thought I'd go downtown and buy a new dress for tonight. All the women will be dressed up and I don't want to go looking like a frump."

"Watch out for the department stores," he reminded her. "They can be dangerous. Don't take any crowded elevators and check the dressing room before you try anything on."

She locked and double-locked the door after him, then fastened the chain before she had her own breakfast. Standing at the window while she drank her coffee, she thought how ridiculous it was the way they went through the same routine each morning as if the very fact that they had to take precautions was making them nervous. When they were first married two years ago, it would never have occurred to either of them that there was any reason for worry.

It must be because we're so much in love, she told herself, stacking the dishes in the washer. Love breeds its own vulnerability, its own fear.

When the signal flashed on the wall, Althea had just finished dressing. She watched it for a moment. It was their code, all right. Three lights in a row, the flickering pause, and then the slow, deliberate hold. She pressed the button that buzzed downstairs.

"Who is it?" she said, her mouth against the intercom.

"It's all right," said a woman's voice, clear and high and a bit too shrill. "I've already shown my identification to your doorman. I'm Sally Milford—Cary Milford's wife. My husband works in your husband's office."

"What do you want?" said Althea cautiously. "I'm much too busy to see anyone this morning. Besides, I'm on my way out." She bit her lip. George would be right if he scolded her for being careless. Why had she told this woman she was going out?

"I'll only take a moment of your time. It's important."

"Can't you tell me what it is over the intercom?"

"If I wanted to talk this way, I could have called you on the phone. I must see you. Please."

"All right," said Althea, reluctantly, knowing she was being foolish, "you can come up."

She checked her own gun even though she knew it was loaded and she palmed the small dagger—the one her mother had given her as a wedding present—the one with the jeweled handle.

"Things are so different now," her mother had said, sighing. She had lifted the dagger from the tissue paper and had studied it for a moment before she handed it to Althea. "In my day we could walk the streets without this sort of thing."

"That's not true," Althea reminded her. "You told me you used to wear stilt-like heels and you always carried a whistle in your purse."

"But that's not the same. It still wasn't like this," said her mother. "Did you know we weren't allowed to carry weapons?"

"You weren't?" said Althea, startled.

"That was before everyone realized that our laws were lagging behind our customs and public opinion. That was before the Citizen's Defense Act was passed."

"There is only one crime," Althea said firmly, "and that is to be a victim. Nothing makes sense otherwise."

"I suppose not." Her mother shook her head. "I guess I'm just being sentimental," she added wistfully. "Sometimes I miss the policemen we used to have. They would wear blue uniforms and they would drive around with sirens blaring and lights flashing. It seems a shame they became obsolete. Why I can even remember the time when we could take a walk in the park."

"In the park?" said Althea, incredulous. "You could actually do that?"

Now Althea bit her lip. There was no point in daydreaming. She stationed herself at the oneway peephole. The woman who now came within her range of vision was thin of face and well-dressed. She blinked her eyes nervously and hesitated before she knocked.

"Just a moment," said Althea. She unfastened the chain and the two locks, and then stepped back so that when the door opened she would be behind it. "Come in," she said.

"Where are you?"

"Right behind you," said Althea, her hand on her gun. "You're not very smart to walk right in like that, are you?"

"But I know who you are," said Sally Milford, her eyes wide with fright. "My husband and your husband are good friends."

"The first thing you have to learn," said Althea, "is not to trust anyone."

She kicked the door shut. "Hold up your hands." She found a small acid gun in Sally's purse and a knife in the pocket of her jacket. "Just put them on the table," Althea directed, "and then sit down. Would you like some coffee?"

Sally shook her head, "Look," she said, her mouth trembling, "I wouldn't trouble you like this—I wouldn't have come at all if I didn't, in a way, know you. You see that, don't you?"

"No," said Althea firmly, "I don't see anything. Suppose you tell me what you want."

Sally clasped her hands on the edge of the table. "I have a brother-in-law who knows someone on the Board of Commissioners," she said, leaning forward in her eagerness, "and we heard that your apartment house has been chosen."

"These things are supposed to be a secret," Althea said sharply. "No one except the people involved is supposed to know. Don't you realize what can happen to you if they find out? And what can happen to me?"

"I'm sorry but I just couldn't help it. When I heard about it—all I could think was that I simply had to go. I have never been to a performance and, the way things look, I'll never have a chance."

"Where do you live?" Althea asked, putting the gun away.

"On the East Side. You know how safe it's getting to be over there. We haven't had an incident in months."

"That doesn't mean they won't choose your building eventually."

"Do you really think they will?"

"Why not?" said Althea.

"Then, in that case, why can't you make believe that we're visiting you or something? They do have special passes for visitors and then, when we're finally chosen, we could reciprocate. Cary and I could invite you and George. That way we could each see two performances."

"It wouldn't work," said Althea. "In the first place, we have the perfect setting for this sort of thing. That's why we picked this particular apartment building. We could have had a much better place to live but both George and I agreed that our best chance was being here. We had to wait two years for this day, and if they ever suspect that was a put-up thing, you know what would happen to us."

"I suppose I was foolish to even hope." Sally stood up. "I thought it would work out."

"It won't," said Althea, feeling a sudden pity for her. "Believe me, Sally, it won't. I happen to know that Mrs. Tremont, who lives on the third floor, has her sister-in-law staying with her; that, of course, makes it possible for her sister-in-law to go tonight, but if she had just arrived today someone would be sure to report it and Mrs. Tremont would get into trouble."

"You said you were going out," said Sally. "Do you want a ride with me?"

"I'm going downtown," said Althea. "I thought I'd buy a new dress for tonight."

"I haven't been shopping in ages," said Sally. "Cary won't let me go without him and he's been much too busy on Saturdays. We could shop together and maybe have lunch."

"Just remember one thing," Althea warned as she reached for her coat and hat. "No matter what you say, I won't change my mind. You can spend the whole day with me if you like but I still won't change my mind."

"I know you're right," said Sally as they pressed the button for the elevator. "It's just that I'm glad to have some company on the subway."

"Are you still taking the subway?" Althea stared at her, amazed. "George insists that I take the bus. Not taxis—they're not too reliable anymore but a bus is still fine."

"It takes too long," said Sally. "The subway is much quicker. I have my own system. I never wait on a platform if I'm alone and I usually ride in the first car where the motorman is and, just in case anyone is following me, I change at every other stop."

"Now," said Althea, watching as the elevator stopped at their floor, "run!"

They pounded through the corridor and down one flight of steps. Then they rang for the elevator again. When it arrived, it was empty and they rode it the rest of the way down.

It turned out to be, Althea told George later, a rather pleasant day. With the two of them together, the shopping proved much easier. Sally stood watch while Althea tried on dresses and Althea stood guard while Sally shopped. When they finally parted, it was after four.

Althea took a bus uptown again and got off three blocks before her destination. She glanced behind to make sure she wasn't being followed; then she bought a steak at the meat market. Steak would be the quickest thing to cook for dinner and she didn't want to load her arms with too many packages. It was difficult enough carrying the dress, although she had insisted that the clerk put it in a shopping bag instead of a box. With a shopping bag she would feel less clumsy and have one hand free.

The doorman beamed at her when she entered the lobby.

"This is a great day for us," he said.

Althea nodded. "I bought a new dress," she told him happily, "a black sheath."

"I'll ride the elevator with you if you like," he offered generously. "Most of the tenants are home by now."

"You're not supposed to leave your post," Althea reminded him. "Anyone could come in while you were away. You know what happened to the last doorman we had?"

"You're right," he admitted. "For a moment I forgot."

"By the way," she whispered, "do you know who will be giving the performance?"

He shook his head. "No one knows," he said. "I've been asking but no one knows for sure. I think it's a young one. They usually are."

"You'd think those kids could learn," said Althea, ringing for the elevator. "My parents were pretty strict with me—I can tell you that."

"That's the best way," the doorman said. "You have to be firm with them. I always say that from the time they can walk, they can be taught. Now, you take that kid of Mrs. Hammond. You know the Hammonds on the fifth floor? He got his first slash today and was sent home from school in disgrace."

"Oh, no," said Althea, in horror. "He's only eleven. He's only allowed two more mistakes."

"The way Mrs. Hammond spanked him, he'll learn," the doorman said. "That'll never happen to him again, I can tell you that."

"Who was the other boy?"

"It was a girl," said the doorman. "A pretty little thing, I understand. Well, she'll get her first gold star for that."

"I got a gold star when I was twelve," said Althea, stepping into the elevator.

She rode it to the fourth floor and got out. She took the stairs the rest of the way, then stood before her own front door for a moment, listening. When she was positive it was safe, she inserted her key in the lock.

At precisely six o'clock George came home and, by seven thirty, they had finished dinner and were dressed.

"I'd like to go now," said Althea, impatiently.

"It won't get dark until eight," George said. "You know how it is this time of year. Even then, we'll have to wait a while."

"I can see the stands from here," said Althea, craning her neck as she peered out of the window. "People are beginning to arrive now. Please, darling, let's go."

"You're like a child," he said, hugging her. "Just an anxious little kid."

"I can't help it," she said. "I'm excited. Aren't you thrilled, George?"

"Come on," he said, indulgently. He looked at her, chic and lovely in her new black sheath. "No pockets," he said, shaking his head. "What made you buy a dress without any pockets? I didn't know they made them that way anymore."

"I'll only wear it when I'm with you," she said. "Besides, I have a knife in my purse."

"Just see that you keep it handy." He held the door for her. "I'm glad you used your head this morning."

"For a moment I was tempted," Althea confessed. "Sally seems like a sweet person and it might be fun if we could go there sometimes, but then I realized we'd be taking a chance."

"It doesn't pay to take chances," said George. "Otherwise you can end up giving the performance instead of watching it."

"The doorman told me it was a young one. Probably a girl."

"It usually is," said George.

"Do you know what she did?" Althea asked as they walked through the back of the lobby and out into the courtyard. "No one seems to know what she did."

"Probably something stupid," said George, looking around and waving to their neighbors. "You know, honey, you were right. The stands are filling up."

The stands had been placed next to their building. They were permanent, sturdily built of brick and stone, and erected when the building itself had been new. Optimistically every building had its stands ready for the day when it would be chosen, and Althea looked around proudly as she and George found seats in the second row.

Mr. and Mrs. Hammond were there and seated between them was their son, Timmy. Timmy's right arm was bandaged and he huddled close to his mother.

"I heard about it," said Althea, with sympathy. "I'm sure Timmy will never let it happen again."

"Because she was pretty. Because it was a girl," said Mrs. Hammond bitterly. "She called to him and he ran right over, leaving his knife in his pocket as if a knife ever did anybody any good in a pocket. Just because it was a little girl, he trusted her. But he's learned his lesson, haven't you, Timmy?" she said, slapping him across the face.

"No more," Timmy wept, putting his bandaged arm across his eyes. "Please, Mommy, don't hit me anymore."

He'll never amount to anything, Althea thought, staring at him in dismay. Only three chances and he's used up one already. He's too soft. When I have a child—

She thought about it for a moment, longing for a child but the apartment they were in was too small and they hadn't wanted to move until they had a chance at a performance. Maybe now—maybe now that they were finally spectators—perhaps now that the longed-for, dreamed-about moment had finally arrived, they could move to a larger place and she would have a child.

"You have to train them from the beginning," she whispered to George.

"Sure," he said, knowing what she meant. "It won't happen to us."

"It won't happen to us," she agreed, seeing the way George, even now, even at this moment of pleasure and relaxation, kept his hand in his pocket; George's hand curled over the bulge of his gun.

Althea leaned back. She had known, of course, what the stage setting would be but, just the same, sitting there, part of the expectant, eager audience, she had to admire its reality.

It represented a street scene. It could have been Althea's own street with its middle-class, red-brick buildings, the old-fashioned canopies extending from wide entrances to the edge of the curb. Behind the lighted windows of the buildings, Althea could see the people, all the families together, having dinner, watching television, reading, talking, laughing—all the people of the city settling down for the night.

In the center of the stage was a street lamp, still unlit although it was twilight now; on the far right, there was a fire hydrant. The first floor of the center building was occupied by a shop. The sign said, "ANTIQUES," and Althea could see the lovely things in the window—the paintings in the carved, ornate frames, the delicate crystal goblets, a curved brass bowl. Suddenly the street light went on, dominating the center of the stage with its soft, gentle glow.

The curtain is rising, thought Althea, taking a deep breath. She always loved that moment in the theatre, that magic moment when all the murmuring and the movement and the whispering stopped, the hush and wonder when the curtain rose and the stage lay there before them, the play ready to begin.

Someone somewhere in the back coughed and Althea drew a deep, sighing gasp of impatience.

The stage became alive. From the center building a man emerged, a nondescript man walking his dog at night. The dog tugged and the man whistled softly between his teeth as the two of them walked down the street. The stage became empty again and Althea clasped her hands in her lap, amazed to discover that they were shaking.

At the far right two shadows blurred, moved, took form. Now a girl and a boy strolled down the street. His arm was flung around her shoulders and, from the way she smiled at him, Althea knew they were in love. They moved slowly across the stage. They stopped before the antique shop and the girl pointed to the brass bowl and the boy nodded and gestured expansively showing her there was nothing in the world he wouldn't get for her. They disappeared on the far left and the stage was empty again.

Althea unclasped her hands and, because her palms were wet, she rubbed them furtively together. Beside her she could hear the sound of George's breathing, slow, heavy, as if each breath were an effort.

Onstage, in the lighted backdrop, in the center building, some of the windows began to darken as if the occupants were retiring for the night.

It's getting late, thought Althea, watching. The lights are dimming all over the city. People are yawning and stretching and getting into bed and even the sounds of the distant traffic seem muted as if someone had muffled all the rolling wheels.

A shadow, part of the shadow of the building, almost part of the square shape of the center building, took on form, and Althea saw that it was a man, a man who had been there all the time, hiding there without her being conscious of his presence.

From the far right she could hear the clicking of high heels on the pavement. Someone else, she thought, will walk down this street this night.

There was a rustle and a stir in the stands.

"Please, Mommy," Timmy whispered. "I don't want to stay here."

"Oh, you'll stay all right," said Mrs. Hammond grimly. "You just open your eyes wide. You watch everything, Timmy Hammond, if you know what's good for you."

"Be quiet down there," someone hissed. "Do you want to spoil everything?"

Althea gripped George's arm.

The footsteps grew louder and a girl came into view, entering downstage from the right. The shadow that was the man moved, and then became very still, waiting.

The girl moved across the stage. She paused under the street light. She touched the lamppost as if the feel of it under her fingers gave her some sort of reassurance. She hesitated, reluctant to leave the light.

Althea could see her clearly now. She was very young. She could be no more than nineteen—perhaps twenty. She wore a red suit and a little red beret with a feather stuck jauntily in it and her handbag was tucked under her arm. Her hair was blond and it tumbled loose over her shoulders.

Althea watched absorbed as the second figure moved again, the man crouching and then straightening as he ran toward the light, toward the girl in the red suit. At the clear view of his black-jacketed, black-clad figure, there was a sudden roar of applause. Althea clapped until her hands ached.

Out of the dark, into the light, he moved. The girl had her back toward him, not seeing him as the watchers saw him—sinuous, beautiful in his grace, tall, broad of shoulder, his hair allowed to grow long in back and his black cap set on the back of his head. The knife in his hand caught the light and sparkled.

He ran and then stopped. Deliberately, he stalked her. Professional that he was, he began to move slowly, coming down light on the balls of his feet.

The girl whirled around and, at the sight of him, she made a little whimpering sound in her throat. Her back now to the audience, she darted to the left and, as if they were part of a rigid dance pattern, the man stepped after her. She turned and ran to the right, her heels clicking frantically but he was there before her.

"Please," said the girl in the red suit. She darted back to the lamppost, back where the light was the brightest, where she could be seen most clearly. She turned and faced the backdrop, faced the buildings, the windows where the people were. Her right hand still clutched her purse, her left was now at her throat.

"Oh, please." Her voice rose to a keening wail of terror and anguish.

"Please," she screamed, her voice begging, her body begging. Then blindly she turned again and ran.

This cry in the night had awakened the sleepers. It had roused the dreamers. The darkened windows in the backdrop were illuminated again. Figures moved; there were silhouettes framed in the windows. The sleepers were awake. The dreamers had stopped dreaming and the city was alert and watching.

"Help me."

The city held its breath and listened.

"Please, help me."

But, Althea saw, she couldn't run far enough. She couldn't run fast enough. The man had her pinned against the wall now, pinned against the lighted, listening backdrop of the building and her handbag fell to the ground.

"I beg you." She was almost hidden by the man's bulk as he bent over her. "Won't someone help me?"

The man in the black jacket raised his arm and the knife flashed. The girl screamed in agony, her cheek now as crimson as her suit. Dodging under his arm, she ran again, the slowing rhythm of her clicking heels the only sound to be heard.

The man watched her for a moment. The quiet, lighted windows watched and the filled stands watched. The man stood very still as if he were resting and then, gracefully, quickly, easily, he caught her again.

That does it, thought Althea, her heart pounding; that does it.

The knife gleamed and Althea held her breath. The arm lifted. The black-draped arm lifted and fell, lifted and fell. The red suit crumpled, falling as if it were empty, the red suit only a splotch now on the pavement. Then the man moved toward the hushed, absorbed watchers.

And there he stood, bowing and smiling, the knife dripping red at his side. Over and over again he took his bow while they all gave him the ultimate, the supreme tribute of their silence.

BY WAY OF DISCUSSION

Although this story has an obvious protagonist, Althea, and a cluster of supporting characters—George, Althea's husband and confidant; Sally Milford, an acquaintance; the doorman of the apartment building; Mr. and Mrs. Hammond and their delicate son Timmy from upstairs; all the unnamed spectators at the grisly play; and even the actors and actresses—it is not primarily from character that the theme arises. Nor is it from plot, although the story is carefully and traditionally plotted in a chronological sequence and includes considerable action. Suspense, also an important element in the story, is not the basic source of the theme either.

The theme in ''The Watchers'' arises from a technique that has recently become very popular in fiction. The author simply observes a condition or set of circumstances existing in contemporary society. Usually the condition is not a pleasant one. Then, by enlarging upon what this condition has a chance of developing into and projecting this development into the not-too-distant future, the author comments thematically about both the seriousness of the present situation and the horror that it may ultimately produce.

Florence Randall began with the current phenomenon of urban vio-lence and citizen apathy toward it and projected what this situation, given the apparent illogic and viciousness of much human behavior, may result in down the road a few years. Recent successful motion pictures such as *Soylent Green, Rollerball,* and *Logan's Run* have made use of the technique. *Soylent Green* expands upon the phenomenon of unlim-ited population growth, the collapse of law and order in the cities, and ultimate human starvation. *Rollerball* combines the current phenom-enon of violence in professional sport with the growing power of giant corporations. And *Logan's Run* begins from the point of our current seeming preoccupation with remaining young all our lives, or from the point of the problems that a society with a very young population is likely to face.

The state of affairs that Randall depicts in "The Watchers" is a possi-ble direct result of our present-day social violence, which has come to infest every segment of this future society. Thematically, the story seems to be saying that as violence escalates, public acceptance and even approval of it are also likely to increase. This situation leads in turn to the belief—perhaps rationalization—that each individual should be responsible for his or her own protection. The final result, after the abo-lition of police departments, is a society in which, as Althea puts it, "There is only one crime, and that is to be a victim."

The point to notice in most stories or films using this technique is that the ultimate situation that may occur down the road is always worse than the current situation from which it is thematically developed and the situation down the road usually returns human beings to a condition that most of us would agree is more primitive or barbarous than the condi-tions under which we now live. In "The Watchers" Florence Randall returns us human creatures to a miniature Roman coliseum where the lions eat the Christians, the Christians being those people who are not by nature as violent as society has legislated that they must be.

FOR ADDITIONAL READING

The following stories, which appear elsewhere in this book, are especially appropriate for an analysis of theme:

Points of View in the Modern Short Story

2

The term *point of view* refers to the physical vantage point from which the author narrates the actions of the story. It is the position or location from which the author speaks to the reader. An understanding of point of view is essential to a thorough analysis of any modern short story because its techniques comprise the fundamental elements with which the writer begins and carries out a tale and establishes her or his artistic authority. An awareness of the author's handling of point of view will greatly increase the reader's ability to understand a story's overall intent. Nothing is of greater importance to the reader than knowing where the author "stands" in relation to the events of the story or, if you will, knowing how the author has tried to camouflage the fact that she or he exists at all.

Narrative presentations may be divided into two broad categories: *subjective narration* and *anonymous narration*. We should keep in mind, however, that all fictional narration is ultimately subjective; some types simply acknowledge their subjectivity more than others. Furthermore, stories displaying anonymous narration are anonymous not because we do not know the real author's name, but rather because the narrator within the story is unnamed and unidentified.

For our purposes, then, all stories in which the narrator refers to himself or herself as "I" may be considered examples of *subjective narration*. This is often called the "first-person point of view." The person telling the story—the ostensible author, as opposed to the real author who has actually written the story—may be a major character, a minor character, or simply an observer. There are several variations on the technique of first-person narration: (1) interior monologue, (2) dramatic monologue, (3) narrator as participant, (4) narrator as observer, (5) simple or untrustworthy narrator, and (6) narrator as diarist or letter writer.

Interior monologue is a type of subjective narration in which the author presents a character thinking or talking to himself or herself. The technique is analogous to the soliloquy in a play. As the reader "overhears" the character, the story is revealed.

There are two forms of interior monologue, the *indirect* and the *direct*. The *indirect*, of which Dorothy Parker's "But the One on the Right" is an example, employs the central character to select and present specific details in a rational, orderly manner as well as to comment on the general situation of the story. In the *direct interior monologue*, however, the central character seems hardly to exist at all. It is as though the reader were privy to a free-flowing stream of thoughts, fantasies, images, and meditations coming from the character's mind. The direct interior monologue is sometimes called "stream of consciousness." Writers like Virginia Woolf, James Joyce, and William Faulkner have employed the technique effectively. Both types of interior monologue may be considered spin-offs of the literary influence of Freudian psychology. Both create an intimacy between reader and central character that is very difficult to achieve with any other device of narrative presentation.

Dramatic monologue, a technique more common in poetry than in short fiction, can nevertheless be used forcefully in the modern short story. Here we have a central character who is actually speaking, not simply thinking or talking to himself or herself. The central character seems to have seized the "stage" and is determined to tell his or her tale. From various references made in the monologue the reader can usually tell where the character is and to whom he or she is speaking. Frequently, the real author of the story will be the person to whom the narrator is speaking.

The dramatic monologue is a particularly effective type of subjective narration because it can provide a variety of dramatic irony somewhat different from the types of irony available with other narrative methods. This is possible because the central character often tells a tale quite different from the one he or she thinks is being told. While trying to convince the silent listener of the rightness of one particular idea or position, the narrator may unwittingly persuade the listener—and thus the reader as well—of quite another position. Such are the circumstances in Katherine Mansfield's "The Lady's Maid."

Subjective narration having the *narrator as participant* may involve a narrator who is either a major character or a minor character. Furthermore, the events of the story may have occurred recently, or they may have taken place many years ago. Sometimes the events of the tale seem to be taking place as the narrator tells us about them. In the most popular and most effective variation of the technique, the narrator is a mature and reflective adult recalling a childhood experience. This form is so effective because it places the now-mature narrator and the reader in virtually identical positions of reflection. Both look back on the narrator's experience with similar understanding, amusement, disdain, or whatever. In Frank O'Connor's "First Confession" we have just such a story.

The technique of *narrator as observer* is, in a sense, a variation on the technique of minor character narrator as participant. The technique is a little like firsthand reporting, with the narrator sitting on the sidelines and telling someone else's story. Sometimes the narrator may be a confidant of the story's protagonist. At other times the narrator may be drawn into the action of the story, particularly at the point of highest tension. The great strength of the technique of narrator as observer is its ability to make the reader a vicarious eyewitness to the events of the story. Doris Lessing's "The Nuisance" makes the reader an eyewitness to a pathetic situation between a husband and wife. Ivan Turgenev's "The Tryst" makes the reader an eyewitness to an emotional scene between a Russian peasant girl and her departing lover.

All creative narration is subjective, but a short story utilizing a *simple or untrustworthy narrator* almost flaunts its subjectivity. The narrator tells the tale, but tells it all wrong. It may be wrong because the narrator is simple-minded, or is deliberately lying or telling a tall tale. In either instance, readers know—or gradually discover—that they can't depend on what they are being told. The narrator is unreliable. If simple-minded, the narrator is likely to tell quite a different story from the one he or she thinks is being told. This discrepancy often renders the whole situation ironic.

The clever, vicious, and untrustworthy narrator is harder to catch. He or she intends to mislead. The reader, then, must read carefully to pick up inconsistencies between what the narrator says are the facts and what the facts are otherwise shown to be.

Students often ask why an author would want to go to the trouble of telling a story through the eyes of an unreliable narrator. Is the technique just a gimmick or trick to mislead the reader? Not at all. Writers use an untrustworthy narrator to draw the reader into the action of the story. Rather than handing the reader a nicely packaged story with reasonable, believable, and correct interpretations, the unreliable narrator makes the reader participate in the story by questioning the validity of the information and judgments being presented.

The unreliable narrator forces the reader to read actively. From this active participation the reader is likely to experience a greater emotional involvement than he or she otherwise would, including a feeling of accomplishment at having caught the narrator in a web of untruths. The narrator in Ring Lardner's "Haircut" seems to be spinning such a web. Later on, you may want to question the reliability of the narrator in Edgar Allan Poe's "The Fall of the House of Usher."

The technique of *narrator as diarist* is a little like the dramatic monologue in that the narrator makes prolonged, although written, speeches. It also resembles the technique of narrator as observer in that the narrator reports on what other people are doing. For a reader who is patient enough to work through a leisurely story in the format of a diary, the rewards can be substantial. The primary reason for this, and the greatest strength of the technique, is that practically all meaning in such stories is dramatized. The narrator has only the most general notion of the consequences of all that is really taking place. Dramatic irony, then, can be a pervasive element of diary narration. Daniel Keyes' "Flowers for Algernon," a few years ago made into an Academy Award–winning motion picture entitled *Charly*, is a splendid example of the technique of narrator as (simple) diarist.

A variation of the technique of narrator as diarist presents the *narrator as letter writer*. This technique is called epistolary narration. ("Epistolary" means "contained in, or pertaining to, letters.") A story using this type of narration consists of a series of fictionalized letters written by one or more characters. One of the oldest techniques in English fiction, epistolary narration has been used in the short story by such notable writers as Henry James, Ambrose Bierce, and Fyodor Dostoevski. Thomas Bailey Aldrich's "Marjorie Daw" is our selection illustrating the technique.

Now let us turn to the second general category of narrative presentation, *anonymous narration*. This is usually called the "third-person point of view." Stories written in the third person do not reveal or name their narrator. Thus the reader may think of the narrator as existing outside the story or as being submerged within it, depending on the specific circumstances of the story. The narrator "speaks" in the third person and may occupy either an omniscient (all-knowing) position or a dramatic position.

The *totally omniscient narrator* exists outside the story and knows everything that can possibly be known about *all* things within the story, including the histories, thoughts, capacities, and emotions of all the characters. There are, however, degrees of narrative omniscience. They are: (1) single character limited omniscience, (2) dual character limited omniscience, and (3) multiple character omniscience.

Single character limited omniscience involves an anonymous narrator who has full knowledge of what goes on inside the head of only one character. The narrator is submerged within this character. The reader is told and shown what this character thinks and how he or she feels and sees the world in general, but the reader is told nothing whatsoever about the thoughts, feelings, or actions of the other characters in the story. The "chosen" character may be a major character, usually the protagonist, or a minor character who may or may not participate in the action.

The great strength of this point of view is that it acquaints the reader with the world as perceived through the mind and senses of only one individual, thus approximating more sensibly than can the totally omniscient point of view the conditions of real life. The author, as a result of restricting himself or herself to the inner experiences of a single person, can employ this point of view as a unifying element in the story. The reader is locked in to the realities of the chosen character. Since this point of view is probably the most popular of all points of view among modern short-story writers, locating examples of it is a very easy task. We have chosen a story that comes close to exaggerating the technique, Gina Berriault's "The Stone Boy."

Dual character limited omniscience allows the anonymous narrator to reveal the inner thoughts, feelings, and perceptions of two characters. This technique is not used nearly as often as single character limited omniscience. When it is employed, the narrator usually treats one of the characters much more thoroughly than the other.

Emotional response from the reader is the primary reason authors use this point of view. When readers can participate in the innermost feelings of two characters—especially sympathetic characters—who are in conflict with each other or with an unjust world or unfeeling universe, the readers' response is likely to be more than doubled. Such will be the case with most perceptive readers of D. H. Lawrence's "The Shadow in the Rose Garden." Sherwood Anderson's "Unlighted Lamps" is also written from the dual character limited omniscient point of view.

Multiple character omniscience gives the anonymous narrator the opportunity to reveal to the reader what goes on inside the heads of a whole community of characters. For all practical purposes, this technique is the same as total omniscience. Although not particularly popular today, multiple character omniscience was enormously popular among nineteenth-century novelists and short-story writers. Its popularity stemmed from the fact that it is the most flexible of all points of view, permitting the author a very broad scope. The omniscient narrator tells the reader far more about the events and characters of the story than the reader could possibly learn through personal observations. However, it is precisely the flexibility of multiple character omniscience that has led to serious abuses among careless writers.

The constant shifting from the viewpoint of one character to that of another not only destroys a story's illusion of reality but also does considerable harm to coherence and unity. The narrative point of view directs so much attention to itself that the flow of the story is often interrupted. Nevertheless, in the hands of a careful and experienced literary artist, multiple character omniscience can be a useful technique. Thomas Mann's "The Infant Prodigy" is a little story effectively narrated from the omniscient point of view.

One additional type of anonymous narration—*dramatic narration*—offers virtually no omniscience. Dramatic narration is also called the "objective point of view" or the "view of the effaced narrator." The author, assuming a combination of the roles of roving motion-picture camera and chorus—as in a classical Greek play—moves about recording and ultimately divulging only what has happened and what has been said. Except for general background information and equally generalized thoughts of groups of people, there is no commenting, no interrupting, no peeking into anyone's head. In a sense, the reader is put in a position similar to that of a spectator at a play or movie. The reader sees what the characters do and hears what they have to say but is given only inferences or suggestions of what anyone other than groups of people thinks.

Dramatic narration, a very popular method today, is excellent for concealing information until the end of the story. It thereby creates suspense for the reader or makes possible a surprise, though not contrived, ending. It also works well in stories that deal with groups of people or relationships rather than with traditional protagonist-antagonist conflicts. Two good stories employing dramatic narration are John Steinbeck's "The Chrysanthemums" and Ernest Hemingway's "The Killers."

As you read stories demonstrating subjective and anonymous narration, keep in mind that an author employs the point of view that will best serve his or her general artistic purposes. Consequently, an examination of point of view is often important for understanding and evaluating a story. You might also keep four questions about point of view in mind when you analyze a short story:

1. Are the events of the story interpreted by the author or by one or more of the characters?
2. Is the author's point of view intended primarily to reveal information to the reader or to conceal information from the reader?
3. Has the author maintained a consistent point of view throughout the story?
4. Has the author's narrative point of view directed attention to itself and thus distracted the reader from the flow of the story?

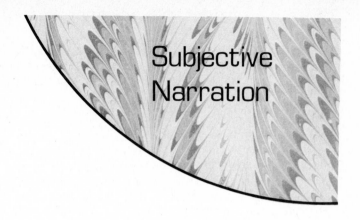

Subjective Narration

DOROTHY PARKER

But the One on the Right

I knew it. I knew if I came to this dinner, I'd draw something like this baby on my left. They've been saving him up for me for weeks. Now, we've simply got to have him—his sister was so sweet to us in London; we can stick him next to Mrs. Parker—she talks enough for two. Oh, I should never have come, never. I'm here against my better judgment, to a decision. That would be a good thing for them to cut on my tombstone: Wherever she went, including here, it was against her better judgment. This is a fine time of the evening to be thinking about tombstones. That's the effect he's had on me, already, and the soup hardly cold yet. I should have stayed at home for dinner. I could have had something on a tray. The head of John the Baptist, or something. Oh, I should not have come.

Well, the soup's over, anyway. I'm that much nearer to my Eternal Home. Now the soup belongs to the ages, and I have said precisely four words to the gentleman on my left. I said, 'Isn't this soup delicious?'; that's four words. And he said, 'Yes, isn't it?'; that's three. He's one up on me.

At any rate, we're in perfect accord. We agree like lambs. We've been all through the soup together, and never a cross word between us. It seems rather a pity to let the subject drop, now we've found something on which we harmonize so admirably. I believe I'll bring it up again; I'll ask him if that wasn't delicious soup. He says, 'Yes, wasn't it?' Look at that, will you; perfect command of his tenses.

Here comes the fish. Goody, goody, goody, we got fish. I wonder if he likes fish. Yes, he does; he says he likes fish. Ah, that's nice. I love that in a man. Look, he's talking! He's chattering away like a veritable magpie! He's asking me if I like fish. Now does he really want to know, or is it only a line? I'd better play it cagey. I'll tell him, 'Oh, pretty well.' Oh, I like fish pretty well; there's a fascinating bit of autobiography for him to study over. Maybe he would rather wrestle with it alone. I'd better steal softly away, and leave him to his thoughts.

I might try my luck with what's on my right. No, not a chance there. The woman on his other side has him cold. All I can see is his shoulder. It's a nice shoulder, too; oh, it's a nice, *nice* shoulder. All my life, I've been a fool for a nice shoulder. Very well, lady; you saw him first. Keep your Greek god, and I'll go back to my Trojan horse.

Let's see, where were we? Oh, we'd got to where he had confessed his liking for fish. I wonder what else he likes. Does he like cucumbers? Yes, he does; he likes cucumbers. And potatoes? Yes, he likes potatoes, too. Why, he's a regular old Nature-lover, that's what he is. I would have to come out to dinner, and sit next to the Boy Thoreau. Wait, he's saying something! Words are simply pouring out of him. He's asking me if I'm fond of potatoes. No, I don't like potatoes. There, I've done it! I've differed from him. It's our first quarrel. He's fallen into a moody silence. Silly boy, have I pricked your bubble? Do you think I am nothing but a painted doll with sawdust for a heart? Ah, don't take it like that. Look, I have something to tell you that will bring back your faith. I do like cucumbers. Why, he's better already. He speaks again. He says, yes, he likes them, too. Now we've got that all straightened out, thank heaven. We both like cucumbers. Only he likes them twice.

I'd better let him alone now, so he can get some food. He ought to try to get his strength back. He's talked himself groggy.

I wish I had something to do. I hate to be a mere drone. People ought to let you know when they're going to sit you next to a thing like this, so you could bring along some means of occupation. Dear Mrs. Parker, do come to us for dinner on Friday next, and don't forget your drawn-work. I could have brought my top bureau drawer and tidied it up, here on my lap. I could have made great strides towards getting those photographs of the groups on the beach pasted up in the album. I wonder if my hostess would think it strange if I asked for a pack of cards. I wonder if there are any old copies of *St. Nicholas* lying about. I wonder if they wouldn't like a little help out in the kitchen. I wonder if anybody would want me to run up to the corner and get a late paper.

I could do a little drinking, of course, all by myself. There's always that. Oh, dear, oh, dear, oh, dear, there's always that. But I don't want to drink. I'll get *vin triste*. I'm melancholy before I even start. I wonder what this stiff on my left would say, if I told him I was in a fair way to get *vin triste*. Oh, look at him, hoeing into his fish! What does he care whether I get *vin triste* or not? His soul can't rise above food. Purely physical, that's all he is. Digging his grave with his teeth, that's what he's doing. Yah, yah, ya-ah! Digging your grave with your tee-eeth! Making a god of your stommick! Yah, yah, ya-ah!

He doesn't care if I get *vin triste*. Nobody cares. Nobody gives a damn. And me so nice. All right, you baskets, I'll drink myself to death, right in front of your eyes, and see how you'll feel. Here I go. . . . Oh, my God, it's Chablis. And of a year when the grapes failed, and they used Summer squash, instead. Fifteen dollars for all you can carry home on your shoulder. Oh, now, listen, where I come from, we feed this to the pigs. I think I'll ask old Chatterbox on my left if this isn't rotten wine. That ought to open up a new school of dialectics for us. Oh, he says he really wouldn't know—he never touches wine. Well, that fairly well ends that. I wonder how he'd like to step to hell, anyway. Yah, yah, ya-ah! Never touches wi-yine! Don't know what you're miss-sing! Yah, yah, ya-ah!

I'm not going to talk to him any more. I'm not going to spend the best years of my life thinking up pearls to scatter before him. I'm going to stick to my Chablis, rotten though it be. From now on, he can go his way, and I'll go mine. I'm better than anybody at this table. Ah, but am I really? Have I, after all, half of what they have? Here I am lonely, unwanted, silent, and me with all my new clothes on. Oh, what would Louiseboulanger say if she saw her gold lamé going unnoticed like this? It's life, I suppose. Poor little things, we dress, and we plan, and we hope—and for what? What is life, anyway? A death sentence. The longest distance between two points. The bunch of hay that's tied to the nose of the tired mule. The——

Well, well, well, here we are at the *entrecôte*. Button up your *entrecôte*, when the wind is free—no, I guess not. Now I'll be damned if I ask old Loquacity if he likes meat. In the first place, his likes and dislikes are nothing to me, and in the second—well, look at him go after it! He must have been playing hard all afternoon; he's Mother's Hungry Boy, tonight. All right, let him worry it all he wants. As for me, I'm on a higher plane. I do not stoop to him. He's less than the dust beneath my chariot wheel. Yah, yah, ya-ah! Less than the du-ust! Before I'd be that way. Yah, yah, ya-ah!

I'm glad there's red wine now. Even if it isn't good, I'm glad. Red wine gives me courage. The Red Badge of Courage. I need courage. I'm in a thin way, here. Nobody knows what a filthy time I'm having. My precious evening, that can never come again, ruined, ruined, ruined, and all because of this Somewhat Different Monologist on my left. But he can't lick me. The night is not yet dead, no, nor dying. You know, this really isn't bad wine.

Now what do you suppose is going on with the Greek God on my right? Ah, no use. There's still only the shoulder—the nice, *nice* shoulder. I wonder what the woman's like, that's got him. I can't see her at all. I wonder if she's beautiful. I wonder if she's Greek, too. When Greek meets immovable body—

you might be able to do something with that, if you only had the time. I'm not going to be spineless any longer. Don't think for a minute, lady, that I've given up. He's still using his knife and fork. While there's hands above the table, there's hope.

Really, I suppose out of obligation to my hostess, I ought to do something about saying a few words to this macaw on my left. What shall I try? Have you been reading anything good lately, do you go much to the play, have you ever been to the Riviera? I wonder if he would like to hear about my Summer on the Riviera; hell, no, that's no good without lantern slides. I bet, though, if I started telling him about That One Night, he'd listen. I won't tell him—it's too good for him. Anybody that never touches wine can't hear that. But the one on the right—he'd like that. He touches wine. Touches it, indeed! He just threw it for a formidable loss.

Oh, look, old Silver Tongue is off again! Why, he's mad with his own perfume! He's rattling away like lightning. He's asking me if I like salad. Yes, I do; what does he want to make of that? He's telling me about salad through the ages. He says it's so good for people. So help me God, if he gives me a talk on roughage, I'll slap his face. Isn't that my life, to sit here, all dressed up in my best, and listen to this thing talk about romaine? And all the time, right on my right—

Well, I thought you were never going to turn around. . . . You haven't? . . . You have? Oh, Lord, I've been having an awful time, too. . . . Was she? . . . Well, you should have seen what I drew. . . . Oh, I don't see how we could. . . . Yes, I know it's terrible, but how can we get out of it? . . . Well. . . . Well, yes, that's true. . . . Look, right after dinner, I'll say I have this horrible headache, and you say you're going to take me home in your car, and—

BY WAY OF DISCUSSION

In the interior monologue the author presents a character (narrator) thinking or talking to himself or herself. In this particular story the author is the central character: by name, Mrs. Parker. We should notice that the central character, as narrator, is not altogether trustworthy. In part, this untrustworthiness stems from her growing a little tipsy as the meal progresses. But it also stems from a general cattiness that seems to color everything she thinks about.

The plot of "But the One on the Right" could hardly be reduced below what it is. Mrs. Parker has come alone to a dinner party that she really didn't want to attend. Partially to amuse herself, she speculates about the characters of the men on her left and right, consistently to the advantage of the latter. He is described as a Greek, even a Greek god; whereas the one on her left is a Trojan, sometimes a Trojan horse. As the meal progresses, Mrs. Parker chatters away, mostly to herself. But at the conclusion she allows herself to be picked up by the Greek god.

Although there is no reason to consider this story a particularly profound one, it does do an effective job of presenting character, and it does suggest a few incisive points concerning the relations between men and women. The first thing one notices about Mrs. Parker is her waggish wit. Indeed, she rips into almost everything in the room: the hostess, the wine, and especially the despised Trojan. Everything except the Greek god, of course. Mrs. Parker possesses other noteworthy and not particularly pleasant traits as well—a certain vainness about clothes and a strong streak of self-pity that is reflected in her maudlin thoughts on loneliness and the meaning of life. But it is her flippant cleverness that makes her really interesting.

Most of the derogatory observations are made at the expense of the man sitting on the narrator's left, and it is the narrator's tone as well as her specific observations that make the presentation so effective. The Trojan is a mere baby. He is anything but a clever conversationalist, and when he does speak he rattles on about such boring topics as soup, cucumbers, potatoes, salad, and perhaps even the importance of roughage in one's diet. Hardly items of philosophical significance, even in the surface world of the 1920s. He never touches wine—a habit that does nothing to improve Mrs. Parker's opinion of him.

On the other hand, the Greek god hardly speaks to her. He just eats, and eats heartily. He also drinks wine; he "touches" it. But the fellow has a nice shoulder, and Mrs. Parker, almost a self-stereotype of the giddy female, is intrigued by and enamored of him. The man who tries to be civil and social annoys her, while the one who seems hardly to notice her at all wins her. Perhaps the fact that she thinks her Greek god is attached to another woman also contributes to Mrs. Parker's interest in him. This brings up the old business of competition between females for the most desirable males.

Finally, the Greek god casually turns toward the fascinated protagonist and without seeming to try, perhaps simply because of his maleness, sizes her up within a matter of moments. How much the wine has helped we can't be sure, but with only a word or two he has her on the edge of her seat, and they will shortly be off to do whatever our imaginations would have them do.

By employing the interior monologue to tell this story, the author has been able to dramatize the character of Mrs. Parker without ever having to "say" a word about her. Mrs. Parker herself has done the job. We know her more intimately than we could possibly have come to know her through the eyes of anyone else—say, a confidant or an antagonist. However, observe how much more accurate is our view of Mrs. Parker than is our view of the poor man seated on her left. We have intentionally been given such a distorted and incomplete picture of this fellow that he comes off as little more than a stereotyped bore. We know what Mrs.

Parker thinks of him, but we really have no idea what he might actually be like if we were to meet him ourselves. Strangely enough, though, because of the convincing facility with which the monologue is presented, we tend to accept Mrs. Parker's evaluation of the man on her left.

KATHERINE MANSFIELD

The Lady's Maid

Eleven o'clock. A knock at the door. . . . I hope I haven't disturbed you, madam. You weren't asleep—were you? But I've just given my lady her tea, and there was such a nice cup over, I thought, perhaps . . .

. . . Not at all, madam. I always make a cup of tea last thing. She drinks it in bed after her prayers to warm her up. I put the kettle on when she kneels down and I say to it, "Now you needn't be in too much of a hurry to say *your* prayers." But it's always boiling before my lady is half through. You see, madam, we know such a lot of people, and they've all got to be prayed for— every one. My lady keeps a list of the names in a little red book. Oh dear! whenever some one new has been to see us and my lady says afterwards, "Ellen, give me my little red book," I feel quite wild, I do. "There's another," I think, "keeping her out of her bed in all weathers." And she won't have a cushion, you know, madam; she kneels on the hard carpet. It fidgets me something dreadful to see her, knowing her as I do. I've tried to cheat her; I've spread out the eiderdown. But the first time I did it—oh, she gave me such a look—holy it was, madam. "Did our Lord have an eiderdown, Ellen?" she said. But—I was younger at the time—I felt inclined to say, "No, but our Lord wasn't your age, and he didn't know what it was to have your lumbago." Wicked—wasn't it? But she's *too* good, you know, madam. When I tucked her up just now and seen—saw her lying back, her hands outside and her head on the pillow—so pretty—I couldn't help thinking, "Now you look just like your dear mother when I laid her out!"

. . . Yes, madam, it was all left to me. Oh, she did look sweet. I did her hair, soft-like, round her forehead, all in dainty curls, and just to one side of her neck I put a bunch of most beautiful purple pansies. Those pansies made a picture of her, madam! I shall never forget them. I thought to-night, when I looked at my lady, "Now, if only the pansies was there no one could tell the difference."

. . . Only the last year, madam. Only after she'd got a little—well—feeble as you might say. Of course, she was never dangerous; she was the sweetest old lady. But how it took her was—she thought she'd lost something. She couldn't keep still, she couldn't settle. All day long she'd be up and down, up and down; you'd meet her everywhere—on the stairs, in the porch, making for the kitchen. And she'd look up at you, and she'd say—just like a child, "I've lost it, I've lost it." "Come along," I'd say, "come along, and I'll lay out your patience for you." But she'd catch me by the hand—I was a favourite of hers—and whisper, "Find it for me, Ellen. Find it for me." Sad, wasn't it?

. . . No, she never recovered, madam. She had a stroke at the end. Last words she ever said was—very slow, "Look in—the—— Look—in——" And then she was gone.

. . . No, madam, I can't say I noticed it. Perhaps some girls. But you see, it's like this, I've got nobody but my lady. My mother died of consumption when I was four, and I lived with my grandfather, who kept a hair-dresser's shop. I used to spend all my time in the shop under a table dressing my doll's hair— copying the assistants, I suppose. They were ever so kind to me. Used to make me little wigs, all colours, the latest fashions and all. And there I'd sit all day, quiet as quiet—the customers never knew. Only now and again I'd take my peep from under the table-cloth.

. . . But one day I managed to get a pair of scissors and—would you believe it, madam? I cut off all my hair; snipped it off all in bits, like the little monkey I was. Grandfather was *furious!* He caught hold of the tongs—I shall never forget it—grabbed me by the hand and shut my fingers in them. "That'll teach you!" he said. It was a fearful burn. I've got the mark of it to-day.

. . . Well, you see, madam, he'd taken such pride in my hair. He used to sit me up on the counter, before the customers came, and do it something beau- tiful—big, soft curls and waved over the top. I remember the assistants stand- ing round, and me ever so solemn with the penny grandfather gave me to hold while it was being done. . . . But he always took the penny back afterwards. Poor grandfather! Wild, he was, at the fright I'd made of myself. But he frightened me that time. Do you know what I did, madam? I ran away. Yes, I did, round the corners, in and out, I don't know how far I didn't run. Oh, dear, I must have looked a sight, with my hand rolled up in my pinny and my hair sticking out. People must have laughed when they saw me. . . .

. . . No, madam, grandfather never got over it. He couldn't bear the sight of me after. Couldn't eat his dinner, even, if I was there. So my aunt took me. She was a cripple, an upholstress. Tiny! She had to stand on the sofas when she wanted to cut out the backs. And it was helping her I met my lady. . . .

. . . Not so very, madam. I was thirteen, turned. And I don't remember ever feeling—well—a child, as you might say. You see there was my uniform, and one thing and another. My lady put me into collars and cuffs from the first. Oh yes—once I did! That was—funny! It was like this. My lady had her two little nieces staying with her—we were at Sheldon at the time—and there was a fair on the common.

"Now, Ellen," she said, "I want you to take the two young ladies for a ride on the donkeys." Off we went; solemn little loves they were; each had a hand. But when we came to the donkeys they were too shy to go on. So we stood and watched instead. Beautiful those donkeys were! They were the first I'd seen out of a cart—for pleasure as you might say. They were a lovely silver-grey, with little red saddles and blue bridles and bells jing-a-jingling on their ears. And quite big girls—older than me, even—were riding them, ever so gay. Not at all common, I don't mean, madam, just enjoying themselves. And I don't know what it was, but the way the little feet went, and the eyes—so gentle—and the soft ears—made me want to go on a donkey more than any-thing in the world!

. . . Of course, I couldn't. I had my young ladies. And what would I have looked like perched up there in my uniform? But all the rest of the day it was donkeys—donkeys on the brain with me. I felt I should have burst if I didn't tell some one; and who was there to tell? But when I went to bed—I was sleeping in Mrs. James's bedroom, our cook that was, at the time—as soon as the lights was out, there they were, my donkeys, jingling along, with their neat little feet and sad eyes. . . . Well, madam, would you believe it, I waited for a long time and pretended to be asleep, and then suddenly I sat up and called out as loud as I could, "*I do want to go on a donkey. I do want a donkey-ride!*" You see, I had to say it, and I thought they wouldn't laugh at me if they knew I was only dreaming. Artful—wasn't it? Just what a silly child would think. . . .

. . . No, madam, never now. Of course, I did think of it at one time. But it wasn't to be. He had a little flower-shop just down the road and across from where we was living. Funny—wasn't it? And me such a one for flowers. We were having a lot of company at the time, and I was in and out of the shop more often than not, as the saying is. And Harry and I (his name was Harry) got to quarrelling about how things ought to be arranged—and that began it. Flowers! you wouldn't believe it, madam, the flowers he used to bring me. He'd stop at nothing. It was lilies-of-the-valley more than once, and I'm not exaggerating! Well, of course, we were going to be married and live over the shop, and it was all going to be just so, and I was to have the window to arrange. . . . Oh, how I've done that window of a Saturday! Not really, of course, madam, just dreaming, as you might say. I've done it for Christmas—motto in holly, and all—and I've had my Easter lilies with a gorgeous star all daffodils in the middle. I've hung—well, that's enough of that. The day came he was to call for me to choose the furniture. Shall I ever forget it? It was a Tuesday. My lady wasn't quite herself that afternoon. Not that she'd said anything, of course; she never does or will. But I knew by the way that she kept wrapping herself up and asking me if it was cold—and her little nose looked . . . pinched. I didn't like leaving her; I knew I'd be worrying all the time. At last I asked her if she'd rather I put it off. "Oh no, Ellen," she said, "you mustn't mind about me. You mustn't disappoint your young man." And so cheerful, you know, madam, never thinking about herself. It made me feel worse than ever. I began to wonder . . . then she dropped her handkerchief and began to stoop down to pick it up herself—a thing she never did. "Whatever are you doing!" I cried, running to stop her. "Well," she said, smiling, you know, madam, "I shall have to begin to practise." Oh, it was all I could do not to burst out crying. I went over to the dressing-table and made believe to rub up the silver, and I couldn't keep myself in, and I asked her if she'd rather I . . . didn't get married. "No, Ellen," she said—that was her voice, madam, like I'm giving you—"No, Ellen, not for the *wide world!*" But while she said it, madam—I was looking in her glass; of course, she didn't know I could see her—she put her little hand on her heart just like her dear mother used to, and lifted her eyes. . . . Oh, *madam!*

When Harry came I had his letters all ready, and the ring and a ducky little brooch he'd given me—a silver bird it was, with a chain in its beak, and on the end of the chain a heart with a dagger. Quite the thing! I opened the door to him. I never gave him time for a word. "There you are," I said. "Take them all back," I said, "it's all over. I'm not going to marry you," I said, "I can't leave my lady." White! he turned as white as a woman. I had to slam the door, and there I stood, all of a tremble, till I knew he had gone. When I opened the door—believe me or not, madam—that man *was* gone! I ran out into the road just as I was, in my apron and my house-shoes, and there I stayed in the middle of the road . . . staring. People must have laughed if they saw me. . . .

. . . Goodness gracious!—What's that? It's the clock striking! And here I've been keeping you awake. Oh, madam, you ought to have stopped me. . . . Can I tuck in your feet? I always tuck in my lady's feet, every night, just the same. And she says, "Good night, Ellen. Sleep sound and wake early!" I don't know what I should do if she didn't say that, now.

. . . Oh dear, I sometimes think . . . whatever should I do if anything were to . . . But, there, thinking's no good to any one—is it, madam? Thinking won't help. Not that I do it often. And if ever I do I pull myself up sharp, "Now, then, Ellen. At it again—you silly girl! If you can't find anything better to do than to start thinking! . . ."

BY WAY OF DISCUSSION

"The Lady's Maid" is a particularly interesting example of a dramatic monologue. The narrator, Ellen, tells her story—a highly condensed version of her life's story—by answering a series of questions asked by an unnamed listener. In fact, we are not given the questions directly; we must figure them out from the answers that Ellen gives.

In the dramatic monologue there is usually a listener, someone present—named or unnamed—who hears all that the narrator tells. This character occupies a position that is at once the reader's and ultimately the author's. In "The Lady's Maid," we get the feeling that it is Katherine Mansfield herself who is propped up in bed listening to what Ellen has to say.

The narrator in the dramatic monologue often tells a story somewhat different from the one he or she intends to tell. Ellen thinks she is saying one thing, but in fact she is telling us and the listener something quite different. The *implied story*, the one that peeks out from between the lines, is often the "real" story of an effective dramatic monologue.

What is the real story in "The Lady's Maid"? It is one of a woman who, throughout her life, has been treated not as an individual but as a thing that exists only to please and serve others. This story is consistently reinforced by a series of broadly Freudian symbols—hair of various lengths, a uniform, Ellen's wanting to ride a donkey, flowers of several varieties, and a little silver bird with a chain in its beak and a dagger in its heart.

To her grandfather, Ellen is little more than a doll, something to play with in exactly the same way that Ellen herself plays with her own doll— an inanimate object that can be used and then ignored or put aside when not desired. Ellen's cutting her hair hardly represents nothing more than the willful act of a "little monkey." Rather, it is the natural cry of the heart for a relationship based upon closeness and love. All it earns her, however, are burns and banishment. Ellen's desire to ride the gentle-eyed, soft-eared donkey represents the same sort of subconscious wish. This time, though, she is thwarted not by the callous grandfather but by her own mistaken sense of propriety and her unwillingness to leave the young ladies' side for even a few minutes. This reluctance, of course, foreshadows what is to come later on. Without love, Ellen's spirit has withered, and she is well on her way to losing all of her individuality and independence. Unlike the younger Ellen, this one cannot conceive of running away; she can only lie in bed and call out: "*I do want to go on a donkey. I do want a donkey-ride.*"

For a brief time, Harry offers Ellen a chance for fulfillment, both personal and sexual in the fullest sense. By then, however, the process of depersonalization has almost run its course, and her mistress finds it shamefully easy to thwart Ellen's marriage plans. A dropped handkerchief, a few theatrical gestures, and Ellen has soon sent Harry packing with his letters and the silver brooch. The brooch symbolizes to perfection the pervasiveness of Ellen's bondage. Ellen's final gesture of rebellion occurs when she rushes outside, subconsciously hoping that Harry has remained to free her from her mental and psychological bondage. But, of course, Harry isn't there. Ellen, then, is a slave; and she will quite likely always be one. She has even arrived at the point where she refuses to think: "thinking's no good to any one—is it, madam?" But what about the part of Ellen's psyche that lies beyond conscious thought, the part of her being that actually gives rise to the story? In telling her narrative about tucking up her mistress, Ellen says,

> When I tucked her up just now and seen—saw her lying back, her hands outside and her head on the pillow—so pretty—I couldn't help thinking, "Now you look just like your dear mother when I laid her out!"

Incredibly, Ellen may even yet possess at least a subconscious desire to break free from her bondage, to become a total human being. In any event, for those of us who do not like to see human beings enslaved, it would be nice to think so. Shouldn't everyone have the opportunity to go on life's donkey ride, however precarious the experience may be?

FRANK O'CONNOR

First Confession

All the trouble began when my grandfather died and my grandmother—my father's mother—came to live with us. Relations in the one house are a strain at the best of times, but, to make matters worse, my grandmother was a real old countrywoman and quite unsuited to the life in town. She had a fat, wrinkled old face, and, to Mother's great indignation, went round the house in bare feet—the boots had her crippled, she said. For dinner she had a jug of porter and a pot of potatoes with—sometimes—a bit of salt fish, and she poured out the potatoes on the table and ate them slowly, with great relish, using her fingers by way of a fork.

Now, girls are supposed to be fastidious, but I was the one who suffered most from this. Nora, my sister, just sucked up to the old woman for the penny she got every Friday out of the old-age pension, a thing I could not do. I was too honest, that was my trouble; and when I was playing with Bill Connell, the sergeant-major's son, and saw my grandmother steering up the path with the jug of porter sticking out from beneath her shawl I was mortified. I made excuses not to let him come into the house, because I could never be sure what she would be up to when we went in.

When Mother was at work and my grandmother made the dinner I wouldn't touch it. Nora once tried to make me, but I hid under the table from her and took the bread-knife with me for protection. Nora let on to be very indignant (she wasn't, of course, but she knew Mother saw through her, so she sided with Gran) and came after me. I lashed out at her with the bread-knife, and after that she left me alone. I stayed there till Mother came in from work and made my dinner, but when Father came in later Nora said in a shocked voice: "Oh, Dadda, do you know what Jackie did at dinnertime?" Then, of course, it all came out; Father gave me a flaking; Mother interfered, and for days after that he didn't speak to me and Mother barely spoke to Nora. And all because of that old woman! God knows, I was heart-scalded.

Then, to crown my misfortunes, I had to make my first confession and communion. It was an old woman called Ryan who prepared us for these. She was about the one age with Gran; she was well-to-do, lived in a big house on Montenotte, wore a black cloak and bonnet, and came every day to school at three o'clock when we should have been going home, and talked to us of hell. She may have mentioned the other place as well, but that could only have been by accident, for hell had the first place in her heart.

She lit a candle, took out a new half-crown, and offered it to the first boy who would hold one finger—only one finger!—in the flame for five minutes by the school clock. Being always very ambitious I was tempted to volunteer, but I thought it might look greedy. Then she asked were we afraid of holding one finger—only one finger!—in a little candle flame for five minutes and not afraid of burning all over in roasting hot furnaces for all eternity. "All eternity! Just think of that! A whole lifetime goes by and it's nothing, not even a drop in the ocean of your sufferings." The woman was really interesting about hell, but my attention was all fixed on the half-crown. At the end of the lesson she put it back in her purse. It was a great disappointment; a religious woman like that, you wouldn't think she'd bother about a thing like a half-crown.

Another day she said she knew a priest who woke one night to find a fellow he didn't recognize leaning over the end of his bed. The priest was a bit frightened—naturally enough—but he asked the fellow what he wanted, and the fellow said in a deep, husky voice that he wanted to go to confession. The priest said it was an awkward time and wouldn't it do in the morning, but the fellow said that last time he went to confession, there was one sin he kept back, being ashamed to mention it, and now it was always on his mind. Then the priest knew it was a bad case, because the fellow was after making a bad confession and committing a mortal sin. He got up to dress, and just then the cock crew in the yard outside, and—lo and behold!—when the priest looked round there was no sign of the fellow, only a smell of burning timber, and when the priest looked at his bed didn't he see the print of two hands burned in it? That was because the fellow had made a bad confession. This story made a shocking impression on me.

But the worst of all was when she showed us how to examine our conscience. Did we take the name of the Lord, our God, in vain? Did we honour our father and our mother? (I asked her did this include grandmothers and she said it did.) Did we love our neighbours as ourselves? Did we covet our neighbour's goods? (I thought of the way I felt about the penny that Nora got every Friday.) I decided that, between one thing and another, I must have broken the whole ten commandments, all on account of that old woman, and so far as

I could see, so long as she remained in the house I had no hope of ever doing anything else.

I was scared to death of confession. The day the whole class went I let on to have a toothache, hoping my absence wouldn't be noticed; but at three o'clock, just as I was feeling safe, along comes a chap with a message from Mrs. Ryan that I was to go to confession myself on Saturday and be at the chapel for communion with the rest. To make it worse, Mother couldn't come with me and sent Nora instead.

Now, that girl had ways of tormenting me that Mother never knew of. She held my hand as we went down the hill, smiling sadly and saying how sorry she was for me, as if she were bringing me to the hospital for an operation.

"Oh, God help us!" she moaned. "Isn't it a terrible pity you weren't a good boy? Oh, Jackie, my heart bleeds for you! How will you ever think of all your sins? Don't forget you have to tell him about the time you kicked Gran on the shin."

"Lemme go!" I said, trying to drag myself free of her. "I don't want to go to confession at all."

"But sure, you'll have to go to confession, Jackie," she replied in the same regretful tone. "Sure, if you didn't, the parish priest would be up to the house, looking for you. 'Tisn't, God knows, that I'm not sorry for you. Do you remember the time you tried to kill me with the bread-knife under the table? And the language you used to me? I don't know what he'll do with you at all, Jackie. He might have to send you up to the bishop."

I remember thinking bitterly that she didn't know the half of what I had to tell—if I told it. I knew I couldn't tell it, and understood perfectly why the fellow in Mrs. Ryan's story made a bad confession; it seemed to me a great shame that people wouldn't stop criticizing him. I remember that steep hill down to the church, and the sunlit hillsides beyond the valley of the river, which I saw in the gaps between the houses like Adam's last glimpse of Paradise.

Then, when she had manœuvred me down the long flight of steps to the chapel yard, Nora suddenly changed her tone. She became the raging malicious devil she really was.

"There you are!" she said with a yelp of triumph, hurling me through the church door. "And I hope he'll give you the penitential psalms, you dirty little caffler."

I knew then I was lost, given up to eternal justice. The door with the coloured-glass panels swung shut behind me, the sunlight went out and gave place to deep shadow, and the wind whistled outside so that the silence within seemed to crackle like ice under my feet. Nora sat in front of me by the confession box. There were a couple of old women ahead of her, and then a miserable-looking poor devil came and wedged me in at the other side, so that I couldn't escape even if I had the courage. He joined his hands and rolled his eyes in the direction of the roof, muttering aspirations in an anguished tone, and I wondered had he a grandmother too. Only a grandmother could account for a fellow behaving in that heartbroken way, but he was better off than I, for he at least could go and confess his sins; while I would make a bad confession and then die in the night and be continually coming back and burning people's furniture.

Nora's turn came, and I heard the sound of something slamming, and then her voice as if butter wouldn't melt in her mouth, and then another slam, and out she came. God, the hypocrisy of women! Her eyes were lowered, her head was bowed, and her hands were joined very low down on her stomach, and she walked up the aisle to the side altar looking like a saint. You never saw such an exhibition of devotion; and I remembered the devilish malice with which she had tormented me all the way from our door, and wondered were all religious people like that, really. It was my turn now. With the fear of damnation in my soul I went in, and the confessional door closed of itself behind me.

It was pitch-dark and I couldn't see priest or anything else. Then I really began to be frightened. In the darkness it was a matter between God and me, and He had all the odds. He knew what my intentions were before I even started; I had no chance. All I had ever been told about confession got mixed up in my mind, and I knelt to one wall and said: "Bless me, father, for I have sinned; this is my first confession." I waited for a few minutes, but nothing happened, so I tried it on the other wall. Nothing happened there either. He had me spotted all right.

It must have been then that I noticed the shelf at about one height with my head. It was really a place for grown-up people to rest their elbows, but in my distracted state I thought it was probably the place you were supposed to kneel. Of course, it was on the high side and not very deep, but I was always good at climbing and managed to get up all right. Staying up was the trouble. There was room only for my knees, and nothing you could get a grip on but a sort of wooden moulding a bit above it. I held on to the moulding and repeated the words a little louder, and this time something happened all right. A slide was slammed back; a little light entered the box, and a man's voice said: "Who's there?"

" 'Tis me, father," I said for fear he mightn't see me and go away again. I couldn't see him at all. The place the voice came from was under the moulding, about level with my knees, so I took a good grip of the moulding and swung myself down till I saw the astonished face of a young priest looking up at me. He had to put his head on one side to see me, and I had to put mine on one side to see him, so we were more or less talking to one another upside-down. It struck me as a queer way of hearing confessions, but I didn't feel it my place to criticize.

"Bless me, father, for I have sinned; this is my first confession," I rattled off all in one breath, and swung myself down the least shade more to make it easier for him.

"What are you doing up there?" he shouted in an angry voice, and the strain the politeness was putting on my hold of the moulding, and the shock of being addressed in such an uncivil tone, were too much for me. I lost my grip, tumbled, and hit the door an unmerciful wallop before I found myself flat on my back in the middle of the aisle. The people who had been waiting stood up with their mouths open. The priest opened the door of the middle box and came out, pushing his biretta back from his forehead; he looked something terrible. Then Nora came scampering down the aisle.

"Oh, you dirty little caffler!" she said. "I might have known you'd do it. I might have known you'd disgrace me. I can't leave you out of my sight for one minute."

Before I could even get to my feet to defend myself she bent down and gave me a clip across the ear. This reminded me that I was so stunned I had even forgotten to cry, so that people might think I wasn't hurt at all, when in fact I was probably maimed for life. I gave a roar out of me.

"What's all this about?" the priest hissed, getting angrier than ever and pushing Nora off me. "How dare you hit the child like that, you little vixen?"

"But I can't do my penance with him, father," Nora cried, cocking an outraged eye up at him.

"Well, go and do it, or I'll give you some more to do," he said, giving me a hand up. "Was it coming to confession you were, my poor man?" he asked me.

" 'Twas, father," said I with a sob.

"Oh," he said respectfully, "a big hefty fellow like you must have terrible sins. Is this your first?"

" 'Tis, father," said I.

"Worse and worse," he said gloomily. "The crimes of a lifetime. I don't know will I get rid of you at all today. You'd better wait now till I'm finished with these old ones. You can see by the looks of them they haven't much to tell."

"I will, father," I said with something approaching joy.

The relief of it was really enormous. Nora stuck out her tongue at me from behind his back, but I couldn't even be bothered retorting. I knew from the very moment that man opened his mouth that he was intelligent above the ordinary. When I had time to think, I saw how right I was. It only stood to reason that a fellow confessing after seven years would have more to tell than people that went every week. The crimes of a lifetime, exactly as he said. It was only what he expected, and the rest was the cackle of old women and girls with their talk of hell, the bishop, and the penitential psalms. That was all they knew. I started to make my examination of conscience, and barring the one bad business of my grandmother it didn't seem so bad.

The next time, the priest steered me into the confession box himself and left the shutter back the way I could see him get in and sit down at the further side of the grille from me.

"Well, now," he said, "what do they call you?"

"Jackie, father," said I.

"And what's a-trouble to you, Jackie?"

"Father," I said, feeling I might as well get it over while I had him in good humour, "I had it all arranged to kill my grandmother."

He seemed a bit shaken by that, all right, because he said nothing for quite a while.

"My goodness," he said at last, "that'd be a shocking thing to do. What put that into your head?"

"Father," I said, feeling very sorry for myself, "she's an awful woman."

"Is she?" he asked. "What way is she awful?"

"She takes porter, father," I said, knowing well from the way Mother talked of it that this was a mortal sin, and hoping it would make the priest take a more favourable view of my case.

"Oh, my!" he said, and I could see he was impressed.

"And snuff, father," said I.

"That's a bad case, sure enough, Jackie," he said.

"And she goes round in her bare feet, father," I went on in a rush of self-pity, "and she knows I don't like her, and she gives pennies to Nora and none to me, and my da sides with her and flakes me, and one night I was so heart-scalded I made up my mind I'd have to kill her."

"And what would you do with the body?" he asked with great interest.

"I was thinking I could chop that up and carry it away in a barrow I have," I said.

"Begor, Jackie," he said, "do you know you're a terrible child?"

"I know, father," I said, for I was just thinking the same thing myself. "I tried to kill Nora too with a bread-knife under the table, only I missed her."

"Is that the little girl that was beating you just now?" he asked.

" 'Tis, father."

"Someone will go for her with a bread-knife one day, and he won't miss her," he said rather cryptically. "You must have great courage. Between ourselves, there's a lot of people I'd like to do the same to but I'd never have the nerve. Hanging is an awful death."

"Is it, father?" I asked with the deepest interest—I was always very keen on hanging. "Did you ever see a fellow hanged?"

"Dozens of them," he said solemnly. "And they all died roaring."

"Jay!" I said.

"Oh, a horrible death!" he said with great satisfaction. "Lots of the fellows I saw killed their grandmothers too, but they all said 'twas never worth it."

He had me there for a full ten minutes talking, and then walked out the chapel yard with me. I was genuinely sorry to part with him, because he was the most entertaining character I'd ever met in the religious line. Outside, after the shadow of the church, the sunlight was like the roaring of waves on a beach; it dazzled me; and when the frozen silence melted and I heard the screech of trams on the road my heart soared. I knew now I wouldn't die in the night and come back, leaving marks on my mother's furniture. It would be a great worry to her, and the poor soul had enough.

Nora was sitting on the railing, waiting for me, and she put on a very sour puss when she saw the priest with me. She was mad jealous because a priest had never come out of the church with her.

"Well," she asked coldly, after he left me, "what did he give you?"

"Three Hail Marys," I said.

"Three Hail Marys," she repeated incredulously. "You mustn't have told him anything."

"I told him everything," I said confidently.

"About Gran and all?"

"About Gran and all."

(All she wanted was to be able to go home and say I'd made a bad confession.)

"Did you tell him you went for me with the bread-knife?" she asked with a frown.

"I did to be sure."

"And he only gave you three Hail Marys?"

"That's all."

She slowly got down from the railing with a baffled air. Clearly, this was beyond her. As we mounted the steps back to the main road she looked at me suspiciously.

"What are you sucking?" she asked.

"Bullseyes."

"Was it the priest gave them to you?"

" 'Twas."

"Lord God," she wailed bitterly, "some people have all the luck! 'Tis no advantage to anybody trying to be good. I might just as well be a sinner like you."

BY WAY OF DISCUSSION

The use of the central character of a story as the subjective (first-person) narrator places the reader in the middle of the action, keeps the reader's attention focused on the experiences of a single character, and brings an air of plausibility to the proceedings. The technique is especially well suited for exploring some significant event in the life of the protagonist. Such is the case in our present story, as well as in an earlier example of the technique, John Updike's "A & P."

Jackie, the seven-year-old boy of "First Confession," is the central character and narrator-participant, but he is much older when he tells the tale. He has had years to look back on the incident. But, clearly, the circumstances surrounding his first confession remain important to his adult mind; otherwise, he would not be able to recall them in such detail.

In plot, "First Confession" includes most of the elements we have discussed before. Jackie is the protagonist, and his sister Nora is the primary antagonist. The death of the boy's grandfather and the subsequent coming of his grandmother to live with the family provide the precipitating incident. As the conflict intensifies to the crisis level, we have a clear climax in which a wise priest is able to deal with every one of the young boy's problems. Afterward, Jackie is a much-relieved person. In fact, in the denouement he is in a perfect position to score off his nasty sister.

"First Confession" is a humorous story, one that accomplishes its comic impact in several ways. To begin, we might mention the slapstick episode in the confessional, when Jackie climbs up on the shelf and then falls out of the booth and into the church aisle. On a more sophisticated level, we have Jackie's precocious ability to recognize hypocrisy and roast it with piquant wit. This ability gives us two gems of character assessment, one of old Mrs. Ryan and the other of Nora, that "raging malicious devil."

Humor also arises from Jackie's changing emotional state as the story proceeds. Thus, sitting in the pitch-dark confessional, he reflects gloomily that his sins are "a matter between God and me, and He had all the odds." Later, after absolution, his heart soars at the thought that "I wouldn't die in the night and come back, leaving marks on my mother's furniture." Finally, there is also ironic humor, reflected in such things as the priest's mock-serious tone with the young penitent and the latter's final victory over Nora, who almost certainly had less to confess than did Jackie.

Despite the light-hearted tone in which the story is narrated, Jackie's experience has taught him—and us as well, hopefully—a serious lesson about sin and expiation. The first thing we learn is that once a sin has been committed, guilt and fear quickly take over, assuming an aspect all out of proportion to the offense. To illustrate this, we see Jackie at one point convinced that he has broken all the Ten Commandments. At another point he believes that he is "lost, given up to eternal justice." At the latter point, O'Connor symbolically dramatizes Jackie's state of mind by having the boy move from the sunlight into the "deep shadow" of the church. After forgiveness has been accomplished, however, guilt and fear vanish and are replaced by a feeling of psychological release. Symbolically—and in Jackie's eyes, literally—one steps from the shadows into the sunlight once again.

The Irish writer Seán O'Faoláin once wrote about Frank O'Connor, author of "First Confession": "He was like a man who takes a machine gun into a shooting gallery. Everybody falls flat on his face, the proprietor at once takes for the hills, and when it is all over, and you cautiously peep up, you find that he has wrecked the place but got three perfect bull's-eyes." How apt a statement, for in "First Confession" it is literally bullseyes—hard candy—that the priest gives Jackie after hearing his "good" confession. The boy has scored a direct hit with the sympathetic man.

We should not ignore the machine-gun quality of O'Connor's writing. By the end of the story, O'Connor, speaking through his youthful narrator-protagonist, has pretty well blasted Jackie's sister, grandmother, father, mother, and even the other people in the church.

Only Jackie and the priest come off as sympathetic characters.

DORIS LESSING

The Nuisance

Two narrow tracks, one of them deepened to a smooth dusty groove by the incessant padding of bare feet, wound from the farm compound to the old well through half a mile of tall blond grass that was soiled and matted because of the nearness of the clustering huts: the compound had been on that ridge for twenty years.

The native women with their children used to loiter down the track, and their shrill laughter and chattering sounded through the trees as if one might suddenly have come on a flock of brilliant noisy parrots. It seemed as if fetching water was more of a social event to them than a chore. At the well itself they would linger half the morning, standing in groups to gossip, their arms raised in that graceful, eternally moving gesture to steady glittering or rusted petrol tins balanced on head-rings woven of grass; kneeling to slap bits of bright cloth on slabs of stone blasted long ago from the depths of earth. Here they washed and scolded and dandled their children. Here they scrubbed their pots. Here they sluiced themselves and combed their hair.

Coming upon them suddenly there would be sharp exclamations; a glimpse of soft brown shoulders and thighs withdrawing to the bushes, or annoyed and resentful eyes. It was their well. And while they were there, with their laughter, and gossip and singing, their folded draperies, bright armbands, earthenware jars and metal combs, grouped in attitudes of head-slowed indolence, it seemed as if the bellowing of distant cattle, drone of tractor, all the noises of the farm, were simply lending themselves to form a background to this antique scene: Women, drawing water at the well.

When they left the ground would be scattered with the bright-pink, fleshy skins of the native wild-plum which contracts the mouth shudderingly with its astringency, or with the shiny green fragments of the shells of kaffir oranges.

Without the women the place was ugly, paltry. The windlass, coiled with greasy rope, propped for safety with a forked stick, was sheltered by a tiny cock of thatch that threw across the track a long, intensely black shadow. For the rest, veld; the sere, flattened, sun-dried veld.

They were beautiful, these women. But she whom I thought of vaguely as "The cross-eyed one," offended the sight. She used to lag behind the others on the road, either by herself, or in charge of the older children. Not only did she suffer from a painful squint, so that when she looked towards you it was with a confused glare of white eyeball; but her body was hideous. She wore the traditional dark-patterned blue stuff looped at the waist, and above it her breasts were loose, flat crinkling triangles.

She was a solitary figure at the well, doing her washing unaided and without laughter. She would strain at the windlass during the long slow ascent of the swinging bucket that clanged sometimes, far below, against the sides of naked rock until at that critical moment when it hung vibrating at the mouth of the well, she would set the weight of her shoulder in the crook of the handle and with a fearful snatching movement bring the water to safety. It would slop over, dissolving in a shower of great drops that fell tinkling to disturb the surface of that tiny, circular, dully-gleaming mirror which lay at the bottom of the plunging rock tunnel. She was clumsy. Because of her eyes her body lumbered.

She was the oldest wife of "The Long One," who was our most skilful driver.

"The Long One" was not so tall as he was abnormally thin. It was the leanness of those driven by inner restlessness. He could never keep still. His hands plucked at pieces of grass, his shoulder twitched to a secret rhythm of the nerves. Set a-top of that sinewy, narrow, taut body was a narrow head, with wide-pointed ears, which gave him an appearance of alert caution. The expression of the face was always violent, whether he was angry, laughing, or—most usually—sardonically critical. He had a tongue that was feared by every labourer of the farm. Even my father would smile ruefully after an altercation with his driver and say: "He's a man, that native. One must respect him, after all. He never lets you get away with anything."

In his own line he was an artist—his line being cattle. He handled oxen with a delicate brutality that was fascinating and horrifying to watch. Give him a bunch of screaming, rearing three-year-olds, due to take their first taste of the yoke, and he would fight them for hours under a blistering sun with the sweat running off him, his eyes glowing with a wicked and sombre satisfaction. Then he would use his whip, grunting savagely as the lash cut down into flesh, his tongue stuck calculatingly between his teeth as he measured the exact weight of the blow. But to watch him handle a team of sixteen fat tamed oxen was a different thing. It was like watching a circus act; there was the same suspense in it: it was a matter of pride to him that he did not need to use the whip. This did not by any means imply that he wished to spare the beasts pain, not at all; he liked to feed his pride on his own skill. Alongside the double line of ponderous cattle that strained across acres of heavy clods, danced, raved and screamed the Long One, with his twelve-foot-long lash circling in black patterns over their backs; and though his threatening yells were the yells of an inspired madman, and the heavy whip could be heard clean across the farm, so that on a moonlight night when they were ploughing late it sounded like the crack and whine of a rifle, never did the dangerous metal-tipped lash so much as touch a hair of their hides. If you examined the oxen as they were outspanned, they might be exhausted, driven to staggering-point, so that my father had to remonstrate, but there was never a mark on them.

"He knows how to handle oxen, but he can't handle his women."

We gave our natives labels such as that, since it was impossible ever to know them as their fellows knew them, in the round. That phrase summarised for us what the Long One offered in entertainment during the years he was with us. Coming back to the farm, after an absence, one would say in humorous anticipation: "And what has the Long One been up to now, with his harem?"

There was always trouble with his three wives. He used to come up to the house to discuss with my father, man to man, how the youngest wife was flirting with the boss-boy from the neighbouring compound, six miles off; or how she had thrown a big pot of smoking mealie-pap at the middle wife, who was jealous of her.

We grew accustomed to the sight of the Long One standing at the back door, at the sunset hour, when my father held audience after work. He always wore long khaki trousers that slipped down over thin bony hips and went bare-chested, and there would be a ruddy gleam on his polished black skin, and his spindly gesticulating form would be outlined against a sea of fiery colours. At the end of his tale of complaint he would relapse suddenly into a pose of resignation that was self-consciously weary. My father used to laugh until his face was wet and say: "That man is a natural-born comedian. He would have been on the stage if he had been born another colour."

But he was no buffoon. He would play up to my father's appreciation of the comic, but he would never play the ape, as some Africans did, for our amusement. And he was certainly no figure of fun to his fellows. That same thing in him that sat apart, watchfully critical, even of himself, gave his humour its mordancy, his tongue its sting. And he was terribly attractive to his women. I have seen him slouch down the road on his way from one team to another, his whip trailing behind in the dust, his trousers sagging in folds from hip-bone to ankle, his eyes broodingly directed in front of him, merely nodding as he passed a group of women among whom might be his wives. And it was as if he had lashed them with that whip. They would bridle and writhe; and then call provocatively after him, but with a note of real anger, to make him notice them. He would not so much as turn his head.

When the real trouble started, though, my father soon got tired of it. He liked to be amused, not seriously implicated in his labourers' problems. The

Long One took to coming up not occasionally, as he had been used to do, but every evening. He was deadly serious, and very bitter. He wanted my father to persuade the old wife, the cross-eyed one, to go back home to her own people. The woman was driving him crazy. A nagging woman in your house was like having a flea on your body; you could scratch but it always moved to another place, and there was no peace till you killed it.

"But you can't send her back, just because you are tired of her."

The Long One said his life had become insupportable. She grumbled, she sulked, she spoilt his food.

"Well, then your other wives can cook for you."

But it seemed there were complications. The two younger women hated each other, but they were united in one thing, that the old wife should stay, for she was so useful. She looked after the children; she did the hoeing in the garden; she picked relishes from the veld. Besides, she provided endless amusement with her ungainliness. She was the eternal butt, the fool, marked by fate for the entertainment of the whole-limbed and the comely.

My father referred at this point to a certain handbook on native lore, which stated definitively that an elder wife was entitled to be waited on by a young wife, perhaps as compensation for having to give up the pleasures of her lord's favour. The Long One and his ménage cut clean across this amiable theory. And my father, being unable to find a prescribed remedy (as one might look for a cure of a disease in a pharmacopoeia), grew angry. After some weeks of incessant complaint from the Long One he was told to hold his tongue and manage his women himself. That evening the man stalked furiously down the path, muttering to himself between teeth clenched on a grass-stem, on his way home to his two giggling younger wives and the ugly sour-faced old woman, the mother of his elder children, the drudge of his household and the scourge of his life.

It was some weeks later that my father asked casually one day: "And by the way, Long One, how are things with you? All right again?"

And the Long One answered simply: "Yes, baas. She's gone away."

"What do you mean, gone away?"

The Long One shrugged. She had just gone. She had left suddenly, without saying anything to anyone.

Now, the woman came from Nyasaland, which was days and days of weary walking away. Surely she hadn't gone by herself? Had a brother or an uncle come to fetch her? Had she gone with a band of passing Africans on their way home?

My father wondered a little, and then forgot about it. It wasn't his affair. He was pleased to have his most useful native back at work with an unharassed mind. And he was particularly pleased that the whole business was ended before the annual trouble over the water-carrying.

For there were two wells. The new one, used by ourselves, had fresh sparkling water that was sweet in the mouth; but in July of each year it ran dry. The water of the old well had a faintly unpleasant taste and was pale brown, but there was always plenty of it. For three or four months of the year, depending on the rains, we shared that well with the compound.

Now, the Long One hated fetching water three miles, four times a week, in the water-cart. The women of the compound disliked have to arrange their visits to the well so as not to get in the way of the water-carriers. There was always grumbling.

This year we had not even begun to use the old well when complaints started that the water tasted bad. The big baas must get the well cleaned.

My father said vaguely that he would clean the well when he had time.

Next day there came a deputation from the women of the compound. Half a dozen of them stood at the back door, arguing that if the well wasn't cleaned soon, all their children would be sick.

"I'll do it next week," he promised, with bad grace.

The following morning the Long One brought our first load of the season from the old well; and as we turned the taps on the barrels a foetid smell began to pervade the house. As for drinking it, that was out of the question.

"Why don't you keep the cover on the well?" my father said to the women, who were still loitering resentfully at the back door. He was really angry. "Last time the well was cleaned there were fourteen dead rats and a dead snake. We never get things in our well because we remember to keep the lid on."

But the women appeared to consider the lid being on, or off, was an act of God, and nothing to do with them.

We always went down to watch the well-emptying, which had the fascination of a ritual. Like the mealie-shelling, or the first rains, it marked a turning-point in the year. It seemed as if a besieged city were laying plans for the conservation of supplies. The sap was falling in tree and grass-root; the sun was withdrawing high, high, behind a veil of smoke and dust; the fierce dryness of the air was a new element, parching foliage as the heat cauterized it. The well-emptying was an act of faith, and of defiance. For a whole afternoon there would be no water on the farm at all. One well was completely dry. And this one would be drained, dependent on the mysterious ebbing and flowing of underground rivers. What if they should fail us? There was an anxious evening, every year; and in the morning, when the Long One stood at the back door and said, beaming, that the bucket was bringing up fine new water, it was like a festival.

But this afternoon we could not stick it out. The smell was intolerable. We saw the usual complement of bloated rats, laid out on the stones around the well, and there was even the skeleton of a small buck that must have fallen in the dark. Then we left, along the road that was temporarily a river whose source was that apparently endless succession of buckets filled by greyish, evil water.

It was the Long One himself that came to tell us the news. Afterwards we tried to remember what look that always expressive face wore as he told it.

It seemed that in the last bucket but one had floated a human arm, or rather the fragments of one. Piece by piece they had fetched her up, the Cross-eyed

Woman, his own first wife. They recognised her by her bangles. Last of all, the Long One went down to fetch up her head, which was missing.

"I thought you said your wife had gone home?" said my father.

"I thought she had. Where else could she have gone?"

"Well," said my father at last, disgusted by the whole thing, "if she had to kill herself, why couldn't she hang herself on a tree, instead of spoiling the well?"

"She might have slipped and fallen," said the Long One.

My father looked up at him suddenly. He stared for a few moments. Then: "Ye-yes," he said, "I suppose she might."

Later, we talked about the thing, saying how odd it was that natives should commit suicide; it seemed almost like an impertinence, as if they were claiming to have the same delicate feelings as ours.

But later still, apropos of nothing in particular, my father was heard to remark: "Well, I don't know, I'm damned if I know, but in any case he's a damned good driver."

BY WAY OF DISCUSSION

Doris Lessing's "The Nuisance" is a miniature masterpiece of the technique of narrator as observer. The narrator-observer, a sort of firsthand reporter, stands on the sidelines and tells someone else's story. Employing this point of view allows the author to present the reactions of both the narrator and the characters involved in the action. Sometimes, as in our present selection, these reactions are identical. At other times, they may be different. The technique permits the author to make some point, often ironic, that goes beyond the narrative situation.

The Long One is the protagonist of "The Nuisance," his cross-eyed wife the antagonist. Violent, sardonic, cruel, a man who "never lets you get away with anything," the Long One is the last person who would put up with a woman who refuses to make the traditional concessions in a male-dominated social system. To him, a nagging wife is like "a flea on your body; . . . there was no peace until you killed it." Of course, he takes no account of the aggravations that have probably helped make the cross-eyed one the shrew she is.

As for the narrator of the story and her father, their response to the whole tragic affair is painfully bland and casual. When the trouble begins, the father is at first amused; but soon he tires of the constant complaining of the Long One and tells him to hold his tongue. Later, he all too readily accepts the improbable story of the wife's disappearance and the verdict of suicide. After everything has been concluded, narrator and father remark about "how odd it was that natives should commit suicide; it seemed almost like an impertinence, as if they were claiming to have the same delicate feelings as ours." The grindingly ironic point is, of course, that these white people have no delicate feelings at all; they are as callous as the Long One.

The pervasive irony of the story is that it treats a complex personal situation by presenting what many white Western people—as exemplified by the narrator's father—would view as a simple, almost primitive, social system. And in showing the essential similarity between whites and blacks—or any other people, for that matter—the author can be viewed as offering an oblique reminder that we of the so-called civilized and cosmopolitan world have come up with no better ways of dealing with problems such as the one faced by the Long One. Although it may seem a brutal solution for him to simply eliminate his wife, a look at our own handling of people who refuse to conform to accepted patterns of behavior might show that often we are equally brutal.

So, here in "The Nuisance" is the carefully modulated "nuisance" voice of Lessing coming to us from the Dark Continent, saying something like: "Do these people seem like simple children to you? They do? How are you any different from them?" The use of the narrator-observer is particularly appropriate in a story that seeks to pose such questions indirectly and therefore unobtrusively.

RING LARDNER

Haircut

I got another barber that comes over from Carterville and helps me out Saturdays, but the rest of the time I can get along all right alone. You can see for yourself that this ain't no New York City and besides that, the most of the boys works all day and don't have no leisure to drop in here and get themselves prettied up.

You're a newcomer, ain't you? I thought I hadn't seen you round before. I hope you like it good enough to stay. As I say, we ain't no New York City or Chicago, but we have pretty good times. Not as good, though, since Jim Kendall got killed. When he was alive, him and Hod Meyers used to keep this town in an uproar. I bet they was more laughin' done here than any town its size in America.

Jim was comical, and Hod was pretty near a match for him. Since Jim's gone, Hod tries to hold his end up just the same as ever, but it's tough goin' when you ain't got nobody to kind of work with.

They used to be plenty fun in here Saturdays. This place is jam-packed Saturdays, from four o'clock on. Jim and Hod would show up right after their supper, round six o'clock. Jim would set himself down in that big chair, nearest the blue spittoon. Whoever had been settin' in that chair, why they'd get up when Jim come in and give it to him.

You'd of thought it was a reserved seat like they have sometimes in a theayter. Hod would generally always stand or walk up and down, or some Saturdays, of course, he'd be settin' in this chair part of the time, gettin' a haircut.

Well, Jim would set there a w'ile without openin' his mouth only to spit, and then finally he'd say to me, "Whitey,"—my right name, that is, my right first name, is Dick, but everybody round here calls me Whitey—Jim would say, "Whitey, your nose looks like a rosebud tonight. You must of been drinkin' some of your aw de cologne."

So I'd say, "No, Jim, but you look like you'd been drinkin' somethin' of that kind or somethin' worse."

Jim would have to laugh at that, but then he'd speak up and say, "No, I ain't had nothin' to drink, but that ain't sayin' I wouldn't like somethin'. I wouldn't even mind if it was wood alcohol."

Then Hod Meyers would say, "Neither would your wife." That would set everybody to laughin' because Jim and his wife wasn't on very good terms. She'd of divorced him only they wasn't no chance to get alimony and she didn't have no way to take care of herself and the kids. She couldn't never understand Jim. He *was* kind of rough, but a good fella at heart.

Jim and Hod had all kinds of sport with Milt Sheppard. I don't suppose you've seen Milt. Well, he's got an Adam's apple that looks more like a mushmelon. So I'd be shavin' Milt and when I'd start to shave down here on his neck, Hod would holler, "Hey, Whitey, wait a minute! Before you cut into it, let's make up a pool and see who can guess closest to the number of seeds."

And Jim would say, "If Milt hadn't of been so hoggish, he'd of ordered a half a cantaloupe instead of a whole one and it might not of stuck in his throat."

All the boys would roar at this and Milt himself would force a smile, though the joke was on him. Jim certainly was a card!

There's his shavin' mug, settin' on the shelf, right next to Charley Vail's. "Charles M. Vail." That's the druggist. He comes in regular for his shave, three times a week. And Jim's is the cup next to Charley's. "James H. Kendall." Jim won't need no shavin' mug no more, but I'll leave it there just the same for old time's sake. Jim certainly was a character!

Years ago, Jim used to travel for a canned goods concern over in Carterville. They sold canned goods. Jim had the whole northern half of the State and was on the road five days out of every week. He'd drop in here Saturdays and tell his experiences for that week. It was rich.

I guess he paid more attention to playin' jokes than makin' sales. Finally the concern let him out and he come right home here and told everybody he'd been fired instead of sayin' he'd resigned like most fellas would of.

It was a Saturday and the shop was full and Jim got up out of that chair and says, "Gentlemen, I got an important announcement to make. I been fired from my job."

Well, they asked him if he was in earnest and he said he was and nobody could think of nothin' to say till Jim finally broke the ice himself. He says, "I been sellin' canned goods and now I'm canned goods myself."

You see, the concern he'd been workin' for was a factory that made canned goods. Over in Carterville. And now Jim said he was canned himself. He was certainly a card!

Jim had a great trick that he used to play w'ile he was travelin'. For instance, he'd be ridin' on a train and they'd come to some little town like, well, like, we'll say, like Benton. Jim would look out the train window and read the signs on the stores.

For instance, they'd be a sign, "Henry Smith, Dry Goods." Well, Jim would write down the name and the name of the town and when he got to wherever he was goin' he'd mail back a postal card to Henry Smith at Benton and not sign no name to it, but he'd write on the card, well, somethin' like "Ask your wife about that book agent that spent the afternoon last week," or "Ask your Missus who kept her from gettin' lonesome the last time you was in Carterville." And he'd sign the card, "A Friend."

Of course, he never knew what really come of none of these jokes, but he could picture what *probably* happened and that was enough.

Jim didn't work very steady after he lost his position with the Carterville people. What he did earn, doin' odd jobs round town, why he spent pretty near all of it on gin and his family might of starved if the stores hadn't of carried them along. Jim's wife tried her hand at dressmakin', but they ain't nobody goin' to get rich makin' dresses in this town.

As I say, she'd of divorced Jim, only she seen that she couldn't support herself and the kids and she was always hopin' that some day Jim would cut out his habits and give her more than two or three dollars a week.

They was a time when she would go to whoever he was workin' for and ask them to give her his wages, but after she done this once or twice, he beat her to it by borrowin' most of his pay in advance. He told it all round town, how he had outfoxed his Missus. He certainly was a caution!

But he wasn't satisfied with just outwittin' her. He was sore the way she had acted, tryin' to grab off his pay. And he made up his mind he'd get even. Well, he waited till Evans's Circus was advertised to come to town. Then he told his wife and two kiddies that he was goin' to take them to the circus. The day of the circus, he told them he would get the tickets and meet them outside the entrance to the tent.

Well, he didn't have no intentions of bein' there or buyin' tickets or nothin'. He got full of gin and laid round Wright's poolroom all day. His wife and the kids waited and waited and of course he didn't show up. His wife didn't have a dime with her, or nowhere else, I guess. So she finally had to tell the kids it was all off and they cried like they wasn't never goin' to stop.

Well, it seems, w'ile they was cryin', Doc Stair came along and he asked what was the matter, but Mrs. Kendall was stubborn and wouldn't tell him, but the kids told him and he insisted on takin' them and their mother in the show. Jim found this out afterwards and it was one reason why he had it in for Doc Stair.

Doc Stair come here about a year and a half ago. He's a mighty handsome young fella and his clothes always look like he has them made to order. He goes to Detroit two or three times a year and w'ile he's there he must have a tailor take his measure and then make him a suit to order. They cost pretty near twice as much, but they fit a whole lot better than if you just bought them in a store.

For a w'ile everybody was wonderin' why a young doctor like Doc Stair should come to a town like this where we already got old Doc Gamble and Doc Foote that's both been here for years and all the practice in town was always divided between the two of them.

Then they was a story got round that Doc Stair's gal had throwed him over, a gal up in the Northern Peninsula somewheres, and the reason he come here was to hide himself away and forget it. He said himself that he thought they wasn't nothin' like general practice in a place like ours to fit a man to be a good all round doctor. And that's why he'd came.

Anyways, it wasn't long before he was makin' enough to live on, though they tell me that he never dunned nobody for what they owed him, and the folks here certainly has got the owin' habit, even in my business. If I had all that was comin' to me for just shaves alone, I could go to Carterville and put up at the Mercer for a week and see a different picture every night. For instance, they's old George Purdy—but I guess I shouldn't ought to be gossipin'.

Well, last year, our coroner died, died of the flu. Ken Beatty, that was his name. He was the coroner. So they had to choose another man to be coroner in his place and they picked Doc Stair. He laughed at first and said he didn't want it, but they made him take it. It ain't no job that anybody would fight for and what a man makes out of it in a year would just about buy seeds for their garden. Doc's the kind, though, that can't say no to nothin' if you keep at him long enough.

But I was goin' to tell you about a poor boy we got here in town—Paul Dickson. He fell out of a tree when he was about ten years old. Lit on his head and it done somethin' to him and he ain't never been right. No harm in him, but just silly. Jim Kendall used to call him cuckoo; that's a name Jim had for anybody that was off their head, only he called people's head their bean. That was another of his gags, callin' head bean and callin' crazy people cuckoo. Only poor Paul ain't crazy, but just silly.

You can imagine that Jim used to have all kinds of fun with Paul. He'd send him to the White Front Garage for a left-handed monkey wrench. Of course they ain't no such a thing as a left-handed monkey wrench.

And once we had a kind of a fair here and they was a baseball game between the fats and the leans and before the game started Jim called Paul over and sent him way down to Schrader's hardware store to get a key for the pitcher's box.

They wasn't nothin' in the way of gags that Jim couldn't think up, when he put his mind to it.

Poor Paul was always kind of suspicious of people, maybe on account of how Jim had kept foolin' him. Paul wouldn't have much to do with anybody only his own mother and Doc Stair and a girl here in town named Julie Gregg. That is, she ain't a girl no more, but pretty near thirty or over.

When Doc first come to town, Paul seemed to feel like here was a real friend and he hung around Doc's office most of the w'ile; the only time he wasn't there was when he'd go home to eat or sleep or when he seen Julie Gregg doin' her shoppin'.

When he looked out Doc's window and seen her, he'd run downstairs and join her and tag along with her to the different stores. The poor boy was crazy about Julie and she always treated him mighty nice and made him feel like he was welcome, though of course it wasn't nothin' but pity on her side.

Doc done all he could to improve Paul's mind and he told me once that he really thought the boy was gettin' better, that they was times when he was as bright and sensible as anybody else.

But I was goin' to tell you about Julie Gregg. Old Man Gregg was in the lumber business, but got to drinkin' and lost the most of his money and when he died, he didn't leave nothin' but the house and just enough insurance for the girl to skimp along on.

Her mother was a kind of a half invalid and didn't hardly ever leave the house. Julie wanted to sell the place and move somewheres else after the old man died, but the mother said she was born here and would die here. It was tough on Julie, as the young people round this town—well, she's too good for them.

She's been away to school and Chicago and New York and different places and they ain't no subject she can't talk on, where you take the rest of the young folks here and you mention anything to them outside of Gloria Swanson or Tommy Meighan and they think you're delirious. Did you see Gloria in Wages of Virtue? You missed somethin'!

Well, Doc Stair hadn't been here more than a week when he come in one day to get shaved and I recognized who he was as he had been pointed out to me, so I told him about my old lady. She's been ailin' for a couple of years and either Doc Gamble or Doc Foote, neither one, seemed to be helpin' her. So he said he would come out and see her, but if she was able to get out herself, it would be better to bring her to his office where he could make a completer examination.

So I took her to his office and w'ile I was waitin' for her in the reception room, in come Julie Gregg. When somebody comes in Doc Stair's office, they's a bell that rings in his inside office so as he can tell they's somebody to see him.

So he left my old lady inside and come out to the front office and that's the first time him and Julie met and I guess it was what they call love at first sight. But it wasn't fifty-fifty. This young fella was the slickest lookin' fella she'd ever seen in this town and she went wild over him. To him she was just a young lady that wanted to see the doctor.

She'd came on about the same business I had. Her mother had been doctorin' for years with Doc Gamble and Doc Foote and without no results. So she'd heard they was a new doc in town and decided to give him a try. He promised to call and see her mother that same day.

I said a minute ago that it was love at first sight on her part. I'm not only judgin' by how she acted afterwards but how she looked at him that first day in his office. I ain't no mind reader, but it was wrote all over her face that she was gone.

Now Jim Kendall, besides bein' a jokesmith and a pretty good drinker, well, Jim was quite a lady-killer. I guess he run pretty wild durin' the time he was on the road for them Carterville people, and besides that, he'd had a couple little affairs of the heart right here in town. As I say, his wife could of divorced him, only she couldn't.

But Jim was like the majority of men, and women, too, I guess. He wanted what he couldn't get. He wanted Julie Gregg and worked his head off tryin' to land her. Only he'd of said bean instead of head.

Well, Jim's habits and his jokes didn't appeal to Julie and of course he was a married man, so he didn't have no more chance than, well, than a rabbit. That's an expression of Jim's himself. When somebody didn't have no chance to get elected or somethin', Jim would always say they didn't have no more chance than a rabbit.

He didn't make no bones about how he felt. Right in here, more than once, in front of the whole crowd, he said he was stuck on Julie and anybody that could get her for him was welcome to his house and his wife and kids included. But she wouldn't have nothin' to do with him; wouldn't even speak to him on the street. He finally seen he wasn't gettin' nowheres with his usual line so he decided to try the rough stuff. He went right up to her house one evenin' and when she opened the door he forced his way in and grabbed her. But she broke loose and before he could stop her, she run in the next room and locked the door and phoned to Joe Barnes. Joe's the marshal. Jim could hear who she was phonin' to and he beat it before Joe got there.

Joe was an old friend of Julie's pa. Joe went to Jim the next day and told him what would happen if he ever done it again.

I don't know how the news of this little affair leaked out. Chances is that Joe Barnes told his wife and she told somebody else's wife and they told their husband. Anyways, it did leak out and Hod Meyers had the nerve to kid Jim about it, right here in this shop. Jim didn't deny nothin' and kind of laughed it off and said for us all to wait; that lots of people had tried to make a monkey out of him, but he always got even.

Meanw'ile everybody in town was wise to Julie's bein' wild mad over the Doc. I don't suppose she had any idear how her face changed when him and her was together; of course she couldn't of, or she'd of kept away from him. And she didn't know that we was all noticin' how many times she made excuses to go up to his office or pass it on the other side of the street and look up in his window to see if he was there. I felt sorry for her and so did most other people.

Hod Meyers kept rubbin' it into Jim about how the Doc had cut him out. Jim didn't pay no attention to the kiddin' and you could see he was plannin' one of his jokes.

One trick Jim had was the knack of changin' his voice. He could make you think he was a girl talkin' and he could mimic any man's voice. To show you how good he was along this line, I'll tell you the joke he played on me once.

You know, in most towns of any size, when a man is dead and needs a shave, why the barber that shaves him soaks him five dollars for the job; that is, he don't soak *him*, but whoever ordered the shave. I just charge three dollars because personally I don't mind much shavin' a dead person. They lay a whole lot stiller than live customers. The only thing is that you don't feel like talkin' to them and you get kind of lonesome.

Well, about the coldest day we ever had here, two years ago last winter, the phone rung at the house w'ile I was home to dinner and I answered the phone and it was a woman's voice and she said she was Mrs. John Scott and her husband was dead and would I come out and shave him.

Old John had always been a good customer of mine. But they live seven miles out in the country, on the Streeter road. Still I didn't see how I could say no.

So I said I would be there, but would have to come in a jitney and it might cost three or four dollars besides the price of the shave. So she, or the voice, it said that was all right, so I got Frank Abbott to drive me out to the place and when I got there, who should open the door but old John himself! He wasn't no more dead than, well, than a rabbit.

It didn't take no private detective to figure out who had played me this little joke. Nobody could of thought it up but Jim Kendall. He certainly was a card!

I tell you this incident just to show you how he could disguise his voice and make you believe it was somebody else talkin'. I'd of swore it was Mrs. Scott had called me. Anyways, some woman.

Well, Jim waited till he had Doc Stair's voice down pat; then he went after revenge.

He called Julie up on a night when he knew Doc was over in Carterville. She never questioned but what it was Doc's voice. Jim said he must see her that night; he couldn't wait no longer to tell her somethin'. She was all excited and told him to come to the house. But he said he was expectin' an important long distance call and wouldn't she please forget her manners for once and come to his office. He said they couldn't nothin' hurt her and nobody would see her and he just *must* talk to her a little w'ile. Well, poor Julie fell for it.

Doc always keeps a night light in his office, so it looked to Julie like they was somebody there.

Meanw'ile Jim Kendall had went to Wright's poolroom, where they was a whole gang amusin' themselves. The most of them had drank plenty of gin, and they was a rough bunch even when sober. They was always strong for Jim's jokes and when he told them to come with him and see some fun they give up their card games and pool games and followed along.

Doc's office is on the second floor. Right outside his door they's a flight of stairs leadin' to the floor above. Jim and his gang hid in the dark behind these stairs.

Well, Julie come up to Doc's door and rung the bell and they was nothin' doin'. She rung it again and rung it seven or eight times. Then she tried the door and found it locked. Then Jim made some kind of noise and she heard it and waited a minute, and then she says, "Is that you, Ralph?" Ralph is Doc's first name.

They was no answer and it must of came to her all of a sudden that she'd been bunked. She pretty near fell downstairs and the whole gang after her. They chased her all the way home, hollerin', "Is that you, Ralph?" and "Oh, Ralphie, dear, is that you?" Jim says he couldn't holler it himself, as he was laughin' too hard.

Poor Julie! She didn't show up here on Main Street for a long, long time afterward.

And of course Jim and his gang told everybody in town, everybody but Doc Stair. They was scared to tell him, and he might of never knowed only for Paul Dickson. The poor cuckoo, as Jim called him, he was here in the shop one night when Jim was still gloatin' yet over what he'd done to Julie. And Paul took in as much of it as he could understand and he run to Doc with the story.

It's a cinch Doc went up in the air and swore he'd make Jim suffer. But it was a kind of a delicate thing, because if it got out that he had beat Jim up, Julie was bound to hear of it and then she'd know that Doc knew and of course knowin' that he knew would make it worse for her than ever. He was goin' to do somethin', but it took a lot of figurin'.

Well, it was a couple days later when Jim was here in the shop again, and so was the cuckoo. Jim was goin' duck-shootin' the next day and had came in lookin' for Hod Meyers to go with him. I happened to know that Hod had went over to Carterville and wouldn't be home till the end of the week. So Jim said he hated to go alone and he guessed he would call it off. Then poor Paul spoke up and said if Jim would take him he would go along. Jim thought a w'ile and then he said, well, he guessed a half-wit was better than nothin'.

I suppose he was plottin' to get Paul out in the boat and play some joke on him, like pushin' him in the water. Anyways, he said Paul could go. He asked him had he ever shot a duck and Paul said no, he'd never even had a gun in his hands. So Jim said he could set in the boat and watch him and if he behaved himself, he might lend him his gun for a couple of shots. They made a date to meet in the mornin' and that's the last I seen of Jim alive.

Next mornin', I hadn't been open more than ten minutes when Doc Stair come in. He looked kind of nervous. He asked me had I seen Paul Dickson. I said no, but I knew where he was, out duck-shootin' with Jim Kendall. So Doc says that's what he had heard, and he couldn't understand it because Paul had told him he wouldn't never have no more to do with Jim as long as he lived.

He said Paul had told him about the joke Jim had played on Julie. He said Paul had asked him what he thought of the joke and the Doc had told him that anybody that would do a thing like that ought not to be let live.

I said it had been a kind of a raw thing, but Jim just couldn't resist no kind of a joke, no matter how raw. I said I thought he was all right at heart, but just bubblin' over with mischief. Doc turned and walked out.

At noon he got a phone call from old John Scott. The lake where Jim and Paul had went shootin' is on John's place. Paul had come runnin' up to the house a few minutes before and said they'd been an accident. Jim had shot a few ducks and then give the gun to Paul and told him to try his luck. Paul hadn't never handled a gun and he was nervous. He was shakin' so hard that he couldn't control the gun. He let fire and Jim sunk back in the boat, dead.

Doc Stair, bein' the coroner, jumped in Frank Abbott's flivver and rushed out to Scott's farm. Paul and old John was down on the shore of the lake. Paul had rowed the boat to shore, but they'd left the body in it, waitin' for Doc to come.

Doc examined the body and said they might as well fetch it back to town. They was no use leavin' it there or callin' a jury, as it was a plain case of accidental shootin'.

Personally I wouldn't never leave a person shoot a gun in the same boat I was in unless I was sure they knew somethin' about guns. Jim was a sucker to leave a new beginner have his gun, let alone a half-wit. It probably served Jim right, what he got. But still we miss him round here. He certainly was a card!

Comb it wet or dry?

BY WAY OF DISCUSSION

"Haircut" is an example of a short story told by an untrustworthy narrator. Authors employ this type of narrator to draw readers into the action of the story, to make them read actively, and to make them think about what they have read. The story is a long dramatic monologue, but the narrator, Whitey, is hardly the same type of servile character as Ellen, the narrator in "The Lady's Maid." One of the key points to understanding and evaluating "Haircut" is knowing just how clever or how simpleminded Whitey really is. Is he nothing more than a small-town barber who runs off at the mouth, unwittingly relating the tale of a deliberate murder that he himself does not realize was a murder? Does he know that the death of Jim Kendall was a deliberate murder and cleverly relate this intelligence to the customer-listener in the chair? Or, in fact, is Whitey the consummate untrustworthy narrator who enjoys occupying slow days in his shop by spinning incredible yarns at the expense of incredulous newcomers to the town?

Traditionally, Whitey has been judged a simple-minded character who tells the tale of a local murder without understanding the irony of his narrative. Some later interpretations have grudgingly allowed that Whitey is not so dumb after all, that he understands Paul deliberately murdered Kendall but doesn't want to come right out and say so. Our position is that both views give Whitey—and, indirectly, Lardner—too little credit. We believe that Whitey may be concocting a false yarn or a grisly tall tale, an action far more devious than just hinting that he knows the truth about Kendall's death. A devious untrustworthy narrator, as opposed to a simple-minded one, knows precisely what he is up to, and this fact often leaves the reader, as well as the narrative listener, at the narrator's mercy.

In evaluating the degree of Whitey's deviousness as a narrator, let's begin by looking at the circumstances surrounding the telling of the tale. First, Whitey is a small-town barber in his own shop, and barbershops have long been known as arenas for the spinning of tall tales. Indeed, one might well argue that the barbershop is the oldest theater-in-the-round in the land. As Whitey says of Kendall's regular seat in the shop: "You'd of thought it was a reserved seat like they have sometimes in a theayter." And the performances one can view in such a "theayter" often boggle the minds of all but the thoroughly initiated. Furthermore, the major player in the barbershop-theater is almost always the first barber himself—the owner or the man at the first chair. Whitey, then, may be viewed as an accomplished provincial thespian performing in his own playhouse. The customer-listener is a newcomer, a person out of his element and uninitiated. And the reader of the story is placed in a similar position.

Next, let's consider Whitey's motivation for delivering such a long and complex narrative. No one asks him to tell the story, and at no point in the narrative does the customer-listener encourage him to go on. At the outset we are told that no one is likely to come into the shop on such a slow day to interrupt, or perhaps give away, the tale. Whitey is performing alone. Notice that Jim Kendall and Hod Meyers, Jim's supposed confidant, are presented as having done their best work in the shop on Saturdays. But since Jim is gone, "Hod tries to hold his end up just the same as ever, but it's tough goin' when you ain't got nobody to kind of work with.'' By implication, then, Whitey may be saying that his own Saturday performances in the barbershop-theater are even better than the one he is about to do solo, made better by the rest of the cast—the barber from Carterville and the slate of local customers. The motivation for Whitey's telling his tale, at least a part of his motivation, may be simply to keep his art honed for those Saturdays when he has a full house.

If you take the time to consider the complexity of Whitey's tale, the way he weaves so many people and so many incidents together for a single dramatic impact, it becomes a little difficult to view him as a naïve or simple-minded narrator who is trying to recount an actual occurrence. And when you consider the similarities between Whitey himself and Kendall, it becomes even easier to believe that Kendall is actually Whitey's creation. Notice, for example, how Whitey sometimes uses the same words and phrases that he assigns to Kendall. Kendall calls Paul ''cuckoo'' and ''half-wit,'' something the barber also does a couple of times. Then, too, both appear to have a fondness for the word ''rabbit.'' Kendall, we are told, was very good at changing his voice to sound like someone else, and at one point while describing the men hooting at Julie, Whitey betrays some talent for mimicry himself. Perhaps most telling of all is the unwarranted fondness Whitey has for Kendall. Several times he refers to Kendall as a ''card.'' At other times he characterizes him as ''kind of rough, but a good fellow at heart'' and ''all right at heart, but just bubblin' over with mischief.'' Once Whitey even calls Kendall a ''character.'' Whitey's feeling for Kendall seems, in fact, much like the feeling an author might have for a singular character he or she has worked hard at creating.

But Whitey's art, as competent as it may be, is far from flawless. From time to time he slips up and tells us things that he could not, as a first-person narrator, really know. And at least once this results in a false note in what he says about one of his characters. When Paul went to Doc Stair with the story of Kendall's trick on Julie, Whitey says:

> It's a cinch Doc went up in the air and swore he'd make Jim suffer. But it was a kind of a delicate thing, because if it got out that he had beat Jim up, Julie was bound to hear of it and then she'd know that Doc knew and of course knowin' that he knew would make it worse for her than ever. He was goin' to do somethin', but it took a lot of figurin'.

Clearly, there would be no way for Whitey to know just what thoughts went through Doc Stair's mind and whether or not he planned to take any action. As for the doctor's swearing he would make Jim suffer, this seems completely at variance with his character as Whitey has presented it before. At this point, indeed, the doctor seems almost like another Jim Kendall, who, as Whitey has told us, made a practice of getting even with people who angered him.

Another possible slip occurs when Whitey retells the story of the hunting accident:

> At noon he [Doc Stair] got a phone call from old John Scott. The lake where Jim and Paul had went shootin' is on John's place. Paul had came runnin' up to the house a few minutes before and said they'd been an accident. Jim had shot a few ducks and then give the gun to Paul and told him to try his luck. Paul hadn't never handled a gun and he was nervous. He was shakin' so hard that he couldn't control the gun. He let fire and Jim sunk back in the boat, dead.
>
> Doc Stair, bein' the coroner, jumped in Frank Abbott's flivver and rushed out to Scott's farm.

There are several problems here. How would Whitey have known just what Kendall said to Paul and just how Doc Stair got to the scene of the shooting? For that matter, how can he know that Paul was "shakin' so hard that he couldn't control the gun"? The barber was not at the lakeside when Paul told his story, nor apparently was he around when the doctor was notified, and it seems unlikely that any of these stray bits of information would have figured in later accounts of the incident. Perhaps more importantly, it is hard to imagine the Jim Kendall described to us by Whitey allowing himself to be shot by a nervous simpleton who had never before fired a gun.

One final bit of weakness in Whitey's story lies in Doc Stair's peculiar behavior between the time Paul tells him of Kendall's joke on Julie and the time he learns that Paul and Jim have gone hunting. At first, according to Whitey, the doctor flies into a rage, swears to make Kendall suffer, and says he "ought not to be let live." Once the doctor has heard about the hunting trip, he suddenly becomes nervous, yet makes no effort to go after Paul, even though he clearly suspects something terrible may be about to happen. The lake, after all, is nearby. If the doctor really wants Kendall dead, why the nervousness? As coroner he could easily cover up for Paul—as he indeed does, again according to Whitey. If, on the other hand, the doctor didn't mean what he said, why didn't he head for the lake right away? Faulty characterization on Whitey's part seems a very plausible explanation for all this.

What we cannot know about Whitey's tale is the extent to which it is pure fiction. Do these people really exist? Is the tale based upon some incident that has occurred in the community? We simply don't know. Of course, there is the shaving mug with "James H. Kendall" emblazoned on its side. So there is little doubt that someone by that name is, or has been, in the town. However, we cannot take his mere existence as proof that Whitey's story is true. Perhaps it is, but perhaps Whitey is using the mug as a convenient stage prop to help convince the incredulous customer-listener of the truth of a made-up story. Whether the customer is indeed convinced we cannot tell. What we do know, though, is that over the years many readers have accepted the tale at face value, and volumes of criticism have been written about what a shameful character poor Jim Kendall was.

For our part, though, viewing Whitey as a clever, devious, and untrust-worthy narrator, we would like to have seen what he could have done with the other mug, the one with "Charles M. Vail" inscribed on it. But perhaps a mug isn't really necessary; perhaps Whitey could have worked with an old lock of hair just as well.

DANIEL KEYES

Flowers for Algernon

progris riport 1—martch 5, 1965

Dr. Strauss says I shud rite down what I think and evrey thing that happins to me from now on. I dont know why but he says its importint so they will see if they will use me. I hope they use me. Miss Kinnian says maybe they can make me smart. I want to be smart. My name is Charlie Gordon. I am 37 years old and 2 weeks ago was my birthday. I have nuthing more to rite now so I will close for today.

progris riport 2—martch 6

I had a test today. I think I faled it. and I think that maybe now they wont use me. What happind is a nice young man was in the room and he had some white cards with ink spillled all over them. He sed Charlie what do you see on this card. I was very skared even tho I had my rabits foot in my pockit because when I was a kid I always faled tests in school and I spillled ink to.

I told him I saw a inkblot. He said yes and it made me feel good. I thot that was all but when I got up to go he stopped me. He said now sit down Charlie we are not thru yet. Then I don't remember so good but he wantid me to say what was in the ink. I dint see nuthing in the ink but he said there was picturs there other pepul saw some picturs. I couldn't see any picturs. I reely tryed to see. I held the card close up and then far away. Then I said if I had my glases I coud see better I usally only ware my glases in the movies or TV but I said they are in the closit in the hall. I got them. Then I said let me see that card agen I bet Ill find it now.

I tryed hard but I still coudnt find the pictures I only saw the ink. I told him maybe I need new glases. He rote somthing down on a paper and I got skared of faling the test. I told him it was a very nice inkblot with little points all around the edges. He looked very sad so that wasnt it. I said please let me try agen. Ill get it in a few minits becaus Im not so fast somtimes. Im a slow reeder too in Miss Kinnians class for slow adults but Im trying very hard.

He gave me a chance with another card that had 2 kinds of ink spillled on it red and blue.

He was very nice and talked slow like Miss Kinnian does and he explaned it to me that it was a *raw shok*. He said pepul see things in the ink. I said show me where. He said think. I told him I think a inkblot but that wasnt rite eather. He said what does it remind you—pretend something. I closd my eyes for a long time to pretend. I told him I pretned a fowntan pen with ink leeking all over a table cloth. Then he got up and went out.

I dont think I passd the *raw shok* test.

progris report 3—martch 7

Dr Strauss and Dr Nemur say it dont matter about the inkblots. I told them I dint spill the ink on the cards and I coudnt see anything in the ink. They said that maybe they will still use me. I said Miss Kinnian never gave me tests like that one only spelling and reading. They said Miss Kinnian told that I was her bestist pupil in the adult nite scool becaus I tryed the hardist and I reely wantid to lern. They said how come you went to the adult nite scool all by yourself Charlie. How did you find it. I said I askd pepul and sumbody told me where I shud go to lern to read and spell good. They said why did you want to. I told them becaus all my life I wantid to be smart and not dumb. But its very hard to be smart. They said you know it will probly be tempirery. I said yes. Miss Kinnian told me. I dont care if it herts.

Later I had more crazy tests today. The nice lady who gave it me told me the name and I asked her how do you spellit so I can rite it in my progris riport. THEMATIC APPERCEPTION TEST. I dont know the frist 2 words but I know what *test* means. You got to pass it or you get bad marks. This test lookd easy becaus I coud see the picturs. Only this time she dint want me to tell her the picturs. That mixd me up. I said the man yesterday said I shoud tell him what I saw in the ink she said that dont make no difrence. She said make up storys about the pepul in the picturs.

I told her how can you tell storys about pepul you never met. I said why shud I make up lies. I never tell lies any more becaus I always get caut.

She told me this test and the other one the raw-shok was for getting personalty. I laffed so hard. I said how can you get that thing from inkblots and fotos. She got sore and put her picturs away. I dont care. It was sily. I gess I faled that test too.

Later some men in white coats took me to a difernt part of the hospitil and gave me a game to play. It was like a race with a white mouse. They called the mouse Algernon. Algernon was in a box with a lot of twists and turns like all kinds of walls and they gave me a pencil and a paper with lines and lots of boxes. On one side it said START and on the other end it said FINISH. They said it was *amazed* and that Algernon and me had the same *amazed* to do. I dint see how we could have the same *amazed* if Algernon had a box and I had a paper but I dint say nothing. Anyway there wasnt time because the race started.

One of the men had a watch he was trying to hide so I woudnt see it so I tryed not to look and that made me nervus.

Anyway that test made me feel worser than all the others because they did it over 10 times with difernt *amazeds* and Algernon won every time. I dint know that mice were so smart. Maybe thats because Algernon is a white mouse. Maybe white mice are smarter than other mice.

progris riport 4—Mar 8

Their going to use me! Im so exited I can hardly write. Dr Nemur and Dr Strauss had a 'argament about it first. Dr Nemur was in the office when Dr Strauss brot me in. Dr Nemur was worryed about using me but Dr Strauss told him Miss Kinnian rekemmended me the best from all the people who was teaching. I like Miss Kinnian becaus shes a very smart teacher. And she said Charlie your going to have a second chance. If you volenteer for this experament you mite get smart. They dont know if it will be perminint but theirs a chance. Thats why I said ok even when I was scared because she said it was an operashun. She said dont be scared Charlie you done so much with so little I think you deserv it most of all.

So I got scaird when Dr Nemur and Dr Strauss argud about it. Dr Strauss said I had something that was very good. He said I had a good *motor-vation*. I never even knew I had that. I felt proud when he said that not every body with an eye-q of 68 had that thing. I dont know what it is or where I got it but he said Algernon had it too. Algernons *motor-vation* is the cheese they put in his box. But it cant be that because I didnt eat any cheese this week.

Then he told Dr Nemur something I dint understand so while they were talking I wrote down some of the words.

He said Dr Nemur I know Charlie is not what you had in mind as the first of your new brede of intelek**(coudnt get the word) superman. But most people of his low ment** are host** and uncoop** they are usualy dull apath** and hard to reach. He has a good natcher hes intristed and eager to please.

Dr Nemur said remember he will be the first human beeng ever to have his intelijence trippled by surgicle meens.

Dr Strauss said exakly. Look at how well hes lerned to read and write for his low mentel age its as grate an acheve** as you and I lerning einstines therey of **vity without help. That shows the intenss motor-vation. Its comparat** a tremen** achev** I say we use Charlie.

I dint get all the words and they were talking to fast but it sounded like Dr Strauss was on my side and like the other one wasnt.

Then Dr Nemur nodded he said all right maybe your right. We will use Charlie. When he said that I got so exited I jumped up and shook his hand for being so good to me. I told him thank you doc you wont be sorry for giving me a second chance. And I mean it like I told him. After the operashun Im gonna try to be smart. Im gonna try awful hard.

progris ript 5—Mar 10

Im skared. Lots of people who work here and the nurses and the people who gave me the tests came to bring me candy and wish me luck. I hope I have luck. I got my rabits foot and my lucky penny and my horse shoe. Only a black cat crossed me when I was comming to the hospitil. Dr Strauss says dont be supersitis Charlie this is sience. Anyway Im keeping my rabits foot with me.

I asked Dr Strauss if Ill beat Algernon in the race after the operashun and he said maybe. If the operashun works Ill show that mouse I can be as smart as he is. Maybe smarter. Then Ill be abel to read better and spell the words good and know lots of things and be like other people. I want to be smart like other people. If it works perminint they will make everybody smart all over the wurld.

They dint give me anything to eat this morning. I dont know what that eating has to do with getting smart. Im very hungry and Dr Nemur took away my box of candy. That Dr Nemur is a grouch. Dr Strauss says I can have it back after the operashun. You cant eat befor a operashun . . .

Progress Report 6—Mar 15

The operashun dint hurt. He did it while I was sleeping. They took off the bandijis from my eyes and my head today so I can make a PROGRESS REPORT. Dr Nemur who looked at some of my other ones sayd I spell PROGRESS wrong and he told me how to spell it and REPORT too. I got to try and remember that.

I have a very bad memary for spelling. Dr Strauss says its ok to tell about all the things that happin to me but he says I shoud tell more about what I feel and what I think. When I told him I dont know how to think he said try. All the time when the bandijis were on my eyes I tryed to think. Nothing happened. I dont know what to think about. Maybe if I ask him he will tell me how I can think now that Im suppose to get smart. What do smart people think about. Fancy things I suppose. I wish I knew some fancy things alredy.

Progress Report 7—mar 19

Nothing is happining. I had lots of tests and different kinds of races with Algernon. I hate that mouse. He always beats me. Dr Strauss said I got to play those games. And he said some time I got to take those tests over again. Thse inkblots are stupid. And those pictures are stupid too. I like to draw a picture of a man and a woman but I wont make up lies about people.

I got a headache from trying to think so much. I thot Dr Strauss was my frend but he dont help me. He dont tell me what to think or when Ill get smart. Miss Kinnian dint come to see me. I think writing these progress reports are stupid too.

Progress Report 8—Mar 23

Im going back to work at the factery. They said it was better I shud go back to work but I cant tell anyone what the operashun was for and I have to come to the hospitil for an hour evry night after work. They are gonna pay me mony every month for lerning to be smart.

Im glad Im going back to work because I miss my job and all my frends and all the fun we have there.

Dr Strauss says I shud keep writing things down but I dont have to do it every day just when I think of something or something speshul happins. He says dont get discoridged because it takes time and it happins slow. He says it took a long time with Algernon before he got 3 times smarter then he was before. Thats why Algernon beats me all the time because he had that operashun too. That makes me feel better. I coud probly do that *amazed* faster than a reglar mouse. Maybe some day Ill beat Algernon. Boy that would be something. So far Algernon looks like he mite be smart perminent.

Mar 25 (I dont have to write PROGRESS REPORT on top any more just when I hand it in once a week for Dr Nemur to read. I just have to put the date on. That saves time.)

We had a lot of fun at the factery today. Joe Carp said hey look where Charlie had his operashun what did they do Charlie put some brains in. I was going to tell him but I remembered Dr Strauss said no. Then Frank Reilly said what did you do Charlie forget your key and open your door the hard way. That made me laff. Their really my friends and they like me.

Sometimes somebody will say hey look at Joe or Frank or George he really pulled a Charlie Gordon. I dont know why they say that but they always laff. This morning Amos Borg who is the 4 man at Donnegans used my name when he shouted at Ernie the office boy. Ernie lost a packige. He said Ernie for godsake what are you trying to be a Charlie Gordon. I dont understand why he said that. I never lost any packiges.

Mar 28 Dr Strauss came to my room tonight to see why I dint come in like I was suppose to. I told him I dont like to race with Algernon any more. He said I dont have to for a while but I shud come in. He had a present for me only it wasnt a present but just for lend. I thot it was a little television but it wasnt. He said I got to turn it on when I go to sleep. I said your kidding why shud I turn it on when Im going to sleep. Who ever herd of a thing like that. But he said if I want to get smart I got to do what he says. I told him I dont think I was going to get smart and he put his hand on my sholder and said Charlie you dont know it yet but your getting smarter all the time. You wont notice for a while. I think he was just being nice to make me feel good because I dont look any smarter.

Oh yes I almost forgot. I asked him when I can go back to the class at Miss Kinnians school. He said I wont go their. He said that soon Miss Kinnian will come to the hospitil to start and teach me speshul. I was mad at her for not comming to see me when I got the operashun but I like her so maybe we will be frends again.

Mar 29 That crazy TV kept me up all night. How can I sleep with something yelling crazy things all night in my ears. And the nutty pictures. Wow. I dont know what it says when Im up so how am I going to know when Im sleeping.

Dr Strauss says its ok. He says my brains are lerning when I sleep and that will help me when Miss Kinnian starts my lessons in the hospitl (only I found out it isnt a hospitil its a labatory). I think its all crazy. If you can get smart when your sleeping why do people go to school. That thing I dont think will work. I use to watch the late show and the late late show on TV all the time and it never made me smart. Maybe you have to sleep while you watch it.

PROGRESS REPORT 9—*April 3*

Dr Strauss showed me how to keep the TV turned low so now I can sleep. I dont hear a thing. And I still dont understand what it says. A few times I play it over in the morning to find out what I lerned when I was sleeping and I dont think so. Miss Kinnian says Maybe its another langwidge or something. But most times it sounds american. It talks so fast faster then even Miss Gold who was my teacher in 6 grade and I remember she talked so fast I coudnt understand her.

I told Dr Strauss what good is it to get smart in my sleep. I want to be smart when Im awake. He says its the same thing and I have two minds. Theres the *subconscious* and the *conscious* (that's how you spell it). And one dont tell the other one what its doing. They dont even talk to each other. Thats why I dream. And boy have I been having crazy dreams. Wow. Ever since that night TV. The late late late late late show.

I forgot to ask him if it was only me or if everybody had those two minds.

(I just looked up the word in the dictionary Dr Strauss gave me. The word is *subconscious. adj. Of the nature of mental operations yet not present in consciousness; as, subconscious conflict of desires.*) Theres more but I still don't know what it means. This isnt a very good dictionary for dumb people like me.

Anyway the headache is from the party. My frends from the factery Joe Carp and Frank Reilly invited me to go with them to Muggsys Saloon for some drinks. I dont like to drink but they said we will have lots of fun. I had a good time.

Joe Carp said I shoud show the girls how I mop out the toilet in the factery and he got me a mop. I showed them and everyone laffed when I told that Mr Donnegan said I was the best janiter he ever had because I like my job and do it good and never come late or miss a day except for my operashun.

I said Miss Kinnian always said Charlie be proud of your job because you do it good.

Everybody laffed and we had a good time and they gave me lots of drinks and Joe said Charlie is a card when hes potted. I dont know what that means but everybody likes me and we have fun. I cant wait to be smart like my best frends Joe Carp and Frank Reilly.

I dont remember how the party was over but I think I went out to buy a newspaper and coffe for Joe and Frank and when I came back there was no one their. I looked for them all over till late. Then I dont remember so good but I think I got sleepy or sick. A nice cop brot me back home. Thats what my landlady Mrs Flynn says.

But I got a headache and a big lump on my head and black and blue all over. I think maybe I fell but Joe Carp says it was the cop they beat up drunks some times. I don't think so. Miss Kinnian says cops are to help people. Anyway I got a bad headache and Im sick and hurt all over. I dont think Ill drink anymore.

April 6 I beat Algernon! I dint even know I beat him until Burt the tester told me. Then the second time I lost because I got so exited I fell off the chair before I finished. But after that I beat him 8 more times. I must be getting smart to beat a smart mouse like Algernon. But I dont *feel* smarter.

I wanted to race Algernon some more but Burt said thats enough for one day. They let me hold him for a minit. Hes not so bad. Hes soft like a ball of cotton. He blinks and when he opens his eyes their black and pink on the eges.

I said can I feed him because I felt bad to beat him and I wanted to be nice and make frends. Burt said no Algernon is a very specshul mouse with an operashun like mine, and he was the first of all the animals to stay smart so long. He told me Algernon is so smart that every day he has to solve a test to get his food. Its a thing like a lock on a door that changes every time Algernon goes in to eat so he has to lern something new to get his food. That made me sad because if he coudnt lern he would be hungry.

I dont think its right to make you pass a test to eat. How woud Dr Nemur like it to have to pass a test every time he wants to eat. I think Ill be frends with Algernon.

April 9 Tonight after work Miss Kinnian was at the laboratory. She looked like she was glad to see me but scared. I told her dont worry Miss Kinnian Im not smart yet and she laffed. She said I have confidence in you Charlie the way you struggled so hard to read and right better than all the others. At werst you will have it for a littel wile and your doing somthing for sience.

We are reading a very hard book. I never read such a hard book before. Its called *Robinson Crusoe* about a man who gets merooned on a dessert Iland. Hes smart and figers out all kinds of things so he can have a house and food and hes a good swimmer. Only I feel sorry because hes all alone and has no frends. But I think their must be somebody else on the iland because theres a picture with his funny umbrella looking at footprints. I hope he gets a frend and not be lonly.

April 10 Miss Kinnian teaches me to spell better. She says look at a word and close your eyes and say it over and over until you remember. I have lots of truble with *through* that you say *threw* and *enough* and *tough* that you dont say *new* and *tew*. You got to say *enuff* and *tuff*. Thats how I use to write it before I started to get smart. Im confused but Miss Kinnian says theres no reason in spelling.

Apr 14 Finished *Robinson Crusoe*. I want to find out more about what happens to him but Miss Kinnian says thats all there is. *Why*

April 15 Miss Kinnian says Im lerning fast. She read some of the Progress Reports and she looked at me kind of funny. She says Im a fine person and Ill show them all. I asked her why. She said never mind but I shoudnt feel bad if I find out that everybody isnt nice like I think. She said for a person who god gave so little to you done more then a lot of people with brains they never even used. I said all my frends are smart people but there good. They like me and they never did anything that wasnt nice. Then she got something in her eye and she had to run out to the ladys room.

Apr 16 Today, I lerned, the *comma,* this is a comma (,) a period, with a tail, Miss Kinnian, says its importent, because, it makes writing, better, she said, some-body, coud lose, a lot of money, if a comma, isnt, in the, right place, I dont have, any money, and I dont see, how a comma, keeps you, from losing it,
    But she says, everybody, uses commas, so Ill use, them too,

Apr 17 I used the comma wrong. Its punctuation. Miss Kinnian told me to look up long words in the dictionary to lern to spell them. I said whats the differ-ence if you can read it anyway. She said its part of your education so now on Ill look up all the words Im not sure how to spell. It takes a long time to write that way but I think Im remembering. I only have to look up once and after that I get it right. Anyway thats how come I got the word *punctuation* right. (Its that way in the dictionary). Miss Kinnian says a period is punctuation too, and there are lots of other marks to lern. I told her I thot all the periods had to have tails but she said no.
    You got to mix them up, she showed? me" how. to mix! them (up,. and now; I can! mix up all kinds" of punctuation, in! my writing? There, are lots! of rules? to lern; but I'm gettin'g them in my head.
    One thing I? like about, Dear Miss Kinnian: (thats the way it goes in a business letter if I ever go into business) is she, always gives me' a reason" when—I ask. She's a gen'ius! I wish! I cou'd be smart" like, her;
    (Punctuation, is; fun!)

April 18 What a dope I am! I didn't even understand what she was talking about. I read the grammar book last night and it explanes the whole thing. Then I saw it was the same way as Miss Kinnian was trying to tell me, but I didn't get it. I got up in the middle of the night, and the whole thing straightened out in my mind.

Miss Kinnian said that the TV working in my sleep helped out. She said I reached a plateau. Thats like the flat top of a hill.

After I figgered out how punctuation worked, I read over all my old Progress Reports from the beginning. Boy, did I have crazy spelling and punctuation! I told Miss Kinnian I ought to go over the pages and fix all the mistakes but she said, "No, Charlie, Dr. Nemur wants them just as they are. That's why he let you keep them after they were photostated, to see your own progress. You're coming along fast, Charlie."

That made me feel good. After the lesson I went down and played with Algernon. We don't race any more.

April 20 I feel sick inside. Not sick like for a doctor, but inside my chest it feels empty like getting punched and a heartburn at the same time.

I wasn't going to write about it, but I guess I got to, because it's important. Today was the first time I ever stayed home from work.

Last night Joe Carp and Frank Reilly invited me to a party. There were lots of girls and some men from the factory. I remembered how sick I got last time I drank too much, so I told Joe I didn't want anything to drink. He gave me a plain Coke instead. It tasted funny, but I thought it was just a bad taste in my mouth.

We had a lot of fun for a while. Joe said I should dance with Ellen and she would teach me the steps. I fell a few times and I couldn't understand why because no one else was dancing besides Ellen and me. And all the time I was tripping because somebody's foot was always sticking out.

Then when I got up I saw the look on Joe's face and it gave me a funny feeling in my stomack. "He's a scream," one of the girls said. Everybody was laughing.

Frank said, "I ain't laughed so much since we sent him off for the newspaper that night at Muggsy's and ditched him."

"Look at him. His face is red."

"He's blushing. Charlie is blushing."

"Hey, Ellen, what'd you do to Charlie? I never saw him act like that before."

I didn't know what to do or where to turn. Everyone was looking at me and laughing and I felt naked. I wanted to hide myself. I ran out into the street and I threw up. Then I walked home. It's a funny thing I never knew that Joe and Frank and the others liked to have me around all the time to make fun of me.

Now I know what it means when they say "to pull a Charlie Gordon." I'm ashamed.

PROGRESS REPORT 11

April 21 Still didn't go into the factory. I told Mrs. Flynn my landlady to call and tell Mr. Donnegan I was sick. Mrs. Flynn looks at me very funny lately like she's scared of me.

I think it's a good thing about finding out how everybody laughs at me. I thought about it a lot. It's because I'm so dumb and I don't even know when I'm doing something dumb. People think it's funny when a dumb person can't do things the same way they can.

Anyway, now I know I'm getting smarter every day. I know punctuation and I can spell good. I like to look up all the hard words in the dictionary and I remember them. I'm reading a lot now, and Miss Kinnian says I read very fast. Sometimes I even understand what I'm reading about, and it stays in my mind. There are times when I can close my eyes and think of a page and it all comes back like a picture.

Besides history, geography, and arithmetic, Miss Kinnian said I should start to learn a few foreign languages. Dr. Strauss gave me some more tapes to play while I sleep. I still don't understand how that conscious and unconscious mind works, but Dr. Strauss says not to worry yet. He asked me to promise that when I start learning college subjects next week I wouldn't read any books on psychology—that is, until he gives me permission.

I feel a lot better today, but I guess I'm still a little angry that all the time people were laughing and making fun of me because I wasn't so smart. When I become intelligent like Dr. Strauss says, with three times my I.Q. of 68, then maybe I'll be like everyone else and people will like me and be friendly.

I'm not sure what an I.Q. is. Dr. Nemur said it was something that measured how intelligent you were—like a scale in the drugstore weighs pounds. But Dr. Strauss had a big argument with him and said an I.Q. didn't weigh intelligence at all. He said an I.Q. showed how much intelligence you could get, like the numbers on the outside of a measuring cup. You still had to fill the cup up with stuff.

Then when I asked Burt, who gives me my intelligence tests and works with Algernon, he said that both of them were wrong (only I had to promise not to tell them he said so). Burt says that the I.Q. measures a lot of different things including some of the things you learned already, and it really isn't any good at all.

So I still don't know what I.Q. is except that mine is going to be over 200 soon. I didn't want to say anything, but I don't see how if they don't know *what* it is, or *where* it is—I don't see how they know *how much* of it you've got.

Dr. Nemur says I have to take a *Rorshach Test* tomorrow. I wonder what *that* is.

April 22 I found out what a *Rorschach* is. It's the test I took before the operation—the one with the inkblots on the pieces of cardboard. The man who gave me the test was the same one.

I was scared to death of those inkblots. I knew he was going to ask me to find the pictures and I knew I wouldn't be able to. I was thinking to myself, if only there was some way of knowing what kind of pictures were hidden there. Maybe there weren't any pictures at all. Maybe it was just a trick to see if I was dumb enough to look for something that wasn't there. Just thinking about that made me sore at him.

"All right, Charlie," he said, "you've seen these cards before, remember?"
"Of course I remember."

The way I said it, he knew I was angry, and he looked surprised. "Yes, of course. Now I want you to look at this one. What might this be? What do you see on this card? People see all sorts of things in these inkblots. Tell me what it might be for you—what it makes you think of."

I was shocked. That wasn't what I had expected him to say at all. "You mean there are no pictures hidden in those inkblots?"

He frowned and took off his glasses. "What?"

"Pictures. Hidden in the inkblots. Last time you told me that everyone could see them and you wanted me to find them too."

He explained to me that the last time he had used almost the exact same words he was using now. I didn't believe it, and I still have the suspicion that he misled me at the time just for the fun of it. Unless—I don't know any more—could I have been *that* feeble-minded?

We went through the cards slowly. One of them looked like a pair of bats tugging at something. Another one looked like two men fencing with swords. I imagined all sorts of things. I guess I got carried away. But I didn't trust him any more, and I kept turning them around and even looking on the back to see if there was anything there I was supposed to catch. While he was making his notes, I peeked out of the corner of my eye to read it. But it was all in code that looked like this:

WF + A DdF − Ad orig. WF − A SF + obj

The test still doesn't make sense to me. It seems to me that anyone could make up lies about things that they didn't really see. How could he know I wasn't making a fool of him by mentioning things that I didn't really imagine? Maybe I'll understand it when Dr. Strauss lets me read up on psychology.

April 25 I figured out a new way to line up the machines in the factory, and Mr. Donnegan says it will save him ten thousand dollars a year in labor and increased production. He gave me a twenty-five-dollar bonus.

I wanted to take Joe Carp and Frank Reilly out to lunch to celebrate, but Joe said he had to buy some things for his wife, and Frank said he was meeting his cousin for lunch. I guess it'll take a little time for them to get used to the changes in me. Everybody seems to be frightened of me. When I went over to Amos Borg and tapped him on the shoulder, he jumped up in the air.

People don't talk to me much any more or kid around the way they used to. It makes the job kind of lonely.

April 27 I got up the nerve today to ask Miss Kinnian to have dinner with me tomorrow night to celebrate my bonus.

At first she wasn't sure it was right, but I asked Dr. Strauss and he said it was okay. Dr. Strauss and Dr. Nemur don't seem to be getting along so well. They're arguing all the time. This evening when I came in to ask Dr. Strauss about having dinner with Miss Kinnian, I heard him shouting. Dr. Nemur was saying that it was *his* experiment and *his* research, and Dr. Strauss was shouting back that he contributed just as much, because he found me through Miss Kinnian and he performed the operation. Dr. Strauss said that someday thousands of neurosurgeons might be using his technique all over the world.

Dr. Nemur wanted to publish the results of the experiment at the end of this month. Dr. Strauss wanted to wait a while longer to be sure. Dr. Strauss said that Dr. Nemur was more interested in the Chair of Psychology at Princeton than he was in the experiment. Dr. Nemur said that Dr. Strauss was nothing but an opportunist who was trying to ride to glory on *his* coattails.

When I left afterwards, I found myself trembling. I don't know why for sure, but it was as if I'd seen both men clearly for the first time. I remember hearing Burt say that Dr. Nemur had a shrew of a wife who was pushing him all the time to get things published so that he could become famous. Burt said that the dream of her life was to have a bigshot husband.

Was Dr. Strauss really trying to ride on his coattails?

April 28 I don't understand why I never noticed how beautiful Miss Kinnian really is. She has brown eyes and feathery brown hair that comes to the top of her neck. She's only thirty-four! I think from the beginning I had the feeling that she was an unreachable genius—and very, very old. Now, every time I see her she grows younger and more lovely.

We had dinner and a long talk. When she said that I was coming along so fast that soon I'd be leaving her behind, I laughed.

"It's true, Charlie. You're already a better reader than I am. You can read a whole page at a glance while I can take in only a few lines at a time. And you remember every single thing you read. I'm lucky if I can recall the main thoughts and the general meaning."

"I don't feel intelligent. There are so many things I don't understand."

She took out a cigarette and I lit it for her. "You've got to be a *little* patient. You're accomplishing in days and weeks what it takes normal people to do in half a lifetime. That's what makes it so amazing. You're like a giant sponge now, soaking things in. Facts, figures, general knowledge. And soon you'll begin to connect them, too. You'll see how the different branches of learning are related. There are many levels, Charlie, like steps on a giant ladder that take you up higher and higher to see more and more of the world around you.

"I can see only a little bit of that, Charlie, and I won't go much higher than I am now, but you'll keep climbing up and up, and see more and more, and each step will open new worlds that you never even knew existed." She frowned. "I hope . . . I just hope to God—"

"What?"

"Never mind, Charles. I just hope I wasn't wrong to advise you to go into this in the first place."

I laughed. "How could that be? It worked, didn't it? Even Algernon is still smart."

We sat there silently for a while and I knew what she was thinking about as

The room grew silent. I cursed myself for losing control and creating a scene. I tried not to look at the boy as I paid my check and walked out without touching my food. I felt ashamed for both of us.

How strange it is that people of honest feelings and sensibility, who would not take advantage of a man born without arms or legs or eyes—how such people think nothing of abusing a man born with low intelligence. It infuriated me to think that not too long ago I, like this boy, had foolishly played the clown.

And I had almost forgotten.

I'd hidden the picture of the old Charlie Gordon from myself because now that I was intelligent it was something that had to be pushed out of my mind. But today in looking at that boy, for the first time I saw what I had been. I was just like him!

Only a short time ago, I learned that people laughed at me. Now I can see that unknowingly I joined with them in laughing at myself. That hurts most of

have often reread my progress reports and seen the illiteracy, the childish naiveté, the mind of low intelligence peering from a dark room, through the hole, at the dazzling light outside. I see that even in my dullness I knew I was inferior, and that other people had something I lacked—something denied me. In my mental blindness, I thought that it was somehow connected with the ability to read and write, and I was sure that if I could get those skills I would automatically have intelligence too.

Even a feeble-minded man wants to be like other men.

A child may not know how to feed itself, or what to eat, yet it knows of hunger.

This then is what I was like, I never knew. Even with my gift of intellectual awareness, I never really knew.

This day was good for me. Seeing the past more clearly, I have decided to use my knowledge and skills to work in the field of increasing human intelligence levels. Who is better equipped for this work? Who else has lived in both worlds? These are my people. Let me use my gift to do something for them. Tomorrow, I will discuss with Dr. Strauss the manner in which I can work in this area. I may be able to help him work out the problems of widespread use of the technique which was used on me. I have several good ideas of my own.

There is so much that might be done with this technique. If I could be made into a genius, what about thousands of others like myself? What fantastic things might be achieved by using this technique on normal people? On geniuses?

There are so many doors to open. I am impatient to begin.

PROGRESS REPORT 13

happened today. Algernon bit me. I visited the lab to see him as I do occasionally, and when I took him out of his cage, he snapped at my hand. I

she watched me toying with the chain of my rabbit's foot and my keys. I didn't want to think of that possibility any more than elderly people want to think of death. I *knew* that this was only the beginning. I knew what she meant about levels because I'd seen some of them already. The thought of leaving her behind made me sad.

I'm in love with Miss Kinnian.

PROGRESS REPORT 12

April 30 I've quit my job with Donnegan's Plastic Box Company. Mr. Donnegan insisted that it would be better for all concerned if I left. What did I do to make them hate me so?

The first I knew of it was when Mr. Donnegan showed me the petition. Eight hundred and forty names, everyone connected with the factory, except Fanny Girden. Scanning the list quickly, I saw at once that hers was the only missing name. All the rest demanded that I be fired.

Joe Carp and Frank Reilly wouldn't talk to me about it. No one else would either, except Fanny. She was one of the few people I'd known who set her mind to something and believed it no matter what the rest of the world proved, said, or did—and Fanny did not believe that I should have been fired. She had been against the petition on principle and despite the pressure and threats she'd held out.

"Which don't mean to say," she remarked, "that I don't think there's something mighty strange about you, Charlie. Them changes. I don't know. You used to be a good, dependable, ordinary man—not too bright maybe, but honest. Who knows what you done to yourself to get so smart all of a sudden. Like everybody around here's been saying, Charlie, it's not right."

"But how can you say that, Fanny? What's wrong with a man becoming intelligent and wanting to acquire knowledge and understanding of the world around him?"

She stared down at her work and I turned to leave. Without looking at me, she said: "It was evil when Eve listened to the snake and ate from the tree of knowledge. It was evil when she saw that she was naked. If not for that none of us would ever have to grow old and sick, and die."

Once again now I have the feeling of shame burning inside me. This intelligence has driven a wedge between me and all the people I once knew and loved. Before, they laughed at me and despised me for my ignorance and dullness; now, they hate me for my knowledge and understanding. What in God's name do they want of me?

They've driven me out of the factory. Now I'm more alone than ever before . . .

May 15 Dr. Strauss is very angry at me for not having written any progress reports in two weeks. He's justified because the lab is now paying me a regular salary. I told him I was too busy thinking and reading. When I pointed out that writing was such a slow process that it made me impatient with my poor handwriting, he suggested that I learn to type. It's much easier to write now because I can type nearly seventy-five words a minute. Dr. Strauss continually reminds me of the need to speak and write simply so that people will be able to understand me.

I'll try to review all the things that happened to me during the last two weeks. Algernon and I were presented to the American Psychological Association sitting in convention with the World Psychological Association last Tuesday. We created quite a sensation. Dr. Nemur and Dr. Strauss were proud of us.

I suspect that Dr. Nemur, who is sixty—ten years older than Dr. Strauss—finds it necessary to see tangible results of his work. Undoubtedly the result of pressure by Mrs. Nemur.

Contrary to my earlier impressions of him I realize that Dr Nemur is not at all a genius. He has a very good mind, but it struggles under the spectre of self-doubt. He wants people to take him for a genius. Therefore, it is important for him to feel that his work is accepted by the world. I believe that Dr. Nemur was afraid of further delay because he worried that someone else might make a discovery along these lines and take the credit from him.

Dr. Strauss on the other hand might be called a genius, although I feel that his areas of knowledge are too limited. He was educated in the tradition of narrow specialization; the broader aspects of background were neglected far more than necessary—even for a neurosurgeon.

I was shocked to learn that the only ancient languages he could read were Latin, Greek, and Hebrew, and that he knows almost nothing of mathematics beyond the elementary levels of the calculus of variations. When he admitted this to me, I found myself almost annoyed. It was as if he'd hidden this part of himself in order to deceive me, pretending—as do many people I've discovered—to be what he is not. No one I've ever known is what he appears to be on the surface.

Dr. Nemur appears to be uncomfortable around me. Sometimes when I try to talk to him, he just looks at me strangely and turns away. I was angry at first when Dr. Strauss told me I was giving Dr. Nemur an inferiority complex. I thought he was mocking me and I'm oversensitive at being made fun of.

How was I to know that a highly respected psychoexperimentalist like Nemur was unacquainted with Hindustani and Chinese? It's absurd when you consider the work that is being done in India and China today in the very field of his study.

I asked Dr. Strauss how Nemur could refute Rahajamati's attack on his method and results if Nemur couldn't even read them in the first place. That strange look on Dr. Strauss' face can mean only one of two things. Either he doesn't want to tell Nemur what they're saying in India, or else—and this worries me—Dr. Strauss doesn't know either. I must be careful to speak and write clearly and simply so that people won't laugh.

May 18 I am very disturbed. I saw Miss Kinnian last night for the first time in

over a week. I tried to avoid all discussions of intellectual concep the conversation on a simple, everyday level, but she just stared and asked me what I meant about the mathematical varianc Dobermann's *Fifth Concerto*.

When I tried to explain she stopped me and laughed. I guess I suspect I'm approaching her on the wrong level. No matt discuss with her, I am unable to communicate. I must review tions on *Levels of Semantic Progression*. I find that I don't c people much any more. Thank God for books and music think about. I am alone in my apartment at Mrs. Flynn's b of the time and seldom speak to anyone.

May 20 I would not have noticed the new dishwasher, a b at the corner diner where I take my evening meals if not f broken dishes.

They crashed to the floor, shattering and sending bits the tables. The boy stood there, dazed and frightened, h in his hand. The whistles and catcalls from the custon there go the profits!" . . . "*Mazeltov!*" . . . and "well, h long . . ." which invariably seem to follow the breakin a public restaurant) all seemed to confuse him.

When the owner came to see what the excitem cowered as if he expected to be struck and threw up the blow.

"All right! All right, you dope," shouted the own Get the broom and sweep that mess up. A broom in the kitchen. Sweep up all the pieces."

The boy saw that he was not going to be puni sion disappeared and he smiled and hummed as I to sweep the floor. A few of the rowdier cust amusing themselves at his expense.

"Here, sonny, over here there's a nice piece

"C'mon, do it again . . ."

"He's not so dumb. It's easier to break 'em

As his vacant eyes moved across the crowd mirrored their smiles and finally broke int which he obviously did not understand.

I felt sick inside as I looked at his dull, va of a child, uncertain but eager to please. T he was mentally retarded.

And I had been laughing at him too.

Suddenly, I was furious at myself and I jumped up and shouted, "Shut up! Leav understand! He can't help what he is! Bu being!"

put him back and watched him for a while. He was unusually disturbed and vicious.

May 24 Burt, who is in charge of the experimental animals, tells me that Algernon is changing. He is less co-operative; he refuses to run the maze any more; general motivation has decreased. And he hasn't been eating. Everyone is upset about what this may mean.

May 25 They've been feeding Algernon, who now refuses to work the shifting-lock problem. Everyone identifies me with Algernon. In a way we're both the first of our kind. They're all pretending that Algernon's behavior is not necessarily significant for me. But it's hard to hide the fact that some of the other animals who were used in this experiment are showing strange behavior.

Dr. Strauss and Dr. Nemur have asked me not to come to the lab any more. I know what they're thinking but I can't accept it. I am going ahead with my plans to carry their research forward. With all due respect to both of these fine scientists, I am well aware of their limitations. If there is an answer, I'll have to find it out for myself. Suddenly, time has become very important to me.

May 29 I have been given a lab of my own and permission to go ahead with the research. I'm on to something. Working day and night. I've had a cot moved into the lab. Most of my writing time is spent on the notes which I keep in a separate folder, but from time to time I feel it necessary to put down my moods and my thoughts out of sheer habit.

I find the *calculus of intelligence* to be a fascinating study. Here is the place for the application of all the knowledge I have acquired. In a sense it's the problem I've been concerned with all my life.

May 31 Dr. Strauss thinks I'm working too hard. Dr. Nemur says I'm trying to cram a lifetime of research and thought into a few weeks. I know I should rest, but I'm driven on by something inside that won't let me stop. I've got to find the reason for the sharp regression in Algernon. I've got to know *if* and *when* it will happen to me.

June 4
LETTER TO DR. STRAUSS (*copy*)
Dear Dr. Strauss:

Under separate cover I am sending you a copy of my report entitled, "The Algernon-Gordon Effect: A Study of Structure and Function of Increased Intelligence," which I would like to have you read and have published.

As you see, my experiments are completed. I have included in my report all of my formulae, as well as mathematical analysis in the appendix. Of course, these should be verified.

Because of its importance to both you and Dr. Nemur (and need I say to myself, too?) I have checked and rechecked my results a dozen times in the hope of finding an error. I am sorry to say the results must stand. Yet for the sake of science, I am grateful for the little bit that I here add to the knowledge of the function of the human mind and of the laws governing the artificial increase of human intelligence.

I recall your once saying to me that an experimental *failure* or the *disproving* of a theory was as important to the advancement of learning as a success would be. I know now that this is true. I am sorry, however, that my own contribution to the field must rest upon the ashes of the work of two men I regard so highly.

Yours truly,
Charles Gordon

encl.: rept.

June 5 I must not become emotional. The facts and the results of my experiments are clear, and the more sensational aspects of my own rapid climb cannot obscure the fact that the tripling of intelligence by the surgical technique developed by Drs. Strauss and Nemur must be viewed as having little or no practical applicability (at the present time) to the increase of human intelligence.

As I review the records and data on Algernon, I see that although he is still in his physical infancy, he has regressed mentally. Motor activity is impaired; there is a general reduction of glandular activity; there is an accelerated loss of co-ordination.

There are also strong indications of progressive amnesia.

As will be seen by my report, these and other physical and mental deterioration syndromes can be predicted with statistically significant results by the application of my formula.

The surgical stimulus to which we were both subjected has resulted in an intensification and acceleration of all mental processes. The unforeseen development, which I have taken the liberty of calling the *Algernon-Gordon Effect,* is the logical extention of the entire intelligence speed-up. The hypothesis here proven may be described simply in the following terms: Artificially increased intelligence deteriorates at a rate of time directly proportional to the quantity of the increase.

I feel that this, in itself, is an important discovery.

As long as I am able to write, I will continue to record my thoughts in these progress reports. It is one of my few pleasures. However, by all indications, my own mental deterioration will be very rapid.

I have already begun to notice signs of emotional instability and forgetfulness, the first symptoms of the burnout.

June 10 Deterioration progressing. I have become absentminded. Algernon died two days ago. Dissection shows my predictions were right. His brain had decreased in weight and there was a general smoothing out of cerebral convolutions as well as a deepening and broadening of brain fissures.

I guess the same thing is or will soon be happening to me. Now that it's definite, I don't want it to happen.

I put Algernon's body in a cheese box and buried him in the back yard. I cried.

June 15 Dr. Strauss came to see me again. I wouldn't open the door and I told him to go away. I want to be left to myself. I have become touchy and irritable. I feel the darkness closing in. It's hard to throw off thoughts of suicide. I keep telling myself how important this introspective journal will be.

It's a strange sensation to pick up a book that you've read and enjoyed just a few months ago and discover that you don't remember it. I remembered how great I thought John Milton was, but when I picked up *Paradise Lost* I couldn't understand it at all. I got so angry I threw the book across the room.

I've got to try to hold on to some of it. Some of the things I've learned. Oh, God, please don't take it all away.

June 19 Sometimes, at night, I go out for a walk. Last night I couldn't remember where I lived. A policeman took me home. I have the strange feeling that this has all happened to me before—a long time ago. I keep telling myself I'm the only person in the world who can describe what's happening to me.

June 21 Why can't I remember? I've got to fight. I lie in bed for days and I don't know who or where I am. Then it all comes back to me in a flash. Fugues of amnesia. Symptoms of senility—second childhood. I can watch them coming on. It's so cruelly logical. I learned so much and so fast. Now my mind is deteriorating rapidly. I won't let it happen. I'll fight it. I can't help thinking of the boy in the restaurant, the blank expression, the silly smile, the people laughing at him. No—please—not that again . . .

June 22 I'm forgetting things that I learned recently. It seems to be following the classic pattern—the last things learned are the first things forgotten. Or is that the pattern? I'd better look it up again. . . .

I reread my paper on the *Algernon-Gordon Effect* and I get the strange feeling that it was written by someone else. There are parts I don't even understand.

Motor activity impaired. I keep tripping over things, and it becomes increasingly difficult to type.

June 23 I've given up using the typewriter completely. My co-ordination is bad. I feel that I'm moving slower and slower. Had a terrible shock today. I picked up a copy of an article I used in my research, Krueger's *Uber psychische Ganzheit*, to see if it would help me understand what I had done. First I thought there was something wrong with my eyes. Then I realized I could no longer read German. I tested myself in other languages. All gone.

June 30 A week since I dared to write again. It's slipping away like sand through my fingers. Most of the books I have are too hard for me now. I get angry with them because I know that I read and understood them just a few weeks ago.

I keep telling myself I must keep writing these reports so that somebody will know what is happening to me. But it gets harder to form the words and remember spellings. I have to look up even simple words in the dictionary now and it makes me impatient with myself.

Dr. Strauss comes around almost every day, but I told him I wouldn't see or speak to anybody. He feels guilty. They all do. But I don't blame anyone. I knew what might happen. But how it hurts.

July 7 I don't know where the week went. Todays Sunday I know because I can see through my window people going to church. I think I stayed in bed all week but I remember Mrs. Flynn bringing food to me a few times. I keep saying over and over Ive got to do something but then I forget or maybe its just easier not to do what I say Im going to do.

I think of my mother and father a lot these days. I found a picture of them with me taken at a beach. My father has a big ball under his arm and my mother is holding me by the hand. I dont remember them the way they are in the picture. All I remember is my father drunk most of the time and arguing with mom about money.

He never shaved much and he used to scratch my face when he hugged me. My mother said he died but Cousin Miltie said he heard his mom and dad say that my father ran away with another woman. When I asked my mother she slapped my face and said my father was dead. I don't think I ever found out which was true but I don't care much. (He said he was going to take me to see cows on a farm once but he never did. He never kept his promises . . .)

July 10 My landlady Mrs Flynn is very worried about me. She says the way I lay around all day and dont do anything I remind her of her son before she threw him out of the house. She said she doesnt like loafers. If Im sick its one thing, but if Im a loafer thats another thing and she wont have it. I told her I think Im sick.

I try to read a little bit every day, mostly stories, but sometimes I have to read the same thing over and over again because I dont know what it means. And its hard to write. I know I should look up all the words in the dictionary but its so hard and Im so tired all the time.

Then I got the idea that I would only use the easy words instead of the long hard ones. That saves time. I put flowers on Algernons grave about once a week. Mrs. Flynn thinks Im crazy to put flowers on a mouses grave but I told her that Algernon was special.

July 14 Its sunday again. I dont have anything to do to keep me busy now because my television set is broke and I dont have any money to get it fixed. (I think I lost this months check from the lab. I dont remember)

I get awful headaches and asperin doesnt help me much. Mrs Flynn knows Im really sick and she feels very sorry for me. Shes a wonderful woman whenever someone is sick.

July 22 Mrs Flynn called a strange doctor to see me. She was afraid I was going to die. I told the doctor I wasnt too sick and that I only forget sometimes. He asked me did I have any friends or relatives and I said no I dont have any. I told him I had a friend called Algernon once but he was a mouse and we used to run races together. He looked at me kind of funny like he thought I was crazy.

He smiled when I told him I used to be a genius. He talked to me like I was a baby and he winked at Mrs Flynn. I got mad and chased him out because he was making fun of me the way they all used to.

July 24 I have no more money and Mrs. Flynn says I got to go to work somewhere and pay the rent because I havent paid for over two months. I dont know any work but the job I used to have at Donnegans Plastic Box Company. I dont want to go back there because they all knew me when I was smart and maybe theyll laugh at me. But I dont know what else to do to get money.

July 25 I was looking at some of my old progress reports and its very funny but I cant read what I wrote. I can make out some of the words but they dont make sense.

Miss Kinnian came to the door but I said go away I dont want to see you. She cried and I cried too but I wouldn't let her in because I didn't want her to laugh at me. I told her I didn't like her any more. I told her I didn't want to be smart any more. Thats not true. I still love her and I still want to be smart but I had to say that so shed go away. She gave Mrs Flynn money to pay the rent. I dont want that. I got to get a job.

Please . . . please let me not forget how to read and write . . .

July 27 Mr Donnegan was very nice when I came back and asked him for my old job of janitor. First he was very suspicious but I told him what happened to me then he looked very sad and put his hand on my shoulder and said Charlie Gordon you got guts.

Everybody looked at me when I came downstairs and started working in the toilet sweeping it out like I used to. I told myself Charlie if they make fun of you dont get sore because you remember their not so smart as you once thot they were. And besides they were once your friends and if they laughed at you that doesnt mean anything because they liked you too.

One of the new men who came to work there after I went away made a nasty crack he said hey Charlie I hear your a very smart fella a real quiz kid. Say something intelligent. I felt bad but Joe Carp came over and grabbed him by the shirt and said leave him alone you lousy cracker or Ill break your neck. I didn't expect Joe to take my part so I guess hes really my friend.

Later Frank Reilly came over and said Charlie if anybody bothers you or trys to take advantage you call me or Joe and we will set em straight. I said thanks Frank and I got choked up so I had to turn around and go into the supply room so he wouldnt see me cry. Its good to have friends.

July 28 I did a dumb thing today I forgot I wasnt in Miss Kinnians class at the adult center any more like I use to be. I went in and sat down in my old seat in the back of the room and she looked at me funny and she said Charles. I dint remember she ever called me that before only Charlie so I said hello Miss Kinnian Im redy for my lesin today only I lost my reader that we was using. She startid to cry and run out of the room and everybody looked at me and I saw they wasnt the same pepul who used to be in my class.

Then all of a sudden I remember some things about the operashun and me getting smart and I said holy smoke I reely pulled a Charlie Gordon that time. I went away before she come back to the room.

Thats why Im going away from New York for good. I dont want to do nothing like that agen. I dont want Miss Kinnian to feel sorry for me. Evry body feels sorry at the factery and I dont want that eather so Im going some-place where nobody knows that Charlie Gordon was once a genus and now he cant even reed a book or rite good.

Im taking a cuple of books along and even if I cant reed them Ill practise hard and maybe I wont forget every thing I lerned. If I try reel hard maybe Ill be a littel bit smarter then I was before the operashun. I got my rabits foot and my luky penny and maybe they will help me.

If you ever reed this Miss Kinnian dont be sorry for me Im glad I got a second chanse to be smart becaus I lerned a lot of things that I never even new were in this world and Im grateful that I saw it all for a little bit. I dont know why Im dumb agen or what I did wrong maybe its becaus I dint try hard enuff. But if I try and practis very hard maybe Ill get a little smarter and know what all the words are. I remember a littel bit how nice I had a feeling with the blue book that has the torn cover when I red it. Thats why Im gonna keep trying to get smart so I can have that feeling agen. Its a good feeling to know things and be smart. I wish I had it rite now if I did I would sit down and reed all the time. Anyway I bet Im the first dumb person in the world who ever found out somthing importent for sience. I remember I did somthing but I dont remem-ber what. So I gess its like I did it for all the dumb pepul like me.

Good-by Miss Kinnian and Dr Strauss and evreybody. And P.S. please tell Dr Nemur not to be such a grouch when pepul laff at him and he would have more frends. Its easy to make frends if you let pepul laff at you. Im going to have lots of frends where I go.

P.P.S. Please if you get a chanse put some flowrs on Algernons grave in the bak yard . . .

BY WAY OF DISCUSSION

Diary narration is an effective technique for exploring the innermost thoughts and feelings of the narrator without sacrificing a strong story line. "Flowers for Algernon" offers us a well-developed, interesting plot and a most unusual narrator-protagonist, a feeble-minded janitor whose temporary transformation into a super-genius provides a disturbing look at the problems of human isolation.

Charlie begins the story as a simple-minded narrator and does not achieve full awareness until well over a month after his operation. Evidence of his mental incapacity abounds throughout the early passages of the diary: in his near-illiterate writing, in the reasons he offers for his poor performance with the Rorschach inkblots and against Algernon, in his hostility toward the sleep-teaching device, and, saddest of all, in his failure to recognize the cruelty of those people he regards as his friends. Throughout most of these entries Charlie remains like a child "peering from a dark room, through the keyhole, and into the dazzling light outside," a child barred by lack of intelligence from all normal relationships with his fellow humans.

However, one vital quality distinguishes Charlie from others of his sort, an intense and unflagging determination to shatter the walls that isolate him in mental darkness. Spurred by this ambition, Charlie has worked a small miracle of self-improvement. Indeed, as Dr. Strauss tells Dr. Nemur, Charlie's accomplishments in reading and writing represent "as great an achievement as you or I learning Einstein's Theory of Relativity without help." It is this personal determination that finally wins Charlie the operation.

For some three weeks after the operation, there are few substantive signs that the surgery has helped Charlie at all. But then the intellectual floodgates burst open, and within a matter of days Charlie finds himself able to grasp simple abstract concepts. Soon he starts winning his contests against Algernon, embarks upon a course of adult reading, and gains a thorough grasp of proper spelling, punctuation, and grammar. Like Adam, Charlie has eaten of the fruit of the Tree of Knowledge. However, he hasn't yet learned anything about the dark intricacies of human behavior. His first lesson comes when he attends the party with Frank and Joe and discovers how his supposed friends really feel about him. The experience leaves Charlie sickened and ashamed, but he is still naïvely hopeful that people will like him when his I.Q. has tripled.

But, of course, people do not like him. When Charlie figures out a money-saving way to rearrange the machines in the factory, Frank and Joe find excuses to turn down his luncheon invitation, and shortly thereafter his co-workers force him out of his job. At the same time, Charlie is learning some unpleasant truths about Dr. Strauss and Dr. Nemur.

Until this point he has regarded these two men as disinterested truth-seekers, idols without the clay feet of ordinary people. Now, looking at them from the perspective of his newly matured genius, Charlie realizes with shocked sadness that they, no less than others, feel the inner ragings of pride, greed, and envy. They, too, suffer pangs of self-doubt and inferiority. They are not even above pretending to have knowledge that they do not really possess. Both appear to be as uncomfortable around him as were his fellow employees at the factory.

Worst of all, Charlie finds it impossible to communicate with Miss Kinnian, who, in a manner uncomfortably reminiscent of the behavior of

Frank and Joe, laughs when he attempts to explain the mathematical variance equivalent in a musical composition. Ironically, Charlie is now even more isolated than he was in the days before his operation, when he lacked the intelligence to recognize his true situation. Out of his agony, Charlie writes:

> This intelligence has driven a wedge between me and all the people I once knew and loved. Before, they laughed at me and despised me for my ignorance and dullness; now they hate me for my knowledge and understanding. What in God's name do they want from me?

What they want, of course, is a Charlie exactly like themselves, a Charlie who never was and never will be.

Despite the bitterness he feels, Charlie never loses his humanity. This is made clear by the diner episode, in which a retarded boy smashes some dishes. Because of this incident, Charlie makes an important decision: he will devote his new-found genius to the task of "increasing human intelligence levels." He concludes the entry of the episode by writing, "There are so many doors to open. I am impatient to begin."

Although Charlie does not realize it, his own mental doors are about to close again, isolating him once more in the prison of feeble-mindedness. The first sign of this impending tragedy occurs when a newly disturbed and vicious Algernon bites Charlie's finger. Within little more than two weeks, Algernon has regressed and died, and—through an ironical bit of research—Charlie has proved that he is fated to undergo a similar intellectual deterioration. The tragedy plays itself out swiftly, and soon the diary notations assume their old near-illiterate character. The wheel of isolation has turned full circle for Charlie: he is back in the "dark room" he occupied before the operation. For a brief time, he returns to his old job, but he soon leaves both the job and New York rather than cause the woman he loves any unnecessary suffering.

"Flowers for Algernon" almost begs the reader to ask a specific question: Can any ethical justification be offered for the experiment on Charlie? If we consider only the mixed motives of Dr. Strauss and Dr. Nemur, the uncertain prognosis, and the disastrous outcome, the whole affair seems indefensible. However, there is another side of the matter: the tremendous potential benefits if the operation were a success and the humanizing effect of Charlie's experience on Frank and Joe, who end up wanting to protect the man they once mocked. Then, too, Charlie himself is eager to undergo the operation, and even after it is ultimately a failure he shows no regrets, as the final entry in the diary demonstrates:

> dont be sorry for me Im glad I got a second chanse to be smart becaus I lerned a lot of things that I never even new were in this world and Im grateful that I saw it all for a little bit. . . . I remember a littel bit how nice I had a feeling with the blue book that has the torn cover when I red it. Thats why Im gonna keep trying to get smart so I can have that feeling agen Its a good feeling to know things and be smart.

The ethical question is not a simple one. Like so many of the real issues we face today—issues like experimentation with radical surgical procedures and biological engineering—the question of tampering with a human brain in the hope of artificially increasing intelligence will have to be given careful thought over a considerable period of time. The great virtue of the author's employing diary narration in this story is that the technique allows the reader the unique chance to ''hear'' the human guinea pig in such an experiment relate what happens to him.

THOMAS BAILEY ALDRICH

Marjorie Daw

I

Dr. Dillon to Edward Delaney, Esq., at the Pines, Near Rye, N. H.

August 8, 1872

My Dear Sir: I am happy to assure you that your anxiety is without reason. Flemming will be confined to the sofa for three or four weeks, and will have to be careful at first how he uses his leg. A fracture of this kind is always a tedious affair. Fortunately the bone was very skilfully set by the surgeon who chanced to be in the drugstore where Flemming was brought after his fall, and I apprehend no permanent inconvenience from the accident. *Flemming is doing perfectly well physically*; but I must confess that the irritable and morbid state of mind into which he has fallen causes me a great deal of uneasiness. He is the last man in the world who ought to break his leg. You know how impetuous our friend is ordinarily, what a soul of restlessness and energy, never content unless he is rushing at some object, like a sportive bull at a red shawl; but amiable withal. He is no longer amiable. His temper has become something frightful. Miss Fanny Flemming came up from Newport, where the family are staying for the summer, to nurse him; but he packed her off the next morning in tears. He has a complete set of Balzac's works, twenty-seven volumes, piled up near his sofa, to throw at Watkins whenever that exemplary serving-man appears with his meals. Yesterday I very innocently brought Flemming a small basket of lemons. You know it was a strip of lemon-peel on the curbstone that caused our friend's mischance. Well, he no sooner set his eyes upon these lemons than he fell into such a rage as I cannot adequately describe. This is only one of his moods, and the least distressing. At other times he sits with bowed head regarding his splintered limb, silent, sullen, despairing. When this fit is on him—and it sometimes lasts all day—nothing can distract his melancholy. He refuses to eat, does not even read the newspapers; books, except as projectiles for Watkins, have no charms for him. His state is truly pitiable.

Now, if he were a poor man, with a family depending on his daily labor, this irritability and despondency would be natural enough. But in a young fellow of twenty-four, with plenty of money and seemingly not a care in the world, the thing is monstrous. If he continues to give way to his vagaries in this manner, he will end by bringing on an inflammation of the fibula. It was the fibula he broke. I am at my wits' end to know what to prescribe for him. I have anæsthetics and lotions, to make people sleep and to soothe pain; but I've no medicine that will make a man have a little common sense. That is beyond my skill, but maybe it is not beyond yours. You are Flemming's intimate friend, his *fidus Achates*. Write to him, write to him frequently, distract his mind, cheer him up, and prevent him from becoming a confirmed case of melancholia. Perhaps he has some important plans disarranged by his present confinement. If he has you will know, and will know how to advise him judiciously. I trust your father finds the change beneficial? I am, my dear sir, with great respect, etc.

II

Edward Delaney to John Flemming, West 38th Street, New York

August 9, 1872

My Dear Jack: I had a line from Dillon this morning, and was rejoiced to learn that your hurt is not so bad as reported. Like a certain personage, you are not so black and blue as you are painted. Dillon will put you on your pins again in two or three weeks, if you will only have patience and follow his counsels. Did you get my note of last Wednesday? I was greatly troubled when I heard of the accident.

I can imagine how tranquil and saintly you are with your leg in a trough! It is deuced awkward, to be sure, just as we had promised ourselves a glorious month together at the sea-side; but we must make the best of it. It is unfortunate, too, that my father's health renders it impossible for me to leave him. I think he has much improved; the sea air is his native element; but he still needs my arm to lean upon in his walks, and requires some one more careful than a servant to look after him. I cannot come to you, dear Jack, but I have hours of unemployed time on hand, and I will write you a whole post-office full of letters, if that will divert you. Heaven knows, I haven't anything to write about. It isn't as if we were living at one of the beach houses; then I could do you some character studies, and fill your imagination with groups of sea-goddesses, with their (or somebody else's) raven and blond manes hanging down their shoulders. You should have Aphrodite in morning wrapper, in evening costume, and in her prettiest bathing suit. But we are far from all that here. We have rooms in a farm-house, on a cross-road, two miles from the hotels, and lead the quietest of lives.

I wish I were a novelist. This old house, with its sanded floors and high wainscots, and its narrow windows looking out upon a cluster of pines that turn themselves into æolian-harps every time the wind blows, would be the place in which to write a summer romance. It should be a story with the odors of the forest and the breath of the sea in it. It should be a novel like one of that Russian fellow's—what's his name?—Tourguénieff, Turguenef, Turgenif, Toorguniff, Turgénjew—nobody knows how to spell him. Yet I wonder if even a Liza or an Alexandra Paulovna could stir the heart of a man who has constant twinges in his leg. I wonder if one of our own Yankee girls of the best type, haughty and *spirituelle*, would be of any comfort to you in your present deplorable condition. If I thought so, I would hasten down to the Surf House and catch one for you; or, better still, I would find you one over the way.

Picture to yourself a large white house just across the road, nearly opposite our cottage. It is not a house, but a mansion, built, perhaps, in the colonial period, with rambling extensions, and gambrel roof, and a wide piazza on three sides—a self-possessed, high-bred piece of architecture, with its nose in the air. It stands back from the road, and has an obsequious retinue of fringed elms and oaks and weeping willows. Sometimes in the morning, and oftener in the afternoon, when the sun has withdrawn from that part of the mansion, a young woman appears on the piazza with some mysterious Penelope web of embroidery in her hand, or a book. There is a hammock over there—of pine-apple fibre, it looks from here. A hammock is very becoming when one is eighteen, and has golden hair, and dark eyes, and an emerald-colored illusion dress looped up after the fashion of a Dresden china shepherdess, and is *chaussée* like a belle of the time of Louis Quatorze. All this splendor goes into that hammock, and sways there like a pond-lily in the golden afternoon. The window of my bedroom looks down on that piazza—and so do I.

But enough of this nonsense, which ill becomes a sedate young attorney taking his vacation with an invalid father. Drop me a line, dear Jack, and tell me how you really are. State your case. Write me a long, quiet letter. If you are violent or abusive, I'll take the law to you.

III

John Flemming to Edward Delaney

August 11, 1872

Your letter, dear Ned, was a godsend. Fancy what a fix I am in—I, who never had a day's sickness since I was born. My left leg weighs three tons. It is embalmed in spices and smothered in layers of fine linen, like a mummy. I can't move. I haven't moved for five thousand years. I'm of the time of Pharaoh.

I lie from morning till night on a lounge, staring into the hot street. Everybody is out of town enjoying himself. The brown-stone-front houses across the street resemble a row of particularly ugly coffins set up on end. A green mould is settling on the names of the deceased, carved on the silver door-plates. Sardonic spiders have sewed up the key-holes. All is silence and dust and desolation—I interrupt this a moment, to take a shy at Watkins with the second volume of César Birotteau. Missed him! I think I could bring him down with a copy of Sainte-Beuve or the Dictionnaire Universel, if I had it. These small Balzac books somehow don't quite fit my hand; but I shall fetch him yet. I've an idea Watkins is tapping the old gentleman's Château Yquem. Dupli-cate key of the wine-cellar. Hibernian swarries in the front basement. Young Cheops up-stairs, snug in his cerements. Watkins glides into my chamber, with that colorless, hypocritical face of his drawn out long like an accordion; but I know he grins all the way down-stairs, and is glad I have broken my leg. Was not my evil star in the very zenith when I ran up to town to attend that dinner at Delmonico's? I didn't come up altogether for that. It was partly to buy Frank Livingstone's roan mare Margot. And now I shall not be able to sit in the saddle these two months. I'll send the mare down to you at The Pines— is that the name of the place?

Old Dillon fancies that I have something on my mind. He drives me wild with lemons. Lemons for a mind diseased! Nonsense. I am only as restless as the devil under this confinement—a thing I'm not used to. Take a man who has never had so much as a headache or a toothache in his life, strap one of his legs in a section of water-spout, keep him in a room in the city for weeks, with the hot weather turned on, and then expect him to smile and purr and be happy! It is preposterous. I can't be cheerful or calm.

Your letter is the first consoling thing I have had since my disaster, ten days ago. It really cheered me up for half an hour. Send me a screed, Ned, as often as you can, if you love me. Anything will do. Write me more about that little girl in the hammock. That was very pretty, all that about the Dresden china shepherdess and the pond-lily; the imagery a little mixed, perhaps, but very pretty. I didn't suppose you had so much sentimental furniture in your upper story. It shows how one may be familiar for years with the reception-room of his neighbor, and never suspect what is directly under his mansard. I sup-posed your loft stuffed with dry legal parchments, mortgages and affidavits; you take down a package of manuscript, and lo! there are lyrics and sonnets and canzonettas. You really have a graphic descriptive touch, Edward Delaney, and I suspect you of anonymous love-tales in the magazines.

I shall be a bear until I hear from you again. Tell me all about your pretty inconnue across the road. What is her name? Who is she? Who's her father? Where's her mother? Who's her lover? You cannot imagine how this will occupy me. The more trifling the better. My imprisonment has weakened me intellectually to such a degree that I find your epistolary gifts quite consider-able. I am passing into my second childhood. In a week or two I shall take to India-rubber rings and prongs of coral. A silver cup, with an appropriate inscription, would be a delicate attention on your part. In the mean time, write!

IV

Edward Delaney to John Flemming

August 12, 1872

The sick pasha shall be amused. *Bismillah!* he wills it so. If the story-teller becomes prolix and tedious—the bow-string and the sack, and two Nubians to drop him into the Piscataqua! But, truly, Jack, I have a hard task. There is literally nothing here—except the little girl over the way. She is swinging in the hammock at this moment. It is to me compensation for many of the ills of life to see her now and then put out a small kid boot, which fits like a glove, and set herself going. Who is she, and what is her name? Her name is Daw. Only daughter of Mr. Richard W. Daw, ex-colonel and banker. Mother dead. One brother at Harvard, elder brother killed at the battle of Fair Oaks, ten years ago. Old, rich family, the Daws. This is the homestead, where father and daughter pass eight months of the twelve; the rest of the year in Baltimore and Washington. The New England winter too many for the old gentleman. The daughter is called Marjorie—Marjorie Daw. Sounds odd at first, doesn't it? But after you say it over to yourself half a dozen times, you like it. There's a pleasing quaintness to it, something prim and pansy-like. Must be a nice sort of girl to be called Marjorie Daw.

I had mine host of The Pines in the witness-box last night, and drew the foregoing testimony from him. He has charge of Mr. Daw's vegetable-garden, and has known the family these thirty years. Of course I shall make the acquaintance of my neighbors before many days. It will be next to impossible for me not to meet Mr. Daw or Miss Daw in some of my walks. The young lady has a favorite path to the sea-beach. I shall intercept her some morning, and touch my hat to her. Then the princess will bend her fair head to me with courteous surprise not unmixed with haughtiness. Will snub me, in fact. All this for thy sake, O Pasha of the Snapt Axle-tree! . . . How oddly things fall out! Ten minutes ago I was called down to the parlor—you know the kind of parlors in farm-houses on the coast, a sort of amphibious parlor, with sea-shells on the mantel-piece and spruce branches in the chimney-place—where I found my father and Mr. Daw doing the antique polite to each other. He had come to pay his respects to his new neighbors. Mr. Daw is a tall, slim gentleman of about fifty-five, with a florid face and snow-white mustache and side-whiskers. Looks like Mr. Dombey, or as Mr. Dombey would have looked if he had served a few years in the British Army. Mr. Daw was a colonel in the late war, commanding the regiment in which his son was a lieutenant. Plucky old boy, backbone of New Hampshire granite. Before taking his leave, the colonel delivered himself of an invitation as if he were issuing a general order. Miss Daw has a few friends coming, at 4 P.M., to play croquet on the lawn (parade-ground) and have tea (cold rations) on the piazza. Will we honor them with our company? (or be sent to the guard-house.) My father declines on the plea of ill-health. My father's son bows with as much suavity as he knows, and accepts.

In my next I shall have something to tell you. I shall have seen the little beauty face to face. I have a presentiment, Jack, that this Daw is a *rara avis!* Keep up your spirits, my boy, until I write you another letter—and send me along word how's your leg.

V

Edward Delaney to John Flemming

August 13, 1872

The party, my dear Jack, was as dreary as possible. A lieutenant of the navy, the rector of the Episcopal church at Stillwater, and a society swell from Nahant. The lieutenant looked as if he had swallowed a couple of his buttons, and found the bullion rather indigestible; the rector was a pensive youth, of the daffydowndilly sort; and the swell from Nahant was a very weak tidal wave indeed. The women were much better, as they always are; the two Miss Kingsburys of Philadelphia, staying at the Sea-shell House, two bright and engaging girls. But Marjorie Daw!

The company broke up soon after tea, and I remained to smoke a cigar with the colonel on the piazza. It was like seeing a picture to see Miss Marjorie hovering around the old soldier, and doing a hundred gracious little things for him. She brought the cigars and lighted the tapers with her own delicate fingers, in the most enchanting fashion. As we sat there, she came and went in the summer twilight, and seemed, with her white dress and pale gold hair, like some lovely phantom that had sprung into existence out of the smoke-wreaths. If she had melted into air, like the statue of Galatea in the play, I should have been more sorry than surprised.

It was easy to perceive that the old colonel worshipped her, and she him. I think the relation between the elderly father and a daughter just blooming into womanhood the most beautiful possible. There is in it a subtle sentiment that cannot exist in the case of mother and daughter, or that of son and mother. But this is getting into deep water.

I sat with the Daws until half past ten, and saw the moon rise on the sea. The ocean, that had stretched motionless and black against the horizon, was changed by magic into a broken field of glittering ice, interspersed with marvellous silvery fjords. In the far distance the Isles of Shoals loomed up like a group of huge bergs drifting down on us. The Polar Regions in a June thaw! It was exceedingly fine. What did we talk about? We talked about the weather—and *you!* The weather has been disagreeable for several days past—and so have you. I glided from one topic to the other very naturally. I told my friends of your accident; how it had frustrated all our summer plans, and what our plans were. I played quite a spirited solo on the fibula. Then I described you; or, rather, I didn't. I spoke of your amiability, of your patience under this severe affliction; of your touching gratitude when Dillon brings you little presents of fruit; of your tenderness to your sister Fanny, whom you would not allow to stay in town to nurse you, and how you heroically sent her back to Newport, preferring to remain alone with Mary, the cook, and your man Watkins, to whom, by the way, you were devotedly attached. If you had been there, Jack, you wouldn't have known yourself. I should have excelled as a criminal lawyer, if I had not turned my attention to a different branch of jurisprudence.

Miss Marjorie asked all manner of leading questions concerning you. It did not occur to me then, but it struck me forcibly afterwards, that she evinced a singular interest in the conversation. When I got back to my room, I recalled how eagerly she leaned forward, with her full, snowy throat in strong moon-light, listening to what I said. Positively, I think I made her like you!

Miss Daw is a girl whom you would like immensely, I can tell you that. A beauty without affectation, a high and tender nature—if one can read the soul in the face. And the old colonel is a noble character, too.

I am glad the Daws are such pleasant people. The Pines is an isolated spot, and my resources are few. I fear I should have found life here somewhat monotonous before long, with no other society than that of my excellent sire. It is true, I might have made a target of the defenceless invalid; but I haven't a taste for artillery, *moi*.

VI

John Flemming to Edward Delaney

August 17, 1872

For a man who hasn't a taste for artillery, it occurs to me, my friend, you are keeping up a pretty lively fire on my inner works. But go on. Cynicism is a small brass field-piece that eventually bursts and kills the artilleryman.

You may abuse me as much as you like, and I'll not complain; for I don't know what I should do without your letters. They are curing me. I haven't hurled anything at Watkins since last Sunday, partly because I have grown more amiable under your teaching, and partly because Watkins captured my ammunition one night, and carried it off to the library. He is rapidly losing the habit he had acquired of dodging whenever I rub my ear, or make any slight motion with my right arm. He is still suggestive of the wine-cellar, however. You may break, you may shatter Watkins, if you will, but the scent of the Roederer will hang round him still.

Ned, that Miss Daw must be a charming person. I should certainly like her. I like her already. When you spoke in your first letter of seeing a young girl swinging in a hammock under your chamber window, I was somehow strangely drawn to her. I cannot account for it in the least. What you have subsequently written of Miss Daw has strengthened the impression. You seem to be describing a woman I have known in some previous state of existence, or dreamed of in this. Upon my word, if you were to send me her photograph, I believe I should recognize her at a glance. Her manner, that listening attitude, her traits of character, as you indicate them, the light hair and the dark eyes—they are all familiar things to me. Asked a lot of questions, did she? Curious about me? That is strange.

You would laugh in your sleeve, you wretched old cynic, if you knew how I lie awake nights, with my gas turned down to a star, thinking of The Pines and the house across the road. How cool it must be down there! I long for the salt smell in the air. I picture the colonel smoking his cheroot on the piazza. I send you and Miss Daw off on afternoon rambles along the beach. Sometimes I let you stroll with her under the elms in the moonlight, for you are great friends by this time, I take it, and see each other every day. I know your ways and your manners! Then I fall into a truculent mood, and would like to destroy somebody. Have you noticed anything in the shape of a lover hanging around the colonial Lares and Penates? Does that lieutenant of the horse-marines or that young Stillwater parson visit the house much? Not that I am pining for news of them, but any gossip of the kind would be in order. I wonder, Ned, you don't fall in love with Miss Daw. I am ripe to do it myself. Speaking of photographs, couldn't you manage to slip one of her *cartes-de-visite* from her album—she must have an album, you know—and send it to me? I will return it before it could be missed. That's a good fellow! Did the mare arrive safe and sound? It will be a capital animal this autumn for Central Park.

O—my leg? I forgot about my leg. It's better.

VII

Edward Delaney to John Flemming

August 20, 1872

You are correct in your surmises. I am on the most friendly terms with our neighbors. The colonel and my father smoke their afternoon cigar together in our sitting-room or on the piazza opposite, and I pass an hour or two of the day or the evening with the daughter. I am more and more struck by the beauty, modesty, and intelligence of Miss Daw.

You ask me why I do not fall in love with her. I will be frank, Jack: I have thought of that. She is young, rich, accomplished, uniting in herself more attractions, mental and personal, than I can recall in any girl of my acquaint-ance; but she lacks the something that would be necessary to inspire in me that kind of interest. Possessing this unknown quantity, a woman neither beautiful nor wealthy nor very young could bring me to her feet. But not Miss Daw. If we were shipwrecked together on an uninhabited island—let me suggest a tropical island, for it costs no more to be picturesque—I would build her a bamboo hut, I would fetch her bread-fruit and cocoanuts. I would fry yams for her, I would lure the ingenuous turtle and make her nourishing soups, but I wouldn't make love to her—not under eighteen months. I would like to have her for a sister, that I might shield her and counsel her, and spend half my income on thread-lace and camel's-hair shawls. (We are off the island now.) If such were not my feeling, there would still be an obstacle to my loving Miss Daw. A greater misfortune could scarcely befall me than to love her. Flemming, I am about to make a revelation that will astonish you. I may be all wrong in my premises and consequently in my conclusions; but you shall judge.

That night when I returned to my room after the croquet party at the Daws', and was thinking over the trivial events of the evening, I was suddenly impressed by the air of eager attention with which Miss Daw had followed my account of your accident. I think I mentioned this to you. Well, the next morning, as I went to mail my letter, I overtook Miss Daw on the road to Rye, where the post-office is, and accompanied her thither and back, an hour's walk. The conversation again turned on you, and again I remarked that inexplicable look of interest which had lighted up her face the previous evening. Since then, I have seen Miss Daw perhaps ten times, perhaps oftener, and on each occasion I found that when I was not speaking of you, or your sister, or some person or place associated with you, I was not holding her attention. She would be absent-minded, her eyes would wander away from me to the sea, or to some distant object in the landscape; her fingers would play with the leaves of a book in a way that convinced me she was not listening. At these moments if I abruptly changed the theme—I did it several times as an experiment—and dropped some remark about my friend Flemming, then the sombre blue eyes would come back to me instantly.

Now, is not this the oddest thing in the world? No, not the oddest. The effect which you tell me was produced on you by my casual mention of an unknown girl swinging in a hammock is certainly as strange. You can conjecture how that passage in your letter of Friday startled me. Is it possible, then, that two people who have never met, and who are hundreds of miles apart, can exert a magnetic influence on each other? I have read of such psychological phenomena, but never credited them. I leave the solution of the problem to you. As for myself, all other things being favorable, it would be impossible for me to fall in love with a woman who listens to me only when I am talking of my friend!

I am not aware that any one is paying marked attention to my fair neighbor. The lieutenant of the navy—he is stationed at Rivermouth—sometimes drops in of an evening, and some times the rector from Stillwater; the lieutenant the oftener. He was there last night. I should not be surprised if he had an eye to the heiress; but he is not formidable. Mistress Daw carries a neat little spear of irony, and the honest lieutenant seems to have a particular facility for impaling himself on the point of it. He is not dangerous, I should say; though I have known a woman to satirize a man for years, and marry him after all. Decidedly, the lowly rector is not dangerous; yet, again, who has not seen Cloth of Frieze victorious in the lists where Cloth of Gold went down?

As to the photograph. There is an exquisite ivorytype of Marjorie, in passe-partout, on the drawing-room mantel-piece. It would be missed at once if taken. I would do anything reasonable for you, Jack; but I've no burning desire to be hauled up before the local justice of the peace, on a charge of petty larceny.

P.S.—Enclosed is a spray of mignonette, which I advise you to treat tenderly. Yes, we talked of you again last night, as usual. It is becoming a little dreary for me.

VIII

Edward Delaney to John Flemming

August 22, 1872

Your letter in reply to my last has occupied my thoughts all the morning. I do not know what to think. Do you mean to say that you are seriously half in love with a woman whom you have never seen—with a shadow, a chimera? for what else can Miss Daw be to you? I do not understand it at all. I understand neither you nor her. You are a couple of ethereal beings moving in finer air than I can breathe with my commonplace lungs. Such delicacy of sentiment is something I admire without comprehending. I am bewildered. I am of the earth earthy, and I find myself in the incongruous position of having to do with mere souls, with natures so finely tempered that I run some risk of shattering them in my awkwardness. I am as Caliban among the spirits!

Reflecting on your letter, I am not sure that it is wise in me to continue this correspondence. But no, Jack; I do wrong to doubt the good sense that forms the basis of your character. You are deeply interested in Miss Daw; you feel that she is a person whom you may perhaps greatly admire when you know her: at the same time you bear in mind that the chances are ten to five that, when you do come to know her, she will fall far short of your ideal, and you will not care for her in the least. Look at it in this sensible light, and I will hold back nothing from you.

Yesterday afternoon my father and myself rode over to Rivermouth with the Daws. A heavy rain in the morning had cooled the atmosphere and laid the dust. To Rivermouth is a drive of eight miles, along a winding road lined all the way with wild barberry-bushes. I never saw anything more brilliant than these bushes, the green of the foliage and the pink of the coral berries intensified by the rain. The colonel drove, with my father in front, Miss Daw and I on the back seat. I resolved that for the first five miles your name should not pass my lips. I was amused by the artful attempts she made, at the start, to break through my reticence. Then a silence fell upon her; and then she became suddenly gay. That keenness which I enjoyed so much when it was exercised on the lieutenant was not so satisfactory directed against myself. Miss Daw has great sweetness of disposition, but she can be disagreeable. She is like the young lady in the rhyme, with the curl on her forehead—

> *"When she is good,*
> *She is very, very good,*
> *And when she is bad, she is horrid!"*

I kept to my resolution, however; but on the return home I relented, and talked of your mare! Miss Daw is going to try a side-saddle on Margot some morning. The animal is a trifle too light for my weight. By the bye, I nearly forgot to say that Miss Daw sat for a picture yesterday to a Rivermouth artist. If the negative turns out well, I am to have a copy. So our ends will be accomplished without crime. I wish, though, I could send you the ivorytype in the drawing-room; it is cleverly colored, and would give you an idea of her hair and eyes, which of course the other will not.

No, Jack, the spray of mignonette did not come from me. A man of twenty-eight doesn't enclose flowers in his letters—to another man. But don't attach too much significance to the circumstance. She gives sprays of mignonette to the rector, sprays to the lieutenant. She has even given a rose from her bosom to your slave. It is her jocund nature to scatter flowers, like Spring.

If my letters sometimes read disjointedly, you must understand that I never finish one at a sitting, but write at intervals, when the mood is on me.

The mood is not on me now.

IX

Edward Delaney to John Flemming

August 23, 1872

I have just returned from the strangest interview with Marjorie. She has all but confessed to me her interest in you. But with what modesty and dignity! Her words elude my pen as I attempt to put them on paper; and, indeed, it was not so much what she said as her manner; and that I cannot reproduce. Perhaps it was of a piece with the strangeness of this whole business, that she should tacitly acknowledge to a third party the love she feels for a man she has never beheld! But I have lost, through your aid, the faculty of being surprised. I accept things as people do in dreams. Now that I am again in my room, it all appears like an illusion—the black masses of Rembrandtish shadow under the trees, the fire-flies whirling in Pyrrhic dances among the shrubbery, the sea over there, Marjorie sitting on the hammock!

It is past midnight, and I am too sleepy to write more.

Thursday Morning

My father has suddenly taken it into his head to spend a few days at the Shoals. In the meanwhile you will not hear from me. I see Marjorie walking in the garden with the colonel. I wish I could speak to her alone, but shall probably not have an opportunity before we leave.

X

Edward Delaney to John Flemming

August 28, 1872

You were passing into your second childhood, were you? Your intellect was so reduced that my epistolary gifts seemed quite considerable to you, did they? I rise superior to the sarcasm in your favor of the 11th instant, when I notice that five days' silence on my part is sufficient to throw you into the depths of despondency.

We returned only this morning from Appledore, that enchanted island—at four dollars per day. I find on my desk three letters from you! Evidently there is no lingering doubt in *your* mind as to the pleasure I derive from your correspondence. These letters are undated, but in what I take to be the latest are two passages that require my consideration. You will pardon my candor, dear Flemming, but the conviction forces itself upon me that as your leg grows stronger your head becomes weaker. You ask my advice on a certain point. I will give it. In my opinion you could do nothing more unwise than to address a note to Miss Daw, thanking her for the flower. It would, I am sure, offend her delicacy beyond pardon. She knows you only through me; you are to her an abstraction, a figure in a dream—a dream from which the faintest shock would awaken her. Of course, if you enclose a note to me and insist on its delivery, I shall deliver it; but I advise you not to do so.

You say you are able, with the aid of a cane, to walk about your chamber, and that you purpose to come to The Pines the instant Dillon thinks you strong enough to stand the journey. Again I advise you not to. Do you not see that, every hour you remain away, Marjorie's glamour deepens, and your influence over her increases? You will ruin everything by precipitancy. Wait until you are entirely recovered; in any case, do not come without giving me warning. I fear the effect of your abrupt advent here—under the circumstances.

Miss Daw was evidently glad to see us back again, and gave me both hands in the frankest way. She stopped at the door a moment this afternoon in the carriage; she had been over to Rivermouth for her pictures. Unluckily the photographer had spilt some acid on the plate, and she was obliged to give him another sitting. I have an intuition that something is troubling Marjorie. She had an abstracted air not usual with her. However, it may be only my fancy. . . . I end this, leaving several things unsaid, to accompany my father on one of those long walks which are now his chief medicine—and mine!

XI

Edward Delaney to John Flemming

August 29, 1872

I write in great haste to tell you what has taken place here since my letter of last night. I am in the utmost perplexity. Only one thing is plain—*you* must not dream of coming to The Pines. Marjorie has told her father everything! I saw her for a few minutes, an hour ago, in the garden; and, as near as I could gather from her confused statement, the facts are these: Lieutenant Bradley— that's the naval officer stationed at Rivermouth—has been paying court to Miss Daw for some time past, but not so much to her liking as to that of the colonel, who it seems is an old friend of the young gentleman's father. Yesterday (I knew she was in some trouble when she drove up to our gate) the colonel spoke to Marjorie of Bradley—urged his suit, I infer. Marjorie expressed her dislike for the lieutenant with characteristic frankness, and finally confessed to her father—well, I really do not know what she confessed. It must have been the vaguest of confessions, and must have sufficiently puzzled the colonel. At any rate, it exasperated him. I suppose I am implicated in that matter, and that the colonel feels bitterly towards me. I do not see why: I have carried no messages between you and Miss Daw; I have behaved with the greatest discretion. I can find no flaw anywhere in my proceeding. I do not see that anybody has done anything—except the colonel himself.

It is probable, nevertheless, that the friendly relations between the two houses will be broken off. "A plague o' both your houses," say you. I will keep you informed, as well as I can, of what occurs over the way. We shall remain here until the second week in September. Stay where you are, or, at all events, do not dream of joining me. . . . Colonel Daw is sitting on the piazza looking rather wicked. I have not seen Marjorie since I parted with her in the garden.

XII

Edward Delaney to Thomas Dillon, M.D., Madison Square, New York

August 30, 1872

My Dear Doctor: If you have any influence over Flemming, I beg of you to exert it to prevent his coming to this place at present. There are circumstances which I will explain to you before long, that make it of the first importance that he should not come into this neighborhood. His appearance here, I speak advisedly, would be disastrous to him. In urging him to remain in New York, or to go to some inland resort, you will be doing him and me a real service. Of course you will not mention my name in this connection. You know me well enough, my dear doctor, to be assured that, in begging your secret cooperation, I have reasons that will meet your entire approval when they are made plain to you. We shall return to town on the 15th of next month, and my first duty will be to present myself at your hospitable door and satisfy your curiosity, if I have excited it. My father, I am glad to state, has so greatly improved that he can no longer be regarded as an invalid. With great esteem, I am, etc., etc.

XIII

Edward Delaney to John Flemming

August 31, 1872

Your letter, announcing your mad determination to come here, has just reached me. I beseech you to reflect a moment. The step would be fatal to your interests and hers. You would furnish just cause for irritation to R. W. D.; and, though he loves Marjorie tenderly, he is capable of going to any lengths if opposed. You would not like, I am convinced, to be the means of causing him to treat *her* with severity. That would be the result of your presence at The Pines at this juncture. I am annoyed to be obliged to point out these things to you. We are on very delicate ground, Jack; the situation is critical, and the slightest mistake in a move would cost us the game. If you consider it worth the winning, be patient. Trust a little to my sagacity. Wait and see what happens. Moreover, I understand from Dillon that you are in no condition to take so long a journey. He thinks the air of the coast would be the worst thing possible for you; that you ought to go inland, if anywhere. Be advised by me. Be advised by Dillon.

XIV

Telegrams

September 1, 1872

1—To Edward Delaney
Letter received. Dillon be hanged. I think I ought to be on the ground.

J.F.

2—To John Flemming
Stay where you are. You would only complicate matters. Do not move until you hear from me.

E.D.

3—To Edward Delaney
My being at The Pines could be kept secret. I must see her.

J.F.

4—To John Flemming

Do not think of it. It would be useless. R. W. D. has locked M. in her room. You would not be able to effect an interview.

E.D.

5—To Edward Delaney

Locked in her room. Good God. That settles the question. I shall leave by the twelve-fifteen express.

J.F.

XV

The Arrival

On the second of September, 1872, as the down express due at 3.40 left the station at Hampton, a young man, leaning on the shoulder of a servant, whom he addressed as Watkins, stepped from the platform into a hack, and requested to be driven to The Pines. On arriving at the gate of a modest farmhouse, a few miles from the station, the young man descended with difficulty from the carriage, and, casting a hasty glance across the road, seemed much impressed by some peculiarity in the landscape. Again leaning on the shoulder of the person Watkins, he walked to the door of the farm-house and inquired for Mr. Edward Delaney. He was informed by the aged man who answered his knock, that Mr. Edward Delaney had gone to Boston the day before, but that Mr. Jonas Delaney was within. This information did not appear satisfactory to the stranger, who inquired if Mr. Edward Delaney had left any message for Mr. John Flemming. There *was* a letter for Mr. Flemming, if he were that person. After a brief absence the aged man reappeared with a Letter.

XVI

Edward Delaney to John Flemming

September 1, 1872

I am horror-stricken at what I have done! When I began this correspondence I had no other purpose than to relieve the tedium of your sick-chamber. Dillon told me to cheer you up. I tried to. I thought you entered into the spirit of the thing. I had no idea, until within a few days, that you were taking matters *au grand sérieux*.

What can I say? I am in sackcloth and ashes. I am a pariah, a dog of an outcast. I tried to make a little romance to interest you, something soothing and idyllic, and, by Jove! I have done it only too well! My father doesn't know a word of this, so don't jar the old gentleman any more than you can help. I fly from the wrath to come—when you arrive! For oh, dear Jack, there isn't any colonial mansion on the other side of the road, there isn't any piazza, there isn't any hammock—there isn't any Marjorie Daw!

BY WAY OF DISCUSSION

It would be difficult to think of another story whose general intent and ultimate impact are more a result of its method of narration than is Thomas Bailey Aldrich's "Marjorie Daw." Trying to imagine the story being written from any point of view other than a series of fictionalized letters seems impossible. In fact, the epistolary method of narration so completely controls the whole production that it is quite easy for the reader to forget that it is Aldrich who has written these fictionalized letters and not Dr. Dillon, John Flemming, and Edward Delaney. Furthermore, not a few readers are almost as surprised as John Flemming is at the story's conclusion to learn that "there isn't any Marjorie Daw!"

Every element in "Marjorie Daw"—plot, character, emotion, symbolism, and theme—is dramatized, and the method of dramatization consists of the careful presentation of the letters. A few specific questions are worth discussing, however. First, can we believe that a young man like John Flemming would come to think that Marjorie Daw actually exists? Dr. Dillon describes Flemming's condition in this way:

> *Flemming is doing perfectly well physically*; but I must confess that the irritable and morbid state of mind into which he has fallen causes me a great deal of uneasiness. . . . His temper has become something frightful.

The man broods for hours at a time, refuses to eat or read, and has given himself over to fits of melancholy. The answer, then, seems to be yes: Flemming is likely to grasp at anything that promises to break the tedium of having to convalesce in his New York apartment at the time of year when everyone else is "out of town enjoying himself."

Next, does the author unfairly mislead the reader into thinking that Marjorie Daw exists? To answer this question, let's look at Delaney's first letter to Flemming. Delaney is responding to Dr. Dillon's letter in which Dillon says, "Write to him, write to him frequently, distract his mind, cheer him up, and prevent him from becoming a confirmed case of melancholia." So, Delaney writes to Flemming. He tells Flemming that he really has nothing much to say but that if it will help, "I will write you a whole post-office full of letters." He goes on to make the following comments:

> I wish I were a novelist. This old house . . . would be the place in which to write a summer romance. . . . Yet I wonder if even a Liza or an Alexandra Paulovna could stir the heart of a man who has constant twinges in his leg. I wonder if one of our own Yankee girls . . . would be of any comfort to you in your present deplorable condition. If I thought so, I would hasten down to the Surf House and catch one for you; or, better still, I would find you one over the way.

Then Delaney launches into his description of the mansion and its pretty occupant. Significantly, this description begins with the word "picture," a word often used to mean "imagine" or "suppose," and ends with the phrase "But enough of this nonsense." We can conclude, then, that the careful reader will not be misled into believing that Marjorie and the mansion actually exist.

But there is a greater question to be considered: Do Delaney's motives in creating the fictional Marjorie Daw remain as pure as they were at the beginning of the correspondence? To answer this question, we must take note of just how well Delaney succeeds in his original goal of diverting Flemming from a state of intense melancholia. By August 17, Flemming is clearly intrigued by the mythical Marjorie:

> Ned, that Miss Daw must be a charming person. I should certainly like her. I like her already. When you spoke in your first letter of seeing a young girl swinging in a hammock under your chamber window, I was somehow strangely drawn to her. I cannot account for it in the least. What you have subsequently written of Miss Daw has strengthened the impression. You seem to be describing a woman I have known in some previous state of existence, or dreamed of in this.

Near the end of this same letter, Flemming suggests that Delaney send him a photograph of Miss Daw:

> Speaking of photographs, couldn't you manage to slip one of her *cartes-de-visite* from her album—she must have an album, you know—and send it to me? I will return it before it could be missed.

Shortly thereafter, in a letter that does not actually appear in the story, Flemming confesses that he is "half in love" with Marjorie.

From this point on, it is clear that Flemming is in deep emotional trouble. Unfortunately, however, Delaney cannot confess his trickery: doing so would probably cause his friend to suffer a second, and more severe, attack of melancholia. Delaney's only recourse, then, is to continue the deception until Flemming is more nearly recovered and at the same time try to prepare him psychologically for the inevitable revelation. Thus, in his August 22 letter we find Delaney chiding Flemming for falling "half in love with a woman you have never seen—with a shadow, a chimera." He tells Flemming that "the chances are ten to five that, when you do come to know her, she will fall far short of your ideal, and you will not care for her in the least."

Although finding it necessary to inform Flemming that Marjorie "has all but confessed to me her interest in you," Delaney manages to compound the ambiguity of this already ambiguous statement by suggesting that Marjorie's supposed confession may not in fact have been made at all: "Now that I am back again in my room, it all appears like an illusion." Later, in advising Flemming not to write to Marjorie, Delaney says, "She knows you only through me; you are to her an abstraction, a figure in a dream."

To this point, Delaney's course of action, although perhaps less than prudent, has made good sense. But how can we account for his behavior when Flemming announces that he will visit Marjorie? Are Delaney's motives still as pure as they were at the start of the deception? After all, more than three weeks have elapsed since Flemming's accident, and he is now able to move about with the help of his servant. Presumably, then, Delaney can confess the truth without triggering more melancholia in his friend. Presumably, too, such a confession would be less distressing to Flemming than would allowing him to discover the truth for himself after a long trip. Nonetheless, Delaney makes desperate and complicated efforts to halt Flemming's visit to The Pines; and when these efforts fail, Delaney flees rather than stay and face the music.

Even if we admit that Delaney's motives for creating the mythical Marjorie may have at first been pure, there is a definite question about what they later become. Is it possible that Delaney's behavior at the story's end is motivated by the egotistical desire to play the part of successful tale-spinner as long as possible? Early in the exchange of letters, Flemming flattered his friend's literary ability:

> I supposed your loft stuffed with dry legal parchments, mortgages and affidavits; you take down a package of manuscript, and lo! there are lyrics and sonnets and canzonettas. You really have a graphic descriptive touch, Edward Delaney, and I suspect you of anonymous love-tales in the magazines.

Perhaps there is an even darker side of Edward Delaney's character. Maybe, for some unknown and perhaps subconscious reason, he even comes to the point of trying to punish his old friend. Given the story's ending, there seems ample cause to suspect that this may be exactly the case.

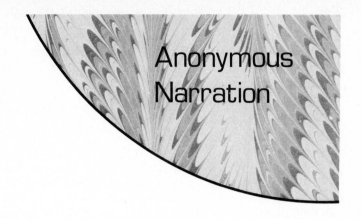

Anonymous Narration

GINA BERRIAULT

The Stone Boy

Arnold drew his overalls and raveling gray sweater over his naked body. In the other narrow bed his brother Eugene went on sleeping, undisturbed by the alarm clock's rusty ring. Arnold, watching his brother sleeping, felt a peculiar dismay; he was nine, six years younger than Eugie, and in their waking hours it was he who was subordinate. To dispel emphatically his uneasy advantage over his sleeping brother, he threw himself on the hump of Eugie's body.

"Get up! Get up!" he cried.

Arnold felt his brother twist away and saw the blankets lifted in a great wing, and, all in an instant, he was lying on his back under the covers with only his face showing, like a baby, and Eugie was sprawled on top of him.

"Whassa matter with you?" asked Eugie in sleepy anger, his face hanging close.

"Get up," Arnold repeated. "You said you'd pick peas with me."

Stupidly, Eugie gazed around the room as if to see if morning had come into it yet. Arnold began to laugh derisively, making soft, snorting noises, and was thrown off the bed. He got up from the floor and went down the stairs, the laughter continuing, like hiccups, against his will. But when he opened the staircase door and entered the parlor, he hunched up his shoulders and was quiet because his parents slept in the bedroom downstairs.

Arnold lifted his .22-caliber rifle from the rack on the kitchen wall. It was an old lever-action Winchester that his father had given him because nobody else used it any more. On their way down to the garden he and Eugie would go by the lake, and if there were any ducks on it he'd take a shot at them. Standing on the stool before the cupboard, he searched on the top shelf in the confusion of medicines and ointments for man and beast and found a small yellow box of .22 cartridges. Then he sat down on the stool and began to load his gun.

It was cold in the kitchen so early, but later in the day, when his mother canned the peas, the heat from the wood stove would be almost unbearable. Yesterday she had finished preserving the huckleberries that the family had picked along the mountain, and before that she had canned all the cherries his father had brought from the warehouse in Corinth. Sometimes, on these summer days, Arnold would deliberately come out from the shade where he was playing and make himself as uncomfortable as his mother was in the kitchen by standing in the sun until the sweat ran down his body.

Eugie came clomping down the stairs and into the kitchen, his head drooping with sleepiness. From his perch on the stool Arnold watched Eugie slip on his green knit cap. Eugie didn't really need a cap; he hadn't had a haircut in a long time and his brown curls grew thick and matted, close around his ears and down his neck, tapering there to a small whorl. Eugie passed his left hand through his hair before he set his cap down with his right. The very way he slipped his cap on was an announcement of his status; almost everything he did was a reminder that he was eldest—first he, then Nora, then Arnold—and called attention to how tall he was (almost as tall as his father), how long his legs were, how small he was in the hips, and what a neat dip above his buttocks his thick-soled logger's boots gave him. Arnold never tired of watching Eugie offer silent praise unto himself. He wondered, as he sat enthralled, if when he got to be Eugie's age he would still be undersized and his hair still straight.

Eugie eyed the gun. "Don't you know this ain't duck-season?" he asked gruffly, as if he were the sheriff.

"No, I don't know," Arnold said with a snigger.

Eugie picked up the tin washtub for the peas, unbolted the door with his free hand and kicked it open. Then, lifting the tub to his head, he went clomping down the back steps. Arnold followed, closing the door behind him.

The sky was faintly gray, almost white. The mountains behind the farm made the sun climb a long way to show itself. Several miles to the south, where the range opened up, hung an orange mist, but the valley in which the farm lay was still cold and colorless.

Eugie opened the gate to the yard and the boys passed between the barn and the row of chicken houses, their feet stirring up the carpet of brown feathers dropped by the molting chickens. They paused before going down the slope to the lake. A fluky morning wind ran among the shocks of wheat that covered the slope. It sent a shimmer northward across the lake, gently moving the rushes that formed an island in the center. Killdeer, their white markings flashing, skimmed the water, crying their shrill, sweet cry. And there at the south end of the lake were four wild ducks, swimming out from the willows into open water.

Arnold followed Eugie down the slope, stealing, as his brother did, from one shock of wheat to another. Eugie paused before climbing through the wire fence that divided the wheatfield from the marshy pasture around the lake. They were screened from the ducks by the willows along the lake's edge.

"If you hit your duck, you want me to go in after it?" Eugie said.

"If you want," Arnold said.

Eugie lowered his eyelids, leaving slits of mocking blue. "You'd drown 'fore you got to it, them legs of yours are so puny," he said.

He shoved the tub under the fence and, pressing down the center wire, climbed through into the pasture.

Arnold pressed down the bottom wire, thrust a leg through and leaned forward to bring the other leg after. His rifle caught on the wire and he jerked at it. The air was rocked by the sound of the shot. Feeling foolish, he lifted his face, baring it to an expected shower of derision from his brother. But Eugie did not turn around. Instead, from his crouching position, he fell to his knees and then pitched forward onto his face. The ducks rose up crying from the lake, cleared the mountain background and beat away northward across the pale sky.

Arnold squatted beside his brother. Eugie seemed to be climbing the earth, as if the earth ran up and down, and when he found he couldn't scale it he lay still.

"Eugie?"

Then Arnold saw it, under the tendril of hair at the nape of the neck—a slow rising of bright blood. It had an obnoxious movement, like that of a parasite.

"Hey, Eugie," he said again. He was feeling the same discomfort he had felt when he had watched Eugie sleeping; his brother didn't know that he was lying face down in the pasture.

Again he said, "Hey, Eugie," an anxious nudge in his voice. But Eugie was as still as the morning about them.

Arnold set his rifle on the ground and stood up. He picked up the tub and, dragging it behind him, walked along by the willows to the garden fence and climbed through. He went down on his knees among the tangled vines. The pods were cold with the night, but his hands were strange to him, and not until some time had passed did he realize that the pods were numbing his fingers. He picked from the top of the vine first, then lifted the vine to look underneath for pods and then moved on to the next.

It was a warmth on his back, like a large hand laid firmly there, that made him raise his head. Way up the slope the gray farmhouse was struck by the sun. While his head had been bent the land had grown bright around him.

When he got up his legs were so stiff that he had to go down on his knees again to ease the pain. Then, walking sideways, he dragged the tub, half full of peas, up the slope.

The kitchen was warm now; a fire was roaring in the stove with a closed-up, rushing sound. His mother was spooning eggs from a pot of boiling water and putting them into a bowl. Her short brown hair was uncombed and fell forward across her eyes as she bent her head. Nora was lifting a frying pan full of trout from the stove, holding the handle with a dish towel. His father had just come in from bringing the cows from the north pasture to the barn, and was sitting on the stool, unbuttoning his red plaid Mackinaw.

"Did you boys fill the tub?" his mother asked.

"They ought of by now," his father said. "They went out of the house an hour ago. Eugie woke me up comin' downstairs. I heard you shootin'—did you get a duck?"

"No," Arnold said. They would want to know why Eugie wasn't coming in for breakfast, he thought. "Eugie's dead," he told them.

They stared at him. The pitch cracked in the stove.

"You kids playin' a joke?" his father asked.

"Where's Eugene?" his mother asked scoldingly. She wanted, Arnold knew, to see his eyes, and when he had glanced at her she put the bowl and spoon down on the stove and walked past him. His father stood up and went out the door after her. Nora followed them with little skipping steps, as if afraid to be left alone.

Arnold went into the barn, down along the foddering passage past the cows waiting to be milked, and climbed into the loft. After a few minutes he heard a terrifying sound coming toward the house. His parents and Nora were returning from the willows, and sounds sharp as knives were rising from his mother's breast and carrying over the sloping fields. In a short while he heard his father go down the back steps, slam the car door and drive away.

Arnold lay still as a fugitive, listening to the cows eating close by. If his parents never called him, he thought, he would stay up in the loft forever, out of the way. In the night he would sneak down for a drink of water from the faucet over the trough and for whatever food they left for him by the barn.

The rattle of his father's car as it turned down the lane recalled him to the present. He heard voices of his Uncle Andy and Aunt Alice as they and his father went past the barn to the lake. He could feel the morning growing heavier with sun. Someone, probably Nora, had let the chickens out of their coops and they were cackling in the yard.

After a while another car turned down the road off the highway. The car drew to a stop and he heard the voices of strange men. The men also went past the barn and down to the lake. The undertakers, whom his father must have phoned from Uncle Andy's house, had arrived from Corinth. Then he heard everybody come back and heard the car turn around and leave.

"Arnold!" It was his father calling from the yard.

He climbed down the ladder and went out into the sun, picking wisps of hay from his overalls.

Corinth, nine miles away, was the county seat. Arnold sat in the front seat of the old Ford between his father, who was driving, and Uncle Andy; no one spoke. Uncle Andy was his mother's brother, and he had been fond of Eugie because Eugie had resembled him. Andy had taken Eugie hunting and had given him a knife and a lot of things, and now Andy, his eyes narrowed, sat tall and stiff beside Arnold.

Arnold's father parked the car before the courthouse. It was a two-story brick building with a lamp on each side of the bottom step. They went up the wide stone steps, Arnold and his father going first, and entered the darkly paneled hallway. The shirt-sleeved man in the sheriff's office said that the sheriff was at Carlson's Parlor examining the Curwing boy.

Andy went off to get the sheriff while Arnold and his father waited on a bench in the corridor. Arnold felt his father watching him, and he lifted his eyes with painful casualness to the announcement, on the opposite wall, of the Corinth County Annual Rodeo, and then to the clock with its loudly clucking pendulum. After he had come down from the loft his father and Uncle Andy had stood in the yard with him and asked him to tell them everything, and he had explained to them how the gun had caught on the wire. But when they had asked him why he hadn't run back to the house to tell his parents, he had had no answer—all he could say was that he had gone down into the garden to pick the peas. His father had stared at him in a pale, puzzled way, and it was then that he had felt his father and the others set their cold, turbulent silence against him. Arnold shifted on the bench, his only feeling a small one of compunction imposed by his father's eyes.

At a quarter past nine Andy and the sheriff came in. They all went into the sheriff's private office, and Arnold was sent forward to sit in the chair by the sheriff's desk; his father and Andy sat down on the bench against the wall.

The sheriff lumped down into his swivel chair and swung toward Arnold. He was an old man with white hair like wheat stubble. His restless green eyes made him seem not to be in his office but to be hurrying and bobbing around somewhere else.

"What did you say your name was?" the sheriff asked.

"Arnold," he replied; but he could not remember telling the sheriff his name before.

"Curwing?"

"Yes."

"What were you doing with a .22, Arnold?"

"It's mine," he said.

"Okay. What were you going to shoot?"

"Some ducks," he replied.

"Out of season?"

He nodded.

"That's bad," said the sheriff. "Were you and your brother good friends?"

What did he mean—good friends? Eugie was his brother. That was different from a friend, Arnold thought. A best friend was his own age, but Eugie was almost a man. Eugie had had a way of looking at him, slyly and mockingly and yet confidentially, that had summed up how they both felt about being brothers. Arnold had wanted to be with Eugie more than with anybody else but he couldn't say they had been good friends.

"Did they ever quarrel?" the sheriff asked his father.

"Not that I know," his father replied. "It seemed to me that Arnold cared a lot for Eugie."

"Did you?" the sheriff asked Arnold.

If it seemed so to his father, then it was so. Arnold nodded.

"Were you mad at him this morning?"

"No."

"How did you happen to shoot him?"

"We was crawlin' through the fence."

"Yes?"

"An' the gun got caught on the wire."

"Seems the hammer must of caught," his father put in.

"All right, that's what happened," said the sheriff. "But what I want you to tell me is this. Why didn't you go back to the house and tell your father right away? Why did you go and pick peas for an hour?"

Arnold gazed over his shoulder at his father, expecting his father to have an answer for this also. But his father's eyes, larger and even lighter blue than usual, were fixed upon him curiously. Arnold picked at a callus in his right palm. It seemed odd now that he had not run back to the house and wakened his father, but he could not remember why he had not. They were all waiting for him to answer.

"I come down to pick peas," he said.

"Didn't you think," asked the sheriff, stepping carefully from word to word, "that it was more important for you to go tell your parents what had happened?"

"The sun was gonna come up," Arnold said.

"What's that got to do with it?"

"It's better to pick peas while they're cool."

The sheriff swung away from him, laid both hands flat on his desk. "Well, all I can say is," he said across to Arnold's father and Uncle Andy, "he's either a moron or he's so reasonable that he's way ahead of us." He gave a challenging snort. "It's come to my notice that the most reasonable guys are mean ones. They don't feel nothing."

For a moment the three men sat still. Then the sheriff lifted his hand like a man taking an oath. "Take him home," he said.

Andy uncrossed his legs. "You don't want him?"

"Not now," replied the sheriff. "Maybe in a few years."

Arnold's father stood up. He held his hat against his chest. "The gun ain't his no more," he said wanly.

Arnold went first through the hallway, hearing behind him the heels of his father and Uncle Andy striking the floor boards. He went down the steps ahead of them and climbed into the back seat of the car. Andy paused as he was getting into the front seat and gazed back at Arnold, and Arnold saw that his uncle's eyes had absorbed the knowingness from the sheriff's eyes. Andy and his father and the sheriff had discovered what made him go down into the garden. It was because he was cruel, the sheriff had said, and didn't care about his brother. Was that the reason? Arnold lowered his eyelids meekly against his uncle's stare.

The rest of the day he did his tasks around the farm, keeping apart from the family. At evening, when he saw his father stomp tiredly into the house, Arnold did not put down his hammer and leave the chicken coop he was repairing. He was afraid that they did not want him to eat supper with them. But in a few minutes another fear that they would go to the trouble of calling him and that he would be made conspicuous by his tardiness made him follow his father into the house. As he went through the kitchen he saw the jars of peas standing in rows on the workbench, a reproach to him.

No one spoke at supper, and his mother, who sat next to him, leaned her head in her hand all through the meal, curving her fingers over her eyes so as not to see him. They were finishing their small, silent supper when the visitors began to arrive, knocking hard on the back door. The men were coming from their farms now that it was growing dark and they could not work any more.

Old Man Matthews, gray and stocky, came first, with his two sons, Orion, the elder, and Clint, who was Eugie's age. As the callers entered the parlor, where the family ate, Arnold sat down in a rocking chair. Even as he had been undecided before supper whether to remain outside or take his place at the table, he now thought that he should go upstairs, and yet he stayed to avoid being conspicuous by his absence. If he stayed, he thought, as he always stayed and listened when visitors came, they would see that he was only Arnold and not the person the sheriff thought he was. He sat with his arms crossed and his hands tucked into his armpits and did not lift his eyes.

The Matthews men had hardly settled down around the table, after Arnold's mother and Nora had cleared away the dishes, when another car rattled down the road and someone else rapped on the back door. This time it was Sullivan, a spare and sandy man, so nimble of gesture and expression that Arnold had never been able to catch more than a few of his meanings. Sullivan, in dusty jeans, sat down in the other rocker, shot out his skinny legs and began to talk in his fast way, recalling everything that Eugene had ever said to him. The other men interrupted to tell of occasions they remembered, and after a time Clint's young voice, hoarse like Eugene's had been, broke in to tell about the time Eugene had beat him in a wrestling match.

Out in the kitchen the voices of Orion's wife and of Mrs. Sullivan mingled with Nora's voice but not, Arnold noticed, his mother's. Then dry little Mr. Cram came, leaving large Mrs. Cram in the kitchen, and there was no chair left for Mr. Cram to sit in. No one asked Arnold to get up and he was unable to rise. He knew that the story had got around to them during the day about how he had gone and picked peas after he had shot his brother, and he knew that although they were talking only about Eugie they were thinking about him and if he got up, if he moved even his foot, they would all be alerted. Then Uncle Andy arrived and leaned his tall, lanky body against the door-jamb and there were two men standing.

Presently Arnold was aware that the talk had stopped. He knew without looking up that the men were watching him.

"Not a tear in his eye," said Andy, and Arnold knew that it was his uncle who had gestured the men to attention.

"He don't give a hoot, is that how it goes?" asked Sullivan, trippingly.

"He's a reasonable fellow," Andy explained. "That's what the sheriff said. It's us who ain't reasonable. If we'd of shot our brother, we'd of come runnin' back to the house, cryin' like a baby. Well, we'd of been unreasonable. What would of been the use of actin' like that? If your brother is shot dead, he's shot dead. What's the use of gettin' emotional about it? The thing to do is go down to the garden and pick peas. Am I right?"

The men around the room shifted their heavy, satisfying weight of unreasonableness.

Matthews' son Orion said: "If I'd of done what he done, Pa would've hung my pelt by the side of that big coyote's in the barn."

Arnold sat in the rocker until the last man had filed out. While his family was out in the kitchen bidding the callers good night and the cars were driving away down the dirt lane to the highway, he picked up one of the kerosene lamps and slipped quickly up the stairs. In his room he undressed by lamp-light, although he and Eugie had always undressed in the dark, and not until he was lying in his bed did he blow out the flame. He felt nothing, not any grief. There was only the same immense silence and crawling inside of him; it was the way the house and fields felt under a merciless sun.

He awoke suddenly. He knew that his father was out in the yard, closing the doors of the chicken houses so that the chickens could not roam out too early and fall prey to the coyotes that came down from the mountains at daybreak. The sound that had wakened him was the step of his father as he got up from the rocker and went down the back steps. And he knew that his mother was awake in her bed.

Throwing off the covers, he rose swiftly, went down the stairs and across the dark parlor to his parents' room. He rapped on the door.

"Mother?"

From the closed room her voice rose to him, a seeking and retreating voice. "Yes?"

"Mother?" he asked insistently. He had expected her to realize that he wanted to go down on his knees by her bed and tell her that Eugie was dead. She did not know it yet, nobody knew it, and yet she was sitting up in bed, waiting to be told, waiting for him to confirm her dread. He had expected her to tell him to come in, to allow him to dig his head into her blankets and tell her about the terror he had felt when he had knelt beside Eugie. He had come to clasp her in his arms and, in his terror, to pommel her breasts with his head. He put his hand upon the knob.

"Go back to bed, Arnold," she called sharply.

But he waited.

"Go back! Is night when you get afraid?"

At first he did not understand. Then, silently, he left the door and for a stricken moment stood by the rocker. Outside everything was still. The fences, the shocks of wheat seen through the window before him were so still it was as if they moved and breathed in the daytime and had fallen silent with the lateness of the hour. It was a silence that seemed to observe his father, a figure moving alone around the yard, his lantern casting a circle of light by his feet. In a few minutes his father would enter the dark house, the lantern still lighting his way.

Arnold was suddenly aware that he was naked. He had thrown off his blankets and come down the stairs to tell his mother how he felt about Eugie, but she had refused to listen to him and his nakedness had become unpardonable. At once he went back up the stairs, fleeing from his father's lantern.

At breakfast he kept his eyelids lowered as if to deny the humiliating night. Nora, sitting at his left, did not pass the pitcher of milk to him and he did not ask for it. He would never again, he vowed, ask them for anything, and he ate his fried eggs and potatoes only because everybody ate meals—the cattle ate, and the cats; it was customary for everybody to eat.

"Nora, you gonna keep that pitcher for yourself?" his father asked.

Nora lowered her head unsurely.

"Pass it on to Arnold," his father said.

Nora put her hands in her lap.

His father picked up the metal pitcher and set it down at Arnold's plate.

Arnold, pretending to be deaf to the discord, did not glance up but relief rained over his shoulders at the thought that his parents recognized him again. They must have lain awake after his father had come in from the yard: had they realized together why he had come down the stairs and knocked at their door?

"Bessie's missin' this morning," his father called out to his mother, who had gone into the kitchen. "She went up the mountain last night and had her calf, most likely. Somebody's got to go up and find her 'fore the coyotes get the calf."

That had been Eugie's job, Arnold thought. Eugie would climb the cattle trails in search of a newborn calf and come down the mountain carrying the calf across his back, with the cow running down along behind him, mooing in alarm.

Arnold ate the few more forkfuls of his breakfast, put his hands on the edge of the table and pushed back his chair. If he went for the calf he'd be away from the farm all morning. He could switch the cow down the mountain slowly, and the calf would run along at its mother's side.

When he passed through the kitchen his mother was setting a kettle of water on the stove. "Where you going?" she asked awkwardly.

"Up to get the calf," he replied, averting his face.

"Arnold?"

At the door he paused reluctantly, his back to her, knowing that she was seeking him out, as his father was doing, and he called upon his pride to protect him from them.

"Was you knocking at my door last night?"

He looked over his shoulder at her, his eyes narrow and dry.

"What'd you want?" she asked humbly.

"I didn't want nothing," he said flatly.

Then he went out the door and down the back steps, his legs trembling from the fright his answer gave him.

BY WAY OF DISCUSSION

"The Stone Boy" employs the narrative technique called single character limited omniscience. Consequently, nothing in the story is presented from the "I" point of view. In fact, we do not know who the real storyteller is, because the narrator is submerged within the mind of Arnold Curwing, the young protagonist. Narrative omniscience is thus limited to Arnold, and from the first we see, hear, and feel everything that happens through his senses. As the story progresses, Arnold experiences two severe mental and emotional traumas, each of which is sharply reflected in his thoughts as they are presented.

During the part of the story preceding the accidental shooting, Arnold clearly shows his love and admiration for his elder brother. In fact, there exists an easy camaraderie between the two, with Arnold playing the role of little brother and Eugie playing the role of big brother. This relationship is demonstrated by Arnold's knowing that he can throw himself upon his sleeping big brother without any serious reprisals. The playful banter between the two boys, Arnold's easy laughter, and the fact that Arnold thinks of his brother as Eugie rather than as Eugene are further signs of the closeness between the boys.

Between the time of the shooting and Arnold's attempt to visit his mother in her bedroom, Arnold is in a state of shock that temporarily robs him of the ability to demonstrate his feelings. This condition causes his family, his relatives, and the sheriff to mistakenly regard Arnold as some sort of little monster. The emotional paralysis is dramatized at many points. For example, let's consider Arnold's inner reactions as he and his father are waiting for the sheriff:

> Arnold felt his father watching him, and he lifted his eyes with painful casualness to the announcement, on the opposite wall, of the Corinth County Annual Rodeo, and then to the clock with its loudly clucking pendulum. . . . Arnold shifted on the bench, his only feeling a small one of compunction imposed by his father's eyes.

Throughout the remainder of the day and up until the time he goes to bed, Arnold remains in a state of shock:

> In his room he undressed by lamplight, although he and Eugie had always undressed in the dark, and not until he was lying in his bed did he blow out the flame. He felt nothing, not any grief. There was only the same immense silence and crawling inside of him; it was the way the house and fields felt under a merciless sun.

The story's climax occurs when sleep finally releases Arnold from his emotional straitjacket. He awakens suddenly and with grief flooding his mind, he makes his way downstairs to unburden himself to his mother:

> He had expected her to realize that he wanted to go down on his knees by her bed and tell her that Eugie was dead. . . . He had expected her to tell him to come in, to allow him to dig his head into her blankets and tell her about the terror he had felt when he had knelt beside Eugie. He had come to clasp her in his arms and, in his terror, to pommel her breasts with his head.

But this catharsis is not to be. Convinced that Arnold is some sort of emotionless robot, she refuses to admit him to her room, thus ironically transforming him into the very creature she believes he already is. The mother's actions also lend a note of ironic prophecy to the sheriff's earlier remark that he might want Arnold in a few years. If, as the sheriff says, the meanest people are those without feelings, Arnold may well commit some terrible crime in future years.

To conclude our discussion, we might ask why Gina Berriault chose the third-person point of view in telling this story rather than narration in the first person, which would have provided a much closer identification with the workings of Arnold's mind. Actually, she chose the third person because she had to. Given Arnold's emotional paralysis at the story's conclusion, it would seem completely implausible for the boy to be telling anyone about his own condition.

D. H. LAWRENCE

The Shadow in the Rose Garden

A rather small young man sat by the window of a pretty seaside cottage trying to persuade himself that he was reading the newspaper. It was about half-past eight in the morning. Outside, the glory roses hung in the morning sunshine like little bowls of fire tipped up. The young man looked at the table, then at the clock, then at his own big silver watch. An expression of stiff endurance came on to his face. Then he rose and reflected on the oil-paintings that hung on the walls of the room, giving careful but hostile attention to 'The Stag at Bay'. He tried the lid of the piano, and found it locked. He caught sight of his own face in a little mirror, pulled his brown moustache, and an alert interest sprang into his eyes. He was not ill-favoured. He twisted his moustache. His figure was rather small, but alert and vigorous. As he turned from the mirror a look of self-commiseration mingled with his appreciation of his own physiognomy.

In a state of self-suppression, he went through into the garden. His jacket, however, did not look dejected. It was new, and had a smart and self-confident air, sitting upon a confident body. He contemplated the Tree of Heaven that flourished by the lawn, then sauntered on to the next plant. There was more promise in a crooked apple tree covered with brown-red fruit. Glancing round, he broke off an apple and, with his back to the house, took a clean, sharp bite. To his surprise the fruit was sweet. He took another. Then again he turned to survey the bedroom windows overlooking the garden. He started, seeing a woman's figure; but it was only his wife. She was gazing across to the sea, apparently ignorant of him.

For a moment or two he looked at her, watching her. She was a good-looking woman, who seemed older than he, rather pale, but healthy, her face yearning. Her rich auburn hair was heaped in folds on her forehead. She looked apart from him and his world, gazing away to the sea. It irked her husband that she should continue abstracted and in ignorance of him; he pulled poppy fruits and threw them at the window. She started, glanced at him with a wild smile, and looked away again. Then almost immediately she left the window. He went indoors to meet her. She had a fine carriage, very proud, and wore a dress of soft white muslin.

"I've been waiting long enough," he said.

"For me or for breakfast?" she said lightly. "You know we said nine o'clock. I should have thought you could have slept after the journey."

"You know I'm always up at five, and I couldn't stop in bed after six. You might as well be in pit as in bed, on a morning like this."

"I shouldn't have thought the pit would occur to you, here."

She moved about examining the room, looking at the ornaments under glass covers. He, planted on the hearth-rug, watched her rather uneasily, and grudgingly indulgent. She shrugged her shoulders at the apartment.

"Come," she said, taking his arm, "let us go into the garden till Mrs. Coates brings the tray."

"I hope she'll be quick," he said, pulling his moustache. She gave a short laugh, and leaned on his arm as they went. He had lighted a pipe.

Mrs. Coates entered the room as they went down the steps. The delightful, erect old lady hastened to the window for a good view of her visitors. Her china-blue eyes were bright as she watched the young couple go down the path, he walking in an easy, confident fashion, with his wife on his arm. The landlady began talking to herself in a soft, Yorkshire accent.

"Just of a height they are. She wouldn't ha' married a man less than herself in stature, I think, though he's not her equal otherwise." Here her grand-daughter came in, setting a tray on the table. The girl went to the old woman's side.

"He's been eating the apples, Gran'," she said.

"Has he, my pet? Well, if he's happy, why not?"

Outside, the young, well-favoured man listened with impatience to the chink of the tea-cups. At last, with a sigh of relief, the couple came in to breakfast. After he had eaten for some time, he rested a moment and said:

"Do you think it's any better place than Bridlington?"

"I do," she said, "infinitely! Besides, I am at home here—it's not like a strange sea-side place to me."

"How long were you here?"

"Two years."

He ate reflectively.

"I should ha' thought you'd rather go to a fresh place," he said at length. She sat very silent, and then, delicately, put out a feeler.

"Why?" she said. "Do you think I shan't enjoy myself?"

He laughed comfortably, putting the marmalade thick on his bread.

"I hope so," he said.

She again took no notice of him.

"But don't say anything about it in the village, Frank," she said casually. "Don't say who I am, or that I used to live here. There's nobody I want to meet, particularly, and we should never feel free if they knew me again."

"Why did you come, then?"

" 'Why?' Can't you understand why?"

"Not if you don't want to know anybody."

"I came to see the place, not the people."

He did not say any more.

"Women," she said, "are different from men. I don't know why I wanted to come—but I did."

She helped him to another cup of coffee, solicitously.

"Only," she resumed, "don't talk about me in the village." She laughed shakily. "I don't want my past brought up against me, you know." And she moved the crumbs on the cloth with her finger-tip.

He looked at her as he drank his coffee; he sucked his moustache, and putting down his cup, said phlegmatically:

"I'll bet you've had a lot of past."

She looked with a little guiltiness, that flattered him, down at the table-cloth.

"Well," she said, caressive, "you won't give me away, who I am, will you?"

"No," he said, comforting, laughing, "I won't give you away."

He was pleased.

She remained silent. After a moment or two she lifted her head, saying:

"I've got to arrange with Mrs. Coates, and do various things. So you'd better go out by yourself this morning—and we'll be in to dinner at one."

"But you can't be arranging with Mrs. Coates all morning," he said.

"Oh, well—then I've got some letters to write, and I must get that mark out of my skirt. I've got plenty of little things to do this morning. You'd better go out by yourself."

He perceived that she wanted to be rid of him, so that when she went upstairs, he took his hat and lounged out on to the cliffs, suppressedly angry.

Presently she too came out. She wore a hat with roses, and a long lace scarf hung over her white dress. Rather nervously, she put up her sunshade, and her face was half hidden in its coloured shadow. She went along the narrow track of flagstones that were worn hollow by the feet of the fishermen. She seemed to be avoiding her surroundings, as if she remained safe in the little obscurity of her parasol.

She passed the church, and went down the lane till she came to a high wall by the wayside. Under this she went slowly, stopping at length by an open doorway, which shone like a picture of light in the dark wall. There in the magic beyond the doorway, patterns of shadow lay on the sunny court, on the blue and white sea-pebbles of its paving, while a green lawn glowed beyond, wherea bay tree glittered at the edges. She tiptoed nervously into the court-yard, glancing at the house that stood in shadow. The uncurtained windows looked black and soulless, the kitchen door stood open. Irresolutely she took a step forward, and again forward, leaning, yearning, towards the garden be-yond.

She had almost gained the corner of the house when a heavy step came crunching through the trees. A gardener appeared before her. He held a wicker tray on which were rolling great, dark red gooseberries, over-ripe. He moved slowly.

"The garden isn't open to-day," he said quietly to the attractive woman, who was poised for retreat.

For a moment she was silent with surprise. How should it be public at all?

"When is it open?" she asked, quick-witted.

"The rector lets visitors in on Fridays and Tuesdays."

She stood still, reflecting. How strange to think of the rector opening his garden to the public!

"But everybody will be at church," she said coaxingly to the man. "There'll be nobody here, will there?"

He moved, and the big gooseberries rolled.

"The rector lives at the new rectory," he said.

The two stood still. He did not like to ask her to go. At last she turned to him with a winning smile.

"Might I have *one* peep at the roses?" she coaxed, with pretty wilfulness.

"I don't suppose it would matter," he said, moving aside; "you won't stop long——"

She went forward, forgetting the gardener in a moment. Her face became strained, her movements eager. Glancing round, she saw all the windows giving on to the lawn were curtainless and dark. The house had a sterile appearance, as if it were still used, but not inhabited. A shadow seemed to go over her. She went across the lawn towards the garden, through an arch of crimson ramblers, a gate of colour. There beyond lay the soft blue sea within the bay, misty with morning, and the farthest headland of black rock jutting dimly out between blue and blue of the sky and water. Her face began to shine, transfigured with pain and joy. At her feet the garden fell steeply, all a confusion of flowers, and away below was the darkness of tree-tops covering the beck.

She turned to the garden that shone with sunny flowers around her. She knew the little corner where was the seat beneath the yew tree. Then there was the terrace where a great host of flowers shone, and from this, two paths went down, one at each side of the garden. She closed her sunshade and walked slowly among the many flowers. All round were rose bushes, big banks of roses, then roses hanging and tumbling from pillars, or roses balanced on the standard bushes. By the open earth were many other flowers. If she lifted her head, the sea was upraised beyond, and the Cape.

Slowly she went down one path, lingering like one who has gone back into the past. Suddenly she was touching some heavy crimson roses that were soft as velvet, touching them thoughtfully, without knowing, as a mother sometimes fondles the hand of her child. She leaned slightly forward to catch the scent. Then she wandered on in abstraction. Sometimes a flame-coloured, scentless rose would hold her arrested. She stood gazing at it as if she could not understand it. Again the same softness of intimacy came over her, as she stood before a tumbling heap of pink petals. Then she wondered over the white rose, that was greenish, like ice, in the centre. So, slowly, like a white, pathetic butterfly, she drifted down the path, coming at last to a tiny terrace all full of roses. They seemed to fill the place, a sunny, gay throng. She was shy of them, they were so many and so bright. They seemed to be conversing and laughing. She felt herself in a strange crowd. It exhilarated her, carried her out of herself. She flushed with excitement. The air was pure scent.

Hastily, she went to a little seat among the white roses, and sat down. Her scarlet sunshade made a hard blot of colour. She sat quite still, feeling her own existence lapse. She was no more than a rose, a rose that could not quite come into blossom, but remained tense. A little fly dropped on her knee, on her white dress. She watched it, as if it had fallen on a rose. She was not herself.

Then she started cruelly as a shadow crossed her and a figure moved into her sight. It was a man who had come in slippers, unheard. He wore a linen coat. The morning was shattered, the spell vanished away. She was only afraid of being questioned. He came forward. She rose. Then, seeing him, the strength went from her and she sank on the seat again.

He was a young man, military in appearance, growing slightly stout. His black hair was brushed smooth and bright, his moustache was waxed. But there was something rambling in his gait. She looked up, blanched to the lips, and saw his eyes. They were black, and stared without seeing. They were not a man's eyes. He was coming towards her.

He stared at her fixedly, made an unconscious salute, and sat down beside her on the seat. He moved on the bench, shifted his feet, saying, in a gentlemanly, military voice:

"I don't disturb you—do I?"

She was mute and helpless. He was scrupulously dressed in dark clothes and a linen coat. She could not move. Seeing his hands, with the ring she knew so well upon the little finger, she felt as if she were going dazed. The whole world was deranged. She sat unavailing. For his hands, her symbols of passionate love, filled her with horror as they rested now on his strong thighs.

"May I smoke?" he asked intimately, almost secretly, his hand going to his pocket.

She could not answer, but it did not matter, he was in another world. She wondered, craving, if he recognised her—if he could recognise her. She sat pale with anguish. But she had to go through it.

"I haven't got any tobacco," he said thoughtfully.

But she paid no heed to his words, only she attended to him. Could he recognise her, or was it all gone? She sat still in a frozen kind of suspense.

"I smoke John Cotton," he said, "and I must economise with it, it is expensive. You know, I'm not very well off while these law-suits are going on."

"No," she said, and her heart was cold, her soul kept rigid.

He moved, made a loose salute, rose, and went away. She sat motionless. She could see his shape, the shape she had loved with all her passion: his compact, soldier's head, his fine figure now slackened. And it was not he. It only filled her with horror too difficult to know.

Suddenly he came again, his hand in his jacket pocket.

"Do you mind if I smoke?" he said. "Perhaps I shall be able to see things more clearly."

He sat down beside her again, filling a pipe. She watched his hands with the fine strong fingers. They had always inclined to tremble slightly. It had surprised her, long ago, in such a healthy man. Now they moved inaccurately, and the tobacco hung raggedly out of the pipe.

"I have legal business to attend to. Legal affairs are always so uncertain. I tell my solicitor exactly, precisely what I want, but I can never get it done."

She sat and heard him talking. But it was not he. Yet those were the hands she had kissed, there were the glistening, strange black eyes that she had loved. Yet it was not he. She sat motionless with horror and silence. He dropped his tobacco-pouch, and groped for it on the ground. Yet she must wait to see if he would recognise her. Why could she not go! In a moment he rose.

"I must go at once," he said. "The owl is coming." Then he added confidentially: "His name isn't really the owl, but I call him that. I must go and see if he has come."

She rose too. He stood before her, uncertain. He was a handsome, soldierly fellow, and a lunatic. Her eyes searched him, and searched him, to see if he would recognise her, if she could discover him.

"You don't know me?" she asked, from the terror of her soul, standing alone.

He looked back at her quizzically. She had to bear his eyes. They gleamed on her, but with no intelligence. He was drawing nearer to her.

"Yes, I do know you," he said, fixed, intent, but mad, drawing his face nearer hers. Her horror was too great. The powerful lunatic was coming too near to her.

A man approached, hastening.

"The garden isn't open this morning," he said.

The deranged man stopped and looked at him. The keeper went to the seat and picked up the tobacco-pouch left lying there.

"Don't leave your tobacco, sir," he said, taking it to the gentleman in the linen coat.

"I was just asking this lady to stay to lunch," the latter said politely. "She is a friend of mine."

The woman turned and walked swiftly, blindly, between the sunny roses, out from the garden, past the house with the blank, dark windows, through the sea-pebbled courtyard to the street. Hastening and blind, she went forward without hesitating, not knowing whither. Directly she came to the house she went upstairs, took off her hat, and sat down on the bed. It was as if some membrane had been torn in two in her, so that she was not an entity that could think and feel. She sat staring across at the window, where an ivy spray waved slowly up and down in the sea wind. There was some of the uncanny luminousness of the sunlit sea in the air. She sat perfectly still, without any being. She only felt she might be sick, and it might be blood that was loose in her torn entrails. She sat perfectly still and passive.

After a time she heard the hard tread of her husband on the floor below, and, without herself changing, she registered his movement. She heard his rather disconsolate footsteps go out again, then his voice speaking, answering, growing cheery, and his solid tread drawing near.

He entered, ruddy, rather pleased, an air of complacency about his alert, sturdy figure. She moved stiffly. He faltered in his approach.

"What's the matter?" he asked, a tinge of impatience in his voice. "Aren't you feeling well?"

This was torture to her.

"Quite," she replied.

His brown eyes became puzzled and angry.

"What is the matter?" he said.

"Nothing."

He took a few strides, and stood obstinately, looking out of the window.

"Have you run up against anybody?" he asked.

"Nobody who knows me," she said.

His hands began to twitch. It exasperated him, that she was no more sensible of him than if he did not exist. Turning on her at length, driven, he asked:

"Something has upset you, hasn't it?"

"No, why?" she said, neutral. He did not exist for her, except as an irritant.

His anger rose, filling the veins of his throat.

"It seems like it," he said, making an effort not to show his anger, because there seemed no reason for it. He went away downstairs. She sat still on the bed, and with the residue of feeling left to her, she disliked him because he tormented her. The time went by. She could smell the dinner being served, the smoke of her husband's pipe from the garden. But she could not move. She had no being. There was a tinkle of the bell. She heard him come indoors. And then he mounted the stairs again. At every step her heart grew tight in her. He opened the door.

"Dinner is on the table," he said.

It was difficult for her to endure his presence, for he would interfere with her. She could not recover her life. She rose stiffly and went down. She could neither eat nor talk during the meal. She sat absent, torn, without any being of her own. He tried to go on as if nothing were the matter. But at last he became silent with fury. As soon as it was possible, she went upstairs again, and locked the bedroom door. She must be alone. He went with his pipe into the garden. All his suppressed anger against her who held herself superior to him filled and blackened his heart. Though he had not known it, yet he had never really won her, she had never loved him. She had taken him on sufferance. This had foiled him. He was only a labouring electrician in the mine, she was superior to him. He had always given way to her. But all the while, the injury and ignominy had been working in his soul because she did not hold him seriously. And now all his rage came up against her.

He turned and went indoors. The third time, she heard him mounting the stairs. Her heart stood still. He turned the catch and pushed the door—it was locked. He tried it again, harder. Her heart was standing still.

"Have you fastened the door?" he asked quietly, because of the landlady.
"Yes. Wait a minute."

She rose and turned the lock, afraid he would burst in. She felt hatred towards him, because he did not leave her free. He entered, his pipe between his teeth, and she returned to her old position on the bed. He closed the door and stood with his back to it.

"What's the matter?" he asked determinedly.

She was sick with him. She could not look at him.

"Can't you leave me alone?" she replied, averting her face from him.

He looked at her quickly, fully, wincing with ignominy. Then he seemed to consider for a moment.

"There's something up with you, isn't there?" he asked definitely.

"Yes," she said, "but that's no reason why you should torment me."

"I don't torment you. What's the matter?"

"Why should you know?" she cried, in hate and desperation.

Something snapped. He started and caught his pipe as it fell from his mouth. Then he pushed forward the bitten-off mouthpiece with his tongue, took it from off his lips, and looked at it. Then he put out his pipe, and brushed the ash from his waistcoat. After which he raised his head.

"I want to know," he said. His face was greyish pale, and set uglily.

Neither looked at the other. She knew he was fired now. His heart was pounding heavily. She hated him, but she could not withstand him. Suddenly she lifted her head and turned on him.

"What right have you to know?" she asked.

He looked at her. She felt a pang of surprise for his tortured eyes and his fixed face. But her heart hardened swiftly. She had never loved him. She did not love him now.

But suddenly she lifted her head again swiftly, like a thing that tries to get free. She wanted to be free of it. It was not him so much, but it, something she had put on herself, that bound her so horribly. And having put the bond on herself, it was hardest to take it off. But now she hated everything and felt destructive. He stood with his back to the door, fixed, as if he would oppose her eternally, till she was extinguished. She looked at him. Her eyes were cold and hostile. His workman's hands spread on the panels of the door behind him.

"You know I used to live here?" she began, in a hard voice, as if wilfully to wound him. He braced himself against her, and nodded.

"Well, I was companion to Miss Birch of Torill Hall—she and the rector were friends, and Archie was the rector's son." There was a pause. He listened without knowing what was happening. He stared at his wife. She was squatted in her white dress on the bed, carefully folding and re-folding the hem of her skirt. Her voice was full of hostility.

"He was an officer—a sub-lieutenant—then he quarrelled with his colonel and came out of the army. At any rate"—she plucked at her skirt hem, her husband stood motionless, watching her movements which filled his veins with madness—"he was awfully fond of me, and I was of him—awfully."

"How old was he?" asked the husband.

"When—when I first knew him? Or when he went away——?"

"When you first knew him."

"When I first knew him, he was twenty-six—he's thirty-one—nearly thirty-two—because I'm twenty-nine, and he is nearly three years older——"

She lifted her head and looked at the opposite wall.

"And what then?" said her husband.

She hardened herself, and said callously:

"We were as good as engaged for nearly a year, though nobody knew—at least—they talked—but—it wasn't open. Then he went away——"

"He chucked you?" said the husband brutally, wanting to hurt her into contact with himself. Her heart rose wildly with rage. Then "Yes," she said, to anger him. He shifted from one foot to the other, giving a "Pah!" of rage. There was silence for a time.

"Then," she resumed, her pain giving a mocking note to her words, "he suddenly went out to fight in Africa, and almost the very day I first met you, I heard from Miss Birch he'd got sunstroke—and two months after, that he was dead——"

"That was before you took on with me?" said the husband.

There was no answer. Neither spoke for a time. He had not understood. His eyes were contracted uglily.

"So you've been looking at your old courting places!" he said. "That was what you wanted to go out by yourself for this morning."

Still she did not answer him anything. He went away from the door to the window. He stood with his hands behind him, his back to her. She looked at him. His hands seemed gross to her, the back of his head paltry.

At length, almost against his will, he turned round, asking:

"How long were you carrying on with him?"

"What do you mean?" she replied coldly.

"I mean how long were you carrying on with him?"

She lifted her head, averting her face from him. She refused to answer. Then she said:

"I don't know what you mean, by carrying on. I loved him from the first days I met him—two months after I went to stay with Miss Birch."

"And do you reckon he loved you?" he jeered.

"I know he did."

"How do you know, if he'd have no more to do with you?"

There was a long silence of hate and suffering.

"And how far did it go between you?" he asked at length, in a frightened, stiff voice.

"I hate your not-straightforward questions," she cried, beside herself with his baiting. "We loved each other, and we *were* lovers—we were. I don't care what *you* think: what have you got to do with it? We were lovers before I knew you——"

"Lovers—lovers," he said, white with fury. "You mean you had your fling with an army man, and then came to me to marry you when you'd done——"

She sat swallowing her bitterness. There was a long pause.

"Do you mean to say you used to go—the whole hogger?" he asked, still incredulous.

"Why, what else do you think I mean?" she cried brutally.

He shrank, and became white, impersonal. There was a long, paralysed silence. He seemed to have gone small.

"You never thought to tell me all this before I married you," he said, with bitter irony, at last.

"You never asked me," she replied.

"I never thought there was any need."

"Well, then, you *should* think."

He stood with expressionless, almost child-like set face, revolving many thoughts, whilst his heart was mad with anguish.

Suddenly she added:

"And I saw him to-day," she said. "He is not dead, he's mad."

"Mad!" he said involuntarily.

"A lunatic," she said. It almost cost her her reason to utter the word. There was a pause.

"Did he know you?" asked the husband, in a small voice.

"No," she said.

He stood and looked at her. At last he had learned the width of the breach between them. She still squatted on the bed. He could not go near her. It would be violation to each of them to be brought into contact with the other. The thing must work itself out. They were both shocked so much, they were impersonal, and no longer hated each other. After some minutes he left her and went out.

BY WAY OF DISCUSSION

Dual character limited omniscience, the narrative point of view in "The Shadow in the Rose Garden," allows the reader to focus on the thoughts and feelings of two central characters. It lends itself especially well to the examination of conflicts between individuals with differing backgrounds and temperaments, as well as to showing differing perceptions of a variety of situations and events. In "The Shadow in the Rose Garden" the conflict involves a working-class husband with matter-of-fact sensibilities and his socially superior wife who seems preoccupied with a past love affair. The conflict is rooted in the wife's lingering emotional attachment to her former lover.

As Frank, the husband, awaits his wife's morning appearance, his behavior offers several clues about his character. From his posturing before the mirror, it is evident that he is a man who holds himself in considerable esteem. Although not entirely without an aesthetic sense, as is shown by his disapproving reaction to an overly sentimental painting on the cottage wall, Frank exhibits only a generalized appreciation of the beauties of nature. Thus, although he likes to get up early "on a morning like this," he ignores the glory roses that hang outside the cottage window "like little bowls of fire tipped up"—a reaction completely different from that of his wife later on when she is in the vicar's garden—and he gives only passing contemplation to the Tree of Heaven before turning his attention to the "crooked apple tree" and the fruit it bears. In eating an apple from the tree—ironically the fruit is sweet—Frank symbolically reenacts a variation of the Biblical transgression of Adam, and the incident foreshadows the death of his yet infant marriage, suggesting the unhappiness that will soon enter his own little world.

Other perhaps less subtle signs also point toward the coming marital breakdown between Frank and his wife. As he glances at his watch, Frank is irked by his wife's late sleeping habits. They are totally unlike his own early-to-rise conditioning, a clear indication of the social gulf between the two. Moments later, Frank displays further irritation when his wife, wearing a preoccupied look, appears at the bedroom window but remains oblivious to his presence below. Even after he attracts her attention, he receives only a fleeting smile before she turns away. Disturbed by his wife's distant manner, Frank greets her uneasily and is further puzzled by her desire to steer clear of the villagers. For a brief moment, as she pleads with him not to give her away, Frank feels a resurgence of self-confidence. But once it becomes clear that she wishes the morning to herself, this feeling evaporates, and Frank departs for the cliffside in a state of suppressed rage.

The wife's preoccupation and her rejection of her husband's company stem from her desire to renew the past, and they bode no good for the couple's future together. As soon as Frank is well away, she emerges from the house, puts up her parasol to hide her identity, and hastens guiltily toward the true objective of her vacation trip—the garden in which her old romance had once blossomed. To her, the garden's open doorway, shining like "a picture of light," appears a magic casement into an enchanted land of glowing lawns and glittering trees. Only one thing mars this enchantment, the rectory itself, whose "black and soulless" windows symbolize the destroyed mind of the man she once loved.

Once within the portals of the garden, she becomes "transfigured with pain and joy" and moves among the mossed banks and flowers like a sleepwalker. Pausing before the red and pink roses, she feels once again the old stirrings of tenderness and passion but experiences only bemused puzzlement at the scentless roses with icelike centers. These characteristics reflect the coldness and sterility of her marriage, and as she takes a seat among the flowers she feels a sense of self-estrangement, likening herself to "a rose that could not quite come into blossom." Her thoughts are interrupted when a shadow falls across her face, and she glances up to confront Archie, the lover she thought dead.

A sunstroke has transformed this once passionate fellow into a shambling madman who stares unseeingly out of glistening eyes, talks incoherently of lawsuits and tobacco, and cannot even fill his pipe properly. In the past, the woman had looked upon Archie's hands, with their "fine strong fingers," as "her symbols of passionate love." Now, bereft of all Freudian significance, they fill her with a horror that overwhelms her as she senses the possibility of violence. Emotionally shattered, she rushes like some mortally wounded animal past the flowers, through the gate, and along the village street, away from the shadow in the rose garden and back to Frank, who no longer exists for her "except as an irritant."

The moment he sees his wife again, Frank realizes, despite her denials, that something has upset her badly. As she sits unspeaking through dinner, and afterward as he walks in the cottage garden, Frank is gripped by a silent rage at the thought that his wife considers herself superior to a mere "labouring electrician in the mine" and has "taken him on sufferance." Returning to their room, Frank again tries to talk with his wife, and what he learns is that she has once loved the rector's son. The couple now feel only intense hatred for each other.

Gazing at Frank's frozen face, the wife realizes that she has never loved him. His "workman's" hands, far from being a symbol of passion, appear gross to her, arousing only disgust. For Frank's part, he wishes to hurt his wife as she has hurt him. Jeeringly, he asks her how long she "carried on" her affair and why she is so certain that Archie had truly cared for her, only to be stunned into anguished silence by her admission that she had gone the "whole hogger" with Archie. At this point the couple have completely lost contact and are incapable of feeling anything for each other, even hatred:

> He stood and looked at her. At last he had learned the width of the breach between them. She still squatted on the bed. He could not go near her. It would be a violation to each of them to be brought into contact with the other. The thing must work itself out. They were both shocked so much, they were impersonal, and no longer hated each other. After some minutes he left her and went out.

When reading a story written from the dual character limited omniscience point of view in which the two central characters are in conflict with each other, one must be very careful about deciding which character is to be sympathized with. If the story is a good one, as often as not both characters will deserve at least a measure of our sympathy. In "The Shadow in the Rose Garden," we may at first be inclined to be more sympathetic toward the wife, who has lost her lover, than toward Frank. Almost unconsciously, we are willing to concentrate more on her emotional state than his. But a careful reading of the story will show that Frank is just as deserving of happiness as is his wife, and he loses just as much in the way of desired romance and companionship (with his wife) as his wife has lost. He has played no more unfairly or behaved no more unreasonably with her than she has with him. In another woman's eyes Frank may be preferred over Archie, in Archie's best day. Both characters, then, require our understanding. It is a mistake to sympathize with one and blame the other.

THOMAS MANN

The Infant Prodigy

The infant prodigy entered. The hall became quiet.

It became quiet and then the audience began to clap, because somewhere at the side a leader of mobs, a born organizer, clapped first. The audience had heard nothing yet, but they applauded; for a mighty publicity organization had heralded the prodigy and people were already hypnotized, whether they knew it or not.

The prodigy came from behind a splendid screen embroidered with Empire garlands and great conventionalized flowers, and climbed nimbly up the steps to the platform, diving into the applause as into a bath; a little chilly and shivering, but yet as though into a friendly element. He advanced to the edge of the platform and smiled as though he were about to be photographed; he made a shy, charming gesture of greeting, like a little girl.

He was dressed entirely in white silk, which the audience found enchanting. The little white jacket was fancifully cut, with a sash underneath it, and even his shoes were made of white silk. But against the white socks his bare little legs stood out quite brown; for he was a Greek boy.

He was called Bibi Saccellaphylaccas. And such indeed was his name. No one knew what Bibi was the pet name for, nobody but the impresario, and he regarded it as a trade secret. Bibi had smooth black hair reaching to his shoulders; it was parted on the side and fastened back from the narrow domed forehead by a little silk bow. His was the most harmless childish countenance in the world, with an unfinished nose and guileless mouth. The area beneath his pitch-black mouselike eyes was already a little tired and visibly lined. He looked as though he were nine years old but was really eight and given out for seven. It was hard to tell whether to believe this or not. Probably everybody knew better and still believed it, as happens about so many things. The average man thinks that a little falseness goes with beauty. Where should we get any excitement out of our daily life if we were not willing to pretend a bit? And the average man is quite right, in his average brains!

The prodigy kept on bowing until the applause died down, then he went up to the grand piano, and the audience cast a last look at its programmes. First came a *Marche solonnelle*, then a *Rêverie*, and then *Le Hibou et les moineaux*—all by Bibi Saccellaphylaccas. The whole programme was by him, they were all his compositions. He could not score them, of course, but he had them all in his extraordinary little head and they possessed real artistic significance, or so it said, seriously and objectively, in the programme. The programme sounded as though the impresario had wrested these concessions from his critical nature after a hard struggle.

The prodigy sat down upon the revolving stool and felt with his feet for the pedals, which were raised by means of a clever device so that Bibi could reach them. It was Bibi's own piano, he took it everywhere with him. It rested upon wooden trestles and its polish was somewhat marred by the constant transportation—but all that only made things more interesting.

Bibi put his silk-shod feet on the pedals; then he made an artful little face, looked straight ahead of him, and lifted his right hand. It was a brown, childish little hand; but the wrist was strong and unlike a child's, with well-developed bones.

Bibi made his face for the audience because he was aware that he had to entertain them a little. But he had his own private enjoyment in the thing too, an enjoyment which he could never convey to anybody. It was that prickling delight, that secret shudder of bliss, which ran through him every time he sat at an open piano—it would always be with him. And here was the keyboard again, these seven black and white octaves, among which he had so often lost himself in abysmal and thrilling adventures—and yet it always looked as clean and untouched as a newly washed blackboard. This was the realm of music that lay before him. It lay spread out like an inviting ocean, where he might plunge in and blissfully swim, where he might let himself be borne and carried away, where he might go under in night and storm, yet keep the mastery: control, ordain—he held his right hand poised in the air.

A breathless stillness reigned in the room—the tense moment before the first note came. . . . How would it begin? It began so. And Bibi, with his index finger, fetched the first note out of the piano, a quite unexpectedly powerful first note in the middle register, like a trumpet blast. Others followed, an introduction developed—the audience relaxed.

The concert was held in the palatial hall of a fashionable first-class hotel. The walls were covered with mirrors framed in gilded arabesques, between frescoes of the rosy and fleshly school. Ornamental columns supported a ceiling that displayed a whole universe of electric bulbs, in clusters darting a brilliance far brighter than day and filling the whole space with thin, vibrating golden light. Not a seat was unoccupied, people were standing in the side aisles and at the back. The front seats cost twelve marks; for the impresario believed that anything worth having was worth paying for. And they were occupied by the best society, for it was in the upper classes, of course, that the greatest enthusiasm was felt. There were even some children, with their legs hanging down demurely from their chairs and their shining eyes staring at their gifted little white-clad contemporary.

Down in front on the left side sat the prodigy's mother, an extremely obese woman with a powdered double chin and a feather on her head. Beside her was the impresario, a man of oriental appearance with large gold buttons on his conspicuous cuffs. The princess was in the middle of the front row—a wrinkled, shrivelled little old princess but still a patron of the arts, especially everything full of sensibility. She sat in a deep, velvet-upholstered arm-chair, and a Persian carpet was spread before her feet. She held her hands folded over her grey striped-silk breast, put her head on one side, and presented a picture of elegant composure as she sat looking up at the performing prodigy. Next her sat her lady-in-waiting, in a green striped-silk gown. Being only a lady-in-waiting she had to sit up very straight in her chair.

Bibi ended in a grand climax. With what power this wee manikin belaboured the keyboard! The audience could scarcely trust its ears. The march theme, an infectious, swinging tune, broke out once more, fully harmonized, bold and showy; with every note Bibi flung himself back from the waist as though he were marching in a triumphal procession. He ended *fortissimo*, bent over, slipped sideways off the stool, and stood with a smile awaiting the applause.

And the applause burst forth, unanimously, enthusiastically; the child made his demure little maidenly curtsy and people in the front seat thought: "Look what slim little hips he has! Clap, clap! Hurrah, bravo, little chap, Saccophylax or whatever your name is! Wait, let me take off my gloves—what a little devil of a chap he is!"

Bibi had to come out three times from behind the screen before they would stop. Some late-comers entered the hall and moved about looking for seats. Then the concert continued. Bibi's *Rêverie* murmured its numbers, consisting almost entirely of arpeggios, above which a bar of melody rose now and then, weak-winged. Then came *Le Hibou et les moineaux*. This piece was brilliantly successful, it made a strong impression; it was an effective childhood fantasy, remarkably well envisaged. The bass represented the owl, sitting morosely rolling his filmy eyes; while in the treble the impudent, half-frightened sparrows chirped. Bibi received an ovation when he finished, he was called out four times. A hotel page with shiny buttons carried up three great laurel wreaths onto the stage and proffered them from one side while Bibi nodded and expressed his thanks. Even the princess shared in the applause, daintily and noiselessly pressing her palms together.

Ah, the knowing little creature understood how to make people clap! He stopped behind the screen, they had to wait for him; lingered a little on the steps of the platform, admired the long streamers on the wreaths—although actually such things bored him stiff by now. He bowed with the utmost charm, he gave the audience plenty of time to rave itself out, because applause is valuable and must not be cut short. "*Le Hibou* is my drawing card," he thought—this expression he had learned from the impresario. "Now I will play the fantasy, it is a lot better than *Le Hibou*, of course, especially the C-sharp passage. But you idiots dote on the *Hibou*, though it is the first and silliest thing I wrote." He continued to bow and smile.

Next came a *Méditation* and then an *Étude*—the programme was quite comprehensive. The *Méditation* was very like the *Rêverie*—which was nothing against it—and the *Étude* displayed all of Bibi's virtuosity, which naturally fell a little short of his inventiveness. And then the *Fantaisie*. This was his favourite; he varied it a little each time, giving himself free rein and sometimes surprising even himself, on good evenings, by his own inventiveness.

He sat and played, so little, so white and shining, against the great black grand piano, elect and alone, above that confused sea of faces, above the heavy, insensitive mass soul, upon which he was labouring to work with his individual, differentiated soul. His lock of soft black hair with the white silk bow had fallen over his forehead, his trained and bony little wrists pounded away, the muscles stood out visibly on his brown childish cheeks.

Sitting there he sometimes had moments of oblivion and solitude, when the gaze of his strange little mouselike eyes with the big rings beneath them would lose itself and stare through the painted stage into space that was peopled with strange vague life. Then out of the corner of his eye he would give a quick look back into the hall and be once more with his audience.

"Joy and pain, the heights and the depths—that is my *Fantaisie*," he thought lovingly. "Listen, here is the C-sharp passage." He lingered over the approach, wondering if they would notice anything. But no, of course not, how should they? And he cast his eyes up prettily at the ceiling so that at least they might have something to look at.

All these people sat there in their regular rows, looking at the prodigy and thinking all sorts of things in their regular brains. An old gentleman with a white beard, a seal ring on his finger and a bulbous swelling on his bald spot, a growth if you like, was thinking to himself: "Really, one ought to be ashamed." He had never got any further than "Ah, thou dearest Augustin" on the piano, and here he sat now, a grey old man, looking on while this little hop-o'-my-thumb performed miracles. Yes, yes, it is a gift of God, we must remember that. God grants His gifts, or He withholds them, and there is no shame in being an ordinary man. Like with the Christ Child.—Before a child one may kneel without feeling ashamed. Strange that thoughts like these should be so satisfying—he would even say so sweet, if it was not too silly for a tough old man like him to use the word. That was how he felt, anyhow.

Art . . . the business man with the parrot-nose was thinking. "Yes, it adds something cheerful to life, a little good white silk and a little tumty-ti-ti-tum. Really he does not play so badly. Fully fifty seats, twelve marks apiece, that makes six hundred marks—and everything else besides. Take off the rent of the hall, the lighting and the programmes, you must have fully a thousand marks profit. That is worth while."

That was Chopin he was just playing, thought the piano-teacher, a lady with a pointed nose; she was of an age when the understanding sharpens as the hopes decay. "But not very original—I will say that afterwards, it sounds well. And his hand position is entirely amateur. One must be able to lay a coin on the back of the hand—I would use a ruler on him."

Then there was a young girl, at that self-conscious and chlorotic time of life when the most ineffable ideas come into the mind. She was thinking to herself: "What is it he is playing? It is expressive of passion, yet he is a child. If he kissed me it would be as though my little brother kissed me—no kiss at all. Is there such a thing as passion all by itself, without any earthly object, a sort of child's-play of passion? What nonsense! If I were to say such things aloud they would just be at me with some more cod-liver oil. Such is life."

An officer was leaning against a column. He looked on at Bibi's success and thought: "Yes, you are something and I am something, each in his own way." So he clapped his heels together and paid to the prodigy the respect which he felt to be due to all the powers that be.

Then there was a critic, an elderly man in a shiny black coat and turned-up trousers splashed with mud. He sat in his free seat and thought: "Look at him, this young beggar of a Bibi. As an individual he has still to develop, but as a type he is already quite complete, the artist *par excellence*. He has in himself all the artist's exaltation and his utter worthlessness, his charlatanry and his sacred fire, his burning contempt and his secret raptures. Of course I can't write all that, it is too good. Of course, I should have been an artist myself if I had not seen through the whole business so clearly."

Then the prodigy stopped playing and a perfect storm arose in the hall. He had to come out again and again from behind his screen. The man with the shiny buttons carried up more wreaths: four laurel wreaths, a lyre made of violets, a bouquet of roses. He had not arms enough to convey all these tributes, the impresario himself mounted the stage to help him. He hung a laurel wreath round Bibi's neck, he tenderly stroked the black hair—and suddenly as though overcome he bent down and gave the prodigy a kiss, a resounding kiss, square on the mouth. And then the storm became a hurricane. That kiss ran through the room like an electric shock, it went direct to peoples' marrow and made them shiver down their backs. They were carried away by a helpless compulsion of sheer noise. Loud shouts mingled with the hysterical clapping of hands. Some of Bibi's commonplace little friends down there waved their handkerchiefs. But the critic thought: "Of course that kiss had to come—it's a good old gag. Yes, good Lord, if only one did not see through everything quite so clearly—"

And so the concert drew to a close. It began at half past seven and finished at half past eight. The platform was laden with wreaths and two little pots of flowers stood on the lamp-stands of the piano. Bibi played as his last number his *Rhapsodie grecque*, which turned into the Greek national hymn at the end. His fellow-countrymen in the audience would gladly have sung it with him if the company had not been so august. They made up for it with a powerful noise and hullabaloo, a hot-blooded national demonstration. And the aging critic was thinking: "Yes, the hymn had to come too. They have to exploit

every vein—publicity cannot afford to neglect any means to its end. I think I'll criticize that as inartistic. But perhaps I am wrong, perhaps that is the most artistic thing of all. What is the artist? A jack-in-the-box. Criticism is on a higher plane. But I can't say that." And away he went in his muddy trousers.

After being called out nine or ten times the prodigy did not come any more from behind the screen but went to his mother and the impresario down in the hall. The audience stood about among the chairs and applauded and pressed forward to see Bibi close at hand. Some of them wanted to see the princess too. Two dense circles formed, one round the prodigy, the other round the princess, and you could actually not tell which of them was receiving more homage. But the court lady was commanded to go over to Bibi; she smoothed down his silk jacket a bit to make it look suitable for a court function, led him by the arm to the princess, and solemnly indicated to him that he was to kiss the royal hand. "How do you do it, child?" asked the princess. "Does it come into your head of itself when you sit down?" "Oui, madame," answered Bibi. To himself he thought: "Oh, what a stupid old princess!" Then he turned round shyly and uncourtier-like and went back to his family.

Outside in the cloak-room there was a crowd. People held up their numbers and received with open arms furs, shawls, and galoshes. Somewhere among her acquaintances the piano-teacher stood making her critique. "He is not very original," she said audibly and looked about her.

In front of one of the great mirrors an elegant young lady was being arrayed in her evening cloak and fur shoes by her brothers, two lieutenants. She was exquisitely beautiful, with her steel-blue eyes and her clean-cut, well-bred face. A really noble dame. When she was ready she stood waiting for her brothers. "Don't stand so long in front of the glass, Adolf," she said softly to one of them, who could not tear himself away from the sight of his simple, good-looking young features. But Lieutenant Adolf thinks: What cheek! He would button his overcoat in front of the glass, just the same. Then they went out on the street where the arc-lights gleamed cloudily through the white mist. Lieutenant Adolf struck up a little nigger-dance on the frozen snow to keep warm, with his hands in his slanting overcoat pockets and his collar turned up.

A girl with untidy hair and swinging arms, accompanied by a gloomy-faced youth, came out just behind them. A child! she thought. A charming child. But in there he was an awe-inspiring . . . and aloud in a toneless voice she said: "We are all infant prodigies, we artists."

"Well, bless my soul!" thought the old gentleman who had never got further than Augustin on the piano, and whose boil was now concealed by a top hat. "What does all that mean? She sounds very oracular." But the gloomy youth understood. He nodded his head slowly.

Then they were silent and the untidy-haired girl gazed after the brothers and sister. She rather despised them, but she looked after them until they had turned the corner.

BY WAY OF DISCUSSION

The technique of multiple character omniscience, or narrative omniscience, allows the author to go into the heads of a whole community of characters. In Thomas Mann's "The Infant Prodigy," a story reminiscent of a nineteenth-century literary sketch, we see the narrator-author presenting little snatches of thought from a series of characters, most of whom are developed very little otherwise. The thoughts of the prodigy himself are presented most fully, but the thoughts of other characters are also revealed: an old gentleman with a white beard, a businessman with a parrot-nose, a piano teacher, a pubescent young girl, an aging music critic.

What can we say about these concert-goers' thoughts? Two points seem obvious. First, all are self-serving in one way or another. Second, most betray various kinds of musical ignorance. The old gentleman excuses his own failure as a pianist by telling himself that musical talent is a gift of God. The music teacher, who mistakenly thinks she is hearing Chopin when the prodigy is actually playing one of his own compositions, mentally attacks the young performer's technique and resolves to criticize it in order to make herself look good. Only the music critic fathoms Bibi's true nature, but he occupies part of his thoughts with excuses for his own artistic failures.

The music critic's judgment is accurate, however. The prodigy does possess a degree of charlatanry, contempt, and secret rapture. Indeed his very name, Bibi Saccellaphylaccas, suggests psychological complexity. The first two of these qualities are reflected in his white satin garb, his "artful little face" as he sits down to play, and his reflections on his audience's musical preferences. Beyond all these, though, lies the quality that sets Bibi apart:

> an enjoyment which he could never convey to anybody. It was that prickling delight, that secret shudder of bliss, which ran through him every time he sat at an open piano . . .

This bliss and prickling delight are also utterly beyond the perception of the ordinary concert-goer.

Although Mann "speaks" mostly through the thoughts of his characters, he sometimes emerges from the story to play the role of the *obtrusive narrator* and make certain editorial comments. He does this when he remarks that "the knowing little creature understood how to make people clap!" and when he makes this observation about ordinary people:

> The average man thinks that a little falseness goes with beauty. Where should we get any excitement out of our daily life if we were not willing to pretend a bit? And the average man is quite right, in his average brains!

Such editorializing is not uncommon in stories presented from the point of view of narrative omniscience.

Thematically, "The Infant Prodigy" is a story treating the nature of art and the artistic temperament. The plot is simple, a one-hour concert; the characterizations are brief, generally limited to passing thoughts; the conflict, if there is any, is of a very general nature; and nothing has been resolved at the story's conclusion. Everyone leaves the hall pretty much as he or she came in. The entire work is rather like a dramatized personal essay in which the narrator-author offers some thoughts for the reader's consideration.

JOHN STEINBECK

The Chrysanthemums

The high grey-flannel fog of winter closed off the Salinas Valley from the sky and from all the rest of the world. On every side it sat like a lid on the mountains and made of the great valley a closed pot. On the broad, level land floor the gang plows bit deep and left the black earth shining like metal where the shares had cut. On the foothill ranches across the Salinas River, the yellow stubble fields seemed to be bathed in pale cold sunshine, but there was no sunshine in the valley now in December. The thick willow scrub along the river flamed with sharp and positive yellow leaves.

It was a time of quiet and of waiting. The air was cold and tender. A light wind blew up from the southwest so that the farmers were mildly hopeful of a good rain before long; but fog and rain do not go together.

Across the river, on Henry Allen's foothill ranch there was little work to be done, for the hay was cut and stored and the orchards were plowed up to receive the rain deeply when it should come. The cattle on the higher slopes were becoming shaggy and rough-coated.

Elisa Allen, working in her flower garden, looked down across the yard and saw Henry, her husband, talking to two men in business suits. The three of them stood by the tractor shed, each man with one foot on the side of the little Fordson. They smoked cigarettes and studied the machine as they talked.

Elisa watched them for a moment and then went back to her work. She was thirty-five. Her face was lean and strong and her eyes were as clear as water. Her figure looked blocked and heavy in her gardening costume, a man's black hat pulled down low over her eyes, clodhopper shoes, a figured print dress almost completely covered by a big corduroy apron with four big pockets to hold the snips, the trowel and scratcher, the seeds and the knife she worked with. She wore heavy leather gloves to protect her hands while she worked.

She was cutting down the old year's chrysanthemum stalks with a pair of short and powerful scissors. She looked down toward the men by the tractor shed now and then. Her face was eager and mature and handsome; even her work with the scissors was over-eager, over-powerful. The chrysanthemum stems seemed too small and easy for her energy.

She brushed a cloud of hair out of her eyes with the back of her glove, and left a smudge of earth on her cheek in doing it. Behind her stood the neat white farm house with red geraniums close-banked around it as high as the windows. It was a hard-swept looking little house, with hard-polished windows, and a clean mud-mat on the front steps.

Elisa cast another glance toward the tractor shed. The strangers were getting into their Ford coupe. She took off a glove and put her strong fingers down into the forest of new green chrysanthemum sprouts that were growing around the old roots. She spread the leaves and looked down among the close-growing stems. No aphids were there, no sowbugs or snails or cutworms. Her terrier fingers destroyed such pests before they could get started.

Elisa started at the sound of her husband's voice. He had come near quietly, and he leaned over the wire fence that protected her flower garden from cattle and dogs and chickens.

"At it again," he said. "You've got a strong new crop coming."

Elisa straightened her back and pulled on the gardening glove again. "Yes. They'll be strong this coming year." In her tone and on her face there was a little smugness.

"You've got a gift with things," Henry observed. "Some of those yellow chrysanthemums you had this year were ten inches across. I wish you'd work out in the orchard and raise some apples that big."

Her eyes sharpened. "Maybe I could do it, too. I've a gift with things, all right. My mother had it. She could stick anything in the ground and make it grow. She said it was having planters' hands that knew how to do it."

"Well, it sure works with flowers," he said.

"Henry, who were those men you were talking to?"

"Why, sure, that's what I came to tell you. They were from the Western Meat Company. I sold those thirty head of three-year-old steers. Got nearly my own price, too."

"Good," she said. "Good for you."

"And I thought," he continued, "I thought how it's Saturday afternoon, and we might go into Salinas for dinner at a restaurant, and then go to a picture-show—to celebrate, you see."

"Good," she repeated. "Oh, yes. That will be good."

Henry put on his joking tone. "There's fights tonight. How'd you like to go to the fights?"

"Oh, no," she said breathlessly. "No, I wouldn't like fights."

"Just fooling, Elisa. We'll go to a movie. Let's see. It's two now. I'm going to take Scotty and bring down those steers from the hill. It'll take us maybe two hours. We'll go in town about five and have dinner at the Cominos Hotel. Like that?"

"Of course I'll like it. It's good to eat away from home."

"All right, then. I'll go get up a couple of horses."

She said, "I'll have plenty of time to transplant some of these sets, I guess."

She heard her husband calling Scotty down by the barn. And a little later she saw the two men ride up the pale yellow hillside in search of the steers.

There was a little square sandy bed kept for rooting the chrysanthemums. With her trowel she turned the soil over and over, and smoothed it and patted it firm. Then she dug ten parallel trenches to receive the sets. Back at the chrysanthemum bed she pulled out the little crisp shoots, trimmed off the leaves of each one with her scissors and laid it on a small orderly pile.

A squeak of wheels and plod of hoofs came from the road. Elisa looked up. The country road ran along the dense bank of willows and cottonwoods that bordered the river, and up this road came a curious vehicle, curiously drawn. It was an old spring-wagon, with a round canvas top on it like the cover of a prairie schooner. It was drawn by an old bay horse and a little grey-and-white burro. A big stubble-bearded man sat between the cover flaps and drove the crawling team. Underneath the wagon, between the hind wheels, a lean and rangy mongrel dog walked sedately. Words were painted on the canvas, in clumsy, crooked letters. "Pots, pans, knives, sisors, lawn mores, Fixed." Two rows of articles, and the triumphantly definitive "Fixed" below. The black paint had run down in little sharp points beneath each letter.

Elisa, squatting on the ground, watched to see the crazy, loose-jointed wagon pass by. But it didn't pass. It turned into the farm road in front of her house, crooked old wheels skirling and squeaking. The rangy dog darted from between the wheels and ran ahead. Instantly the two ranch shepherds flew out at him. Then all three stopped, and with stiff and quivering tails, with taut straight legs, with ambassadorial dignity, they slowly circled, sniffing daintily. The caravan pulled up to Elisa's wire fence and stopped. Now the newcomer dog, feeling out-numbered, lowered his tail and retired under the wagon with raised hackles and bared teeth.

The man on the wagon seat called out, "That's a bad dog in a fight when he gets started."

Elisa laughed. "I see he is. How soon does he generally get started?"

The man caught up her laughter and echoed it heartily. "Sometimes not for weeks and weeks," he said. He climbed stiffly down, over the wheel. The horse and the donkey drooped like unwatered flowers.

Elisa saw that he was a very big man. Although his hair and beard were greying, he did not look old. His worn black suit was wrinkled and spotted with grease. The laughter had disappeared from his face and eyes the moment his laughing voice ceased. His eyes were dark, and they were full of the brooding that gets in the eyes of teamsters and of sailors. The calloused hands he rested on the wire fence were cracked, and every crack was a black line. He took off his battered hat.

"I'm off my general road, ma'am," he said. "Does this dirt road cut over across the river to the Los Angeles highway?"

Elisa stood up and shoved the thick scissors in her apron pocket. "Well, yes, it does, but it winds around and then fords the river. I don't think your team could pull through the sand."

He replied with some asperity, "It might surprise you what them beasts can pull through."

"When they get started?" she asked.

He smiled for a second. "Yes. When they get started."

"Well," said Elisa, "I think you'll save time if you go back to the Salinas road and pick up the highway there."

He drew a big finger down the chicken wire and made it sing. "I ain't in any hurry, ma'am. I go from Seattle to San Diego and back every year. Takes all my time. About six months each way. I aim to follow nice weather."

Elisa took off her gloves and stuffed them in the apron pocket with the scissors. She touched the under edge of her man's hat, searching for fugitive hairs. "That sounds like a nice kind of way to live," she said.

He leaned confidentially over the fence. "Maybe you noticed the writing on my wagon. I mend pots and sharpen knives and scissors. You got any of them things to do?"

"Oh, no," she said quickly. "Nothing like that." Her eyes hardened with resistance.

"Scissors is the worst thing," he explained. "Most people just ruin scissors trying to sharpen 'em, but I know how. I got a special tool. It's a little bobbit kind of thing, and patented. But it sure does the trick."

"No. My scissors are all sharp."

"All right, then. Take a pot," he continued earnestly, "a bent pot, or a pot with a hole. I can make it like new so you don't have to buy no new ones. That's a saving for you."

"No," she said shortly. "I tell you I have nothing like that for you to do."

His face fell to an exaggerated sadness. His voice took on a whining undertone. "I ain't had a thing to do today. Maybe I won't have no supper tonight. You see I'm off my regular road. I know folks on the highway clear from Seattle to San Diego. They save their things for me to sharpen up because they know I do it so good and save them money."

"I'm sorry," Elisa said irritably. "I haven't anything for you to do."

His eyes left her face and fell to searching the ground. They roamed about until they came to the chrysanthemum bed where she had been working. "What's them plants, ma'am?"

The irritation and resistance melted from Elisa's face. "Oh, those are chrysanthemums, giant whites and yellows. I raise them every year, bigger than anybody around here."

"Kind of a long-stemmed flower? Looks like a quick puff of colored smoke?" he asked.

"That's it. What a nice way to describe them."

"They smell kind of nasty till you get used to them," he said.

"It's a good bitter smell," she retorted, "not nasty at all."

He changed his tone quickly. "I like the smell myself."

"I had ten-inch blooms this year," she said.

The man leaned farther over the fence. "Look. I know a lady down the road a piece, has got the nicest garden you ever seen. Got nearly every kind of flower but no chrysanthemums. Last time I was mending a copper-bottom washtub for her (that's a hard job but I do it good), she said to me, 'If you ever run acrost some nice chrysanthemums I wish you'd try to get me a few seeds.' That's what she told me."

Elisa's eyes grew alert and eager. "She couldn't have known much about chrysanthemums. You *can* raise them from seed, but it's much easier to root the little sprouts you see there."

"Oh," he said. "I s'pose I can't take none to her, then."

"Why yes you can," Elisa cried. "I can put some in damp sand, and you can carry them right along with you. They'll take root in the pot if you keep them damp. And then she can transplant them."

"She'd sure like to have some, ma'am. You say they're nice ones?"

"Beautiful," she said. "Oh, beautiful." Her eyes shone. She tore off the battered hat and shook out her dark pretty hair. "I'll put them in a flower pot, and you can take them right with you. Come into the yard."

While the man came through the picket gate Elisa ran excitedly along the geranium-bordered path to the back of the house. And she returned carrying a big red flower pot. The gloves were forgotten now. She kneeled on the ground by the starting bed and dug up the sandy soil with her fingers and scooped it into the bright new flower pot. Then she picked up the little pile of shoots she had prepared. With her strong fingers she pressed them into the sand and tamped around them with her knuckles. The man stood over her. "I'll tell you what to do," she said. "You remember so you can tell the lady."

"Yes, I'll try to remember."

"Well, look. These will take root in about a month. Then she must set them out, about a foot apart in good rich earth like this, see?" She lifted a handful of dark soil for him to look at. "They'll grow fast and tall. Now remember this: In July tell her to cut them down, about eight inches from the ground."

"Before they bloom?" he asked.

"Yes, before they bloom." Her face was tight with eagerness. "They'll grow right up again. About the last of September the buds will start."

She stopped and seemed perplexed. "It's the budding that takes the most care," she said hesitantly. "I don't know how to tell you." She looked deep into his eyes, searchingly. Her mouth opened a little, and she seemed to be listening. "I'll try to tell you," she said. "Did you ever hear of planting hands?"

"Can't say I have, ma'am."

"Well, I can only tell you what it feels like. It's when you're picking off the buds you don't want. Everything goes right down into your fingertips. You watch your fingers work. They do it themselves. You can feel how it is. They pick and pick the buds. They never make a mistake. They're with the plant. Do you see? Your fingers and the plant. You can feel that, right up your arm. They know. They never make a mistake. You can feel it. When you're like that you can't do anything wrong. Do you see that? Can you understand that?"

She was kneeling on the ground looking up at him. Her breast swelled passionately.

The man's eyes narrowed. He looked away self-consciously. "Maybe I know," he said. "Sometimes in the night in the wagon there———"

Elisa's voice grew husky. She broke in on him. "I've never lived as you do, but I know what you mean. When the night is dark—why, the stars are sharp-pointed, and there's quiet. Why, you rise up and up! Every pointed star gets driven into your body. It's like that. Hot and sharp and—lovely."

Kneeling there, her hand went out toward his legs in the greasy black trousers. Her hesitant fingers almost touched the cloth. Then her hand dropped to the ground. She crouched low like a fawning dog.

He said, "It's nice, just like you say. Only when you don't have no dinner, it ain't."

She stood up then, very straight, and her face was ashamed. She held the flower pot out to him and placed it gently in his arms. "Here. Put it in your wagon, on the seat, where you can watch it. Maybe I can find something for you to do."

At the back of the house she dug in the can pile and found two old and battered aluminum saucepans. She carried them back and gave them to him. "Here, maybe you can fix these."

His manner changed. He became professional. "Good as new I can fix them." At the back of his wagon he set a little anvil, and out of an oily tool box dug a small machine hammer. Elisa came through the gate to watch him while he pounded out the dents in the kettles. His mouth grew sure and knowing. At a difficult part of the work he sucked his under-lip.

"You sleep right in the wagon?" Elisa asked.

"Right in the wagon, ma'am. Rain or shine I'm dry as a cow in there."

"It must be nice," she said. "It must be very nice. I wish women could do such things."

"It ain't the right kind of life for a woman."

Her upper lip raised a little, showing her teeth. "How do you know? How can you tell?" she said.

"I don't know, ma'am," he protested. "Of course I don't know. Now here's your kettles, done. You don't have to buy no new ones."

"How much?"

"Oh, fifty cents'll do. I keep my prices down and my work good. That's why I have all them satisfied customers up and down the highway."

Elisa brought him a fifty-cent piece from the house and dropped it in his hand. "You might be surprised to have a rival some time. I can sharpen scissors, too. And I can beat the dents out of little pots. I could show you what a woman might do."

He put his hammer back in the oily box and shoved the little anvil out of sight. "It would be a lonely life for a woman, ma'am, and a scarey life, too, with animals creeping under the wagon all night." He climbed over the singletree, steadying himself with a hand on the burro's white rump. He settled himself in the seat, picked up the lines. "Thank you kindly, ma'am," he said. "I'll do like you told me; I'll go back and catch the Salinas road."

"Mind," she called, "if you're long in getting there, keep the sand damp."

"Sand, ma'am? . . . Sand? Oh, sure. You mean around the chrysanthemums. Sure I will." He clucked his tongue. The beasts leaned luxuriously into their collars. The mongrel dog took his place between the back wheels. The wagon turned and crawled out the entrance road and back the way it had come, along the river.

Elisa stood in front of her wire fence watching the slow progress of the caravan. Her shoulders were straight, her head thrown back, her eyes half-closed, so that the scene came vaguely into them. Her lips moved silently, forming the words "Good-bye—good-bye." Then she whispered, "That's a bright direction. There's a glowing there." The sound of her whisper startled her. She shook herself free and looked about to see whether anyone had been listening. Only the dogs had heard. They lifted their heads toward her from their sleeping in the dust, and then stretched out their chins and settled asleep again. Elisa turned and ran hurriedly into the house.

In the kitchen she reached behind the stove and felt the water tank. It was full of hot water from the noonday cooking. In the bathroom she tore off her soiled clothes and flung them into the corner. And then she scrubbed herself with a little block of pumice, legs and thighs, loins and chest and arms, until her skin was scratched and red. When she had dried herself she stood in front of a mirror in her bedroom and looked at her body. She tightened her stomach and threw out her chest. She turned and looked over her shoulder at her back.

After a while she began to dress, slowly. She put on her newest underclothing and her nicest stockings and the dress which was the symbol of her prettiness. She worked carefully on her hair, penciled her eyebrows and rouged her lips.

Before she was finished she heard the little thunder of hoofs and the shouts of Henry and his helper as they drove the red steers into the corral. She heard the gate bang shut and set herself for Henry's arrival.

His step sounded on the porch. He entered the house calling, "Elisa, where are you?"

"In my room, dressing. I'm not ready. There's hot water for your bath. Hurry up. It's getting late."

When she heard him splashing in the tub, Elisa laid his dark suit on the bed, and shirt and socks and tie beside it. She stood his polished shoes on the floor beside the bed. Then she went to the porch and sat primly and stiffly down. She looked toward the river road where the willow-line was still yellow with frosted leaves so that under the high grey fog they seemed a thin band of sunshine. This was the only color in the grey afternoon. She sat unmoving for a long time. Her eyes blinked rarely.

Henry came banging out of the door, shoving his tie inside his vest as he came. Elisa stiffened and her face grew tight. Henry stopped short and looked at her. "Why—why, Elisa. You look so nice!"

"Nice? You think I look nice? What do you mean by 'nice'?"

Henry blundered on. "I don't know. I mean you look different, strong and happy."

"I am strong? Yes, strong. What do you mean 'strong'?"

He looked bewildered. "You're playing some kind of a game," he said helplessly. "It's a kind of a play. You look strong enough to break a calf over your knee, happy enough to eat it like a watermelon."

For a second she lost her rigidity. "Henry! Don't talk like that. You didn't know what you said." She grew complete again. "I'm strong," she boasted. "I never knew before how strong."

Henry looked down toward the tractor shed, and when he brought his eyes back to her, they were his own again. "I'll get out the car. You can put on your coat while I'm starting."

Elisa went into the house. She heard him drive to the gate and idle down his motor, and then she took a long time to put on her hat. She pulled it here and pressed it there. When Henry turned the motor off she slipped into her coat and went out.

The little roadster bounced along on the dirt road by the river, raising the birds and driving the rabbits into the brush. Two cranes flapped heavily over the willow-line and dropped into the river-bed.

Far ahead on the road Elisa saw a dark speck. She knew.

She tried not to look as they passed it, but her eyes would not obey. She whispered to herself sadly, "He might have thrown them off the road. That wouldn't have been much trouble, not very much. But he kept the pot," she explained. "He had to keep the pot. That's why he couldn't get them off the road."

The roadster turned a bend and she saw the caravan ahead. She swung full around toward her husband so she could not see the little covered wagon and the mismatched team as the car passed them.

In a moment it was over. The thing was done. She did not look back.

She said loudly, to be heard above the motor, "It will be good, tonight, a good dinner."

"Now you're changed again," Henry complained. He took one hand from the wheel and patted her knee. "I ought to take you in to dinner oftener. It would be good for both of us. We get so heavy out on the ranch."

"Henry," she asked, "could we have wine at dinner?"

"Sure we could. Say! That will be fine."

She was silent for a while; then she said, "Henry, at those prize fights, do the men hurt each other very much?"

"Sometimes a little, not often. Why?"

"Well, I've read how they break noses, and blood runs down their chests. I've read how the fighting gloves get heavy and soggy with blood."

He looked around at her. "What's the matter, Elisa? I didn't know you read things like that." He brought the car to a stop, then turned to the right over the Salinas River bridge.

"Do any women ever go to the fights?" she asked.

"Oh, sure, some. What's the matter, Elisa? Do you want to go? I don't think you'd like it, but I'll take you if you really want to go."

She relaxed limply in the seat. "Oh, no. No. I don't want to go. I'm sure I don't." Her face was turned away from him. "It will be enough if we can have wine. It will be plenty." She turned up her coat collar so he could not see that she was crying weakly—like an old woman.

BY WAY OF DISCUSSION

As one reads John Steinbeck's story "The Chrysanthemums," it is apparent that the author intended to use dramatic narration in telling this tale. "The Chysanthemums" is told in the third person, but Steinbeck carefully avoids going directly into anyone's mind and telling the reader what thoughts are there. At the beginning of the story, Henry comes to Elisa in the flower garden and comments, "You've got a strong new crop coming." Elisa's response is described in this way: "In her tone and on her face there was a little smugness." A tone is something that can be heard, and a facial expression is something that can be seen. Thus, Steinbeck avoids telling the reader that there is smugness in Elisa's mind, that she actually feels pride in what she is doing.

Similarly, when the tinker shows up in his rickety wagon and asks Elisa whether she has anything for him to mend and she tells him that she hasn't, the reader is told, "His face fell to an exaggerated sadness. His voice took on a whining undertone." Once again, a face is something that can be seen, and a voice is something that can be heard. Both are items that the modern motion-picture camera could record.

Why would Steinbeck want to go to all the trouble of not telling the reader the actual thoughts of his characters, especially when it would have been easy to do so here and there throughout the story? There are two major reasons in this particular story. First, by dramatizing thoughts, through the presentation of words, actions, and facial expressions, Steinbeck avoids the direct revelation of the personalities of his characters. This technique increases the plausibility of the dramatic situations of the story, because in real life we seldom know the actual thoughts of the people we encounter. Then, by not detailing the thoughts of his characters, Steinbeck is able to shift the emphasis of the story to other things, such as conversational exchanges, graphic descriptions, and an array of symbols.

It is, in fact, largely through the use of descriptive images and recurrent symbols that the thematic intent of the story is revealed. Without question, "The Chrysanthemums" is a careful study of feminine frustration, the frustration that a woman experiences in living—perhaps "surviving" would be a better word—in a world of men. The theme is suggested in the story's opening lines:

> The high grey-flannel fog of winter closed off the Salinas Valley from the sky and from all the rest of the world. On every side it sat like a lid on the mountains and made of the great valley a closed pot.

Elisa is a trapped woman. Her surroundings, as well as her life, are like "a closed pot." Furthermore, the garden in which she spends so much time is encircled by a "wire fence that protected her . . . from cattle and dogs and chickens." She is thus symbolically isolated and cut off from the real world of action, activity, and accomplishment. She has no suitable outlet for her vigor—for what in a man might be called the "natural juices." She cannot deal in cattle as her husband does. "Got nearly my own price," Henry says. Nor can she drift about the country as the traveling tinker does. "I wish women could do such things," she tells the tinker. And when the tinker tells her that a rover's life is not suitable for a woman, Elisa responds by saying, "I could show you what a woman might do." Clearly, this affirmation shows Elisa's frustrations and her desire to take advantage of the more dynamic opportunities open to men in the world of men.

In addition to being barred from so-called masculine activities, Elisa is also sexually repressed. Steinbeck points this out in several ways. For one thing, Elisa is passionately devoted to growing her chrysanthemums. Because flowers, symbolically, have feminine connotations in our culture, her activity can be taken as symbolically reflecting the desire for the flowering of her womanhood. And then there is Henry, who can best be dubbed a romantic dullard, even if he is a successful farmer. Notice that he lacks even the rudiments of chivalric inclinations. After Elisa has bathed, he tells her, "You look so nice!" But when pressed to explain what he means by "nice," all he can manage to say is, "You look strong enough to break a calf over your knee, happy enough to eat it like a watermelon." Hardly the sort of compliment to stir one's tenderer emotions! Even Elisa's appearance belies her natural femininity:

Her figure looked blocked and heavy in her gardening costume, a man's black hat pulled low down over her eyes, clodhopper shoes, a figured print dress almost completely covered by a big corduroy apron with four big pockets to hold the snips, the trowel and scratcher, the seeds and the knife she worked with. She wore heavy leather gloves to protect her hands while she worked.

However, things change when the tinker appears, feigns an interest in her flowers, and likens them to "a quick puff of colored smoke." This meeting with a man who by comparison with Henry seems romantic, even poetic, arouses Elisa's long-dormant sexuality. The intensity of the arousal is made clear by Elisa's unconsciously erotic (Freudian) description of her feelings about the stars:

"When the night is dark—why, the stars are sharp-pointed, and there is quiet. Why, you rise up and up! Every pointed star gets driven into your body. It's like that. Hot and sharp and—lovely."

Moments later, Elisa reaches out and almost touches the tinker's greasy trousers; but then, suddenly aware of what she is doing, she bows her head and looks ashamed.

Elisa's desire to cast away her repressions and reassert her womanliness is also especially well dramatized in the scene where she prepares herself for the trip into town with Henry:

In the bathroom she tore off her soiled clothes and flung them into the corner. And then she scrubbed herself with a little block of pumice, legs and thighs, loins and chest and arms, until her skin was scratched and red. When she had dried herself she stood in front of a mirror in her bedroom and looked at her body. She tightened her stomach and threw out her chest. She turned and looked over her shoulder at her back.

However, Henry's crudely humorous comment about his wife's great strength, "You look strong enough to break a calf over your knee, happy enough to eat it like a watermelon" ironically signals Elisa's final decline. Her decline concludes when she, sitting in the roadster on the way into town, "turned up her coat collar so he could not see that she was crying weakly—like an old woman."

The central conflict of the story is between Elisa and Henry. The tinker serves only to point up this conflict. When Elisa discovers that the tinker has thrown away the plants she gave him and kept the pot—notice the recurring image of the pot—her mood apparently becomes one of wanting revenge against all men. She wishes to attend the prize fights that Henry had mentioned earlier, where there is a chance that "men hurt each other." Perhaps they "break noses, and blood runs down their chests." She tells Henry, "I've read how the fighting gloves get heavy and soggy with blood." But this mood soon passes—"alas," some might say—and she settles for wine with dinner: "It will be enough if we can have wine. It will be plenty." It might be argued that in rejecting the idea of attending the fights Elisa has somehow identified herself with the pugilists who lose, a condition that symbolically mirrors her own defeated condition.

Keep in mind that chrysanthemums are flowers often associated with funerals. Appropriately, we may have been witnessing the death of whatever personal strength Elisa may have possessed. She has been overwhelmed by men in a man's world, one of the legitimate complaints many modern-day women make about the structure of our society.

FOR ADDITIONAL READING

The following stories, which appear elsewhere in this book, are especially appropriate for an analysis of point of view:

1. Sherwood Anderson, "Unlighted Lamps" (p. 484)
2. Virginia Woolf, "The String Quartet" (p. 497)
3. Honoré de Balzac, "A Passion in the Desert" (p. 367)
4. Edgar Allan Poe, "The Fall of the House of Usher" (p. 353)
5. Ernest Hemingway, "The Killers" (p. 511)
6. Jessamyn West, "Love, Death, and the Ladies' Drill Team" (p. 568)

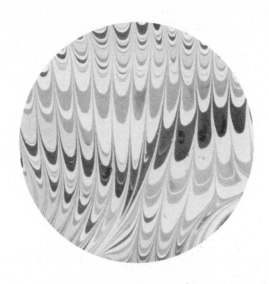

Historical Evolution of the
Modern Short Story

Nineteenth-Century Origin and Development

The modern short story emerged as a distinct literary genre during the early decades of the nineteenth century. It developed more or less simultaneously in Germany, the United States, France, and Russia. Prior to this time, short stories had generally taken the form of simple narratives with loosely constructed plots, shallow characterization, and escapist themes. These early stories, now usually called tales or sketches, represented little real advancement over the fourteenth-century efforts of Boccaccio and the imitators who followed him. As late as 1795, for example, the German writer Johann Wolfgang von Goethe (1749–1832) wrote *Roman Elegies*, a series of poetic stories clearly patterned after Boccaccio's *Decameron*.

Three factors seem particularly responsible for the emergence of the modern short story: (1) a steady increase in the number of people who could read, (2) growing literary sophistication among readers, and (3) a rapid increase in the number of popular magazines and newspapers published in America and throughout Europe. Of these factors, the last is, statistically at least, the most important. During the first thirty years of the nineteenth century, for example, the number of newspapers being published in America jumped tenfold, and this increase was equaled or exceeded by American magazines. Within one eighteen-year period, the annual newspaper circulation rose from 22 million copies to 68 million copies. Although many of these early publications had short lives, as quickly as one fell by the wayside others usually sprang up to take its place. In 1829 this situation led the *New York Mirror* to remark:

> The United States are fertile in most things, but in periodicals they are extremely luxuriant. They spring up as fast as mushrooms in every corner, and like all rapid vegetation bear the seeds of early decay within them . . . but hundreds more are found to supply their place.

Similar growth was taking place in Europe, so it is not surprising that by the end of the third decade of the century the modern short story had completely overshadowed its simpler predecessor. Goethe himself took note of this development, drawing a clear distinction between the new form and the old by stating that many an older work was "not a short story at all but merely a tale."

The new short story of the nineteenth century is clearly a more carefully crafted work of art than are the earlier forms. The new stories contain a well-developed plot with various devices to arouse the reader's interest. Conflict builds to a climax, at which point emotion reaches a peak and the action takes a decisive turn. After the climax there is a general falling-off of intensity, followed by a resolution of some sort. The characters, although sometimes far from ordinary, are well drawn and usually believable. Often they are deeply affected by the experiences they undergo or the events they witness. Incidents and events are carefully selected and arranged to advance the action smoothly; character is more and more often dramatized; and the statement of theme requires progressively more complex interpretations.

The earliest practitioners of the modern short story are clearly identified with the literary and intellectual movement called *romanticism*. The romantic movement was a late-eighteenth-century reaction against the rationalistic outlook that had held sway in educated circles for more than a hundred years.

Rationalism—a product of the ideas and scientific findings of such sixteenth- and seventeenth-century figures as Sir Francis Bacon, Johannes Kepler, René Descartes, and Sir Isaac Newton—exalted human reason, rejected all forms of emotionalism, and denied the existence of the miraculous and the supernatural. The rationalists viewed matter as a mass of innumerable tiny particles. The universe, they were sure, was a place of order and harmony operating in accordance with uniform and unchanging mathematical laws that regulated the planets in their orbits and the stars in their courses. God was regarded as a benevolent being Who, having created the universe, did not interfere with its operation. Humans, as creatures of God, were seen as rational and good. By studying the laws of nature, they could come to know God and achieve happiness.

Of the numerous thinkers who helped pave the way for romanticism, two eighteenth-century philosophers, Jean Jacques Rousseau and Immanuel Kant, merit our special attention. Rousseau (1712–1778), an extreme individualist, argued that humans have an emotional component that is more deeply rooted than is their rationality. Rousseau believed that instinct, emotion, and first impressions are more trustworthy than are thought, caution, or the experience gained from dealing with other people. Humans, Rousseau said, are at their best when living a primitive life amid natural surroundings; then they are happy, virtuous, and possess a wisdom that goes beyond rational understanding. Furthermore, Rousseau saw the repressive societies of his day as breeding grounds of vice and corruption, and he declared that these societies ought to be replaced by democratic governments that would allow the natural goodness of humans to come into play.

Kant (1724–1804) believed that reason and science are valid tools for describing the world we perceive through our senses. However, he insisted, they are incapable of showing us how the world would really appear if it were not screened through a selective instrument such as the human mind. Thus, we cannot know how the world would appear to a perfect mind, one free from all human limitations, such as the mind of God. As evidence of a higher reality than that described by reason and science, Kant pointed to the experiences of conscience, beauty, and the religious impulse, all of which he said are far too strong to be dismissed as mere illusion. Kant maintained that humans act out of a sense of moral obligation, respond to beauty in a way that cannot be rationally explained, and feel a natural impulse to worship a deity. Kant's philosophy helped open the way to a nonscientific view of human nature.

Events as well as people helped set the stage for the romantic movement. In 1789, a mob stormed and destroyed the Bastille, a prison in Paris, ending the power of a monarchy that to many symbolized the height of absolutism in government. Six years earlier, America had successfully concluded its revolution against England and embarked on a completely new and promising political course. To thousands of young idealists, these happenings demonstrated the great power of the human imagination and pointed toward the general collapse of outmoded institutions and philosophies. The later failure of the French Revolution served only to weaken, not destroy, this optimism.

The romantics rejected the rationalists' theoretical interest in humankind and replaced it with an interest in individual women and men. They glorified individualism and devoted much time to exploring the personalities of particular people. Fictional characters run the gamut from the simple farmer or villager to the eccentric or demented nobleman. Imagination and emotion ranked high on the romantic's scale of values. Romantic stories—often set in the remote past—abound with castle ruins, wild forests, possessed people, rushing cataracts, and supernatural creatures. Many romantic writers, although not necessarily the best short-story writers, had a passion for social reform and felt that by communing mystically with nature one could gain an intuitive understanding of God.

Although romanticism may have gotten an earlier start in England, particularly among the theoreticians and poets, the movement was ultimately more intense in Germany. The French Revolution and the prolonged Napoleonic Wars slowed all literary activity in France, and the very notion of viewing the world through romantic eyes seems to have been alien to most Russians. Important among the German writers of later romantic tales—precursors of the modern short story—were Heinrich von Kleist, Ludwig Tieck, and E. T. A Hoffmann.

The stories of Hoffmann (1776–1822) have been called the culmination of German romanticism. They are crowded with grotesque and supernatural events, and various psychological problems and complexities are recurring themes. Although by and large Hoffmann's stories lack the stylistic elegance of other late romantic writers, the characters, settings, and events are rendered with a clear-eyed matter-of-factness. Many times the reader feels that Hoffmann has actually experienced the events that he describes. Writers in both France and America were influenced by Hoffmann's work. Washington Irving and Edgar Allan Poe were particularly indebted to Hoffmann.

Washington Irving (1783–1859), America's first master of the short story, personifies the romantic tradition. Irving created a series of stories set in earlier times and making use of faraway places, unusual settings, and supernatural or mock-supernatural personages. The action of "The Spectre Bridegroom," for example, takes place "many, many years since" in a castle located in "a wild and romantic tract of Upper Germany." The story has as its chief characters an eccentric baron and a supposed ghost.

Irving's best-known works, "Rip Van Winkle" and "The Legend of Sleepy Hollow," feature far humbler characters: a village ne'er-do-well and a country schoolmaster respectively. Nevertheless, the settings are romantic, and supernaturalism—real or fancied—plays a prominent part. In writing these and other stories with American settings, Irving deliberately set out to create a group of native legends, further evidence of a romantic's love of the imagined past.

Although Edgar Allan Poe (1809–1849) was clearly within the romantic camp, he had a rational inclination that showed itself in several ways. Like the rationalists, he believed the universe possessed a mathematical beauty that reflected the work of God. In his essay "Eureka" he declares, "The plots of God are perfect. The universe is a plot of God." Rationalism likewise stamps Poe's stories of ratiocination—that is, stories that pose a problem or mystery and then solve it by the rigorous application of logic. A number of these detective stories, a genre Poe invented almost single-handedly, have become classics.

Poe adopted a thoroughly methodical approach to the writing of short fiction. A short story, he felt, should strive to achieve a single unique and preconceived effect. When reviewing Nathaniel Hawthorne's *Twice-Told Tales* in 1842, Poe wrote:

> A skilful artist has constructed a tale. If wise, he has not fashioned his thoughts to accommodate his incidents; but having conceived, with deliberate care, a certain unique or single *effect* to be wrought out, he then invents such incidents—he then combines such events as may best aid him in establishing this preconceived effect. If his very initial sentence tend not to be outbringing of this effect, then he has failed in his first step. In the whole composition there should be no word written, of which the tendency, direct or indirect, is not to the one pre-established design.

Additionally, Poe suggested that a story not be too long for reading at a single sitting. Moreover, a reader who finishes a story should be so satisfied that he or she does not wish the work to be any longer. Such observations have positioned Poe as the first to define the modern short story, and many of his precepts have had a long-lasting effect on the criticism of the genre.

Despite all this, however, Poe's chief claim to literary fame is probably his Gothic, or horror, stories. Such stories crowded the popular maga-

zines of the day and were devoured by readers who displayed a seemingly insatiable appetite for decaying mansions, dank catacombs, secret
passageways, and other Gothic trappings. Poe fed this appetite, but in
his hands the Gothic story became something new: a tool for probing the
workings of psychologically warped minds.

Often Poe tells his story from within the character's head, allowing an
awareness of creeping insanity gradually to grow upon the reader. True
to his own theories, Poe constructed each story carefully to create one
particular impression—fear, suspense, melancholy, horror. Thus, he
was able to strengthen a story's dramatic impact.

Nathaniel Hawthorne (1804–1864), also within the romantic camp,
likewise utilized supernatural motifs and analyzed character, but not for
the purpose of depicting the picturesque or creating a mood. He was
more interested in exploring ideas, particularly ideas about the nature of
evil. Although Hawthorne had rejected the Puritan belief that all people—except for a few lucky individuals especially chosen by God—are
totally depraved, he did feel that far too often men and women are cold,
selfish, spiteful, and strangely drawn to evil. "Man must feel," Hawthorne once said, "that when he shall come to knock at the gate of
heaven no semblance of an unspoiled life can entitle him to enter there."

Hawthorne came to believe that isolation—the deliberate segregation
of the individual from the everyday concerns of life—causes much of the
world's evil. Hawthorne believed that isolation results from many things.
An individual seeking greater self-reliance may reject the popular philosophies and conventions by which others live, thereby depriving herself or
himself of the ordinary ways of coping with disappointment and tragedy.
The obsessive and ultimately futile pursuit of ideal beauty may lead an
artist to sacrifice the chance for personal or financial security and thus
bring tragedy to the people who care for him or her.

The worst evil of all, Hawthorne said, arises from overweening pride,
which drives its possessor to treat others as objects rather than as people in order to satisfy intellectual curiosity or the lust for power. Hawthorne called such pride "the unforgivable sin." Without the transforming power of love, Hawthorne warned, without rejecting self-
centeredness, one cannot hope to escape the consequences of evil—
isolation.

Like Hawthorne, Herman Melville (1819–1891) rejected a Calvinist
background but spent much of his writing life grappling with the question of evil, both in its abstract form and as it is evidenced in human
relationships. Melville's views on evil in the abstract receive their fullest
treatment in *Moby Dick*, a novel in which the white whale that gives the
book its title represents evil made flesh. To Melville, evil is part of the
nature of things and can never be eradicated. People who actively try to
wipe it out are especially likely to meet with disaster. Thus, Captain
Ahab, a monomaniac whose sole purpose in life is to kill the white whale,
thereby eliminating evil, meets a brutal end when he goes out of his way
to find his great nemesis. Elsewhere, Melville makes the related point
that humans are imperfect creatures and that any attempt to live by
"heavenly" absolutes will also bring personal disaster.

In considering human nature, Melville did not rule out depravity, not even total depravity. However, he felt that social evil is far less a product of innate human badness than of society's institutions. Cities in particular he regarded as sinkholes of suffering and alienation. Melville's descriptions of cities abound with images of physical and spiritual darkness. For example, in the novel *Redburn* Liverpool is "sooty and begrimed," enveloped in "a shroud of coal smoke." In *Pierre*, New York has "empty, heartless, ceremonial ways." And in *Moby Dick*, New Bedford has "dreary streets, blocks of blackness," while New York is a place where men are "tied to counters, nailed to benches, clinched to desks."

The indictment becomes harshest when Melville turns his attention from places to people: to such representatives of the urban hell as prostitutes, drunken sailors, prisoners in a police station, and—above all else—to the maimed and starving people in Liverpool. The creatures from this last group are mute in their misery. A man injured by a machine solicits alms by displaying a picture of his accident. Another man tells passersby, through a message written on the sidewalk, that he and his family are dying of starvation. The picture and message serve as symbols of total human isolation, the inability of urban dwellers to communicate except in a superficial and impersonal fashion.

As the nineteenth century approached its midpoint, a new literary movement called *realism* appeared and gradually gained influence. By 1900 realism and its various derivatives clearly dominated the works of serious short-story writers, although thousands of romantic stories, most of them of an inferior quality, continued to appear in popular magazines.

Realism was the product of several forces coming together at the same time. Partly, it no doubt represented a simple desire among imaginative literary artists to try something new. Also, particularly in America, it reflected a growing democratic distaste for the aristocratic or unusual characters who peopled so much romantic fiction. Too many eccentric barons bore both the reader and the writer after a time.

The English novel of the eighteenth and early nineteenth centuries also helped to foster the growth of realism, especially on the European continent. From its beginnings with writers such as Henry Fielding, Tobias Smollett, and Laurence Stern, the English novel was a popular art form intended to appeal primarily to middle-class tastes and concerns. As a result, although many early offerings are sensational and overly sentimental, the genre—except for the Gothic novels—shuns the distant, the miraculous, and the romantic past to focus on believable events in the here-and-now, the everyday world of the time. Although the characters range from aristocrats to humbler folks such as footmen, serving girls, farmers, and country parsons, it is the humble people more often than not who get top billing. Events, characters, and settings are well detailed in a matter-of-fact manner, with much attention being given to personality and human motivation.

Of the philosophies that helped to nurture the realistic movement, the positivism of the French thinker Auguste Comte (1798–1857) registers larger than any other. Comte held that the only worthwhile knowledge is positive knowledge, the kind derived from science and mathematics. He rejected metaphysical speculation—that is, speculation into the ultimate nature of things—as totally useless and said that philosophy should concern itself with determining general scientific principles. Once determined, these principles should serve as guides to personal conduct and social organization. Although positivism bears obvious resemblances to the earlier rationalism, its chief roots lay in the rapid growth of science and technology that brought about the Industrial Revolution and gradually transformed Great Britain, America, and the nations of western Europe into industrialized societies.

The Industrial Revolution took definite form in the late eighteenth century, which saw in quick succession the invention of the spinning jenny, the power loom, the rolling mill, and the steam engine. The early nineteenth century marked the appearance of the steamboat, the railroad locomotive, and the telegraph. In 1830, steam-powered ships began crossing the Atlantic Ocean on regular schedules. By 1840, public train transportation was a fact of life, and cities had started taking the first steps toward improving sanitation and providing the services that we now take for granted.

The Industrial Revolution affected different people in different ways. To a comparatively small but always growing body of workers, it brought a life of misery lived out in what later came to be dubbed "dark satanic mills." At the same time, though, it brought a veritable flood of low-priced goods to the marketplace, easing and enriching the lives of millions of working-class and middle-class people. Thus it is hardly surprising that many people, philosophers and ordinary people alike, came almost to worship at the shrine of science and technology.

Realist writers rejected the faraway, the dreamy, the strange, and the supernatural; they concentrated on characters, settings, and situations that conveyed a clear sense of everyday life. Their tone was generally objective and unemotional, and their stories, almost as methodical as a scientific experiment, often contained detailed and sustained observations. The thematic range of the stories was gradually broadened, though most writers steered clear of dealing explicitly with sex. In considering various social evils—often related to the changing conditions of the day—some writers focused on the reactions of the characters to their problems and misfortunes; others, usually not of the first rank, crusaded for one type of reform or another. The stories of the second group were forerunners of later propaganda stories.

From the beginning, it was the Russian writers who were the most consistently realistic, especially in the short story. Ivan Krylov (1768–1844), a widely read writer of fables, helped to set the stage by making short fiction popular in Russia. Then came Alexander Pushkin (1799–1873), generally considered Russia's greatest poet as well as the man who brought Russian literature into the nineteenth century. Pushkin's stories became progressively more realistic, culminating in what was later called psychological realism.

Ivan Turgenev (1818–1883), known primarily for his novels, is one of the foremost Russian short-story writers of the nineteenth century. Turgenev's realism—apparent in "The Tryst"—is tempered with a genuine interest in people and how they behave toward one another. Many of his stories can be viewed as carefully thought-out sociological documents indicting the cruelty and oppression of Russian serfdom. Others take as their subject damaging personal relationships. Natural settings are often described in a vibrantly lyrical prose that gives the reader a sense of being on the scene.

Among the French practitioners of the short story, Honoré de Balzac (1799–1850) stands as the chief transitional figure between romanticism and realism. Like the realists, Balzac delineates his settings and characters with great exactness, but his plots often include the melodramatic and the improbable. Many of his stories have an urban setting and deal with the transformation of preindustrial localities into chaotic modern metropolises. Some, however, are set in far-off, romantic places and have themes dealing with the impact of unusual settings, and their attendant pressures, on traditional behavior.

French realism found its most brilliant expression in the stories of Guy de Maupassant (1850–1893), probably the most influential short-story writer France has produced. Maupassant's stories combine fast-moving plots, often with a surprise twist, and a notable economy of descriptive detail. His characters are commonplace peasants, priests, prostitutes, and civil servants; and he depicts them in an unpitying light that seldom leaves a shortcoming, spiritual or physical, unexposed. The stories turn upon incidents that at first glance appear common and unremarkable. In the hands of Maupassant, however, they take on a significance, a previously hidden or unknown quality, that often escapes the attention of less astute observers.

Maupassant held a grimly pessimistic view of human beings, saying, ''I seem to see in them the horror of their souls as one sees a monstrous fetus in . . . a glass jar.'' True to his vision, Maupassant rarely deals with such virtues as love and compassion. Rather, he offers a pageant of evil characters and case studies of pride, greed, lust, and envy. Although well aware of the general moral corruption he is dealing with, Maupassant maintains a hands-off attitude toward his material, offering few moral judgments and even fewer attempts to delve into the psychology of his characters. He simply tells the story as he sees it, letting his readers form their own judgments.

The stories of the Russian realist Anton Chekhov (1860–1904) both resemble and differ from those of Maupassant. Like his French contemporary, Chekhov wrote about ordinary people and events, avoided spectacular themes and language, pruned away all extraneous detail, and sought to maintain a reserved demeanor toward his characters. Unlike Maupassant, however, Chekhov possessed compassion—a forever-flickering belief in the possibility of human progress.

Again and again, Chekhov was drawn to explore the effects of isolation and petty vice upon the human psyche. Sometimes isolation results from the gradual breakdown of communication between formerly close friends; sometimes it stems from simple indifference on the part of one person to the troubles of others. In either instance the result is, as Chekhov saw it, a sort of spiritual death. Petty vices—jealousy, disloyalty, ill temper, self-indulgence, hypocrisy—pose a special danger. Because they are so easy both to commit and to conceal, they may quickly become an ingrained and permanent part of the personality, preventing us from developing our full human potential.

Chekhov's desire for absolute honesty led him to reject the neat, carefully orchestrated plots of both Maupassant and the early romantics. Life, Chekhov thought, was much more formless than rigidly structured plots, and he sought to demonstrate this notion in his own stories, even at the expense of narrative interest. This has led many readers to conclude that nothing happens in Chekhov's stories. Actually, considerable conflict does occur, but because it is often psychological rather than physical it may not always be grasped without a close reading.

The Chekhovian approach to plot, although foreshadowed in many of the earlier stories of Gogol and Turgenev, made few converts among the popular writers of the day. They continued to churn out thousands of plot-dominated stories, often with a "clever" twist at the end. Such stories dominated the periodical market—much to the detriment of the genre generally—until a decade or two into the twentieth century, when the inevitable reaction finally set in.

The closing decades of the nineteenth century marked the appearance of two additional intellectual and literary movements: naturalism and psychological realism. Both would profoundly affect the continuing development of the short story.

Naturalism, sometimes called determinism, can be thought of as an intense and pessimistic form of realism. Naturalism dealt with a greater diversity of topics and often with lower and coarser human types than did realism. It did not hesitate to present unpleasant material if the story required such a presentation. Perhaps most important, naturalism depicted human beings without dignity or strength, devoid of free will and ethical responsibility, adrift in a vast indifferent universe that they could not begin to understand.

The naturalistic movement was in part a reaction to industrialization and the findings of the English biologist Charles Darwin (1809–1882). Industrialization gave rise to social and political problems that worsened as time passed. To operate their great factories, industrial entrepreneurs found it necessary to recruit armies of workers, most of whom had been simple farmers and who had little technical skill. As these people swarmed into the cities where the factories were located, serious problems of housing, sanitation, and crime arose, placing new burdens on city governments. Within the factories themselves, conditions were dangerous. Employees frequently worked from twelve to sixteen hours a day, six or seven days a week. And the workers, who often included women and small children, were paid a pittance—just enough *not* to be able to keep body and soul together.

Darwin's initial theory was first published in 1859 in his *On the Origin of Species*. Darwin noted that organisms tend to produce an excess of offspring, some of which—usually a very small percentage—are likely to vary slightly from their parents. When the deviant individuals are, because of some accident of circumstance, better suited to the environment, they tend to survive in greater numbers, passing their deviant (superior) characteristics on to their offspring. This process Darwin called "natural selection" or the "survival of the fittest." Through the continued operation of the process of selection, new species are not only produced, they are constantly revised and "improved." Darwin described the matter succinctly:

> Natural selection is daily and hourly scrutinising, throughout the world, the slightest variations; rejecting those that are bad, preserving and adding up all that are good; silently and insensibly working, *whenever and wherever opportunity offers*, at the improvement of each organic being in relation to the organic and inorganic conditions of life.

The social impact of Darwinism was little less than devastating. These theories challenged the first teaching of Christianity, the belief that God had created humans in the Creator's own image. If Darwin's ideas were true, then the human race, over eons of time, had developed willy-nilly from simple animal origins. Darwinism also undermined traditional morality by substituting the operation of blind chance for precepts based upon Biblical teachings. The result was to make humans seem much less important in the scheme of things than they had in the past. The human being had become a human animal.

Other developments with religious implications added to the impact of Darwinism. Linguists and Biblical scholars were able to show that the Bible is a collection of individual and sometimes contradictory writings produced over a millennium rather than the literal and infallible word of God that many Christians held it to be. At about the same time, anthropologists were demonstrating that accounts of worldwide floods, virgin births, and resurrections occur in the ancient writings of many religions. In astronomy, Sir John Herschel discovered that star clusters and nebulae are not stable entities but instead undergo constant evolutionary change. At Yale University, Willard Gibbs formulated the second law of thermodynamics: all matter loses energy at a constant rate, even when energy is not being expended as work; thus all energy will eventually be distributed evenly throughout the universe. Taken together, these findings seemed to refute the notion that Christianity is divinely inspired and that God created the universe in a fixed and final form.

Before long, many thinkers began to apply evolutionary principles to the social and political spheres. Herbert Spencer, the most influential of these people, taught that society, as well as the individual, undergoes an evolutionary development from the simple to the complex and that the survival-of-the-fittest doctrine operates within human society just as it does in nature. Spencer denounced all types of social reform as unwarranted interference with the workings of natural law, which by itself would in time produce a utopian society.

Capitalists everywhere seized upon the teachings of the Social Darwinists to justify the status quo, the status quo being the making of enormous fortunes and the holding of masses of workers in conditions of grinding poverty. Capitalism, they argued, provided an example of Darwinism in action. The strong workers would survive, the weak perish. The whole process, however grim it might appear from the inside, was operating in accordance with natural law, and any attempt to meddle with the system would only delay the advancement of the race.

Humans, however, seem cursed—or blessed—with a perverse disinclination to accept what experts decree is best for them, and the workers of the late nineteenth century proved no exception. Ungraciously refusing to sacrifice themselves for what they were told was the greater good, they banded together in labor unions and sought relief through the legislative process. Eventually, their efforts led to safer factories, shorter working hours, higher wages, and an end to child labor. By and large, though, these improvements came about after 1900 and thus did little to moderate the gloomy outlook of the naturalist writers.

Stephen Crane (1871–1900), the foremost American naturalist, experienced at first hand the realities of slum life when as a youth he lived for a time with several artist friends in New York's Bowery. His stories were strongly influenced by the work of two other naturalists, the French writers Gustave Flaubert (1821–1880) and Émile Zola (1840–1902), whose stories present human beings as little more than pawns of heredity and chance, enslaved by animal appetites.

Like most naturalists, Crane believed in a universe completely indifferent to human struggles and aspirations. Because of the indifference of the universe, humans enjoy a limited measure of freedom. Sometimes they may exercise complete control over situations in which they become involved; at other times they may have no control at all. Most often, however, events are partly under and partly out of human control. Furthermore, no one can hope to grasp the true significance of these events as they occur.

Individuals can best achieve meaningful relationships with one another during periods when a group is faced by a common danger. At those times all selfish desires are swept away—even if only temporarily—and are replaced by feelings of friendship, cooperation, and camaraderie. The individual also gains a clearer understanding of his or her capabilities and limitations. Crane's short story "The Open Boat" stands as a definitive fictional statement of naturalist doctrine.

Henry James (1843–1916) was the originator of psychological realism—a type of realism that places great stress on examining the workings of the human mind. James wrote admiringly about the works of Maupassant, Turgenev, and other realists, several of whom he knew personally. Hawthorne's stories, with their consistent emphasis on the psychological analysis of character, greatly influenced James' own approach to character dramatization. Through his brother, the psychologist William James, Henry kept abreast of developments in the evolving science of the mind.

Henry James was a realist, but a realist of quite a different stripe from those who felt that fiction should merely present an exact reproduction of life. Similarly, he rejected the naturalist view that fiction should depict human character as the hopeless pawn of chance and fate. Although he felt that humans are to some extent shaped by forces beyond their control, James consistently maintained that they could exercise a certain degree of self-determination.

James saw reality as a series of impressions that must be selected and artistically arranged in order to provide a story with a sense of solidity or reality. The artist must strive to select exactly the right background details and time scheme, as well as a center, or point, from which the action can be viewed. Many of his stories make use of what James called a "central intelligence"—sometimes a major character and sometimes a minor character, who views and interprets the significance of the events taking place. This device allowed James to probe deeply into the delicate and shifting relationships among individuals, the growth and degeneration of a personality, and the influence of heredity and environment on human lives.

Reality, to James, included anything that had an effect on an individual, whether or not it had objective existence. Thus, in James' ghost stories the ghosts are real enough to those who see them, but the reader never knows for certain whether they actually exist. James, along with Sigmund Freud, influenced the work of James Joyce, Sherwood Anderson, D. H. Lawrence, and almost every other twentieth-century literary investigator of the human psyche.

E. T. A. HOFFMANN

The Story of Serapion

"You know that some years ago I spent a considerable time in B——, a place in one of the pleasantest districts of the South of Germany. As my habit is, I used to take long walks in the surrounding country by myself, without any guide, though I should often have been the better for one. On one of these occasions I got into a piece of thickly wooded country and lost my way; the farther I went, the less could I discover the smallest vestige of a human footstep. At last the wood grew less thick, and I saw, not far from me, a man in a hermit's brown robe, with a broad straw hat on his head, and a long, wild black beard, sitting on a rock by the side of a deep ravine, gazing, with folded hands, thoughtfully into the distance. This sight had something so strange, unexpected, and out of the common about it that I felt a shiver of eeriness and awe. One can scarcely help such a feeling when what one has only heretofore seen in pictures, or read of in books, suddenly appears before one's eyes in actual, everyday life. Here was an anchorite of the early ages of Christianity, in the body, seated in one of Salvator Rosa's wild mountain scenes. But it soon occurred to me that probably a monk on his peregrinations was nothing uncommon in that part of the country. So I walked up to him, and asked if he could tell me the shortest way out of the wood to the high road leading to

B——. He looked at me from head to foot with a gloomy glance, and said, in a hollow and solemn voice:

" 'I know well that it is merely an idle curiosity to see me, and to hear me speak which has led you to this desert. But you must perceive that I have no time to talk with you now. My friend Ambrosius of Camaldoli is returning to Alexandria. Travel with him.'

"With which he arose and walked down into the ravine.

"I felt as if I must be in a dream. Presently I heard the sound of wheels close by. I made my way through the thickets, and found myself in a forest track, where I saw a countryman going along in a cart. I overtook him, and he shortly brought me to a high road leading to B——. As we went along I told him my adventure, and asked if he knew who the extraordinary man in the forest was.

" 'Oh, sir,' he said, 'that was the worthy man who calls himself Priest Serapion, and who has been living in these woods for some years, in a little hut which he built himself. People say he's not quite right in his head, but he is a nice, good gentleman, never does any harm, and edifies us of the village with pious discourses, giving us all the good advice that he can.'

"I had come across the anchorite some six or eight miles from B——, so I concluded that something must be known of him there, and this proved to be the case. Dr. S—— told me all the story. This hermit had once been one of the most brilliant intellects, one of the most universally accomplished men in M——; and belonging, as he did, to a very distinguished family, he was naturally appointed to an important diplomatic post as soon as he had completed his studies: the duties of this office he discharged with great ability and energy. Moreover, he had remarkable poetical gifts, and everything he wrote was inspired by a most brilliant fancy, a mind and imagination which sounded the profoundest depths of all subjects. His incomparable humor, and the unusual charm of his character made him the most delightful of companions imaginable. He had risen from step to step of his career, and was on the point of being despatched on an important diplomatic mission, when he disappeared, in the most incomprehensible fashion, from M——. All search for him was fruitless, and conjecture and inquiry were baffled by a combination of circumstances.

"After a time there appeared amongst the villages, in the depths of the Tyrolese mountains, a man in a brown robe, who preached in these hamlets, and then went away into the wildest parts of the forest, where he lived the life of a hermit. It chanced one day that Count P—— saw this man (who called himself Priest Serapion), and at once recognized him as his unfortunate nephew, who had disappeared from M——. He was taken into custody, became violent, and all the skill of the best doctors in M—— could do nothing to alleviate his terrible condition. He was taken to the lunatic asylum at B——, and there the methodical system, based upon profound psychological knowledge, pursued by the medical men then in charge of that institution, succeeded in bringing about a condition of much less excitement, and greater quietness in the form of his malady. Whether this doctor, true to his theory, gave the patient an opportunity of escaping, or whether he himself found the means of doing so, escape he did, and was lost sight of for a considerable time.

"Serapion appeared, ultimately, in the country some eight miles from B——, where I had seen him; and the doctor declared that if any true compassion was to be shown him, he should not be again driven into a condition of wild excitement; but that, if he was to be at peace, and, after his fashion, happy, he should be left in these woods in perfect freedom, to do just as he liked; in which case he, the said doctor, would be responsible for the consequences. Accordingly, the police authorities were content to leave him to a distant and imperceptible supervision by the officials of the nearest village, and the result bore out what the doctor had said. Serapion built himself a little hut, pretty, and, under the circumstances, comfortable. He made chairs and tables, wove mats of rushes to lie upon, and laid out a garden where he grew flowers and vegetables. In all that did not touch the idea that he was the hermit Serapion who fled into the Theban desert in the days of the Emperor Decius, and suffered martyrdom in Alexandria, his mind was completely unaffected. He could carry on the most intellectual conversation, and often showed traces of the brilliant humor and charming individuality of character for which he had been remarkable in his former life. The aforesaid doctor declared him to be completely incurable, and strongly deprecated all attempts to restore him to the world and to his former pursuits and duties.

"You will readily understand that I could not drive this anchorite of mine out of my thoughts, and that I experienced an irresistible longing to see him again. But just picture to yourselves the excess of my folly! I had no less an undertaking in my mind than that of attacking Serapion's fixed idea at its very roots. I read Pinel, Reil, every conceivable book on insanity which I could lay my hands on. I fondly believed that it might be reserved for me, an amateur psychologist and doctor, to cast some rays of light into Serapion's darkened intelligence. And I did not omit, either, to make myself acquainted with the stories of all the Serapions (there were no fewer than eight of them) treated of in the histories of saints and martyrs.

"Thus equipped, I set out one fine morning in search of my anchorite.

"I found him working in his garden with hoe and spade, singing a devotional song. Wild pigeons, for which he had strewed an abundant supply of food, were fluttering and cooing around him, and a young deer was peeping through the leaves on the trellis. He was evidently living in the closest intimacy with the woodland creatures. Not the faintest trace of insanity was visible in his face; it bore a quiet expression of remarkable serenity and happiness; and all this confirmed what Dr. S—— in B—— had told me. When he heard of my projected visit to the anchorite, he advised me to go some fine, bright, pleasant morning, because, he said, his mind would be less troubled then and he would be more inclined to talk to a stranger, whereas at evening he would shun all intercourse with mankind.

"As soon as he saw me he laid down his spade, and came toward me in a kind and friendly manner. I said that, being weary with a longish journey, I should be glad if he would allow me to rest with him for a little while.

" 'You are heartily welcome,' he said. 'The little which I can offer you in the shape of refreshment is at your service.'

"And he took me to a seat of moss in front of his hut, brought out a little table, set on bread, magnificent grapes, and a can of wine, and hospitably begged me to eat and drink. He sat down opposite me, and ate bread with much appetite, washing it down with draughts of water.

"In good sooth I did not see how I was to lead the conversation to my subject—how I was to bring my psychological science to bear upon this peaceful, happy man. At last I pulled myself together and began:

" 'You style yourself Serapion, reverend sir?'

" 'Yes, certainly,' he answered. 'The Church has given me that name.'

" 'Ancient ecclesiastical history,' I continued, 'mentions several celebrated holy men of that name. An abbot Serapion, known for his good works—the learned Bishop Serapion alluded to by Hieronimus in his book *De Viris Illustribus*. There was also a monk Serapion, who (as Heraclides relates in his *Paradise*) on one occasion, coming from the Theban desert to Rome, ordered a virgin, who had joined him—saying she had renounced the world and its pleasures—to prove this by walking with him naked in the streets of Rome, and repulsed her when she hesitated, saying, "You still live the life of Nature, and are careful for the opinions of mankind. Think not that you are anything great or have overcome the world." If I am not mistaken, reverend sir, this was the "filthy monk" (Heraclides himself so styles him) who suffered a terrible martyrdom under the Emperor Decius—his limbs being torn asunder at the joints, and his body thrown down from a lofty rock.'

" 'That was so,' said Serapion, turning pale, and his eyes glowing with a somber fire. 'But Serapion the martyr had no connection with that monk, who, in the fury of his asceticism, did battle against human nature. I am Serapion the martyr, to whom you allude.'

" 'What?' I cried, with feigned surprise, 'You believe that you are that Serapion who suffered such hideous martyrdom so many hundred years ago?'

" 'That,' said Serapion with much calmness, 'may appear incredible to you, and I admit that it must sound very wonderful to many who cannot see further than the points of their own noses. However, it is as I tell you. God's omnipotence permitted me to survive my martyrdom, and to recover from its effects, because it was ordained, in His mysterious providence, that I had still to pass a certain period of my existence, to His praise and glory, here in the Theban desert. There is nothing now to remind me of the tortures which I suffered except sometimes a severe headache, and occasional violent cramps and twitching in my limbs.

" 'Now,' thought I, 'is the time to commence my cure.'

"I made a wide circumbendibus, and talked in an erudite style concerning the malady of 'Fixed Idea,' which attacks people, marring, like one single discord, the otherwise harmonious organisms. I spoke of the scientific man who could not be induced to rise from his chair for fear he would break the windows across the street with his nose. I mentioned the Abbot Molanus, who conversed most rationally upon every subject, but would not leave his room because he thought he was a barleycorn and the hens would swallow him. I came to the fact that to confound oneself with some historical character was a frequent form of Fixed Idea. 'Nothing more absurd and preposterous,' I said, 'could possibly be imagined than that a little bit of woodland country eight miles from B——, daily frequented by country folk, sportsmen, and people walking for exercise was the Theban desert, and he himself that ascetic who suffered martyrdom many centuries ago.'

"Serapion listened in silence. He seemed to feel what I said, and to be struggling with himself in deep reflection. So that I thought it was time to strike my decisive blow. I stood up, took him by both hands, and cried, loudly and emphatically:

" 'Count P——, awake from the pernicious dream which is enthralling you; throw off that abominable dress, and come back to your family, which mourns your loss, and to the world where you have such important duties to discharge.'

"Serapion gazed at me with a somber, penetrating gaze. Then a sarcastic smile played about his lips and cheeks, and he said, slowly and solemnly:

" 'You have spoken, sir, long, and, as you consider, wisely and well. Allow me, in turn, to say a few words in reply. Saint Anthony, and all the men of the Church who have withdrawn from the world into solitude, were often visited by vexing spirits, who, envying the inward peace and contentment of their souls, carried on with them lengthy contest, until they had to lie down conquered in the dust. And such is my fortune also. Every now and then there appear to me emissaries, sent by Satan, who try to persuade me that I am Count P—— of M——, and that I ought to betake myself to the life of Courts, and all sorts of unholiness. Were it not for the efficacy of prayer, I should take these people by the shoulders, turn them out of my little garden, and carefully barricade it against them. But I need not do so in your case; for you are, most unmistakably, the very feeblest of all the adversaries who have ever come to me, and I can vanquish you with your own weapons—those of ratiocination. It is insanity that is in question between us. But if one of us two is suffering from that sad malady, it is evident that you are so in a much greater degree than I. You maintain that it is a case of Fixed Idea that I believe myself to be Serapion the martyr—and I am quite aware that many persons hold the same opinion, or pretend that they do. Now, if I am really insane, none but a lunatic can think that he could argue me out of the Fixed Idea which insanity has engendered in me. Were such a proceeding possible, there would soon be no madmen on the face of the earth, for men would be able to rule, and command, their mental power, which is not their own, but merely lent to them for a time by a Higher Power which disposes of them. But if I am not mad, and if I am really Serapion the martyr, it is insane to set about arguing me out of that, and leading me to adopt the Fixed Idea that I am Count P—— of M——. You say that Serapion the martyr lived several centuries ago, and that, consequently, I cannot be that martyr, presumably for the reason that human beings cannot remain so long on this earth. Well, as regards this, the notion of time is just as relative a notion as that of number; and I may say to you that, according to the notion of time which I have in me, it is scarcely three hours (or whatever appellation you may choose to give to the divisions of time) since I was put to martyrdom by the Emperor Decius. But, leaving this on one side, can you assert, in opposition to me, that a life of such length as I say I have lived, is unexampled and contrary to human nature? Have you cognizance of the precise length of the life of every human being who has existed in all this wide world, that you can employ the expression "unexampled" in this pert and decisive manner? Do you compare God's omnipotence to the wretched art of the clockmaker, who can't save his lifeless machinery from destruction? You say this place where we are is not the Theban desert, but a little woodland district eight miles from B——, daily frequented by country folk, sportsmen, and others. Prove that to me.'

"Here I thought I had my man.

" 'Come with me,' said I, 'and in a couple of hours we shall be in B——, and what I assert will be proved.'

" 'Poor blinded fool,' said Serapion. 'What a wide distance lies between us and B——! But put the case that I went with you to some town which you call B——; would you be able to convince me that we had been traveling for two hours only, and the place we had arrived at was really B——? If I were to assert that you were insane, and suppose the Theban desert is a little bit of wooded country, and far-away Alexandria the town of B—— in the south of Germany, what would you say in reply? Our old discussion would go on forever. Then there is another point which you ought seriously to consider. You must, I should suppose, perceive that I, who am talking with you, am leading the peaceful and happy life of a man reconciled with God. It is only after having passed through martyrdom that such a life dawns upon the soul. And if it has pleased the Almighty to cast a veil over what happened before my martyrdom, is it not a terrible and diabolical action to try to tear that veil away?'

"With all my wisdom, I stood confounded and silenced in the presence of this insane man! With the very rationality of his irrationality he had beaten me completely out of the field, and I saw the folly of my undertaking in all its fulness. Still more than that, I felt the reproach contained in what he had last said as deeply as I was astounded at the dim remembrance of his previous life which shone through it like some lofty, invulnerable higher spirit.

"Serapion seemed to be reading my thoughts, and, looking me full in the face with an expression of the greatest kindliness, he said:

" 'I never took you for an evil-disposed adversary, and I see I was not mistaken. You may have been instigated by somebody—perhaps by the Evil One himself—to come here to vex and try me, but I am sure it was not a spontaneous act of yours. And perhaps the fact that you found me other than you expected may have strengthened you in your expression of the doubts which you have suggested. Although I in no sense deviate from the devoutness beseeming him who has given up his life to God and the Church, the cynicism of asceticism into which many of my brethren have fallen—thereby giving proof of the weakness, nay, utter destruction of their mental vigor, instead of its boasted strength—is utterly foreign to me! You expected to find the Monk Serapion pale and haggard, wasted with fast and vigil, all the horror of visions, terrible as those which drove even Saint Anthony to despair, in his somber face, with quivering knees scarce able to support him, in a filthy robe, stained with his blood. You find a placid, cheerful man. But I, too, have passed through those tortures, and have overcome them and survived. And when I awoke with shattered limbs and fractured skull, the spirit dawned, and shone bright within me, restoring my mind and my body to health. May it please Heaven speedily to grant to you also, my brother, even here on earth, a peace and happiness such as those which daily refresh and strengthen me. Have no dread of the terror of the deepest solitude. It is only there that a life like this can dawn upon the pious soul.'

"Serapion, who had spoken with genuine priestly unction, raised, in silence, his eyes to Heaven with an expression of blissful gratitude. How could I feel otherwise than awe-struck! A madman, congratulating himself on his condition, looking upon it as a priceless gift from Heaven, and, from the depths of his heart, wishing me a similar fate!

"I was on the point of leaving him, but he began in an altered tone, saying:

" 'You would, probably, scarcely suppose that this wild inhospitable desert is often almost too full of the noise and bustle of life to be suitable for my silent meditations. Every day I receive visits from the most remarkable people of the most diverse kinds. Ariosto was here yesterday, and Dante and Petrarch afterwards. And this evening I expect Evagrus, the celebrated father, with whom I shall discuss the most recent ecclesiastical affairs, as I did poetry yesterday. I often go up to the top of that hill there, whence the towers of Alexandria are to be seen distinctly in clear weather, and the most wonderful and interesting events happen before my eyes. Many people have thought that incredible, too, and considered that I only fancy I see before me, in actual life, what is merely born in my mind and imagination. Now I say that is the most incomprehensible piece of folly that can exist. What is it, except the mind, which takes cognizance of what happens around us in time and space? What is it that hears, and feels, and sees? Is it the lifeless mechanism which we call eyes, ears, hands, etc., and not the mind? Does the mind give form and shape to that peculiar world of its own which has space and time for its conditions of existence, and then hand over the functions of seeing, hearing, etc., to some other principle inherent in us? How illogical! Therefore, if it is the mind only which takes cognizance of events around us, it follows that that which it has taken cognizance of has actually occurred. Last evening only, Ariosto was speaking of the images of his fancy, and saying he had created in his brain forms and events which had never existed in time and space. I at once denied the possibility of this, and he was obliged to allow that it was only from lack of a higher knowledge that a poet would box up within the narrow limits of his brain that which, by virtue of his peculiar seer gift, he was enabled to see in full life before him. But the complete acquirement of this higher knowledge only comes after martyrdom, and is strengthened by the life in profound solitude. You don't appear to agree with me; probably you don't understand me here. Indeed how could a child of this world, however well disposed, understand an anchorite consecrated in all his works and ways to God. Let me tell you what happened before my eyes, as I was standing this morning at sunrise at the top of that hill.'

"He then related a regular romance, with a plot and incidents such as only the most imaginative poet could have constructed. The characters and events stood out with such a vivid, plastic relief, that it was impossible—carried away as one was by the magic spell of them—to help believing, as if in a species of dream, that Serapion had actually witnessed them from the hilltop. This romance was succeeded by another, and that by another, by which time the sun stood high above us in the noontide sky. Serapion then rose from his seat, and looking into the distance, said: 'Yonder comes my brother Hilarion, who, in his overstrictness, always blames me for being too much given to the society of strangers.'

"I understood the hint, and took my leave, asking if I should be allowed to pay him another visit. Serapion answered with a gentle smile, 'My friend, I thought you would be eager to get away from this wilderness, so little adapted to your mode of life. But if it is your pleasure to take up your abode for a time in my neighborhood, you will always be welcome to my cottage and my little garden. Perhaps it may be granted to me to convert him who came to me as an adversary. Farewell, my friend.'

"I am wholly unable to characterize the impression which my visit to him had made upon me. Whilst his condition, his methodical madness in which he found the joy of his life, produced the weirdest effect upon me, his extraordinary poetical genius filled me with amazement, and his kindly, peaceful happiness, instinct with the quietest resignation of the purest mind, touched me unspeakably. I thought of Ophelia's sorrowful words:

'O what a noble mind is here o'erthrown,' etc.

Yet I could not make plaint against the Omnipotence, which probably had, in this mysterious fashion, steered his bark away from reefs, which might have wrecked it, into this secure haven.

"The oftener I went to see him, the more attached to him I became. I always found him happy, and disposed to converse, and I took great care never again to essay my role of the psychological doctor. It was wonderful with what acuteness and penetration he spoke of life in all its aspects, and most remarkable of all, how he deduced historical events from causes wholly remote from all ordinary theories on the subject. When sometimes—notwithstanding the striking acuteness of those divinations of his—I took it upon me to object that no work on history made any mention of the circumstances which he alluded to, he would answer, with a quiet smile, that probably no historian in the world knew as much about them as he did, seeing that he had them from the very lips of the people concerned, when they came to see him.

"I was obliged to leave B—— and it was three years before I could go back there. It was late in Autumn, about the middle of November—the 14th, if I do not mistake—when I set out to pay my anchorite a visit. Whilst I was still at a distance, I heard the sound of the little bell which hung above his hut, and was filled with gloomy forebodings, without apparent cause. At last I reached the cottage and went in.

"Serapion was lying on his mat, with his hands folded on his breast. I thought he was sleeping, and went softly up to him. Then I saw that he was dead."

FOR STUDY, DISCUSSION, AND WRITING

1. How do you account for the strange attraction the narrator feels for Serapion? As you read the story, did you share in this attraction?
2. Keeping in mind that individual eccentricity and madness were part and parcel of romanticism, do you think Serapion was really insane?
3. How does the fact that Serapion has taken his name from an early Christian martyr reflect romanticism?
4. How is nineteenth-century German romanticism's interest in abnormal psychology reflected by the narrator and in the conversations between Serapion and the narrator?
5. What is the point of view of the story? How does the point of view contribute to the story?
6. Compare and contrast the self-deception practiced by Serapion and that practiced by Walter Mitty.

WASHINGTON IRVING

The Spectre Bridegroom*

He that supper for is dight,
He lyes full cold, I trow, this night!
Yestreen to chamber I him led,
This night Gray-Steel has made his bed.

SIR EGER, SIR GRAHAME AND SIR GRAY-STEEL

*The erudite reader, well versed in good-for-nothing lore, will perceive that the above Tale must have been suggested to the old Swiss by a little French anecdote, a circumstance said to have taken place at Paris.

On the summit of one of the heights of the Odenwald, a wild and romantic tract of Upper Germany, that lies not far from the confluence of the Main and the Rhine, there stood, many, many, years since, the Castle of the Baron Von Landshort. It is now quite fallen to decay, and almost buried among beech trees and dark firs; above which, however, its old watch-tower may still be seen struggling, like the former possessor I have mentioned, to carry a high head, and look down upon a neighboring country.

The baron was a dry branch of the great family of Katzenellenbogen,† and inherited the relics of the property, and all the pride of his ancestors. Though the warlike disposition of his predecessors had much impaired the family possessions, yet the baron still endeavored to keep up some show of former state. The times were peaceable, and the German nobles, in general, had abandoned their inconvenient old castles, perched like eagles' nests among the mountains, and had built more convenient residences in the valleys: still the baron remained proudly drawn up in his little fortress, cherishing, with hereditary inveteracy, all the old family feuds; so that he was on ill terms with some of his nearest neighbors, on account of disputes that had happened between their great-great-grandfathers.

The baron had but one child, a daughter; but nature, when she grants but one child, always compensates by making it a prodigy; and so it was with the daughter of the baron. All the nurses, gossips, and country cousins, assured her father that she had not her equal for beauty in all Germany; and who should know better than they? She had, moreover, been brought up with great care, under the superintendence of two maiden aunts, who had spent some years of their early life at one of the little German courts, and were skilled in all the branches of knowledge necessary to the education of a fine lady. Under their instructions she became a miracle of accomplishments. By the time she was eighteen, she could embroider to admiration, and had worked whole histories of the saints in tapestry, with such strength of expression in their countenances, that they looked like so many souls in purgatory. She could read without great difficulty, and had spelled her way through several church legends, and almost all the chivalric wonders of the Heldenbuch. She had even made considerable proficiency in writing; could sign her own name without missing a letter, and so legibly, that her aunts could read it without spectacles. She excelled in making little good-for-nothing ladylike nicknacks of all kinds; was versed in the most abstruse dancing of the day; played a number of airs on the harp and guitar; and knew all the tender ballads of the Minnie-lieders by heart.

Her aunts, too, having been great flirts and coquettes in their younger days, were admirably calculated to be vigilant guardians and strict censors of the conduct of their niece; for there is no duenna so rigidly prudent, and inexorably decorous, as a superannuated coquette. She was rarely suffered out of

†i.e., CAT'S-ELBOW. The name of a family of those parts very powerful in former times. The appellation, we are told, was given in compliment to a peerless dame of the family, celebrated for her fine arm.

their sight; never went beyond the domains of the castle, unless well attended, or, rather well watched; had continual lectures read to her about strict decorum and implicit obedience; and, as to the men—pah!—she was taught to hold them at such a distance, and in such absolute distrust, that, unless properly authorized, she would not have cast a glance upon the handsomest cavalier in the world—no, not if he were even dying at her feet.

The good effects of this system were wonderfully apparent. The young lady was a pattern of docility and correctness. While others were wasting their sweetness in the glare of the world, and liable to be plucked and thrown aside by every hand, she was coyly blooming into fresh and lovely womanhood under the protection of those immaculate spinsters, like a rose-bud blushing forth among guardian thorns. Her aunts looked upon her with pride and exultation, and vaunted that though all the other young ladies in the world might go astray, yet, thank Heaven, nothing of the kind could happen to the heiress of Katzenellenbogen.

But, however scantily the Baron Von Landshort might be provided with children, his household was by no means a small one; for Providence had enriched him with abundance of poor relations. They, one and all, possessed the affectionate disposition common to humble relatives; were wonderfully attached to the baron, and took every possible occasion to come in swarms and enliven the castle. All family festivals were commemorated by these good people at the baron's expense; and when they were filled with good cheer, they would declare that there was nothing on earth so delightful as these family meetings, these jubilees of the heart.

The baron, though a small man, had a large soul, and it swelled with satisfaction at the consciousness of being the greatest man in the little world about him. He loved to tell long stories about the stark old warriors whose portraits looked grimly down from the walls around, and he found no listeners equal to those who fed at his expense. He was much given to the marvellous, and a firm believer in all those supernatural tales with which every mountain and valley in Germany abounds. The faith of his guests even exceeded his own; they listened to every tale of wonder with open eyes and mouth, and never failed to be astonished, even though repeated for the hundredth time. Thus lived the Baron Von Landshort, the oracle of his table, the absolute monarch of his little territory, and happy, above all things, in the persuasion that he was the wisest man of the age.

At the time of which my story treats there was a great family gathering at the castle, on an affair of the utmost importance: it was to receive the destined bridegroom of the baron's daughter. A negotiation had been carried on between the father and an old nobleman of Bavaria, to unite the dignity of their houses by the marriage of their children. The preliminaries had been conducted with proper punctilio. The young people were betrothed without seeing each other; and the time was appointed for the marriage ceremony. The young Count Von Altenburg had been recalled from the army for the purpose, and was actually on his way to the baron's to receive his bride. Missives had even been received from him, from Wurtzburg, where he was accidentally detained, mentioning the day and hour when he might be expected to arrive.

The castle was in a tumult of preparation to give him a suitable welcome. The fair bride had been decked out with uncommon care. The two aunts had superintended her toilet, and quarreled the whole morning about every article of her dress. The young lady had taken advantage of their contest to follow the bent of her own taste; and fortunately it was a good one. She looked as lovely as youthful bridegroom could desire; and the flutter of expectation heightened the lustre of her charms.

The suffusions that mantled her face and neck, the gentle heaving of the bosom, the eye now and then lost in reverie, all betrayed the soft tumult that was going on in her little heart. The aunts were continually hovering around her; for maiden aunts are apt to take great interest in affairs of this nature. They were giving her a world of staid counsel how to deport herself, what to say, and in what manner to receive the expected lover.

The baron was no less busied in preparations. He had, in truth, nothing exactly to do: but he was naturally a fuming bustling little man, and could not remain passive when all the world was in a hurry. He worried from top to bottom of the castle with an air of infinite anxiety; he continually called the servants from their work to exhort them to be diligent; and buzzed about every hall and chamber, as idly restless and importunate as a blue-bottle fly of a warm summer's day.

In the mean time the fatted calf had been killed; the forests had rung with the clamor of the huntsmen; the kitchen was crowded with good cheer; the cellars had yielded up whole oceans of *Rhein-wein* and *Ferne-wein*; and even the great Heidelberg tun had been laid under contribution. Every thing was ready to receive the distinguished guest with *Saus und Braus* in the true spirit of German hospitality—but the guest delayed to make his appearance. Hour rolled after hour. The sun that had poured his downward rays upon the rich forest of the Odenwald, now just gleamed along the summits of the mountains. The baron mounted the highest tower, and strained his eyes in hopes of catching a distant sight of the count and his attendants. Once he thought he beheld them; the sound of horns came floating from the valley, prolonged by the mountain echoes. A number of horsemen were seen far below, slowly advancing along the road; but when they had nearly reached the foot of the mountain, they suddenly struck off in a different direction. The last ray of sunshine departed—the bats began to flit by in the twilight—the road grew dimmer and dimmer to the view; and nothing appeared stirring in it but now and then a peasant lagging homeward from his labor.

While the old castle of Landshort was in this state of perplexity, a very interesting scene was transacting in a different part of the Odenwald.

The young Count Von Altenburg was tranquilly pursuing his route in that sober job-trot way, in which a man travels toward matrimony when his friends have taken all the trouble and uncertainty of courtship off his hands, and a bride is waiting for him, as certainly as a dinner at the end of his journey. He had encountered at Wurtzburg, a youthful companion in arms, with whom he had seen some service on the frontiers; Herman Von Starkenfaust, one of the stoutest hands, and worthiest hearts, of German chivalry, who was now returning from the army. His father's castle was not far distant from the old fortress of Landshort, although an hereditary feud rendered the families hostile, and strangers to each other.

In the warm-hearted moment of recognition, the young friends related all their past adventures and fortunes, and the count gave the whole history of his intended nuptials with a young lady whom he had never seen, but of whose charms he had received the most enrapturing descriptions.

As the route of the friends lay in the same direction, they agreed to perform the rest of their journey together; and, that they might do it more leisurely, set off from Wurtzburg at an early hour, the count having given directions for his retinue to follow and overtake him.

They beguiled their wayfaring with recollections of their military scenes and adventures; but the count was apt to be a little tedious, now and then, about the reputed charms of his bride, and the felicity that awaited him.

In this way they had entered among the mountains of the Odenwald, and were traversing one of its most lonely and thickly-wooded passes. It is well known that the forests of Germany have always been as much infested with robbers as its castles by spectres; and, at this time, the former were particularly numerous, from the hordes of disbanded soldiers wandering about the country. It will not appear extraordinary, therefore, that the cavaliers were attacked by a gang of these stragglers in the midst of the forest. They defended themselves with bravery, but were nearly overpowered, when the count's retinue arrived to their assistance. At sight of them the robbers fled, but not until the count had received a mortal wound. He was slowly and carefully conveyed back to the city of Wurtzburg, and a friar summoned from a neighboring convent, who was famous for his skill in administering to both soul and body; but half of his skill was superfluous; the moments of the unfortunate count were numbered.

With his dying breath he entreated his friend to repair instantly to the castle of Landshort, and explain the fatal cause of his not keeping his appointment with his bride. Though not the most ardent of lovers, he was one of the most punctilious of men, and appeared earnestly solicitous that this mission should be speedily and courteously executed. "Unless this is done," said he, "I shall not sleep quietly in my grave!" He repeated these last words with peculiar solemnity. A request, at a moment so impressive, admitted no hesitation. Starkenfaust endeavored to soothe him to calmness; promised faithfully to execute his wish, and gave him his hand in solemn pledge. The dying man pressed it in acknowledgment, but soon lapsed into delirium—raved about his bride—his engagements—his plighted word; ordered his horse, that he might ride to the castle of Landshort; and expired in the fancied act of vaulting into the saddle.

Starkenfaust bestowed a sigh and a soldier's tear on the untimely fate of his comrade; and then pondered on the awkward mission he had undertaken. His heart was heavy, and his head perplexed; for he was to present himself an unbidden guest among hostile people, and to damp their festivity with tidings fatal to their hopes. Still there were certain whisperings of curiosity in his bosom to see this far-famed beauty of Katzenellenbogen, so cautiously shut up from the world; for he was a passionate admirer of the sex, and there was a dash of eccentricity and enterprise in his character that made him fond of all singular adventure.

Previous to his departure he made all due arrangements with the holy fraternity of the convent for the funeral solemnities of his friend, who was to be buried in the cathedral of Wurtzburg, near some of his illustrious relatives; and the mourning retinue of the count took charge of his remains.

It is now high time that we should return to the ancient family of Katzenellenbogen, who were impatient for their guest, and still more for their dinner; and to the worthy little baron, whom we left airing himself on the watchtower.

Night closed in, but still no guest arrived. The baron descended from the tower in despair. The banquet, which had been delayed from hour to hour, could no longer be postponed. The meats were already overdone; the cook in an agony; and the whole household had the look of a garrison that had been reduced by famine. The baron was obliged reluctantly to give orders for the feast without the presence of the guest. All were seated at table, and just on the point of commencing, when the sound of a horn from without the gate gave notice of the approach of a stranger. Another long blast filled the old courts of the castle with its echoes, and was answered by the warder from the walls. The baron hastened to receive his future son-in-law.

The drawbridge had been let down, and the stranger was before the gate. He was a tall gallant cavalier, mounted on a black steed. His countenance was pale, but he had a beaming, romantic eye, and an air of stately melancholy. The baron was a little mortified that he should have come in this simple, solitary style. His dignity for a moment was ruffled, and he felt disposed to consider it a want of proper respect for the important occasion, and the important family with which he was to be connected. He pacified himself, however, with the conclusion that it must have been youthful impatience which had induced him thus to spur on sooner than his attendants.

"I am sorry," said the stranger, "to break in upon you thus unseasonably—"

Here the baron interrupted him with a world of compliments and greetings; for, to tell the truth, he prided himself upon his courtesy and eloquence. The stranger attempted, once or twice, to stem the torrent of words, but in vain, so he bowed his head and suffered it to flow on. By the time the baron had come to a pause, they had reached the inner court of the castle; and the stranger was again about to speak, when he was once more interrupted by the appearance of the female part of the family, leading forth the shrinking and blushing bride. He gazed on her for a moment as one entranced; it seemed as if his whole soul beamed forth in the gaze, and rested upon that lovely form. One of the maiden aunts whispered something in her ear; she made an effort to speak; her moist blue eye was timidly raised; gave a shy glance of inquiry on the stranger; and was cast again to the ground. The words died away; but there was a sweet smile playing about her lips, and a soft dimpling of the cheek that showed her glance had not been unsatisfactory. It was impossible for a girl of the fond age of eighteen, highly predisposed for love and matrimony, not to be pleased with so gallant a cavalier.

The late hour at which the guest had arrived left no time for parley. The baron was peremptory, and deferred all particular conversation until the morning, and led the way to the untasted banquet.

It was served up in the great hall of the castle. Around the walls hung the hard-favored portraits of the heroes of the house of Katzenellenbogen, and the trophies which they had gained in the field and in the chase. Hacked corselets, splintered jousting spears, and tattered banners, were mingled with the spoils of sylvan warfare; the jaws of the wolf, and the tusks of the boar, grinned horribly among crossbows and battle-axes, and a huge pair of antlers branched immediately over the head of the youthful bridegroom.

The cavalier took but little notice of the company or the entertainment. He scarcely tasted the banquet, but seemed absorbed in admiration of his bride. He conversed in a low tone that could not be overheard—for the language of love is never loud; but where is the female ear so dull that it cannot catch the softest whisper of the lover? There was a mingled tenderness and gravity in his manner, that appeared to have a powerful effect upon the young lady. Her color came and went as she listened with deep attention. Now and then she made some blushing reply, and when his eye was turned away, she would steal a sidelong glance at his romantic countenance, and heave a gentle sigh of tender happiness. It was evident that the young couple were completely enamored. The aunts, who were deeply versed in the mysteries of the heart, declared that they had fallen in love with each other at first sight.

The feast went on merrily, or at least noisily, for the guests were all blessed with those keen appetites that attend upon light purses and mountain air. The baron told his best and longest stories, and never had he told them so well, or with such great effect. If there was any thing marvellous, his auditors were lost in astonishment; and if any thing facetious, they were sure to laugh exactly in the right place. The baron, it is true, like most great men, was too dignified to utter any joke but a dull one; it was always enforced, however, by a bumper of excellent Hochheimer; and even a dull joke, at one's own table, served up with jolly old wine, is irresistible. Many good things were said by poorer and keener wits, that would not bear repeating, except on similar occasions; many sly speeches whispered in ladies' ears, that almost convulsed them with suppressed laughter; and a song or two roared out by a poor, but merry and broad-faced cousin of the baron, that absolutely made the maiden aunts hold up their fans.

Amid all this revelry, the stranger guest maintained a most singular and unseasonable gravity. His countenance assumed a deeper cast of dejection as the evening advanced; and, strange as it may appear, even the baron's jokes seemed only to render him the more melancholy. At times he was lost in thought, and at times there was a perturbed and restless wandering of the eye that bespoke a mind but ill at ease. His conversations with the bride became more and more earnest and mysterious. Lowering clouds began to steal over the fair serenity of her brow, and tremors to run through her tender frame.

All this could not escape the notice of the company. Their gayety was chilled by the unaccountable gloom of the bridegroom; their spirits were infected; whispers and glances were interchanged, accompanied by shrugs and dubious shakes of the head. The song and the laugh grew less and less frequent; there were dreary pauses in the conversation, which were at length succeeded by wild tales and supernatural legends. One dismal story produced another still more dismal, and the baron nearly frightened some of the ladies into hysterics with the history of the goblin horseman that carried away the fair Leonora; a dreadful story, which has since been put into excellent verse, and is read and believed by all the world.

The bridegroom listened to this tale with profound attention. He kept his eyes steadily fixed on the baron, and, as the story drew to a close, began gradually to rise from his seat, growing taller and taller, until, in the baron's entranced eye, he seemed almost to tower into a giant. The moment the tale was finished, he heaved a deep sigh, and took a solemn farewell of the company. They were all amazement. The baron was perfectly thunder-struck.

"What! going to leave the castle at midnight? why, every thing was prepared for his reception; a chamber was ready for him if he wished to retire."

The stranger shook his head mournfully and mysteriously; "I must lay my head in a different chamber to-night!"

There was something in this reply, and the tone in which it was uttered, that made the baron's heart misgive him; but he rallied his forces, and repeated his hospitable entreaties.

The stranger shook his head silently, but positively, at every offer; and, waving his farewell to the company, stalked slowly out of the hall. The maiden aunts were absolutely petrified—the bride hung her head, and a tear stole to her eye.

The baron followed the stranger to the great court of the castle, where the black charger stood pawing the earth, and snorting with impatience. When they had reached the portal, whose deep archway was dimly lighted by a cresset, the stranger paused, and addressed the baron in a hollow tone of voice, which the vaulted roof rendered still more sepulchral.

"Now that we are alone," said he, "I will impart to you the reason of my going. I have a solemn, an indispensable engagement—"

"Why," said the baron, "cannot you send some one in your place?"

"It admits of no substitute—I must attend it in person—I must away to Wurtzburg cathedral—"

"Ay," said the baron, plucking up spirit, "but not until to-morrow—to-morrow you shall take your bride there."

"No! no!" replied the stranger, with tenfold solemnity, "my engagement is with no bride—the worms! the worms expect me! I am a dead man—I have been slain by robbers—my body lies at Wurtzburg—at midnight I am to be buried—the grave is waiting for me—I must keep my appointment!"

He sprang on his black charger, dashed over the drawbridge, and the clattering of his horse's hoofs was lost in the whistling of the nightblast.

The baron returned to the hall in the utmost consternation, and related what had passed. Two ladies fainted outright, others sickened at the idea of having banqueted with a spectre. It was the opinion of some, that this might be the wild huntsman, famous in German legend. Some talked of mountain sprites, of wood-demons, and of other supernatural beings, with which the good people of Germany have been so grievously harassed since time immemorial. One of the poor relations ventured to suggest that it might be some sportive evasion of the young cavalier, and that the very gloominess of the caprice seemed to accord with so melancholy a personage. This, however, drew on him the indignation of the whole company, and especially of the baron, who looked upon him as little better than an infidel; so that he was fain to abjure his heresy as speedily as possible, and come into the faith of the true believers.

But whatever may have been the doubts entertained, they were completely put to an end by the arrival, next day, of regular missives confirming the intelligence of the young count's murder, and his interment in Wurtzburg cathedral.

The dismay at the castle may well be imagined. The baron shut himself up in his chamber. The guests, who had come to rejoice with him, could not think of abandoning him in his distress. They wandered about the courts, or collected in groups in the hall, shaking their heads and shrugging their shoulders, at the troubles of so good a man; and sat longer than ever at table, and ate and drank more stoutly than ever, by way of keeping up their spirits. But the situation of the widowed bride was the most pitiable. To have lost a husband before she had even embraced him—and such a husband! If the very spectre could be so gracious and noble, what must have been the living man? She filled the house with lamentations.

On the night of the second day of her widowhood, she had retired to her chamber, accompanied by one of her aunts, who insisted on sleeping with her. The aunt, who was one of the best tellers of ghost stories in all Germany, had just been recounting one of her longest, and had fallen asleep in the very midst of it. The chamber was remote, and overlooked a small garden. The niece lay pensively gazing at the beams of the rising moon, as they trembled on the leaves of an aspen-tree before the lattice. The castle clock had just tolled midnight, when a soft strain of music stole up from the garden. She rose hastily from her bed, and stepped lightly to the window. A tall figure stood among the shadows of the trees. As it raised its head, a beam of moonlight fell upon the countenance. Heaven and earth! She beheld the Spectre Bridegroom! A loud shriek at that moment burst upon her ear, and her aunt, who had been awakened by the music, and had followed her silently to the window, fell into her arms. When she looked again, the spectre had disappeared.

Of the two females, the aunt now required the most soothing, for she was

perfectly beside herself with terror. As to the young lady, there was something, even in the spectre of her lover, that seemed endearing. There was still
the semblance of manly beauty; and though the shadow of a man is but little
calculated to satisfy the affections of a love-sick girl, yet, where the substance
is not to be had, even that is consoling. The aunt declared that she would
never sleep in that chamber again; the niece, for once, was refractory, and
declared as strongly that she would sleep in no other in the castle: the consequence was, that she had to sleep in it alone: but she drew a promise from her
aunt not to relate the story of the spectre, lest she should be denied the only
melancholy pleasure left her on earth—that of inhabiting the chamber over
which the guardian shade of her lover kept its nightly vigils.

How long the good old lady would have observed this promise is uncertain,
for she dearly loved to talk of the marvellous, and there is a triumph in being
the first to tell a frightful story; it is, however, still quoted in the neighborhood, as a memorable instance of female secrecy, that she kept it to herself for
a whole week; when she was suddenly absolved from all further restraint by
intelligence brought to the breakfast table one morning that the young lady
was not to be found. Her room was empty—the bed had not been slept in—
the window was open, and the bird had flown!

The astonishment and concern with which the intelligence was received can
only be imagined by those who have witnessed the agitation which the mis-
haps of a great man cause among his friends. Even the poor relations paused
for a moment from the indefatigable labors of the trencher; when the aunt,
who had at first been struck speechless, wrung her hands, and shrieked out,
"The goblin! the goblin! she's carried away by the goblin."

In a few words she related the fearful scene of the garden, and concluded
that the spectre must have carried off his bride. Two of the domestics corrobo-
rated the opinion, for they had heard the clattering of a horse's hoofs down
the mountain about midnight, and had no doubt that it was the spectre on his
black charger, bearing her away to the tomb. All present were struck with the
direful probability; for events of the kind are extremely common in Germany,
as many well authenticated histories bear witness.

What a lamentable situation was that of the poor baron! What a heart-
rending dilemma for a fond father, and a member of the great family of
Katzenellenbogen! His only daughter had either been rapt away to the grave,
or he was to have some wood-demon for a son-in-law, and, perchance, a troop
of goblin grandchildren. As usual, he was completely bewildered, and all the
castle in an uproar. The men were ordered to take horse and scour every road
and path and glen of the Odenwald. The baron himself had just drawn on his
jack-boots, girded on his sword, and was about to mount his steed to sally
forth on the doubtful quest, when he was brought to a pause by a new
apparition. A lady was seen approaching the castle, mounted on a palfrey,
attended by a cavalier on horseback. She galloped up to the gate, sprang from
her horse, and falling at the baron's feet, embraced his knees. It was his lost
daughter, and her companion—the Spectre Bridegroom! The baron was astounded. He looked at his daughter, then at the spectre, and almost doubted

the evidence of his senses. The latter, too, was wonderfully improved in his appearance since his visit to the world of spirits. His dress was splendid, and set off a noble figure of manly symmetry. He was no longer pale and melancholy. His fine countenance was flushed with the glow of youth, and joy rioted in his large dark eye.

The mystery was soon cleared up. The cavalier (for, in truth, as you must have known all the while, he was no goblin) announced himself as Sir Herman Von Starkenfaust. He related his adventure with the young count. He told how he had hastened to the castle to deliver the unwelcome tidings, but that the eloquence of the baron had interrupted him in every attempt to tell his tale. How the sight of the bride had completely captivated him, and that to pass a few hours near her, he had tacitly suffered the mistake to continue. How he had been sorely perplexed in what way to make a decent retreat, until the baron's goblin stories had suggested his eccentric exit. How, fearing the feudal hostility of the family, he had repeated his visits by stealth—had haunted the garden beneath the young lady's window—had wooed—had won—had borne away in triumph—and, in a word, had wedded, the fair.

Under any other circumstances the baron would have been inflexible, for he was tenacious of paternal authority, and devoutly obstinate in all family feuds; but he loved his daughter; he had lamented her as lost; he rejoiced to find her still alive; and, though her husband was of a hostile house, yet, thank Heaven, he was not a goblin. There was something, it must be acknowledged, that did not exactly accord with his notions of strict veracity, in the joke the knight had passed upon him of his being a dead man; but several old friends present, who had served in the wars, assured him that every stratagem was excusable in love, and that the cavalier was entitled to especial privilege, having lately served as a trooper.

Matters, therefore, were happily arranged. The baron pardoned the young couple on the spot. The revels at the castle were resumed. The poor relations overwhelmed this new member of the family with loving-kindness; he was so gallant, so generous—and so rich. The aunts, it is true, were somewhat scandalized that their system of strict seclusion, and passive obedience should be so badly exemplified, but attributed all to their negligence in not having the windows grated. One of them was particularly mortified at having her marvellous story marred, and that the only spectre she had ever seen should turn out a counterfeit; but the niece seemed perfectly happy at having found him substantial flesh and blood—and so the story ends.

FOR STUDY, DISCUSSION, AND WRITING

1. Discuss specific romantic elements of the story.
2. What is the author's general tone in telling the story? Does the story offer any evidence that Irving is spoofing romanticism?

3. Locate and discuss such plot elements as the precipitating incident, rising action, climax, and denouement. Is this a traditionally plotted story, or could it more correctly be considered experimental?
4. In terms of the story's happenings, why is the title ironic?
5. Discuss the character of Baron Von Landshort. Is he a static or dynamic character?
6. To what extent does Irving rely on dramatization in presenting his characters?
7. Do you see any substantial evidence that Irving was trying to make a thematic point by writing this story?
8. Compare and contrast the supernaturalism of "The Spectre Bridegroom" with that of "The Monkey's Paw."
9. Discuss the presentation of all the women in the story in terms of modern-day ideas of sexism.

NATHANIEL HAWTHORNE

The Birthmark

In the latter part of the last century, there lived a man of science—an eminent proficient in every branch of natural philosophy—who, not long before our story opens, had made experience of a spiritual affinity, more attractive than any chemical one. He had left his laboratory to the care of an assistant, cleared his fine countenance from the furnace-smoke, washed the stain of acids from his fingers, and persuaded a beautiful woman to become his wife. In those days, when the comparatively recent discovery of electricity, and other kindred mysteries of nature, seemed to open paths into the region of miracle, it was not unusual for the love of science to rival the love of woman, in its depth and absorbing energy. The higher intellect, the imagination, the spirit, and even the heart, might all find their congenial aliment in pursuits which, as some of their ardent votaries believed, would ascend from one step of powerful intelligence to another, until the philosopher should lay his hand on the secret of creative force, and perhaps make new worlds for himself. We know not whether Aylmer possessed this degree of faith in man's ultimate control over nature. He had devoted himself, however, too unreservedly to scientific studies, ever to be weaned from them by any second passion. His love for his young wife might prove the stronger of the two; but it could only be by intertwining itself with his love of science, and uniting the strength of the latter to its own.

Such an union accordingly took place, and was attended with truly remarkable consequences, and a deeply impressive moral. One day, very soon after their marriage, Aylmer sat gazing at his wife, with a trouble in his countenance that grew stronger, until he spoke.

"Georgiana," said he, "has it never occurred to you that the mark upon your cheek might be removed?"

"No, indeed," said she, smiling; but perceiving the seriousness of his manner, she blushed deeply. "To tell you the truth, it has been so often called a charm, that I was simple enough to imagine it might be so."

"Ah, upon another face, perhaps it might," replied her husband. "But never on yours! No, dearest Georgiana, you came so nearly perfect from the hand of Nature, that this slightest possible defect—which we hesitate whether to term a defect or a beauty—shocks me, as being the visible mark of earthly imperfection."

"Shocks you, my husband!" cried Georgiana, deeply hurt; at first reddening with momentary anger, but then bursting into tears. "Then why did you take me from my mother's side? You cannot love what shocks you!"

To explain this conversation, it must be mentioned, that, in the centre of Georgiana's left cheek, there was a singular mark, deeply interwoven, as it were, with the texture and substance of her face. In the usual state of her complexion—a healthy, though delicate bloom—the mark wore a tint of deeper crimson, which imperfectly defined its shape amid the surrounding rosiness. When she blushed, it gradually became more indistinct, and finally vanished amid the triumphant rush of blood, that bathed the whole cheek with its brilliant glow. But, if any shifting emotion caused her to turn pale, there was the mark again, a crimson stain upon the snow, in what Aylmer sometimes deemed an almost fearful distinctness. Its shape bore not a little similarity to the human hand, though of the smallest pigmy size. Georgiana's lovers were wont to say, that some fairy, at her birth-hour, had laid her tiny hand upon the infant's cheek, and left this impress there, in token of the magic endowments that were to give her such sway over all hearts. Many a desperate swain would have risked life for the privilege of pressing his lips to the mysterious hand. It must not be concealed, however, that the impression wrought by this fairy sign-manual varied exceedingly, according to the difference of temperament in the beholders. Some fastidious persons—but they were exclusively of her own sex—affirmed that the Bloody Hand, as they chose to call it, quite destroyed the effect of Georgiana's beauty, and rendered her countenance even hideous. But it would be as reasonable to say, that one of those small blue stains, which sometimes occur in the purest statuary marble, would convert the Eve of Powers to a monster. Masculine observers, if the birthmark did not heighten their admiration, contented themselves with wishing it away, that the world might possess one living specimen of ideal loveliness, without the semblance of a flaw. After his marriage—for he thought little or nothing of the matter before—Aylmer discovered that this was the case with himself.

Had she been less beautiful—if Envy's self could have found aught else to sneer at—he might have felt his affection heightened by the prettiness of this mimic hand, now vaguely portrayed, now lost, now stealing forth again, and glimmering to and fro with every pulse of emotion that throbbed within her heart. But, seeing her otherwise so perfect, he found this one defect grow more and more intolerable, with every moment of their united lives. It was the fatal flaw of humanity, which Nature, in one shape or another, stamps ineffaceably on all her productions, either to imply that they are temporary and finite, or that their perfection must be wrought by toil and pain. The Crimson Hand expressed the ineludible gripe, in which mortality clutches the highest and purest of earthly mould, degrading them into kindred with the lowest, and even with the very brutes, like whom their visible frames return to dust. In this manner, selecting it as the symbol of his wife's liability to sin, sorrow, decay, and death, Aylmer's sombre imagination was not long in rendering the birthmark a frightful object, causing him more trouble and horror than ever Georgiana's beauty, whether of soul or sense, had given him delight.

At all the seasons which should have been their happiest, he invariably, and without intending it—nay, in spite of a purpose to the contrary—reverted to this one disastrous topic. Trifling as it at first appeared, it so connected itself with innumerable trains of thought, and modes of feeling, that it became the central point of all. With the morning twilight, Aylmer opened his eyes upon his wife's face, and recognized the symbol of imperfection; and when they sat together at the evening hearth, his eyes wandered stealthily to her cheek, and beheld, flickering with the blaze of the wood fire, the spectral Hand that wrote mortality where he would fain have worshipped. Georgiana soon learned to shudder at his gaze. It needed but a glance, with the peculiar expression that his face often wore, to change the roses of her cheek into a death-like paleness, amid which the Crimson Hand was brought strongly out, like a bas-relief of ruby on the whitest marble.

Late, one night, when the lights were growing dim, so as hardly to betray the stain on the poor wife's cheek, she herself, for the first time, voluntarily took up the subject.

"Do you remember, my dear Aylmer," said she, with a feeble attempt at a smile—"have you any recollection of a dream, last night, about this odious Hand?"

"None! none whatever!" replied Aylmer, starting; but then he added in a dry, cold tone, affected for the sake of concealing the real depth of his emotion: "I might well dream of it; for, before I fell asleep, it had taken a pretty firm hold of my fancy."

"And you did dream of it," continued Georgiana, hastily; for she dreaded lest a gush of tears should interrupt what she had to say—"A terrible dream! I wonder that you can forget it. Is it possible to forget this one expression? 'It is in her heart now—we must have it out!' Reflect, my husband; for by all means I would have you recall that dream."

The mind is in a sad state, when Sleep, the all-involving, cannot confine her spectres within the dim region of her sway, but suffers them to break forth, affrighting this actual life with secrets that perchance belong to a deeper one. Aylmer now remembered his dream. He had fancied himself, with his servant Aminadab, attempting an operation for the removal of the birthmark. But the deeper went the knife, the deeper sank the Hand, until at length its tiny grasp appeared to have caught hold of Georgiana's heart; whence, however, her husband was inexorably resolved to cut or wrench it away.

When the dream had shaped itself perfectly in his memory, Aylmer sat in his wife's presence with a guilty feeling. Truth often finds its way to the mind close-muffled in robes of sleep, and then speaks with uncompromising direct-ness of matters in regard to which we practise an unconscious self-deception, during our waking moments. Until now, he had not been aware of the tyran-nizing influence acquired by one idea over his mind, and of the lengths which he might find in his heart to go, for the sake of giving himself peace.

"Aylmer," resumed Georgiana, solemnly, "I know not what may be the cost to both of us, to rid me of this fatal birthmark. Perhaps its removal may cause cureless deformity. Or, it may be, the stain goes as deep as life itself. Again, do we know that there is a possibility, on any terms, of unclasping the firm gripe of this little Hand, which was laid upon me before I came into the world?"

"Dearest Georgiana, I have spent much thought upon the subject," hastily interrupted Aylmer—"I am convinced of the perfect practicability of its re-moval."

"If there be the remotest possibility of it," continued Georgiana, "let the attempt be made, at whatever risk. Danger is nothing to me; for life—while this hateful mark makes me the object of your horror and disgust—life is a burthen which I would fling down with joy. Either remove this dreadful Hand, or take my wretched life! You have deep science! All the world bears witness of it. You have achieved great wonders! Cannot you remove this little, little mark, which I cover with the tips of two small fingers! Is this beyond your power, for the sake of your own peace, and to save your poor wife from madness?"

"Noblest—dearest—tenderest wife!" cried Aylmer, rapturously. "Doubt not my power. I have already given this matter the deepest thought—thought which might almost have enlightened me to create a being less perfect than yourself. Georgiana, you have led me deeper than ever into the heart of sci-ence. I feel myself fully competent to render this dear cheek as faultless as its fellow; and then, most beloved, what will be my triumph, when I shall have corrected what Nature left imperfect, in her fairest work! Even Pygmalion, when his sculptured woman assumed life, felt not greater ecstasy than mine will be."

"It is resolved, then," said Georgiana, faintly smiling—"And, Aylmer, spare me not, though you should find the birthmark take refuge in my heart at last."

Her husband tenderly kissed her cheek—her right cheek—not that which bore the impress of the Crimson Hand.

The next day, Aylmer apprised his wife of a plan that he had formed, whereby he might have opportunity for the intense thought and constant watchfulness which the proposed operation would require; while Georgiana, likewise, would enjoy the perfect repose essential to its success. They were to seclude themselves in the extensive apartments occupied by Aylmer as a laboratory, and where, during his toilsome youth, he had made discoveries in the elemental powers of Nature, that had roused the admiration of all the learned societies in Europe. Seated calmly in this laboratory, the pale philosopher had investigated the secrets of the highest cloud-region, and of the profoundest mines; he had satisfied himself of the causes that kindled and kept alive the fires of the volcano; and had explained the mystery of fountains, and how it is that they gush forth, some so bright and pure, and others with such rich medicinal virtues, from the dark bosom of the earth. Here, too, at an earlier period, he had studied the wonders of the human frame, and attempted to fathom the very process by which Nature assimilates all her precious influences from earth and air, and from the spiritual world, to create and foster Man, her masterpiece. The latter pursuit, however, Aylmer had long laid aside, in unwilling recognition of the truth, against which all seekers sooner or later stumble, that our great creative Mother, while she amuses us with apparently working in the broadest sunshine, is yet severely careful to keep her own secrets, and, in spite of her pretended openness, shows us nothing but results. She permits us indeed to mar, but seldom to mend, and, like a jealous patentee, on no account to make. Now, however, Aylmer resumed these half-forgotten investigations; not, of course, with such hopes or wishes as first suggested them; but because they involved much physiological truth, and lay in the path of his proposed scheme for the treatment of Georgiana.

As he led her over the threshold of the laboratory, Georgiana was cold and tremulous. Aylmer looked cheerfully into her face, with intent to reassure her, but was so startled with the intense glow of the birthmark upon the whiteness of her cheek, that he could not restrain a strong convulsive shudder. His wife fainted.

"Aminadab! Aminadab!" shouted Aylmer, stamping violently on the floor.

Forthwith, there issued from an inner apartment a man of low stature, but bulky frame, with shaggy hair hanging about his visage, which was grimed with the vapors of the furnace. This personage had been Aylmer's under-worker during his whole scientific career, and was admirably fitted for that office by his great mechanical readiness, and the skill with which, while incapable of comprehending a single principle, he executed all the practical details of his master's experiments. With his vast strength, his shaggy hair, his smoky aspect, and the indescribable earthiness that encrusted him, he seemed to represent man's physical nature; while Aylmer's slender figure, and pale, intellectual face, were no less apt a type of the spiritual element.

"Throw open the door of the boudoir, Aminadab," said Aylmer, "and burn a pastille."

"Yes, master," answered Aminadab, looking intently at the lifeless form of

Georgiana; and then he muttered to himself: "If she were my wife, I'd never part with that birthmark."

When Georgiana recovered consciousness, she found herself breathing an atmosphere of penetrating fragrance, the gentle potency of which had recalled her from her death-like faintness. The scene around her looked like enchantment. Aylmer had converted those smoky, dingy, sombre rooms, where he had spent his brightest years in recondite pursuits, into a series of beautiful apartments, not unfit to be the secluded abode of a lovely woman. The walls were hung with gorgeous curtains, which imparted the combination of grandeur and grace, that no other species of adornment can achieve; and as they fell from the ceiling to the floor, their rich and ponderous folds, concealing all angles and straight lines, appeared to shut in the scene from infinite space. For aught Georgiana knew, it might be a pavilion among the clouds. And Aylmer, excluding the sunshine, which would have interfered with his chemical processes, had supplied its place with perfumed lamps, emitting flames of various hue, but all uniting in a soft, empurpled radiance. He now knelt by his wife's side, watching her earnestly, but without alarm; for he was confident in his science, and felt that he could draw a magic circle round her, within which no evil might intrude.

"Where am I? Ah, I remember!" said Georgiana, faintly; and she placed her hand over her cheek, to hide the terrible mark from her husband's eyes.

"Fear not, dearest!" exclaimed he. "Do not shrink from me! Believe me, Georgiana, I even rejoice in this single imperfection, since it will be such a rapture to remove it."

"Oh, spare me!" sadly replied his wife. "Pray do not look at it again. I never can forget that convulsive shudder."

In order to soothe Georgiana, and, as it were, to release her mind from the burthen of actual things, Aylmer now put in practice some of the light and playful secrets which science had taught him among its profounder lore. Airy figures, absolutely bodiless ideas, and forms of unsubstantial beauty, came and danced before her, imprinting their momentary footsteps on beams of light. Though she had some indistinct idea of the method of these optical phenomena, still the illusion was almost perfect enough to warrant the belief that her husband possessed sway over the spiritual world. Then again, when she felt a wish to look forth from her seclusion, immediately, as if her thoughts were answered, the procession of external existence flitted across a screen. The scenery and the figures of actual life were perfectly represented, but with that bewitching, yet indescribable difference, which always makes a picture, an image, or a shadow, so much more attractive than the original. When wearied of this, Aylmer bade her cast her eyes upon a vessel, containing a quantity of earth. She did so, with little interest at first, but was soon startled, to perceive the germ of a plant, shooting upward from the soil. Then came the slender stalk—the leaves gradually unfolded themselves—and amid them was a perfect and lovely flower.

"It is magical!" cried Georgiana, "I dare not touch it."

"Nay, pluck it," answered Aylmer, "pluck it, and inhale its brief perfume while you may. The flower will wither in a few moments, and leave nothing save its brown seed-vessels—but thence may be perpetuated a race as ephemeral as itself."

But Georgiana had no sooner touched the flower than the whole plant suffered a blight, its leaves turning coal-black, as if by the agency of fire.

"There was too powerful a stimulus," said Aylmer thoughtfully.

To make up for this abortive experiment, he proposed to take her portrait by a scientific process of his own invention. It was to be effected by rays of light striking upon a polished plate of metal. Georgiana assented—but, on looking at the result, was affrighted to find the features of the portrait blurred and indefinable; while the minute figure of a hand appeared where the cheek should have been. Aylmer snatched the metallic plate, and threw it into a jar of corrosive acid.

Soon, however, he forgot these mortifying failures. In the intervals of study and chemical experiment, he came to her, flushed and exhausted, but seemed invigorated by her presence, and spoke in glowing language of the resources of his art. He gave a history of the long dynasty of the Alchemists, who spent so many ages in quest of the universal solvent, by which the Golden Principle might be elicited from all things vile and base. Aylmer appeared to believe, that, by the plainest scientific logic, it was altogether within the limits of possibility to discover this long-sought medium; but, he added, a philosopher who should go deep enough to acquire the power, would attain too lofty a wisdom to stoop to the exercise of it. Not less singular were his opinions in regard to the Elixir Vitae. He more than intimated, that it was at his option to concoct a liquid that should prolong life for years—perhaps interminably— but that it would produce a discord in nature, which all the world, and chiefly the quaffer of the immortal nostrum, would find cause to curse.

"Aylmer, are you in earnest?" asked Georgiana, looking at him with amazement and fear; "it is terrible to possess such power, or even to dream of possessing it!"

"Oh, do not tremble, my love!" said her husband, "I would not wrong either you or myself, by working such inharmonious effects upon our lives. But I would have you consider how trifling, in comparison, is the skill requisite to remove this little Hand."

At the mention of the birthmark, Georgiana, as usual, shrank, as if a red-hot iron had touched her cheek.

Again Aylmer applied himself to his labors. She could hear his voice in the distant furnace-room, giving directions to Aminadab, whose harsh, uncouth, mis-shapen tones were audible in response, more like the grunt or growl of a brute than human speech. After hours of absence, Aylmer reappeared, and proposed that she should now examine his cabinet of chemical products, and natural treasures of the earth. Among the former he showed her a small vial, in which, he remarked, was contained a gentle yet most powerful fragrance, capable of impregnating all the breezes that blow across a kingdom. They were of inestimable value, the contents of that little vial; and, as he said so, he threw some of the perfume into the air, and filled the room with piercing and invigorating delight.

"And what is this?" asked Georgiana, pointing to a small crystal globe, containing a gold-colored liquid. "It is so beautiful to the eye, that I could imagine it the Elixir of Life."

"In one sense it is," replied Aylmer, "or rather the Elixir of Immortality. It is the most precious poison that ever was concocted in this world. By its aid, I could apportion the life-time of any mortal at whom you might point your finger. The strength of the dose would determine whether he were to linger out years, or drop dead in the midst of a breath. No king, on his guarded throne, could keep his life, if I, in my private station, should deem that the welfare of millions justified me in depriving him of it."

"Why do you keep such a terrific drug?" inquired Georgiana in horror.

"Do not mistrust me, dearest!" said her husband, smiling; "its virtuous potency is yet greater than its harmful one. But, see! here is a powerful cosmetic. With a few drops of this, in a vase of water, freckles may be washed away as easily as the hands are cleansed. A stronger infusion would take the blood out of the cheek, and leave the rosiest beauty a pale ghost."

"Is it with this lotion that you intend to bathe my cheek?" asked Georgiana, anxiously.

"Oh, no!" hastily replied her husband—"this is merely superficial. Your case demands a remedy that shall go deeper."

In his interviews with Georgiana, Aylmer generally made minute inquiries as to her sensations, and whether the confinement of the rooms, and the temperature of the atmosphere, agreed with her. These questions had such a particular drift, that Georgiana began to conjecture that she was already subjected to certain physical influences, either breathed in with the fragrant air, or taken with her food. She fancied, likewise—but it might be altogether fancy— that there was a stirring up of her system: a strange, indefinite sensation creeping through her veins, and tingling, half-painfully, half-pleasurably, at her heart. Still, whenever she dared to look into the mirror, there she beheld herself, pale as a white rose, and with the crimson birthmark stamped upon her cheek. Not even Aylmer now hated it so much as she.

To dispel the tedium of the hours which her husband found it necessary to devote to the processes of combination and analysis, Georgiana turned over the volumes of his scientific library. In many dark old tomes, she met with chapters full of romance and poetry. They were the works of the philosophers of the middle ages, such as Albertus Magnus, Cornelius Agrippa, Paracelsus, and the famous friar who created the prophetic Brazen Head. All these antique naturalists stood in advance of their centuries, yet were imbued with some of their credulity, and therefore were believed, and perhaps imagined themselves, to have acquired from the investigation of nature a power above nature, and from physics a sway over the spiritual world. Hardly less curious and imaginative were the early volumes of the Transactions of the Royal Society, in which the members, knowing little of the limits of natural possibility, were continually recording wonders, or proposing methods whereby wonders might be wrought.

But, to Georgiana, the most engrossing volume was a large folio from her husband's own hand, in which he had recorded every experiment of his scientific career, with its original aim, the methods adopted for its development, and its final success or failure, with the circumstances to which either event was attributable. The book, in truth, was both the history and emblem of his ardent, ambitious, imaginative, yet practical and laborious, life. He handled physical details, as if there were nothing beyond them; yet spiritualized them all, and redeemed himself from materialism, by his strong and eager aspiration towards the infinite. In his grasp, the veriest clod of earth assumed a soul. Georgiana, as she read, reverenced Aylmer, and loved him more profoundly than ever, but with a less entire dependence on his judgment than heretofore. Much as he had accomplished, she could not but observe that his most splendid successes were almost invariably failures, if compared with the ideal at which he aimed. His brightest diamonds were the merest pebbles, and felt to be so by himself, in comparison with the inestimable gems which lay hidden beyond his reach. The volume, rich with achievements that had won renown for its author, was yet as melancholy a record as ever mortal hand had penned. It was the sad confession, and continual exemplification, of the short-comings of the composite man—the spirit burthened with clay and working in matter; and of the despair that assails the higher nature, at finding itself so miserably thwarted by the earthly part. Perhaps every man of genius, in whatever sphere, might recognize the image of his own experience in Aylmer's journal.

So deeply did these reflections affect Georgiana, that she laid her face upon the open volume, and burst into tears. In this situation she was found by her husband.

"It is dangerous to read in a sorcerer's books," said he, with a smile, though his countenance was uneasy and displeased. "Georgiana, there are pages in that volume, which I can scarcely glance over and keep my senses. Take heed lest it prove as detrimental to you!"

"It has made me worship you more than ever," said she.

"Ah! wait for this one success," rejoined he, "then worship me if you will. I shall deem myself hardly unworthy of it. But, come! I have sought you for the luxury of your voice. Sing to me, dearest!"

So she poured out the liquid music of her voice to quench the thirst of his spirit. He then took his leave, with a boyish exuberance of gaiety, assuring her that her seclusion would endure but a little longer, and that the result was already certain. Scarcely had he departed, when Georgiana felt irresistibly impelled to follow him. She had forgotten to inform Aylmer of a symptom, which, for two or three hours past, had begun to excite her attention. It was a sensation in the fatal birthmark, not painful, but which induced a restlessness throughout her system. Hastening after her husband, she intruded, for the first time, into the laboratory.

The first thing that struck her eye was the furnace, that hot and feverish worker, with the intense glow of its fire, which, by the quantities of soot clustered above it, seemed to have been burning for ages. There was a distilling apparatus in full operation. Around the room were retorts, tubes, cylinders, crucibles, and other apparatus of chemical research. An electrical machine stood ready for immediate use. The atmosphere felt oppressively close, and was tainted with gaseous odors, which had been tormented forth by the processes of science. The severe and homely simplicity of the apartment, with its naked walls and brick pavement, looked strange, accustomed as Georgiana had become to the fantastic elegance of her boudoir. But what chiefly, indeed almost solely, drew her attention, was the aspect of Aylmer himself.

He was pale as death, anxious, and absorbed, and hung over the furnace as if it depended upon his utmost watchfulness whether the liquid, which it was distilling, should be the draught of immortal happiness or misery. How different from the sanguine and joyous mien that he had assumed for Georgiana's encouragement!

"Carefully now, Aminadab! Carefully, thou human machine! Carefully, thou man of clay!" muttered Aylmer, more to himself than his assistant. "Now, if there be a thought too much or too little, it is all over!"

"Hoh! hoh!" mumbled Aminadab—"look, master, look!"

Aylmer raised his eyes hastily, and at first reddened, then grew paler than ever, on beholding Georgiana. He rushed towards her, and seized her arm with a gripe that left the print of his fingers upon it.

"Why do you come hither? Have you no trust in your husband?" cried he impetuously. "Would you throw the blight of that fatal birthmark over my labors? It is not well done. Go, prying woman, go!"

"Nay, Aylmer," said Georgiana, with the firmness of which she possessed no stinted endowment, "it is not you that have a right to complain. You mistrust your wife! You have concealed the anxiety with which you watch the development of this experiment. Think not so unworthily of me, my husband! Tell me all the risk we run; and fear not that I shall shrink, for my share in it is far less than your own!"

"No, no, Georgiana!" said Aylmer impatiently, "it must not be."

"I submit," replied she calmly. "And, Aylmer, I shall quaff whatever draught you bring me; but it will be on the same principle that would induce me to take a dose of poison, if offered by your hand."

"My noble wife," said Aylmer, deeply moved, "I knew not the height and depth of your nature, until now. Nothing shall be concealed. Know, then, that this Crimson Hand, superficial as it seems, has clutched its grasp into your being, with a strength of which I had no previous conception. I have already administered agents powerful enough to do aught except to change your entire physical system. Only one thing remains to be tried. If that fail us, we are ruined!"

"Why did you hesitate to tell me this?" asked she.

"Because, Georgiana," said Aylmer, in a low voice, "there is danger!"

"Danger? There is but one danger—that this horrible stigma shall be left upon my cheek!" cried Georgiana. "Remove it! remove it!—whatever be the cost—or we shall both go mad!"

"Heaven knows, your words are too true," said Aylmer, sadly. "And now, dearest, return to your boudoir. In a little while, all will be tested."

He conducted her back, and took leave of her with a solemn tenderness, which spoke far more than his words how much was now at stake. After his departure, Georgiana became wrapt in musings. She considered the character of Aylmer, and did it completer justice than at any previous moment. Her heart exulted, while it trembled, at his honorable love, so pure and lofty that it would accept nothing less than perfection, nor miserably make itself contented with an earthlier nature than he had dreamed of. She felt how much more precious was such a sentiment, than that meaner kind which would have borne with the imperfection for her sake, and have been guilty of treason to holy love, by degrading its perfect idea to the level of the actual. And, with her whole spirit, she prayed, that, for a single moment, she might satisfy his highest and deepest conception. Longer than one moment, she well knew, it could not be; for his spirit was ever on the march—ever ascending—and each instant required something that was beyond the scope of the instant before.

The sound of her husband's footsteps aroused her. He bore a crystal goblet, containing a liquor colorless as water, but bright enough to be the draught of immortality. Aylmer was pale; but it seemed rather the consequence of a highly wrought state of mind, and tension of spirit, than of fear or doubt.

"The concoction of the draught has been perfect," said he, in answer to Georgiana's look. "Unless all my science have deceived me, it cannot fail."

"Save on your account, my dearest Aylmer," observed his wife, "I might wish to put off this birthmark of mortality by relinquishing mortality itself, in preference to any other mode. Life is but a sad possession to those who have attained precisely the degree of moral advancement at which I stand. Were I weaker and blinder, it might be happiness. Were I stronger, it might be endured hopefully. But, being what I find myself, methinks I am of all mortals the most fit to die."

"You are fit for heaven without tasting death!" replied her husband. "But why do we speak of dying? The draught cannot fail. Behold its effect upon this plant!"

On the window-seat there stood a geranium, diseased with yellow blotches, which had overspread all its leaves. Aylmer poured a small quantity of the liquid upon the soil in which it grew. In a little time, when the roots of the plant had taken up the moisture, the unsightly blotches began to be extinguished in a living verdure.

"There needed no proof," said Georgiana, quietly. "Give me the goblet. I joyfully stake all upon your word."

"Drink, then, thou lofty creature!" exclaimed Aylmer, with fervid admiration. "There is no taint of imperfection on thy spirit. Thy sensible frame, too, shall soon be all perfect!"

She quaffed the liquid, and returned the goblet to his hand.

"It is grateful," said she, with a placid smile. "Methinks it is like water from a heavenly fountain; for it contains I know not what of unobtrusive fragrance and deliciousness. It allays a feverish thirst, that had parched me for many days. Now, dearest, let me sleep. My earthly senses are closing over my spirit, like the leaves around the heart of a rose, at sunset."

She spoke the last words with a gentle reluctance, as if it required almost more energy than she could command to pronounce the faint and lingering syllables. Scarcely had they loitered through her lips, ere she was lost in slumber. Aylmer sat by her side, watching her aspect with the emotions proper to a man, the whole value of whose existence was involved in the process now to be tested. Mingled with this mood, however, was the philosophic investigation, characteristic of the man of science. Not the minutest symptom escaped him. A heightened flush of the cheek—a slight irregularity of breath—a quiver of the eyelid—a hardly perceptible tremor through the frame—such were the details which, as the moments passed, he wrote down in his folio volume. Intense thought had set its stamp upon every previous page of that volume; but the thoughts of years were all concentrated upon the last.

While thus employed, he failed not to gaze often at the fatal Hand, and not without a shudder. Yet once, by a strange and unaccountable impulse, he pressed it with his lips. His spirit recoiled, however, in the very act, and Georgiana, out of the midst of her deep sleep, moved uneasily and murmured, as if in remonstrance. Again, Aylmer resumed his watch. Nor was it without avail. The Crimson Hand, which at first had been strongly visible upon the marble paleness of Georgiana's cheek now grew more faintly outlined. She remained not less pale than ever; but the birthmark, with every breath that came and went, lost somewhat of its former distinctness. Its presence had been awful; its departure was more awful still. Watch the stain of the rainbow fading out of the sky; and you will know how that mysterious symbol passed away.

"By Heaven, it is well-nigh gone!" said Aylmer to himself, in almost irrepressible ecstasy. "I can scarcely trace it now. Success! Success! And now it is like the faintest rose-color. The slightest flush of blood across her cheek would overcome it. But she is so pale!"

He drew aside the window-curtain, and suffered the light of natural day to fall into the room, and rest upon her cheek. At the same time, he heard a gross, hoarse chuckle, which he had long known as his servant Aminadab's expression of delight.

"Ah, clod! Ah, earthly mass!" cried Aylmer, laughing in a sort of frenzy. "You have served me well! Master and spirit—Earth and Heaven—have both done their part in this! Laugh, thing of the senses! You have earned the right to laugh."

These exclamations broke Georgiana's sleep. She slowly unclosed her eyes, and gazed into the mirror, which her husband had arranged for that purpose. A faint smile flitted over her lips, when she recognized how barely perceptible was now that Crimson Hand, which had once blazed forth with such disastrous brilliancy as to scare away all their happiness. But then her eyes sought

Aylmer's face, with a trouble and anxiety that he could by no means account for.

"My poor Aylmer!" murmured she.

"Poor? Nay, richest! Happiest! Most favored!" exclaimed he. "My peerless bride, it is successful! You are perfect!"

"My poor Aylmer!" she repeated, with a more than human tenderness. "You have aimed loftily! you have done nobly! Do not repent, that, with so high and pure a feeling, you have rejected the best the earth could offer. Aylmer—dearest Aylmer, I am dying!"

Alas, it was too true! The fatal Hand had grappled with the mystery of life, and was the bond by which an angelic spirit kept itself in union with a mortal frame. As the last crimson tint of the birthmark—that sole token of human imperfection—faded from her cheek, the parting breath of the now perfect woman passed into the atmosphere, and her soul, lingering a moment near her husband, took its heavenward flight. Then a hoarse, chuckling laugh was heard again! Thus ever does the gross Fatality of Earth exult in its invariable triumph over the immortal essence, which, in this dim sphere of half-development, demands the completeness of a higher state. Yet, had Aylmer reached a profounder wisdom, he need not thus have flung away the happiness, which would have woven his mortal life of the self-same texture with the celestial. The momentary circumstance was too strong for him; he failed to look beyond the shadowy scope of Time, and living once for all in Eternity, to find the perfect Future in the present.

FOR STUDY, DISCUSSION, AND WRITING

1. Discuss the character of Aylmer. In what respects can he be considered an evil person?
2. Discuss the symbolic meaning of Georgiana's birthmark.
3. In what ways does Hawthorne foreshadow the failure of Aylmer's attempts to eradicate Georgiana's birthmark?
4. Discuss the use of religious symbols and terminology in the story and relate their use to the character of Aylmer.
5. Discuss the role of Aminadab in terms of foil, antagonist, and confidant.
6. Compare and contrast the role of Aminadab in this story with that of Ivan in "The Most Dangerous Game."
7. What evidence can you find that this story is strongly thematic?
8. In terms of the modern-day feminist's distaste for the passive or put-upon woman, analyze Georgiana's portion of guilt in allowing Aylmer to do the things to her that he does.
9. Discuss the antiscience (Frankenstein) motif of the story.

HERMAN MELVILLE

Bartleby, the Scrivener

I am a rather elderly man. The nature of my avocations, for the last thirty years, has brought me into more than ordinary contact with what would seem an interesting and somewhat singular set of men, of whom, as yet, nothing, that I know of, has ever been written—I mean, the law-copyists, or scriveners. I have known very many of them, professionally and privately, and, if I pleased, could relate divers histories, at which good-natured gentlemen might smile, and sentimental souls might weep. But I waive the biographies of all other scriveners, for a few passages in the life of Bartleby, who was a scrivener, the strangest I ever saw, or heard of. While, of other law-copyists, I might write the complete life, of Bartleby nothing of that sort can be done. I believe that no materials exist, for a full and satisfactory biography of this man. It is an irreparable loss to literature. Bartleby was one of those beings of whom nothing is ascertainable, except from the original sources, and, in his case, those are very small. What my own astonished eyes saw of Bartleby, *that* is all I know of him, except, indeed, one vague report, which will appear in the sequel.

Ere introducing the scrivener, as he first appeared to me, it is fit I make some mention of myself, my *employés*, my business, my chambers, and general surroundings; because some such description is indispensable to an adequate understanding of the chief character about to be presented. Imprimis: I am a man who, from his youth upwards, has been filled with a profound conviction that the easiest way of life is the best. Hence, though I belong to a profession proverbially energetic and nervous, even to turbulence, at times, yet nothing of that sort have I ever suffered to invade my peace. I am one of those unambitious lawyers who never address a jury, or in any way draw down public applause; but, in the cool tranquillity of a snug retreat, do a snug business among rich men's bonds, and mortgages, and title-deeds. All who know me, consider me an eminently *safe* man. The late John Jacob Astor, a personage little given to poetic enthusiasm, had no hesitation in pronouncing my first grand point to be prudence; my next, method. I do not speak it in vanity, but simply record the fact, that I was not unemployed in my profession by the late John Jacob Astor; a name which, I admit, I love to repeat; for it hath a rounded and orbicular sound to it, and rings like unto bullion. I will freely add, that I was not insensible to the late John Jacob Astor's good opinion.

Some time prior to the period at which this little history begins, my avocations had been largely increased. The good old office, now extinct in the State of New York, of a Master in Chancery, had been conferred upon me. It was not a very arduous office, but very pleasantly remunerative. I seldom lose my temper; much more seldom indulge in dangerous indignation at wrongs and outrages; but I must be permitted to be rash here and declare, that I consider the sudden and violent abrogation of the office of Master in Chancery, by the new Constitution, as a —— premature act; inasmuch as I had counted upon a life-lease of the profits, whereas I only received those of a few short years. But this is by the way.

My chambers were up stairs, at No. — Wall Street. At one end, they looked upon the white wall of the interior of a spacious sky-light shaft, penetrating the building from top to bottom.

This view might have been considered rather tame than otherwise, deficient in what landscape painters call "life." But, if so, the view from the other end of my chambers offered, at least, a contrast, if nothing more. In that direction, my windows commanded an unobstructed view of a lofty brick wall, black by age and everlasting shade; which wall required no spy-glass to bring out its lurking beauties, but, for the benefit of all nearsighted spectators, was pushed up to within ten feet of my window-panes. Owing to the great height of the surrounding buildings, and my chambers being on the second floor, the interval between this wall and mine not a little resembled a huge square cistern.

At the period just preceding the advent of Bartleby, I had two persons as copyists in my employment, and a promising lad as an office-boy. First, Turkey; second, Nippers; third, Ginger Nut. These may seem names, the like of which are not usually found in the Directory. In truth, they were nicknames, mutually conferred upon each other by my three clerks, and were deemed expressive of their respective persons or characters. Turkey was a short, pursy Englishman, of about my own age—that is, somewhere not far from sixty. In the morning, one might say, his face was of a fine florid hue, but after twelve o'clock, meridian—his dinner hour—it blazed like a grate full of Christmas coals; and continued blazing—but, as it were, with a gradual wane—till six o'clock, P.M., or thereabouts; after which, I saw no more of the proprietor of the face, which, gaining its meridian with the sun, seemed to set with it, to rise, culminate, and decline the following day, with the like regularity and undiminished glory. There are many singular coincidences I have known in the course of my life, not the least among which was the fact, that, exactly when Turkey displayed his fullest beams from his red and radiant countenance, just then, too, at that critical moment, began the daily period when I considered his business capacities as seriously disturbed for the remainder of the twenty-four hours. Not that he was absolutely idle, or averse to business then; far from it. The difficulty was, he was apt to be altogether too energetic. There was a strange, inflamed, flurried, flighty recklessness of activity about him. He would be incautious in dipping his pen into his inkstand. All his blots upon my documents were dropped there after twelve o'clock, meridian. Indeed, not only would he be reckless, and sadly given to making blots in the afternoon, but, some days, he went further, and was rather noisy. At such times, too, his face flamed with augmented blazonry, as if cannel coal had been heaped on anthracite. He made an unpleasant racket with his chair; spilled his sand-box; in mending his pens, impatiently split them all to pieces, and threw them on the floor in a sudden passion; stood up, and leaned over his table, boxing his papers about in a most indecorous manner, very sad to behold in an elderly man like him. Nevertheless, as he was in many ways a most valuable person to me, and all the time before twelve o'clock, meridian, was the quickest, steadiest creature, too, accomplishing a great deal of work in a style not easily to be matched—for these reasons, I was willing to overlook his eccentricities, though, indeed, occasionally, I remonstrated with him. I did this very gently, however, because, though the civilest, nay, the blandest and most reverential of men in the morning, yet, in the afternoon, he was disposed, upon provocation, to be slightly rash with his tongue—in fact, insolent. Now, valuing his morning services as I did, and resolved not to lose them—yet, at the same time, made uncomfortable by his inflamed ways after twelve o'clock—and being a man of peace, unwilling by my admonitions to call forth unseemly retorts from him, I took upon me, one Saturday noon (he was always worse on Saturdays) to hint to him, very kindly, that, perhaps, now that he was growing old, it might be well to abridge his labors; in short, he need not come to my chambers after twelve o'clock, but, dinner over, had best go home to his lodgings, and rest himself till tea-time. But no; he insisted upon his afternoon devotions. His countenance became intolerably fervid, as he oratorically assured me—gesticulating with a long ruler at the other end of the room—that if his services in the morning were useful, how indispensable, then, in the afternoon?

"With submission, sir," said Turkey, on this occasion, "I consider myself your right-hand man. In the morning I but marshal and deploy my columns; but in the afternoon I put myself at their head, and gallantly charge the foe, thus"—and he made a violent thrust with the ruler.

"But the blots, Turkey," intimated I.

"True; but, with submission, sir, behold these hairs! I am getting old. Surely, sir, a blot or two of a warm afternoon is not to be severely urged against gray hairs. Old age—even if it blot the page—is honorable. With submission, sir, we *both* are getting old."

This appeal to my fellow-feeling was hardly to be resisted. At all events, I saw that go he would not. So, I made up my mind to let him stay, resolving, nevertheless, to see to it that, during the afternoon, he had to do with my less important papers.

Nippers, the second on my list, was a whiskered, sallow, and, upon the whole, rather piratical-looking young man, of about five-and-twenty. I always deemed him the victim of two evil powers—ambition and indigestion. The ambition was evinced by a certain impatience of the duties of a mere copyist, an unwarrantable usurpation of strictly professional affairs, such as the original drawing up of legal documents. The indigestion seemed betokened in an occasional nervous testiness and grinning irritability, causing the teeth to audibly grind together over mistakes committed in copying; unnecessary maledictions, hissed, rather than spoken, in the heat of business; and especially by a continual discontent with the height of the table where he worked. Though of a very ingenious mechanical turn, Nippers could never get this table to suit him. He put chips under it, blocks of various sorts, bits of pasteboard, and at last went so far as to attempt an exquisite adjustment, by final pieces of folded blotting-paper. But no invention would answer. If, for the sake of easing his back, he brought the table-lid at a sharp angle well up towards his chin, and wrote there like a man using the steep roof of a Dutch house for his desk, then he declared that it stopped the circulation in his arms. If now he lowered the table to his waistbands, and stooped over it in writing, then there was a sore aching in his back. In short, the truth of the matter was, Nippers knew not what he wanted. Or, if he wanted anything, it was to be rid of a scrivener's table altogether. Among the manifestations of his diseased ambition was a fondness he had for receiving visits from certain ambiguous-looking fellows in seedy coats, whom he called his clients. Indeed, I was aware that not only was he, at times, considerable of a ward-politician, but he occasionally did a little business at the Justices' courts, and was not unknown on the steps of the Tombs. I have good reason to believe, however, that one individual who called upon him at my chambers, and who, with a grand air, he insisted was his client, was no other than a dun, and the alleged title-deed, a bill. But, with all his failings, and the annoyances he caused me, Nippers, like his compatriot Turkey, was a very useful man to me; wrote a neat, swift hand; and, when he chose, was not deficient in a gentlemanly sort of deportment. Added to this, he always dressed in a gentlemanly sort of way; and so, incidentally, reflected credit upon my chambers. Whereas, with respect to Turkey, I had much ado to keep him from being a reproach to me. His clothes were apt to look oily, and smell of eating-houses. He wore his pantaloons very loose and baggy in summer. His coats were execrable; his hat not to be handled. But while the hat was a thing of indifference to me, inasmuch as his natural civility and deference, as a dependent Englishman, always led him to doff it the moment he entered the room, yet his coat was another matter. Concerning his coats, I reasoned with him; but with no effect. The truth was, I suppose, that a man with so small an income could not afford to sport such a lustrous face and a lustrous coat at one and the same time. As Nippers once observed, Turkey's money went chiefly for red ink. One winter day, I presented Turkey with a highly respectable-looking coat of my own—a padded gray coat, of a most comfortable warmth, and which buttoned straight up from the knee to the neck. I thought Turkey would appreciate the favor, and abate his rashness and obstreperousness of afternoons. But no; I verily believe that buttoning himself up in so downy and blanket-like a coat had a pernicious effect upon him— upon the same principle that too much oats are bad for horses. In fact, precisely as a rash, restive horse is said to feel his oats, so Turkey felt his coat. It made him insolent. He was a man whom prosperity harmed.

Though, concerning the self-indulgent habits of Turkey, I had my own private surmises, yet, touching Nippers, I was well persuaded that, whatever might be his faults in other respects, he was, at least, a temperate young man.

But, indeed, nature herself seemed to have been his vintner, and, at his birth, charged him so thoroughly with an irritable, brandy-like disposition, that all subsequent potations were needless. When I consider how, amid the stillness of my chambers, Nippers would sometimes impatiently rise from his seat, and stooping over his table, spread his arms wide apart, seize the whole desk, and move it, and jerk it, with a grim, grinding motion on the floor, as if the table were a perverse voluntary agent, intent on thwarting and vexing him, I plainly perceive that, for Nippers, brandy-and-water were altogether superfluous.

It was fortunate for me that, owing to its peculiar cause—indigestion—the irritability and consequent nervousness of Nippers were mainly observable in the morning, while in the afternoon he was comparatively mild. So that, Turkey's paroxysms only coming on about twelve o'clock, I never had to do with their eccentricities at one time. Their fits relieved each other, like guards. When Nippers's was on, Turkey's was off; and vice versa. This was a good natural arrangement, under the circumstances.

Ginger Nut, the third on my list, was a lad, some twelve years old. His father was a carman, ambitious of seeing his son on the bench instead of a cart, before he died. So he sent him to my office, as student at law, errand-boy, cleaner and sweeper, at the rate of one dollar a week. He had a little desk to himself, but he did not use it much. Upon inspection, the drawer exhibited a great array of the shells of various sorts of nuts. Indeed, to this quick-witted youth, the whole noble science of the law was contained in a nut-shell. Not the least among the employments of Ginger Nut, as well as one which he discharged with the most alacrity, was his duty as cake and apple purveyor for Turkey and Nippers. Copying law-papers being proverbially a dry, husky sort of business, my two scriveners were fain to moisten their mouths very often with Spitzenbergs, to be had at the numerous stalls nigh the Custom House and Post Office. Also, they sent Ginger Nut very frequently for that peculiar cake—small, flat, round, and very spicy—after which he had been named by them. Of a cold morning, when business was but dull, Turkey would gobble up scores of these cakes, as if they were mere wafers—indeed, they sell them at the rate of six or eight for a penny—the scrape of his pen blending with the crunching of the crisp particles in his mouth. Of all the fiery afternoon blunders and flurried rashnesses of Turkey, was his once moistening a ginger-cake between his lips, and clapping it on to a mortgage, for a seal. I came within an ace of dismissing him then. But he mollified me by making an oriental bow, and saying—

"With submission, sir, it was generous of me to find you in stationery on my own account."

Now my original business—that of a conveyancer and title hunter, and drawer-up of recondite documents of all sorts—was considerably increased by receiving the Master's office. There was now great work for scriveners. Not only must I push the clerks already with me, but I must have additional help.

In answer to my advertisement, a motionless young man one morning stood upon my office threshold, the door being open, for it was summer. I can see that figure now—pallidly neat, pitiably respectable, incurably forlorn! It was Bartleby.

After a few words touching his qualifications, I engaged him, glad to have among my corps of copyists a man of so singularly sedate an aspect, which I thought might operate beneficially upon the flighty temper of Turkey, and the fiery one of Nippers.

I should have stated before that ground-glass folding-doors divided my premises into two parts, one of which was occupied by my scriveners, the other by myself. According to my humor, I threw open these doors, or closed them. I resolved to assign Bartleby a corner by the folding-doors, but on my side of them, so as to have this quiet man within easy call, in case any trifling thing was to be done. I placed his desk close up to a small side-window in that part of the room, a window which orginally had afforded a lateral view of certain grimy backyards and bricks, but which, owing to subsequent erections, commanded at present no view at all, though it gave some light. Within three feet of the panes was a wall, and the light came down from far above, between two lofty buildings, as from a very small opening in a dome. Still further to a satisfactory arrangement, I procured a high green folding screen, which might entirely isolate Bartleby from my sight, though not remove him from my voice. And thus, in a manner, privacy and society were conjoined.

At first Bartleby did an extraordinary quantity of writing. As if long famishing for something to copy, he seemed to gorge himself on my documents. There was no pause for digestion. He ran a day and night line, copying by sunlight and by candle-light. I should have been quite delighted with his application, had he been cheerfully industrious. But he wrote on silently, palely, mechanically.

It is, of course, an indispensable part of a scrivener's business to verify the accuracy of his copy, word by word. Where there are two or more scriveners in an office, they assist each other in this examination, one reading from the copy, the other holding the original. It is a very dull, wearisome, and lethargic affair. I can readily imagine that, to some sanguine temperaments, it would be altogether intolerable. For example, I cannot credit that the mettlesome poet, Byron, would have contentedly sat down with Bartleby to examine a law document of, say five hundred pages, closely written in a crimpy hand.

Now and then, in the haste of business, it had been my habit to assist in comparing some brief document myself, calling Turkey or Nippers for this purpose. One object I had, in placing Bartleby so handy to me behind the screen, was, to avail myself of his services on such trivial occasions. It was on the third day, I think, of his being with me, and before any necessity had arisen for having his own writing examined, that, being much hurried to complete a small affair I had in hand, I abruptly called to Bartleby. In my haste and natural expectancy of instant compliance, I sat with my head bent over the original on my desk, and my right hand sideways, and somewhat nervously extended with the copy, so that, immediately upon emerging from his retreat, Bartleby might snatch it and proceed to business without the least delay.

In this very attitude did I sit when I called to him, rapidly stating what it was I wanted him to do—namely, to examine a small paper with me. Imagine my surprise, nay, my consternation, when, without moving from his privacy, Bartleby, in a singularly mild, firm voice, replied, "I would prefer not to."

I sat awhile in perfect silence, rallying my stunned faculties. Immediately it occurred to me that my ears had deceived me, or Bartleby had entirely misunderstood my meaning. I repeated my request in the clearest tone I could assume; but in quite as clear a one came the previous reply, "I would prefer not to."

"Prefer not to," echoed I, rising in high excitement, and crossing the room with a stride. "What do you mean? Are you moon-struck? I want you to help me compare this sheet here—take it," and I thrust it towards him.

"I would prefer not to," said he.

I looked at him steadfastly. His face was leanly composed; his gray eye dimly calm. Not a wrinkle of agitation rippled him. Had there been the least uneasiness, anger, impatience or impertinence in his manner; in other words, had there been anything ordinarily human about him, doubtless I should have violently dismissed him from the premises. But as it was, I should have as soon thought of turning my pale plaster-of-paris bust of Cicero out of doors. I stood gazing at him awhile, as he went on with his own writing, and then reseated myself at my desk. This is very strange, thought I. What had one best do? But my business hurried me. I concluded to forget the matter for the present, reserving it for my future leisure. So, calling Nippers from the other room, the paper was speedily examined.

A few days after this, Bartleby concluded four lengthy documents, being quadruplicates of a week's testimony taken before me in my High Court of Chancery. It became necessary to examine them. It was an important suit, and great accuracy was imperative. Having all things arranged, I called Turkey, Nippers and Ginger Nut, from the next room, meaning to place the four copies in the hands of my four clerks, while I should read from the original. Accordingly, Turkey, Nippers, and Ginger Nut had taken their seats in a row, each with his document in his hand, when I called to Bartleby to join this interesting group.

"Bartleby! quick, I am waiting."

I heard a slow scrape of his chair legs on the uncarpeted floor, and soon he appeared standing at the entrance of his hermitage.

"What is wanted?" said he, mildly.

"The copies, the copies," said I, hurriedly. "We are going to examine them. There"—and I held towards him the fourth quadruplicate.

"I would prefer not to," he said, and gently disappeared behind the screen.

For a few moments I was turned into a pillar of salt, standing at the head of my seated column of clerks. Recovering myself, I advanced towards the screen, and demanded the reason for such extraordinary conduct.

"Why do you refuse?"

"I would prefer not to."

With any other man I should have flown outright into a dreadful passion, scorned all further words, and thrust him ignominiously from my presence. But there was something about Bartleby that not only strangely disarmed me, but, in a wonderful manner, touched and disconcerted me. I began to reason with him.

"These are your own copies we are about to examine. It is labor saving to you, because one examination will answer for your four papers. It is common usage. Every copyist is bound to help examine his copy. Is it not so? Will you not speak? Answer!"

"I prefer not to," he replied in a flute-like tone. It seemed to me that, while I had been addressing him, he carefully revolved every statement that I made; fully comprehended the meaning; could not gainsay the irresistible conclusion; but, at the same time, some paramount consideration prevailed with him to reply as he did.

"You are decided, then, not to comply with my request—a request made according to common usage and common sense?"

He briefly gave me to understand, that on that point my judgment was sound. Yes: his decision was irreversible.

It is not seldom the case that, when a man is browbeaten in some unprecedented and violently unreasonable way, he begins to stagger in his own plainest faith. He begins, as it were, vaguely to surmise that, wonderful as it may be, all the justice and all the reason is on the other side. Accordingly, if any disinterested persons are present, he turns to them for some reinforcement for his own faltering mind.

"Turkey," said I, "what do you think of this? Am I not right?"

"With submission, sir," said Turkey, in his blandest tone, "I think that you are."

"Nippers," said I, "what do *you* think of it?"

"I think I should kick him out of the office."

(The reader of nice perceptions will here perceive that, it being morning, Turkey's answer is couched in polite and tranquil terms, but Nippers's replies in ill-tempered ones. Or, to repeat a previous sentence, Nippers's ugly mood was on duty, and Turkey's off.)

"Ginger Nut," said I, willing to enlist the smallest suffrage in my behalf, "what do *you* think of it?"

"I think, sir, he's a little *luny*," replied Ginger Nut, with a grin.

"You hear what they say," said I, turning towards the screen, "come forth and do your duty."

But he vouchsafed no reply. I pondered a moment in sore perplexity. But once more business hurried me. I determined again to postpone the consideration of this dilemma to my future leisure. With a little trouble we made out to examine the papers without Bartleby, though at every page or two Turkey deferentially dropped his opinion, that this proceeding was quite out of the common; while Nippers, twitching in his chair with a dyspeptic nervousness, ground out, between his set teeth, occasional hissing maledictions against the stubborn oaf behind the scene. And for his (Nippers's) part, this was the first and the last time he would do another man's business without pay.

Meanwhile Bartleby sat in his hermitage, oblivious to everything but his own peculiar business there.

Some days passed, the scrivener being employed upon another lengthy work. His late remarkable conduct led me to regard his ways narrowly. I observed that he never went to dinner; indeed, that he never went anywhere. As yet I had never, of my personal knowledge, known him to be outside of my office. He was a perpetual sentry in the corner. At about eleven o'clock though, in the morning, I noticed that Ginger Nut would advance toward the opening in Bartleby's screen, as if silently beckoned thither by a gesture invisible to me where I sat. The boy would then leave the office, jingling a few pence, and reappear with a handful of ginger-nuts, which he delivered in the hermitage, receiving two of the cakes for his trouble.

He lives, then, on ginger-nuts, thought I; never eats a dinner, properly speaking; he must be a vegetarian, then, but no; he never eats even vegetables, he eats nothing but ginger-nuts. My mind then ran on in reveries concerning the probable effects upon the human constitution of living entirely on ginger-nuts. Ginger-nuts are so called, because they contain ginger as one of their peculiar constituents, and the final flavoring one. Now, what was ginger? A hot, spicy thing. Was Bartleby hot and spicy? Not at all. Ginger, then, had no effect upon Bartleby. Probably he preferred it should have none.

Nothing so aggravates an earnest person as a passive resistance. If the individual so resisted be of a not inhumane temper, and the resisting one perfectly harmless in his passivity, then, in the better moods of the former, he will endeavor charitably to construe to his imagination what proves impossible to be solved by his judgment. Even so, for the most part, I regarded Bartleby and his ways. Poor fellow! thought I, he means no mischief; it is plain he intends no insolence; his aspect sufficiently evinces that his eccentricities are involuntary. He is useful to me. I can get along with him. If I turn him away, the chances are he will fall in with some less indulgent employer, and then he will be rudely treated, and perhaps driven forth miserably to starve. Yes. Here I can cheaply purchase a delicious self-approval. To befriend Bartleby; to humor him in his strange wilfulness, will cost me little or nothing, while I lay up in my soul what will eventually prove a sweet morsel for my conscience. But this mood was not invariable with me. The passiveness of Bartleby sometimes irritated me. I felt strangely goaded on to encounter him in new opposition— to elicit some angry spark from him answerable to my own. But, indeed, I might as well have essayed to strike fire with my knuckles against a bit of Windsor soap. But one afternoon the evil impulse in me mastered me, and the following little scene ensued:

"Bartleby," said I, "when those papers are all copied, I will compare them with you."

"I would prefer not to."

"How? Surely you do not mean to persist in that mulish vagary?"

No answer.

I threw open the folding-doors near by, and, turning upon Turkey and Nippers, exclaimed:

"Bartleby a second time says, he won't examine his papers. What do you think of it, Turkey?"

It was afternoon, be it remembered. Turkey sat glowing like a brass boiler; his bald head steaming; his hands reeling among his blotted papers.

"Think of it?" roared Turkey. "I think I'll just step behind his screen, and black his eyes for him!"

So saying, Turkey rose to his feet and threw his arms into a pugilistic position. He was hurrying away to make good his promise, when I detained him, alarmed at the effect of incautiously rousing Turkey's combativeness after dinner.

"Sit down, Turkey," said I, "and hear what Nippers has to say. What do you think of it, Nippers? Would I not be justified in immediately dismissing Bartleby?"

"Excuse me, that is for you to decide, sir. I think his conduct quite unusual, and, indeed, unjust, as regards Turkey and myself. But it may only be a passing whim."

"Ah," exclaimed I, "you have strangely changed your mind, then—you speak very gently of him now."

"All beer,"cried Turkey; "gentleness is effects of beer—Nippers and I dined together to-day. You see how gentle *I* am, sir. Shall I go and black his eyes?"

"You refer to Bartleby, I suppose. No, not to-day, Turkey," I replied; "pray, put up your fists."

I closed the doors, and again advanced towards Bartleby. I felt additional incentives tempting me to my fate. I burned to be rebelled against again. I remembered that Bartleby never left the office.

"Bartleby," said I, "Ginger Nut is away; just step around to the Post-Office, won't you?" (it was but a three minutes' walk) "and see if there is anything for me."

"I would prefer not to."

"You *will* not?"

"I *prefer* not."

I staggered to my desk, and sat there in a deep study. My blind inveteracy returned. Was there any other thing in which I could procure myself to be ignominiously repulsed by this lean, penniless wight?—my hired clerk? What added thing is there, perfectly reasonable, that he will be sure to refuse to do?

"Bartleby!'

No answer.

"Bartleby," in a louder tone.

No answer.

"Bartleby," I roared.

Like a very ghost, agreeably to the laws of magical invocation, at the third summons, he appeared at the entrance of his hermitage.

"Go to the next room, and tell Nippers to come to me."

"I prefer not to," he respectfully and slowly said, and mildly disappeared.

"Very good, Bartleby," said I, in a quiet sort of serenely-severe self-possessed tone, intimating the unalterable purpose of some terrible retribution very close at hand. At the moment I half intended something of the kind. But upon the whole, as it was drawing towards my dinner-hour, I thought it best to put on my hat and walk home for the day, suffering much from perplexity and distress of mind.

Shall I acknowledge it? The conclusion of this whole business was, that it soon became a fixed fact of my chambers, that a pale young scrivener, by the name of Bartleby, had a desk there; that he copied for me at the usual rate of four cents a folio (one hundred words); but he was permanently exempt from examining the work done by him, that duty being transferred to Turkey and Nippers, out of compliment, doubtless, to their superior acuteness; moreover, said Bartleby was never, on any account, to be dispatched on the most trivial errand of any sort; and that even if entreated to take upon him such a matter, it was generally understood that he would '"prefer not to"—in other words, that he would refuse point-blank.

As days passed on, I became considerably reconciled to Bartleby. His steadiness, his freedom from all dissipation, his incessant industry (except when he chose to throw himself into a standing revery behind his screen), his great stillness, his unalterableness of demeanor under all circumstances, made him a valuable acquisition. One prime thing was this—*he was always there*—first in the morning, continually through the day, and the last at night. I had a singular confidence in his honesty. I felt my most precious papers perfectly safe in his hands. Sometimes, to be sure, I could not, for the very soul of me, avoid falling into sudden spasmodic passions with him. For it was exceeding difficult to bear in mind all the time those strange peculiarities, privileges, and unheard-of exemptions, forming the tacit stipulations on Bartleby's part under which he remained in my office. Now and then, in the eagerness of dispatching pressing business, I would inadvertently summon Bartleby, in a short, rapid tone, to put his finger, say, on the incipient tie of a bit of red tape with which I was about compressing some papers. Of course, from behind the screen the usual answer, "I prefer not to," was sure to come; and then, how could a human creature, with the common infirmities of our nature, refrain from bitterly exclaiming upon such perverseness—such unreasonableness? However, every added repulse of this sort which I received only tended to lessen the probability of my repeating the inadvertence.

Here it must be said, that, according to the custom of most legal gentlemen occupying chambers in densely-populated law buildings, there were several keys to my door. One was kept by a woman residing in the attic, which person weekly scrubbed and daily swept and dusted my apartments. Another was kept by Turkey for convenience sake. The third I sometimes carried in my own pocket. The fourth I knew not who had.

Now, one Sunday morning I happened to go to Trinity Church, to hear a celebrated preacher, and finding myself rather early on the ground I thought I would walk round to my chambers for a while. Luckily I had my key with me; but upon applying it to the lock, I found it resisted by something inserted from the inside. Quite surprised, I called out; when to my consternation a key was turned from within; and thrusting his lean visage at me, and holding the door ajar, the apparition of Bartleby appeared, in his shirt-sleeves, and otherwise in a strangely tattered deshabille, saying quietly that he was sorry, but he was deeply engaged just then, and—preferred not admitting me at present. In a brief word or two, he moreover added, that perhaps I had better walk round the block two or three times, and by that time he would probably have concluded his affairs.

Now, the utterly unsurmised appearance of Bartleby, tenanting my law-chambers of a Sunday morning, with his cadaverously gentlemanly *nonchalance*, yet withal firm and self-possessed, had such a strange effect upon me, that incontinently I slunk away from my own door, and did as desired. But not without sundry twinges of impotent rebellion against the mild effrontery of this unaccountable scrivener. Indeed, it was his wonderful mildness chiefly, which not only disarmed me, but unmanned me, as it were. For I consider that one, for the time, is a sort of unmanned when he tranquilly permits his hired clerk to dictate to him, and order him away from his own premises. Furthermore, I was full of uneasiness as to what Bartleby could possibly be doing in my office in his shirt-sleeves, and in an otherwise dismantled condition of a Sunday morning. Was anything amiss going on? Nay, that was out of the question. It was not to be thought of for a moment that Bartleby was an immoral person. But what could he be doing there?—copying? Nay again, whatever might be his eccentricities, Bartleby was an eminently decorous person. He would be the last man to sit down to his desk in any state approaching to nudity. Besides, it was Sunday; and there was something about Bartleby that forbade the supposition that he would by any secular occupation violate the proprieties of the day.

Nevertheless, my mind was not pacified; and full of restless curiosity, at last I returned to the door. Without hindrance I inserted my key, opened it, and entered. Bartleby was not to be seen. I looked round anxiously, peeped behind his screen; but it was very plain that he was gone. Upon more closely examining the place, I surmised that for an indefinite period Bartleby must have ate, dressed, and slept in my office, and that too without plate, mirror, or bed. The cushioned seat of a rickety old sofa in one corner bore the faint impress of a lean, reclining form. Rolled away under his desk, I found a blanket; under the empty grate, a blacking box and brush; on a chair, a tin basin, with soap and a ragged towel; in a newspaper a few crumbs of ginger-nuts and a morsel of cheese. Yes, thought I, it is evident enough that Bartleby has been making his home here, keeping bachelor's hall all by himself. Immediately then the thought came sweeping across me, what miserable friendlessness and loneliness are here revealed! His poverty is great; but his solitude, how horrible! Think of it. Of a Sunday, Wall Street is deserted as Petra; and every night of every day it is an emptiness. This building, too, which of week-days hums with industry and life, at nightfall echoes with sheer vacancy, and all through Sunday is forlorn. And here Bartleby makes his home; sole spectator of a solitude which he has seen all populous—a sort of innocent and transformed Marius brooding among the ruins of Carthage!

For the first time in my life a feeling of overpowering stinging melancholy seized me. Before, I had never experienced aught but a not unpleasing sadness. The bond of a common humanity now drew me irresistibly to gloom. A fraternal melancholy! For both I and Bartleby were sons of Adam. I remembered the bright silks and sparkling faces I had seen that day, in gala trim, swan-like sailing down the Mississippi of Broadway; and I contrasted them with the pallid copyist, and thought to myself, Ah, happiness courts the light, so we deem the world is gay; but misery hides aloof, so we deem that misery there is none. These sad fancyings—chimeras, doubtless, of a sick and silly brain—led on to other and more special thoughts, concerning the eccentricities of Bartleby. Presentiments of strange discoveries hovered round me. The scrivener's pale form appeared to me laid out, among uncaring strangers, in its shivering winding-sheet.

Suddenly I was attracted by Bartleby's closed desk, the key in open sight left in the lock.

I mean no mischief, seek the gratification of no heartless curiosity, thought I; besides, the desk is mine, and its contents, too, so I will make bold to look within. Everything was methodically arranged, the papers smoothly placed. The pigeon-holes were deep, and removing the files of documents, I groped into their recesses. Presently I felt something there, and dragged it out. It was an old bandanna handkerchief, heavy and knotted. I opened it, and saw it was a saving's bank.

I now recalled all the quiet mysteries which I had noted in the man. I remembered that he never spoke but to answer; that, though at intervals he had considerable time to himself, yet I had never seen him reading—no, not even a newspaper; that for long periods he would stand looking out, at his pale window behind the screen, upon the dead brick wall; I was quite sure he never visited any refectory or eating-house; while his pale face clearly indicated that he never drank beer like Turkey, or tea and coffee even, like other men; that he never went anywhere in particular that I could learn; never went out for a walk, unless, indeed, that was the case at present; that he had declined telling who he was, or whence he came, or whether he had any relatives in the world; that though so thin and pale, he never complained of ill-health. And more than all, I remembered a certain unconscious air of pallid—how shall I call it?—of pallid haughtiness, say, or rather an austere reserve about him, which had positively awed me into my tame compliance with his eccentricities, when I had feared to ask him to do the slightest incidental thing for me, even though I might know, from his long-continued motionlessness, that behind his screen he must be standing in one of those dead-wall reveries of his.

Revolving all these things, and coupling them with the recently discovered fact, that he made my office his constant abiding place and home, and not forgetful of his morbid moodiness; revolving all these things, a prudential feeling began to steal over me. My first emotions had been those of pure melancholy and sincerest pity; but just in proportion as the forlornness of Bartleby grew and grew to my imagination, did that same melancholy merge into fear, that pity into repulsion. So true it is, and so terrible, too, that up to a certain point the thought or sight of misery enlists our best affections; but, in certain special cases, beyond that point it does not. They err who would assert that invariably this is owing to the inherent selfishness of the human heart. It rather proceeds from a certain hopelessness of remedying excessive and organic ill. To a sensitive being, pity is not seldom pain. And when at last it is perceived that such pity cannot lead to effectual succor, common sense bids the soul be rid of it. What I saw that morning persuaded me that the scrivener was the victim of innate and incurable disorder. I might give alms to his body; but his body did not pain him; it was his soul that suffered, and his soul I could not reach.

I did not accomplish the purpose of going to Trinity Church that morning. Somehow, the things I had seen disqualified me for the time from church-going. I walked homeward, thinking what I would do with Bartleby. Finally, I resolved upon this—I would put certain calm questions to him the next morning, touching his history, etc., and if he declined to answer them openly and unreservedly (and I supposed he would prefer not), then to give him a twenty dollar bill over and above whatever I might owe him, and tell him his services were no longer required; but that if in any other way I could assist him, I would be happy to do so, especially if he desired to return to his native place, wherever that might be, I would willingly help to defray the expenses. Moreover, if, after reaching home, he found himself at any time in want of aid, a letter from him would be sure of a reply.

The next morning came.

"Bartleby," said I, gently calling to him behind his screen.

No reply.

"Bartleby," said I, in a still gentler tone, "come here; I am not going to ask you to do anything you would prefer not to do—I simply wish to speak to you."

Upon this he noiselessly slid into view.

"Will you tell me, Bartleby, where you were born?"

"I would prefer not to."

"Will you tell me *anything* about yourself?"

"I would prefer not to."

"But what reasonable objection can you have to speak to me? I feel friendly towards you."

He did not look at me while I spoke, but kept his glance fixed upon my bust of Cicero, which, as I then sat, was directly behind me, some six inches above my head.

"What is your answer, Bartleby?" said I, after waiting a considerable time for a reply, during which his countenance remained immovable, only there was the faintest conceivable tremor of the white attenuated mouth.

"At present I prefer to give no answer," he said, and retired into his hermitage.

It was rather weak in me I confess, but his manner, on this occasion, nettled me. Not only did there seem to lurk in it a certain calm disdain, but his perverseness seemed ungrateful, considering the undeniable good usage and indulgence he had received from me.

Again I sat ruminating what I should do. Mortified as I was at his behavior, and resolved as I had been to dismiss him when I entered my office, nevertheless I strangely felt something superstitious knocking at my heart, and forbidding me to carry out my purpose, and denouncing me for a villain if I dared to breathe one bitter word against this forlornest of mankind. At last, familiarly drawing my chair behind his screen, I sat down and said: "Bartleby, never mind, then, about revealing your history; but let me entreat you, as a friend, to comply as far as may be with the usages of this office. Say now, you will help to examine papers to-morrow or next day: in short, say now, that in a day or two you will begin to be a little reasonable:—say so, Bartleby."

"At present I would prefer not to be a little reasonable," was his mildly cadaverous reply.

Just then the folding-doors opened, and Nippers approached. He seemed suffering from an unusually bad night's rest, induced by severer indigestion than common. He overheard those final words of Bartleby.

"*Prefer not,* eh?" gritted Nippers—"I'd *prefer* him, if I were you, sir," addressing me—"I'd *prefer* him; I'd give him preferences, the stubborn mule! What is it, sir, pray, that he *prefers* not to do now?"

Bartleby moved not a limb.

"Mr. Nippers," said I, "I'd prefer that you would withdraw for the present."

Somehow, of late, I had got into the way of involuntarily using this word "prefer" upon all sorts of not exactly suitable occasions. And I trembled to think that my contact with the scrivener had already and seriously affected me in a mental way. And what further and deeper aberration might it not yet produce? This apprehension had not been without efficacy in determining me to summary measures.

As Nippers, looking very sour and sulky, was departing, Turkey blandly and deferentially approached.

"With submission, sir," said he, "yesterday I was thinking about Bartleby here, and I think that if he would but prefer to take a quart of good ale every day, it would do much towards mending him, and enabling him to assist in examining his papers."

"So you have got the word, too," said I, slightly excited.

"With submission, what word, sir?" asked Turkey, respectfully crowding himself into the contracted space behind the screen, and by so doing, making me jostle the scrivener. "What word, sir?"

"I would prefer to be left alone here," said Bartleby, as if offended at being mobbed in his privacy.

"*That's* the word, Turkey," said I—*"that's it."*

"Oh, *prefer?* oh yes—queer word. I never use it myself. But sir, as I was saying, if he would but prefer—"

"Turkey," interrupted I, "you will please withdraw."

"Oh certainly, sir, if you prefer that I should."

As he opened the folding-door to retire, Nippers at his desk caught a glimpse of me, and asked whether I would prefer to have a certain paper copied on blue paper or white. He did not in the least roguishly accent the word "prefer." It was plain that it involuntarily rolled from his tongue. I thought to myself, surely I must get rid of a demented man, who already has in some degree turned the tongues, if not the heads of myself and clerks. But I thought it prudent not to break the dismission at once.

The next day I noticed that Bartleby did nothing but stand at his window in his dead-wall revery. Upon asking him why he did not write, he said that he had decided upon doing no more writing.

"Why, how now? what next?" exclaimed I, "do no more writing?"

"No more."

"And what is the reason?"

"Do you not see the reason for yourself?" he indifferently replied.

I looked steadfastly at him, and perceived that his eyes looked dull and glazed. Instantly it occurred to me, that his unexampled diligence in copying by his dim window for the first few weeks of his stay with me might have temporarily impaired his vision.

I was touched. I said something in condolence with him. I hinted that of course he did wisely in abstaining from writing for a while; and urged him to embrace that opportunity of taking wholesome exercise in the open air. This, however, he did not do. A few days after this, my other clerks being absent, and being in a great hurry to dispatch certain letters by the mail, I thought that, having nothing else earthly to do, Bartleby would surely be less inflexible than usual, and carry these letters to the post-office. But he blankly declined. So, much to my inconvenience, I went myself.

Still added days went by. Whether Bartleby's eyes improved or not, I could not say. To all appearance, I thought they did. But when I asked him if they did, he vouchsafed no answer. At all events, he would do no copying. At last, in reply to my urgings, he informed me that he had permanently given up copying.

"What!" exclaimed I; "suppose your eyes should get entirely well—better than ever before—would you not copy then?"

"I have given up copying," he answered, and slid aside.

He remained as ever, a fixture in my chamber. Nay—if that were possible—he became still more of a fixture than before. What was to be done? He would do nothing in the office; why should he stay there? In plain fact, he had now become a millstone to me, not only useless as a necklace, but afflictive to bear. Yet I was sorry for him. I speak less than truth when I say that, on his own account, he occasioned me uneasiness. If he would but have named a single relative or friend, I would instantly have written, and urged their taking the poor fellow away to some convenient retreat. But he seemed alone, absolutely alone in the universe. A bit of wreck in the mid-Atlantic. At length, necessities connected with my business tyrannized over all other considerations. Decently as I could, I told Bartleby that in six days' time he must unconditionally leave the office. I warned him to take measures, in the interval, for procuring some other abode. I offered to assist him in this endeavor, if he himself would but take the first step towards a removal. "And when you finally quit me, Bartleby," added I, "I shall see that you go not away entirely unprovided. Six days from this hour, remember."

At the expiration of that period, I peeped behind the screen, and lo! Bartleby was there.

I buttoned up my coat, balanced myself; advanced slowly towards him, touched his shoulder, and said, "The time has come; you must quit this place; I am sorry for you; here is money; but you must go."

"I would prefer not," he replied, with his back still towards me.

"You *must*."

He remained silent.

Now I had an unbounded confidence in this man's common honesty. He had frequently restored to me sixpences and shillings carelessly dropped upon the floor, for I am apt to be very reckless in such shirt-button affairs. The proceeding, then, which followed will not be deemed extraordinary.

"Bartleby," said I, "I owe you twelve dollars on account; here are thirty-two; the odd twenty are yours—Will you take it?" and I handed the bills towards him.

But he made no motion.

"I will leave them here, then," putting them under a weight on the table. Then taking my hat and cane and going to the door, I tranquilly turned and added—"After you have removed your things from these offices, Bartleby, you will of course lock the door—since every one is now gone for the day but you—and if you please, slip your key underneath the mat, so that I may have it in the morning. I shall not see you again; so good-bye to you. If, hereafter, in your new place of abode, I can be of any service to you, do not fail to advise me by letter. Good-bye, Bartleby, and fare you well."

But he answered not a word; like the last column of some ruined temple, he remained standing mute and solitary in the middle of the otherwise deserted room.

As I walked home in a pensive mood, my vanity got the better of my pity. I could not but highly plume myself on my masterly management in getting rid of Bartleby. Masterly I call it, and such it must appear to any dispassionate thinker. The beauty of my procedure seemed to consist in its perfect quietness. There was no vulgar bullying, no bravado of any sort, no choleric hectoring, and striding to and fro across the apartment, jerking out vehement commands for Bartleby to bundle himself off with his beggarly traps. Nothing of the kind. Without loudly bidding Bartleby depart—as an inferior genius might have done—I *assumed* the ground that depart he must; and upon that assumption built all I had to say. The more I thought over my procedure, the more I was charmed with it. Nevertheless, next morning, upon awakening, I had my doubts—I had somehow slept off the fumes of vanity. One of the coolest and wisest hours a man has, is just after he awakes in the morning. My procedure seemed as sagacious as ever—but only in theory. How it would prove in practice—there was the rub. It was truly a beautiful thought to have assumed Bartleby's departure; but, after all, that assumption was simply my own, and none of Bartleby's. The great point was, not whether I had assumed that he would quit me, but whether he would prefer so to do. He was more a man of preferences than assumptions.

After breakfast, I walked down town, arguing the probabilities *pro* and *con*. One moment I thought it would prove a miserable failure, and Bartleby would be found all alive at my office as usual; the next moment it seemed certain that I should find his chair empty. And so I kept veering about. At the corner of Broadway and Canal Street, I saw quite an excited group of people standing in earnest conversation.

"I'll take odds he doesn't," said a voice as I passed.

"Doesn't go?—done!" said I, "put up your money."

I was instinctively putting my hand in my pocket to produce my own, when I remembered that this was an election day. The words I had overheard bore no reference to Bartleby, but to the success or non-success of some candidate for the mayoralty. In my intent frame of mind, I had, as it were, imagined that all Broadway shared in my excitement, and were debating the same question with me. I passed on, very thankful that the uproar of the street screened my momentary absent-mindedness.

As I had intended, I was earlier than usual at my office door. I stood listening for a moment. All was still. He must be gone. I tried the knob. The door was locked. Yes, my procedure had worked to a charm; he indeed must be vanished. Yet a certain melancholy mixed with this: I was almost sorry for my brilliant success. I was fumbling under the door mat for the key, which Bartleby was to have left there for me, when accidentally my knee knocked against a panel, producing a summoning sound, and in response a voice came to me from within—"Not yet; I am occupied."

It was Bartleby.

I was thunderstruck. For an instant I stood like the man who, pipe in mouth, was killed one cloudless afternoon long ago in Virginia, by summer lightning; at his own warm open window he was killed, and remained leaning out there upon the dreamy afternoon, till some one touched him, when he fell.

"Not gone!" I murmured at last. But again obeying that wondrous ascendancy which the inscrutable scrivener had over me, and from which ascendancy, for all my chafing, I could not completely escape, I slowly went down stairs and out into the street, and while walking round the block, considered what I should next do in this unheard-of perplexity. Turn the man out by an actual thrusting I could not; to drive him away by calling him hard names would not do; calling in the police was an unpleasant idea; and yet, permit him to enjoy his cadaverous triumph over me—this, too, I could not think of. What was to be done? or, if nothing could be done, was there anything further that I could *assume* in the matter? Yes, as before I had prospectively assumed that Bartleby would depart, so now I might retrospectively assume that departed he was. In the legitimate carrying out of this assumption, I might enter my office in a great hurry, and pretending not to see Bartleby at all, walk straight against him as if he were air. Such a proceeding would in a singular degree have the appearance of a home-thrust. It was hardly possible that Bartleby could withstand such an application of the doctrine of assumptions. But upon second thoughts the success of the plan seemed rather dubious. I resolved to argue the matter over with him again.

"Bartleby," said I, entering the office, with a quietly severe expression, "I am seriously displeased. I am pained, Bartleby. I had thought better of you. I had imagined you of such a gentlemanly organization, that in any delicate dilemma a slight hint would suffice—in short, an assumption. But it appears I am deceived. Why," I added, unaffectedly starting, "you have not even touched that money yet," pointing to it, just where I had left it the evening previous.

He answered nothing.

"Will you, or will you not, quit me?" I now demanded in a sudden passion, advancing close to him.

"I would prefer *not* to quit you," he replied, gently emphasizing the *not*.

"What earthly right have you to stay here? Do you pay any rent? Do you pay my taxes? Or is this property yours?"

He answered nothing.

"Are you ready to go on and write now? Are your eyes recovered? Could you copy a small paper for me this morning? or help examine a few lines? or step round to the post-office? In a word, will you do anything at all, to give a coloring to your refusal to depart the premises?"

He silently retired into his hermitage.

I was now in such a state of nervous resentment that I thought it but prudent to check myself at present from further demonstrations. Bartleby and

I were alone. I remembered the tragedy of the unfortunate Adams and the still more unfortunate Colt in the solitary office of the latter; and how poor Colt, being dreadfully incensed by Adams, and imprudently permitting himself to get wildly excited, was at unawares hurried into his fatal act—an act which certainly no man could possibly deplore more than the actor himself. Often it had occurred to me in my ponderings upon the subject that had that altercation taken place in the public street, or at a private residence, it would not have terminated as it did. It was the circumstance of being alone in a solitary office, up stairs, of a building entirely unhallowed by humanizing domestic associations—an uncarpeted office, doubtless, of a dusty, haggard sort of appearance—this it must have been, which greatly helped to enhance the irritable desperation of the hapless Colt.

But when this old Adam of resentment rose in me and tempted me concerning Bartleby, I grappled him and threw him. How? Why, simply by recalling the divine injunction: "A new commandment give I unto you, that ye love one another." Yes, this it was that saved me. Aside from higher considerations, charity often operates as a vastly wise and prudent principle—a great safeguard to its possessor. Men have committed murder for jealousy's sake, and anger's sake, and hatred's sake, and selfishness' sake, and spiritual pride's sake; but no man, that ever I heard of, ever committed a diabolical murder for sweet charity's sake. Mere self-interest, then, if no better motive can be enlisted, should, especially with high-tempered men, prompt all beings to charity and philanthropy. At any rate, upon the occasion in question, I strove to drown my exasperated feelings towards the scrivener by benevolently construing his conduct. Poor fellow, poor fellow! thought I, he don't mean anything; and besides, he has seen hard times, and ought to be indulged.

I endeavored, also, immediately to occupy myself, and at the same time to comfort my despondency. I tried to fancy, that in the course of the morning, at such time as might prove agreeable to him, Bartleby, of his own free accord, would emerge form his hermitage and take up some decided line of march in the direction of the door. But no. Half-past twelve o'clock came; Turkey began to glow in the face, overturn his inkstand, and become generally obstreperous; Nippers abated down into quietude and courtesy; Ginger Nut munched his noon apple; and Bartleby remained standing at his window in one of his profoundest dead-wall reveries. Will it be credited? Ought I to acknowledge it? That afternoon I left the office without saying one further word to him.

Some days now passed, during which, at leisure intervals I looked a little into "Edwards on the Will," and "Priestley on Necessity." Under the circumstances, those books induced a salutary feeling. Gradually I slid into the persuasion that these troubles of mine, touching the scrivener, had been all predestinated from eternity, and Bartleby was billeted upon me for some mysterious purpose of an all-wise Providence, which it was not for a mere mortal like me to fathom. Yes, Bartleby, stay there behind your screen, thought I; I shall persecute you no more; you are harmless and noiseless as any of these old chairs; in short, I never feel so private as when I know you are here. At last I see it, I feel it; I penetrate to the predestinated purpose of my life. I am content. Others may have loftier parts to enact; but my mission in this world, Bartleby, is to furnish you with office-room for such period as you may see fit to remain.

I believe that this wise and blessed frame of mind would have continued with me, had it not been for the unsolicited and uncharitable remarks obtruded upon me by my professional friends who visited the rooms. But thus it often is, that the constant friction of illiberal minds wears out at last the best resolves of the more generous. Though to be sure, when I reflected upon it, it was not strange that people entering my office should be struck by the peculiar aspect of the unaccountable Bartleby, and so be tempted to throw out some sinister observations concerning him. Sometimes an attorney, having business with me, and calling at my office, and finding no one but the scrivener there, would undertake to obtain some sort of precise information from him touching my whereabouts; but without heeding his idle talk, Bartleby would remain standing immovable in the middle of the room. So after contemplating him in that position for a time, the attorney would depart, no wiser than he came.

Also, when a reference was going on, and the room full of lawyers and witnesses, and business driving fast, some deeply-occupied legal gentleman present, seeing Bartleby wholly unemployed, would request him to run round to his (the legal gentleman's) office and fetch some papers for him. Thereupon, Bartleby would tranquilly decline, and yet remain idle as before. Then the lawyer would give a great stare, and turn to me. And what could I say? At last I was made aware that all through the circle of my professional acquaintance, a whisper of wonder was running round, having reference to the strange creature I kept at my office. This worried me very much. And as the idea came upon me of his possibly turning out a long-lived man, and keep occupying my chambers, and denying my authority; and perplexing my visitors; and scandalizing my professional reputation; and casting a general gloom over the premises; keeping soul and body together to the last upon his savings (for doubtless he spent but half a dime a day), and in the end perhaps outlive me, and claim possession of my office by right of his perpetual occupancy: as all these dark anticipations crowded upon me more and more, and my friends continually intruded their relentless remarks upon the apparition in my rooms; a great change was wrought in me. I resolved to gather all my faculties together, and forever rid me of this intolerable incubus.

Ere revolving any complicated project, however, adapted to this end, I first simply suggested to Bartleby the propriety of his permanent departure. In a calm and serious tone, I commended the idea to his careful and mature consideration. But, having taken three days to meditate upon it, he apprised me, that his original determination remained the same; in short, that he still preferred to abide with me.

What shall I do? I now said to myself, buttoning up my coat to the last button. What shall I do? what ought I to do? what does conscience say I *should* do with this man, or, rather, ghost. Rid myself of him, I must; go, he shall. But how? You will not thrust him, the poor, pale, passive mortal—you will not thrust such a helpless creature out of your door? you will not dishonor yourself by such cruelty? No, I will not, I cannot do that. Rather would I let him live and die here, and then mason up his remains in the wall. What, then, will you do? For all your coaxing, he will not budge. Bribes he leaves under your own paper-weight on your table; in short, it is quite plain that he prefers to cling to you.

Then something severe, something unusual must be done. What! Surely you will not have him collared by a constable, and commit his innocent pallor to the common jail? And upon what ground could you procure such a thing to be done?—a vagrant, is he? What! he a vagrant, a wanderer, who refuses to budge? It is because he will *not* be a vagrant, then, that you seek to count him *as* a vagrant. That is too absurd. No visible means of support: there I have him. Wrong again: for indubitably he *does* support himself, and that is the only unanswerable proof that any man can show of his possessing the means so to do. No more, then. Since he will not quit me, I must quit him. I will change my offices; I will move elsewhere, and give him fair notice, that if I find him on my new premises I will then proceed against him as a common trespasser.

Acting accordingly, next day I thus addressed him: "I find these chambers too far from the City Hall; the air is unwholesome. In a word, I propose to remove my offices next week, and shall no longer require your services. I tell you this now, in order that you may seek another place."

He made no reply, and nothing more was said.

On the appointed day I engaged carts and men, proceeded to my chambers, and, having but little furniture, everything was removed in a few hours. Throughout, the scrivener remained standing behind the screen, which I directed to be removed the last thing. It was withdrawn; and, being folded up like a huge folio, left him the motionless occupant of a naked room. I stood in the entry watching him a moment, while something from within me upbraided me.

I re-entered, with my hand in my pocket—and—and my heart in my mouth.

"Good-bye, Bartleby; I am going—good-bye, and God some way bless you; and take that," slipping something in his hand. But it dropped upon the floor, and then—strange to say—I tore myself from him whom I had so longed to be rid of.

Established in my new quarters, for a day or two I kept the door locked, and started at every footfall in the passages. When I returned to my rooms, after any little absence, I would pause at the threshold for an instant, and attentively listen, ere applying my key. But these fears were needless. Bartleby never came nigh me.

I thought all was going well, when a perturbed-looking stranger visited me, inquiring whether I was the person who had recently occupied rooms at No. —Wall Street.

Full of forebodings, I replied that I was.

"Then, sir," said the stranger, who proved a lawyer, "you are responsible for the man you left there. He refuses to do any copying; he refuses to do anything; he says he prefers not to; and he refuses to quit the premises."

"I am very sorry, sir," said I, with assumed tranquillity, but an inward tremor, "but, really, the man you allude to is nothing to me—he is no relation or apprentice of mine, that you should hold me responsible for him."

"In mercy's name, who is he?"

"I certainly cannot inform you. I know nothing about him. Formerly I employed him as a copyist; but he has done nothing for me now for some time past."

"I shall settle him, then—good morning, sir."

Several days passed, and I heard nothing more; and, though I often felt a charitable prompting to call at the place and see poor Bartleby, yet a certain squeamishness, of I know not what, withheld me.

All is over with him, by this time, thought I, at last, when, through another week, no further intelligence reached me. But, coming to my room the day after, I found several persons waiting at my door in a high state of nervous excitement.

"That's the man—here he comes," cried the foremost one, whom I recognized as the lawyer who had previously called upon me alone.

"You must take him away, sir, at once," cried a portly person among them, advancing upon me, and whom I knew to be the landlord of No. — Wall Street. "These gentlemen, my tenants, cannot stand it any longer; Mr. B——," pointing to the lawyer, "has turned him out of his room, and he now persists in haunting the building generally, sitting upon the banisters of the stairs by day, and sleeping in the entry by night. Everybody is concerned; clients are leaving the offices; some fears are entertained of a mob; something you must do, and that without delay."

Aghast at this torrent, I fell back before it, and would fain have locked myself in my new quarters. In vain I persisted that Bartleby was nothing to me—no more than to any one else. In vain—I was the last person known to have anything to do with him, and they held me to the terrible account. Fearful, then, of being exposed in the papers (as one person present obscurely threatened), I considered the matter, and, at length, said, that if the lawyer would give me a confidential interview with the scrivener, in his (the lawyer's) own room, I would, that afternoon, strive my best to rid them of the nuisance they complained of.

Going up stairs to my old haunt, there was Bartleby silently sitting upon the banister at the landing.

"What are you doing here, Bartleby?" said I.

"Sitting upon the banister," he mildly replied.

I motioned him into the lawyer's room, who then left us.

"Bartleby," said I, "are you aware that you are the cause of great tribulation to me, by persisting in occupying the entry after being dismissed from the office?"

No answer.

"Now one of two things must take place. Either you must do something, or something must be done to you. Now what sort of business would you like to engage in? Would you like to re-engage in copying for some one?"

"No; I would prefer not to make any change."

"Would you like a clerkship in a dry-goods store?"

"There is too much confinement about that. No, I would not like a clerkship; but I am not particular."

"Too much confinement," I cried, "why, you keep yourself confined all the time!"

"I would prefer not to take a clerkship," he rejoined, as if to settle that little item at once.

"How would a bar-tender's business suit you? There is no trying of the eyesight in that."

"I would not like it at all; though, as I said before, I am not particular."

His unwonted wordiness inspirited me. I returned to the charge.

"Well, then, would you like to travel through the country collecting bills for the merchants? That would improve your health."

"No, I would prefer to be doing something else."

"How, then, would going as a companion to Europe, to entertain some young gentleman with your conversation—how would that suit you?"

"Not at all. It does not strike me that there is anything definite about that. I like to be stationary. But I am not particular."

"Stationary you shall be, then," I cried, now losing all patience, and, for the first time in all my exasperating connection with him, fairly flying into a passion. "If you do not go away from these premises before night, I shall feel bound—indeed, I *am* bound—to—to—to quit the premises myself!" I rather absurdly concluded, knowing not with what possible threat to try to frighten his immobility into compliance. Despairing of all further efforts, I was precipitately leaving him, when a final thought occurred to me—one which had not been wholly unindulged before.

"Bartleby," said I, in the kindest tone I could assume under such exciting circumstances, "will you go home with me now—not to my office, but my dwelling—and remain there till we can conclude upon some convenient arrangement for you at our leisure? Come, let us start now, right away."

"No: at present I would prefer not to make any change at all."

I answered nothing; but, effectually dodging every one by the suddenness and rapidity of my flight, rushed from the building, ran up Wall Street towards Broadway, and, jumping into the first omnibus, was soon removed from pursuit. As soon as tranquillity returned, I distinctly perceived that I had now done all that I possibly could, both in respect to the demands of the landlord and his tenants, and with regard to my own desire and sense of duty, to benefit Bartleby, and shield him from rude persecution. I now strove to be entirely care-free and quiescent; and my conscience justified me in the attempt; though, indeed, it was not so successful as I could have wished. So fearful was I of being again hunted out by the incensed landlord and his exasperated tenants, that, surrendering my business to Nippers, for a few days, I drove about the upper part of the town and through the suburbs, in my rockaway; crossed over to Jersey City and Hoboken, and paid fugitive visits to Manhattanville and Astoria. In fact, I almost lived in my rockaway for the time.

When again I entered my office, lo, a note from the landlord lay upon the desk. I opened it with trembling hands. It informed me that the writer had sent to the police, and had Bartleby removed to the Tombs as a vagrant. Moreover, since I knew more about him than any one else, he wished me to appear at that place, and make a suitable statement of the facts. These tidings had a conflicting effect upon me. At first I was indignant; but at last, almost approved. The landlord's energetic, summary disposition, had led him to adopt a procedure which I do not think I would have decided upon myself; and yet, as a last resort, under such peculiar circumstances, it seemed the only plan.

As I afterward learned, the poor scrivener, when told that he must be conducted to the Tombs, offered not the slightest obstacle, but, in his pale, unmoving way, silently acquiesced.

Some of the compassionate and curious by-standers joined the party; and headed by one of the constables arm-in-arm with Bartleby, the silent procession filed its way through all the noise, and heat, and joy of the roaring thoroughfares at noon.

The same day I received the note, I went to the Tombs, or, to speak more properly, the Halls of Justice. Seeking the right officer, I stated the purpose of my call, and was informed that the individual I described was, indeed, within. I then assured the functionary that Bartleby was a perfectly honest man, and greatly to be compassionated, however unaccountably eccentric. I narrated all I knew, and closed by suggesting the idea of letting him remain in as indulgent confinement as possible, till something less harsh might be done—though, indeed, I hardly knew what. At all events, if nothing else could be decided upon, the alms-house must receive him. I then begged to have an interview.

Being under no disgraceful charge, and quite serene and harmless in all his ways, they had permitted him freely to wander about the prison, and, especially, in the inclosed grass-platted yards thereof. And so I found him there, standing all alone in the quietest of the yards, his face towards a high wall, while all around, from the narrow slits of the jail windows, I thought I saw peering out upon him the eyes of murderers and thieves.

"Bartleby!"

"I know you," he said, without looking round—"and I want nothing to say to you."

"It was not I that brought you here, Bartleby," said I, keenly pained at his implied suspicion. "And to you, this should not be so vile a place. Nothing reproachful attaches to you by being here. And see, it is not so sad a place as one might think. Look, there is the sky, and here is the grass."

"I know where I am," he replied, but would say nothing more, and so I left him.

As I entered the corridor again, a broad meat-like man, in an apron, accosted me, and, jerking his thumb over his shoulder, said—"Is that your friend?"

"Yes."

"Does he want to starve? If he does, let him live on the prison fare, that's all."

"Who are you?" asked I, not knowing what to make of such an unofficially speaking person in such a place.

"I am the grub-man. Such gentlemen as have friends here, hire me to provide them with something good to eat."

"Is this so?" said I, turning to the turnkey.

He said it was.

"Well, then," said I, slipping some silver into the grub-man's hands (for so they called him), "I want you to give particular attention to my friend there; let him have the best dinner you can get. And you must be as polite to him as possible."

"Introduce me, will you?" said the grub-man, looking at me with an expression which seemed to say he was all impatience for an opportunity to give a specimen of his breeding.

Thinking it would prove of benefit to the scrivener, I acquiesced; and, asking the grub-man his name, went up with him to Bartleby.

"Bartleby, this is a friend; you will find him very useful to you."

"Your sarvant, sir, your sarvant," said the grub-man, making a low salutation behind his apron. "Hope you find it pleasant here, sir; nice grounds—cool apartments—hope you'll stay with us some time—try to make it agreeable. What will you have for dinner to-day?"

"I prefer not to dine to-day," said Bartleby, turning away. "It would disagree with me; I am unused to dinners." So saying, he slowly moved to the other side of the inclosure, and took up a position fronting the dead-wall.

"How's this?" said the grub-man, addressing me with a stare of astonishment. "He's odd, ain't he?"

"I think he is a little deranged," said I, sadly.

"Deranged? deranged is it? Well, now, upon my word, I thought that friend of yourn was a gentleman forger; they are always pale and genteel-like, them forgers. I can't help pity 'em—can't help it, sir. Did you know Monroe Edwards?" he added, touchingly, and paused. Then, laying his hand piteously on my shoulder, sighed, "he died of consumption at Sing-Sing. So you weren't acquainted with Monroe?"

"No, I was never socially acquainted with any forgers. But I cannot stop longer. Look to my friend yonder. You will not lose by it. I will see you again."

Some few days after this, I again obtained admission to the Tombs, and went through the corridors in quest of Bartleby; but without finding him.

"I saw him coming from his cell not long ago," said a turnkey, "may be he's gone to loiter in the yards."

So I went in that direction.

"Are you looking for the silent man?" said another turnkey, passing me. "Yonder he lies—sleeping in the yard there. 'Tis not twenty minutes since I saw him lie down."

The yard was entirely quiet. It was not accessible to the common prisoners. The surrounding walls, of amazing thickness, kept off all sounds behind them.The Egyptian character of the masonry weighed upon me with its gloom. But a soft imprisoned turf grew under foot. The heart of the eternal pyramids, it seemed, wherein, by some strange magic, through the clefts, grass-seed, dropped by birds, had sprung.

Strangely huddled at the base of the wall, his knees drawn up, and lying on his side, his head touching the cold stones, I saw the wasted Bartleby. But nothing stirred. I paused; then went close up to him; stooped over, and saw that his dim eyes were open; otherwise he seemed profoundly sleeping. Something prompted me to touch him. I felt his hand, when a tingling shiver ran up my arm and down my spine to my feet.

The round face of the grub-man peered upon me now. "His dinner is ready. Won't he dine to-day, either? Or does he live without dining?"

"Lives without dining," said I, and closed the eyes.

"Eh!—He's asleep, ain't he?"

"With kings and counselors," murmured I.

*　　*　　*

There would seem little need for proceeding further in this history. Imagination will readily supply the meagre recital of poor Bartleby's interment. But, ere parting with the reader, let me say, that if this little narrative has sufficiently interested him to awaken curiosity as to who Bartleby was, and what manner of life he led prior to the present narrator's making his acquaintance, I can only reply, that in such curiosity I fully share, but am wholly unable to gratify it. Yet here I hardly know whether I should divulge one little item of rumor, which came to my ear a few months after the scrivener's decease. Upon what basis it rested, I could never ascertain; and hence, how true it is I cannot now tell. But, inasmuch as this vague report has not been without a certain suggestive interest to me, however sad, it may prove the same with some others; and so I will briefly mention it. The report was this: that Bartleby had been a subordinate clerk in the Dead Letter Office at Washington, from which he had been suddenly removed by a change in the administration. When I think over this rumor, hardly can I express the emotions which seize me. Dead letters! does it not sound like dead men? Conceive a man by nature and misfortune prone to a pallid hopelessness, can any business seem more fitted to heighten it than that of continually handling these dead letters, and assorting them for the flames? For by the cart-load they are annually burned. Sometimes from out the folded paper the pale clerk takes a ring—the finger it was meant for, perhaps, moulders in the grave; a bank-note sent in swiftest charity—he whom it would relieve, nor eats nor hungers any more; pardon for those who died despairing; hope for those who died unhoping; good tidings for those who died stifled by unrelieved calamities. On errands of life, these letters speed to death.

Ah, Bartleby! Ah, humanity!

FOR STUDY, DISCUSSION, AND WRITING

1. Discuss the changing character of the lawyer-narrator as it relates to his feelings for and thoughts about Bartleby.
2. Many readers of this story see Bartleby somewhat differently than the narrator apparently views him. Comment on the possible unreliability of the narrator.
3. What do you think is Bartleby's real problem? What brings him to a state of virtual inactivity? Why does he so casually discard his life?
4. For how many characters in the story are we given a proper name? Do you see any possible significance in the number?
5. What possible reasons can you think of for Bartleby's refusing to accept the lawyer's many offers of help?
6. Discuss the recurring symbol of the wall.
7. Using Ginger Nut, Nippers, Turkey, and Bartleby as examples, comment on the situation of the nineteenth-century urban worker as depicted in the story.
8. What is the possible symbolic significance of Nippers' constant attempts to adjust the height of his writing table?
9. In the future, who will most likely have a lasting effect on the lawyer-narrator's attitudes and behavior, Bartleby or the lawyer's business associates?
10. Discuss the plight of Bartleby as an allegory about the position of the innovative (literary) artist in society.

EDGAR ALLAN POE

The Fall of the House of Usher

Son cœur est un luth suspendu;
Sitôt qu'on le touche il résonne.*

DE BERANGER

During the whole of a dull, dark, and soundless day in the autumn of the year, when the clouds hung oppressively low in the heavens, I had been passing alone, on horseback, through a singularly dreary tract of country; and at length found myself, as the shades of the evening drew on, within view of the melancholy House of Usher. I know not how it was—but, with the first glimpse of the building, a sense of insufferable gloom pervaded my spirit. I say insufferable; for the feeling was unrelieved by any of that half-pleasurable, because poetic, sentiment, with which the mind usually receives even the sternest natural images of the desolate or terrible. I looked upon the scene before me—upon the mere house, and the simple landscape features of the domain—upon the bleak walls—upon the vacant eye-like windows—upon a few rank sedges—and upon a few white trunks of decayed trees—with an utter depression of soul which I can compare to no earthly sensation more properly than to the after-dream of the reveller upon opium—the bitter lapse into everyday life—the hideous dropping off of the veil. There was an iciness, a sinking, a sickening of the heart—an unredeemed dreariness of thought which no goading of the imagination could torture into aught of the sublime. What was it—I paused to think—what was it that so unnerved me in the contemplation of the House of Usher? It was a mystery all insoluble; nor could I grapple with the shadowy fancies that crowded upon me as I pondered. I was forced to fall back upon the unsatisfactory conclusion, that while, beyond doubt, there *are* combinations of very simple natural objects which have the power of thus affecting us, still the analysis of this power lies among considerations beyond our depth. It was possible, I reflected, that a mere different arrangement of the particulars of the scene, of the details of the picture, would be sufficient to modify, or perhaps to annihilate its capacity for sorrowful impression; and, acting upon this idea, I reined my horse to the precipitous brink of a black and lurid tarn that lay in unruffled lustre by the dwelling, and gazed down—but with a shudder even more thrilling than before—upon the remodelled and inverted images of the gray sedge, and the ghastly tree-stems, and the vacant and eye-like windows.

*His heart is a suspended lute;
Whenever one touches it, it resounds.

Nevertheless, in this mansion of gloom I now proposed to myself a sojourn of some weeks. Its proprietor, Roderick Usher, had been one of my boon companions in boyhood; but many years had elapsed since our last meeting. A letter, however, had lately reached me in a distant part of the country—a letter from him—which, in its wildly importunate nature, had admitted of no other than a personal reply. The MS. gave evidence of nervous agitation. The writer spoke of acute bodily illness—of a mental disorder which oppressed him—and of an earnest desire to see me, as his best, and indeed his only personal friend, with a view of attempting, by the cheerfulness of my society, some alleviation of his malady. It was the manner in which all this, and much more, was said—it was the apparent *heart* that went with his request—which allowed me no room for hesitation; and I accordingly obeyed forthwith what I still considered a very singular summons.

Although, as boys, we had been even intimate associates, yet I really knew little of my friend. His reserve had been always excessive and habitual. I was aware, however, that his very ancient family had been noted, time out of mind, for a peculiar sensibility of temperament, displaying itself, through long ages, in many works of exalted art, and manifested, of late, in repeated deeds of munificent yet unobtrusive charity, as well as in a passionate devotion to the intricacies, perhaps even more than to the orthodox and easily recognis-able beauties, of musical science. I had learned, too, the very remarkable fact, that the stem of the Usher race, all time-honoured as it was, had put forth, at no period, any enduring branch; in other words, that the entire family lay in the direct line of descent, and had always, with very trifling and very tempo-rary variation, so lain. It was this deficiency, I considered, while running over in thought the perfect keeping of the character of the premises with the ac-credited character of the people, and while speculating upon the possible in-fluence which the one, in the long lapse of centuries, might have exercised upon the other—it was this deficiency, perhaps of collateral issue, and the consequent undeviating transmission, from sire to son, of the patrimony with the name, which had, at length, so identified the two as to merge the original title of the estate in the quaint and equivocal appellation to the "House of Usher"—an appellation which seemed to include, in the minds of the peas-antry who used it, both the family and the family mansion.

I have said that the sole effect of my somewhat childish experiment—that of looking down within the tarn—had been to deepen the first singular impres-sion. There can be no doubt that the consciousness of the rapid increase of my superstition—for why should I not so term it?—served mainly to accelerate the increase itself. Such, I have long known, is the paradoxical law of all sentiments having terror as a basis. And it might have been for this reason only, that, when I again uplifted my eyes to the house itself, from its image in the pool, there grew in my mind a strange fancy—a fancy so ridiculous, in-deed, that I but mention it to show the vivid force of the sensations which oppressed me. I had so worked upon my imagination as really to believe that about the whole mansion and domain there hung an atmosphere peculiar to themselves and their immediate vicinity—an atmosphere which had no affinity with the air of heaven, but which had reeked up from the decayed trees, and the gray wall, and the silent tarn—a pestilent and mystic vapour, dull, sluggish, faintly discernible, and leaden-hued.

Shaking off from my spirit what *must* have been a dream, I scanned more narrowly the real aspect of the building. Its principal feature seemed to be that of an excessive antiquity. The discoloration of ages had been great. Minute fungi overspread the whole exterior, hanging in a fine tangled web-work from the eaves. Yet all this was apart from any extraordinary dilapidation. No portion of the masonry had fallen; and there appeared to be a wild inconsistency between its still perfect adaptation of parts, and the crumbling condition of the individual stones. In this there was much that reminded me of the specious totality of old wood-work which has rotted for long years in some neglected vault, with no disturbance from the breath of the external air. Beyond this indication of extensive decay, however, the fabric gave little token of instability. Perhaps the eye of a scrutinising observer might have discovered a barely perceptible fissure, which, extending from the roof of the building in front, made its way down the wall in a zigzag direction, until it became lost in the sullen waters of the tarn.

Noticing these things, I rode over a short causeway to the house. A servant in waiting took my horse, and I entered the Gothic archway of the hall. A valet, of stealthy step, thence conducted me, in silence, through many dark and intricate passages in my progress to the *studio* of his master. Much that I encountered on the way contributed, I know not how, to heighten the vague sentiments of which I have already spoken. While the objects around me— while the carvings of the ceilings, the sombre tapestries of the walls, the ebon blackness of the floors, and the phantasmagoric armorial trophies which rattled as I strode, were but matters to which, or to such as which, I had been accustomed from my infancy—while I hesitated not to acknowledge how familar was all this—I still wondered to find how unfamiliar were the fancies which ordinary images were stirring up. On one of the staircases, I met the physician of the family. His countenance, I thought, wore a mingled expression of low cunning and perplexity. He accosted me with trepidation and passed on. The valet now threw open a door and ushered me into the presence of his master.

The room in which I found myself was very large and lofty. The windows were long, narrow, and pointed, and at so vast a distance from the black oaken floor as to be altogether inaccessible from within. Feeble gleams of encrimsoned light made their way through the trellised panes, and served to render sufficiently distinct the more prominent objects around; the eye, however, struggled in vain to reach the remoter angles of the chamber, or the recesses of the vaulted and fretted ceiling. Dark draperies hung upon the walls. The general furniture was profuse, comfortless, antique, and tattered. Many books and musical instruments lay scattered about, but failed to give any vitality to the scene. I felt that I breathed an atmosphere of sorrow. An air of stern, deep, and irredeemable gloom hung over and pervaded all.

Upon my entrance, Usher arose from a sofa on which he had been lying at full length, and greeted me with a vivacious warmth which had much in it, I at first thought, of an overdone cordiality—of the constrained effort of the *ennuyé* man of the world. A glance, however, at his countenance, convinced me of his perfect sincerity. We sat down; and for some moments, while he spoke not, I gazed upon him with a feeling half of pity, half of awe. Surely, man had never before so terribly altered, in so brief a period, as had Roderick Usher! It was with difficulty that I could bring myself to admit the identity of the wan being before me with the companion of my early boyhood. Yet the character of his face had been at all times remarkable. A cadaverousness of complexion; an eye large, liquid, and luminous beyond comparison; lips somewhat thin and very pallid, but of a surpassingly beautiful curve; a nose of delicate Hebrew model, but with a breadth of nostril unusual in similar formations; a finely moulded chin, speaking, in its want of prominence, of a want of moral energy; hair of a more than web-like softness and tenuity; these features, with an inordinate expansion above the regions of the temple, made up altogether a countenance not easily to be forgotten. And now in the mere exaggeration of the prevailing character of these features, and of the expression they were wont to convey, lay so much of change that I doubted to whom I spoke. The now ghastly pallor of the skin, and the now miraculous lustre of the eye, above all things startled and even awed me. The silken hair, too, had been suffered to grow all unheeded, and as, in its wild gossamer texture, it floated rather than fell about the face, I could not, even with effort, connect its Arabesque expression with any idea of simple humanity.

In the manner of my friend I was at once struck with an incoherence—an inconsistency; and I soon found this to arise from a series of feeble and futile struggles to overcome an habitual trepidancy—an excessive nervous agitation. For something of this nature I had indeed been prepared, no less by his letter, than by reminiscences of certain boyish traits, and by conclusions deduced from his peculiar physical conformation and temperament. His action was alternately vivacious and sullen. His voice varied rapidly from a tremulous indecision (when the animal spirits seemed utterly in abeyance) to that species of energetic concision—that abrupt, weighty, unhurried, and hollow-sounding enunciation—that leaden, self-balanced and perfectly modulated guttural utterance, which may be observed in the lost drunkard, or the irreclaimable eater of opium, during the periods of his most intense excitement.

It was thus that he spoke of the object of my visit, of his earnest desire to see me, and of the solace he expected me to afford him. He entered, at some length, into what he conceived to be the nature of his malady. It was, he said, a constitutional and a family evil, and one for which he despaired to find a remedy—a mere nervous affection, he immediately added, which would undoubtedly soon pass off. It displayed itself in a host of unnatural sensations.

Some of these, as he detailed them, interested and bewildered me; although, perhaps, the terms, and the general manner of the narration had their weight. He suffered much from a morbid acuteness of the senses; the most insipid food was alone endurable; he could wear only garments of certain texture; the odours of all flowers were oppressive; his eyes were tortured by even a faint light; and there were but peculiar sounds, and these from stringed instruments, which did not inspire him with horror.

To an anomalous species of terror I found him a bounden slave. "I shall perish," said he, "I *must* perish in this deplorable folly. Thus, thus, and not otherwise, shall I be lost. I dread the events of the future, not in themselves, but in their results. I shudder at the thought of any, even the most trivial, incident, which may operate upon this intolerable agitation of soul. I have, indeed, no abhorrence of danger, except in its absolute effect—in terror. In this unnerved—in this pitiable condition—I feel that the period will sooner or later arrive when I must abandon life and reason together, in some struggle with the grim phantasm, FEAR."

I learned, moreover, at intervals, and through broken and equivocal hints, another singular feature of his mental condition. He was enchained by certain superstitious impressions in regard to the dwelling which he tenanted, and whence, for many years, he had never ventured forth—in regard to an influence whose superstitious force was conveyed in terms too shadowy here to be re-stated—an influence which some peculiarities in the mere form and substance of his family mansion, had, by dint of long sufferance, he said, obtained over his spirit—an effect which the *physique* of the gray walls and turrets, and of the dim tarn into which they all looked down, had, at length, brought about upon the *morale* of his existence.

He admitted, however, although with hesitation, that much of the peculiar gloom which thus afflicted him could be traced to a more natural and far more palpable origin—to the severe and long-continued illness—indeed to the evidently approaching dissolution—of a tenderly beloved sister—his sole companion for long years—his last and only relative on earth. "Her decease," he said, with a bitterness which I can never forget, "would leave him (him the hopeless and the frail) the last of the ancient race of the Ushers." While he spoke, the lady Madeline (for so was she called) passed slowly through a remote portion of the apartment, and, without having noticed my presence, disappeared. I regarded her with an utter astonishment not unmingled with dread—and yet I found it impossible to account for such feelings. A sensation of stupor oppressed me, as my eyes followed her retreating steps. When a door, at length, closed upon her, my glance sought instinctively and eagerly the countenance of the brother—but he had buried his face in his hands, and I could only perceive that a far more than ordinary wanness had overspread the emaciated fingers through which trickled many passionate tears.

The disease of the lady Madeline had long baffled the skill of her physicians. A settled apathy, a gradual wasting away of the person, and frequent although transient affections of a partially cataleptical character, were the unusual diagnosis. Hitherto she had steadily borne up against the pressure of her malady, and had not betaken herself finally to bed; but, on the closing in of the evening of my arrival at the house, she succumbed (as her brother told me at night with inexpressible agitation) to the prostrating power of the destroyer; and I learned that the glimpse I had obtained of her person would thus probably be the last I should obtain—that the lady, at least while living, would be seen by me no more.

For several days ensuing, her name was unmentioned by either Usher or myself: and during this period I was busied in earnest endeavours to alleviate the melancholy of my friend. We painted and read together; or I listened, as if in a dream, to the wild improvisations of his speaking guitar. And thus, as a closer and still closer intimacy admitted me more unreservedly into the recesses of his spirit, the more bitterly did I perceive the futility of all attempt at cheering a mind from which darkness, as if an inherent positive quality, poured forth upon all objects of the moral and physical universe, in one unceasing radiation of gloom.

I shall ever bear about me a memory of the many solemn hours I thus spent alone with the master of the House of Usher. Yet I should fail in any attempt to convey an idea of the exact character of the studies, or of the occupations, in which he involved me, or led me the way. An excited and highly distempered ideality threw a sulphureous lustre over all. His long improvised dirges will ring forever in my ears. Among other things, I hold painfully in mind a certain singular perversion and amplification of the wild air of the last waltz of Von Weber. From the paintings over which his elaborate fancy brooded, and which grew, touch by touch, into vaguenesses at which I shuddered the more thrillingly, because I shuddered knowing not why;—from these paintings (vivid as their images now are before me) I would in vain endeavour to educe more than a small portion which should lie within the compass of merely written words. By the utter simplicity, by the nakedness of his designs, he arrested and overawed attention. If ever mortal painted an idea, that mortal was Roderick Usher. For me at least—in the circumstances then surrounding me—there arose out of the pure abstractions which the hypochondriac contrived to throw upon his canvas, an intensity of intolerable awe, no shadow of which felt I ever yet in the contemplation of the certainly glowing yet too concrete reveries of Fuseli.

One of the phantasmagoric conceptions of my friend, partaking not so rigidly of the spirit of abstraction, may be shadowed forth, although feebly, in words. A small picture presented the interior of an immensely long and rectangular vault or tunnel, with low walls, smooth, white, and without interruption or device. Certain accessory points of the design served well to convey the idea that this excavation lay at an exceeding depth below the surface of the earth. No outlet was observed in any portion of its vast extent, and no torch, or other artificial source of light was discernible; yet a flood of intense rays rolled throughout, and bathed the whole in a ghastly and inappropriate splendour.

I have just spoken of that morbid condition of the auditory nerve which rendered all music intolerable to the sufferer, with the exception of certain effects of stringed instruments. It was, perhaps, the narrow limits to which he thus confined himself upon the guitar, which gave birth, in great measure, to the fantastic character of his performances. But the fervid *facility* of his *impromptus* could not be so accounted for. They must have been, and were, in the notes, as well as in the words of his wild fantasias (for he not unfrequently accompanied himself with rhymed verbal improvisations), the result of that intense mental collectedness and concentration to which I have previously alluded as observable only in particular moments of the highest artificial excitement. The words of one of these rhapsodies I have easily remembered. I was, perhaps, the more forcibly impressed with it, as he gave it, because, in the under or mystic current of its meaning, I fancied that I perceived, and for the first time, a full consciousness on the part of Usher, of the tottering of his lofty reason upon her throne. The verses, which were entitled "The Haunted Palace," ran very nearly, if not accurately, thus:

> In the greenest of our valleys,
>   By good angels tenanted,
> Once a fair and stately palace—
>   Radiant palace—reared its head.
> In the monarch Thought's dominion—
>   It stood there!
> Never seraph spread a pinion
>   Over fabric half so fair.
>
> Banners yellow, glorious, golden,
>   On its roof did float and flow;
> (This—all this—was in the olden
>   Time long ago)
> And every gentle air that dallied,
>   In that sweet day,
> Along the ramparts plumed and pallid,
>   A winged odour went away.
>
> Wanderers in that happy valley
>   Through two luminous windows saw
> Spirits moving musically
>   To a lute's well-tunèd law,
> Round about a throne, where sitting
>   (Porphyrogene!)
> In state his glory well befitting,
>   The ruler of the realm was seen.

> *And all with pearl and ruby glowing*
>   *Was the fair palace door,*
> *Through which came flowing, flowing, flowing*
>   *And sparkling evermore,*
> *A troop of Echoes whose sweet duty*
>   *Was but to sing,*
> *In voices of surpassing beauty,*
>   *The wit and wisdom of their king.*
>
> *But evil things, in robes of sorrow,*
>   *Assailed the monarch's high estate;*
> *(Ah, let us mourn, for never morrow*
>   *Shall dawn upon him, desolate!)*
> *And, round about his home, the glory*
>   *That blushed and bloomed*
> *Is but a dim-remembered story*
>   *Of the old time entombed.*
>
> *And travellers now within that valley,*
>   *Through the red-litten windows, see*
> *Vast forms that move fantastically*
>   *To a discordant melody;*
> *While, like a rapid ghastly river,*
>   *Through the pale door,*
> *A hideous throng rush out forever,*
>   *And laugh—but smile no more.*

I well remember that suggestions arising from this ballad, led us into a train of thought wherein there became manifest an opinion of Usher's which I mention not so much on account of its novelty, (for other men have thought thus,) as on account of the pertinacity with which he maintained it. This opinion, in its general form, was that of the sentience of all vegetable things. But, in his disordered fancy, the idea had assumed a more daring character, and trespassed, under certain conditions, upon the kingdom of inorganization. I lack words to express the full extent, or the earnest *abandon* of his persuasion. The belief, however, was connected (as I have previously hinted) with the gray stones of the home of his forefathers. The conditions of the sentience had been here, he imagined, fulfilled in the method of collocation of these stones—in the order of their arrangement, as well as in that of the many *fungi* which overspread them, and of the decayed trees which stood around—above all, in the long undisturbed endurance of this arrangement, and in its reduplication in the still waters of the tarn. Its evidence—the evidence of the sentience—was to be seen, he said, (and I here started as he spoke,) in the gradual yet certain condensation of an atmosphere of their own about the waters and the walls. The result was discoverable, he added, in that silent, yet importunate and terrible influence which for centuries had moulded the destinies of his family, and which made *him* what I now saw him—what he was. Such opinions need no comment, and I will make none.

Our books—the books which, for years, had formed no small portion of the mental existence of the invalid—were, as might be supposed, in strict keeping with this character of phantasm. We pored together over such works as the *Ververt et Chartreuse* of Gresset; the *Belphegor* of Machiavelli; the *Heaven and Hell* of Swedenborg; the *Subterranean Voyage of Nicholas Klimm* by Holberg; the *Chiromancy* of Robert Flud, of Jean D'Indaginé, and of De la Chambre; the *Journey into the Blue Distance of Tieck;* and the *City of the Sun* by Campanella. One favorite volume was a small octavo edition of the *Directorium Inquisitorum,* by the Dominican Eymeric de Gironne; and there were passages in Pomponius Mela, about the old African Satyrs and Ægipans, over which Usher would sit dreaming for hours. His chief delight, however, was found in the perusal of an exceedingly rare and curious book in quarto Gothic—the manual of a forgotten church—the *Vigiliæ Mortuorum secundum Chorum Ecclesiæ Maguntinæ.*

I could not help thinking of the wild ritual of this work, and of its probable influence upon the hypochondriac, when, one evening, having informed me abruptly that the lady Madeline was no more, he stated his intention of preserving her corpse for a fortnight, (previously to its final interment,) in one of the numerous vaults within the main walls of the building. The worldly reason, however, assigned for this singular proceeding, was one which I did not feel at liberty to dispute. The brother had been led to his resolution (so he told me) by consideration of the unusual character of the malady of the deceased, of certain obtrusive and eager inquiries on the part of her medical men, and of the remote and exposed situation of the burial-ground of the family. I will not deny that when I called to mind the sinister countenance of the person whom I met upon the staircase, on the day of my arrival at the house, I had no desire to oppose what I regarded as at best but a harmless, and by no means an unnatural, precaution.

At the request of Usher, I personally aided him in the arrangements for the temporary entombment. The body having been encoffined, we two alone bore it to its rest. The vault in which we placed it (and which had been so long unopened that our torches, half smothered in its oppressive atmosphere, gave us little opportunity for investigation) was small, damp, and entirely without means of admission for light; lying, at great depth, immediately beneath that portion of the building in which was my own sleeping apartment. It had been used, apparently, in remote feudal times, for the worst purposes of a donjon-keep, and, in later days, as a place of deposit for powder, or some other highly combustible substance, as a portion of its floor, and the whole interior of a long archway through which we reached it, were carefully sheathed with copper. The door, of massive iron, had been, also, similarly protected. Its immense weight caused an unusually sharp grating sound, as it moved upon its hinges.

Having deposited our mournful burden upon tressels within this region of horror, we partially turned aside the yet unscrewed lid of the coffin, and looked upon the face of the tenant. A striking similitude between the brother and sister now first arrested my attention; and Usher, divining, perhaps, my thoughts, murmured out some few words from which I learned that the deceased and himself had been twins, and that sympathies of a scarcely intelligible nature had always existed between them. Our glances, however, rested not long upon the dead—for we could not regard her unawed. The disease which had thus entombed the lady in the maturity of youth, had left, as usual in all maladies of a strictly cataleptical character, the mockery of a faint blush upon the bosom and the face, and that suspiciously lingering smile upon the lip which is so terrible in death. We replaced and screwed down the lid, and, having secured the door of iron, made our way, with toil, into the scarcely less gloomy apartments of the upper portion of the house.

And now, some days of bitter grief having elapsed, an observable change came over the features of the mental disorder of my friend. His ordinary manner had vanished. His ordinary occupations were neglected or forgotten. He roamed from chamber to chamber with hurried, unequal, and objectless step. The pallor of his countenance had assumed, if possible, a more ghastly hue—but the luminousness of his eye had utterly gone out. The once occasional huskiness of his tone was heard no more; and a tremulous quaver, as if of extreme terror, habitually characterized his utterance. There were times, indeed, when I thought his unceasingly agitated mind was labouring with some oppressive secret, to divulge which he struggled for the necessary courage. At times, again, I was obliged to resolve all into the mere inexplicable vagaries of madness, for I beheld him gazing upon vacancy for long hours, in an attitude of the profoundest attention, as if listening to some imaginary sound. It was no wonder that his condition terrified—that it infected me. I felt creeping upon me, by slow yet certain degrees, the wild influences of his own fantastic yet impressive superstitions.

It was, especially, upon retiring to bed late in the night of the seventh or eighth day after the placing of the lady Madeline within the donjon, that I experienced the full power of such feelings. Sleep came not near my couch— while the hours waned and waned away. I struggled to reason off the nervousness which had dominion over me. I endeavoured to believe that much, if not all of what I felt, was due to the bewildering influence of the gloomy furniture of the room—of the dark and tattered draperies, which, tortured into motion by the breath of a rising tempest, swayed fitfully to and fro upon the walls, and rustled uneasily about the decorations of the bed. But my efforts were fruitless. An irrepressible tremour gradually pervaded my frame; and, at length, there sat upon my very heart an incubus of utterly causeless alarm. Shaking this off with a gasp and a struggle, I uplifted myself upon the pillows, and, peering earnestly within the intense darkness of the chamber, hearkened—I know not why, except that an instinctive spirit prompted me—to certain low and indefinite sounds which came, through the pauses of the storm, at long intervals, I knew not whence. Overpowered by an intense sentiment of horror, unaccountable yet unendurable, I threw on my clothes with haste (for I felt that I should sleep no more during the night), and endeavoured to arouse myself from the pitiable condition into which I had fallen, by pacing rapidly to and fro through the apartment.

I had taken but few turns in this manner, when a light step on an adjoining staircase arrested my attention. I presently recognised it as that of Usher. In an instant afterward he rapped, with a gentle touch, at my door, and entered, bearing a lamp. His countenance was, as usual, cadaverously wan—but, more-over, there was a species of mad hilarity in his eyes—an evidently restrained *hysteria* in his whole demeanour. His air appalled me—but anything was pref-erable to the solitude which I had so long endured, and I even welcomed his presence as a relief.

"And you have not seen it?" he said abruptly, after having stared about him for some moments in silence—"you have not then seen it?—but, stay! you shall." Thus speaking, and having carefully shaded his lamp, he hurried to one of the casements, and threw it freely open to the storm.

The impetuous fury of the entering gust nearly lifted us from our feet. It was, indeed, a tempestuous yet sternly beautiful night, and one wildly singu-lar in its terror and its beauty. A whirlwind had apparently collected its force in our vicinity; for there were frequent and violent alterations in the direction of the wind; and the exceeding density of the clouds (which hung so low as to press upon the turrets of the house) did not prevent our perceiving the life-like velocity with which they flew careering from all points against each other, without passing away into the distance. I say that even their exceeding density did not prevent our perceiving this—yet we had no glimpse of the moon or stars—nor was there any flashing forth of the lightning. But the under sur-faces of the huge masses of agitated vapour, as well as all terrestrial objects immediately around us, were glowing in the unnatural light of a faintly lumi-nous and distinctly visible gaseous exhalation which hung about and en-shrouded the mansion.

"You must not—you shall not behold this!" said I, shudderingly, to Usher, as I led him, with a gentle violence, from the window to a seat. "These appear-ances, which bewilder you, are merely electrical phenomena not uncommon— or it may be that they have their ghastly origin in the rank miasma of the tarn. Let us close this casement; the air is chilling and dangerous to your frame. Here is one of your favourite romances. I will read, and you shall listen; and so we will pass away this terrible night together."

The antique volume which I had taken up was the *Mad Trist* of Sir Launce-lot Canning; but I had called it a favourite of Usher's more in sad jest than in earnest; for, in truth, there is little in its uncouth and unimaginative prolixity which could have had interest for the lofty and spiritual ideality of my friend. It was, however, the only book immediately at hand; and I indulged a vague hope that the excitement which now agitated the hypochondriac, might find relief (for the history of mental disorder is full of similar anomalies) even in the extremeness of the folly which I should read. Could I have judged, indeed, by the wild overstrained air of vivacity with which he hearkened, or apparently hearkened, to the words of the tale, I might well have congratulated myself upon the success of my design.

I had arrived at that well-known portion of the story where Ethelred, the hero of the Trist, having sought in vain for peaceable admission into the dwelling of the hermit, proceeds to make good an entrance by force. Here, it will be remembered, the words of the narrative run thus:

"And Ethelred, who was by nature of a doughty heart, and who was now mighty withal, on account of the powerfulness of the wine which he had drunken, waited no longer to hold parley with the hermit, who, in sooth, was of an obstinate and maliceful turn, but, feeling the rain upon his shoulders, and fearing the rising of the tempest, uplifted his mace outright, and, with blows, made quickly room in the plankings of the door for his gauntleted hand; and now pulling therewith sturdily, he so cracked, and ripped, and tore all asunder, that the noise of the dry and hollow-sounding wood alarumed and reverberated throughout the forest."

At the termination of this sentence I started, and for a moment, paused; for it appeared to me (although I at once concluded that my excited fancy had deceived me)—it appeared to me that, from some very remote portion of the mansion, there came, indistinctly, to my ears, what might have been, in its exact similarity of character, the echo (but a stifled and dull one certainly) of the very cracking and ripping sound which Sir Launcelot had so particularly described. It was, beyond doubt, the coincidence alone which had arrested my attention; for, amid the rattling of the sashes of the casements, and the ordinary commingled noises of the still increasing storm, the sound, in itself, had nothing, surely, which would have interested or disturbed me. I continued the story:

"But the good champion Ethelred, now entering within the door, was sore enraged and amazed to perceive no signal of the maliceful hermit; but, in the stead thereof, a dragon of a scaly and prodigious demeanour, and of a fiery tongue, which sate in guard before a palace of gold, with a floor of silver; and upon the wall there hung a shield of shining brass with this legend enwritten—

> Who entereth herein, a conqueror hath bin;
> Who slayeth the dragon, the shield he shall win.

And Ethelred uplifted his mace, and struck upon the head of the dragon, which fell before him, and gave up his pesty breath, with a shriek so horrid and harsh, and withal so piercing, that Ethelred had fain to close his ears with his hands against the dreadful noise of it, the like whereof was never before heard."

Here again I paused abruptly, and now with a feeling of wild amazement—for there could be no doubt whatever that, in this instance, I did actually hear (although from what direction it proceeded I found it impossible to say) a low and apparently distant, but harsh, protracted, and most unusual screaming or grating sound—the exact counterpart of what my fancy had already conjured up for the dragon's unnatural shriek as described by the romancer.

Oppressed, as I certainly was, upon the occurrence of the second and most extraordinary coincidence, by a thousand conflicting sensations, in which wonder and extreme terror were predominant, I still retained sufficient presence of mind to avoid exciting, by any observation, the sensitive nervousness of my companion. I was by no means certain that he had noticed the sounds in question; although, assuredly, a strange alteration had, during the last few minutes, taken place in his demeanour. From a position fronting my own, he had gradually brought round his chair, so as to sit with his face to the door of the chamber; and thus I could but partially perceive his features, although I saw that his lips trembled as if he were murmuring inaudibly. His head had dropped upon his breast—yet I knew that he was not asleep, from the wide and rigid opening of the eye as I caught a glance of it in profile. The motion of his body, too, was at variance with this idea—for he rocked from side to side with a gentle yet constant and uniform sway. Having rapidly taken notice of all this, I resumed the narrative of Sir Launcelot, which thus proceeded:

"And now, the champion, having escaped from the terrible fury of the dragon, bethinking himself of the brazen shield, and of the breaking up of the enchantment which was upon it, removed the carcass from out of the way before him, and approached valorously over the silver pavement of the castle to where the shield was upon the wall; which in sooth tarried not for his full coming, but fell down at his feet upon the silver floor, with a mighty great and terrible ringing sound."

No sooner had these syllables passed my lips, than—as if a shield of brass had indeed, at the moment, fallen heavily upon a floor of silver—I became aware of a distinct, hollow, metallic, and clangorous, yet apparently muffled reverberation. Completely unnerved, I leaped to my feet; but the measured rocking movement of Usher was undisturbed. I rushed to the chair in which he sat. His eyes were bent fixedly before him, and throughout his whole countenance there reigned a stony rigidity. But, as I placed my hand upon his shoulder, there came a strong shudder over his whole person; a sickly smile quivered about his lips; and I saw that he spoke in a low, hurried, and gibbering murmur, as if unconscious of my presence. Bending closely over him, I at length drank in the hideous import of his words.

"Not hear it?—yes, I hear it, and *have* heard it. Long—long—long—many minutes, many hours, many days, have I heard it—yet I dared not—oh, pity me, miserable wretch that I am!—I dared not—I *dared* not speak! *We have put her living in the tomb!* Said I not that my senses were acute? I *now* tell you that I heard her first feeble movements in the hollow coffin. I heard them—many, many days ago—yet I dared not—*I dared not speak!* And now—to-night—Ethelred—ha! ha! the breaking of the hermit's door, and the death-cry of the dragon, and the clangour of the shield!—say, rather, the rending of her coffin, and grating of the iron hinges of her prison, and her struggles within the coppered archway of the vault! Oh whither shall I fly? Will she not be here anon? Is she not hurrying to upbraid me for my haste? Have I not heard her footstep on the stair? Do I not distinguish that heavy and horrible beating of her heart? MADMAN!" here he sprang furiously to his feet, and shrieked out his syllables, as if in the effort he were giving up his soul—"MADMAN! I TELL YOU THAT SHE NOW STANDS WITHOUT THE DOOR!"

As if in the superhuman energy of his utterance there had been found the potency of a spell—the huge antique panels to which the speaker pointed, threw slowly back, upon the instant, their ponderous and ebony jaws. It was the work of the rushing gust—but then without those doors there DID stand the lofty and enshrouded figure of the lady Madeline of Usher. There was blood upon her white robes, and the evidence of some bitter struggle upon every portion of her emaciated frame. For a moment she remained trembling and reeling to and fro upon the threshold, then, with a low moaning cry, fell heavily inward upon the person of her brother, and in her violent and now final death-agonies, bore him to the floor a corpse, and a victim to the terrors he had anticipated.

From that chamber, and from that mansion, I fled aghast. The storm was still abroad in all its wrath as I found myself crossing the old causeway. Suddenly there shot along the path a wild light, and I turned to see whence a gleam so unusual could have issued; for the vast house and its shadows were alone behind me. The radiance was that of the full, setting, and blood-red moon which now shone vividly through that once barely-discernible fissure of which I have before spoken as extending from the roof of the building, in a zigzag direction, to the base. While I gazed, this fissure rapidly widened—there came a fierce breath of the whirlwind—the entire orb of the satellite burst at once upon my sight—my brain reeled as I saw the mighty walls rushing asunder—there was a long tumultuous shouting sound like the voice of a thousand waters—and the deep and dank tarn at my feet closed sullenly and silently over the fragments of the "HOUSE OF USHER."

FOR STUDY, DISCUSSION, AND WRITING

1. What do you learn about the narrator's personality in the opening paragraphs of the story? Does anything that you learn suggest that he may be an unreliable narrator?

2. What early evidence is there of Usher's coming madness?

3. What are the parallels between Usher and his mansion, Usher and Madeline, Usher and the narrator, Usher's song "The Haunted Palace" and the deterioration of Usher's personality? What narrative purpose do these parallels serve?

4. Was the lady Madeline buried dead or alive? In any event, does she really escape from the dungeon and come back up into the house?

5. What narrative purpose do the details of the *Mad Trist* serve?

6. When the reader is told that Madeline reappears outside the narrator's room, why does Usher call the narrator a madman? Is this a matter of simple irony, or is the narrator indeed mad?

7. Comment on the possible symbolic significance of the name Madeline.

8. After the narrator's initial lengthy viewing of the House of Usher and its environs, he finds himself "shaking off from my spirit what *must* have been a dream." What other evidence can you find in the story that suggests the narrator's subsequent experiences may all have been a mad dream?

9. In writing about short fiction, Poe indicated that a short story should strive to achieve a single unique and preconceived effect. Does "The Fall of the House of Usher" adhere to this precept?

HONORÉ DE BALZAC

A Passion in the Desert

"The whole show is dreadful," she cried, coming out of the menagerie of M. Martin. She had just been looking at that daring speculator "working with his hyena"—to speak in the style of the program.

"By what means," she continued, "can he have tamed these animals to such a point as to be certain of their affection for——."

"What seems to you a problem," said I, interrupting, "is really quite natural."

"Oh!" she cried, letting an incredulous smile wander over her lips.

"You think that beasts are wholly without passions?" I asked her. "Quite the reverse; we can communicate to them all the vices arising in our own state of civilization."

She looked at me with an air of astonishment.

"Nevertheless," I continued, "the first time I saw M. Martin, I admit, like you, I did give vent to an exclamation of surprise. I found myself next to an old soldier with the right leg amputated, who had come in with me. His face had struck me. He had one of those intrepid heads, stamped with the seal of warfare, and on which the battles of Napoleon are written. Besides, he had that frank good-humored expression which always impresses me favorably.

He was without doubt one of those troopers who are surprised at nothing, who find matter for laughter in the contortions of a dying comrade, who bury or plunder him quite light-heartedly, who stand intrepidly in the way of bullets; in fact, one of those men who waste no time in deliberation, and would not hesitate to make friends with the devil himself. After looking very attentively at the proprietor of the menagerie getting out of his box, my companion pursed up his lips with an air of mockery and contempt, with that peculiar and expressive twist which superior people assume to show they are not taken in. Then when I was expatiating on the courage of M. Martin, he smiled, shook his head knowingly, and said, 'Well known.'

"How 'well known'?" I said. "If you would only explain to me the mystery I should be vastly obliged."

"After a few minutes, during which we made acquaintance, we went to dine at the first restaurateur's whose shop caught our eye. At dessert a bottle of champagne completely refreshed and brightened up the memories of this odd old soldier. He told me his story, and I said he had every reason to exclaim, 'Well known.' "

When she got home, she teased me to that extent and made so many promises, that I consented to communicate to her the old soldier's confidences. Next day she received the following episode of an epic which one might call "The Frenchman in Egypt."

During the expedition in Upper Egypt under General Desaix, a Provençal soldier fell into the hands of the Mangrabins, and was taken by these Arabs into the deserts beyond the falls of the Nile.

In order to place a sufficient distance between themselves and the French army, the Mangrabins made forced marches, and only rested during the night. They camped round a well overshadowed by palm trees under which they had previously concealed a store of provisions. Not surmising that the notion of flight would occur to their prisoner, they contented themselves with binding his hands, and after eating a few dates, and giving provender to their horses, went to sleep.

When the brave Provençal saw that his enemies were no longer watching him, he made use of his teeth to steal a scimitar, fixed the blade between his knees, and cut the cords which prevented using his hands; in a moment he was free. He at once seized a rifle and dagger, then taking the precaution to provide himself with a sack of dried dates, oats, and powder and shot, and to fasten a scimitar to his waist he leaped onto a horse, and spurred on vigorously in the direction where he thought to find the French army. So impatient was he to see a bivouac again that he pressed on the already tired courser at such speed that its flanks were lacerated with his spurs, and at last the poor animal died, leaving the Frenchman alone in the desert. After walking some time in the sand with all the courage of an escaped convict, the soldier was obliged to stop, as the day had already ended. In spite of the beauty of an oriental sky at night, he felt he had not strength enough to go on. Fortunately he had been able to find a small hill, on the summit of which a few palm trees shot up into the air; it was their verdure seen from afar which had brought hope and consolation to his heart. His fatigue was so great that he lay down upon a rock of granite, capriciously cut out like a camp-bed; there he fell asleep without taking any precaution to defend himself while he slept. He had made the sacrifice of his life. His last thought was one of regret. He repented having left the Mangrabins, whose nomad life seemed to smile on him now that he was afar from them and without help. He was awakened by the sun, whose pitiless rays fell with all their force on the granite and produced an intolerable heat— for he had had the stupidity to place himself inversely to the shadow thrown by the verdant majestic heads of the palm trees. He looked at the solitary trees and shuddered—they reminded him of the graceful shafts crowned with foliage which characterize the Saracen columns in the cathedral of Aries.

But when, after counting the palm trees, he cast his eye around him, the most horrible despair was infused into his soul. Before him stretched an ocean without limit. The dark sand of the desert spread farther than sight could reach in every direction, and glittered like steel struck with a bright light. It might have been a sea of looking-glass, or lakes melted together in a mirror. A fiery vapor carried up in streaks made a perpetual whirlwind over the quivering land. The sky was lit with an oriental splendor of insupportable purity, leaving naught for the imagination to desire. Heaven and earth were on fire.

The silence was awful in its wild and terrible majesty. Infinity, immensity, closed in upon the soul from every side. Not a cloud in the sky, not a breath in the air, not a flaw on the bosom of the sand, ever moving in diminutive waves; the horizon ended as at sea on a clear day, with one line of light, definite as the cut of a sword.

The Provençal threw his arms around the trunk of one of the palm trees, as though it were the body of a friend, and then in the shelter of the thin straight shadow that the palm cast upon the granite, he wept. Then sitting down he remained as he was, contemplating with profound sadness the implacable scene, which was all he had to look upon. He cried aloud, to measure the solitude. His voice, lost in the hollows of the hill, sounded faintly, and aroused no echo—the echo was in his own heart. The Provençal was twenty-two years old;—he loaded his carbine.

"There'll be time enough," he said to himself, laying on the ground the weapon which alone could bring him deliverance.

Looking by turns at the black expanse and the blue expanse, the soldier dreamed of France—he smelt with delight the gutters of Paris—he remembered the towns through which he had passed, the faces of his fellow-soldiers, the most minute details of his life. His southern fancy soon showed him the stones of his beloved Provence, in the play of the heat which waved over the spread sheet of the desert. Fearing the danger of this cruel mirage, he went down the opposite side of the hill to that by which he had come up the day before. The remains of a rug showed that this place of refuge had at one time been inhabited; at a short distance he saw some palm trees full of dates. Then the instinct which binds us to life awoke again in his heart. He hoped to live long enough to await the passing of some Arabs, or perhaps he might hear the sound of cannon; for at this time Bonaparte was traversing Egypt.

This thought gave him new life. The palm tree seemed to bend with the weight of the ripe fruit. He shook some of it down. When he tasted this unhoped-for manna, he felt sure that the palms had been cultivated by a former inhabitant—the savory, fresh meat of the dates was proof of the care of his predecessor. He passed suddenly from dark despair to an almost insane joy. He went up again to the top of the hill, and spent the rest of the day in cutting down one of the sterile palm trees, which the night before had served him for shelter. A vague memory made him think of the animals of the desert; and in case they might come to drink at the spring, visible from the base of the rocks but lost farther down, he resolved to guard himself from their visits by placing a barrier at the entrance of his hermitage.

In spite of his diligence, and the strength which the fear of being devoured asleep gave him, he was unable to cut the palm in pieces, though he succeeded in cutting it down. At eventide the king of the desert fell; the sound of its fall resounded far and wide, like a sign in the solitude; the soldier shuddered as though he had heard some voice predicting woe.

But like an heir who does not long bewail a deceased parent, he tore off from this beautiful tree the tall broad green leaves which are its poetic adornment, and used them to mend the mat on which he was to sleep.

Fatigued by the heat and his work, he fell asleep under the red curtains of his wet cave.

In the middle of the night his sleep was troubled by an extraordinary noise; he sat up, and the deep silence around him allowed him to distinguish the alternative accents of a respiration whose savage energy could not belong to a human creature.

A profound terror, increased still further by the darkness, the silence, and his waking images, froze his heart within him. He almost felt his hair stand on end, when by straining his eyes to their utmost he perceived through the shadows two faint yellow lights. At first he attributed these lights to the reflection of his own pupils, but soon the vivid brilliance of the night aided him gradually to distinguish the objects around him in the cave, and he beheld a huge animal lying but two steps from him. Was it a lion, a tiger, or a crocodile?

The Provençal was not educated enough to know under what species his enemy ought to be classed; but his fright was all the greater, as his ignorance led him to imagine all terrors at once; he endured a cruel torture, noting every variation of the breathing close to him without daring to make the slightest movement. An odor, pungent like that of a fox, but more penetrating, profounder—so to speak—filled the cave, and when the Provençal became sensible of this, his terror reached its height, for he could no longer doubt the proximity of a terrible companion, whose royal dwelling served him for shelter.

Presently the reflection of the moon, descending on the horizon, lit up the den, rendering gradually visible and resplendent the spotted skin of a panther.

The lion of Egypt slept, curled up like a big dog, the peaceful possessor of a sumptuous niche at the gate of an hotel; its eyes opened for a moment and closed again; its face was turned toward the man. A thousand confused thoughts passed through the Frenchman's mind; first he thought of killing it with a bullet from his gun, but he saw there was not enough distance between them for him to take proper aim—the shot would miss the mark. And if it were to wake!—the thought made his limbs rigid. He listened to his own heart beating in the midst of the silence, and cursed the too violent pulsations which the flow of blood brought on, fearing to disturb that sleep which allowed him time to think of some means of escape.

Twice he placed his hand on his scimitar, intending to cut off the head of the enemy; but the difficulty of cutting the stiff, short hair compelled him to abandon this daring project. To miss would be to die for certain, he thought; he preferred the chances of fair fight, and made up his mind to wait till morning; the morning did not leave him long to wait.

He could now examine the panther at ease; its muzzle was smeared with blood.

"She's had a good dinner," he thought, without troubling himself as to whether her feast might have been on human flesh. "She won't be hungry when she gets up."

It was a female. The fur on her belly and flanks was glistening white; many small marks like velvet formed beautiful bracelets round her feet; her sinuous tail was also white, ending with black rings; the overpart of her dress, yellow like unburnished gold, very lissome and soft, had the characteristic blotches in the form of rosettes, which distinguish the panther from every other feline species.

This tranquil and formidable hostess snored in an attitude as graceful as that of a cat lying on a cushion. Her blood-stained paws, nervous and well-armed, were stretched out before her face, which rested upon them, and from which radiated her straight, slender whiskers, like threads of silver.

If she had been like that in a cage, the Provençal would doubtless have admired the grace of the animal, and the vigorous contrasts of vivid color which gave her robe an imperial splendor; but just then his sight was troubled by her sinister appearance.

The presence of the panther, even asleep, could not fail to produce the effect which the magnetic eyes of the serpent are said to have on the nightingale.

For a moment the courage of the soldier began to fail before this danger, though no doubt it would have risen at the mouth of a cannon charged with shell. Nevertheless, a bold thought brought daylight to his soul and sealed up the source of the cold sweat which sprang forth on his brow. Like men driven to bay who defy death and offer their body to the smiter, so he, seeing in this merely a tragic episode, resolved to play his part with honor to the last.

"The day before yesterday the Arabs would have killed me perhaps," he said; so considering himself as good as dead already, he waited bravely, with excited curiosity, his enemy's awakening.

When the sun appeared, the panther suddenly opened her eyes; then she put out her paws with energy, as if to stretch them and get rid of cramp. At last she yawned, showing the formidable apparatus of her teeth and pointed tongue, rough as a file.

"A regular *petite maîtresse,*"thought the Frenchman, seeing her roll herself about so softly and coquettishly. She licked off the blood which stained her paws and muzzle, and scratched her head with reiterated gestures full of prettiness. "All right, make a little toilet," the Frenchman said to himself, beginning to recover his gaiety with his courage; "we'll say good morning to each other presently," and he seized the small, short dagger which he had taken from the Mangrabins. At this moment the panther turned her head toward the man and looked at him fixedly without moving.

The rigidity of her metallic eyes and their insupportable luster made him shudder, especially when the animal walked toward him. But he looked at her caressingly, staring into her eyes in order to magnetize her, and let her come quite close to him; then with a movement both gentle and amorous, as though he were caressing the most beautiful of women, he passed his hand over her whole body, from the head to the tail, scratching the flexible vertebrae which divided the panther's yellow back. The animal waved her tail voluptuously, and her eyes grew gentle; and when for the third time the Frenchman accomplished this interesting flattery, she gave forth one of those purrings by which our cats express their pleasure; but this murmur issued from a throat so powerful and so deep, that it resounded through the cave like the last vibrations of an organ in a church. The man, understanding the importance of his caresses, redoubled them in such a way as to surprise and stupefy his imperious courtesan. When he felt sure of having extinguished the ferocity of his capricious companion, whose hunger had so fortunately been satisfied the day before, he got up to go out of the cave; the panther let him go out, but when he had reached the summit of the hill she sprang with the lightness of a sparrow hopping from twig to twig, and rubbed herself against his legs, putting up her back after the manner of all the race of cats. Then regarding her guest with eyes whose glare had softened a little, she gave vent to that wild cry which naturalists compare to the grating of a saw.

"She is exacting," said the Frenchman, smilingly.

He was bold enough to play with her ears; he caressed her belly and scratched her head as hard as he could.

When he saw that he was successful, he tickled her skull with the point of his dagger, watching for the right moment to kill her, but the hardness of her bones made him tremble for his success.

The sultana of the desert showed herself gracious to her slave; she lifted her head, stretched out her neck, and manifested her delight by the tranquillity of her attitude. It suddenly occurred to the soldier that to kill this savage princess with one blow he must poignard her in the throat.

He raised the blade, when the panther, satisfied no doubt, laid herself gracefully at his feet, and cast up at him glances in which, in spite of their natural fierceness, was mingled confusedly a kind of good-will. The poor Provençal ate his dates, leaning against one of the palm trees, and casting his eyes alternately on the desert in quest of some liberator and on his terrible companion to watch her uncertain clemency.

The panther looked at the place where the date stones fell, and every time that he threw one down her eyes expressed an incredible mistrust.

She examined the man with an almost commercial prudence. However, this examination was favorable to him, for when he had finished his meager meal she licked his boots with her powerful rough tongue, brushing off with marvellous skill the dust gathered in the creases.

"Ah, but when she's really hungry!" thought the Frenchman. In spite of the shudder this thought caused him, the soldier began to measure curiously the proportions of the panther, certainly one of the most splendid specimens of its race. She was three feet high and four feet long without counting her tail; this powerful weapon, rounded like a cudgel, was nearly three feet long. The head, large as that of a lioness, was distinguished by a rare expression of refinement. The cold cruelty of a tiger was dominant, it was true, but there was also a vague resemblance to the face of a sensual woman. Indeed, the face of this solitary queen had something of the gaiety of a drunken Nero: she had satiated herself with blood, and she wanted to play.

The soldier tried if he might walk up and down, and the panther left him free, contenting herself with following him with her eyes, less like a faithful dog than a big Angora cat, observing everything, and every movement of her master.

When he looked around, he saw, by the spring, the remains of his horse; the panther had dragged the carcass all that way; about two-thirds of it had been devoured already. The sight reassured him.

It was easy to explain the panther's absence, and the respect she had had for him while he slept. The first piece of good luck emboldened him to tempt the future, and he conceived the wild hope of continuing on good terms with the panther during the entire day, neglecting no means of taming her, and remaining in her good graces.

He returned to her, and had the unspeakable joy of seeing her wag her tail with an almost imperceptible movement at his approach. He sat down then, without fear, by her side, and they began to play together; he took her paws and muzzle, pulled her ears, rolled her over on her back, stroked her warm, delicate flanks. She let him do whatever he liked, and when he began to stroke the hair on her feet she drew her claws in carefully.

The man, keeping the dagger in one hand, thought to plunge it into the belly of the too-confiding panther, but he was afraid that he would be immediately strangled in her last conclusive struggle; besides, he felt in his heart a sort of remorse which bid him respect a creature that had done him no harm. He seemed to have found a friend, in a boundless desert; half unconsciously he thought of his first sweetheart, whom he had nicknamed "Mignonne" by way of contrast, because she was so atrociously jealous that all the time of their love he was in fear of the knife with which she had always threatened him.

This memory of his early days suggested to him the idea of making the young panther answer to this name, now that he began to admire with less terror her swiftness, suppleness, and softness. Toward the end of the day he had familiarized himself with his perilous position; he now almost like the painfulness of it. At last his companion had got into the habit of looking up at him whenever he cried in a falsetto voice, "Mignonne."

At the setting of the sun Mignonne gave, several times running, a profound melancholy cry. "She's been well brought up," said the light-hearted soldier; "she says her prayers." But this mental joke only occurred to him when he noticed what a pacific attitude his companion remained in."Come, ma petite blonde, I'll let you go to bed first," he said to her, counting on the activity of his own legs to run away as quickly as possible, directly she was asleep, and seek another shelter for the night.

The soldier waited with impatience the hour of his flight, and when it had arrived he walked vigorously in the direction of the Nile; but hardly had he made a quarter of a league in the sand when he heard the panther bounding after him, crying with that saw-like cry more dreadful even than the sound of her leaping.

"Ah!" he said, "then she's taken a fancy to me; she has never met any one before, and it is really quite flattering to have her first love." That instant the man fell into one of those movable quicksands so terrible to travellers and from which it is impossible to save oneself. Feeling himself caught, he gave a shriek of alarm; the panther seized him with her teeth by the collar, and, springing vigorously backward, drew him as if by magic out of the whirling sand.

"Ah, Mignonne!" cried the soldier, caressing her enthusiastically; "we're bound together for life and death—but no jokes, mind!" and he retraced his steps.

From that time the desert seemed inhabited. It contained a being to whom the man could talk, and whose ferocity was rendered gentle by him, though he could not explain to himself the reason for their strange friendship. Great as was the soldier's desire to stay upon guard, he slept.

On awakening he could not find Mignonne; he mounted the hill, and in the distance saw her springing toward him after the habit of these animals, who cannot run on account of the extreme flexibility of the vertebral column. Mignonne arrived, her jaws covered with blood; she received the wonted caress of her companion, showing with much purring how happy it made her. Her eyes, full of languor, turned still more gently than the day before toward the Provençal who talked to her as one would to a tame animal.

"Ah! Mademoiselle, you are a nice girl, aren't you? Just look at that! so we like to be made much of, don't we? Aren't you ashamed of yourself? So you have been eating some Arab or other, have you? that doesn't matter. They're animals just the same as you are; but don't you take to eating Frenchmen, or I shan't like you any longer."

She played like a dog with its master, letting herself be rolled over, knocked about, and stroked, alternately; sometimes she herself would provoke the soldier, putting up her paw with a soliciting gesture.

Some days passed in this manner. This companionship permitted the Provençal to appreciate the sublime beauty of the desert; now that he had a living thing to think about, alternations of fear and quiet, and plenty to eat, his mind became filled with contrast and his life began to be diversified.

Solitude revealed to him all her secrets, and enveloped him in her delights. He discovered in the rising and setting of the sun sights unknown to the world. He knew what it was to tremble when he heard over his head the hiss of a bird's wing, so rarely did they pass, or when he saw the clouds, changing and many-colored travellers, melt one into another. He studied in the night time the effect of the moon upon the ocean of sand, where the simoom made waves swift of movement and rapid in their change. He lived the life of the Eastern day, marvelling at its wonderful pomp; then, after having revelled in the sight of a hurricane over the plain where the whirling sands made red, dry mists and death-bearing clouds, he would welcome the night with joy, for then fell the healthful freshness of the stars, and he listened to imaginary music in the skies. Then solitude taught him to unroll the treasures of dreams. He passed whole hours in remembering mere nothings, and comparing his present life with his past.

At last he grew passionately fond of the panther; for some sort of affection was a necessity.

Whether it was that his will powerfully projected had modified the character of his companion, or whether, because she found abundant food in her predatory excursions in the desert, she respected the man's life, he began to fear for it no longer, seeing her so well tamed.

He devoted the greater part of his time to sleep, but he was obliged to watch like a spider in its web that the moment of his deliverance might not escape him, if any one should pass the line marked by the horizon. He had sacrificed his shirt to make a flag with, which he hung at the top of a palm tree, whose foliage he had torn off. Taught by necessity, he found the means of keeping it spread out, by fastening it with little sticks; for the wind might not be blowing at the moment when the passing traveller was looking through the desert.

It was during the long hours, when he had abandoned hope, that he amused himself with the panther. He had come to learn the different inflections of her voice, the expressions of her eyes; he had studied the capricious patterns of all the rosettes which marked the gold of her robe. Mignonne was not even angry when he took hold of the tuft at the end of her tail to count her rings, those graceful ornaments which glittered in the sun like jewelry. It gave him pleasure to contemplate the supple, fine outlines of her form, the whiteness of her belly, the graceful pose of her head. But it was especially when she was playing that he felt most pleasure in looking at her; the agility and youthful lightness of her movements were a continual surprise to him; he wondered at the supple way in which she jumped and climbed, washed herself and arranged her fur, crouched down and prepared to spring. However rapid her spring might be, however slippery the stone she was on, she would always stop short at the word "Mignonne."

One day, in a bright mid-day sun, an enormous bird coursed through the air. The man left his panther to look at this new guest; but after waiting a moment the deserted sultana growled deeply.

"My goodness! I do believe she's jealous," he cried, seeing her eyes become hard again; "the soul of Virginie has passed into her body; that's certain."

The eagle disappeared into the air, while the soldier admired the curved contour of the panther.

But there was such youth and grace in her form! she was beautiful as a woman! the blond fur of her robe mingled well with the delicate tints of faint white which marked her flanks.

The profuse light cast down by the sun made this living gold, these russet markings, to burn in a way to give them an indefinable attraction.

The man and the panther looked at one another with a look full of meaning; the coquette quivered when she felt her friend stroke her head; her eyes flashed like lightning—then she shut them tightly.

"She has a soul," he said, looking at the stillness of this queen of the sands, golden like them, white like them, solitary and burning like them.

"Well," she said, "I have read your plea in favor of beasts; but how did two so well adapted to understand each other end?"

"Ah, well! you see, they ended as all great passions do end—by a misunderstanding. For some reason *one* suspects the other of treason; they don't come to an explanation through pride, and quarrel and part from sheer obstinacy."

"Yet sometimes at the best moments a single word or a look is enough—but anyhow go on with your story."

"It's horribly difficult, but you will understand, after what the old villain told me over his champagne.

"He said—'I don't know if I hurt her, but she turned round, as if enraged, and with her sharp teeth caught hold of my leg—gently, I daresay; but I, thinking she would devour me, plunged my dagger into her throat. She rolled over, giving a cry that froze my heart; and I saw her dying, still looking at me without anger. I would have given all the world—my cross even, which I had not got then—to have brought her to life again. It was as though I had murdered a real person; and the soldiers who had seen my flag, and were come to my assistance, found me in tears.'

"'Well sir,' he said, after a moment of silence, 'since then I have been in war in Germany, in Spain, in Russia, in France; I've certainly carried my carcass about a good deal, but never have I seen anything like the desert. Ah! yes, it is very beautiful!'

"'What did you feel there?' I asked him.

"'Oh! that can't be described, young man. Besides, I am not always regretting my palm trees and my panther. I should have to be very melancholy for that. In the desert, you see, there is everything, and nothing.'

" 'Yes, but explain——'
" 'Well,' he said, with an impatient gesture, 'it is God without mankind.' "

FOR STUDY, DISCUSSION, AND WRITING

1. What observations about romantic love does this story make?
2. Why does the soldier name the panther Mignonne? In what ways does the panther resemble a woman?
3. Would "A Passion in the Desert" have been as effective if Balzac had substituted a nonfeline animal for the panther?
4. Why do you think Balzac chose to tell this story through a second party, the soldier, rather than presenting it directly as an experience of his own?
5. Why does Balzac probe the thoughts of the soldier but none of the other characters in the story?
6. Why do you think Balzac has the soldier rescued immediately after the death of the panther?
7. Discuss the story's concluding statement about the desert: "It is God without mankind."

IVAN TURGENEV

The Tryst*

I was sitting in a birch grove in autumn, about the middle of September. A fine drizzling rain had been descending ever since dawn, interspersed at times with warm sunshine; the weather was inconstant. Now the sky would be completely veiled in porous white clouds; again, all of a sudden, it would clear up in spots for a moment, and then, from behind the parted thunderclouds, the clear and friendly azure would show itself, like a beautiful eye. I sat, and gazed about me, and listened. The leaves were rustling in a barely audible manner overhead; from their sound alone one could tell what season of the year it was. It was not the cheerful, laughing rustle of springtime, not

*An appointment or meeting, as one made by lovers.

the soft whispering, not the long conversation of summer, not the cold and timid stammering of late autumn, but a barely audible, dreamy chatter. A faint breeze swept feebly across the treetops. The interior of the grove, moist with the rain, kept changing incessantly, according to whether the sun shone forth, or was covered with a cloud; now it was all illuminated, as though everything in it were suddenly smiling; the slender boles of the not too thickly set birches suddenly assumed the tender gleam of white silk, the small leaves which lay on the ground suddenly grew variegated and lighted up with the golden hue of ducats, and the handsome stalks of the tall, curly ferns, already stained with their autumnal hue, like the colour of over-ripe grapes, seemed fairly transparent, as they intertwined interminably and crossed one another before one's eyes; now, of a sudden, everything round about would turn slightly blue: the brilliant hues were extinguished for a moment, the birches stood there all white, devoid of reflections, white as newly fallen snow, which has not yet been touched by the sparkling rays of the winter sun; and the fine rain began stealthily, craftily, to sprinkle and whisper through the forest. The foliage on the trees was still almost entirely green, although it had faded perceptibly; only here and there stood one, some young tree, all scarlet, or all gold, and you should have seen how brilliantly it flamed up in the sun, when the rays gliding and changing, suddenly pierced through the thick network of the slender branches, only just washed clean by the glittering rain. Not a single bird was to be heard; they had all taken refuge, and fallen silent; only now and then did the jeering little voice of the tom-tit ring out like a tiny steel bell. Before I had come to a halt in this birch-forest I and my dog had traversed a grove of lofty aspens. I must confess that I am not particularly fond of that tree, the aspen, with its pale-lilac trunk, and greyish-green, metallic foliage, which it elevates as high aloft as possible, and spreads forth to the air in a trembling fan; I do not like the eternal rocking of its round, dirty leaves, awkwardly fastened to their long stems. It is a fine tree only on some summer evenings when, rising isolated amid a plot of low-growing bushes, it stands directly in the line of the glowing rays of the setting sun, and glistens and quivers from its root to its crest, all deluged with a uniform reddish-yellow stain,—or when, on a bright, windy day, it is all noisily rippling and lisping against the blue sky, and its every leaf, caught in the current, seems to want to wrench itself free, fly off and whirl away into the distance. But, on the whole, I do not like that tree, and therefore, without halting to rest in that grove, I wended my way to the little birch-coppice, nestled down under one small tree, whose boughs began close to the ground, and, consequently, could protect me from the rain, and after having admired the surrounding view, I sank into that untroubled and benignant slumber which is known to sportsmen alone.

I cannot tell how long I slept, but when I opened my eyes,—the whole interior of the forest was filled with sunlight, and in all directions, athwart the joyously rustling foliage, the bright-blue sky seemed to be sparkling: the clouds had vanished, dispersed by the sportive breeze; the weather had cleared, and in the atmosphere was perceptible that peculiar, dry chill which, filling the heart with a sort of sensation of alertness, almost always is the harbinger of a clear evening after a stormy day. I was preparing to rise to my feet, and try my luck again, when suddenly my eyes halted on a motionless human form. I took a more attentive look; it was a young peasant maiden. She was sitting twenty paces distant from me, with her head drooping thoughtfully, and both arms lying idly on her knees; on one of them, which was half bare, lay a thick bunch of field flowers, which went slipping softly down her plaid petticoat at each breath she drew. Her clean white chemise, unbuttoned at the throat and wrists, fell in short, soft folds about her figure: two rows of large yellow pearl-beads depended from her neck upon her breast. She was very comely. Her thick, fair hair, of a fine ash-blond hue, fell in two carefully brushed semi-circles from beneath a narrow, red band which was pulled down almost on her very brow, as white as ivory; the rest of her face was slightly sunburned to that golden tint which only a fine skin assumes. I could not see her eyes—she did not raise them; but I did see her high, slender eyebrows, her long eyelashes; they were moist, and on one of her cheeks there glittered in the sunlight the dried trace of a tear, that had stopped short close to her lips, which had grown slightly pale. Her whole little head was extremely charming; even her rather thick and rounded nose did not spoil it. I was particularly pleased with the expression of her face: it was so simple and gentle, so sad and so full of childish surprise at its own sadness. She was evidently waiting for some one; something crackled faintly in the forest. She immediately raised her head and looked about her; in the transparent shadow her eyes flashed swiftly before me—large, clear, timorous eyes, like those of a doe. She listened for several moments, without taking her widely opened eyes from the spot where the faint noise had resounded, sighed, gently turned away her head, bent down still lower than before, and began slowly to sort over her flowers. Her eyelids reddened, her lips moved bitterly, and a fresh tear rolled from beneath her thick eyelashes, halting and glittering radiantly on her cheek. Quite a long time passed in this manner; the poor girl did not stir,—only now and then she moved her hands about and listened, listened still. . . . Again something made a noise in the forest,—she gave a start. The noise did not cease, grew more distinct, drew nearer; at last brisk, decided footsteps made themselves audible. She drew herself up, and seemed to be frightened; her attentive glance wavered, with expectation, apparently. A man's figure flitted swiftly through the thicket. She glanced at it, suddenly flushed up, smiled joyously and happily, tried to rise to her feet, and immediately bent clear over once more, grew pale and confused,—and only raised her palpitating, almost beseeching glance to the approaching man when the latter had come to a halt by her side.

I gazed at him with interest from my ambush. I must confess that he did not produce a pleasant impression on me. From all the signs, he was the petted valet of a young, wealthy gentleman. His clothing betrayed pretensions to taste and foppish carelessness: he wore a short overcoat of bronze hue, probably the former property of his master, buttoned to the throat, a small pink neckerchief with lilac ends, and a black velvet cap, with gold galloon, pulled down to his very eyebrows. The round collar of his white shirt propped up his ears, and ruthlessly sawed his cheeks, and his starched cuffs covered the whole of his hands down to his red, crooked fingers, adorned with gold and silver rings with turquoise forget-me-nots. His fresh, rosy, bold face belonged to the category of visages which, so far as I have been able to observe, almost always irritate men and, unfortunately, very often please women. He was, obviously, trying to impart to his somewhat coarse features a scornful and bored expression; he kept incessantly screwing up his little milky-grey eyes, which were small enough without that, knitting his brows, drawing down the corners of his lips, constrainedly yawning, and with careless, although not quite skilful ease of manner he now adjusted with his hand his sandy, dashingly upturned temple-curls, now plucked at the small yellow hairs which stuck out on his thick upper lip,—in a word, he put on intolerable airs. He began to put on airs as soon as he caught sight of the young peasant girl who was waiting for him; slowly, with a swaggering stride, he approached her, stood for a moment, shrugged his shoulders, thrust both hands into the pockets of his coat, and, barely vouchsafing the poor girl a fugitive and indifferent glance, he dropped down on the ground.

"Well,"—he began, continuing to gaze off somewhere to one side, dangling his foot and yawning:—"hast thou been here long?"

The girl could not answer him at once.

"A long time, sir, Viktór Alexándrovitch,"—she said at last, in a barely audible voice.

"Ah!" (He removed his cap, passed his hand majestically over his thick, tightly curled hair, which began almost at his very eyebrows, and after glancing around him with dignity, he carefully covered his precious head again.) "Why, I came pretty near forgetting all about it. And then, there was the rain, you know!" (He yawned again.)—"I have a lot of things to do: I can't attend to them all, and he scolds into the bargain. To-morrow we are going away. . . ."

"To-morrow?"—ejaculated the girl, and fixed a frightened glance on him.

"Yes, to-morrow. . . . Come, come, come, pray,"—he interposed hastily and with vexation, seeing that she was beginning to tremble, and had softly dropped her head:—"Pray, don't cry, Akulína. Thou knowest that I cannot endure that." (And he wrinkled up his stubby nose.)—"If thou dost, I'll go away instantly. . . . How stupid it is to whimper!"

"Well, I won't, I won't,"—hastily articulated Akulína, swallowing her tears with an effort—"So you are going away to-morrow?"— she added after a short silence:—"When will God grant me to see you again, Viktór Alexándrovitch?"

"We shall see each other again, we shall see each other again. If not next year, then later on. I think the master intends to enter the government service in Petersburg,"—he went on, uttering his words carelessly and somewhat through his nose:—"and perhaps we shall go abroad."

"You will forget me, Viktór Alexándrovitch,"—said Akulína sadly.

"No, why should I? I will not forget thee: only, thou must be sensible, don't

make a fool of thyself, heed thy father. . . . And I won't forget thee—no-o-o."
(And he calmly stretched himself and yawned again.)

"Do not forget me, Viktór Alexándrovitch," she continued, in a tone of
entreaty. "I think that I have loved you to such a degree, it always seems as
though for you, I would . . . you say, I must obey my father, Viktór Alexándrovitch. . . . But how am I to obey my father. . . ."

"But why not?" (He uttered these words as though from his stomach, as he
lay on his back, with his arms under his head.)

"But what do you mean, Viktór Alexándrovitch . . . you know yourself. . . ."
She stopped short, Viktór toyed with the steel chain of his watch.

"Thou art not a stupid girl, Akulína,"—he began at last:—"therefore, don't
talk nonsense. I desire thy welfare, dost understand me? Of course, thou art
not stupid, not a regular peasant, so to speak; and thy mother also was not
always a peasant. All the same, thou hast no education—so thou must obey
when people give thee orders."

"But I'm afraid, Viktór Alexándrovitch."

"I-i, what nonsense, my dear creature! What hast thou to be afraid of?
What's that thou hast there,"—he added, moving toward her:—"flowers?"

"Yes,"—replied Akulína, dejectedly.—"I have been plucking some wild
tansy,"—she went on, after a brief pause:—" 'T is good for the calves. And
this here is a good remedy for scrofula. See, what a wonderfully beautiful
flower! I have never seen such a beautiful flower in my life. Here are forget-
me-nots, and here is a violet. . . . And this, here, I got for you,"—she added,
drawing from beneath the yellow tansy a small bunch of blue corn-flowers,
bound together with a slender blade of grass:—"Will you take them?"

Viktór languidly put out his hand, took the flowers, smelled of them carelessly, and began to twist them about in his fingers, staring pompously upward. Akulína glanced at him. . . . In her sorrowful gaze there was a great deal
of devotion, of adoring submission to him. And she was afraid of him also,
and did not dare to cry, and was bidding him farewell and gloating upon him
for the last time; but he lay there, sprawling out like a sultan, and tolerated
her adoration with magnanimous patience and condescension. I must confess,
that I gazed with indignation at his red face, whereon, athwart the feignedly-
scornful indifference, there peered forth satisfied, satiated self-conceit. Akulína was so fine at that moment: her whole soul opened confidingly, passionately before him, reached out to him, fawned upon him, and he . . . he
dropped the corn-flowers on the grass, pulled a round monocle in a bronze
setting from the side-pocket of his paletot, and began to stick it into his eye;
but try as he would to hold it fast with his frowning brows, the monocle kept
tumbling out and falling into his hand.

"What is that?"—inquired the amazed Akulína at last.

"A lorgnette,"—he replied pompously.

"What is it for?"

"To see better with."

"Pray let me see it."

Viktór frowned, but gave her the monocle.

"Look out, see that thou dost not break it."

"Never fear, I won't break it." (She raised it timidly to her eye.) "I can see nothing,"—she said innocently.

"Why, pucker up thine eye,"—he retorted in the tone of a displeased preceptor. (She screwed up the eye in front of which she was holding the glass.)

"Not that one, not that one, the other one!"—shouted Viktór, and without giving her a chance to repair her mistake, he snatched the lorgnette away from her.

Akulína blushed scarlet, smiled faintly, and turned away.

"Evidently, it is not suited to the like of me,"—said she.

"I should say not!"

The poor girl made no reply, and sighed deeply.

"Akh, Viktór Alexándrovitch; what shall I do without you!"—she suddenly said. Viktór wiped the lorgnette with the tail of his coat, and put it back in his pocket.

"Yes, yes,"—he said at last:—"thou wilt really find it very hard at first." (He patted her condescendingly on the shoulder; she softly removed his hand from her shoulder, and kissed it timidly.)—"Well, yes, yes, thou really art a good girl,"—he went on, with a conceited smile; "but what can one do? Judge for thyself! the master and I cannot remain here; winter will soon be here, and the country in winter—thou knowest it thyself—is simply vile. 'Tis quite another matter in Petersburg! There are simply such marvels there as thou, silly, canst not even imagine in thy dreams. Such houses, such streets, and society, culture—simply astounding! . . ." (Akulína listened to him with devouring attention, her lips slightly parted, like those of a child.)—"But what am I telling thee all this for?"—he added, turning over on the ground. "Of course, thou canst not understand!"

"Why not, Viktór Alexándrovitch? I have understood—I have understood everything."

"Did any one ever see such a girl!"

Akulína dropped her eyes.

"You did not use to talk to me formerly in that way, Viktór Alexándrovitch,"—she said, without raising her eyes.

"Formerly? . . . formerly! Just see there, now! . . . Formerly!"—he remarked, as though vexed.

Both maintained silence for a while.

"But I must be off,"—said Viktór, and began to raise himself on his elbow. . . .

"Wait a little longer,"—articulated Akulína, in a beseeching voice.

"What's the use of waiting? . . . I have already bade thee farewell, haven't I?"

"Wait,"—repeated Akulína.

Viktór stretched himself out again, and began to whistle. Still Akulína never took her eyes from him. I could perceive that she had grown somewhat agitated; her lips were twitching, her pale cheeks had taken on a faint flush. . . .

"Viktór Alexándrovitch,"—she said at last, in a broken voice:—" 't is sinful of you . . . sinful of you, Viktór Alexándrovitch: by heaven, it is!"

"What's sinful?"—he asked, knitting his brows, and he half rose and turned toward her.

" 'T is sinful, Viktór Alexándrovitch. You might at least speak a kind word to me at parting; you might at least say one little word to me, an unhappy orphan. . . ."

"But what am I to say to thee?"

"I don't know; you know that better than I do, Viktór Alexándrovitch. Here you are going away, and not a single word. . . . How have I deserved such treatment?"

"What a queer creature thou art! What can I do?"

"You might say one little word. . . ."

"Come, thou'rt wound up to say the same thing over and over,"—he said testily, and rose to his feet.

"Don't be angry, Viktór Alexándrovitch,"—she added hurriedly, hardly able to repress her tears.

"I'm not angry, only thou art so stupid. . . . What is it thou wantest? I can't marry thee, can I? I can't, can I? Well, then, what is it thou dost want? What?" (He turned his face toward her, as though awaiting an answer, and spread his fingers far apart.)

"I want nothing . . . nothing,"—she replied, stammering, and barely venturing to stretch out to him her trembling arms:—"but yet, if you would say only one little word in farewell. . . ."

And the tears streamed down her face in a torrent.

"Well, there she goes! She's begun to cry," said Viktór coldly, pulling his cap forward over his eyes.

"I want nothing,"—she went on, sobbing, and covering her face with both hands;—"but how do I stand now with my family, what is my position? and what will happen to me, what will become of me, unhappy one? They will marry off the poor deserted one to a man she does not love. . . . Woe is me!"

"O, go on, go on,"—muttered Viktór in an undertone, shifting from foot to foot where he stood.

"And if he would say only one word, just one . . . such as: 'Akulína, I. . . .' "

Sudden sobs, which rent her breast, prevented her finishing her sentence—she fell face downward on the grass, and wept bitterly, bitterly. . . . Her whole body was convulsively agitated, the back of her neck fairly heaved. . . . Her long-suppressed woe had burst forth, at last, in a flood. Viktór stood over her, stood there a while, and shrugged his shoulders, then wheeled round, and marched off with long strides.

Several minutes elapsed. . . . She quieted down, raised her head, glanced around, and clasped her hands; she tried to run after him, but her limbs gave way under her—she fell on her knees. . . . I could not restrain myself, and rushed to her; but no sooner had she glanced at me than strength from some source made its appearance,—she rose to her feet with a faint shriek, and vanished behind the trees, leaving her flowers scattered on the ground.

I stood there for a while, picked up the bunch of corn-flowers, and emerged from the grove into the fields. The sun hung low in the palely-clear sky, its rays, too, seemed to have grown pallid, somehow, and cold; they did not beam, they disseminated an even, almost watery light. Not more than half an hour remained before night-fall, and the sunset glow was only just beginning to kindle. A gusty breeze dashed swiftly to meet me across the yellow, dried-up stubble-field; small, warped leaves rose hastily before it, and darted past, across the road, along the edge of the woods; the side of the grove, turned toward the field like a wall, was all quivering and sparkling with a drizzling glitter, distinct but not brilliant; on the reddish turf, on the blades of grass, on the straws, everywhere around, gleamed and undulated the innumerable threads of autumnal spiders' webs. I halted. . . . I felt sad: athwart the cheerful though chilly smile of fading nature, the mournful terror of not far-distant winter seemed to be creeping up. High above me, cleaving the air heavily and sharply with its wings, a cautious raven flew past, cast a sidelong glance at me, soared aloft and, floating on outstretched wings, disappeared behind the forest, croaking spasmodically; a large flock of pigeons fluttered sharply from the threshing-floor and, suddenly rising in a cloud, eagerly dispersed over the fields—a sign of autumn! Some one was driving past behind the bare hill, his empty cart rumbling loudly. . . .

I returned home; but the image of poor Akulína did not leave my mind for a long time, and her corn-flowers, long since withered, I have preserved to this day. . . .

FOR STUDY, DISCUSSION, AND WRITING

1. What role does the narrator play in the story?
2. What symbolic purpose do you see in the lengthy descriptions of the birch and aspen trees?
3. What do we learn about the characters of Alexándrovitch and Akulína from the way they dress?
4. In what ways does Alexándrovitch resemble the aspen tree?
5. Compare the descriptions of Akulína's and Alexándrovitch's eyes. What do these descriptions reveal about the character of each?
6. At several points in the story, Turgenev makes use of metallic terms in

describing Alexándrovitch. In light of Alexándrovitch's reason for meeting with Akulína, why do you think Turgenev employed these terms?

7. How does Akulína show her love for Alexándrovitch?

8. At one point, Akulína looks through Alexándrovitch's monocle but says
she can't see anything. What symbolic significance can you attribute to
this remark? How clever is Alexándrovitch with the monocle?

9. Compare the point of view employed in this story with that used in Doris
Lessing's "The Nuisance."

GUY DE MAUPASSANT

The Piece of String

It was market-day, and over all the roads around Goderville the peasants and their wives were coming towards the town. The men walked easily,
lurching the whole body forward at every step. Their long legs were twisted
and deformed by the slow, painful labors of the country:—by bending over to
plough, which is what also makes their left shoulders too high and their
figures crooked; and by reaping corn, which obliges them for steadiness' sake
to spread their knees too wide. Their starched blue blouses, shining as though
varnished, ornamented at collar and cuffs with little patterns of white stitch-
work, and blown up big around their bony bodies, seemed exactly like balloons about to soar, but putting forth a head, two arms, and two feet.

Some of these fellows dragged a cow or a calf at the end of a rope. And just
behind the animal, beating it over the back with a leaf-covered branch to
hasten its pace, went their wives, carrying large baskets from which came
forth the heads of chickens or the heads of ducks. These women walked with
steps far shorter and quicker than the men; their figures, withered and upright, were adorned with scanty little shawls pinned over their flat bosoms;
and they enveloped their heads each in a white cloth, close fastened round the
hair and surmounted by a cap.

Now a char-à-banc passed by, drawn by a jerky-paced nag. It shook up
strangely the two men on the seat. And the woman at the bottom of the cart
held fast to its sides to lessen the hard joltings.

In the market-place at Goderville was a great crowd, a mingled multitude of
men and beasts. The horns of cattle, the high and long-napped hats of wealthy
peasants, the head-dresses of the women, came to the surface of that sea. And
voices clamorous, sharp, shrill, made a continuous and savage din. Above it a

huge burst of laughter from the sturdy lungs of a merry yokel would sometimes sound, and sometimes a long bellow from a cow tied fast to the wall of
a house.

It all smelled of the stable, of milk, of hay, and of perspiration, giving off
that half-human, half-animal odor which is peculiar to the men of the fields.

Maître Hauchecorne, of Bréauté, had just arrived at Goderville, and was
taking his way towards the square, when he perceived on the ground a little
piece of string. Maître Hauchecorne, economical, like all true Normans, reflected that everything was worth picking up which could be of any use; and
he stooped down—but painfully, because he suffered from rheumatism. He
took the bit of thin cord from the ground, and was carefully preparing to roll
it up when he saw Maître Malandain, the harness-maker, on his door-step,
looking at him. They had once had a quarrel about a halter, and they had
remained angry, bearing malice on both sides. Maître Hauchecorne was overcome with a sort of shame at being seen by his enemy looking in the dirt so
for a bit of string. He quickly hid his find beneath his blouse; then in the
pocket of his breeches; then pretended to be still looking for something on the
ground which he did not discover; and at last went off towards the market-
place, with his head bent forward, and a body almost doubled in two by
rheumatic pains.

He lost himself immediately in the crowd, which was clamorous, slow, and
agitated by interminable bargains. The peasants examined the cows, went off,
came back, always in great perplexity and fear of being cheated, never quite
daring to decide, spying at the eye of the seller, trying ceaselessly to discover
the tricks of the man and the defect in the beast.

The women, having placed their great baskets at their feet, had pulled out
the poultry, which lay upon the ground, tied by the legs, with eyes scared,
with combs scarlet.

They listened to propositions, maintaining their prices, with a dry manner,
with an impassible face; or, suddenly, perhaps, deciding to take the lower
price which was offered, they cried out to the customer, who was departing
slowly:

"All right, I'll let you have them, Maît' Anthime."

Then, little by little, the square became empty, and when the *Angelus* struck
mid-day those who lived at a distance poured into the inns.

At Jourdain's the great room was filled with eaters, just as the vast court was
filled with vehicles of every sort—wagons, gigs, char-à-bancs, tilburys, tilt-
carts which have no name, yellow with mud, misshapen, pieced together,
raising their shafts to heaven like two arms, or it may be with their nose in the
dirt and their rear in the air.

Just opposite to where the diners were at table the huge fireplace, full of
clear flame, threw a lively heat on the backs of those who sat along the right.
Three spits were turning, loaded with chickens, with pigeons, and with joints
of mutton; and a delectable odor of roast meat, and of gravy gushing over

crisp brown skin, took wing from the hearth, kindled merriment, caused mouths to water.

All the aristocracy of the plough were eating there, at Maît' Jourdain's, the innkeeper's, a dealer in horses also, and a sharp fellow who had made a pretty penny in his day.

The dishes were passed round, were emptied, with jugs of yellow cider. Every one told of his affairs, of his purchases and his sales. They asked news about the crops. The weather was good for green stuffs, but a little wet for wheat.

All of a sudden the drum rolled in the court before the house. Every one, except some of the most indifferent, was on his feet at once, and ran to the door, to the windows, with his mouth still full and his napkin in his hand.

When the public crier had finished his tattoo he called forth in a jerky voice, making his pauses out of time:

"Be it known to the inhabitants of Goderville, and in general to all—persons present at the market, that there has been lost this morning, on the Beuzeville road, between—nine and ten o'clock, a pocket-book of black leather, containing five hundred francs and business papers. You are requested to return it—to the mayor's office, at once, or to Maître Fortuné Houlbrèque, of Manneville. There will be twenty francs reward."

Then the man departed. They heard once more at a distance the dull beatings on the drum and the faint voice of the crier.

Then they began to talk of this event, reckoning up the chances which Maître Houlbrèque had of finding or not finding his pocket-book again.

And the meal went on.

They were finishing their coffee when the corporal of gendarmes appeared on the threshold.

He asked:

"Is Maître Hauchecorne, of Bréauté, here?"

Maître Hauchecorne, seated at the other end of the table, answered:

"Here I am."

And the corporal resumed:

"Maître Hauchecorne, will you have the kindness to come with me to the mayor's office? M. le Maire would like to speak to you."

The peasant, surprised and uneasy, gulped down his little glass of cognac, got up, and, even worse bent over than in the morning, since the first steps after a rest were always particularly difficult, started off, repeating:

"Here I am, here I am."

And he followed the corporal.

The mayor was waiting for him, seated in an arm-chair. He was the notary of the place, a tall, grave man of pompous speech.

"Maître Hauchecorne," said he, "this morning, on the Beuzeville road, you were seen to pick up the pocket-book lost by Maître Houlbrèque, of Manneville."

The countryman, speechless, regarded the mayor, frightened already by this suspicion which rested on him he knew not why.

"I, I picked up that pocket-book?"

"Yes, you."

"I swear I didn't even know nothing about it at all."

"You were seen."

"They saw me, me? Who is that who saw me?"

"M. Malandain, the harness-maker."

Then the old man remembered, understood, and, reddening with anger:

"Ah! he saw me, did he, the rascal? He saw me picking up this string here, M'sieu' le Maire."

And, fumbling at the bottom of his pocket, he pulled out of it the little end of string.

But the mayor incredulously shook his head:

"You will not make me believe, Maître Hauchecorne, that M. Malandain, who is a man worthy of credit, has mistaken this string for a pocket-book."

The peasant, furious, raised his hand and spit as if to attest his good faith, repeating:

"For all that, it is the truth of the good God, the blessed truth, M'sieu' le Maire. There! on my soul and my salvation I repeat it."

The mayor continued:

"After having picked up the thing in question, you even looked for some time in the mud to see if a piece of money had not dropped out of it."

The good man was suffocated with indignation and with fear:

"If they can say!—if they can say . . . such lies as that to slander an honest man! If they can say!—"

He might protest, he was not believed.

He was confronted with M. Malandain, who repeated and sustained his testimony. They abused one another for an hour. At his own request Maître Hauchecorne was searched. Nothing was found upon him.

At last, the mayor, much perplexed, sent him away, warning him that he would inform the public prosecutor, and ask for orders.

The news had spread. When he left the mayor's office, the old man was surrounded, interrogated with a curiosity which was serious or mocking as the case might be, but into which no indignation entered. And he began to tell the story of the string. They did not believe him. They laughed.

He passed on, button-holed by every one, himself button-holing his acquaintances, beginning over and over again his tale and his protestations, showing his pockets turned inside out to prove that he had nothing.

They said to him:

"You old rogue, va!"

And he grew angry, exasperated, feverish, in despair at not being believed, and always telling his story.

The night came. It was time to go home. He set out with three of his neighbors, to whom he pointed out the place where he had picked up the end of string; and all the way he talked of his adventure.

That evening he made the round in the village of Bréauté, so as to tell every one. He met only unbelievers.

He was ill of it all night long.

The next day, about one in the afternoon, Marius Paumelle, a farm hand of Maître Breton, the market-gardener at Ymauville, returned the pocket-book and its contents to Maître Houlbrèque, of Manneville.

This man said, indeed, that he had found it on the road; but not knowing how to read, he had carried it home and given it to his master.

The news spread to the environs. Maître Hauchecorne was informed. He put himself at once upon the go, and began to relate his story as completed by the *dénouement*. He triumphed.

"What grieved me," said he, "was not the thing itself, do you understand; but it was the lies. There's nothing does you so much harm as being in disgrace for lying."

All day he talked of his adventure, he told it on the roads to the people who passed; at the cabaret to the people who drank; and the next Sunday, when they came out of church. He even stopped strangers to tell them about it. He was easy, now, and yet something worried him without his knowing exactly what it was. People had a joking manner while they listened. They did not seem convinced. He seemed to feel their tittle-tattle behind his back.

On Tuesday of the next week he went to market at Goderville, prompted entirely by the need of telling his story.

Malandain, standing on his door-step, began to laugh as he saw him pass. Why?

He accosted a farmer of Criquetot, who did not let him finish, and, giving him a punch in the pit of his stomach, cried in his face:

"Oh you great rogue, *va!*" Then turned his heel upon him.

Maître Hauchecorne remained speechless, and grew more and more uneasy. Why had they called him "great rogue"?

When seated at table in Jourdain's tavern he began again to explain the whole affair.

A horse-dealer of Montivilliers shouted at him:

"Get out, get out you old scamp; I know all about your string!"

Hauchecorne stammered:

"But since they found it again, the pocket-book!"

But the other continued:

"Hold your tongue, daddy; there's one who finds it and there's another who returns it. And no one the wiser."

The peasant was choked. He understood at last. They accused him of having had the pocket-book brought back by an accomplice, by a confederate.

He tried to protest. The whole table began to laugh.

He could not finish his dinner, and went away amid a chorus of jeers.

He went home, ashamed and indignant, choked with rage, with confusion, the more cast-down since from his Norman cunning, he was, perhaps, capable of having done what they accused him of, and even of boasting of it as a good trick. His innocence dimly seemed to him impossible to prove, his craftiness being so well known. And he felt himself struck to the heart by the injustice of the suspicion.

Then he began anew to tell of his adventure, lengthening his recital every day, each time adding new proofs, more energetic protestations, and more solemn oaths which he thought of, which he prepared in his hours of solitude, his mind being entirely occupied by the story of the string. The more complicated his defence, the more artful his arguments, the less he was believed.

"Those are liar's proofs," they said behind his back.

He felt this; it preyed upon his heart. He exhausted himself in useless efforts.

He was visibly wasting away.

The jokers now made him tell the story of "The Piece of String" to amuse them, just as you make a soldier who has been on a campaign tell his story of the battle. His mind, struck at the root, grew weak.

About the end of December he took to his bed.

He died early in January, and, in the delirium of the death-agony, he protested his innocence, repeating:

"A little bit of string—a little bit of string—see, here it is, M'sieu' le Maire."

FOR STUDY, DISCUSSION, AND WRITING

1. What is the story's precipitating incident?
2. How do the events of "The Piece of String" reflect Guy de Maupassant's pessimistic view of human nature?
3. One of the early paragraphs of the story deals with the thought processes of the peasants as they bargain with one another. What narrative purpose is served by this paragraph?
4. Why does Hauchecorne obsessively continue to proclaim his innocence even after he has been officially cleared of any wrongdoing?
5. Why does Maître Malandain charge Hauchecorne with finding and keeping the pocket-book?
6. Why do the other peasants persist in disbelieving that Hauchecorne is innocent even after the pocket-book has been returned?
7. Clearly, this is a story with a single dominating symbol, the piece of string. What do you think this object symbolizes?

ANTON CHEKHOV

Gooseberries*

The sky had been covered with rain-clouds ever since the early morning; it was a still day, cool and dull, one of those misty days when the clouds have long been lowering overhead and you keep thinking it is just going to rain, and the rain holds off. Ivan Ivanich, the veterinary surgeon, and Burkin, the high-school teacher, had walked till they were tired, and the way over the fields seemed endless to them. Far ahead they could just make out the windmill of the village of Mironositskoye, and what looked like a range of low hills at the right extending well beyond the village, and they both knew that this range was really the bank of the river, and that further on were meadows, green willow-trees, country-estates; if they were on top of these hills, they knew they would see the same boundless fields and telegraph-posts, and the train, like a crawling caterpillar in the distance, while in fine weather even the town would be visible. On this still day, when the whole of nature seemed kindly and pensive, Ivan Ivanich and Burkin felt a surge of love for this plain, and thought how vast and beautiful their country was.

"The last time we stayed in Elder Prokofy's hut," said Burkin, "you said you had a story to tell me."

"Yes. I wanted to tell you the story of my brother."

Ivan Ivanich took a deep breath and lighted his pipe as a preliminary to his narrative, but just then the rain came. Five minutes later it was coming down in torrents and nobody could say when it would stop. Ivan Ivanich and Burkin stood still, lost in thought. The dogs, already soaked, stood with drooping tails, gazing at them wistfully.

"We must try and find shelter," said Burkin. "Let's go to Alekhin's. It's quite near."

"Come on, then."

They turned aside and walked straight across the newly reaped field, veering to the right till they came to a road. Very soon poplars, an orchard, and the red roofs of barns came into sight. The surface of a river gleamed, and they had a view of an extensive reach of water, a windmill and a whitewashed bathing-shed. This was Sofyino, where Alekhin lived.

The mill was working, and the noise made by its sails drowned the sound of the rain; the whole dam trembled. Horses, soaking wet, were standing near some carts, their heads drooping, and people were moving about with sacks over their heads and shoulders. It was wet, muddy, bleak, and the water looked cold and sinister. Ivan Ivanich and Burkin were already experiencing

*The fruit of a shrub of the rose family.

the misery of dampness, dirt, physical discomfort, their boots were caked with mud, and when, having passed the mill-dam, they took the upward path to the landowner's barns, they fell silent, as if vexed with one another.

The sound of winnowing came from one of the barns; the door was open, and clouds of dust issued from it. Standing in the door-way was Alekhin himself, a stout man of some forty years, with longish hair, looking more like a professor or an artist than a landed proprietor. He was wearing a white shirt, greatly in need of washing, belted with a piece of string, and long drawers with no trousers over them. His boots, too, were caked with mud and straw. His eyes and nose were ringed with dust. He recognized Ivan Ivanich and Burkin, and seemed glad to see them.

"Go up to the house, gentlemen," he said, smiling. "I'll be with you in a minute."

It was a large two-storey house. Alekhin occupied the ground floor, two rooms with vaulted ceilings and tiny windows, where the stewards had lived formerly. They were poorly furnished, and smelled of rye-bread, cheap vodka, and harness. He hardly ever went into the upstairs rooms, excepting when he had guests. Ivan Ivanich and Burkin were met by a maid-servant, a young woman of such beauty that they stood still involuntarily and exchanged glances.

"You have no idea how glad I am to see you here, dear friends," said Alekhin, overtaking them in the hall. "It's quite a surprise! Pelageya," he said, turning to the maid, "find the gentlemen a change of clothes. And I might as well change, myself. But I must have a wash first, for I don't believe I've had a bath since the spring. Wouldn't you like to go and have a bathe while they get things ready here?"

The beauteous Pelageya, looking very soft and delicate, brought them towels and soap, and Alekhin and his guests set off for the bathing-house.

"Yes, it's a long time since I had a wash," he said, taking off his clothes. "As you see I have a nice bathing-place, my father had it built, but somehow I never seem to get time to wash."

He sat on the step, soaping his long locks and his neck, and all round him the water was brown.

"Yes, you certainly . . ." remarked Ivan Ivanich, with a significant glance at his host's head.

"It's a long time since I had a wash . . ." repeated Alekhin, somewhat abashed, and he soaped himself again, and now the water was dark-blue, like ink.

Ivan Ivanich emerged from the shed, splashed noisily into the water, and began swimming beneath the rain, spreading his arms wide, making waves all round him, and the white water-lilies rocked on the waves he made. He swam into the very middle of the river and then dived, a moment later came up at another place and swam further, diving constantly, and trying to touch the bottom. "Ah, my God," he kept exclaiming in his enjoyment. "Ah, my God. . . ." He swam up to the mill, had a little talk with some peasants there and turned back, but when he got to the middle of the river, he floated, holding his face up to the rain. Burkin and Alekhin were dressed and ready to go, but he went on swimming and diving.

"God! God!" he kept exclaiming. "Dear God!"

"Come out!" Burkin shouted to him.

They went back to the house. And only after the lamp was lit in the great drawing-room on the upper floor, and Burkin and Ivan Ivanich, in silk dressing-gowns and warm slippers, were seated in arm-chairs, while Alekhin, washed and combed, paced the room in his new frock-coat, enjoying the warmth, the cleanliness, his dry clothes and comfortable slippers, while the fair Pelageya, smiling benevolently, stepped noiselessly over the carpet with her tray of tea and preserves, did Ivan Ivanich embark upon his yarn, the ancient dames, young ladies, and military gentlemen looking down at them severely from the gilded frames, as if they, too, were listening.

"There were two of us brothers," he began. "Ivan Ivanich (me), and my brother Nikolai Ivanich, two years younger than myself. I went in for learning and became a veterinary surgeon, but Nikolai started working in a government office when he was only nineteen. Our father, Chimsha-Himalaisky, was educated in a school for the sons of private soldiers, but was later promoted to officer's rank, and was made a hereditary nobleman and given a small estate. After his death the estate had to be sold for debts, but at least our childhood was passed in the freedom of the country-side, where we roamed the fields and the woods like peasant children, taking the horses to graze, peeling bark from the trunks of lime-trees, fishing, and all that sort of thing. And anyone who has once in his life fished for perch, or watched the thrushes fly south in the autumn, rising high over the village on clear, cool days, is spoilt for town life, and will long for the country-side for the rest of his days. My brother pined in his government office. The years passed and he sat in the same place every day, writing out the same documents and thinking all the time of the same thing—how to get back to the country. And these longings of his gradually turned into a definite desire, into a dream of purchasing a little estate somewhere on the bank of a river or the shore of a lake.

"He was a meek, good-natured chap, I was fond of him, but could feel no sympathy with the desire to lock oneself up for life in an estate of one's own. They say man only needs six feet of earth. But it is a corpse, and not man, which needs these six feet. And now people are actually saying that it is a good sign for our intellectuals to yearn for the land and try to obtain country-dwellings. And yet these estates are nothing but those same six feet of earth. To escape from the town, from the struggle, from the noise of life, to escape and hide one's head on a country-estate, is not life, but egoism, idleness, it is a sort of renunciation, but renunciation without faith. It is not six feet of earth, not a country-estate, that man needs, but the whole globe, the whole of nature, room to display his qualities and the individual characteristics of his soul.

"My brother Nikolai sat at his office-desk, dreaming of eating soup made from his own cabbages, which would spread a delicious smell all over his own

HISTORICAL EVOLUTION OF THE MODERN SHORT STORY

yard, of eating out of doors, on the green grass, of sleeping in the sun, sitting for hours on a bench outside his gate, and gazing at the fields and woods. Books on agriculture, and all those hints printed on calendars were his delight, his favourite spiritual nourishment. He was fond of reading newspapers, too, but all he read in them was advertisements of the sale of so many acres of arable and meadowland, with residence attached, a river, an orchard, a mill, and ponds fed by springs. His head was full of visions of garden paths, flowers, fruit, nesting-boxes, carp-ponds, and all that sort of thing. These visions differed according to the advertisements he came across, but for some reason gooseberry bushes invariably figured in them. He could not picture to himself a single estate or picturesque nook that did not have gooseberry bushes in it.

" 'Country life has its conveniences,' he would say. 'You sit on the verandah, drinking tea, with your own ducks floating on the pond, and everything smells so nice, and . . . and the gooseberries ripen on the bushes.'

"He drew up plans for his estate, and every plan showed the same features: a) the main residence, b) the servant's wing, c) the kitchen-garden, d) gooseberry bushes. He lived thriftily, never ate or drank his fill, dressed anyhow, like a beggar, and saved up all his money in the bank. He became terribly stingy. I could hardly bear to look at him, and whenever I gave him a little money, or sent him a present on some holiday, he put that away, too. Once a man gets an idea into his head, there's no doing anything with him.

"The years passed, he was sent to another gubernia,* he was over forty, and was still reading advertisements in the papers, and saving up. At last I heard he had married. All for the same purpose, to buy himself an estate with gooseberry bushes on it, he married an ugly elderly widow, for whom he had not the slightest affection, just because she had some money. After his marriage he went on living as thriftily as ever, half-starving his wife, and putting her money in his own bank account. Her first husband had been a postmaster, and she was used to pies and cordials, but with her second husband she did not even get enough black bread to eat. She began to languish under such a regime, and three years later yielded up her soul to God. Of course my brother did not for a moment consider himself guilty of her death. Money, like vodka, makes a man eccentric. There was a merchant in our town who asked for a plate of honey on his deathbed and ate up all his bank-notes and lottery tickets with the honey, so that no one else should get it. And one day when I was examining a consignment of cattle at a railway station, a drover fell under the engine and his leg was severed from his body. We carried him all bloody into the waiting-room, a terrible sight, and he did nothing but beg us to look for his leg, worrying all the time—there were twenty rubles in the boot, and he was afraid they would be lost."

"You're losing the thread," put in Burkin.

Ivan Ivanich paused for a moment, and went on: "After his wife's death my brother began to look about for an estate. You can search for five years, of

*Province.

course, and in the end make a mistake and buy something quite different from what you dreamed of. My brother Nikolai bought three hundred acres, complete with gentleman's house, servants' quarters, and a park, as well as a mortgage to be paid through an agent, but there were neither an orchard, gooseberry bushes, nor a pond with ducks on it. There was a river, but it was as dark as coffee, owing to the fact that there was a brick-works on one side of the estate, and bone-kilns on the other. Nothing daunted, however, my brother Nikolai Ivanich ordered two dozen gooseberry bushes and settled down as a landed proprietor.

"Last year I paid him a visit. I thought I would go and see how he was getting on there. In his letters my brother gave his address as Chumbaroklova Pustosh or Himalaiskoye. I arrived at Himalaiskoye in the afternoon. It was very hot. Everywhere were ditches, fences, hedges, rows of fir-trees, and it was hard to drive into the yard and find a place to leave one's carriage. As I went a fat ginger-coloured dog, remarkably like a pig, came out to meet me. It looked as if it would have barked if it were not so lazy. The cook, who was also fat and like a pig, came out of the kitchen, barefoot, and said her master was having his after-dinner rest. I made my way to my brother's room, and found him sitting up in bed, his knees covered by a blanket. He had aged, and grown stout and flabby. His cheeks, nose and lips protruded—I almost expected him to grunt into the blanket.

"We embraced and wept—tears of joy, mingled with melancholy—because we had once been young and were now both grey-haired and approaching the grave. He put on his clothes and went out to show me over his estate.

" 'Well, how are you getting on here?' I asked.

" 'All right, thanks be, I'm enjoying myself.' "

"He was no longer the poor, timid clerk, but a true proprietor, a gentleman. He had settled down, and was entering with zest into country life. He ate a lot, washed in the bath-house, and put on flesh. He had already got into litigation with the village commune, the brick-works and the bone-kilns, and took offence if the peasants failed to call him 'Your Honour.' He went in for religion in a solid, gentlemanly way, and there was nothing casual about his pretentious good works. And what were these good works? He treated all the diseases of the peasants with bicarbonate of soda and castor-oil, and had a special thanksgiving service held on his name-day, after which he provided half a pail of vodka, supposing that this was the right thing to do. Oh, those terrible half pails! Today the fat landlord hauls the peasants before the Zemstvo representative* for letting their sheep graze on his land, tomorrow, on the day of rejoicing, he treats them to half a pail of vodka, and they drink and sing and shout hurrah, prostrating themselves before him when they are drunk. Any improvement in his conditions, anything like satiety or idleness, develops the most insolent complacency in a Russian. Nikolai Ivanich, who had been afraid of having an opinion of his own when he was in the government service, was

*Country or rural police officer.

now continually coming out with axioms, in the most ministerial manner: 'Education is essential, but the people are not ready for it yet,' 'corporal punishment is an evil, but in certain cases it is beneficial and indispensable.'

" 'I know the people and I know how to treat them,' he said. 'The people love me. I only have to lift my little finger, and the people will do whatever I want.'

"And all this, mark you, with a wise, indulgent smile. Over and over again he repeated: 'We the gentry,' or 'speaking as a gentleman,' and seemed to have quite forgotten that our grandfather was a peasant, and our father a common soldier. Our very surname—Chimsha-Himalaisky—in reality so absurd, now seemed to him a resounding, distinguished, and euphonious name.

"But it is of myself, and not of him, that I wish to speak. I should like to describe to you the change which came over me in those few hours I spent on my brother's estate. As we were drinking tea in the evening, the cook brought us a full plate of gooseberries. These were not gooseberries bought for money, they came from his own garden, and were the first fruits of the bushes he had planted. Nikolai Ivanich broke into a laugh and gazed at the gooseberries, in tearful silence for at least five minutes. Speechless with emotion, he popped a single gooseberry into his mouth, darted at me the triumphant glance of a child who has at last gained possession of a longed-for toy, and said:

" 'Delicious!'

"And he ate them greedily, repeating over and over again:

" 'Simply delicious! You try them.'

"They were hard and sour, but, as Pushkin says: 'The lie which elates us is dearer than a thousand sober truths.' I saw before me a really happy man, one whose dearest wish had come true, who had achieved his aim in life, got what he wanted, and was content with his lot and with himself. There had always been a tinge of melancholy in my conception of human happiness, and now, confronted by a happy man, I was overcome by a feeling of sadness bordering on desperation. This feeling grew strongest of all in the night. A bed was made up for me in the room next to my brother's bedroom, and I could hear him moving about restlessly, every now and then getting up to take a gooseberry from a plate. How many happy, satisfied people there are, after all, I said to myself! What an overwhelming force! Just consider this life—the insolence and idleness of the strong, the ignorance and bestiality of the weak, all around intolerable poverty, cramped dwellings, degeneracy, drunkenness, hypocrisy, lying. . . . And yet peace and order apparently prevail in all those homes and in the streets. Of the fifty thousand inhabitants of a town, not one will be found to cry out, to proclaim his indignation aloud. We see those who go to the market to buy food, who eat in the day-time and sleep at night, who prattle away, marry, grow old, carry their dead to the cemeteries. But we neither hear nor see those who suffer, and the terrible things in life are played out behind the scenes. All is calm and quiet, only statistics, which are dumb, protest: so many have gone mad, so many barrels of drink have been consumed, so many children died of malnutrition. . . . And apparently this is as it should be. Apparently those who are happy can only enjoy themselves because the unhappy bear their burdens in silence, and but for this silence happiness would be impossible. It is a kind of universal hypnosis. There ought to be a man with a hammer behind the door of every happy man, to remind him by his constant knocks that there are unhappy people, and that happy as he himself may be, life will sooner or later show him its claws, catastrophe will overtake him—sickness, poverty, loss—and nobody will see it, just as he now neither sees nor hears the misfortunes of others. But there is no man with a hammer, the happy man goes on living and the petty vicissitudes of life touch him lightly, like the wind in an aspen-tree, and all is well.

"That night I understood that I, too, was happy and content," continued Ivan Ivanich, getting up. "I, too, while out hunting, or at the dinner table, have held forth on the right way to live, to worship, to manage the people. I, too, have declared that without knowledge there can be no light, that education is essential, but that bare literacy is sufficient for the common people. Freedom is a blessing, I have said, one can't get on without it, any more than without air, but we must wait. Yes, that is what I said, and now I ask: In the name of what must we wait?" Here Ivan Ivanich looked angrily at Burkin. "In the name of what must we wait, I ask you. What is there to be considered? Don't be in such a hurry, they tell me, every idea materializes gradually, in its own time. But who are they who say this? What is the proof that it is just? You refer to the natural order of things, to the logic of facts, but according to what order, what logic do I, a living, thinking individual, stand on the edge of a ditch and wait for it to be gradually filled up, or choked with silt, when I might leap across it or build a bridge over it? And again, in the name of what must we wait? Wait, when we have not the strength to live, though live we must and to live we desire!

"I left my brother early the next morning, and ever since I have found town life intolerable. The peace and order weigh on my spirits, and I am afraid to look into windows, because there is now no sadder spectacle for me than a happy family seated around the tea-table. I am old and unfit for the struggle, I am even incapable of feeling hatred. I can only suffer inwardly, and give way to irritation and annoyance, at night my head burns from the rush of thoughts, and I am unable to sleep. . . . Oh, if only I were young!"

Ivan Ivanich began pacing backwards and forwards, repeating:

"If only I were young still!"

Suddenly he went up to Alekhin and began pressing first one of his hands, and then the other.

"Pavel Konstantinich," he said in imploring accents. "Don't *you* fall into apathy, don't *you* let your conscience be lulled to sleep! While you are still young, strong, active, do not be weary of well-doing. There is no such thing as happiness, nor ought there to be, but if there is any sense or purpose in life, this sense and purpose are to be found not in our own happiness, but in something greater and more rational. Do good!"

Ivan Ivanich said all this with a piteous, imploring smile, as if he were asking for something for himself.

Then they all three sat in their arm-chairs a long way apart from one another, and said nothing. Ivan Ivanich's story satisfied neither Burkin or Ale-khin. It was not interesting to listen to the story of a poor clerk who ate gooseberries, when from the walls generals and fine ladies, who seemed to come to life in the dark, were looking down from their gilded frames. It would have been much more interesting to hear about elegant people, lovely women. And the fact that they were sitting in a drawing-room in which everything— the swathed chandeliers, the arm-chairs, the carpet on the floor, proved that the people now looking out of the frames had once moved about here, sat in the chairs, drunk tea, where the fair Pelageya was now going noiselessly to and fro, was better than any story.

Alekhin was desperately sleepy. He had got up early, at three o'clock in the morning, to go about his work on the estate, and could now hardly keep his eyes open. But he would not go to bed, for fear one of his guests would relate something interesting after he was gone. He could not be sure whether what Ivan Ivanich had just told them was wise or just, but his visitors talked of other things besides grain, hay, or tar, of things which had no direct bearing on his daily life, and he liked this, and wanted them to go on. . . .

"Well, time to go to bed," said Burkin, getting up. "Allow me to wish you a good night."

Alekhin said good night and went downstairs to his own room, the visitors remaining on the upper floor. They were allotted a big room for the night, in which were two ancient bedsteads of carved wood, and an ivory crucifix in one corner. There was a pleasant smell of freshly laundered sheets from the wide, cool beds which the fair Pelageya made up for them.

Ivan Ivanich undressed in silence and lay down.

"Lord have mercy on us, sinners," he said, and covered his head with the sheet.

There was a strong smell of stale tobacco from his pipe, which he put on the table, and Burkin lay awake a long time, wondering where the stifling smell came from.

The rain tapped on the window-panes all night.

FOR STUDY, DISCUSSION, AND WRITING

1. Like Galsworthy's "The Japanese Quince" or Maupassant's "The Piece of String," this story has a single dominant symbol, the gooseberry bush. What do you think the gooseberries symbolize?

2. How is Chekhov's rejection of the traditional, neatly orchestrated plot reflected in the plot of this story?

3. "Gooseberries" contains a story within a story. Point out some of the similarities between the two narratives. Why do you think these similarities are employed?

4. What is ironic about Ivan's apparent condemnation of human happiness, especially in terms of the swimming scene?
5. Despite Ivan's advocacy of social reform, is he any less a class snob than his brother Nikolai?
6. Considering Ivan's demonstrated physical vigor, can we believe that he really is too old to involve himself in a struggle for revolutionary social change?
7. Can you attribute any significance to the fact that it rains throughout the story?
8. In what ways might Ivan be compared to what is today often called a pseudoliberal?

STEPHEN CRANE

The Open Boat

A Tale Intended to be after the Fact: Being
the Experience of Four Men from the
Sunk Steamer "COMMODORE"

I

None of them knew the color of the sky. Their eyes glanced level, and were fastened upon the waves that swept toward them. These waves were of the hue of slate, save for the tops, which were of foaming white, and all of the men knew the colors of the sea. The horizon narrowed and widened, and dipped and rose, and at all times its edge was jagged with waves that seemed thrust up in points like rocks.

Many a man ought to have a bathtub larger than the boat which here rode upon the sea. These waves were most wrongfully and barbarously abrupt and tall, and each froth-top was a problem in small-boat navigation.

The cook squatted in the bottom, and looked with both eyes at the six inches of gunwale which separated him from the ocean. His sleeves were rolled over his fat forearms, and the two flaps of his unbuttoned vest dangled as he bent to bail out the boat. Often he said, "Gawd! that was a narrow clip." As he remarked it he invariably gazed eastward over the broken sea.

The oiler, steering with one of the two oars in the boat, sometimes raised himself suddenly to keep clear of water that swirled in over the stern. It was a thin little oar, and it seemed often ready to snap.

The correspondent, pulling at the other oar, watched the waves and wondered why he was there.

The injured captain, lying in the bow, was at this time buried in that profound dejection and indifference which comes, temporarily at least, to even the bravest and most enduring when, willy-nilly, the firm fails, the army loses, the ship goes down. The mind of the master of a vessel is rooted deep in the timbers of her, though he command for a day or a decade; and this captain had on him the stern impression of a scene in the grays of dawn of seven turned faces, and later a stump of a topmast with a white ball on it, that slashed to and fro at the waves, went low and lower, and down. Thereafter there was something strange in his voice. Although steady, it was deep with mourning, and of a quality beyond oration or tears.

"Keep'er a little more south, Billie," said he.

"A little more south, sir," said the oiler in the stern.

A seat in this boat was not unlike a seat upon a bucking broncho, and by the same token a broncho is not much smaller. The craft pranced and reared and plunged like an animal. As each wave came, and she rose for it, she seemed like a horse making at a fence outrageously high. The manner of her scramble over these walls of water is a mystic thing, and, moreover, at the top of them were ordinarily these problems in white water, the foam racing down from the summit of each wave requiring a new leap, and a leap from the air. Then, after scornfully bumping a crest, she would slide and race and splash down a long incline, and arrive bobbing and nodding in front of the next menace.

A singular disadvantage of the sea lies in the fact that after successfully surmounting one wave you discover that there is another behind it just as important and just as nervously anxious to do something effective in the way of swamping boats. In a ten-foot dinghy one can get an idea of the resources of the sea in the line of waves that is not probable to the average experience, which is never at sea in a dinghy. As each slaty wall of water approached, it shut all else from the view of the men in the boat, and it was not difficult to imagine that this particular wave was the final outburst of the ocean, the last effort of the grim water. There was a terrible grace in the move of the waves, and they came in silence, save for the snarling of the crests.

In the wan light the faces of the men must have been gray. Their eyes must have glinted in strange ways as they gazed steadily astern. Viewed from a balcony, the whole thing would, doubtless, have been weirdly picturesque. But the men in the boat had no time to see it, and if they had had leisure, there were other things to occupy their minds. The sun swung steadily up the sky, and they knew it was broad day because the color of the sea changed from slate to emerald-green streaked with amber lights, and the foam was like tumbling snow. The process of the breaking day was unknown to them. They were aware only of this effect upon the color of the waves that rolled toward them.

In disjointed sentences the cook and the correspondent argued as to the difference between a life-saving station and a house of refuge. The cook had said: "There's a house of refuge just north of the Mosquito Inlet Light, and as soon as they see us they'll come off in their boat and pick us up."

"As soon as who see us?" said the correspondent.

"The crew," said the cook.

"Houses of refuge don't have crews," said the correspondent. "As I understand them, they are only places where clothes and grub are stored for the benefit of shipwrecked people. They don't carry crews."

"Oh, yes, they do," said the cook.

"No, they don't," said the correspondent.

"Well, we're not there yet, anyhow," said the oiler, in the stern.

"Well," said the cook, "perhaps it's not a house of refuge that I'm thinking of as being near Mosquito Inlet Light; perhaps it's a life-saving station."

"We're not there yet," said the oiler in the stern.

II

As the boat bounced from the top of each wave the wind tore through the hair of the hatless men, and as the craft plopped her stern down again the spray slashed past them. The crest of each of these waves was a hill, from the top of which the men surveyed for a moment a broad tumultuous expanse, shining and wind-riven. It was probably splendid, it was probably glorious, this play of the free sea, wild with lights of emerald and white and amber.

"Bully good thing it's an on-shore wind," said the cook. "If not, where would we be? Wouldn't have a show."

"That's right," said the correspondent.

The busy oiler nodded his assent.

Then the captain, in the bow, chuckled in a way that expressed humor, contempt, tragedy, all in one. "Do you think we've got much of a show now, boys?" said he.

Whereupon the three were silent, save for a trifle of hemming and hawing. To express any particular optimism at this time they felt to be childish and stupid, but they all doubtless possessed this sense of the situation in their minds. A young man thinks doggedly at such times. On the other hand, the ethics of their condition was decidedly against any open suggestion of hopelessness. So they were silent.

"Oh, well," said the captain, soothing his children, "we'll get ashore all right."

But there was that in his tone which made them think; so the oiler quoth, "Yes! if this wind holds."

The cook was bailing. "Yes! if we don't catch hell in the surf."

Canton-flannel gulls flew near and far. Sometimes they sat down on the sea, near patches of brown seaweed that rolled over the waves with a movement like carpets on a line in a gale. The birds sat comfortably in groups, and they were envied by some in the dinghy, for the wrath of the sea was no more to them than it was to a covey of prairie chickens a thousand miles inland. Often they came very close and stared at the men with black bead-like eyes. At these times they were uncanny and sinister in their unblinking scrutiny, and the men hooted angrily at them, telling them to be gone. One came, and evidently decided to alight on the top of the captain's head. The bird flew parallel to the boat and did not circle, but made short sidelong jumps in the air in chicken fashion. His black eyes were wistfully fixed upon the captain's head. "Ugly brute," said the oiler to the bird. "You look as if you were made with a jackknife." The cook and the correspondent swore darkly at the creature. The captain naturally wished to knock it away with the end of the heavy painter, but he did not dare do it, because anything resembling an emphatic gesture would have capsized this freighted boat; and so, with his open hand, the captain gently and carefully waved the gull away. After it had been discouraged from the pursuit the captain breathed easier on account of his hair, and others breathed easier because the bird struck their minds at this time as being somehow gruesome and ominous.

In the meantime the oiler and the correspondent rowed; and also they rowed. They sat together in the same seat, and each rowed an oar. Then the oiler took both oars; then the correspondent took both oars, then the oiler; then the correspondent. They rowed and they rowed. The very ticklish part of the business was when the time came for the reclining one in the stern to take his turn at the oars. By the very last star of truth, it is easier to steal eggs from under a hen than it was to change seats in the dinghy. First the man in the stern slid his hand along the thwart and moved with care, as if he were of Sèvres. Then the man in the rowing-seat slid his hand along the other thwart. It was all done with the most extraordinary care. As the two sidled past each other, the whole party kept watchful eyes on the coming wave, and the captain cried: "Look out, now! Steady, there!"

The brown mats of seaweed that appeared from time to time were like islands, bits of earth. They were travelling, apparently, neither one way nor the other. They were, to all intents, stationary. They informed the men in the boat that it was making progress slowly toward the land.

The captain, rearing cautiously in the bow after the dinghy soared on a great swell, said that he had seen the lighthouse at Mosquito Inlet. Presently the cook remarked that he had seen it. The correspondent was at the oars then, and for some reason he too wished to look at the lighthouse; but his back was toward the far shore, and the waves were important, and for some time he could not seize an opportunity to turn his head. But at last there came a wave more gentle than the others, and when at the crest of it he swiftly scoured the western horizon.

"See it?" said the captain.

"No," said the correspondent, slowly; "I didn't see anything."

"Look again," said the captain. He pointed. "It's exactly in that direction."

At the top of another wave the correspondent did as he was bid, and this time his eyes chanced on a small, still thing on the edge of the swaying horizon. It was precisely like the point of a pin. It took an anxious eye to find a lighthouse so tiny.

"Think we'll make it, Captain?"

"If this wind holds and the boat don't swamp, we can't do much else," said the captain.

The little boat, lifted by each towering sea and splashed viciously by the crests, made progress that in the absence of seaweed was not apparent to those in her. She seemed just a wee thing wallowing, miraculously top up, at the mercy of five oceans. Occasionally a great spread of water, like white flames, swarmed into her.

"Bail her, cook," said the captain, serenely.

"All right, Captain," said the cheerful cook.

III

It would be difficult to describe the subtle brotherhood of men that was here established on the seas. No one said that it was so. No one mentioned it. But it dwelt in the boat, and each man felt it warm him. They were a captain, an oiler, a cook, and a correspondent, and they were friends—friends in a more curiously iron-bound degree than may be common. The hurt captain, lying against the water-jar in the bow, spoke always in a low voice and calmly; but he could never command a more ready and swiftly obedient crew than the motley three of the dinghy. It was more than a mere recognition of what was best for the common safety. There was surely in it a quality that was personal and heart-felt. And after this devotion to the commander of the boat, there was this comradeship, that the correspondent, for instance, who had been taught to be cynical of men, knew even at the time was the best experience of his life. But no one said that it was so. No one mentioned it.

"I wish we had a sail," remarked the captain. "We might try my overcoat on the end of an oar, and give you two boys a chance to rest." So the cook and the correspondent held the mast and spread wide the overcoat; the oiler steered; and the little boat made good way with her new rig. Sometimes the oiler had to scull sharply to keep a sea from breaking into the boat, but otherwise sailing was a success.

Meanwhile the lighthouse had been growing slowly larger. It had now almost assumed color, and appeared like a little gray shadow on the sky. The man at the oars could not be prevented from turning his head rather often to try for a glimpse of this little gray shadow.

At last, from the top of each wave, the men in the tossing boat could see land. Even as the lighthouse was an upright shadow on the sky, this land seemed but a long black shadow on the sea. It certainly was thinner than paper. "We must be about opposite New Smyrna," said the cook, who had coasted this shore often in schooners. "Captain, by the way, I believe they abandoned that life-saving station there about a year ago."

"Did they?" said the captain.

The wind slowly died away. The cook and the correspondent were not now obliged to slave in order to hold high the oar. But the waves continued their old impetuous swooping at the dinghy, and the little craft, no longer under way, struggled woundily over them. The oiler or the correspondent took the oars again.

Shipwrecks are *apropos* of nothing. If men could only train for them and have them occur when the men had reached pink condition, there would be less drowning at sea. Of the four in the dinghy none had slept any time worth mentioning for two days and two nights previous to embarking in the dinghy, and in the excitement of clambering about the deck of a foundering ship they had also forgotten to eat heartily.

For these reasons, and for others, neither the oiler nor the correspondent was fond of rowing at this time. The correspondent wondered ingenuously how in the name of all that was sane could there be people who thought it amusing to row a boat. It was not an amusement; it was a diabolical punishment, and even a genius of mental aberrations could never conclude that it was anything but a horror to the muscles and a crime against the back. He mentioned to the boat in general how the amusement of rowing struck him, and the weary-faced oiler smiled in full sympathy. Previously to the foundering, by the way, the oiler had worked a double watch in the engine-room of the ship.

"Take her easy now, boys," said the captain. "Don't spend yourselves. If we have to run a surf you'll need all your strength, because we'll sure have to swim for it. Take your time."

Slowly the land arose from the sea. From a black line it became a line of black and a line of white—trees and sand. Finally the captain said that he could make out a house on the shore. "That's the house of refuge, sure," said the cook. "They'll see us before long, and come out after us."

The distant lighthouse reared high. "The keeper ought to be able to make us out now, if he's looking through a glass," said the captain. "He'll notify the life-saving people."

"None of those other boats could have got ashore to give word of this wreck," said the oiler, in a low voice, "else the life-boat would be out hunting us."

Slowly and beautifully the land loomed out of the sea. The wind came again. It had veered from the northeast to the southeast. Finally a new sound struck the ears of the men in the boat. It was the low thunder of the surf on the shore. "We'll never be able to make the lighthouse now," said the captain. "Swing her head a little more north, Billie."

"A little more north, sir," said the oiler.

Whereupon the little boat turned her nose once more down the wind, and all but the oarsman watched the shore grow. Under the influence of this expansion doubt and direful apprehension were leaving the minds of the men. The management of the boat was still most absorbing, but it could not prevent a quiet cheerfulness. In an hour, perhaps, they would be ashore.

Their backbones had become thoroughly used to balancing in the boat, and they now rode this wild colt of a dinghy like circus men. The correspondent thought that he had been drenched to the skin, but happening to feel in the top pocket of his coat, he found therein eight cigars. Four of them were soaked with sea-water; four were perfectly scatheless. After a search, somebody produced three dry matches; and thereupon the four waifs rode impudently in their little boat and, with an assurance of an impending rescue shining in their eyes, puffed at the big cigars, and judged well and ill of all men. Everybody took a drink of water.

IV

"Cook," remarked the captain, "there don't seem to be any signs of life about your house of refuge."

"No," replied the cook. "Funny they don't see us!"

A broad stretch of lowly coast lay before the eyes of the men. It was of low dunes topped with dark vegetation. The roar of the surf was plain, and sometimes they could see the white lip of a wave as it spun up the beach. A tiny house was blocked out black upon the sky. Southward, the slim lighthouse lifted its little gray length.

Tide, wind, and waves were swinging the dinghy northward. "Funny they don't see us," said the men.

The surf's roar was here dulled, but its tone was nevertheless thunderous and mighty. As the boat swam over the great rollers the men sat listening to this roar. "We'll swamp sure," said everybody.

It is fair to say here that there was not a life-saving station within twenty miles in either direction; but the men did not know this fact, and in consequence they made dark and opprobrious remarks concerning the eyesight of the nation's life-savers. Four scowling men sat in the dinghy and surpassed records in the invention of epithets.

"Funny they don't see us."

The light-heartedness of a former time had completely faded. To their sharpened minds it was easy to conjure pictures of all kinds of incompetency and blindness and, indeed, cowardice. There was the shore of the populous land, and it was bitter and bitter to them that from it came no sign.

"Well," said the captain, ultimately, "I suppose we'll have to make a try for ourselves. If we stay out here too long, we'll none of us have strength left to swim after the boat swamps."

And so the oiler, who was at the oars, turned the boat straight for the shore. There was a sudden tightening of muscles. There was some thinking.

"If we don't all get ashore," said the captain—"if we don't all get ashore, I suppose you fellows know where to send news of my finish?"

They then briefly exchanged some addresses and admonitions. As for the reflections of the men, there was a great deal of rage in them. Perchance they might be formulated thus: "If I am going to be drowned—if I am going to be drowned—if I am going to be drowned, why, in the name of the seven mad gods who rule the sea, was I allowed to come thus far and contemplate sand and trees? Was I brought here merely to have my nose dragged away as I was about to nibble the sacred cheese of life? It is preposterous. If this old ninny-woman, Fate, cannot do better than this, she should be deprived of the management of men's fortunes. She is an old hen who knows not her intention. If she has decided to drown me, why did she not do it in the beginning and save me all this trouble? The whole affair is absurd. . . . But no; she cannot mean to drown me. She dare not drown me. She cannot drown me. Not after all this work." Afterward the man might have had an impulse to shake his fist at the clouds. "Just you drown me, now, and then hear what I call you!"

The billows that came at this time were more formidable. They seemed always just about to break and roll over the little boat in a turmoil of foam. There was a preparatory and long growl in the speech of them. No mind unused to the sea would have concluded that the dinghy could ascend these sheer heights in time. The shore was still afar. The oiler was a wily surfman. "Boys," he said swiftly, "she won't live three minutes more, and we're too far out to swim. Shall I take her to sea again, Captain?"

"Yes; go ahead!" said the captain.

This oiler, by a series of quick miracles and fast and steady oarsmanship, turned the boat in the middle of the surf and took her safely to sea again.

There was a considerable silence as the boat bumped over the furrowed sea to deeper water. Then somebody in gloom spoke: "Well, anyhow, they must have seen us from the shore by now."

The gulls went in slanting flight up the wind toward the gray, desolate east. A squall, marked by dingy clouds and clouds brick-red, like smoke from a burning building, appeared from the southeast.

"What do you think of those life-saving people? Ain't they peaches?"

"Funny they haven't seen us."

"Maybe they think we're out here for sport! Maybe they think we're fishin'. Maybe they think we're damned fools."

It was a long afternoon. A changed tide tried to force them southward, but wind and wave said northward. Far ahead, where coast-line, sea, and sky formed their mighty angle, there were little dots which seemed to indicate a city on the shore.

"St. Augustine?"

The captain shook his head. "Too near Mosquito Inlet."

And the oiler rowed, and then the correspondent rowed; then the oiler rowed. It was a weary business. The human back can become the seat of more aches and pains than are registered in books for the composite anatomy of a regiment. It is a limited area, but it can become the theater of innumerable muscular conflicts, tangles, wrenches, knots, and other comforts.

"Did you ever like to row, Billie?" asked the correspondent.

"No," said the oiler; "hang it!"

When one exchanged the rowing-seat for a place in the bottom of the boat, he suffered a bodily depression that caused him to be careless of everything save an obligation to wiggle one finger. There was cold sea-water swashing to and fro in the boat, and he lay in it. His head, pillowed on a thwart, was within an inch of the swirl of a wave-crest, and sometimes a particularly obstreperous sea came inboard and drenched him once more. But these matters did not annoy him. It is almost certain that if the boat had capsized he would have tumbled comfortably out upon the ocean as if he felt sure that it was a great soft mattress.

"Look! There's a man on the shore!"

"Where?"

"There! See 'im? See 'im?"

"Yes, sure! He's walking along."

"Now he's stopped. Look! He's facing us!"

"He's waving at us!"

"So he is! By thunder!"

"Ah, now we're all right! Now we're all right! There'll be a boat out here for us in half an hour."

"He's going on. He's running. He's going up to that house there."

The remote beach seemed lower than the sea, and it required a searching glance to discern the little black figure. The captain saw a floating stick, and they rowed to it. A bath towel was by some weird chance in the boat, and, tying this on the stick, the captain waved it. The oarsman did not dare turn his head, so he was obliged to ask questions.

"What's he doing now?"

"He's standing still again. He's looking, I think. . . . There he goes again—toward the house. . . . Now he's stopped again."

"Is he waving at us?"

"No, not now; he was, though."

"Look! There comes another man!"

"He's running."

"Look at him go, would you!"

"Why, he's on a bicycle. Now he's met the other man. They're both waving at us. Look!"

"There comes something up the beach."

"What the devil is that thing?"

"Why, it looks like a boat."

"Why, certainly, it's a boat."

"No; it's on wheels."

"Yes, so it is. Well, that must be the life-boat. They drag them along shore on a wagon."

"That's the life-boat, sure."

"No, by God, it's—it's an omnibus."

"I tell you it's a life-boat."

"It is not! It's an omnibus. I can see it plain. See? One of these big hotel omnibuses."

"By thunder, you're right. It's an omnibus, sure as fate. What do you suppose they are doing with an omnibus? Maybe they are going around collecting the life-crew, hey?"

"That's it, likely. Look! There's a fellow waving a little black flag. He's standing on the steps of the omnibus. There come those other two fellows. Now they're all talking together. Look at the fellow with the flag. Maybe he ain't waving it!"

"That ain't a flag, is it? That's his coat. Why, certainly, that's his coat."

"So it is; it's his coat. He's taken it off and is waving it around his head. But would you look at him swing it!"

"Oh, say, there isn't any life-saving station there. That's just a winter-resort hotel omnibus that has brought over some of the boarders to see us drown."

"What's that idiot with the coat mean? What's he signalling, anyhow?"

"It looks as if he were trying to tell us to go north. There must be a life-saving station up there."

"No; he thinks we're fishing. Just giving us a merry hand. See? Ah, there, Willie!"

"Well, I wish I could make something out of those signals. What do you suppose he means?"

"He don't mean anything; he's just playing."

"Well, if he'd just signal us to try the surf again, or to go to sea and wait, or go north, or go south, or go to hell, there would be some reason in it. But look at him! He just stands there and keeps his coat revolving like a wheel! The ass!"

"There come more people."

"Now there's quite a mob. Look! Isn't that a boat?"

"Where? Oh, I see where you mean. No, that's no boat."

"That fellow is still waving his coat."

"He must think we like to see him do that. Why don't he quit it? It don't mean anything."

"I don't know. I think he is trying to make us go north. It must be that there's a life-saving station there somewhere."

"Say, he ain't tired yet. Look at 'im wave!"

"Wonder how long he can keep that up. He's been revolving his coat ever since he caught sight of us. He's an idiot. Why aren't they getting men to bring a boat out? A fishing-boat—one of those big yawls—could come out here all right. Why don't he do somethng?"

"Oh, it's all right now."

"They'll have a boat out here for us in less than no time, now that they've seen us."

A faint yellow tone came into the sky over the low land. The shadows on the sea slowly deepened. The wind bore coldness with it, and the men began to shiver.

"Holy smoke!" said one, allowing his voice to express his impious mood, "if we keep on monkeying out here! If we've got to flounder out here all night!"

"Oh, we'll never have to stay here all night! Don't you worry. They've seen us now, and it won't be long before they'll come chasing out after us."

The shore grew dusky. The man waving a coat blended gradually into this gloom, and it swallowed in the same manner the omnibus and the group of people. The spray, when it dashed uproariously over the side, made the voyagers shrink and swear like men who were being branded.

"I'd like to catch the chump who waved the coat. I feel like socking him one, just for luck."

"Why? What did he do?"

"Oh, nothing, but then he seemed so damned cheerful."

In the meantime the oiler rowed, and then the correspondent rowed, and then the oiler rowed. Gray-faced and bowed forward, they mechanically, turn by turn, plied the leaden oars. The form of the lighthouse had vanished from the southern horizon, but finally a pale star appeared, just lifting from the sea. The streaked saffron in the west passed before the all-merging darkness, and the sea to the east was black. The land had vanished, and was expressed only by the low and drear thunder of the surf.

"If I am going to be drowned—if I am going to be drowned—if I am going to be drowned, why, in the name of the seven mad gods who rule the sea, was I allowed to come thus far and contemplate sand and trees? Was I brought here merely to have my nose dragged away as I was about to nibble the sacred cheese of life?"

The patient captain, drooped over the water-jar, was sometimes obliged to speak to the oarsman.

"Keep her head up! Keep her head up!"

"Keep her head up, sir." The voices were weary and low.

This was surely a quiet evening. All save the oarsman lay heavily and listlessly in the boat's bottom. As for him, his eyes were just capable of noting the tall black waves that swept forward in a most sinister silence, save for an occasional subdued growl of a crest.

The cook's head was on a thwart, and he looked without interest at the water under his nose. He was deep in other scenes. Finally he spoke. "Billie," he murmured dreamfully, "what kind of pie do you like best?"

V

"Pie!" said the oiler and the correspondent, agitatedly. "Don't talk about those things, blast you!"

"Well," said the cook, "I was just thinking about ham sandwiches, and—"

A night on the sea in an open boat is a long night. As darkness settled finally, the shine of the light, lifting from the sea in the south, changed to full gold. On the northern horizon a new light appeared, a small bluish gleam on the edge of the waters. These two lights were the furniture of the world. Otherwise there was nothing but waves.

Two men huddled in the stern, and distances were so magnificent in the dinghy that the rower was enabled to keep his feet partly warm by thrusting them under his companions. Their legs indeed extended far under the rowing-seat until they touched the feet of the captain forward. Sometimes, despite the efforts of the tired oarsman, a wave came piling into the boat, an icy wave of the night, and the chilling water soaked them anew. They would twist their bodies for a moment and groan, and sleep the dead sleep once more, while the water in the boat gurgled about them as the craft rocked.

The plan of the oiler and the correspondent was for one to row until he lost the ability, and then arouse the other from his sea-water couch in the bottom of the boat.

The oiler plied the oars until his head drooped forward and the overpowering sleep blinded him; and he rowed yet afterward. Then he touched a man in the bottom of the boat, and called his name. "Will you spell me for a little while?" he said meekly.

"Sure, Billie," said the correspondent, awaking and dragging himself to a sitting position. They exchanged places carefully, and the oiler, cuddling down in the sea-water at the cook's side, seemed to go to sleep instantly.

The particular violence of the sea had ceased. The waves came without snarling. The obligation of the man at the oars was to keep the boat headed so that the tilt of the rollers would not capsize her, and to preserve her from filling when the crests rushed past. The black waves were silent and hard to be seen in the darkness. Often one was almost upon the boat before the oarsman was aware.

In a low voice the correspondent addressed the captain. He was not sure that the captain was awake, although this iron man seemed to be always awake. "Captain, shall I keep her making for that light north, sir?"

The same steady voice answered him. "Yes. Keep it about two points off the port bow."

The cook had tied a life-belt around himself in order to get even the warmth which this clumsy cork contrivance could donate, and he seemed almost stove-like when a rower, whose teeth invariably chattered wildly as soon as he ceased his labor, dropped down to sleep.

The correspondent, as he rowed, looked down at the two men sleeping underfoot. The cook's arm was around the oiler's shoulders, and, with their fragmentary clothing and haggard faces, they were the babes of the sea—a grotesque rendering of the old babes in the wood.

Later he must have grown stupid at his work, for suddenly there was a growling of water, and a crest came with a roar and a swash into the boat, and it was a wonder that it did not set the cook afloat in his life-belt. The cook continued to sleep, but the oiler sat up, blinking his eyes and shaking with the new cold.

"Oh, I'm awful sorry, Billie," said the correspondent, contritely.

"That's all right, old boy," said the oiler, and lay down again and was asleep.

Presently it seemed that even the captain dozed, and the correspondent thought that he was the one man afloat on all the ocean. The wind had a voice as it came over the waves, and it was sadder than the end.

There was a long, loud swishing astern of the boat, and a gleaming trail of phosphorescence, like blue flame, was furrowed on the black waters. It might have been made by a monstrous knife.

Then there came a stillness, while the correspondent breathed with open mouth and looked at the sea.

Suddenly there was another swish and another long flash of bluish light, and this time it was alongside the boat, and might almost have been reached with an oar. The correspondent saw an enormous fin speed like a shadow through the water, hurling the crystalline spray and leaving the long glowing trail.

The correspondent looked over his shoulder at the captain. His face was hidden, and he seemed to be asleep. He looked at the babes of the sea. They certainly were asleep. So, being bereft of sympathy, he leaned a little way to one side and swore softly into the sea.

But the thing did not then leave the vicinity of the boat. Ahead or astern, on one side or the other, at intervals long or short, fled the long sparkling streak, and there was to be heard the *whirroo* of the dark fin. The speed and power of the thing was greatly to be admired. It cut the water like a gigantic and keen projectile.

The presence of this biding thing did not affect the man with the same horror that it would if he had been a picnicker. He simply looked at the sea dully and swore in an undertone.

Nevertheless, it is true that he did not wish to be alone with the thing. He wished one of his companions to be awake by chance and keep him company with it. But the captain hung motionless over the water-jar, and the oiler and the cook in the bottom of the boat were plunged in slumber.

VI

"If I am going to be drowned—if I am going to be drowned—if I am going to be drowned, why, in the name of the seven mad gods who rule the sea, was I allowed to come thus far and contemplate sand and trees?"

During this dismal night, it may be remarked that a man would conclude that it was really the intention of the seven mad gods to drown him, despite the abominable injustice of it. For it was certainly an abominable injustice to drown a man who had worked so hard, so hard. The man felt it would be a crime most unnatural. Other people had drowned at sea since galleys swarmed with painted sails, but still—

When it occurs to a man that nature does not regard him as important, and that she feels she would not maim the universe by disposing of him, he at first wishes to throw bricks at the temple, and he hates deeply the fact that there are no bricks and no temples. Any visible expression of nature would surely be pelleted with his jeers.

Then, if there be no tangible thing to hoot, he feels, perhaps, the desire to confront a personification and indulge in pleas, bowed to one knee, and with hands supplicant, saying, "Yes, but I love myself."

A high cold star on a winter's night is the word he feels that she says to him. Thereafter he knows the pathos of his situation.

The men in the dinghy had not discussed these matters, but each had, no doubt, reflected upon them in silence and according to his mind. There was seldom any expression upon their faces save the general one of complete weariness. Speech was devoted to the business of the boat.

To chime the notes of his emotion, a verse mysteriously entered the correspondent's head. He had even forgotten that he had forgotten this verse, but it suddenly was in his mind.

> *A soldier of the Legion lay dying in Algiers;*
> *There was lack of woman's nursing, there was dearth of woman's tears;*
> *But a comrade stood beside him, and he took that comrade's hand,*
> *And he said, "I never more shall see my own, my native land."*

In his childhood the correspondent had been made acquainted with the fact that a soldier of the Legion lay dying in Algiers, but he had never regarded it as important. Myriads of his school-fellows had informed him of the soldier's plight, but the dinning had naturally ended by making him perfectly indifferent. He had never considered it his affair that a soldier of the Legion lay dying in Algiers, nor had it appeared to him as a matter for sorrow. It was less to him than the breaking of a pencil's point.

Now, however, it quaintly came to him as a human, living thing. It was no longer merely a picture of a few throes in the breast of a poet, meanwhile drinking tea and warming his feet at the grate; it was an actuality—stern, mournful, and fine.

The correspondent plainly saw the soldier. He lay on the sand with his feet out straight and still. While his pale left hand was upon his chest in an attempt to thwart the going of his life, the blood came between his fingers. In the far Algerian distance, a city of low square forms was set against a sky that was faint with the last sunset hues. The correspondent, plying the oars and dreaming of the slow and slower movements of the lips of the soldier, was moved by a profound and perfectly impersonal comprehension. He was sorry for the soldier of the Legion who lay dying in Algiers.

The thing which had followed the boat and waited had evidently grown bored at the delay. There was no longer to be heard the slash of the cutwater, and there was no longer the flame of the long trail. The light in the north still glimmered, but it was apparently no nearer to the boat. Sometimes the boom of the surf rang in the correspondent's ears, and he turned the craft seaward then and rowed harder. Southward, some one had evidently built a watch-fire on the beach. It was too low and too far to be seen, but it made a shimmering, roseate reflection upon the bluff in back of it, and this could be discerned from the boat. The wind came stronger, and sometimes a wave suddenly raged out like a mountain cat, and there was to be seen the sheen and sparkle of a broken crest.

The captain, in the bow, moved on his water-jar and sat erect. "Pretty long night," he observed to the correspondent. He looked at the shore. "Those life-saving people take their time."

"Did you see that shark playing around?"

"Yes, I saw him. He was a big fellow, all right."

"Wish I had known you were awake."

Later the correspondent spoke into the bottom of the boat. "Billie!" There was a slow and gradual disentanglement. "Billie, will you spell me?"

"Sure," said the oiler.

As soon as the correspondent touched the cold, comfortable sea-water in the bottom of the boat and had huddled close to the cook's life-belt he was deep in sleep, despite the fact that his teeth played all the popular airs. This sleep was so good to him that it was but a moment before he heard a voice call his name in a tone that demonstrated the last stages of exhaustion. "Will you spell me?"

"Sure, Billie."

The light in the north had mysteriously vanished, but the correspondent took his course from the wide-awake captain.

Later in the night they took the boat farther out to sea, and the captain directed the cook to take one oar at the stern and keep the boat facing the seas. He was to call out if he should hear the thunder of the surf. This plan enabled the oiler and the correspondent to get respite together. "We'll give those boys a chance to get into shape again," said the captain. They curled down and, after a few preliminary chatterings and trembles, slept once more the dead sleep. Neither knew they had bequeathed to the cook the company of another shark, or perhaps the same shark.

As the boat caroused on the waves, spray occasionally bumped over the side and gave them a fresh soaking, but this had no power to break their repose. The ominous slash of the wind and the water affected them as it would have affected mummies.

"Boys," said the cook, with the notes of every reluctance in his voice, "she's drifted in pretty close. I guess one of you had better take her to sea again." The correspondent, aroused, heard the crash of the toppled crests.

As he was rowing, the captain gave him some whiskey-and-water, and this steadied the chills out of him. "If I ever get ashore and anybody shows me even a photograph of an oar—"

At last there was a short conversation.

"Billie! . . . Billie, will you spell me?"

"Sure," said the oiler.

VII

When the correspondent again opened his eyes, the sea and the sky were each of the gray hue of the dawning. Later, carmine and gold was painted upon the waters. The morning appeared finally, in its splendor, with a sky of pure blue, and the sunlight flamed on the tips of the waves.

On the distant dunes were set many little black cottages, and a tall white windmill reared above them. No man, nor dog, nor bicycle appeared on the beach. The cottages might have formed a deserted village.

The voyagers scanned the shore. A conference was held in the boat. "Well," said the captain, "if no help is coming, we might better try a run through the surf right away. If we stay out here much longer we will be too weak to do anything for ourselves at all." The others silently acquiesced in this reasoning. The boat was headed for the beach. The correspondent wondered if none ever ascended the tall wind-tower, and if then they never looked seaward. This tower was a giant, standing with its back to the plight of the ants. It represented in a degree, to the correspondent, the serenity of nature amid the struggles of the individual—nature in the wind, and nature in the vision of men. She did not seem cruel to him then, nor beneficent, nor treacherous, nor wise. But she was indifferent, flatly indifferent. It is, perhaps, plausible that a man in this situation, impressed with the unconcern of the universe, should see the innumerable flaws of his life, and have them taste wickedly in his mind, and wish for another chance. A distinction between right and wrong seems absurdly clear to him, then, in this new ignorance of the grave-edge, and he understands that if he were given another opportunity he would mend his conduct and his words, and be better and brighter during an introduction or at a tea.

"Now, boys," said the captain, "she is going to swamp sure. All we can do is to work her in as far as possible, and then when she swamps, pile out and scramble for the beach. Keep cool now, and don't jump until she swamps sure."

The oiler took the oars. Over his shoulders he scanned the surf. "Captain," he said, "I think I'd better bring her about and keep her head-on to the seas and back her in."

"All right, Billie," said the captain. "Back her in." The oiler swung the boat then, and, seated in the stern, the cook and the correspondent were obliged to look over their shoulders to contemplate the lonely and indifferent shore.

The monstrous inshore rollers heaved the boat high until the men were again enabled to see the white sheets of water scudding up the slanted beach. "We won't get in very close," said the captain. Each time a man could wrest his attention from the rollers, he turned his glance toward the shore, and in the expression of the eyes during this contemplation there was a singular quality. The correspondent, observing the others, knew that they were not afraid, but the full meaning of their glances was shrouded.

As for himself, he was too tired to grapple fundamentally with the fact. He tried to coerce his mind into thinking of it, but the mind was dominated at this time by the muscles, and the muscles said they did not care. It merely occurred to him that if he should drown it would be a shame.

There were no hurried words, no pallor, no plain agitation. The men simply looked at the shore. "Now, remember to get well clear of the boat when you jump," said the captain.

Seaward the crest of a roller suddenly fell with a thunderous crash, and the long white comber came roaring down upon the boat.

"Steady now," said the captain. The men were silent. They turned their eyes from the shore to the comber and waited. The boat slid up the incline, leaped at the furious top, bounced over it, and swung down the long back of the wave. Some water had been shipped, and the cook bailed it out.

But the next crest crashed also. The tumbling, boiling flood of white water caught the boat and whirled it almost perpendicular. Water swarmed in from all sides. The correspondent had his hands on the gunwale at this time, and when the water entered at that place he swiftly withdrew his fingers, as if he objected to wetting them.

The little boat, drunken with this weight of water, reeled and snuggled deeper into the sea.

"Bail her out, cook! Bail her out!" said the captain.

"All right, Captain," said the cook.

"Now, boys, the next one will do us for sure," said the oiler. "Mind to jump clear of the boat."

The third wave moved forward, huge, furious, implacable. It fairly swallowed the dinghy, and almost simultaneously, the men tumbled into the sea. A piece of life-belt had lain in the bottom of the boat, and as the correspondent went overboard he held this to his chest with his left hand.

The January water was icy, and reflected immediately that it was colder than he had expected to find it off the coast of Florida. This appeared to his dazed mind as a fact important enough to be noted at the time. The coldness of the water was sad; it was tragic. This fact was somehow mixed and confused with his opinion of his own situation, so that it seemed almost a proper reason for tears. The water was cold.

When he came to the surface he was conscious of little but the noisy water. Afterward he saw his companions in the sea. The oiler was ahead in the race. He was swimming strongly and rapidly. Off to the correspondent's left, the cook's great white and corked back bulged out of the water; and in the rear the captain was hanging with his one good hand to the keel of the overturned dinghy.

There is a certain immovable quality to a shore, and the correspondent wondered at it amid the confusion of the sea.

It seemed also very attractive; but the correspondent knew that it was a long journey, and he paddled leisurely. The piece of life-preserver lay under him, and sometimes he whirled down the incline of a wave as if he were on a hand-sled.

But finally he arrived at a place in the sea where travel was beset with difficulty. He did not pause swimming to inquire what manner of current had caught him, but there his progress ceased. The shore was set before him like a bit of scenery on a stage, and he looked at it and understood with his eyes each detail of it.

As the cook passed, much farther to the left, the captain was calling to him, "Turn over on your back, cook! Turn over on your back and use the oar."

"All right, sir." The cook turned on his back, and, paddling with an oar, went ahead as if he were a canoe.

Presently the boat also passed to the left of the correspondent, with the captain clinging with one hand to the keel. He would have appeared like a man raising himself to look over a board fence if it were not for the extraordinary gymnastics of the boat. The correspondent marvelled that the captain could still hold to it.

They passed on nearer to shore—the oiler, the cook, the captain—and following them went the water-jar, bouncing gaily over the seas.

The correspondent remained in the grip of this strange new enemy, a current. The shore, with its white slope of sand and its green bluff topped with little silent cottages, was spread like a picture before him. It was very near to him then, but he was impressed as one who, in a gallery, looks at a scene from Brittany or Algiers.

He thought: "I am going to drown? Can it be possible? Can it be possible? Can it be possible?" Perhaps an individual must consider his own death to be the final phenomenon of nature.

But later a wave perhaps whirled him out of this small deadly current, for he found suddenly that he could again make progress toward the shore. Later still he was aware that the captain, clinging with one hand to the keel of the dinghy, had his face turned away from the shore and toward him, and was calling his name. "Come to the boat! Come to the boat!"

In his struggle to reach the captain and the boat, he reflected that when one gets properly wearied drowning must really be a comfortable arrangement—a cessation of hostilities accompanied by a large degree of relief; and he was glad of it, for the main thing in his mind for some moments had been horror of the temporary agony; he did not wish to be hurt.

Presently he saw a man running along the shore. He was undressing with most remarkable speed. Coat, trousers, shirt, everything flew magically off him.

"Come to the boat!" called the captain.

"All right, Captain." As the correspondent paddled, he saw the captain let himself down to bottom and leave the boat. Then the correspondent performed his one little marvel of the voyage. A large wave caught him and flung him with ease and supreme speed completely over the boat and far beyond it. It struck him even then as an event in gymnastics and a true miracle of the sea. An overturned boat in the surf is not a plaything to a swimming man.

The correspondent arrived in water that reached only to his waist, but his condition did not enable him to stand for more than a moment. Each wave knocked him into a heap, and the undertow pulled at him.

Then he saw the man who had been running and undressing, and undressing and running, come bounding into the water. He dragged ashore the cook, and then waded toward the captain; but the captain waved him away and sent him to the correspondent. He was naked—naked as a tree in winter; but a halo was about his head, and he shone like a saint. He gave a strong pull, and a long drag, and a bully heave at the correspondent's hand. The correspondent, schooled in the minor formulae, said, "Thanks, old man." But suddenly the man cried, "What's that?" He pointed a swift finger. The correspondent said, "Go."

In the shallows, face downward, lay the oiler. His forehead touched sand that was periodically, between each wave, clear of the sea.

The correspondent did not know all that transpired afterward. When he achieved safe ground he fell, striking the sand with each particular part of his body. It was as if he had dropped from a roof, but the thud was grateful to him.

It seems that instantly the beach was populated with men with blankets, clothes, and flasks, and women with coffee-pots and all the remedies sacred to their minds. The welcome of the land to the men from the sea was warm and generous; but a still and dripping shape was carried slowly up the beach, and the land's welcome for it could only be the different and sinister hospitality of the grave.

When it came night, the white waves paced to and fro in the moonlight, and the wind brought the sound of the great sea's voice to the men on the shore, and they felt that they could then be interpreters.

FOR STUDY, DISCUSSION, AND WRITING

1. What significance can you assign to the story's opening line: "None of them knew the color of the sky"?
2. At what points in the story can you find evidence of Crane's belief that humans are often unable to interpret situations or events accurately?
3. Explain the tone and meaning of the expression "nibble the sacred cheese of life."
4. What specific symbolic items indicating the indifference of the universe can you find in the story? Explain each.
5. In what ways do the men show consideration for one another?
6. What narrative purpose is served by the episode in which the correspondent recalls the verses about the soldier in Algiers?
7. How does the correspondent's brush with death in the small boat on the open sea affect his attitude toward the other men and toward humanity in general? What evidence does the story provide that the attitudes of the other men are similarly affected?
8. What is ironic about the fact that the oiler is the only person who drowns?
9. Discuss the significance of the story's final paragraph.

The Real Thing

I

When the porter's wife (she used to answer the house-bell) announced "A gentleman—with a lady, sir," I had, as I often had in those days, for the wish was father to the thought, an immediate vision of sitters. Sitters my visitors in this case proved to be; but not in the sense I should have preferred. However, there was nothing at first to indicate that they might not have come for a portrait. The gentleman, a man of fifty, very high and very straight, with a moustache slightly grizzled and a dark grey walking-coat admirably fitted, both of which I noted professionally—I don't mean as a barber or yet as a tailor—would have struck me as a celebrity if celebrities often were striking. It was a truth of which I had for some time been conscious that a figure with a good deal of frontage was, as one might say, almost never a public institution. A glance at the lady helped to remind me of this paradoxical law: she also looked too distinguished to be a "personality." Moreover one would scarcely come across two variations together.

Neither of the pair spoke immediately—they only prolonged the preliminary gaze which suggested that each wished to give the other a chance. They were visibly shy; they stood there letting me take them in—which, as I afterwards perceived, was the most practical thing they could have done. In this way their embarrassment served their cause. I had seen people painfully reluctant to mention that they desired anything so gross as to be represented on canvas; but the scruples of my new friends appeared almost insurmountable. Yet the gentleman might have said "I should like a portrait of my wife," and the lady might have said "I should like a portrait of my husband." Perhaps they were not husband and wife—this naturally would make the matter more delicate. Perhaps they wished to be done together—in which case they ought to have brought a third person to break the news.

"We come from Mr Rivet," the lady said at last, with a dim smile which had the effect of a moist sponge passed over a "sunk" piece of painting, as well as of a vague allusion to vanished beauty. She was as tall and straight, in her degree, as her companion, and with ten years less to carry. She looked as sad as a woman could look whose face was not charged with expression; that is her tinted oval mask showed friction as an exposed surface shows it. The hand of time had played over her freely, but only to simplify. She was slim and stiff, and so well-dressed, in dark blue cloth, with lappets and pockets and buttons, that it was clear she employed the same tailor as her husband. The couple had an indefinable air of prosperous thrift—they evidently got a good deal of luxury for their money. If I was to be one of their luxuries it would behove me to consider my terms.

"Ah, Claude Rivet recommended me?" I inquired; and I added that it was very kind of him, though I could reflect that, as he only painted landscape, this was not a sacrifice.

The lady looked very hard at the gentleman, and the gentleman looked round the room. Then staring at the floor a moment and stroking his moustache, he rested his pleasant eyes on me with the remark: "He said you were the right one."

"I try to be, when people want to sit."

"Yes, we should like to," said the lady anxiously.

"Do you mean together?"

My visitors exchanged a glance. "If you could do anything with *me*, I suppose it would be double," the gentleman stammered.

"Oh yes, there's naturally a higher charge for two figures than for one."

"We should like to make it pay," the husband confessed.

"That's very good of you," I returned, appreciating so unwonted a sympathy—for I supposed he meant pay the artist.

A sense of strangeness seemed to dawn on the lady. "We mean for the illustrations—Mr Rivet said you might put one in."

"Put one in—an illustration?" I was equally confused.

"Sketch her off, you know," said the gentleman, colouring.

It was only then that I understood the service Claude Rivet had rendered me; he had told them that I worked in black and white, for magazines, for story-books, for sketches of contemporary life, and consequently had frequent employment for models. These things were true, but it was not less true (I may confess it now—whether because the aspiration was to lead to everything or to nothing I leave the reader to guess), that I couldn't get the honours, to say nothing of the emoluments, of a great painter of portraits out of my head. My "illustrations" were my pot-boilers; I looked to a different branch of art (far and away the most interesting it had always seemed to me), to perpetuate my fame. There was no shame in looking to it also to make my fortune; but that fortune was by so much further from being made from the moment my visitors wished to be "done" for nothing. I was disappointed; for in the pictorial sense I had immediately *seen* them. I had seized their type—I had already settled what I would do with it. Something that wouldn't absolutely have pleased them, I afterwards reflected.

"Ah, you're—you're—a—?" I began, as soon as I had mastered my surprise. I couldn't bring out the dingy word "models"; it seemed to fit the case so little.

"We haven't had much practice," said the lady.

"We've got to *do* something, and we've thought that an artist in your line might perhaps make something of us," her husband threw off. He further mentioned that they didn't know many artists and that they had gone first, on the off-chance (he painted views of course, but sometimes put in figures—

perhaps I remembered), to Mr Rivet, whom they had met a few years before at a place in Norfolk where he was sketching.

"We used to sketch a little ourselves," the lady hinted.

"It's very awkward, but we absolutely *must* do something," her husband went on.

"Of course, we're not so *very* young," she admitted, with a wan smile.

With the remark that I might as well know something more about them, the husband had handed me a card extracted from a neat new pocket-book (their appurtenances were all of the freshest) and inscribed with the words "Major Monarch." Impressive as these words were they didn't carry my knowledge much further; but my visitor presently added: "I've left the army, and we've had the misfortune to lose our money. In fact our means are dreadfully small."

"It's an awful bore," said Mrs Monarch.

They evidently wished to be discreet—to take care not to swagger because they were gentlefolks. I perceived they would have been willing to recognise this as something of a drawback, at the same time that I guessed at an underlying sense—their consolation in adversity—that they *had* their points. They certainly had; but these advantages struck me as preponderantly social; such for instance as would help to make a drawing-room look well. However, a drawing-room was always, or ought to be, a picture.

In consequence of his wife's allusion to their age Major Monarch observed: "Naturally, it's more for the figure that we thought of going in. We can still hold ourselves up." On the instant I saw that the figure was indeed their strong point. His "naturally" didn't sound vain, but it lighted up the question. "*She* has got the best," he continued, nodding at his wife, with a pleasant after-dinner absence of circumlocution. I could only reply, as if we were in fact sitting over our wine, that this didn't prevent his own from being very good; which led him in turn to rejoin: "We thought that if you ever have to do people like us, we might be something like it. *She*, particularly—for a lady in a book, you know."

I was so amused by them that, to get more of it, I did my best to take their point of view; and though it was an embarrassment to find myself appraising physically, as if they were animals on hire or useful blacks, a pair whom I should have expected to meet only in one of the relations in which criticism is tacit, I looked at Mrs Monarch judicially enough to be able to exclaim, after a moment, with conviction: "Oh yes, a lady in a book!" She was singularly like a bad illustration.

"We'll stand up, if you like," said the Major; and he raised himself before me with a really grand air.

I could take his measure at a glance—he was six feet two and a perfect gentleman. It would have paid any club in process of formation and in want of a stamp to engage him at a salary to stand in the principal window. What struck me immediately was that in coming to me they had rather missed their vocation; they could surely have been turned to better account for advertising purposes. I couldn't of course see the thing in detail, but I could see them make someone's fortune—I don't mean their own. There was something in them for a waistcoat-maker, an hotel-keeper or a soap-vendor. I could imagine "We always use it" pinned on their bosoms with the greatest effect; I had a vision of the promptitude with which they would launch a table d'hôte.

Mrs Monarch sat still, not from pride but from shyness, and presently her husband said to her: "Get up my dear and show how smart you are." She obeyed, but she had no need to get up to show it. She walked to the end of the studio, and then she came back blushing, with her fluttered eyes on her husband. I was reminded of an incident I had accidentally had a glimpse of in Paris—being with a friend there, a dramatist about to produce a play—when an actress came to him to ask to be intrusted with a part. She went through her paces before him, walked up and down as Mrs Monarch was doing. Mrs Monarch did it quite as well, but I abstained from applauding. It was very odd to see such people apply for such poor pay. She looked as if she had ten thousand a year. Her husband had used the word that described her: she was, in the London current jargon, essentially and typically "smart." Her figure was, in the same order of ideas, conspicuously and irreproachably "good." For a woman of her age her waist was surprisingly small; her elbow moreover had the orthodox crook. She held her head at the conventional angle; but why did she come to *me*? She ought to have tried on jackets at a big shop. I feared my visitors were not only destitute, but "artistic"—which would be a great complication. When she sat down again I thanked her, observing that what a draughtsman most valued in his model was the faculty of keeping quiet.

"Oh, *she* can keep quiet," said Major Monarch. Then he added, jocosely: "I've always kept her quiet."

"I'm not a nasty fidget, am I?" Mrs Monarch appealed to her husband.

He addressed his answer to me. "Perhaps it isn't out of place to mention—because we ought to be quite businesslike, oughtn't we?—that when I married her she was known as the Beautiful Statue."

"Oh dear!" said Mrs Monarch, ruefully.

"Of course I should want a certain amount of expression," I rejoined.

"Of *course!*" they both exclaimed.

"And then I suppose you know that you'll get awfully tired."

"Oh, we *never* get tired!" they eagerly cried.

"Have you had any kind of practice?"

They hesitated—they looked at each other. "We've been photographed, *immensely*," said Mrs Monarch.

"She means the fellows have asked us," added the Major.

"I see—because you're so good-looking."

"I don't know what they thought, but they were always after us."

"We always got our photographs for nothing," smiled Mrs Monarch.

"We might have brought some, my dear," her husband remarked.

"I'm not sure we have any left. We've given quantities away," she explained to me.

"With our autographs and that sort of thing," said the Major.

"Are they to be got in the shops?" I inquired, as a harmless pleasantry.

"Oh, yes; hers—they used to be."

"Not now," said Mrs Monarch, with her eyes on the floor.

II

I could fancy the "sort of thing" they put on the presentation-copies of their photographs, and I was sure they wrote a beautiful hand. It was odd how quickly I was sure of everything that concerned them. If they were now so poor as to have to earn shillings and pence, they never had had much of a margin. Their good looks had been their capital, and they had good-humour-edly made the most of the career that this resource marked out for them. It was in their faces, the blankness, the deep intellectual repose of the twenty years of country-house visiting which had given them pleasant intonations. I could see the sunny drawing-rooms, sprinkled with periodicals she didn't read, in which Mrs Monarch had continuously sat; I could see the wet shrub-beries in which she had walked, equipped to admiration for either exercise. I could see the rich covers the Major had helped to shoot and the wonderful garments in which, late at night, he repaired to the smoking-room to talk about them. I could imagine their leggings and waterproofs, their knowing tweeds and rugs, their rolls of sticks and cases of tackle and neat umbrellas; and I could evoke the exact appearance of their servants and the compact variety of their luggage on the platforms of country stations.

They gave small tips, but they were liked; they didn't do anything them-selves, but they were welcome. They looked so well everywhere; they gratified the general relish for stature, complexion and "form." They knew it without fatuity or vulgarity, and they respected themselves in consequence. They were not superficial; they were thorough and kept themselves up—it had been their line. People with such a taste for activity had to have some line. I could feel how, even in a dull house, they could have been counted upon for cheerful-ness. At present something had happened—it didn't matter what, their little income had grown less, it had grown least—and they had to do something for pocket-money. Their friends liked them, but didn't like to support them. There was something about them that represented credit—their clothes, their manners, their type; but if credit is a large empty pocket in which an occa-sional chink reverberates, the chink at least must be audible. What they wanted of me was to help to make it so. Fortunately they had no children—I soon divined that. They would also perhaps wish our relations to be kept secret: this was why it was "for the figure"—the reproduction of the face would betray them.

I liked them—they were so simple; and I had no objection to them if they would suit. But, somehow, with all their perfections I didn't easily believe in them. After all they were amateurs, and the ruling passion of my life was the detestation of the amateur. Combined with this was another perversity—an innate preference for the represented subject over the real one: the defect of the real one was so apt to be a lack of representation. I liked things that appeared; then one was sure. Whether they *were* or not was a subordinate and almost always a profitless question. There were other considerations, the first of which was that I already had two or three people in use, notably a young person with big feet, in alpaca, from Kilburn, who for a couple of years had come to me regularly for my illustrations and with whom I was still—perhaps ignobly—satisfied. I frankly explained to my visitors how the case stood; but they had taken more precautions than I supposed. They had reasoned out their opportunity, for Claude Rivet had told them of the projected *édition de luxe* of one of the writers of our day—the rarest of the novelists—who, long neglected by the multitudinous vulgar and dearly prized by the attentive (need I mention Philip Vincent?) had had the happy fortune of seeing, late in life, the dawn and then the full light of a higher criticism—an estimate in which, on the part of the public, there was something really of expiation. The edition in question, planned by a publisher of taste, was practically an act of high reparation; the wood-cuts with which it was to be enriched were the homage of English art to one of the most independent representatives of English letters. Major and Mrs Monarch confessed to me that they had hoped I might be able to work *them* into my share of the enterprise. They knew I was to do the first of the books, "Rutland Ramsay," but I had to make clear to them that my participation in the rest of the affair—this first book was to be a test—was to depend on the satisfaction I should give. If this should be limited my employers would drop me without a scruple. It was therefore a crisis for me, and naturally I was making special preparations, looking about for new people, if they should be necessary, and securing the best types. I admitted however that I should like to settle down to two or three good models who would do for everything.

"Should we have often to—a—put on special clothes?" Mrs Monarch timidly demanded.

"Dear, yes—that's half the business."

"And should we be expected to supply our own costumes?"

"Oh, no; I've got a lot of things. A painter's models put on—or put off—anything he likes."

"And do you mean—a—the same?"

"The same?"

Mrs Monarch looked at her husband again.

"Oh, she was just wondering," he explained, "if the costumes are in *general* use." I had to confess that they were, and I mentioned further that some of them (I had a lot of genuine, greasy last-century things), had served their time, a hundred years ago, on living, world-stained men and women. "We'll put on anything that *fits*," said the Major.

"Oh, I arrange that—they fit in the pictures."

"I'm afraid I should do better for the modern books. I would come as you like," said Mrs Monarch.

"She has got a lot of clothes at home: they might do for contemporary life," her husband continued.

"Oh, I can fancy scenes in which you'd be quite natural." And indeed I could see the slipshod rearrangements of stale properties—the stories I tried to produce pictures for without the exasperation of reading them—whose sandy tracts the good lady might help to people. But I had to return to the fact that for this sort of work—the daily mechanical grind—I was already equipped; the people I was working with were fully adequate.

"We only thought we might be more like *some* characters," said Mrs Monarch mildly, getting up.

Her husband also rose; he stood looking at me with a dim wistfulness that was touching in so fine a man. "Wouldn't it be rather a pull sometimes to have—a—to have—?" He hung fire; he wanted me to help him by phrasing what he meant. But I couldn't—I didn't know. So he brought it out, awkwardly: "The *real* thing; a gentleman, you know, or a lady." I was quite ready to give a general assent—I admitted that there was a great deal in that. This encouraged Major Monarch to say, following up his appeal with an unacted gulp: "It's awfully hard—we've tried everything." The gulp was communicative; it proved too much for his wife. Before I knew it Mrs Monarch had dropped again upon a divan and burst into tears. Her husband sat down beside her, holding one of her hands; whereupon she quickly dried her eyes with the other, while I felt embarrassed as she looked up at me. "There isn't a confounded job I haven't applied for—waited for—prayed for. You can fancy we'd be pretty bad first. Secretaryships and that sort of thing? You might as well ask for a peerage. I'd be *anything*—I'm strong; a messenger or a coal-heaver. I'd put on a gold-laced cap and open carriage-doors in front of the haberdasher's; I'd hang about a station, to carry portmanteaus; I'd be a postman. But they won't *look* at you; there are thousands, as good as yourself, already on the ground. *Gentlemen*, poor beggars, who have drunk their wine, who have kept their hunters!"

I was as reassuring as I knew how to be, and my visitors were presently on their feet again while, for the experiment, we agreed on an hour. We were discussing it when the door opened and Miss Churm came in with a wet umbrella. Miss Churm had to take the omnibus to Maida Vale and then walk half-a-mile. She looked a trifle blowsy and slightly splashed. I scarcely ever saw her come in without thinking afresh how odd it was that, being so little in herself, she should yet be so much in others. She was a meagre little Miss Churm, but she was an ample heroine of romance. She was only a freckled cockney, but she could represent everything, from a fine lady to a shepherdess; she had the faculty, as she might have had a fine voice or long hair. She couldn't spell, and she loved beer, but she had two or three "points," and practice, and a knack, and mother-wit, and a kind of whimsical sensibility, and a love of the theatre, and seven sisters, and not an ounce of respect, especially for the *h*. The first thing my visitors saw was that her umbrella was wet, and in their spotless perfection they visibly winced at it. The rain had come on since their arrival.

"I'm all in a soak; there *was* a mess of people in the 'bus. I wish you lived near a stytion," said Miss Churm. I requested her to get ready as quickly as possible, and she passed into the room in which she always changed her dress. But before going out she asked me what she was to get into this time.

"It's the Russian princess, don't you know?" I answered; "the one with the 'golden eyes,' in black velvet, for the long thing in the *Cheapside.*"

"Golden eyes? I *say!*" cried Miss Churm, while my companions watched her with intensity as she withdrew. She always arranged herself, when she was late, before I could turn round; and I kept my visitors a little, on purpose, so that they might get an idea, from seeing her, what would be expected of themselves. I mentioned that she was quite my notion of an excellent model— she was really very clever.

"Do you think she looks like a Russian princess?" Major Monarch asked, with lurking alarm.

"When I make her, yes."

"Oh, if you have to *make* her—!" he reasoned, acutely.

"That's the most you can ask. There are so many that are not makeable."

"Well now, *here's* a lady"—and with a persuasive smile he passed his arm into his wife's—"who's already made!"

"Oh, I'm not a Russian princess," Mrs Monarch protested, a little coldly. I could see that she had known some and didn't like them. There, immediately, was a complication of a kind that I never had to fear with Miss Churm.

This young lady came back in black velvet—the gown was rather rusty and very low on her lean shoulders—and with a Japanese fan in her red hands. I reminded her that in the scene I was doing she had to look over someone's head. "I forget whose it is; but it doesn't matter. Just look over a head."

"I'd rather look over a stove," said Miss Churm; and she took her station near the fire. She fell into position, settled herself into a tall attitude, gave a certain backward inclination to her head and a certain forward droop to her fan, and looked, at least to my prejudiced sense, distinguished and charming, foreign and dangerous. We left her looking so, while I went down-stairs with Major and Mrs Monarch.

"I think I could come about as near it as that," said Mrs Monarch.

"Oh, you think she's shabby, but you must allow for the alchemy of art."

However, they went off with an evident increase of comfort, founded on their demonstrable advantage in being the real thing. I could fancy them shuddering over Miss Churm. She was very droll about them when I went back, for I told her what they wanted.

"Well, if *she* can sit I'll tyke to bookkeeping," said my model.

"She's very lady-like," I replied, as an innocent form of aggravation.

"So much the worse for *you.* That means she can't turn round."

"She'll do for the fashionable novels."

"Oh yes, she'll *do* for them!" my model humorously declared. "Ain't they bad enough without her?" I had often sociably denounced them to Miss Churm.

III

It was for the elucidation of a mystery in one of these works that I first tried Mrs Monarch. Her husband came with her, to be useful if necessary—it was sufficiently clear that as a general thing he would prefer to come with her. At first I wondered if this were for "propriety's" sake—if he were going to be jealous and meddling. The idea was too tiresome, and if it had been confirmed it would speedily have brought our acquaintance to a close. But I soon saw there was nothing in it and that if he accompanied Mrs Monarch it was (in addition to the chance of being wanted), simply because he had nothing else to do. When she was away from him his occupation was gone—she never *had* been away from him. I judged, rightly, that in their awkward situation their close union was their main comfort and that this union had no weak spot. It was a real marriage, an encouragement to the hesitating, a nut for pessimists to crack. Their address was humble (I remember afterwards thinking it had been the only thing about them that was really professional), and I could fancy the lamentable lodgings in which the Major would have been left alone. He could bear them with his wife—he couldn't bear them without her.

He had too much tact to try and make himself agreeable when he couldn't be useful; so he simply sat and waited, when I was too absorbed in my work to talk. But I liked to make him talk—it made my work, when it didn't interrupt it, less sordid, less special. To listen to him was to combine the excitement of going out with the economy of staying at home. There was only one hindrance; that I seemed not to know any of the people he and his wife had known. I think he wondered extremely, during the term of our intercourse, whom the deuce I *did* know. He hadn't a stray sixpence of an idea to fumble for; so we didn't spin it very fine—we confined ourselves to questions of leather and even of liquor (saddlers and breeches-makers and how to get good claret cheap), and matters like "good trains" and the habits of small game. His lore on these last subjects was astonishing, he managed to interweave the stationmaster with the ornithologist. When he couldn't talk about greater things he could talk cheerfully about smaller, and since I couldn't accompany him into reminiscences of the fashionable world he could lower the conversation without a visible effort to my level.

So earnest a desire to please was touching in a man who could so easily have knocked one down. He looked after the fire and had an opinion on the draught of the stove, without my asking him, and I could see that he thought many of my arrangements not half clever enough. I remember telling him that if I were only rich I would offer him a salary to come and teach me how to live. Sometimes he gave a random sigh, of which the essence was: "Give me even such a bare old barrack as *this*, and I'd do something with it!" When I wanted to use him he came alone; which was an illustration of the superior courage of women. His wife could bear her solitary second floor, and she was in general more discreet; showing by various small reserves that she was alive to the propriety of keeping our relations markedly professional—not letting them slide into sociability. She wished it to remain clear that she and the Major were employed, not cultivated, and if she approved of me as a superior, who could be kept in his place, she never thought me quite good enough for an equal.

She sat with great intensity, giving the whole of her mind to it, and was capable of remaining for an hour almost as motionless as if she were before a photographer's lens. I could see she had been photographed often, but somehow the very habit that made her good for that purpose unfitted her for mine. At first I was extremely pleased with her lady-like air, and it was a satisfaction, on coming to follow her lines, to see how good they were and how far they could lead the pencil. But after a few times I began to find her too insurmountably stiff; do what I would with it my drawing looked like a photograph or a copy of a photograph. Her figure had no variety of expression—she herself had no sense of variety. You may say that this was my business, was only a question of placing her. I placed her in every conceivable position, but she managed to obliterate their differences. She was always a lady certainly, and into the bargain was always the same lady. She was the real thing, but always the same thing. There were moments when I was oppressed by the serenity of her confidence that she *was* the real thing. All her dealings with me and all her husband's were an implication that this was lucky for *me*. Meanwhile I found myself trying to invent types that approached her own, instead of making her own transform itself—in the clever way that was not impossible, for instance, to poor Miss Churm. Arrange as I would and take the precautions I would, she always, in my pictures, came out too tall—landing me in the dilemma of having represented a fascinating woman as seven feet high, which, out of respect perhaps to my own very much scantier inches, was far from my idea of such a personage.

The case was worse with the Major—nothing I could do would keep *him* down, so that he became useful only for the representation of brawny giants. I adored variety and range, I cherished human accidents, the illustrative note; I wanted to characterise closely, and the thing in the world I most hated was the danger of being ridden by a type. I had quarrelled with some of my friends about it—I had parted company with them for maintaining that one *had* to be, and that if the type was beautiful (witness Raphael and Leonardo), the servitude was only a gain. I was neither Leonardo nor Raphael; I might only be a presumptuous young modern searcher, but I held that everything was to be sacrificed sooner than character. When they averred that the haunting type in question could easily *be* character, I retorted, perhaps superficially: "Whose?" It couldn't be everybody's—it might end in being nobody's.

After I had drawn Mrs Monarch a dozen times I perceived more clearly than before that the value of such a model as Miss Churm resided precisely in the fact that she had no positive stamp, combined of course with the other fact that what she did have was a curious and inexplicable talent for imitation. Her usual appearance was like a curtain which she could draw up at request for a capital performance. This performance was simply suggestive; but it was a word to the wise—it was vivid and pretty. Sometimes, even, I thought it, though she was plain herself, too insipidly pretty; I made it a reproach to her that the figures drawn from her were monotonously (*bêtement*, as we used to say) graceful. Nothing made her more angry; it was so much her pride to feel that she could sit for characters that had nothing in common with each other. She would accuse me at such moments of taking away her "reputytion."

It suffered a certain shrinkage, this queer quantity, from the repeated visits of my new friends. Miss Churm was greatly in demand, never in want of employment, so I had no scruple in putting her off occasionally, to try them more at my ease. It was certainly amusing at first to do the real thing—it was amusing to do Major Monarch's trousers. They *were* the real thing, even if he did come out colossal. It was amusing to do his wife's back hair (it was so mathematically neat,) and the particular "smart" tension of her tight stays. She lent herself especially to positions in which the face was somewhat averted or blurred; she abounded in lady-like back views and *profils perdus*. When she stood erect she took naturally one of the attitudes in which court-painters represent queens and princesses; so that I found myself wondering whether, to draw out this accomplishment, I couldn't get the editor of the *Cheapside* to publish a really royal romance, "A Tale of Buckingham Palace." Sometimes, however, the real thing and the make-believe came into contact; by which I mean that Miss Churm, keeping an appointment or coming to make one on days when I had much work in hand, encountered her invidious rivals. The encounter was not on their part, for they noticed her no more than if she had been the housemaid; not from intentional loftiness, but simply because, as yet, professionally, they didn't know how to fraternize, as I could guess that they would have liked—or at least that the Major would. They couldn't talk about the omnibus—they always walked; and they didn't know what else to try—she wasn't interested in good trains or cheap claret. Besides, they must have felt—in the air—that she was amused at them, secretly derisive of their ever knowing how. She was not a person to conceal her scepticism if she had had a chance to show it. On the other hand Mrs Monarch didn't think her tidy; for why else did she take pains to say to me (it was going out of the way, for Mrs Monarch), that she didn't like dirty women?

One day when my young lady happened to be present with my other sitters (she even dropped in, when it was convenient, for a chat), I asked her to be so good as to lend a hand in getting tea—a service with which she was familiar and which was one of a class that, living as I did in a small way, with slender domestic resources, I often appealed to my models to render. They liked to lay hands on my property, to break the sitting, and sometimes the china—I made them feel Bohemian. The next time I saw Miss Churm after this incident she surprised me greatly by making a scene about it—she accused me of having wished to humiliate her. She had not resented the outrage at the time, but had seemed obliging and amused, enjoying the comedy of asking Mrs Monarch, who sat vague and silent, whether she would have cream and sugar, and putting an exaggerated simper into the question. She had tried intonations— as if she too wished to pass for the real thing; till I was afraid my other visitors would take offence.

Oh, *they* were determined not to do this; and their touching patience was the measure of their great need. They would sit by the hour, uncomplaining, till I was ready to use them; they would come back on the chance of being wanted and would walk away cheerfully if they were not. I used to go to the door with them to see in what magnificent order they retreated. I tried to find other employment for them—I introduced them to several artists. But they didn't "take," for reasons I could appreciate, and I became conscious, rather anxiously, that after such disappointments they fell back upon me with a heavier weight. They did me the honour to think that it was I who was most *their* form. They were not picturesque enough for the painters, and in those days there were not so many serious workers in black and white. Besides, they had an eye to the great job I had mentioned to them—they had secretly set their hearts on supplying the right essence for my pictorial vindication of our fine novelist. They knew that for this undertaking I should want no costume-effects, none of the frippery of past ages—that it was a case in which everything would be contemporary and satirical and, presumably, genteel. If I could work them into it their future would be assured, for the labour would of course be long and the occupation steady.

One day Mrs. Monarch came without her husband—she explained his absence by his having had to go to the City. While she sat there in her usual anxious stiffness there came, at the door, a knock which I immediately recognised as the subdued appeal of a model out of work. It was followed by the entrance of a young man whom I easily perceived to be a foreigner and who proved in fact an Italian acquainted with no English word but my name, which he uttered in a way that made it seem to include all others. I had not then visited his country, nor was I proficient in his tongue; but as he was not so meanly constituted—what Italian is?—as to depend only on that member for expression he conveyed to me, in familiar but graceful mimicry, that he was in search of exactly the employment in which the lady before me was engaged. I was not struck with him at first, and while I continued to draw I emitted rough sounds of discouragement and dismissal. He stood his ground, however, not importunately, but with a dumb, dog-like fidelity in his eyes which amounted to innocent impudence—the manner of a devoted servant (he might have been in the house for years), unjustly suspected. Suddenly I saw that this very attitude and expression made a picture, whereupon I told him to sit down and wait till I should be free. There was another picture in the way he obeyed me, and I observed as I worked that there were others still in the way he looked wonderingly, with his head thrown back, about the high studio. He might have been crossing himself in St. Peter's. Before I finished I said to myself: "The fellow's a bankrupt orange-monger, but he's a treasure."

When Mrs Monarch withdrew he passed across the room like a flash to open the door for her, standing there with the rapt, pure gaze of the young Dante spellbound by the young Beatrice. As I never insisted, in such situations, on the blankness of the British domestic, I reflected that he had the making of a servant (and I needed one, but couldn't pay him to be only that), as well as of a model; in short I made up my mind to adopt my bright adventurer if he would agree to officiate in the double capacity. He jumped at my offer, and in the event my rashness (for I had known nothing about him), was not brought home to me. He proved a sympathetic though a desultory ministrant, and had in a wonderful degree the *sentiment de la pose*. It was uncultivated, instinctive; a part of the happy instinct which had guided him to my door and helped him to spell out my name on the card nailed to it. He had had no other introduction to me than a guess, from the shape of my high north window, seen outside, that my place was a studio, and that as a studio it would contain an artist. He had wandered to England in search of fortune, like other itinerants, and had embarked, with a partner and a small green handcart, on the sale of penny ices. The ices had melted away and the partner had dissolved in their train. My young man wore tight yellow trousers with reddish stripes and his name was Oronte. He was sallow but fair, and when I put him into some old clothes of my own he looked like an Englishman. He was as good as Miss Churm, who could look, when required, like an Italian.

IV

I thought Mrs Monarch's face slightly convulsed when, on her coming back with her husband, she found Oronte installed. It was strange to have to recognise in a scrap of a lazzarone a competitor to her magnificent Major. It was she who scented danger first, for the Major was anecdotically unconscious. But Oronte gave us tea, with a hundred eager confusions (he had never seen such a queer process), and I think she thought better of me for having at last an "establishment." They saw a couple of drawings that I had made of the establishment, and Mrs Monarch hinted that it never would have struck her that he had sat for them. "Now the drawings you make from *us*, they look exactly like us," she reminded me, smiling in triumph; and I recognised that this was indeed just their defect. When I drew the Monarchs I couldn't, somehow, get away from them—get into the character I wanted to represent; and I had not the least desire my model should be discoverable in my picture. Miss Churm never was, and Mrs Monarch thought I hid her, very properly, because she was vulgar; whereas if she was lost it was only as the dead who go to heaven are lost—in the gain of an angel the more.

By this time I had got a certain start with "Rutland Ramsay," the first novel in the great projected series; that is I had produced a dozen drawings, several with the help of the Major and his wife, and I had sent them in for approval. My understanding with the publishers, as I have already hinted, had been that I was to be left to do my work, in this particular case, as I liked, with the whole book committed to me; but my connection with the rest of the series was only contingent. There were moments when, frankly, it *was* a comfort to have the real thing under one's hand; for there were characters in "Rutland Ramsay" that were very much like it. There were people presumably as straight as the Major and women of as good a fashion as Mrs Monarch. There was a great deal of country-house life—treated, it is true, in a fine, fanciful, ironical, generalised way—and there was a considerable implication of knickerbockers and kilts. There were certain things I had to settle at the outset; such things for instance as the exact appearance of the hero, the particular bloom of the heroine. The author of course gave me a lead, but there was a margin for interpretation. I took the Monarchs into my confidence, I told them frankly what I was about, I mentioned my embarrassments and alternatives. "Oh, take *him!*" Mrs Monarch murmured sweetly, looking at her husband; and "What could you want better than my wife?" the Major inquired, with the comfortable candor that now prevailed between us.

I was not obliged to answer these remarks—I was only obliged to place my sitters. I was not easy in mind, and I postponed, a little timidly perhaps, the solution of the question. The book was a large canvas, the other figures were numerous, and I worked off at first some of the episodes in which the hero and the heroine were not concerned. When once I had set *them* up I should have to stick to them—I couldn't make my young man seven feet high in one place and five feet nine in another. I inclined on the whole to the latter measurement, though the Major more than once reminded me that *he* looked about as young as anyone. It was indeed quite possible to arrange him, for the figure, so that it would have been difficult to detect his age. After the spontaneous Oronte had been with me a month, and after I had given him to understand several different times that his native exuberance would presently constitute an insurmountable barrier to our further intercourse, I waked to a sense of his heroic capacity. He was only five feet seven, but the remaining inches were latent. I tried him almost secretly at first, for I was really rather afraid of the judgment my other models would pass on such a choice. If they regarded Miss Churm as little better than a snare, what would they think of the representation by a person so little the real thing as an Italian streetvendor of a protagonist formed by a public school?

If I went a little in fear of them it was not because they bullied me, because they had got an oppressive foothold, but because in their really pathetic decorum and mysteriously permanent newness they counted on me so intensely. I was therefore very glad when Jack Hawley came home: he was always of such good counsel. He painted badly himself, but there was no one like him for putting his finger on the place. He had been absent from England for a year; he had been somewhere—I don't remember where—to get a fresh eye. I was in a good deal of dread of any such organ, but we were old friends; he had been away for months and a sense of emptiness was creeping into my life. I hadn't dodged a missile for a year.

He came back with a fresh eye, but with the same old black velvet blouse, and the first evening he spent in my studio we smoked cigarettes till the small hours. He had done no work himself, he had only got the eye; so the field was clear for the production of my little things. He wanted to see what I had done for the *Cheapside*, but he was disappointed in the exhibition. That at least seemed the meaning of two or three comprehensive groans which, as he lounged on my big divan, on a folded leg, looking at my latest drawings, issued from his lips with the smoke of the cigarette.

"What's the matter with you?" I asked.

"What's the matter with *you?*"

"Nothing save that I'm mystified."

"You are indeed. You're quite off the hinge. What's the meaning of this new fad?" And he tossed me, with visible irreverence, a drawing in which I happened to have depicted both my majestic models. I asked if he didn't think it good, and he replied that it struck him as execrable, given the sort of thing I had always represented myself to him as wishing to arrive at; but I let that pass, I was so anxious to see exactly what he meant. The two figures in the picture looked colossal, but I supposed this was *not* what he meant, inasmuch as, for aught he knew to the contrary, I might have been trying for that. I maintained that I was working exactly in the same way as when he last had done me the honour to commend me. "Well, there's a big hole somewhere," he answered; "wait a bit and I'll discover it." I depended upon him to do so: where else was the fresh eye? But he produced at last nothing more luminous than "I don't know—I don't like your types." This was lame, for a critic who had never consented to discuss with me anything but the question of execution, the direction of strokes and the mystery of values.

"In the drawings you've been looking at I think my types are very handsome."

"Oh, they won't do!"

"I've had a couple of new models."

"I see you have. *They* won't do."

"Are you very sure of that?"

"Absolutely—they're stupid."

"You mean *I* am—for I ought to get round that."

"You *can't*—with such people. Who are they?"

I told him, as far as was necessary, and he declared, heartlessly: "*Ce sont des gens qu'il faut mettre à la porte.*"

"You've never seen them; they're awfully good," I compassionately objected.

"Not seen them? Why, all this recent work of yours drops to pieces with them. It's all I want to see of them."

"No one else has said anything against it—the *Cheapside* people are pleased."

"Everyone else is an ass, and the *Cheapside* people the biggest asses of all. Come, don't pretend, at this time of day, to have pretty illusions about the public, especially about publishers and editors. It's not for *such* animals you work—it's for those who know, *coloro che sanno*; so keep straight for *me* if you can't keep straight for yourself. There's a certain sort of thing you tried for from the first—and a very good thing it is. But this twaddle isn't *in* it." When I talked with Hawley later about "Rutland Ramsay" and its possible successors he declared that I must get back into my boat again or I would go to the bottom. His voice in short was the voice of warning.

I noted the warning, but I didn't turn my friends out of doors. They bored me a good deal; but the very fact that they bored me admonished me not to sacrifice them—if there was anything to be done with them—simply to irritation. As I look back at this phase they seem to me to have pervaded my life not a little. I have a vision of them as most of the time in my studio, seated, against the wall, on an old velvet bench to be out of the way, and looking like a pair of patient courtiers in a royal ante-chamber. I am convinced that during the coldest weeks of the winter they held their ground because it saved them fire. Their newness was losing its gloss, and it was impossible not to feel that they were objects of charity. Whenever Miss Churm arrived they went away, and after I was fairly launched in "Rutland Ramsay" Miss Churm arrived pretty often. They managed to express to me tacitly that they supposed I wanted her for the low life of the book, and I let them suppose it, since they had attempted to study the work—it was lying about the studio—without discovering that it dealt only with the highest circles. They had dipped into the most brilliant of our novelists without deciphering many passages. I still took an hour from them, now and again, in spite of Jack Hawley's warning: it would be time enough to dismiss them, if dismissal should be necessary, when the rigour of the season was over. Hawley had made their acquaintance—he had met them at my fireside—and thought them a ridiculous pair. Learning that he was a painter they tried to approach him, to show him too that they were the real thing; but he looked at them, across the big room, as if they were miles away: they were a compendium of everything that he most objected to in the social system of his country. Such people as that, all convention and patent-leather, with ejaculations that stopped conversation, had no business in a studio. A studio was a place to learn to see, and how could you see through a pair of feather beds?

The main inconvenience I suffered at their hands was that, at first, I was shy of letting them discover how my artful little servant had begun to sit for me for "Rutland Ramsay." They knew that I had been odd enough (they were prepared by this time to allow oddity to artists,) to pick a foreign vagabond out of the streets, when I might have had a person with whiskers and credentials; but it was some time before they learned how high I rated his accomplishments. They found him in an attitude more than once, but they never doubted I was doing him as an organ-grinder. There were several things they never guessed, and one of them was that for a striking scene in the novel, in which a footman briefly figured, it occurred to me to make use of Major Monarch as the menial. I kept putting this off, I didn't like to ask him to don the livery—besides the difficulty of finding a livery to fit him. At last, one day late in the winter, when I was at work on the despised Oronte (he caught one's idea in an instant), and was in the glow of feeling that I was going very straight, they came in, the Major and his wife, with their society laugh about nothing (there was less and less to laugh at), like country-callers—they always reminded me of that—who have walked across the park after church and are presently persuaded to stay to luncheon. Luncheon was over, but they could stay to tea—I knew they wanted it. The fit was on me, however, and I couldn't let my ardour cool and my work wait, with the fading daylight, while my model prepared it. So I asked Mrs Monarch if she would mind laying it out— a request which, for an instant, brought all the blood to her face. Her eyes were on her husband's for a second, and some mute telegraphy passed between them. Their folly was over the next instant; his cheerful shrewdness put an end to it. So far from pitying their wounded pride, I must add, I was moved to give it as complete a lesson as I could. They bustled about together and got out the cups and saucers and made the kettle boil. I know they felt as if they were waiting on my servant, and when the tea was prepared I said: "He'll have a cup, please—he's tired." Mrs Monarch brought him one where he stood, and he took it from her as if he had been a gentleman at a party, squeezing a crush-hat with an elbow.

Then it came over me that she had made a great effort for me—made it with a kind of nobleness—and that I owed her a compensation. Each time I saw her after this I wondered what the compensation could be. I couldn't go on doing the wrong thing to oblige them. Oh, it *was* the wrong thing, the stamp of the work for which they sat—Hawley was not the only person to say it now. I sent in a large number of the drawings I had made for "Rutland Ramsay," and I received a warning that was more to the point than Hawley's. The artistic adviser of the house for which I was working was of opinion that many of my illustrations were not what had been looked for. Most of these illustrations were the subjects in which the Monarchs had figured. Without going into the question of what *had* been looked for, I saw at this rate I shouldn't get the other books to do. I hurled myself in despair upon Miss Churm, I put her through all her paces. I not only adopted Oronte publicly as my hero, but one morning when the Major looked in to see if I didn't require him to finish a figure for the *Cheapside*, for which he had begun to sit the week before, I told him that I had changed my mind—I would do the drawing from my man. At this my visitor turned pale and stood looking at me. "Is *he* your idea of an English gentleman?" he asked.

I was disappointed, I was nervous, I wanted to get on with my work; so I replied with irritation: "Oh, my dear Major—I can't be ruined for *you!*"

He stood another moment; then, without a word, he quitted the studio. I drew a long breath when he was gone, for I said to myself that I shouldn't see him again. I had not told him definitely that I was in danger of having my work rejected, but I was vexed at his not having felt the catastrophe in the air, read with me the moral of our fruitless collaboration, the lesson that, in the deceptive atmosphere of art, even the highest respectability may fail of being plastic.

I didn't owe my friends money, but I did see them again. They re-appeared together, three days later, and under the circumstances there was something tragic in the fact. It was a proof to me that they could find nothing else in life to do. They had threshed the matter out in a dismal conference—they had digested the bad news that they were not in for the series. If they were not useful to me even for the *Cheapside* their function seemed difficult to determine, and I could only judge at first that they had come, forgivingly, decorously, to take a last leave. This made me rejoice in secret that I had little leisure for a scene; for I had placed both my other models in position together and I was pegging away at a drawing from which I hoped to derive glory. It had been suggested by the passage in which Rutland Ramsay, drawing up a chair to Artemisia's piano-stool, says extraordinary things to her while she ostensibly fingers out a difficult piece of music. I had done Miss Churm at the piano before—it was an attitude in which she knew how to take on an absolutely poetic grace. I wished the two figures to "compose" together, intensely, and my little Italian had entered perfectly into my conception. The pair were vividly before me, the piano had been pulled out; it was a charming picture of blended youth and murmured love, which I had only to catch and keep. My visitors stood and looked at it, and I was friendly to them over my shoulder.

They made no response, but I was used to silent company and went on with my work, only a little disconcerted (even though exhilarated by the sense that *this* was at least the ideal thing), at not having got rid of them after all. Presently I heard Mrs Monarch's sweet voice beside, or rather above me: "I wish her hair was a little better done." I looked up and she was staring with a strange fixedness at Miss Churm, whose back was turned to her. "Do you mind my just touching it?" she went on—a question which made me spring up for an instant, as with the instinctive fear that she might do the young lady a harm. But she quieted me with a glance I shall never forget—I confess I should like to have been able to paint *that*—and went for a moment to my model. She spoke to her softly, laying a hand upon her shoulder and bending over her; and as the girl, understanding, gratefully assented, she disposed her rough curls, with a few quick passes, in such a way as to make Miss Churm's head twice as charming. It was one of the most heroic personal services I have ever seen rendered. Then Mrs Monarch turned away with a low sigh and, looking about her as if for something to do, stooped to the floor with a noble humility and picked up a dirty rag that had dropped out of my paint-box.

The Major meanwhile had also been looking for something to do and, wandering to the other end of the studio, saw before him my breakfast things, neglected, unremoved. "I say, can't I be useful *here*?" he called out to me with an irrepressible quaver. I assented with a laugh that I fear was awkward and for the next ten minutes, while I worked, I heard the light clatter of china and the tinkle of spoons and glass. Mrs Monarch assisted her husband—they washed up my crockery, they put it away. They wandered off into my little scullery, and I afterwards found that they had cleaned my knives and that my slender stock of plate had an unprecedented surface. When it came over me, the latent eloquence of what they were doing, I confess that my drawing was blurred for a moment—the picture swam. They had accepted their failure, but they couldn't accept their fate. They had bowed their heads in bewilderment to the perverse and cruel law in virtue of which the real thing could be so much less precious than the unreal; but they didn't want to starve. If my servants were my models, my models might be my servants. They would reverse the parts—the others would sit for the ladies and gentlemen, and *they* would do the work. They would still be in the studio—it was an intense dumb appeal to me not to turn them out. "Take us on," they wanted to say—"we'll do *anything*."

When all this hung before me the *afflatus* vanished—my pencil dropped from my hand. My sitting was spoiled and I got rid of my sitters, who were also evidently rather mystified and awestruck. Then, alone with the Major and his wife, I had a most uncomfortable moment. He put their prayer into a single sentence: "I say, you know—just let *us* do for you, can't you?" I couldn't—it was dreadful to see them emptying my slops; but I pretended I could, to oblige them, for about a week. Then I gave them a sum of money to go away; and I never saw them again. I obtained the remaining books, but my friend Hawley repeats that Major and Mrs Monarch did me a permanent harm, got me into a second-rate trick. If it be true I am content to have paid the price—for the memory.

FOR STUDY, DISCUSSION AND WRITING

1. Why is James' choice of the artist as narrator appropriate to the theme of the story?
2. How do your own ideas about the character of a true artist square with the personality and attitudes of the artist-narrator of the story?
3. Why are the Monarchs unsuitable models for the artist?
4. Why are Miss Churm and Oronte such good models for the artist?
5. How does Jack Hawley contribute to the narrator's final decision about the Monarchs?
6. Compare and contrast the temperaments of Jack Hawley and the narrator.
7. Is Major Monarch entirely to be blamed for not being able to find employment?
8. From his experience with the Monarchs, what has the artist-narrator lost and what has he gained?
9. Discuss how a thematic statement such as "Art that works only from the 'real thing' becomes little more than paintbrush photography" is reflected in the events of the story.

Twentieth-Century Movement Toward Variety and Experimentation

In the preceding section we traced the nineteenth-century evolution of the modern short story into a sophisticated tool for probing the complexities of society and human character. In the early decades of the twentieth century, however, the potential of the genre was seldom realized. To understand why, we must look briefly at the market for such writing.

By 1900, publishers were offering readers magazines to satisfy almost any taste. At one end of the spectrum were the pulps—magazines printed on rough paper and featuring lurid stories of crime and violence. At the other end of the spectrum were the slicks—magazines printed on glossy paper and aimed at a more sophisticated and urbane audience. Competition within both groups was intense. Thus publishers often chose to play it safe by restricting their offerings to formula stories featuring fast-action plots and surprise endings.

The story with a surprise ending achieved its greatest success in the hands of the American writer O. Henry (1862–1910). With few exceptions, O. Henry's stories are excessively sentimental and display little psychological depth. The typical O. Henry story leads off with a narrative hook intended to catch the reader's attention and then moves swiftly toward a well-marked climax. Although at times the language is crisp, journalistic, or even slangy, too often it displays a sham-poetical theatricality. And every now and then, the omniscient narrator injects little nuggets of homely wisdom. All this, plus characters with whom unsophisticated readers could easily identify, made for a strong popular appeal but did little to advance the short story as a bona-fide literary form.

The opening decades of the twentieth century also witnessed the publication of a spate of so-called handbooks aimed at teaching would-be authors the craft of short-story writing. In general, these publications prescribed a mechanical, step-by-step approach, largely ignoring or downplaying any sort of literary innovation. Thus, these handbooks further stifled artistic creativity.

The creative eclipse did not continue indefinitely, however. Its intensity was lessened by the growth of so-called little magazines—noncommercial publications of limited circulation, featuring experimental writing. These publications proved to be a new and important outlet for writers unwilling to compromise their standards by churning out formula stories. Eventually the more successful slicks began publishing greater numbers of fresh works. By 1930, stereotyped stories no longer monopolized their pages, although many such stories continued to appear.

Three characteristics may consistently be seen in the fresh offerings. First, the writers tend to focus on psychological rather than on external or overt conflicts. Second, characters often behave in seemingly unreasonable and absurd ways. Third, the mood is for the most part questioning, gloomy, and pessimistic.

No single factor can account for these new developments in the short story. In part, they represent a backlash against elements of a form grown stale from repetition and overuse. More importantly, they were a product of multiple new and old forces interacting in complex ways that are not yet completely understood. Some of the older influences have been mentioned in the nineteenth-century section. Of the newer ones, six are of pervasive importance:

1. Freudianism
2. World War I and its aftermath
3. Totalitarianism
4. Existentialism
5. Science and technology
6. Social regimentation

Freudianism has contributed greatly to the generally pessimistic tone of much twentieth-century literature. Its impact has been strongest on the element of character. Sigmund Freud (1856–1939), from whose works literary Freudianism was derived, was an Austrian physician who developed his psychological theories over a twenty-year period while working with emotionally disturbed patients. He published his basic findings in four volumes appearing between 1900 and 1905.

Freud fragmented the human psyche—that is, the total mind as a functioning unit—into three parts: the id, the ego, and the superego. He considered the id to be the reservoir for all instinctual drives, including the libido, or sexual energy. Irrational and impulsive, the id seeks immediate gratification of its urges even when they may not be in the best interest of the human being as a whole.

The superego functions as an internal censor. It is a repository for moral teachings and social ideas. It criticizes the demands of the id by arousing guilt feelings within the ego. The ego, the conscious segment of the psyche, weighs the conflicting claims of the id and the superego. A mature ego, according to Freudians, is cautious and sensible, allowing an urge to be satisfied only when no painful consequences are likely to result. When satisfaction might be harmful, the ego persuades the id to renounce or postpone the urge or to sublimate (transform) it into a socially desirable activity such as the creation of a work of art.

The libido, Freudian theory holds, is the wellspring of all human activity. However, because of years of social and moral training, an individual's libido is often suppressed when he or she is awake. During sleep or reverie, though, the superego is off-guard, and the libido is able to express itself in distorted and seemingly nonsexual images.

Freud was not the first person to point out the symbolic nature of dreams. Although seldom agreeing in their interpretations, people have been pondering the meaning of dreams throughout human history. For example, in 1843, thirteen years before Freud's birth, Nathaniel Hawthorne offered a view very much like the Austrian's own when he wrote in "The Birthmark" that "truth often finds its way to the mind close muffled in robes of sleep, and then speaks with uncompromising directness of matters in regard to which we practice an unconscious self-deception during our waking moments." Freud, however, was the first person to base his interpretations of dreams on extensive clinical evidence.

Freud's research convinced him that if the libido is suppressed during early childhood, neurotic patterns of behavior can later develop. These neuroses can be successfully treated by systematic questioning, dream analysis, or the free-association technique. The therapist using free association allows the patient to speak whatever random thoughts come to mind and listens for clues to suspected difficulties. Once the patient understands the circumstances responsible for the frustration, a cure becomes possible. Such free association foreshadows the literary stream-of-consciousness technique, wherein characters speak their innermost thoughts and feelings, thus revealing important truths about themselves.

Several popularized versions of Freud's teachings appeared during the 1920s and were often used to justify the relaxed moral standards of the day. Since repression can lead to neurosis, the argument ran, one should avoid the risk of mental or psychological damage by enjoying a full and uninhibited sex life. This reasoning would have horrified Freud, who recognized full well the stabilizing effect of inhibition in any society.

Authentic Freudianism made two points with great force. First, humans, to a much greater extent than hitherto imagined, are irrational creatures at the mercy of subconscious forces whose very existence they may be unaware of. Second, a seemingly irrational activity like daydreaming can provide rational insights into the human personality. Freud's findings influenced James Joyce, D. H. Lawrence, Sherwood Anderson, Virginia Woolf, and a host of later writers, who tended more and more to focus on mental processes by making use of the stream-of-consciousness technique, dream visions, and symbolic fantasies. Characters were often grotesque and their behavior just as often irrational. Once the exclusive hallmark of madmen like Poe's Roderick Usher, irrationality now came to characterize all sorts of people.

The reputation of James Joyce (1882–1941) as one of the great modern short-story writers rests upon a single small volume of fifteen stories called *Dubliners*. First appearing in 1914, these are the only short stories he ever published. In describing *Dubliners*, Joyce said, "My intention was to write a moral history of my country [Ireland] and I chose Dublin as the scene for that city seemed to me to be the center of paralysis. . . . I have written it for the most part in a style of scrupulous meanness." Few writers have ever achieved their aim more completely.

The characters who people *Dubliners* exhibit various forms of psychological paralysis. Some are timid or frustrated; some lack moral imagination or fear public opinion; others are given over to annoying vices such as pettiness and hypocrisy. Joyce reveals their paralysis not only through their thoughts and actions but also by making use of a complex system of symbols. The symbols are of many sorts—a paralyzed priest, a broken communion cup, a rusted and useless bicycle pump, a dead-end street, a harp "weary alike of the eyes of strangers and her master's hands," a snow-encrusted statue of an Irish patriot.

Joyce's characters have become captives of their surroundings, a fact symbolically illustrated by the use of motion. Traditionally, the East has represented life and renewal and the West has represented death. Joyce made use of this symbolism. In the early stories in *Dubliners* characters travel eastward to the outskirts of Dublin and beyond, only to return again to the city's center. Later, actual movement is confined to the center of the city, and the characters attempt only imaginary flights. The three lead-off stories deal with childhood, the middle group with adolescence and maturity, and the last group with people in public life. Psychological paralysis, Joyce shows, cuts across age groups and encompasses the public and private spheres alike.

Joyce's stories can be considered representative of a new and enriched form of naturalism. Like the earlier naturalists, Joyce made extensive use of realistic, even sordid, detail and showed his characters as victims of heredity—in this instance, their national and religious heredity. Upon this naturalistic framework he superimposed his system of symbols, thus greatly deepening our perception of the psychological and moral condition of his characters. From time to time in *Dubliners* he momentarily resorted to the stream-of-consciousness technique that he would later employ extensively in his novels. Finally, he introduced a new literary device, the *epiphany*.

The word "epiphany" was originally a religious term signifying the recognition by the Magi, the three wise men, of the infant Christ's divinity. Joyce extended the term to mean the moment when the inner truth—usually an unpleasant truth—about a person, situation, or event is suddenly revealed. Generally, the epiphany is experienced by a character within the story, although sometimes only the reader is enlightened. The literary epiphany can be likened to the moment when a patient undergoing psychoanalysis first gains insight into the cause of his or her difficulty. It also resembles the climax of a conventionally plotted story, but with psychological realization rather than external action supplying the emotional impact. The Joycean epiphany has become a staple device of modern short-story writers.

D. H. Lawrence (1885–1930) knew the works of Freud intimately, and in two book-length studies he criticized a number of Freud's ideas. Nonetheless, his own writings bear a strong stamp of Freudian thought and make extensive use of Freudian symbols. The son of a miner, Lawrence knew firsthand the squalid ugliness that industrialism can spawn. This knowledge left him with a burning hatred for machines and technology, a hatred that later expanded to encompass Christianity, democracy, unionism, and the major political movements of his day—in short, almost the whole of the modern world.

Life in a small English mining town did have its compensations, though; it brought Lawrence into close contact with nature. In fact, he developed an almost mystic identification with nature. Like the nineteenth-century romantics Lawrence became convinced that the best chance for human salvation lay in the emotions, not in the intellect. "My great religion is a belief in the blood, the flesh as wiser than the intellect," he once said. "We can go wrong in our minds. But what our blood feels and believes and says is true."

Modern civilization, Lawrence felt, had created a race of psychological cripples by exalting the intellect and denying the essential importance of emotion and intuition. Sex offered men and women their best chance of becoming attuned to the universe and achieving a higher consciousness. By sex, however, Lawrence meant neither casual promiscuity nor a relationship based solely upon compatible personalities or common views. The sex he had in mind was possible only between two people who are attracted by the animal magnetism that each intuitively senses in the other. For such individuals, sex becomes a transcendent, even ecstatic, experience, creating complete individuals in whom spirit and intellect have struck a harmonious balance.

Many of Lawrence's stories focus on a triangle involving two males and a female. Sometimes he examines a relationship involving a man of feeling (the animal man), a man of intellect (the cerebral man), and a woman who must choose between the two. At other times the triangle is familial, involving an unhappily married couple and their son.

Typically, the family-triangle stories portray a repressed woman of intellect whose husband lacks the sensibility to arouse her slumbering sexuality. Angry and frustrated, she turns to the son, showering him with affection. The son experiences a sexual attraction for his mother, but because such feelings are taboo he suppresses them. Later, as an adult, the son finds it difficult or impossible to maintain satisfying relationships with respectable women, whom he subconsciously likens to his mother, and must find gratification with so-called lower types of women.

Sherwood Anderson (1876–1941) was the first major American writer to respond to Freudian psychology. He first won literary acclaim in 1919 with the publication of his short-story collection entitled *Winesburg, Ohio*. Anderson focused his attention on the social implications of neurosis, repeatedly exploring the disastrous effects of frustration and repression on the residents of small towns. Several forces, he felt, had a hand in distorting the human personality: the machine age with its pervasive emphasis on material goods and surface appearance rather than on human values, the bigotry and hypocrisy of everyday life, economic status and social class. Such forces denied, if only by implication, the complexity of the individual human personality. Together they twisted people into caricatures whose repressions express themselves in bleak loneliness, mental unsoundness, and abnormal behavior. A number of Anderson's stories show repressed sexuality erupting with such force that it cripples or destroys the individual altogether.

Despite the pervading grimness of his stories, Anderson should not be considered a total pessimist, for he believed deeply in human dignity and worth and felt that happiness lay within everyone's grasp. To gain happiness, however, people must break the barriers of isolation separating them and learn to communicate with one another.

Like Chekhov, Anderson rebelled against the idea of a precisely developed plot. He thought that the writer should concentrate on situation. "The plot notion did seem to me to poison all story-telling," he said. "What was wanted, I thought, was form, not plot." Accordingly, his style is often loose and rambling, many stories seeming to have no clearly marked beginning, middle, or end.

Virginia Woolf (1882–1941), like Sherwood Anderson, felt that "plots don't matter." Rejecting objective narration, this English writer sought to give voice to the complex inner world of her characters by utilizing the stream-of-consciousness technique. Never chaotic, Woolf's discourse mingles thoughts, fantasies, images, and meditations, linking them together so deftly that the story moves forward with an almost breathless smoothness. As a result, careful readers seldom lose sight of where they are in the story.

Woolf's short fiction is concerned more with creating impressions than with telling stories. Her writing is lyrical, and the impressions are of many sorts. One piece, for example, attempts to create a word-picture of the colors green and blue; a second seeks to convey both the image of a garden and the mood of the people who stroll its paths; in yet a third, a traveler fashions an imaginary life-portrait of a fellow passenger on a train—a portrait that proves to be totally false. Taken together, the pieces illustrate the power of the imagination, the extent to which reality is the product of individual consciousness, and the extent to which the unrestrained exercise of imagination can lead one astray.

Although it is not evident in her short fiction, Virginia Woolf was an ardent feminist. She believed that male concerns center almost entirely on fighting, money-making, ordering others about, and keeping women in a state of subjugation. These preoccupations she held responsible for most of the world's psychological and social ills. Woolf's explanation for male domination has strong Lawrencian overtones. Western Europe, she felt, had exalted rationalism—which she considered masculine—at the expense of intuition, a feminine attribute. To correct matters, she believed that the feminine principle had to be restored to a position of respect, perhaps through the creation of a new human personality blending rational and intuitive elements. These views, expounded chiefly in the critical works *A Room of One's Own* and *Three Guineas*, have helped shape the thinking of many present-day advocates of women's rights.

World War I helped deepen twentieth-century literary pessimism. This war followed a brief period of political and social development that to a considerable extent had tempered the gloomy outlook of the middle and late nineteenth century. By the early 1900s, for example, labor unions had grown strong enough to challenge capitalist power both on the picket line and in the legislative halls and to win passage of landmark legislation curbing some of the worst abuses of the factory system. In America, a group of investigative journalists—dubbed "muckrakers" by Theodore Roosevelt—documented in overwhelming detail the evil results of cutthroat business competition: the destruction of many small enterprises, the growth of giant monopolies, and the inflation of consumer prices. These exposés helped bring about legislation aimed at curbing the power of monopolies. Other articles by the muckrakers concentrated on exposing political bribery, graft, and corruption and laid the groundwork for various civic reform movements.

A strong international peace movement also fostered a more optimistic climate. Between 1900 and 1913 some well-endowed peace organizations were established, and several significant peace conferences were held. Most notable was the Second Hague Peace Conference in 1907. The guns of 1914, however, blasted this newborn optimism, possibly forever.

America entered the First World War in high spirits, fired by the moral fervor of President Woodrow Wilson. The president, an extreme idealist, had made several unsuccessful attempts to bring about peace before Americans took up arms in 1917. When it became clear that the United States must soon become involved in the hostilities, the president called for a crusade to "make the world safe for democracy." Wilson's peace aims were expressed in a fourteen-point program calling for a settlement free from vindictiveness, a reduction in armaments everywhere, and the establishment of a new world peace organization to be named the League of Nations. These points helped pave the way for Germany's acceptance of an armistice in 1918, and when the guns fell silent, Wilson proclaimed that America and its allies had won everything they had fought for. Subsequent events soon proved him tragically wrong.

World War I, an incredible bloodbath, killed 9 million men, wounded 21 million more, and left one-tenth of France a ruined battlefield. Small wonder, then, that when victor met vanquished to draft a peace treaty, vindictiveness, not reconciliation, ruled the day. The treaty that emerged—called the Versailles Treaty—forced Germany to accept full and complete responsibility for the war, stripped Germany of its overseas colonies, reduced German armed forces to token size while placing no restrictions on the forces of the victors, and held Germany liable for war damages that were later set at an exorbitant $33 billion. Although the treaty did set up the League of Nations, in 1920 America rejected membership, thus weakening the organization fatally and helping smooth Hitler's path to power only thirteen years later.

The rise of the modern totalitarian state strengthened and further deepened the pervading pessimism of the postwar period. Totalitarianism registered its first victory when, following centuries of czarist misrule and oppression, the Bolsheviks seized power in Russia and proclaimed a communist state. The Bolsheviks took their political text from Karl Marx, a nineteenth-century German economist and philosopher. Marx regarded the capitalist system with undisguised horror and hostility and spent his life attacking it. His most notable criticisms appear in the *Communist Manifesto*, a pamphlet coauthored with Friedrich Engels and published in 1848, and the first volume of *Das Kapital*, published in 1867.

Marx (1818–1883) believed that economic forces operating within a society shape the society's social, political, and cultural superstructure, and that individuals are virtually powerless to alter the course of events. Coupled with this view—called historical determinism—is the idea that capitalism creates great numbers of alienated workers, people who feel estranged, cut off, from everything about them. In the modern world such alienation, Marx held, has several roots, most notably the great size of the factories, the repetitive nature of the work performed in the factories, and the workers' lack of control over either the manufacturing operation or the final product.

Marx viewed history as a continuing struggle between a series of economic masters and the masses of workers whom these masters exploit. Eventually, each exploited group revolts, overthrows its masters, and assumes control until it is in turn deposed by a new class of economic underlings. Marx predicted that the whole process would culminate in a final confrontation between the then-current set of contenders: the capitalist factory owners and the exploited workers, or proletariat. The latter group, upon gaining power, would establish common ownership of the means of production, and the political state would wither away, eventually resulting in a utopian society without poverty, vice, crime, or alienation, and operating in accordance with a new Golden Rule: "From each according to his ability, to each according to his need."

Despite such grand and romantic predictions, the Bolshevik takeover did not signal the dawn of a better era in Russia's history. To the contrary, within months the new regime, led by Nikolai Lenin, began savagely repressing its political opponents. In 1924, following Lenin's death, Joseph Stalin took control and instituted a reign of terror that liquidated thousands, perhaps millions, of real and supposed enemies and sent millions more to forced-labor camps. The hoped-for workers' paradise had become a far worse police state than prerevolutionary Russia.

Within a decade of Stalin's rise to power in Russia, two other powerful totalitarian regimes, both of them anticommunist, appeared on the European scene. And for a brief period in the early 1940s, they, along with imperial Japan, seemed destined to impose their philosophy worldwide. The first of these, a Fascist regime headed by Benito Mussolini, seized Italy's governmental reins in 1922, replacing a weak parliamentary body that had proved unable to deal effectively with post–World War I unrest and frustration. The Fascist brand of totalitarianism rested upon the near-mystical belief in the sanctity of a centralized, all-powerful nation headed by a strong leader to whom the people owed unquestioning allegiance. To promote national solidarity and to preserve their position of power, the Fascists banned independent labor unions and all opposition political parties and compelled private business to operate under strict state controls. Unity was also sought by extolling military strength and by the ruthless pursuit of territorial ambitions. This militaristic philosophy led Mussolini to invade and conquer Ethiopia and to ally his nation with Adolf Hitler's Germany in World War II.

Hitler became German chancellor in 1933, following the first-place showing of his Nazi party in a three-way election fought against a background of social unrest and economic dislocation. He entered office fired by a determination to repudiate the Versailles Treaty and restore the glory of the German nation. The Nazi philosophy was similar to that of the Fascists but added an element—a belief in the innate superiority of the "Aryan," or Nordic, peoples.

Once in power, the Nazis put their philosophy into effect by systematically eliminating their political opponents and infiltrating every phase of private and public life. They also began constructing a series of concentration camps that eventually claimed the lives of some nine million Jews and other people considered "undesirable" by the regime. By the end of 1935, military conscription was in effect and a massive military build-up was underway. German forces annexed Austria in 1938. They overran Czechoslovakia in early 1939 and invaded Poland in September of the same year. The invasion of Poland touched off World War II.

By 1945 Hitler and his allies had been defeated and Fascist-Nazi totalitarianism had ceased to be a threat to Western freedom. Its place was taken by Soviet communism, which remains a real force in world affairs. The whole history of totalitarian governments dramatizes with brutal clarity the power that a modern state can wield over its citizens.

The cynicism and disillusionment engendered by World War I found its strongest direct expression in the decade of the 1920s, the period known as the Jazz Age. This disillusionment affected both Europe and America and was especially intense among veterans and thoughtful young people.

The Jazz Age offers a kaleidoscope of shifting impressions: one novelty after another quickly embraced and even more quickly discarded; flappers flaunting bobbed hair and short skirts and flouting the conventions of an earlier day with their smoking, drinking, and swearing; hip flasks and bootleg whiskey; fast cars and coonskin coats; jazz and dancing the Charleston till dawn; restless travel to faraway places and back again. Underlying all was a sense of futility, an uneasy conviction that all the gods were dead.

Perhaps more accurately than any other Jazz Age short-story writer Katharine Brush (1902–1952) dramatized both the feverish gaiety of the 1920s and the wasteland that lay beneath the decade's tinseled surface. Her first story appeared in 1924, and by 1929, when the Great Depression struck, she had become a preeminent chronicler of what may be called the decade's brittle butterfly milieu. The characters who people her stories are fragile, superficial, and in revolt against the cautious morality of their parents. Their lives are taken up with partying and drinking, and they eagerly grasp at anything that offers the pearl of excitement. Unlike lesser writers of the period, in particular those authors who tended to make something of a fantasy of the twenties, Brush writes in an economical and smooth-flowing style that renders characters and events with almost photographic clarity. Her dialogue is so perceptive and lifelike that the reader has the sense of listening in on private conversations. As a result of all this, Brush's stories convey an unmistakable semblance of reality, though (ironically) her characters may not comprehend that reality.

The pessimism of the twentieth century, especially the first half of the century, is nowhere more clearly evident than in the works of Ernest Hemingway (1898–1961). Hemingway learned the horrors of war first-hand as an ambulance driver in France and then as a combat soldier in Italy, where he was seriously wounded. These experiences left a deep mark on his life and on nearly everything he wrote.

Life to Hemingway was brutish—a brief interlude beginning in pain, passed in suffering and sorrow, and ending in oblivion. In the words of one of his characters: life is "all a nothing, and man a nothing too." Hemingway expressed his bleak outlook in a spare, flat prose that reflects the realist tradition. His sentences are short, his words ordinary. His characters speak the clipped dialogue of commonplace people, stripped of repetition and nonessentials. Swiftness and intensity are the result. A number of his stories include epiphany-like moments of illumination, and one, "The Snows of Kilimanjaro," mingles flashbacks with a stream-of-consciousness narrative.

To achieve any sort of salvation, Hemingway believed, one must seek forgetfulness through physical sensation and face the inevitable with courage and resignation. His characters are often outdoorsmen who have embraced a life of green hills and clear waters, of hunting and fishing in the company of a few kindred souls. Typically, they seem driven to seek out and confront death in a battle, bullfight, or on safari. These men follow an unwritten but well-defined code calling for grace under pressure and loyalty to one another. More often than not, violation of the code leads to death, either spiritual or physical.

Like Hemingway, William Faulkner (1897–1962) found World War I to be a deeply disillusioning experience. He expressed these feelings in an early novel, Soldier's Pay, as well as in several shorter works. However, a more important source of Faulkner's pessimism was not the war but rather the spread of modern commercial morality, which in his view had destroyed everything of value in the American South.

With few exceptions, Faulkner's short stories and novels are pieces of a vast mosaic that, like James Joyce's Dubliners, becomes a moral history of the author's region of birth. Faulkner created an imaginary Mississippi county—Yoknapatawpha—and peopled it with families whose fortunes he traces through several generations. In presenting this history, Faulkner employed a shifting focus, concentrating now on this family or individual and later on another individual or family. As a result, much of what we make of any single Faulkner story often depends on what we know about the rest of his work.

Faulkner's mosaic encompasses over a century of Yoknapatawpha history and general Southern history as well. The tales set farthest back in time center upon the slave-based plantation system that dominated the South before the Civil War. Other stories and novels carry us through the war and succeeding decades and into the modern machine age. Faulkner depicts his plantation owners as aristocrats who live by a code stressing honor, courage, fair dealing, and a fierce love of independence, but also as participants in a society doomed by the curse of slavery.

After the Civil War and the destruction of their way of life, these aristocrats are gradually supplanted by individuals of a new breed—some of aristocratic lineage, others the descendants of tenant farmers—shrewd, coldly logical, totally unscrupulous, and dedicated solely to personal gain. To Faulkner, this new type of individual represented the unhappy triumph of mechanical civilization over the more humanistic culture of the antebellum planters.

Faulkner once said that "man's free will functions against a . . . background of fate." Few of Faulkner's characters seem to possess any clear understanding of the forces that move them, nor do they conduct their lives in a way suggesting intellectual freedom. Rather, they order their lives and actions in accordance with conventional community attitudes and behavior.

Faulkner's white characters seldom pay much attention to the historical or psychological forces that have given rise to their attitudes toward black people. To Faulknerian whites, black people are little more than stereotyped abstractions, a part of life's geographical surroundings. In Faulkner's works blacks, individually and as a group, often serve as scapegoats.

The social orthodoxy of Faulkner's characters may help account for another of their traits: their tendency to surrender to current external circumstances without making any real effort to change things for the better. Nevertheless, Faulkner reminds his readers, through a few fictional creations as well as with his own words, that humans do have the power to act freely in the pursuit of some moral aim: "People can always be saved from injustice by some man. . . . Anyone can save anyone from injustice if he just will, if he just tries, just raises his voice."

The stock market crash of 1929 swept the Jazz Age, along with its social and literary preoccupations, onto the scrap heap of history. The depression that followed was the worst economic catastrophe America has experienced. Within a single two-day period in October 1929 the value of the stocks traded on the New York Stock Exchange dropped by $13 billion. By 1933, the national income of the United States had been cut in half. Almost 16 million people had lost their jobs, and breadlines were a fact of life throughout the nation. Europe too was in the grip of economic depression.

Faced with a disaster of so great a magnitude that society itself seemed near collapse, writers by the hundreds turned, with varying degrees of enthusiasm, to Marxism and the Communist party for solutions to economic woes. The fiction of the 1930s reflects both moral indignation and a passionate concern for ordinary working people battling the economic and social chaos that threatened to destroy their lives. Many stories of the period also look toward a postcapitalist world without social classes or human evil. The commitment of the so-called proletarian writers exacted a heavy artistic price, however.

These writers found themselves under great party pressure to produce fiction that delivered a strong and clear social message, even if producing such stories meant sacrificing literary craftsmanship. Because of the movement's great need for publicity, many aspiring writers devoted their time primarily to grinding out propaganda articles for magazines and newspapers. In addition, ideological squabbles within the Communist party consumed time that might better have been spent in polishing literary skills. Taken as a group, the proletarian stories lack finesse; they are peopled with one-dimensional characters and overburdened with emotionalism. Of the few stories that are first-rate, almost all are the work of individuals who remained relatively uninvolved in party affairs.

During the early 1930s, writers sympathetic to the Marxist cause had little difficulty accepting the fact that the Communist party took its direction from Moscow. However, as time passed and the totalitarian nature of the supposed Russian utopia became clearer and clearer, disaffection mounted and more and more writers disassociated themselves from the Communist cause. In May 1939, with the signing of a short-lived nonaggression pact between Stalin and Hitler, this disaffection became all but complete. By then, American industry had begun to gear up for World War II, and the Great Depression was about to join the Jazz Age as a part of history.

The proletarian writing of Albert Maltz (b. 1908) combines a passion for social justice and an artistry that still has the power to stir readers to anger and pity. Although much of his work focuses on the destructive effects of the economic collapse that followed the stock market crash, his thematic range takes in a considerably larger body of concerns. While yet a college student, Maltz and a classmate collaborated on a successful—and briefly suppressed—play that attacked political corruption in New York City. One of his best-known short stories, "A Man on a Road," considers the tragedy of over a hundred men who contracted silicosis (a lung disease caused by inhaling silica dust) while working on a construction project in which the New River was diverted through a tunnel near Gauley Bridge, West Virginia.

Maltz's interest in the health problems of workers had strong familial roots. His father was a victim of painter's lead poisoning. His mother, who had once hoped to become a schoolteacher, fell victim to the eye disease trachoma while working as a seamstress in a sweatshop; she eventually lost the ability to read. Maltz has said that his work is based on one premise: "that individuals live not in a vacuum but in society, and that a writer cannot write truly of people or characters unless the world in which they live is clearly illumined."

Another major literary influence during the 1930s was existentialism. Existentialism, or at least its twentieth-century manifestation, may be regarded as a backlash against naturalism, Freudianism, Marxism, and other schools of thought that diminish or deny the human capacity to exercise meaningful control over life. Existentialism was also a reaction to the horrors of political totalitarianism and war. It first assumed recognizable form in the writings of Sören Kierkegaard, a nineteenth-century Danish theologian, and was further shaped by the German philosophers Friedrich Nietzsche and Martin Heidegger. However, the movement's influence remained minimal until the 1930s.

Existentialism made its broadest literary impact, particularly in America, through the writings of the French philosopher and author Jean-Paul Sartre (1905–1980). The existentialist believes existence precedes essence—that is, we first exist, then create in our own heads all meaning that life may be thought to have. From such notions, certain conclusions seem to follow. To begin with, we human creatures cannot be the creation of a god, for such invention would require the deity to have a prior idea of what was being created. Such a creation, in short, would require that essence precede existence. Furthermore, there can be no universal human nature and no system of moral values that applies to all people at all times. The world, then, is an absurd place, but people are not helpless pawns. They have freedom of choice and are responsible not only for what they make of their lives but also for what they make of society in general.

Convinced of the validity of such concepts, one may be inclined to surrender to despair and passivity. A person of a more resilient disposition, on the other hand, may choose to create a personal set of values, act affirmatively on them, and shape a life that is basically fulfilling. If enough people choose positive social values, real and lasting improvements in human society are not impossible. Existentialism, then, has a real place for optimism—not an exuberant optimism rooted in the old romantic conviction that "God's in his heaven—/All's right with the world," but rather a defiant optimism flung in the face of nothingness.

Sartre himself once stated that "the writer, a free man addressing other free men, has only one subject: liberty." And, directly or indirectly, Sartre's fiction bears upon this notion. His characters, unlike those of the earlier naturalist writers, are not shackled by heredity or environment; they have the freedom to choose their own responses to the situations in which life places them. Those who exercise their freedom can create worlds with purpose, courage, and even love; the others passively condemn themselves to what amounts to a self-made hell.

Although existentialism as a conscious literary movement got its start with Sartre, the existential outlook colors the works of numerous writers whose careers partially or completely preceded Sartre's own. The Hemingway hero who believes life is brutal and meaningless, yet lives by a strict code stressing honor and courage, can be said to reflect the existential outlook. So, too, can the four shipwrecked men cast upon the sea in Crane's "The Open Boat." Although trapped in an empty and apparently unfeeling universe, these men find meaning in human companionship and struggle to save themselves.

Of all the pre-Sartrean writers, none reflects the existential cast more interestingly than Franz Kafka (1883–1924). Kafka's existentialism seems less a product of any specific literary influence than of personal temperament. Kafka, a native of Czechoslovakia, summed up his literary philosophy in this way:

> What seemed most important and attractive was the need to achieve a view of life . . . in which life would still pursue its natural course of ups and downs, but at the same time would be seen just as clearly to be a nothing, a dream, a weightless moment.

Kafka's writings achieve just such a twin effect. The prose is clear and unadorned. Surface details are presented in a flatly realistic manner, and the narrative moves forward smoothly. Beneath the realistic surface, however, lies an absurd and meaningless world that soon becomes apparent to the reader. One man is transformed into a gigantic insect. Another, tried for an unnamed crime by a court meeting in an attic, is executed by a pair of second-rate opera singers. A machine executes condemned prisoners by tattooing their trivial offenses on their naked bodies.

In his fiction, Kafka deals allegorically with a number of themes. Stories such as "A Hunger Artist" are clearly intended to delineate the relationship between the artist—or anyone who is "different"—and the rest of society. Another group of Kafka's stories can be taken either as mirrors reflecting our modern, impersonal, bureaucratic society or as commentaries on humanity's attempt to understand God and attain some sort of divine grace.

Real bureaucracies, like Kafka's imagined ones, often operate in ways that outsiders cannot understand. They show little concern for the people they are supposed to serve, make disastrous mistakes, and yet are accepted by the public as part of the normal pattern of things. God too seems to move in mysterious ways, but only because humans lack the capacity or will to discern the divine scheme of justice underlying the apparent meaninglessness of life. Faith in God's goodness leads people to accept whatever is visited upon them, however capricious it might seem.

Kafka's protagonists react to their predicaments in two ways. Some accept their situation in a spirit of resignation. Others struggle to make some sense of what is happening and win a measure of justice from the powers that be. However, meaningful communication invariably fails, leaving the individual isolated and uncomprehending. At no time does anyone seek to create meaning by formulating a personal set of values and then living by it. Kafka's world has little or no place for Sartre's brand of existential optimism, only for existential despair.

During the early 1940s several changes in literary approach and attitude began to occur, affecting much of the fiction produced over the next two decades. Plot again assumed greater importance. Writers adopted a more straightforward chronology in telling their tales. Flashbacks and the stream-of-consciousness technique were employed less frequently, although neither disappeared entirely. The preoccupation with meaninglessness that had affected all but the Marxist writers gave way to a general concern for human values, although many of the current values were shown to be inadequate or dated. Many stories dealt with the experiences of children or old people—some with both. Eudora Welty, Jessamyn West, Flannery O'Connor, Mordecai Richler, and Gabriel García Márquez are representative of such short-story writers.

With few exceptions, the writings of Eudora Welty (b. 1909) are concerned with the theme of isolation. As Welty sees it, isolation can have many causes: mental retardation, physical disability, old age, poverty, pride, the thoughtlessness of youth, the fear of facing up to the terror and unpredictability of life. Whatever the cause, the sufferers share a common inability or unwillingness to relate to others in a meaningful way. At best, isolation makes self-realization impossible; at worst, it can result in spiritual or physical death.

Love is the key that unlocks the shackles of isolation, allowing individuals to realize more of their potential. In order for love to develop, there must be a desire to reach out toward others, a sense of the mystery and uniqueness of each human being. Love, fully developed and fully realized, must be directed at a special object. However, such love is not to be confined to that object; it must embrace all humanity and all nature, accepting both human variety and the often inscrutable workings of life. Possessiveness, the selfish desire not only to embrace but also to dominate, can have no part in mature love between individuals. The lover who tries to force a relationship into a special mold or to block the independence and growth of the loved one risks losing everything. To keep the relationship healthy, each partner must never lose sight of the ever-changing individuality of the other.

Many of Welty's stories incorporate elements of myth and legend, and several include historical people like Aaron Burr and James Audubon. One character, for example, is called Old Lethy, a name reminiscent of the River Lethe that flows through Hades. A second character, named Phoenix, recalls the mythological bird that is periodically consumed by fire but rises again from the ashes. A third character, Octavia, displays a personality matching the coldness of the Roman empress whose name she bears. Among Welty's mythological motifs, we might point out those of Ulysses, the ancient mariner, and the descent into hell. The use of these elements, of course, adds greater depth of meaning for the knowledgeable reader.

The outlook of Jessamyn West (b. 1907), like that of Eudora Welty, stands in sharp contrast to the pessimism and hopelessness of so many twentieth-century writers. Although violence, unhappiness, cruelty, and tragedy are not strangers to West's pages, her writings taken as a whole leave little doubt that her characters inhabit a moral universe in which one can hope to find intelligent solutions to human problems and thus achieve a measure of happiness. The continuity of life—the eternal cycle of birth, death, and renewal—forms one of the most persistent themes in West's fiction. This theme receives its most extensive treatment in a series of twenty-five stories chronicling three generations of an Indiana Quaker family. But it is also a noticeable undercurrent in her other works. Whenever the theme occurs, it lends an air of rightness to the order of things.

A number of West's stories touch or turn upon unhappy love affairs or unhappy marriages. Such unhappiness may arise from sexual inadequacy or fear, the indifference or thoughtlessness of a lover or spouse, or a mistaken notion of duty to others. Most importantly, though, it results from the failure to trust in and act upon one's innermost tender feelings. To achieve happiness through love, according to West, people must be willing to follow their intuitions even to the point of rejecting the conflicting claims of the intellect. The mind is not always the best defender of the heart.

Flannery O'Connor (1925–1964), a devout Roman Catholic, wrote her stories with the overriding purpose of demonstrating the need for divine grace in a secular world. To O'Connor, "intelligence determined of its own superiority" represented the ultimate evil, and she castigated such a position in story after story. Her evil characters form a menagerie of egomaniacs, narrow-minded, self-deluded, convinced of their own righteousness and superiority as well as their ability to define their own code of values and live life on their own terms. Awakening comes to such characters only when they undergo some devastating, often violent, experience that shatters their illusions and opens their souls to possible redemption and grace.

Physically grotesque characters and fearsome or threatening imagery help reinforce O'Connor's message that life without grace is wretched and lacking in beauty. One story includes a wooden-legged female atheist, another a child genius with a clubfoot. A train conductor has "the face of an ancient bloated bulldog." A prostitute displays a "wide gull grin" and teeth that are "small and pointed and speckled with green." A line of woods is described as gaping "like a dark open mouth," and the sun is likened to a "swollen red ball" that narrows and pales until it looks "like a bullet."

Three images occur again and again in O'Connor's fiction: (1) the treeline, signaling a moment of crisis, usually for the person viewing the scene; (2) the sun, symbolizing enlightenment or the possibility of enlightenment; and (3) the color purple, denoting mental anguish. Eye descriptions occur repeatedly, both to call attention to the personalities of characters and to dramatize their changing perceptions of reality. Within the Christian tradition, the sun has often been employed to represent divine grace, and the color purple has been employed to symbolize penitence. The consistent presence of such symbolism in O'Connor's stories strengthens and deepens their religious significance.

Mordecai Richler (b. 1931), a Canadian writer, uses the weapon of satiric humor to attack hypocrisy, self-importance, and ostentation. During his writing career Richler has done battle with a wide array of institutions and individuals—publishing houses, the film-making industry, resorts in the Catskill Mountains, multinational corporations, the leaders of the Canadian government, to mention just a few. Artistic timidity ranks high on Richler's list of dislikes, and he has taken television to task for fearing to present such characters as "a Negro whoremonger, a contented adulterer, or a Jew who cheats on his income tax, buys a Jag with his ill-gotten gains, and is all the happier for it." Needless to say, Richler's own stories betray no such fear. Stylistically, Richler has been called a "stuntman with language," and he is particularly skillful at depicting embarrassing moments that provide insight into human character.

The stories of the South American writer Gabriel García Márquez (b. 1928), blend fancy and actuality in a manner reminiscent of the writings of Kafka, who in fact greatly influenced García Márquez's literary development. Reading García Márquez, we enter a sharply etched and seemingly realistic world in which surrealistic events are a recurrent fact of life. In this world, a dictator can live 250 years and a child can be transformed into a spider merely because she has sneaked out to attend a dance. A vendor can cure the halt and the blind, and a drowning victim can transform the life of an entire village. Taken together, such happenings suggest that although God and humanity have their dark sides, miracles nonetheless play a real part in human existence.

Innovation has never for long been a stranger to the modern short story. By the 1960s, innovation and experimentation were assuming an ever-greater importance among writers of serious stories. The experimentation was closely tied to science and technology and to social regimentation. Actually, neither of these influences was new. Technology brought about the Industrial Revolution and thus helped pave the way for movements such as realism, naturalism, and Marxism. Various early short-story writers—for example, Balzac and Melville—dealt directly with the effects of industrialization. Turgenev again and again touched upon the horrors of a particularly severe brand of social regimentation: Russian serfdom. Today, however, because of what modern science has wrought, technology and social regimentation are more dominant forces than ever before.

Since the first decade of the twentieth century, science has played a greater role in shaping Western civilization than has any other single force. The changes have had astounding and catastrophic effects on traditional life styles. For most of human history, technological practice has preceded scientific theory. Our ancestors used the wheel long before they understood the mathematics of the circle. Similarly, men and women made and drank wine for several millennia before understanding the mysteries of fermentation and bacteria. But in the twentieth century, all this has changed.

Thanks to the continuing growth of science and its technological applications, we are now able to formulate basic theoretical concepts, utilize them to imagine things that do not exist, and then create what our minds have conjured up. For us, theory precedes practice. We create in the mind, and then in fact, all sorts of things: machines, assembly lines, robots, atomic bombs, spaceships, synthetic products of every description, and soon perhaps clones of ourselves. The modern short story, being a looking-glass of the age, reflects our technology, more often than not with an ominous pessimism.

Why this pessimistic reaction to science and technology? Medical technology, by increasing the human life span, and agricultural technology, by making it possible to feed more and more people, have brought about an enormously expanded world population. At the same time, industrial technology has transformed great sections of the globe, leading to the creation of giant national and multinational corporations, vast, sprawling urban centers, and an array of powerful, highly centralized governments and bureaucracies to cope with all this technological handiwork. As a result, we now inhabit a rigidly organized world, touched on all sides by the deadening hand of social regimentation. It is a world in which vast numbers of people feel the same sense of alienation that Marx called attention to in the nineteenth century.

Science has also fostered a pessimistic outlook through the development of sophisticated weapons that threaten human existence. Increasing numbers of people are coming to realize that any technological advance, whatever its immediate good, may generate severe problems— pollution, energy shortages, social disruptions—that may far outweigh the advance's original benefits. Finally, there is the continuing erosion of traditional scientific certainty under the impact of what has come to be called the New Physics. As a result of the discoveries of Albert Einstein, Max Planck, Louis de Broglie, and Werner Heisenberg, the very structure of the universe seems to have come unglued. Not only are we now to believe that time, space, energy, and matter are no longer independent entities, we are also told that accurate measurements of the structure of various subatomic particles may be beyond our capacity.

Given these social, technological, and scientific developments, it is not surprising that much experimental fiction is grim and that at its farthest extreme the experimental short story presents humans as unthinking, irrational robots and contemporary society as a mega-sized lunatic asylum. Our final stories, written by John Updike, John Cheever, Yukio Mishima, Toni Cade Bambara, Renata Adler, Donald Barthelme, and Mark Strand, may all, except for the Mishima selection, be taken as examples of experimental fiction. These stories deal with us as we are at this point in history. And since, to many writers the times appear out of joint, the stories, taken as a group, often appear disjointed, incoherent, absurd, and strangely convoluted. They require a reader's careful attention.

Like Flannery O'Connor, John Updike (b. 1932) writes from within the Christian camp. However, he approaches his subject matter from a very different perspective than does O'Connor. Often he does not touch directly on traditional religion at all, although in most instances religion is clearly on his mind.

One of Updike's chief concerns is an examination of the moral and spiritual condition of Americans—mostly upper-middle-class suburbanites—who have abandoned the unproved, and perhaps unprovable, assumptions of religion for the supposed certainties of scientific secularism. Updike's major suburbanite characters display a number of attractive traits. They are intelligent, often witty, keenly interested in the arts, and in possession of a social conscience. However, because their faith has fled them, they are lonely and confused, often feeling life to be without real meaning. To ease their spiritual malaise, they have made a fetish of such concerns as money, which they mistakenly equate with riches; possessions, which they mistakenly equate with security; and sex, which they mistakenly equate with love. These characters suffer and doubt, separated from the god they will not seek, yet longing for some belief that will dignify their existence.

A number of Updike's stories do strike a happier note. Some show goodness as an integral part of the human make-up. Others, "A & P" among them, point out that the world abounds in small pleasures such as music, childhood memories, and pretty girls, which help make living worthwhile. Then, there are also stories culminating in mystical or religious enlightenment. Many of these dramatize a conviction that nature is orderly, not chaotic, that God exists, and that humans, however dwarfed by the enormousness of the universe, are after all important in God's eyes.

Literary travelers who journey from Updike's fictional world to that of John Cheever (b. 1912) will not experience a great cultural shock, for both writers focus on much the same upper-middle-class milieu. Cheever has disclaimed the role of social critic, declaring that the middle-class way of life can be "as good and rich" as any other. But his writings reveal that he has indeed weighed contemporary society in the balance and found it wanting. True, his suburbia is not without its material attractions; but beneath the surface pleasantries lurks a darker realm in which adultery, alcoholism, vanity, and cruel social snobbery are all too common. Some of Cheever's stories appear to make the point that the whole suburban life style is designed to mask the realities of change, decay, and death.

As grim as much of his fictional world may be, Cheever sometimes holds out the possibility of spiritual wholeness. Such wholeness, he feels, can be achieved through the time-honored rituals and ceremonies accompanying birth, marriage, and death. These things link past to present and provide a feeling of permanence, even awe. Perhaps more importantly, wholeness can also be achieved through the calm contemplation of the world and its wonders, both natural and man-made.

Like William Faulkner, Japanese writer Yukio Mishima (1925–1970) found modern society wanting and sought his cultural ideal in the vanished past. Mishima rejected not only the current commercial temper but also individualism and democracy, and he regarded contemporary Japanese society as warped and artificial. He blamed this state of affairs on the demise of traditional attitudes following his country's defeat in World War II—a demise that can be likened to the situation in the South after the Civil War.

To Mishima, national salvation lay in a return to the values by which the Samurai warriors of feudal Japan had lived. This code stressed loyalty to one's overlord and death before dishonor. Mishima's beliefs led him to embrace, in Hemingwayesque fashion, the virtues of courage and an active physical life and to produce numerous stories that touch upon the meaninglessness of existence. These beliefs also led him, in 1970, to commit hara-kiri after violently denouncing Japan's self-defense army for its weakness under the post–World War II constitution.

Toni Cade Bambara is the author of stories that have been called "shavings off our Black experience." No other American writer better understands and employs what has come to be labeled the black style of speaking and writing—in Bambara's hands a style that is at once staccato and graceful, hip and human, ironic and generous. Bambara's settings range from metropolitan New York City to the small Southern town, from the crowded ghetto to the swank reaches of Fifth Avenue. A number of her stories feature sassy black girls and cunning, street-wise adults. Taken together, the stories offer an affectionate and respectful portrait of contemporary black America, while at the same time not letting the reader forget the mix of social conditions experienced by black Americans.

The writings of Renata Adler (b. 1938) include journalism, film criticism, short stories, and one novel. In describing Adler's reportage of the contemporary scene, one commentator has noted that she is neither an Old Journalist, who takes delight in describing the handwriting on the wall, nor a New Journalist, who wistfully scribbles graffiti on the wall. Rather she is a Third Journalist, who carefully and sometimes painfully describes the circumstances of the wall itself.

As a film critic, Adler has been accused of overintellectualizing what are intended only as celluloid strips for mass entertainment. As a novelist, she has been charged with ignoring not only plot and character but theme as well. These criticisms, in view of the high quality of her fiction, mark Adler as an experimental writer of the first rank. In her fiction, she deals incisively with the confused potpourri of present-day urban life, which she depicts as banal, dangerous, and fraught with inner anguish.

Donald Barthelme (b. 1931), among the most experimental of all contemporary American writers, consistently focuses on the alienation and dislocations that seem to characterize so much of contemporary life. Absurdities, both of form and of situation, abound in his writings. One story, for example, consists of a single sentence, and that sentence is without a subject. Another consists of a series of questions and answers. In a third, a tribe of Indians besieges a large metropolitan center. In yet another, a herd of porcupines, while being driven toward a large university, is diverted toward New York City after a confrontation between a dean and the herder.

In telling his stories, Barthelme blends exaggeration, parody, fashionable slang, business and academic jargon, and touches of the macabre, creating a carefully structured collage that is often ironic and very funny. Taken as a group, his stories represent a sustained attack on the chaos, lunacy, apathy, and violence of the hierarchical and bureaucratized world in which we find ourselves trying to get along.

Mark Strand (b. 1934), a poet as well as a short-story writer, charges contemporary society with demanding that men and women sacrifice spontaneity and creativity in favor of a sober and unimaginative conformity. As a result of this sacrifice, Strand says, "We learn early on to participate in our own demise." The world is overwhelming, according to Strand, and human beings are insignificant creatures whose little lives end in personal extinction. Nevertheless, despite their insignificance and vulnerability to the pressures of society, people do possess the power to make choices. "We are responsible for our lives in the interim," Strand says—a flicker of optimism in an otherwise black sea of pessimism.

Many of the elements that seem basic to the genre appear to go right out the window with experimental stories. Some of the stories may be virtually plotless. Characterization may be almost nonexistent in others. A single story may include several points of view, several narrators. In fact, some critics have concluded that anything goes. Nevertheless, one basic element does seem to hold. No matter how "far-out" an experimental story may be, the element of conflict remains ever present, and an investigation of the underlying conflict is a good place to begin to understand and analyze an experimental story. From this basic element one can work back to other recognizable elements, no matter how altered they may appear to be.

O. HENRY

The Gift of the Magi

One dollar and eighty-seven cents. That was all. And sixty cents of it was in pennies. Pennies saved one and two at a time by bulldozing the grocer and the vegetable man and the butcher until one's cheeks burned with the silent imputation of parsimony that such close dealing implied. Three times Della counted it. One dollar and eighty-seven cents. And the next day would be Christmas.

There was clearly nothing to do but flop down on the shabby little couch and howl. So Della did it. Which instigates the moral reflection that life is made up of sobs, sniffles, and smiles, with sniffles predominating.

While the mistress of the home is gradually subsiding from the first stage to the second, take a look at the home. A furnished flat at $8 per week. It did not exactly beggar description, but it certainly had that word on the lookout for the mendicancy squad.

In the vestibule below was a letter-box into which no letter would go, and an electric button from which no mortal finger could coax a ring. Also appertaining thereunto was a card bearing the name "Mr. James Dillingham Young."

The "Dillingham" had been flung to the breeze during a former period of prosperity when its possessor was being paid $30 per week. Now, when the income was shrunk to $20, the letters of "Dillingham" looked blurred, as though they were thinking seriously of contracting to a modest and unassuming D. But whenever Mr. James Dillingham Young came home and reached his flat above he was called "Jim" and greatly hugged by Mrs. James Dillingham Young, already introduced to you as Della. Which is all very good.

Della finished her cry and attended to her cheeks with the powder rag. She stood by the window and looked out dully at a grey cat walking a grey fence in a grey backyard. To-morrow would be Christmas Day, and she had only $1.87 with which to buy Jim a present. She had been saving every penny she could for months, with this result. Twenty dollars a week doesn't go far. Expenses had been greater than she had calculated. They always are. Only $1.87 to buy a present for Jim. Her Jim. Many a happy hour she had spent planning for something nice for him. Something fine and rare and sterling— something just a little bit near to being worthy of the honour of being owned by Jim.

There was a pier-glass between the windows of the room. Perhaps you have seen a pier-glass in an $8 flat. A very thin and very agile person may, by observing his reflection in a rapid sequence of longitudinal strips, obtain a fairly accurate conception of his looks. Della, being slender, had mastered the art.

Suddenly she whirled from the window and stood before the glass. Her eyes were shining brilliantly, but her face had lost its colour within twenty seconds. Rapidly she pulled down her hair and let it fall to its full length.

Now, there were two possessions of the James Dillingham Youngs in which they both took a mighty pride. One was Jim's gold watch that had been his father's and his grandfather's. The other was Della's hair. Had the Queen of Sheba lived in the flat across the airshaft, Della would have let her hair hang out the window some day to dry just to depreciate Her Majesty's jewels and gifts. Had King Solomon been the janitor, with all his treasures piled up in the basement, Jim would have pulled out his watch every time he passed, just to see him pluck at his beard from envy.

So now Della's beautiful hair fell about her, rippling and shining like a cascade of brown waters. It reached below her knee and made itself almost a garment for her. And then she did it up again nervously and quickly. Once she faltered for a minute and stood still while a tear or two splashed on the worn red carpet.

On went her old brown jacket; on went her old brown hat. With a whirl of skirts and with the brilliant sparkle still in her eyes, she fluttered out the door and down the stairs to the street.

Where she stopped the sign read: "Mme. Sofronie. Hair Goods of All Kinds." One flight up Della ran, and collected herself, panting. Madame, large, too white, chilly, hardly looked the "Sofronie."

"Will you buy my hair?" asked Della.

"I buy hair," said Madame. "Take yer hat off and let's have a sight at the looks of it."

Down rippled the brown cascade.

"Twenty dollars," said Madame, lifting the mass with a practised hand.

"Give it to me quick," said Della.

Oh, and the next two hours tripped by on rosy wings. Forget the hashed metaphor. She was ransacking the stores for Jim's present.

She found it at last. It surely had been made for Jim and no one else. There was no other like it in any of the stores, and she had turned all of them inside out. It was a platinum fob chain simple and chaste in design, properly proclaiming its value by substance alone and not by meretricious ornamentation—as all good things should do. It was even worthy of The Watch. As soon as she saw it she knew that it must be Jim's. It was like him. Quietness and value—the description applied to both. Twenty-one dollars they took from her for it, and she hurried home with the 87 cents. With that chain on his watch Jim might be properly anxious about the time in any company. Grand as the watch was, he sometimes looked at it on the sly on account of the old leather strap that he used in place of a chain.

When Della reached home her intoxication gave way a little to prudence and reason. She got out her curling irons and lighted the gas and went to work repairing the ravages made by generosity added to love. Which is always a tremendous task, dear friends—a mammoth task.

Within forty minutes her head was covered with tiny, close-lying curls that made her look wonderfully like a truant schoolboy. She looked at her reflection in the mirror long, carefully, and critically.

"If Jim doesn't kill me," she said to herself, "before he takes a second look at me, he'll say I look like a Coney Island chorus girl. But what could I do—oh! what could I do with a dollar and eighty-seven cents?"

At 7 o'clock the coffee was made and the frying-pan was on the back of the stove hot and ready to cook the chops.

Jim was never late. Della doubled the fob chain in her hand and sat on the corner of the table near the door that he always entered.Then she heard his step on the stair away down on the first flight, and she turned white for just a moment. She had a habit of saying little silent prayers about the simplest everyday things, and now she whispered: "Please God, make him think I am still pretty."

The door opened and Jim stepped in and closed it. He looked thin and very serious. Poor fellow, he was only twenty-two—and to be burdened with a family! He needed a new overcoat and he was without gloves.

Jim stopped inside the door, as immovable as a setter at the scent of quail. His eyes were fixed upon Della, and there was an expression in them that she could not read, and it terrified her. It was not anger, nor surprise, nor disapproval, nor horror, nor any of the sentiments that she had been prepared for. He simply stared at her fixedly with that peculiar expression on his face.

Della wriggled off the table and went for him.

"Jim, darling," she cried, "don't look at me that way. I had my hair cut off and sold it because I couldn't have lived through Christmas without giving you a present. It'll grow out again—you won't mind, will you? I just had to do it. My hair grows awfully fast. Say 'Merry Christmas!' Jim, and let's be happy. You don't know what a nice—what a beautiful, nice gift I've got for you."

"You've cut off your hair?" asked Jim, laboriously, as if he had not arrived at that patent fact yet even after the hardest mental labour.

"Cut it off and sold it," said Della. "Don't you like me just as well, anyhow? I'm me without my hair, ain't I?"

Jim looked about the room curiously.

"You say your hair is gone?" he said, with an air almost of idiocy.

"You needn't look for it," said Della. "It's sold, I tell you—sold and gone, too. It's Christmas Eve, boy. Be good to me, for it went for you. Maybe the hairs of my head were numbered," she went on with a sudden serious sweetness, "but nobody could ever count my love for you. Shall I put the chops on, Jim?"

Out of his trance Jim seemed quickly to wake. He enfolded his Della. For ten seconds let us regard with discreet scrutiny some inconsequential object in the other direction. Eight dollars a week or a million a year—what is the difference? A mathematician or a wit would give you the wrong answer. The magi brought valuable gifts, but that was not among them. This dark assertion will be illuminated later on.

Jim drew a package from his overcoat pocket and threw it upon the table.

"Don't make any mistake, Dell," he said, "about me. I don't think there's anything in the way of a haircut or a shave or a shampoo that could make me like my girl any less. But if you'll unwrap that package you may see why you had me going a while at first."

White fingers and nimble tore at the string and paper. And then an ecstatic scream of joy; and then, alas! a quick feminine change to hysterical tears and wails, necessitating the immediate employment of all the comforting powers of the lord of the flat.

For there lay The Combs—the set of combs, side and back, that Della had worshipped for long in a Broadway window. Beautiful combs, pure tortoise shell, with jewelled rims—just the shade to wear in the beautiful vanished hair. They were expensive combs, she knew, and her heart had simply craved and yearned over them without the least hope of possession. And now, they were hers, but the tresses that should have adorned the coveted adornments were gone.

But she hugged them to her bosom, and at length she was able to look up with dim eyes and a smile and say: "My hair grows so fast, Jim!"

And then Della leaped up like a little singed cat and cried, "Oh, oh!"

Jim had not yet seen his beautiful present. She held it out to him eagerly upon her open palm. The dull precious metal seemed to flash with a reflection of her bright and ardent spirit.

"Isn't it a dandy, Jim? I hunted all over town to find it. You'll have to look at the time a hundred times a day now. Give me your watch. I want to see how it looks on it."

Instead of obeying, Jim tumbled down on the couch and put his hands under the back of his head and smiled.

"Dell," said he, "let's put our Christmas presents away and keep 'em a while. They're too nice to use just at present. I sold the watch to get the money to buy your combs. And now suppose you put the chops on."

The magi, as you know, were wise men—wonderfully wise men—who brought gifts to the Babe in the manger. They invented the art of giving Christmas presents. Being wise, their gifts were no doubt wise ones, possibly bearing the privilege of exchange in case of duplication. And here I have lamely related to you the uneventful chronicle of two foolish children in a flat who most unwisely sacrificed for each other the greatest treasures of their house. But in a last word to the wise of these days let it be said that of all who give gifts these two were the wisest. Of all who give and receive gifts, such as they are wisest. Everywhere they are wisest. They are the magi.

FOR STUDY, DISCUSSION, AND WRITING

1. Do you think Della is a well-drawn or poorly drawn character? Does she possess plausibility? Is she dynamic or static?
2. Although "The Gift of the Magi" is unquestionably a sentimental story, do you find the emotions experienced by the characters reasonably restrained and believable?
3. Point out specific instances where O. Henry offers editorial comments outside the flow of the story. Does the fact that O. Henry is an obtrusive narrator help or injure the story?
4. Comment on the maturity of motivation that causes Della to have her hair cut and Jim to sell his watch. Do these two people seem like adults to you?
5. Relate what Della and Jim do to the craziness that often seizes otherwise reasonable people at Christmastime.
6. Do you think that O. Henry convinces the reader that Della places a high value on her hair and Jim places a high value his watch?
7. Does O. Henry adequately foreshadow the story's surprise ending? Or does the double twist seem contrived?

JAMES JOYCE

A Little Cloud

Eight years before he had seen his friend off at the North Wall and wished him godspeed. Gallaher had got on. You could tell that at once by his travelled air, his well-cut tweed suit and fearless accent. Few fellows had talents like his and fewer still could remain unspoiled by such success. Galla-

her's heart was in the right place and he had deserved to win. It was something to have a friend like that.

Little Chandler's thoughts ever since lunch-time had been of his meeting
with Gallaher, of Gallaher's invitation and of the great city London where
Gallaher lived. He was called Little Chandler because, though he was but
slightly under the average stature, he gave one the idea of being a little man.
His hands were white and small, his frame was fragile, his voice was quiet and
his manners were refined. He took the greatest care of his fair silken hair and
moustache and used perfume discreetly on his handerchief. The half-moons
of his nails were perfect and when he smiled you caught a glimpse of a row of
childish white teeth.

As he sat at his desk in the King's Inns he thought what changes those eight
years had brought. The friend whom he had known under a shabby and
necessitous guise had become a brilliant figure on the London Press. He
turned often from his tiresome writing to gaze out of the office window. The
glow of a late autumn sunset covered the grass plots and walks. It cast a
shower of kindly golden dust on the untidy nurses and decrepit old men who
drowsed on the benches; it flickered upon all the moving figures—on the
children who ran screaming along the gravel paths and on everyone who
passed through the gardens. He watched the scene and thought of life; and (as
always happened when he thought of life) he became sad. A gentle melancholy took possession of him. He felt how useless it was to struggle against
fortune, this being the burden of wisdom which the ages had bequeathed to
him.

He remembered the books of poetry upon his shelves at home. He had
bought them in his bachelor days and many an evening, as he sat in the little
room off the hall, he had been tempted to take one down from the bookshelf
and read out something to his wife. But shyness had always held him back;
and so the books had remained on their shelves. At times he repeated lines to
himself and this consoled him.

When his hour had struck he stood up and took leave of his desk and of his
fellow-clerks punctiliously. He emerged from under the feudal arch of the
King's Inns, a neat modest figure, and walked swiftly down Henrietta Street.
The golden sunset was waning and the air had grown sharp. A horde of grimy
children populated the street. They stood or ran in the roadway or crawled up
the steps before the gaping doors or squatted like mice upon the thresholds.
Little Chandler gave them no thought. He picked his way deftly through all
that minute vermin-like life and under the shadow of the gaunt spectral mansions in which the old nobility of Dublin had roistered. No memory of the
past touched him, for his mind was full of a present joy.

He had never been in Corless's but he knew the value of the name. He
knew that people went there after the theatre to eat oysters and drink li-
queurs; and he had heard that the waiters there spoke French and German.
Walking swiftly by at night he had seen cabs drawn up before the door and
richly dressed ladies, escorted by cavaliers, alight and enter quickly. They

wore noisy dresses and many wraps. Their faces were powdered and they caught up their dresses, when they touched earth, like alarmed Atalantas. He had always passed without turning his head to look. It was his habit to walk swiftly in the street even by day and whenever he found himself in the city late at night he hurried on his way apprehensively and excitedly. Sometimes, however, he courted the causes of his fear. He chose the darkest and narrowest streets and, as he walked boldly forward, the silence that was spread about his footsteps troubled him, the wandering silent figures troubled him; and at times a sound of low fugitive laughter made him tremble like a leaf.

He turned to the right towards Capel Street. Ignatius Gallaher on the London Press! Who would have thought it possible eight years before? Still, now that he reviewed the past, Little Chandler could remember many signs of future greatness in his friend. People used to say that Ignatius Gallaher was wild. Of course, he did mix with a rakish set of fellows at that time, drank freely and borrowed money on all sides. In the end he had got mixed up in some shady affair, some money transaction; at least, that was one version of his flight. But nobody denied him talent. There was always a certain . . . something in Ignatius Gallaher that impressed you in spite of yourself. Even when he was out at elbows and at his wits' end for money he kept up a bold face. Little Chandler remembered (and the remembrance brought a slight flush of pride to his cheek) one of Ignatius Gallaher's sayings when he was in a tight corner:

—Half time, now, boys, he used to say light-heartedly. Where's my considering cap?

That was Ignatius Gallaher all out; and, damn it, you couldn't but admire him for it.

Little Chandler quickened his pace. For the first time in his life he felt himself superior to the people he passed. For the first time his soul revolted against the dull inelegance of Capel Street. There was no doubt about it: if you wanted to succeed you had to go away. You could do nothing in Dublin. As he crossed Grattan Bridge he looked down the river towards the lower quays and pitied the poor stunted houses. They seemed to him a band of tramps, huddled together along the river-banks, their old coats covered with dust and soot, stupefied by the panorama of sunset and waiting for the first chill of night to bid them arise, shake themselves and begone. He wondered whether he could write a poem to express his idea. Perhaps Gallaher might be able to get it into some London paper for him. Could he write something original? He was not sure what idea he wished to express but the thought that a poetic moment had touched him took life within him like an infant hope. He stepped onward bravely.

Every step brought him nearer to London, farther from his own sober inartistic life. A light began to tremble on the horizon of his mind. He was not so old—thirty-two. His temperament might be said to be just at the point of maturity. There were so many different moods and impressions that he wished to express in verse. He felt them within him. He tried to weigh his soul to see if it was a poet's soul. Melancholy was the dominant note of his temperament, he thought, but it was a melancholy tempered by recurrences of faith and resignation and simple joy. If he could give expression to it in a book of poems perhaps men would listen. He would never be popular: he saw that. He could not sway the crowd but he might appeal to a little circle of kindred minds. The English critics, perhaps, would recognise him as one of the Celtic school by reason of the melancholy tone of his poems; besides that, he would put in allusions. He began to invent sentences and phrases from the notices which his book would get. *Mr. Chandler has the gift of easy and graceful verse. . . . A wistful sadness pervades these poems. . . . The Celtic note.* It was a pity his name was not more Irish-looking. Perhaps it would be better to insert his mother's name before the surname: Thomas Malone Chandler, or better still: T. Malone Chandler. He would speak to Gallaher about it.

He pursued his revery so ardently that he passed his street and had to turn back. As he came near Corless's his former agitation began to overmaster him and he halted before the door in indecision. Finally he opened the door and entered.

The light and noise of the bar held him at the doorway for a few moments. He looked about him, but his sight was confused by the shining of many red and green wine-glasses. The bar seemed to him to be full of people and he felt that the people were observing him curiously. He glanced quickly to right and left (frowning slightly to make his errand appear serious), but when his sight cleared a little he saw that nobody had turned to look at him: and there, sure enough, was Ignatius Gallaher leaning with his back against the counter and his feet planted far apart.

—Hallo, Tommy, old hero, here you are! What is it to be? What will you have? I'm taking whisky: better stuff than we get across the water. Soda? Lithia? No mineral? I'm the same. Spoils the flavour. . . . Here, *garçon*, bring us two halves of malt whisky, like a good fellow. . . . Well, and how have you been pulling along since I saw you last? Dear God, how old we're getting! Do you see any signs of aging in me—eh, what? A little grey and thin on the top—what?

Ignatius Gallaher took off his hat and displayed a large closely cropped head. His face was heavy, pale and clean-shaven. His eyes, which were of bluish slate-colour, relieved his unhealthy pallor and shone out plainly above the vivid orange tie he wore. Between these rival features the lips appeared very long and shapeless and colourless. He bent his head and felt with two sympathetic fingers the thin hair at the crown. Little Chandler shook his head as a denial. Ignatius Gallaher put on his hat again.

—It pulls you down, he said, Press life. Always hurry and scurry, looking for copy and sometimes not finding it: and then, always to have something new in your stuff. Damn proofs and printers, I say, for a few days. I'm deuced glad, I can tell you, to get back to the old country. Does a fellow good, a bit of a holiday. I feel a ton better since I landed again in dear dirty Dublin. . . . Here you are, Tommy. Water? Say when.

Little Chandler allowed his whisky to be very much diluted.

—You don't know what's good for you, my boy, said Ignatius Gallaher. I drink mine neat.

—I drink very little as a rule, said Little Chandler modestly. An odd half-one or so when I meet any of the old crowd: that's all.

—Ah, well, said Ignatius Gallaher, cheerfully, here's to us and to old times and old acquaintance.

They clinked glasses and drank the toast.

—I met some of the old gang to-day, said Ignatius Gallaher. O'Hara seems to be in a bad way. What's he doing?

—Nothing, said Little Chandler. He's gone to the dogs.

—But Hogan has a good sit, hasn't he?

—Yes; he's in the Land Commission.

—I met him one night in London and he seemed to be very flush. . . . Poor O'Hara! Boose, I suppose?

—Other things, too, said Little Chandler shortly.

Ignatius Gallaher laughed.

—Tommy, he said, I see you haven't changed an atom. You're the very same serious person that used to lecture me on Sunday mornings when I had a sore head and a fur on my tongue. You'd want to knock about a bit in the world. Have you never been anywhere, even for a trip?

—I've been to the Isle of Man, said Little Chandler.

Ignatius Gallaher laughed.

—The Isle of Man! he said. Go to London or Paris: Paris, for choice. That'd do you good.

—Have you seen Paris?

—I should think I have! I've knocked about there a little.

—And is it really so beautiful as they say? asked Little Chandler.

He sipped a little of his drink while Ignatius Gallaher finished his boldly.

—Beautiful? said Ignatius Gallaher, pausing on the word and on the flavour of his drink. It's not so beautiful, you know. Of course, it is beautiful. . . . But it's the life of Paris; that's the thing. Ah, there's no city like Paris for gaiety, movement, excitement. . . .

Little Chandler finished his whisky and, after some trouble, succeeded in catching the barman's eye. He ordered the same again.

—I've been to the Moulin Rouge, Ignatius Gallaher continued when the barman had removed their glasses, and I've been to all the Bohemian cafés. Hot stuff! Not for a pious chap like you, Tommy.

Little Chandler said nothing until the barman returned with the two glasses: then he touched his friend's glass lightly and reciprocated the former toast. He was beginning to feel somewhat disillusioned. Gallaher's accent and way of expressing himself did not please him. There was something vulgar in his friend which he had not observed before. But perhaps it was only the result of living in London amid the bustle and competition of the Press. The old personal charm was still there under this new gaudy manner. And, after all,

Gallaher had lived, he had seen the world. Little Chandler looked at his friend enviously.

—Everything in Paris is gay, said Ignatius Gallaher. They believe in enjoying life—and don't you think they're right? If you want to enjoy yourself properly you must go to Paris. And, mind you, they've a great feeling for the Irish there. When they heard I was from Ireland they were ready to eat me, man.

Little Chandler took four or five sips from his glass.

—Tell me, he said, is it true that Paris is so . . . immoral as they say?

Ignatius Gallaher made a catholic gesture with his right arm.

—Every place is immoral, he said. Of course you do find spicy bits in Paris. Go to one of the students' balls, for instance. That's lively, if you like, when the *cocottes* begin to let themselves loose. You know what they are, I suppose?

—I've heard of them, said Little Chandler.

Ignatius Gallaher drank off his whisky and shook his head.

—Ah, he said, you may say what you like. There's no woman like the Parisienne—for style, for go.

—Then it is an immoral city, said Little Chandler, with timid insistence—I mean, compared with London or Dublin?

—London! said Ignatius Gallaher. It's six of one and half-a-dozen of the other. You ask Hogan, my boy. I showed him a bit about London when he was over there. He'd open your eye. . . . I say, Tommy, don't make punch of that whisky: liquor up.

—No, really. . . .

—O, come on, another one won't do you any harm. What is it? The same again, I suppose?

—Well . . . all right.

—*François*, the same again. . . . Will you smoke, Tommy?

Ignatius Gallaher produced his cigar-case. The two friends lit their cigars and puffed at them in silence until their drinks were served.

—I'll tell you my opinion, said Ignatius Gallaher, emerging after some time from the clouds of smoke in which he had taken refuge, it's a rum world. Talk of immorality! I've heard of cases—what am I saying?—I've known them: cases of . . . immorality. . . .

Ignatius Gallaher puffed thoughtfully at his cigar and then, in a calm historian's tone, he proceeded to sketch for his friend some pictures of the corruption which was rife abroad. He summarised the vices of many capitals and seemed inclined to award the palm to Berlin. Some things he could not vouch for (his friends had told him), but of others he had had personal experience. He spared neither rank nor caste. He revealed many of the secrets of religious houses on the Continent and described some of the practices which were fashionable in high society and ended by telling, with details, a story about an English duchess—a story which he knew to be true. Little Chandler was astonished.

—Ah, well, said Ignatius Gallaher, here we are in old jog-along Dublin where nothing is known of such things.

—How dull you must find it, said Little Chandler, after all the other places you've seen!

—Well, said Ignatius Gallaher, it's a relaxation to come over here, you know. And, after all, it's the old country, as they say, isn't it? You can't help having a certain feeling for it. That's human nature. . . . But tell me something about yourself. Hogan told me you had . . . tasted the joys of connubial bliss. Two years ago, wasn't it?

Little Chandler blushed and smiled.

—Yes, he said. I was married last May twelve months.

—I hope it's not too late in the day to offer my best wishes, said Ignatius Gallaher. I didn't know your address or I'd have done so at the time.

He extended his hand, which Little Chandler took.

—Well, Tommy, he said, I wish you and yours every joy in life, old chap, and tons of money, and may you never die till I shoot you. And that's the wish of a sincere friend, an old friend. You know that?

—I know that, said Little Chandler.

—Any youngsters? said Ignatius Gallaher.

Little Chandler blushed again.

—We have one child, he said.

—Son or daughter?

—A little boy.

Ignatius Gallaher slapped his friend sonorously on the back.

—Bravo, he said, I wouldn't doubt you, Tommy.

Little Chandler smiled, looked confusedly at his glass and bit his lower lip with three childishly white front teeth.

—I hope you'll spend an evening with us, he said, before you go back. My wife will be delighted to meet you. We can have a little music and—

—Thanks awfully, old chap, said Ignatius Gallaher, I'm sorry we didn't meet earlier. But I must leave to-morrow night.

—To-night, perhaps . . . ?

—I'm awfully sorry, old man. You see I'm over here with another fellow, clever young chap he is too, and we arranged to go to a little card-party. Only for that . . .

—O, in that case. . . .

—But who knows? said Ignatius Gallaher considerately. Next year I may take a little skip over here now that I've broken the ice. It's only a pleasure deferred.

—Very well, said Little Chandler, the next time you come we must have an evening together. That's agreed now, isn't it?

—Yes, that's agreed, said Ignatius Gallaher. Next year if I come, *parole d'honneur*.

—And to clinch the bargain, said Little Chandler, we'll just have one more now.

Ignatius Gallaher took out a large gold watch and looked at it.

—Is it to be the last? he said. Because you know, I have an a.p.

—O, yes, positively, said Little Chandler.

—Very well, then, said Ignatius Gallaher, let us have another one as a *deoc an doruis*—that's good vernacular for a small whisky, I believe.

Little Chandler ordered the drinks. The blush which had risen to his face a few moments before was establishing itself. A trifle made him blush at any time: and now he felt warm and excited. Three small whiskies had gone to his head and Gallaher's strong cigar had confused his mind, for he was a delicate and abstinent person. The adventure of meeting Gallaher after eight years, of finding himself with Gallaher in Corless's surrounded by lights and noise, of listening to Gallaher's stories and of sharing for a brief space Gallaher's vagrant and triumphant life, upset the equipoise of his sensitive nature. He felt acutely the contrast between his own life and his friend's, and it seemed to him unjust. Gallaher was his inferior in birth and education. He was sure that he could do something better than his friend had ever done, or could ever do, something higher than mere tawdry journalism if he only got the chance. What was it that stood in his way? His unfortunate timidity! He wished to vindicate himself in some way, to assert his manhood. He saw behind Gallaher's refusal of his invitation. Gallaher was only patronising him by his friendliness just as he was patronising Ireland by his visit.

The barman brought their drinks. Little Chandler pushed one glass towards his friend and took up the other boldly.

—Who knows? he said, as they lifted their glasses. When you come next year I may have the pleasure of wishing long life and happiness to Mr and Mrs Ignatius Gallaher.

Ignatius Gallaher in the act of drinking closed one eye expressively over the rim of his glass. When he had drunk he smacked his lips decisively, set down his glass and said:

—No blooming fear of that, my boy. I'm going to have my fling first and see a bit of life and the world before I put my head in the sack—if I ever do.

—Some day you will, said Little Chandler calmly.

Ignatius Gallaher turned his orange tie and slate-blue eyes full upon his friend.

—You think so? he said.

—You'll put your head in the sack, repeated Little Chandler stoutly, like everyone else if you can find the girl.

He had slightly emphasised his tone and he was aware that he had betrayed himself; but, though the colour had heightened in his cheek, he did not flinch from his friend's gaze. Ignatius Gallaher watched him for a few moments and then said:

—If ever it occurs, you may bet your bottom dollar there'll be no mooning and spooning about it. I mean to marry money. She'll have a good fat account at the bank or she won't do for me.

Little Chandler shook his head.

—Why, man alive, said Ignatius Gallaher, vehemently, do you know what it is? I've only to say the word and to-morrow I can have the woman and the cash. You don't believe it? Well, I know it. There are hundreds—what am I saying?—thousands of rich Germans and Jews, rotten with money, that'd only be too glad. . . . You wait a while, my boy. See if I don't play my cards properly. When I go about a thing I mean business, I tell you. You just wait.

He tossed his glass to his mouth, finished his drink and laughed loudly. Then he looked thoughtfully before him and said in a calmer tone:

—But I'm in no hurry. They can wait. I don't fancy tying myself up to one woman, you know.

He imitated with his mouth the act of tasting and made a wry face.

—Must get a bit stale, I should think, he said.

*   *   *

Little Chandler sat in the room off the hall, holding a child in his arms. To save money they kept no servant but Annie's young sister Monica came for an hour or so in the morning and an hour or so in the evening to help. But Monica had gone home long ago. It was a quarter to nine. Little Chandler had come home late for tea and, moreover, he had forgotten to bring Annie home the parcel of coffee from Bewley's. Of course she was in a bad humour and gave him short answers. She said she would do without any tea but when it came near the time at which the shop at the corner closed she decided to go out herself for a quarter of a pound of tea and two pounds of sugar. She put the sleeping child deftly in his arms and said:

—Here. Don't waken him.

A little lamp with a white china shade stood upon the table and its light fell over a photograph which was enclosed in a frame of crumpled horn. It was Annie's photograph. Little Chandler looked at it, pausing at the thin tight lips. She wore the pale blue summer blouse which he had brought her home as a present one Saturday. It had cost him ten and elevenpence; but what an agony of nervousness it had cost him! How he had suffered that day, waiting at the shop door until the shop was empty, standing at the counter and trying to appear at his ease while the girl piled ladies' blouses before him, paying at the desk and forgetting to take up the odd penny of his change, being called back by the cashier, and, finally, striving to hide his blushes as he left the shop by examining the parcel to see if it was securely tied. When he brought the blouse home Annie kissed him and said it was very pretty and stylish; but when she heard the price she threw the blouse on the table and said it was a regular swindle to charge ten and elevenpence for that. At first she wanted to take it back but when she tried it on she was delighted with it, especially with the make of the sleeves, and kissed him and said he was very good to think of her.

Hm! . . .

He looked coldly into the eyes of the photograph and they answered coldly. Certainly they were pretty and the face itself was pretty. But he found something mean in it. Why was it so unconscious and lady-like? The composure of the eyes irritated him. They repelled him and defied him: there was no passion in them, no rapture. He thought of what Gallaher had said about rich Jewesses. Those dark Oriental eyes, he thought, how full they are of passion, of voluptuous longing! . . . Why had he married the eyes in the photograph?

He caught himself up at the question and glanced nervously round the room. He found something mean in the pretty furniture which he had bought for his house on the hire system. Annie had chosen it herself and it reminded him of her. It too was prim and pretty. A dull resentment against his life awoke within him. Could he not escape from his little house? Was it too late for him to try to live bravely like Gallaher? Could he go to London? There was the furniture still to be paid for. If he could only write a book and get it published, that might open the way for him.

A volume of Byron's poems lay before him on the table. He opened it cautiously with his left hand lest he should waken the child and began to read the first poem in the book:

> Hushed are the winds and still the evening gloom,
>   Not e'en a Zephyr wanders through the grove,
> Whilst I return to view my Margaret's tomb
>   And scatter flowers on the dust I love.

He paused. He felt the rhythm of the verse about him in the room. How melancholy it was! Could he, too, write like that, express the melancholy of his soul in verse? There were so many things he wanted to describe: his sensation of a few hours before on Grattan Bridge, for example. If he could get back again into that mood. . . .

The child awoke and began to cry. He turned from the page and tried to hush it: but it would not be hushed. He began to rock it to and fro in his arms but its wailing cry grew keener. He rocked it faster while his eyes began to read the second stanza:

> Within this narrow cell reclines her clay,
>   That clay where once . . .

It was useless. He couldn't read. He couldn't do anything. The wailing of the child pierced the drum of his ear. It was useless, useless! He was a prisoner for life. His arms trembled with anger and suddenly bending to the child's face he shouted:

—Stop!

The child stopped for an instant, had a spasm of fright and began to scream. He jumped up from his chair and walked hastily up and down the room with the child in his arms. It began to sob piteously, losing its breath for four or five seconds, and then bursting out anew. The thin walls of the room echoed the sound. He tried to soothe it but it sobbed more convulsively. He looked at the contracted and quivering face of the child and began to be alarmed. He counted seven sobs without a break between them and caught the child to his breast in fright. If it died! . . .

The door was burst open and a young woman ran in, panting.

—What is it? What is it? she cried.

The child, hearing its mother's voice, broke out into a paroxysm of sobbing.

—It's nothing, Annie . . . it's nothing . . . . He began to cry . . .

She flung her parcels on the floor and snatched the child from him.

—What have you done to him? she cried, glaring into his face.

Little Chandler sustained for one moment the gaze of her eyes and his heart closed together as he met the hatred in them. He began to stammer.

—It's nothing. . . . He . . . he began to cry. . . . I couldn't . . . I didn't do anything. . . . What?

Giving no heed to him she began to walk up and down the room, clasping the child tightly in her arms and murmuring:

—My little man! My little mannie! Was 'ou frightened, love? . . . There now, love! There now! . . . Lambabaun! Mamma's little lamb of the world! . . . There now!

Little Chandler felt his cheeks suffused with shame and he stood back out of the lamplight. He listened while the paroxysm of the child's sobbing grew less and less; and tears of remorse started to his eyes.

FOR STUDY, DISCUSSION, AND WRITING

1. How does the point of view employed by Joyce contribute to the characterization of Little Chandler? How else is Little Chandler characterized?
2. Does the story offer any evidence that Little Chandler actually possesses "the gift of easy and graceful verse"?
3. How accurately does Little Chandler remember the character of Gallaher?
4. In what ways are Little Chandler and Gallaher alike?
5. What specific symbols does Joyce employ in the characterization of Gallaher?
6. What do you think Gallaher's motives are in telling Little Chandler his lurid stories of life abroad?
7. The whiskey that Little Chandler drinks seems briefly to make him more like Gallaher. Speculate on the possibility that Gallaher (who is drunk throughout the story) when sober might be a bit like Little Chandler.
8. At what point in the story does Little Chandler experience an epiphany? What does he come to realize as a result of the epiphany?
9. Is Annie entirely the cold-eyed and passionless woman that Little Chandler comes to believe she is?
10. Why is Little Chandler crying at the end of the story?

D. H. LAWRENCE

The Shades of Spring

I

It was a mile nearer through the wood. Mechanically, Syson turned up by the forge and lifted the field-gate. The blacksmith and his mate stood still, watching the trespasser. But Syson looked too much a gentleman to be accosted. They let him go on in silence across the small field to the wood.

There was not the least difference between this morning and those of the bright springs, six or eight years back. White and sandy-gold fowls still scratched round the gate, littering the earth and the field with feathers and scratched-up rubbish. Between the two thick holly bushes in the wood-hedge was the hidden gap, whose fence one climbed to get into the wood; the bars were scored just the same by the keeper's boots. He was back in the eternal.

Syson was extraordinarily glad. Like an uneasy spirit he had returned to the country of his past, and he found it waiting for him, unaltered. The hazel still spread glad little hands downwards, the bluebells here were still wan and few, among the lush grass and in shade of the bushes.

The path through the wood, on the very brow of a slope, ran winding easily for a time. All around were twiggy oaks, just issuing their gold, and floor spaces diapered with woodruff, with patches of dog-mercury and tufts of hyacinth. Two fallen trees still lay across the track. Syson jolted down a steep, rough slope, and came again upon the open land, this time looking north as through a great window in the wood. He stayed to gaze over the level fields of the hill-top, at the village which strewed the bare upland as if it had tumbled off the passing wagons of industry, and been forsaken. There was a stiff, modern, grey little church, and blocks and rows of red dwellings lying at random; at the back, the twinkling headstocks of the pit, and the looming pit-hill. All was naked and out-of-doors, not a tree! It was quite unaltered.

Syson turned, satisfied, to follow the path that sheered downhill into the wood. He was curiously elated, feeling himself back in an enduring vision. He started. A keeper was standing a few yards in front, barring the way.

"Where might you be going this road, sir?" asked the man. The tone of his question had a challenging twang. Syson looked at the fellow with an impersonal, observant gaze. It was a young man of four- or five-and-twenty, ruddy and well favoured. His dark blue eyes now stared aggressively at the intruder. His black moustache, very thick, was cropped short over a small, rather soft mouth. In every other respect the fellow was manly and good-looking. He stood just above middle height; the strong forward thrust of his chest, and the perfect ease of his erect, self-sufficient body, gave one the feeling that he was taut with animal life, like the thick jet of a fountain balanced in itself. He stood with the butt of his gun on the ground, looking uncertainly and questioningly at Syson. The dark, restless eyes of the trespasser, examining the man and penetrating into him without heeding his office, troubled the keeper and made him flush.

"Where is Naylor? Have you got his job?" Syson asked.

"You're not from the House, are you?" inquired the keeper. It could not be, since everyone was away.

"No, I'm not from the House," the other replied. It seemed to amuse him.

"Then might I ask where you were making for?" said the keeper, nettled.

"Where I am making for?" Syson repeated. "I am going to Willey-Water Farm."

"This isn't the road."

"I think so. Down this path, past the well, and out by the white gate."

"But that's not the public road."

"I suppose not. I used to come so often, in Naylor's time, I had forgotten. Where is he, by the way?"

"Crippled with rheumatism," the keeper answered reluctantly.

"Is he?" Syson exclaimed in pain.

"And who might you be?" asked the keeper, with a new intonation.

"John Adderley Syson; I used to live in Cordy Lane."

"Used to court Hilda Millership?"

Syson's eyes opened with a pained smile. He nodded. There was an awkward silence.

"And you—who are you?" asked Syson.

"Arthur Pilbeam—Naylor's my uncle," said the other.

"You live here in Nuttall?"

"I'm lodgin' at my uncle's—at Naylor's."

"I see!"

"Did you say you was goin' down to Willey-Water?" asked the keeper. "Yes."

There was a pause of some moments, before the keeper blurted: "I'm courtin' Hilda Millership."

The young fellow looked at the intruder with a stubborn defiance, almost pathetic. Syson opened new eyes.

"Are you?" he said, astonished. The keeper flushed dark.

"She and me are keeping company," he said.

"I didn't know!" said Syson. The other man waited uncomfortably.

"What, is the thing settled?" asked the intruder.

"How, settled?" retorted the other sulkily.

"Are you going to get married soon, and all that?"

The keeper stared in silence for some moments, impotent.

"I suppose so," he said, full of resentment.

"Ah!" Syson watched closely.

"I'm marrried myself," he added, after a time.

"You are?" said the other incredulously.

Syson laughed in his brilliant, unhappy way.

"This last fifteen months," he said.

The keeper gazed at him with wide, wondering eyes, apparently thinking back, and trying to make things out.

"Why, didn't you know?" asked Syson.

"No, I didn't," said the other sulkily.

There was silence for a moment.

"Ah well!" said Syson, "I will go on. I suppose I may." The keeper stood in silent opposition. The two men hesitated in the open, grassy space, set round with small sheaves of sturdy bluebells; a little open platform on the brow of the hill. Syson took a few indecisive steps forward, then stopped.

"I say, how beautiful!" he cried.

He had come in full view of the downslope. The wide path ran from his feet like a river, and it was full of bluebells, save for a green winding thread down the centre, where the keeper walked. Like a stream the path opened into azure shallows at the levels, and there were pools of bluebells, with still the green thread winding through, like a thin current of ice-water through blue lakes. And from under the twig-purple of the bushes swam the shadowed blue, as if the flowers lay in flood water over the woodland.

"Ah, isn't it lovely!" Syson exclaimed; this was his past, the country he had abandoned, and it hurt him to see it so beautiful. Wood-pigeons cooed overhead, and the air was full of the brightness of birds singing.

"If you're married, what do you keep writing to her for, and sending her poetry books and things?" asked the keeper. Syson stared at him, taken aback and humiliated. Then he began to smile.

"Well," he said, "I did not know about you . . ."

Again the keeper flushed darkly.

"But if you are married——" he charged.

"I am," answered the other cynically.

Then, looking down the blue, beautiful path, Syson felt his own humiliation. "What right *have* I to hang on to her?" he thought, bitterly self-contemptuous.

"She knows I'm married and all that," he said.

"But you keep sending her books," challenged the keeper.

Syson, silenced, looked at the other man quizzically, half pitying. Then he turned.

"Good day," he said, and was gone. Now, everything irritated him: the two sallows, one all gold and perfume and murmur, one silver-green and bristly, reminded him that here he had taught her about pollination. What a fool he was! What god-forsaken folly it all was!

"Ah well," he said to himself; "the poor devil seems to have a grudge against me. I'll do my best for him." He grinned to himself, in a very bad temper.

II

The farm was less than a hundred yards from the wood's edge. The wall of trees formed the fourth side to the open quadrangle. The house faced the wood. With tangled emotions, Syson noted the plum blossom falling on the profuse, coloured primroses, which he himself had brought here and set. How they had increased! There were thick tufts of scarlet, and pink, and pale purple primroses under the plum trees. He saw somebody glance at him through the kitchen window, heard men's voices.

The door opened suddenly: very womanly she had grown! He felt himself going pale.

"You?—Addy!" she exclaimed, and stood motionless.

"Who?" called the farmer's voice. Men's low voices answered. Those low voices, curious and almost jeering, roused the tormented spirit in the visitor. Smiling brilliantly at her, he waited.

"Myself—why not?" he said.

The flush burned very deep on her cheek and throat.

"We are just finishing dinner," she said.

"Then I will stay outside." He made a motion to show that he would sit on the red earthenware pipkin that stood near the door among the daffodils, and contained the drinking-water.

"Oh no, come in," she said hurriedly. He followed her. In the doorway, he glanced swiftly over the family, and bowed. Everyone was confused. The farmer, his wife, and the four sons sat at the coarsely laid dinner-table, the men with arms bare to the elbows.

"I am sorry I come at lunch-time," said Syson.

"Hello, Addy!" said the farmer, assuming the old form of address, but his tone cold. "How are you?"

And he shook hands.

"Shall you have a bit?" he invited the young visitor, but taking for granted the offer would be refused. He assumed that Syson was become too refined to eat so roughly. The young man winced at the imputation.

"Have you had any dinner?" asked the daughter.

"No," replied Syson. "It is too early. I shall be back at half-past one."

"You call it lunch, don't you?" asked the eldest son, almost ironical. He had once been an intimate friend of this young man.

"We'll give Addy something when we've finished," said the mother, an invalid, deprecating.

"No—don't trouble. I don't want to give you any trouble," said Syson.

"You could allus live on fresh air an' scenery," laughed the youngest son, a lad of nineteen.

Syson went round the buildings, and into the orchard at the back of the house, where daffodils all along the hedgerow swung like yellow, ruffled birds on their perches. He loved the place extraordinarily, the hills ranging round, with bear-skin woods covering their giant shoulders, and small red farms like brooches clasping their garments; the blue streak of water in the valley, the bareness of the home pasture, the sound of myriad-threaded bird-singing, which went mostly unheard. To his last day, he would dream of this place, when he felt the sun on his face, or saw the small handfuls of snow between the winter twigs, or smelt the coming of spring.

Hilda was very womanly. In her presence he felt constrained. She was twenty-nine, as he was, but she seemed to him much older. He felt foolish, almost unreal beside her. She was so static. As he was fingering some shed plum blossom on a low bough, she came to the back door to shake the table-cloth. Fowls raced from the stack-yard, birds rustled from the trees. Her dark hair was gathered up in a coil like a crown on her head. She was very straight, distant in her bearing. As she folded the cloth, she looked away over the hills.

Presently Syson returned indoors. She had prepared eggs and curd cheese, stewed gooseberries and cream.

"Since you will dine to-night," she said, "I have only given you a light lunch."

"It is awfully nice," he said. "You keep a real idyllic atmosphere—your belt of straw and ivy buds."

Still they hurt each other.

He was uneasy before her. Her brief, sure speech, her distant bearing, were unfamiliar to him. He admired again her grey-black eyebrows, and her lashes. Their eyes met. He saw, in the beautiful grey and black of her glance, tears and a strange light, and at the back of all, calm acceptance of herself, and triumph over him.

He felt himself shrinking. With an effort he kept up the ironic manner.

She sent him into the parlour while she washed the dishes. The long low room was refurnished from the Abbey sale, with chairs upholstered in claret-coloured rep, many years old, and an oval table of polished walnut, and another piano, handsome, though still antique. In spite of the strangeness, he was pleased. Opening a high cupboard let into the thickness of the wall, he found it full of his books, his old lesson-books, and volumes of verse he had sent her, English and German. The daffodils in the white window-bottoms shone across the room, he could almost feel their rays. The old glamour caught him again. His youthful water-colours on the wall no longer made him grin; he remembered how fervently he had tried to paint for her, twelve years before.

She entered, wiping a dish, and he saw again the bright, kernel-white beauty of her arms.

"You are quite splendid here," he said, and their eyes met.

"Do you like it?" she asked. It was the old, low, husky tone of intimacy. He felt a quick change beginning in his blood. It was the old, delicious sublimation, the thinning, almost the vaporising of himself, as if his spirit were to be liberated.

"Aye," he nodded, smiling at her like a boy again. She bowed her head.

"This was the countess's chair," she said in low tones. "I found her scissors down here between the padding."

"Did you? Where are they?"

Quickly, with a lilt in her movement, she fetched her work-basket, and together they examined the long-shanked old scissors.

"What a ballad of dead ladies!" he said, laughing, as he fitted his fingers into the round loops of the countess's scissors.

"I knew you could use them," she said, with certainty. He looked at his fingers, and at the scissors. She meant his fingers were fine enough for the small-looped scissors.

"That is something to be said for me," he laughed, putting the scissors aside. She turned to the window. He noticed the fine, fair down on her cheeks and her upper lip, and her soft, white neck, like the throat of a nettle flower, and her forearms, bright as newly blanched kernels. He was looking at her with new eyes, and she was a different person to him. He did not know her. But he could regard her objectively now.

"Shall we go out awhile?" she asked.

"Yes!" he answered. But the predominant emotion, that troubled the excitement and perplexity of his heart, was fear, fear of that which he saw. There was about her the same manner, the same intonation in her voice, now as then, but she was not what he had known her to be. He knew quite well what she had been for him. And gradually he was realising that she was something quite other, and always had been.

She put no covering on her head, merely took off her apron, saying: "We will go by the larches." As they passed the old orchard, she called him in to show him a blue-tit's nest in one of the apple trees, and a sycock's in the hedge. He rather wondered at her surety, at a certain hardness like arrogance hidden under her humility.

"Look at the apple buds," she said, and he then perceived myriads of little scarlet balls among the drooping boughs. Watching his face, her eyes went hard. She saw the scales were fallen from him, and at last he was going to see her as she was. It was the thing she had most dreaded in the past, and most needed, for her soul's sake. Now he was going to see her as she was. He would not love her, and he would know he never could have loved her. The old illusion gone, they were strangers, crude and entire. But he would give her her due—she would have her due from him.

She was brilliant as he had not known her. She showed him nests: a jenny wren's in a low bush.

"See this jinty's!" she exclaimed.

He was surprised to hear her use the local name. She reached carefully through the thorns, and put her finger in the nest's round door.

"Five!" she said. "Tiny little things."

She showed him nests of robins, and chaffinches, and linnets, and buntings; of a wagtail beside the water.

"And if we go down, nearer the lake, I will show you a kingfisher's. . . ."

"Among the young fir trees," she said, "there's a throstle's or a blackie's on nearly every bough, every ledge. The first day, when I had seen them all, I felt as if I mustn't go in the wood. It seemed a city of birds; and in the morning, hearing them all, I thought of the noisy early markets. I was afraid to go in my own wood."

She was using the language they had both of them invented. Now it was all her own. He had done with it. She did not mind his silence, but was always dominant, letting him see her wood. As they came along a marshy path where forget-me-nots were opening in a rich blue drift: "We know all the birds, but there are many flowers we can't find out," she said. It was half an appeal to him, who had known the names of things.

She looked dreamily across to the open fields that slept in the sun.

"I have a lover as well, you know," she said, with assurance, yet dropping again almost into the intimate tone.

This woke in him the spirit to fight her.

"I think I met him. He is good-looking—also in Arcady."

Without answering, she turned into a dark path that led uphill, where the trees and undergrowth were very thick.

"They did well," she said at length, "to have various altars to various gods, in old days."

"Ah yes!" he agreed. "To whom is the new one?"

"There are no old ones," she said. "I was always looking for this."

"And whose is it?" he asked.

"I don't know," she said, looking full at him.

"I'm very glad, for your sake," he said, "that you are satisfied."

"Aye—but the man doesn't matter so much," she said. There was a pause.

"No!" he exclaimed, astonished, yet recognising her as her real self.

"It is one's self that matters," she said. "Whether one is being one's own self and serving one's own God."

There was silence, during which he pondered. The path was almost flower-less, gloomy. At the side, his heels sank into soft clay.

III

"I," she said, very slowly, "I was married the same night as you."

He looked at her.

"Not legally, of course," she replied. "But—actually."

"To the keeper?" he said, not knowing what else to say.

She turned to him.

"You thought I could not?" she said. But the flush was deep in her cheek and throat, for all her assurance.

Still he would not say anything.

"You see"—she was making an effort to explain—"I had to understand also."

"And what does it amount to, this *understanding*?" he asked.

"A very great deal—does it not to you?" she replied. "One is free."

"And you are not disappointed?"

"Far from it!" Her tone was deep and sincere.

"You love him?"

"Yes, I love him."

"Good!" he said.

This silenced her for a while.

"Here, among his things, I love him," she said.

His conceit would not let him be silent.

"It needs this setting?" he asked.

"It does," she cried. "You were always making me to be not myself."

He laughed shortly.

"But is it a matter of surroundings?" he said. He had considered her all spirit.

"I am like a plant," she replied. "I can only grow in my own soil."

They came to a place where the undergrowth shrank away, leaving a bare, brown space, pillared with the brick-red and purplish trunks of pine trees. On the fringe, hung the sombre green of elder trees, with flat flowers in bud, and below were bright, unfurling pennons of fern. In the midst of the bare space stood a keeper's log hut. Pheasant-coops were lying about, some occupied by a clucking hen, some empty.

Hilda walked over the brown pine-needles to the hut, took a key from among the eaves, and opened the door. It was a bare wooden place with a carpenter's bench and form, carpenter's tools, an axe, snares, traps, some skins pegged down, everything in order. Hilda closed the door. Syson examined the weird flat coats of wild animals, that were pegged down to be cured. She turned some knotch in the side wall, and disclosed a second, small apartment.

"How romantic!" said Syson.

"Yes. He is very curious—he has some of a wild animal's cunning—in a nice sense—and he is inventive, and thoughtful—but not beyond a certain point."

She pulled back a dark green curtain. The apartment was occupied almost entirely by a large couch of heather and bracken, on which was spread an ample rabbit-skin rug. On the floor were patchwork rugs of cat-skin, and a red calf-skin, while hanging from the wall were other furs. Hilda took down one, which she put on. It was a cloak of rabbit-skin and of white fur, with a hood, apparently of the skins of stoats. She laughed at Syson from out of this barbaric mantle, saying:

"What do you think of it?"

"Ah——! I congratulate you on your man," he replied.

"And look!" she said.

In a little jar on a shelf were some sprays, frail and white, of the first honeysuckle.

"They will scent the place at night,"

He looked round curiously.

"Where does he come short, then?" he asked. She gazed at him for a few moments. Then, turning aside:

"The stars aren't the same with him," she said. "You could make them flash and quiver, and the forget-me-nots come up at me like phosphorescence. You could make things *wonderful*. I have found it out—it is true. But I have them all for myself, now."

He laughed, saying:

"After all, stars and forget-me-nots are only luxuries. You ought to make poetry."

"Aye," she assented. "But I have them all now."

Again he laughed bitterly at her.

She turned swiftly. He was leaning against the small window of the tiny, obscure room, and was watching her, who stood in the doorway, still cloaked in her mantle. His cap was removed, so she saw his face and head distinctly in the dim room. His black, straight, glossy hair was brushed clean back from his brow. His black eyes were watching her, and his face, that was clear and cream, and perfectly smooth, was flickering.

"We are very different," she said bitterly.

Again he laughed.

"I see you disapprove of me," he said.

"I disapprove of what you have become," she said.

"You think we might"—he glanced at the hut—"have been like this—you and I?"

She shook her head.

"You! No; never! You plucked a thing and looked at it till you had found out all you wanted to know about it, then you threw it away," she said.

"Did I?" he asked. "And could your way never have been my way? I suppose not."

"Why should it?" she said. "I am a separate being."

"But surely two people sometimes go the same way," he said.

"You took me away from myself," she said.

He knew he had mistaken her, had taken her for something she was not. That was his fault, not hers.

"And did you always know?" he asked.

"No—you never let me know. You bullied me. I couldn't help myself. I was glad when you left me, really."

"I know you were," he said. But his face went paler, almost deathly luminous.

"Yet," he said, "it was you who sent me the way I have gone."

"I!" she exclaimed, in pride.

"You *would* have me take the Grammar School scholarship—and you would have me foster poor little Botell's fervent attachment to me, till he couldn't live without me—and because Botell was rich and influential. You triumphed in the wine-merchant's offer to send me to Cambridge, to befriend his only child. You wanted me to rise in the world. And all the time you were sending me away from you—every new success of mine put a separation between us, and more for you than for me. You never wanted to come with me: you wanted just to send me to see what it was like. I believe you even wanted me to marry a lady. You wanted to triumph over society in me."

"And I am responsible," she said, with sarcasm.

"I distinguished myself to satisfy you," he replied.

"Ah!" she cried, "you always wanted change, change, like a child."

"Very well! And I am a success, and I know it, and I do some good work. But—I thought you were different. What right have you to a man?"

"What do you want?"she said, looking at him with wide, fearful eyes.

He looked back at her, his eyes pointed, like weapons.

"Why, nothing," he laughed shortly.

There was a rattling at the outer latch, and the keeper entered. The woman glanced round, but remained standing, fur-cloaked, in the inner doorway. Syson did not move.

The other man entered, saw, and turned away without speaking. The two also were silent.

Pilbeam attended to his skins.

"I must go," said Syson.

"Yes," she replied.

"Then I give you 'To our vast and varying fortunes.' " He lifted his hand in pledge.

" 'To our vast and varying fortunes,' " she answered gravely, and speaking in cold tones.

"Arthur!" she said.

The keeper pretended not to hear. Syson, watching keenly, began to smile. The woman drew herself up.

"Arthur!" she said again, with a curious upward inflection, which warned the two men that her soul was trembling on a dangerous crisis.

The keeper slowly put down his tool and came to her.

"Yes," he said.

"I wanted to introduce you," she said, trembling.

"I've met him a'ready," said the keeper.

"Have you? It is Addy, Mr. Syson, whom you know about.—This is Arthur, Mr. Pilbeam," she added, turning to Syson. The latter held out his hand to the keeper, and they shook hands in silence.

"I'm glad to have met you," said Syson. "We drop our correspondence, Hilda?"

"Why need we?" she asked.

The two men stood at a loss.

"*Is* there no need?" said Syson.

Still she was silent.

"It is as you will," she said.

They went all three together down the gloomy path.

" 'Qu'il était bleu, le ciel, et grand l'espoir,' " quoted Syson, not knowing what to say.

"What do you mean?" she said. "Besides, *we* can't walk in *our* wild oats—we never sowed any."

Syson looked at her. He was startled to see his young love, his nun, his Botticelli angel, so revealed. It was he who had been the fool. He and she were more separate than any two strangers could be. She only wanted to keep up a correspondence with him—and he, of course, wanted it kept up, so that he could write to her, like Dante to some Beatrice who had never existed save the man's own brain.

At the bottom of the path she left him. He went along with the keeper, towards the open, towards the gate that closed on the wood. The two men walked almost like friends. They did not broach the subject of their thoughts.

*   *   *

Instead of going straight to the high-road gate, Syson went along the woods' edge, where the brook spread out in a little bog, and under the alder trees, among the reeds, great yellow stools and bosses of marigolds shone. Threads of brown water trickled by, touched with gold from the flowers. Suddenly there was a blue flash in the air, as a kingfisher passed.

Syson was extraordinarily moved. He climbed the bank to the gorse bushes, whose sparks of blossom had not yet gathered into a flame. Lying on the dry brown turf, he discovered sprigs of tiny purple milkwort and pink spots of lousewort. What a wonderful world it was—marvellous, for ever new. He felt as if it were underground, like the fields of monotone hell, notwithstanding. Inside his breast was a pain like a wound. He remembered the poem of William Morris, where in the Chapel of Lyonesse a knight lay wounded, with the truncheon of a spear deep in his breast, lying always as dead, yet did not die, while day after day the coloured sunlight dipped from the painted window across the chancel, and passed away. He knew now it never had been true, that which was between him and her, not for a moment. The truth had stood apart all the time.

Syson turned over. The air was full of the sound of larks, as if the sunshine above were condensing and falling in a shower. Amid this bright sound, voices sounded small and distinct.

"But if he's married, an' quite willing to drop it off, what has ter against it?" said the man's voice.

"I don't want to talk about it now. I want to be alone."

Syson looked through the bushes. Hilda was standing in the wood, near the gate. The man was in the field, loitering by the hedge, and playing with the bees as they settled on the white bramble flowers.

There was silence for a while, in which Syson imagined her will among the brightness of the larks. Suddenly the keeper exclaimed "Ah!" and swore. He was gripping at the sleeve of his coat, near the shoulder. Then he pulled off his jacket, threw it on the ground, and absorbedly rolled up his shirt-sleeves right to the shoulder.

"Ah!" he said vindictively, as he picked out the bee and flung it away. He twisted his fine, bright arm, peering awkwardly over his shoulder.

"What is it?" asked Hilda.

"A bee—crawled up my sleeve," he answered.

"Come here to me," she said.

The keeper went to her, like a sulky boy. She took his arm in her hands.

"Here it is—and the sting left in—poor bee!"

She picked out the sting, put her mouth to his arm, and sucked away the drop of poison. As she looked at the red mark her mouth had made, and at his arm, she said, laughing:

"That is the reddest kiss you will ever have."

When Syson next looked up, at the sound of voices, he saw in the shadow the keeper with his mouth on the throat of his beloved, whose head was thrown back, and whose hair had fallen, so that one rough rope of dark brown hair hung across his bare arm.

"No," the woman answered. "I am not upset because he's gone. You won't understand. . . ."

Syson could not distinguish what the man said. Hilda replied, clear and distinct:

"You know I love you. He has gone quite out of my life—don't trouble about him. . . ." He kissed her, murmuring. She laughed hollowly.

"Yes," she said, indulgent. "We will be married, we will be married. But not just yet." He spoke to her again. Syson heard nothing for a time. Then she said:

"You must go home now, dear—you will get no sleep."

Again was heard the murmur of the keeper's voice, troubled by fear and passion.

"But why should we be married at once?" she said. "What more would you have, by being married? It is most beautiful as it is."

At last he pulled on his coat and departed. She stood at the gate, not watching him, but looking over the sunny country.

When at last she had gone, Syson also departed, going back to town.

FOR STUDY, DISCUSSION, AND WRITING

1. In the eyes of the world, is Syson a successful man?
2. Discuss specific ways in which Syson has allowed his intellect to dominate his emotions.
3. Why do you think Syson makes this trip back to the haunts of his youth?
4. Discuss the nature of the reception that Syson receives upon arriving at the Millership farm. Why do you think Hilda reacts the way she does?
5. Discuss specific Freudian symbols in the story as they relate to the characters of Arthur, Hilda, and Syson.
6. What does Hilda mean when she tells Syson that she was married on the same night he was? What does this tell us about her character?
7. Discuss the long standing relationship between Hilda and Syson in terms of Hilda's statement: "The stars aren't the same with him. . . . You could make them flash and quiver, and the forget-me-nots come up at me like phosphorescence."

8. At the conclusion of the story, how is Syson like the wounded knight in the Chapel of Lyonesse, "with the truncheon of a spear deep in his breast, lying always as dead, yet did not die, while day after day the coloured sunlight dipped from the painted window across the chancel, and passed away"?

SHERWOOD ANDERSON

Unlighted Lamps

Mary Cochran went out of the rooms where she lived with her father, Doctor Lester Cochran, at seven o'clock on a Sunday evening. It was June of the year nineteen hundred and eight and Mary was eighteen years old. She walked along Tremont to Main Street and across the railroad tracks to Upper Main, lined with small shops and shoddy houses, a rather quiet cheerless place on Sundays when there were few people about. She had told her father she was going to church but did not intend doing anything of the kind. She did not know what she wanted to do. "I'll get off by myself and think," she told herself as she walked slowly along. The night she thought promised to be too fine to be spent sitting in a stuffy church and hearing a man talk of things that had apparently nothing to do with her own problem. Her own affairs were approaching a crisis and it was time for her to begin thinking seriously of her future.

The thoughtful serious state of mind in which Mary found herself had been induced in her by a conversation had with her father on the evening before. Without any preliminary talk and quite suddenly and abruptly he had told her that he was a victim of heart disease and might die at any moment. He had made the announcement as they stood together in the Doctor's office, back of which were the rooms in which the father and daughter lived.

It was growing dark outside when she came into the office and found him sitting alone. The office and living rooms were on the second floor of an old frame building in the town of Huntersburg, Illinois, and as the Doctor talked he stood beside his daughter near one of the windows that looked down into Tremont Street. The hushed murmur of the town's Saturday night life went on in Main Street just around a corner, and the evening train, bound to Chicago fifty miles to the east, had just passed. The hotel bus came rattling out of Lincoln Street and went through Tremont toward the hotel on Lower Main. A cloud of dust kicked up by the horses' hoofs floated on the quiet air.

A straggling group of people followed the bus and the row of hitching posts on Tremont Street was already lined with buggies in which farmers and their wives had driven into town for the evening of shopping and gossip.

After the station bus had passed three or four more buggies were driven into the street. From one of them a young man helped his sweetheart to alight. He took hold of her arm with a certain air of tenderness, and a hunger to be touched thus tenderly by a man's hand, that had come to Mary many times before, returned at almost the same moment her father made the announcement of his approaching death.

As the Doctor began to speak Barney Smithfield, who owned a livery barn that opened into Tremont Street directly opposite the building in which the Cochrans lived, came back to his place of business from his evening meal. He stopped to tell a story to a group of men gathered before the barn door and a shout of laughter arose. One of the loungers in the street, a strongly built young man in a checkered suit, stepped away from the others and stood before the liveryman. Having seen Mary he was trying to attract her attention. He also began to tell a story and as he talked he gesticulated, waved his arms and from time to time looked over his shoulder to see if the girl still stood by the window and if she were watching.

Doctor Cochran had told his daughter of his approaching death in a cold quiet voice. To the girl it had seemed that everything concerning her father must be cold and quiet. "I have a disease of the heart," he said flatly, "have long suspected there was something of the sort the matter with me and on Thursday when I went into Chicago I had myself examined. The truth is I may die at any moment. I would not tell you but for one reason—I will leave little money and you must be making plans for the future."

The Doctor stepped nearer the window where his daughter stood with her hand on the frame. The announcement had made her a little pale and her hand trembled. In spite of his apparent coldness he was touched and wanted to reassure her. "There now," he said hesitatingly, "it'll likely be all right after all. Don't worry. I haven't been a doctor for thirty years without knowing there's a great deal of nonsense about these pronouncements on the part of experts. In a matter like this, that is to say when a man has a disease of the heart, he may putter about for years." He laughed uncomfortably. "I've even heard it said that the best way to insure a long life is to contract a disease of the heart."

With these words the Doctor had turned and walked out of his office, going down a wooden stairway to the street. He had wanted to put his arm about his daughter's shoulder as he talked to her, but never having shown any feeling in his relations with her could not sufficiently release some tight thing in himself.

Mary had stood for a long time looking down into the street. The young man in the checkered suit, whose name was Duke Yetter, had finished telling his tale and a shout of laughter arose. She turned to look toward the door through which her father had passed and dread took possession of her. In all her life there had never been anything warm and close. She shivered although the night was warm and with a quick girlish gesture passed her hand over her eyes.

The gesture was but an expression of a desire to brush away the cloud of fear that had settled down upon her but it was misinterpreted by Duke Yetter who now stood a little apart from the other men before the livery barn. When he saw Mary's hand go up he smiled and turning quickly to be sure he was unobserved began jerking his head and making motions with his hand as a sign that he wished her to come down into the street where he would have an opportunity to join her.

*   *   *

On the Sunday evening Mary, having walked through Upper Main, turned into Wilmott, a street of workmen's houses. During that year the first sign of the march of factories westward from Chicago into the prairie towns had come to Huntersburg. A Chicago manufacturer of furniture had built a plant in the sleepy little farming town, hoping thus to escape the labor organizations that had begun to give him trouble in the city. At the upper end of town, in Wilmott, Swift, Harrison and Chestnut Streets and in cheap, badly-constructed frame houses, most of the factory workers lived. On the warm summer evening they were gathered on the porches at the front of the houses and a mob of children played in the dusty streets. Red-faced men in white shirts and without collars and coats slept in chairs or lay sprawled on strips of grass or on the hard earth before the doors of the houses.

The laborers' wives had gathered in groups and stood gossiping by the fences that separated the yards. Occasionally the voice of one of the women arose sharp and distinct above the steady flow of voices that ran like a murmuring river through the hot little streets.

In the roadway two children had got into a fight. A thick-shouldered red-haired boy struck another boy who had a pale sharp-featured face, a blow on the shoulder. Other children came running. The mother of the red-haired boy brought the promised fight to an end. "Stop it Johnny, I tell you to stop it. I'll break your neck if you don't," the woman screamed.

The pale boy turned and walked away from his antagonist. As he went slinking along the sidewalk past Mary Cochran his sharp little eyes, burning with hatred, looked up at her.

Mary went quickly along. The strange new part of her native town with the hubbub of life always stirring and asserting itself had a strong fascination for her. There was something dark and resentful in her own nature that made her feel at home in the crowded place where life carried itself off darkly, with a blow and an oath. The habitual silence of her father and the mystery concerning the unhappy married life of her father and mother, that had affected the attitude toward her of the people of the town, had made her own life a lonely one and had encouraged in her a rather dogged determination to in some way think her own way through the things of life she could not understand.

And back of Mary's thinking there was an intense curiosity and a courageous determination toward adventure. She was like a little animal of the forest that has been robbed of its mother by the gun of a sportsman and has been driven by hunger to go forth and seek food. Twenty times during the year she had walked alone at evening in the new and fast growing factory district of her town. She was eighteen and had begun to look like a woman, and she felt that other girls of the town of her own age would not have dared to walk in such a place alone. The feeling made her somewhat proud and as she went along she looked boldly about.

Among the workers in Wilmott Street, men and women who had been brought to town by the furniture manufacturer, were many who spoke in foreign tongues. Mary walked among them and liked the sound of the strange voices. To be in the street made her feel that she had gone out of her town and on a voyage into a strange land. In Lower Main Street or in the residence streets in the eastern part of town where lived the young men and women she had always known and where lived also the merchants, the clerks, the lawyers and the more well-to-do American workmen of Huntersburg, she felt always a secret antagonism to herself. The antagonism was not due to anything in her own character. She was sure of that. She had kept so much to herself that she was in fact but little known. "It is because I am the daughter of my mother," she told herself and did not walk often in the part of town where other girls of her class lived.

Mary had been so often in Wilmott Street that many of the people had begun to feel acquainted with her. "She is the daughter of some farmer and has got into the habit of walking into town," they said. A red-haired, broad-hipped woman who came out of the front door of one of the houses nodded to her. On a narrow strip of grass beside another house sat a young man with his back against a tree. He was smoking a pipe, but when he looked up and saw her he took the pipe from his mouth. She decided he must be an Italian, his hair and eyes were so black. "Ne bella! si fai un onore a passare di qua," he called waving his hand and smiling.

Mary went to the end of Wilmott Street and came out upon a country road. It seemed to her that a long time must have passed since she left her father's presence although the walk had in fact occupied but a few minutes. By the side of the road and on top of a small hill there was a ruined barn, and before the barn a great hole filled with the charred timbers of what had once been a farmhouse. A pile of stones lay beside the hole and these were covered with creeping vines. Between the site of the house and the barn there was an old orchard in which grew a mass of tangled weeds.

Pushing her way in among the weeds, many of which were covered with blossoms, Mary found herself a seat on a rock that had been rolled against the trunk of an old apple tree. The weeds half concealed her and from the road only her head was visible. Buried away thus in the weeds she looked like a quail that runs in the tall grass and that on hearing some unusual sound, stops, throws up its head and looks sharply about.

The doctor's daughter had been to the decayed old orchard many times before. At the foot of the hill on which it stood the streets of the town began, and as she sat on the rock she could hear faint shouts and cries coming out of Wilmott Street. A hedge separated the orchard from the fields on the hillside. Mary intended to sit by the tree until darkness came creeping over the land and to try to think out some plan regarding her future. The notion that her father was soon to die seemed both true and untrue, but her mind was unable to take hold of the thought of him as physically dead. For the moment death in relation to her father did not take the form of a cold inanimate body that was to be buried in the ground, instead it seemed to her that her father was not to die but to go away somewhere on a journey. Long ago her mother had done that. There was a strange hesitating sense of relief in the thought. "Well," she told herself, "when the time comes I also shall be setting out, I shall get out of here and into the world." On several occasions Mary had gone to spend a day with her father in Chicago and she was fascinated by the thought that soon she might be going there to live. Before her mind's eye floated a vision of long streets filled with thousands of people all strangers to herself. To go into such streets and to live her life among strangers would be like coming out of a waterless desert and into a cool forest carpeted with tender young grass.

In Huntersburg she had always lived under a cloud and now she was becoming a woman and the close stuffy atmosphere she had always breathed was becoming constantly more and more oppressive. It was true no direct question had ever been raised touching her own standing in the community life, but she felt that a kind of prejudice against her existed. While she was still a baby there had been a scandal involving her father and mother. The town of Huntersburg had rocked with it and when she was a child people had sometimes looked at her with mocking sympathetic eyes. "Poor child! It's too bad," they said. Once, on a cloudy summer evening when her father had driven off to the country and she sat alone in the darkness by his office window, she heard a man and woman in the street mention her name. The couple stumbled along in the darkness on the sidewalk below the office window. "That daughter of Doc Cochran's is a nice girl," said the man. The woman laughed. "She's growing up and attracting men's attention now. Better keep your eyes in your head. She'll turn out bad. Like mother, like daughter," the woman replied.

For ten or fifteen minutes Mary sat on the stone beneath the tree in the orchard and thought of the attitude of the town toward herself and her father. "It should have drawn us together," she told herself, and wondered if the approach of death would do what the cloud that had for years hung over them had not done. It did not at the moment seem to her cruel that the figure of death was soon to visit her father. In a way Death had become for her and for the time a lovely and gracious figure intent upon good. The hand of death was to open the door out of her father's house and into life. With the cruelty of youth she thought first of the adventurous possibilities of the new life.

Mary sat very still. In the long weeds the insects that had been disturbed in their evening song began to sing again. A robin flew into the tree beneath which she sat and struck a clear sharp note of alarm. The voices of people in the town's new factory district came softly up the hillside. They were like bells of distant cathedrals calling people to worship. Something within the girl's breast seemed to break and putting her head into her hands she rocked slowly back and forth. Tears came accompanied by a warm tender impulse toward the living men and women of Huntersburg.

And then from the road came a call. "Hello there kid," shouted a voice, and Mary sprang quickly to her feet. Her mellow mood passed like a puff of wind and in its place hot anger came.

In the road stood Duke Yetter who from his loafing place before the livery barn had seen her set out for the Sunday evening walk and had followed. When she went through Upper Main Street and into the new factory district he was sure of his conquest. "She doesn't want to be seen walking with me," he had told himself, "that's all right. She knows well enough I'll follow but doesn't want me to put in an appearance until she is well out of sight of her friends. She's a little stuck up and needs to be brought down a peg, but what do I care? She's gone out of her way to give me this chance and maybe she's only afraid of her dad."

Duke climbed the little incline out of the road and came into the orchard, but when he reached the pile of stones covered by vines he stumbled and fell. He arose and laughed. Mary had not waited for him to reach her but had started toward him, and when his laugh broke the silence that lay over the orchard she sprang forward and with her open hand struck him a sharp blow on the cheek. Then she turned and as he stood with his feet tangled in the vines ran out to the road. "If you follow or speak to me I'll get someone to kill you," she shouted.

Mary walked along the road and down the hill toward Wilmott Street. Broken bits of the story concerning her mother that had for years circulated in town had reached her ears. Her mother, it was said, had disappeared on a summer night long ago and a young town rough, who had been in the habit of loitering before Barney Smithfield's Livery Barn, had gone away with her. Now another young rough was trying to make up to her. The thought made her furious.

Her mind groped about striving to lay hold of some weapon with which she could strike a more telling blow at Duke Yetter. In desperation it lit upon the figure of her father already broken in health and now about to die. "My father just wants the chance to kill some such fellow as you," she shouted, turning to face the young man, who having got clear of the mass of vines in the orchard, had followed her into the road. "My father just wants to kill someone because of the lies that have been told in this town about mother."

Having given way to the impulse to threaten Duke Yetter Mary was instantly ashamed of her outburst and walked rapidly along, the tears running from her eyes. With hanging head Duke walked at her heels. "I didn't mean no harm, Miss Cochran," he pleaded. "I didn't mean no harm. Don't tell your father. I was only funning with you. I tell you I didn't mean no harm."

*   *   *

The light of the summer evening had begun to fall and the faces of the people made soft little ovals of light as they stood grouped under the dark porches or by the fences in Wilmott Street. The voices of the children had become subdued and they also stood in groups. They became silent as Mary passed and stood with upturned faces and staring eyes. "The lady doesn't live very far. She must be almost a neighbor," she heard a woman's voice saying in English. When she turned her head she saw only a crowd of dark-skinned men standing before a house. From within the house came the sound of a woman's voice singing a child to sleep.

The young Italian, who had called to her earlier in the evening and who was now apparently setting out on his own Sunday evening's adventures, came along the sidewalk and walked quickly away into the darkness. He had dressed himself in his Sunday clothes and had put on a black derby hat and a stiff white collar, set off by a red necktie. The shining whiteness of the collar made his brown skin look almost black. He smiled boyishly and raised his hat awkwardly but did not speak.

Mary kept looking back along the street to be sure Duke Yetter had not followed but in the dim light could see nothing of him. Her angry excited mood went away.

She did not want to go home and decided it was too late to go to church. From Upper Main Street there was a short street that ran eastward and fell rather sharply down a hillside to a creek and a bridge that marked the end of the town's growth in that direction. She went down along the street to the bridge and stood in the failing light watching two boys who were fishing in the creek.

A broad-shouldered man dressed in rough clothes came down along the street and stopping on the bridge spoke to her. It was the first time she had ever heard a citizen of her home town speak with feeling of her father. "You are Doctor Cochran's daughter?" he asked hesitatingly. "I guess you don't know who I am but your father does." He pointed toward the two boys who sat with fishpoles in their hands on the weed-grown bank of the creek. "Those are my boys and I have four other children," he explained. "There is another boy and I have three girls. One of my daughters has a job in a store. She is as old as yourself." The man explained his relations with Doctor Cochran. He had been a farm laborer, he said, and had but recently moved to town to work in the furniture factory. During the previous winter he had been ill for a long time and had no money. While he lay in bed one of his boys fell out of a barn loft and there was a terrible cut in his head.

"Your father came every day to see us and he sewed up my Tom's head." The laborer turned away from Mary and stood with his cap in his hand looking toward the boys. "I was down and out and your father not only took care of me and the boys but he gave my old woman money to buy the things we had to have from the stores in town here, groceries and medicines." The man spoke in such low tones that Mary had to lean forward to hear his words. Her face almost touched the laborer's shoulder. "Your father is a good man and I don't think he is very happy," he went on. "The boy and I got well and I got work here in town but he wouldn't take any money from me. 'You know how to live with your children and with your wife. You know how to make them happy. Keep your money and spend it on them,' that's what he said to me."

The laborer went on across the bridge and along the creek bank toward the spot where his two sons sat fishing and Mary leaned on the railing of the bridge and looked at the slow moving water. It was almost black in the shadows under the bridge and she thought that it was thus her father's life had been lived. "It has been like a stream running always in shadows and never coming out into the sunlight," she thought, and fear that her own life would run on in darkness gripped her. A great new love for her father swept over her and in fancy she felt his arms about her. As a child she had continually dreamed of caresses received at her father's hands and now the dream came back. For a long time she stood looking at the stream and she resolved that the night should not pass without an effort on her part to make the old dream come true. When she again looked up the laborer had built a little fire of sticks at the edge of the stream. "We catch bullheads here," he called. "The light of the fire draws them close to the shore. If you want to come and try your hand at fishing the boys will lend you one of the poles."

"O, I thank you, I won't do it tonight," Mary said, and then fearing she might suddenly begin weeping and that if the man spoke to her again she would find herself unable to answer, she hurried away. "Good bye!" shouted the man and the two boys. The words came quite spontaneously out of the three throats and created a sharp trumpet-like effect that rang like a glad cry across the heaviness of her mood.

*   *   *

When his daughter Mary went out for her evening walk Doctor Cochran sat for an hour alone in his office. It began to grow dark and the men who all afternoon had been sitting on chairs and boxes before the livery barn across the street went home for the evening meal. The noise of voices grew faint and sometimes for five or ten minutes there was silence. Then from some distant street came a child's cry. Presently church bells began to ring.

The Doctor was not a very neat man and sometimes for several days he forgot to shave. With a long lean hand he stroked his half grown beard. His illness had struck deeper than he had admitted even to himself and his mind had an inclination to float out of his body. Often when he sat thus his hands lay in his lap and he looked at them with a child's absorption. It seemed to him they must belong to someone else. He grew philosophic. "It's an odd thing about my body. Here I've lived in it all these years and how little use I have had of it. Now it's going to die and decay never having been used. I wonder why it did not get another tenant." He smiled sadly over this fancy but went on with it. "Well I've had thoughts enough concerning people and

I've had the use of these lips and a tongue but I've let them lie idle. When my Ellen was here living with me I let her think me cold and unfeeling while something within me was straining and straining trying to tear itself loose."

He remembered how often, as a young man, he had sat in the evening in silence beside his wife in this same office and how his hands had ached to reach across the narrow space that separated them and touch her hands, her face, her hair.

Well, everyone in town had predicted his marriage would turn out badly! His wife had been an actress with a company that came to Huntersburg and got stranded there. At the same time the girl became ill and had no money to pay for her room at the hotel. The young doctor had attended to that and when the girl was convalescent took her to ride about the country in his buggy. Her life had been a hard one and the notion of leading a quiet existence in the little town appealed to her.

And then after the marriage and after the child was born she had suddenly found herself unable to go on living with the silent cold man. There had been a story of her having run away with a young sport, the son of a saloon keeper who had disappeared from town at the same time, but the story was untrue. Lester Cochran had himself taken her to Chicago where she got work with a company going into the far western states. Then he had taken her to the door of her hotel, had put money into her hands and in silence and without even a farewell kiss had turned and walked away.

The Doctor sat in his office living over that moment and other intense moments when he had been deeply stirred and had been on the surface so cool and quiet. He wondered if the woman had known. How many times he had asked himself that question. After he left her that night at the hotel door she never wrote. "Perhaps she is dead," he thought for the thousandth time.

A thing happened that had been happening at odd moments for more than a year. In Doctor Cochran's mind the remembered figure of his wife became confused with the figure of his daughter. When at such moments he tried to separate the two figures, to make them stand out distinct from each other, he was unsuccessful. Turning his head slightly he imagined he saw a white girlish figure coming through a door out of the rooms in which he and his daughter lived. The door was painted white and swung slowly in a light breeze that came in at an open window. The wind ran softly and quietly through the room and played over some papers lying on a desk in a corner. There was a soft swishing sound as of a woman's skirts. The doctor arose and stood trembling. "Which is it? Is it you Mary or is it Ellen?" he asked huskily.

On the stairway leading up from the street there was the sound of heavy feet and the outer door opened. The doctor's weak heart fluttered and he dropped heavily back into his chair.

A man came into the room. He was a farmer, one of the doctor's patients, and coming to the centre of the room he struck a match, held it above his head, and shouted. "Hello!" he called. When the doctor arose from his chair and answered he was so startled that the match fell from his hand and lay burning faintly at his feet.

The young farmer had sturdy legs that were like two pillars of stone supporting a heavy building, and the little flame of the match that burned and fluttered in the light breeze on the floor between his feet threw dancing shadows along the walls of the room. The doctor's confused mind refused to clear itself of his fancies that now began to feed upon this new situation.

He forgot the presence of the farmer and his mind raced back over his life as a married man. The flickering light on the wall recalled another dancing light. One afternoon in the summer during the first year after his marriage his wife Ellen had driven with him into the country. They were then furnishing their rooms and at a farmer's house Ellen had seen an old mirror, no longer in use, standing against a wall in a shed. Because of something quaint in the design the mirror had taken her fancy and the farmer's wife had given it to her. On the drive home the young wife had told her husband of her pregnancy and the doctor had been stirred as never before. He sat holding the mirror on his knees while his wife drove and when she announced the coming of the child she looked away across the fields.

How deeply etched, that scene in the sick man's mind! The sun was going down over young corn and oat fields beside the road. The prairie land was black and occasionally the road ran through short lanes of trees that also looked black in the waning light.

The mirror on his knees caught the rays of the departing sun and sent a great ball of golden light dancing across the fields and among the branches of trees. Now as he stood in the presence of the farmer and as the little light from the burning match on the floor recalled that other evening of dancing lights, he thought he understood the failure of his marriage and of his life. On that evening long ago when Ellen had told him of the coming of the great adventure of their marriage he had remained silent because he had thought no words he could utter would express what he felt. There had been a defense for himself built up. "I told myself she should have understood without words and I've all my life been telling myself the same thing about Mary. I've been a fool and a coward. I've always been silent because I've been afraid of expressing myself—like a blundering fool. I've been a proud man and a coward.

"Tonight I'll do it. If it kills me I'll make myself talk to the girl," he said aloud, his mind coming back to the figure of his daughter.

"Hey! What's that?" asked the farmer who stood with his hat in his hand waiting to tell of his mission.

The doctor got his horse from Barney Smithfield's livery and drove off to the country to attend the farmer's wife who was about to give birth to her first child. She was a slender narrow-hipped woman and the child was large, but the doctor was feverishly strong. He worked desperately and the woman, who was frightened, groaned and struggled. Her husband kept coming in and going out of the room and two neighbor women appeared and stood silently about waiting to be of service. It was past ten o'clock when everything was done and the doctor was ready to depart for town.

The farmer hitched his horse and brought it to the door and the doctor drove off feeling strangely weak and at the same time strong. How simple now seemed the thing he had yet to do. Perhaps when he got home his daughter would have gone to bed but he would ask her to get up and come into the office. Then he would tell the whole story of his marriage and its failure sparing himself no humiliation. "There was something very dear and beautiful in my Ellen and I must make Mary understand that. It will help her to be a beautiful woman," he thought, full of confidence in the strength of his resolution.

He got to the door of the livery barn at eleven o'clock and Barney Smithfield with young Duke Yetter and two other men sat talking there. The liveryman took his horse away into the darkness of the barn and the doctor stood for a moment leaning against the wall of the building. The town's night watchman stood with the group by the barn door and a quarrel broke out between him and Duke Yetter, but the doctor did not hear the hot words that flew back and forth or Duke's loud laughter at the night watchman's anger. A queer hesitating mood had taken possession of him. There was something he passionately desired to do but could not remember. Did it have to do with his wife Ellen or Mary his daughter? The figures of the two women were again confused in his mind and to add to the confusion there was a third figure, that of the woman he had just assisted through child birth. Everything was confusion. He started across the street toward the entrance of the stairway leading to his office and then stopped in the road and stared about. Barney Smithfield having returned from putting his horse in the stall shut the door of the barn and a hanging lantern over the door swung back and forth. It threw grotesque dancing shadows down over the faces and forms of the men standing and quarreling beside the wall of the barn.

*   *   *

Mary sat by a window in the doctor's office awaiting his return. So absorbed was she in her own thoughts that she was unconscious of the voice of Duke Yetter talking with the men in the street.

When Duke had come into the street the hot anger of the early part of the evening had returned and she again saw him advancing toward her in the orchard with the look of arrogant male confidence in his eyes but presently she forgot him and thought only of her father. An incident of her childhood returned to haunt her. One afternoon in the month of May when she was fifteen her father had asked her to accompany him on an evening drive into the country. The doctor went to visit a sick woman at a farmhouse five miles from town and as there had been a great deal of rain the roads were heavy. It was dark when they reached the farmer's house and they went into the kitchen and ate cold food off a kitchen table. For some reason her father had, on that evening, appeared boyish and almost gay. On the road he had talked a little. Even at that early age Mary had grown tall and her figure was becoming womanly. After the cold supper in the farm kitchen he walked with her around the house and she sat on a narrow porch. For a moment her father stood before her. He put his hands into his trouser pockets and throwing back his head laughed almost heartily. "It seems strange to think you will soon be a woman," he said. "When you do become a woman what do you suppose is going to happen, eh? What kind of a life will you lead? What will happen to you?"

The doctor sat on the porch beside the child and for a moment she had thought he was about to put his arm around her. Then he jumped up and went into the house leaving her to sit alone in the darkness.

As she remembered the incident Mary remembered also that on that evening of her childhood she had met her father's advances in silence. It seemed to her that she, not her father, was to blame for the life they had led together. The farm laborer she had met on the bridge had not felt her father's coldness. That was because he had himself been warm and generous in his attitude toward the man who had cared for him in his hour of sickness and misfortune. Her father had said that the laborer knew how to be a father and Mary remembered with what warmth the two boys fishing by the creek had called to her as she went away into the darkness. "Their father has known how to be a father because his children have known how to give themselves," she thought guiltily. She also would give herself. Before the night had passed she would do that. On that evening long ago and as she rode home beside her father he had made another unsuccessful effort to break through the wall that separated them. The heavy rains had swollen the streams they had to cross and when they had almost reached town he had stopped the horse on a wooden bridge. The horse danced nervously about and her father held the reins firmly and occasionally spoke to him. Beneath the bridge the swollen stream made a great roaring sound and beside the road in a long flat field there was a lake of flood water. At that moment the moon had come out from behind clouds and the wind that blew across the water made little waves. The lake of flood water was covered with dancing lights. "I'm going to tell you about your mother and myself," her father said huskily, but at that moment the timbers of the bridge began to crack dangerously and the horse plunged forward. When her father had regained control of the frightened beast they were in the streets of the town and his diffident silent nature had reasserted itself.

Mary sat in the darkness by the office window and saw her father drive into the street. When his horse had been put away he did not, as was his custom, come at once up the stairway to the office but lingered in the darkness before the barn door. Once he started to cross the street and then returned into the darkness.

Among the men who for two hours had been sitting and talking quietly a quarrel broke out. Jack Fisher the town night watchman had been telling the others the story of a battle in which he had fought during the Civil War and Duke Yetter had begun bantering him. The night watchman grew angry. Grasping his nightstick he limped up and down. The loud voice of Duke Yetter cut across the shrill angry voice of the victim of his wit. "You ought to a flanked the fellow, I tell you Jack. Yes sir 'ee, you ought to a flanked that reb and then when you got him flanked you ought to a knocked the stuffings out of the cuss. That's what I would a done," Duke shouted, laughing boisterously. "You would a raised hell, you would," the night watchman answered, filled with ineffectual wrath.

The old soldier went off along the street followed by the laughter of Duke and his companions and Barney Smithfield, having put the doctor's horse away, came out and closed the barn door. A lantern hanging above the door swung back and forth. Doctor Cochran again started across the street and when he had reached the foot of the stairway turned and shouted to the men. "Good night," he called cheerfully. A strand of hair was blown by the light summer breeze across Mary's cheek and she jumped to her feet as though she had been touched by a hand reached out to her from the darkness. A hundred times she had seen her father return from drives in the evening but never before had he said anything at all to the loiterers by the barn door. She became half convinced that not her father but some other man was now coming up the stairway.

The heavy dragging footsteps rang loudly on the wooden stairs and Mary heard her father set down the little square medicine case he always carried. The strange cheerful hearty mood of the man continued but his mind was in a confused riot. Mary imagined she could see his dark form in the doorway. "The woman has had a baby," said the hearty voice from the landing outside the door. "Who did that happen to? Was it Ellen or that other woman or my little Mary?"

A stream of words, a protest came from the man's lips. "Who's been having a baby? I want to know. Who's been having a baby? Life doesn't work out. Why are babies always being born?" he asked.

A laugh broke from the doctor's lips and his daughter leaned forward and gripped the arms of her chair. "A babe has been born," he said again. "It's strange eh, that my hands should have helped a baby be born while all the time death stood at my elbow?"

Doctor Cochran stamped upon the floor of the landing. "My feet are cold and numb from waiting for life to come out of life," he said heavily. "The woman struggled and now I must struggle."

Silence followed the stamping of feet and the tired heavy declaration from the sick man's lips. From the street below came another loud shout of laughter from Duke Yetter.

And then Doctor Cochran fell backward down the narrow stairs to the street. There was no cry from him, just the clatter of his shoes upon the stairs and the terrible subdued sound of the body falling.

Mary did not move from her chair. With closed eyes she waited. Her heart pounded. A weakness complete and overmastering had possession of her and from feet to head ran little waves of feeling as though tiny creatures with soft hair-like feet were playing upon her body.

It was Duke Yetter who carried the dead man up the stairs and laid him on a bed in one of the rooms back of the office. One of the men who had been sitting with him before the door of the barn followed lifting his hands and dropping them nervously. Between his fingers he held a forgotten cigarette the light from which danced up and down in the darkness.

FOR STUDY, DISCUSSION, AND WRITING

1. From what point of view is this story told?
2. What is the author's general tone throughout the story? What devices does he employ to maintain this tone?
3. Why was the doctor's marriage such a complete failure?
4. What evidence in the story suggests that the doctor made the same mistakes in rearing his daughter that he had made in maintaining an intimate relationship with his wife?
5. What is ironic about the doctor's telling Mary, "I have a disease of the heart?"
6. What evidence does the story provide that the doctor, although emotionally repressed, is actually a good and kind-hearted person?
7. Compare and contrast the emotional makeup of the Cochrans with that of the people who live in the factory workers' section of town.
8. Does anything in the doctor's behavior suggest that he takes grim pleasure in the knowledge that his own death is imminent?
9. How do you account for Mary's violent reaction when Duke Yetter tries to approach her?

VIRGINIA WOOLF

The String Quartet

Well, here we are, and if you cast your eye over the room you will see that Tubes and trams and omnibuses, private carriages not a few, even, I venture to believe, landaus with bays in them, have been busy at it, weaving threads from one end of London to the other. Yet I begin to have my doubts—

If indeed it's true, as they're saying, that Regent Street is up, and the Treaty signed, and the weather not cold for the time of year, and even at that rent not a flat to be had, and the worst of influenza its after effects; if I bethink me of having forgotten to write about the leak in the larder, and left my glove in the train; if the ties of blood require me, leaning forward, to accept cordially the hand which is perhaps offered hesitatingly—

"Seven years since we met!"

"The last time in Venice."

"And where are you living now?"

"Well, the late afternoon suits me the best, though, if it weren't asking too much—"

"But I knew you at once!"

"Still, the war made a break—"

If the mind's shot through by such little arrows, and—for human society compels it—no sooner is one launched than another presses forward; if this engenders heat and in addition they've turned on the electric light; if saying one thing does, in so many cases, leave behind it a need to improve and revise, stirring besides regrets, pleasures, vanities, and desires—if it's all the facts I mean, and the hats, the fur boas, the gentlemen's swallow-tail coats, and pearl tie-pins that come to the surface—what chance is there?

Of what? It becomes every minute more difficult to say why, in spite of everything, I sit here believing I can't now say what, or even remember the last time it happened.

"Did you see the procession?"

"The King looked cold."

"No, no, no. But what was it?"

"She's bought a house at Malmesbury."

"How lucky to find one!"

On the contrary, it seems to me pretty sure that she, whoever she may be, is damned, since it's all a matter of flats and hats and sea gulls, or so it seems to be for a hundred people sitting here well dressed, walled in, furred, replete. Not that I can boast, since I too sit passive on a gilt chair, only turning the earth above a buried memory, as we all do, for there are signs, if I'm not mistaken, that we're all recalling something, furtively seeking something. Why fidget? Why so anxious about the sit of cloaks; and gloves—whether to button or unbutton? Then watch that elderly face against the dark canvas, a moment ago urbane and flushed; now taciturn and sad, as if in shadow. Was it the sound of the second violin tuning in the ante-room? Here they come; four black figures, carrying instruments, and seat themselves facing the white squares under the downpour of light; rest the tips of their bows on the music stand; with a simultaneous movement lift them; lightly poise them, and, look-ing across at the player opposite, the first violin counts one, two, three—

Flourish, spring, burgeon, burst! The pear tree on the top of the mountain. Fountains jet; drops descend. But the waters of the Rhone flow swift and deep, race under the arches, and sweep the trailing water leaves, washing shadows over the silver fish, the spotted fish rushed down by the swift waters, now swept into an eddy where—it's difficult this—conglomeration of fish all in a pool; leaping, splashing, scraping sharp fins; and such a boil of current that the yellow pebbles are churned round and round, round and round—free now, rushing downwards, or even somehow ascending in exquisite spirals into the air; curled like thin shavings from under a plane; up and up. . . . How lovely goodness is in those who, stepping lightly, go smiling through the world! Also in jolly old fishwives, squatted under arches, obscene old women, how deeply they laugh and shake and rollick, when they walk, from side to side, hum, hah!

"That's an early Mozart, of course—"

"But the tune, like all his tunes, makes one despair—I mean hope. What do I mean? That's the worst of music! I want to dance, laugh, eat pink cakes, yellow cakes, drink thin, sharp wine. Or an indecent story, now—I could relish that. The older one grows the more one likes indecency. Hah, hah! I'm laughing. What at? You said nothing, nor did the old gentleman opposite. . . . But suppose—suppose—Hush!"

The melancholy river bears us on. When the moon comes through the trailing willow boughs, I see your face, I hear your voice and the bird singing as we pass the osier bed. What are you whispering? Sorrow, sorrow. Joy, joy. Woven together, like reeds in moonlight. Woven together, inextricably commingled, bound in pain and strewn in sorrow—crash!

The boat sinks. Rising, the figures ascend, but now leaf thin, tapering to a dusky wraith, which, fiery tipped, draws its twofold passion from my heart. For me it sings, unseals my sorrow, thaws compassion, floods with love the sunless world, nor, ceasing, abates its tenderness but deftly, subtly, weaves in and out until in this pattern, this consummation, the cleft ones unify; soar, sob, sink to rest, sorrow and joy.

Why then grieve? Ask what? Remain unsatisfied? I say all's been settled; yes; laid to rest under a coverlet of rose leaves, falling. Falling. Ah, but they cease. One rose leaf, falling from an enormous height, like a little parachute dropped from an invisible balloon, turns, flutters waveringly. It won't reach us.

"No, no. I noticed nothing. That's the worst of music—these silly dreams. The second violin was late, you say?"

"There's old Mrs. Munro, feeling her way out—blinder each year, poor woman—on this slippery floor."

Eyeless old age, grey-headed Sphinx. . . . There she stands on the pavement, beckoning, so sternly, the red omnibus.

"How lovely! How well they play! How—how—how!"

The tongue is but a clapper. Simplicity itself. The feathers in the hat next me are bright and pleasing as a child's rattle. The leaf on the plane-tree flashes green through the chink in the curtain. Very strange, very exciting.

"How—how—how!" Hush!

These are the lovers on the grass.

"If, madam, you will take my hand—"

"Sir, I would trust you with my heart. Moreover, we have left our bodies in the banqueting hall. Those on the turf are the shadows of our souls."

"Then these are the embraces of our souls." The lemons nod assent. The swan pushes from the bank and floats dreaming into mid stream.

"But to return. He followed me down the corridor, and, as we turned the corner, trod on the lace of my petticoat. What could I do but cry 'Ah!' and stop to finger it? At which he drew his sword, made passes as if he were stabbing something to death, and cried, 'Mad! Mad! Mad!' Whereupon I screamed, and the Prince, who was writing in the large vellum book in the oriel window, came out in his velvet skull-cap and furred slippers, snatched a rapier from the wall—the King of Spain's gift, you know—on which I escaped, flinging on this cloak to hide the ravages to my skirt—to hide . . . But listen! the horns!"

The gentleman replies so fast to the lady, and she runs up the scale with such witty exchange of compliment now culminating in a sob of passion, that the words are indistinguishable though the meaning is plain enough—love, laughter, flight, pursuit, celestial bliss—all floated out on the gayest ripple of tender endearment—until the sound of the silver horns, at first far distant, gradually sounds more and more distinctly, as if seneschals were saluting the dawn or proclaiming ominously the escape of the lovers. . . . The green garden, moonlit pool, lemons, lovers, and fish are all dissolved in the opal sky, across which, as the horns are joined by trumpets and supported by clarions there rise white arches firmly planted on marble pillars. . . . Tramp and trumpeting. Clang and clangour. Firm establishment. Fast foundations. March of myriads. Confusion and chaos trod to earth. But this city to which we travel has neither stone nor marble; hangs enduring; stands unshakable; nor does a face, nor does a flag greet or welcome. Leave then to perish your hope; droop in the desert my joy; naked advance. Bare are the pillars; auspicious to none; casting no shade; resplendent; severe. Back then I fall, eager no more, desiring only to go, find the street, mark the buildings, greet the applewoman, say to the maid who opens the door: A starry night.

"Good night, good night. You go this way?"

"Alas. I go that."

FOR STUDY, DISCUSSION, AND WRITING

1. The setting for this story is a large hall crowded with concert-goers. What seems to be the attitude of these people toward the evening? Do they appear to be dedicated music lovers?

2. Describe the personality of the narrator. Is she sensitive and imaginative or dull and unromantic?

3. At one point in her musings, the narrator asks herself, "if it's all the facts . . . what chance is there?" Moments later she reflects that "there are signs, if I'm not mistaken, that we're all recalling something, furtively seeking something." Considering all of the narrator's reflections, and her reaction to the music, what do you think that "something" is?

4. What is happening in the story at the point of the passage "as the horns are joined by trumpets and supported by clarions there rise white arches firmly planted on marble pillars. . . . Tramp and trumpeting. Clang and clangour. Firm establishment"?

5. Discuss the possible double meaning of the bit of dialogue that ends the story.

6. How does the stream-of-consciousness technique employed in this story dramatize the narrator's reverie?

KATHARINE BRUSH

Night Club

Promptly at quarter of ten P.M. Mrs. Brady descended the steps of the Elevated. She purchased from the newsdealer in the cubbyhole beneath them a next month's magazine and a tomorrow morning's paper and, with these tucked under one plump arm, she walked. She walked two blocks north on Sixth Avenue; turned and went west. But not far west. Westward half a block only, to the place where the gay green awning marked "Club Français" paints a stripe of shade across the glimmering sidewalk. Under this awning Mrs. Brady halted briefly, to remark to the six-foot doorman that it looked like rain and to await his performance of his professional duty. When the small green door yawned open, she sighed deeply and plodded in.

The foyer was a blackness, an airless velvet blackness like the inside of a jeweler's box. Four drum-shaped lamps of golden silk suspended from the ceiling gave it light (a very little) and formed the jewels: gold signets, those, or cuff-links for a giant. At the far end of the foyer there were black stairs, faintly dusty, rippling upward toward an amber radiance. Mrs. Brady approached and ponderously mounted the stairs, clinging with one fist to the mangy velvet rope that railed their edge.

From the top, Miss Lena Levin observed the ascent. Miss Levin was the checkroom girl. She had dark-at-the-roots blonde hair and slender hips upon which, in moments of leisure, she wore her hands, like buckles of ivory loosely attached.

This was a moment of leisure. Miss Levin waited behind her counter. Row upon row of hooks, empty as yet, and seeming to beckon—wee curved fingers of iron—waited behind her.

"Late," said Miss Levin, "again."

"Go wan!" said Mrs. Brady. "It's only ten to ten. *Whew!* Them *stairs!*"

She leaned heavily, sideways, against Miss Levin's counter, and, applying one palm to the region of her heart, appeared at once to listen and to count. "Feel!" she cried then in a pleased voice.

Miss Levin obediently felt.

"Them stairs," continued Mrs. Brady darkly, "with my bad heart, will be the death of me. Whew! Well, dearie? What's the news?"

"You got a paper," Miss Levin languidly reminded her.

"Yeah!" agreed Mrs. Brady with a sudden vehemence. "I got a paper!" She slapped it upon the counter. "An' a lot of time I'll get to *read* my paper, won't I now? On a Saturday night!" She moaned. "Other nights is bad enough, dear knows—but *Saturday* nights! How I dread 'em! Every Saturday night I say to my daughter, I say, 'Geraldine, I can't,' I say, 'I can't go through it again, an' that's all there is to it,' I say. 'I'll *quit!*' I say. An' I *will*, too!" added Mrs. Brady firmly, if indefinitely.

Miss Levin, in defense of Saturday nights, mumbled some vague something about tips.

"Tips!" Mrs. Brady hissed it. She almost spat it. Plainly money was nothing, nothing at all, to this lady. "I just wish," said Mrs. Brady, and glared at Miss Levin, "I just wish *you* had to spend one Saturday night, just one, in that dressing room! Bein' pushed an' stepped on and near knocked down by that gang of hussies, an' them orderin' an' bossin' you 'round like you was *black*, an' usin' your things an' then sayin' they're sorry, they got no change, they'll be back. Yeah! They *never* come back!"

"There's Mr. Costello," whispered Miss Levin through lips that, like a ventriloquist's, scarcely stirred.

"An' as I was sayin'," Mrs. Brady said at once brightly, "I got to leave you. Ten to ten, time I was on the job."

She smirked at Miss Levin, nodded, and right-about-faced. There, indeed, Mr. Costello was. Mr. Billy Costello, manager, proprietor, monarch of all he surveyed. From the doorway of the big room where the little tables herded in a ring around the waxen floor, he surveyed Mrs. Brady, and in such a way that Mrs. Brady, momentarily forgetting her bad heart, walked fast, scurried faster, almost ran.

The door of her domain was set politely in an alcove, beyond silken curtains looped up at the sides. Mrs. Brady reached it breathless, shouldered it open, and groped for the electric switch. Lights sprang up, a bright white blaze, intolerable for an instant to the eyes, like sun on snow. Blinking, Mrs. Brady shut the door.

The room was a spotless, white-tiled place, half beauty shop, half dressing-room. Along one wall stood washstands, sturdy triplets in a row, with pale-green liquid soap in glass balloons afloat above them. Against the opposite wall there was a couch. A third wall backed an elongated glass-topped dressing table; and over the dressing table and over the washstands long rectangular sheets of mirror reflected lights, doors, glossy tiles, lights multiplied. . . .

Mrs. Brady moved across this glitter like a thick dark cloud in a hurry. At the dressing table she came to a halt, and upon it she laid her newspaper, her magazine, and her purse—a black purse worn gray with much clutching. She divested herself of a rusty black coat and a hat of the mushroom persuasion, and hung both up in a corner cupboard which she opened by means of one of a quite preposterous bunch of keys. From a nook in the cupboard she took down a lace-edged handkerchief with long streamers. She untied the streamers and tied them again around her chunky black alpaca waist. The handkerchief became an apron's baby cousin.

Mrs. Brady relocked the cupboard door, fumbled her key-ring over, and unlocked a capacious drawer of the dressing table. She spread a fresh towel on the plate-glass top, in the geometrical center, and upon the towel she arranged with care a procession of things fished from the drawer. Things for the hair. Things for the complexion. Things for the eyes, the lashes, the brows, the lips, and the finger nails. Things in boxes and things in jars and things in tubes and tins. Also an ash tray, matches, pins, a tiny sewing kit, a pair of scissors. Last of all, a hand-printed sign, a nudging sort of sign:

NOTICE! THESE ARTICLES, PLACED HERE FOR YOUR CONVENIENCE, ARE THE PROPERTY OF THE *MAID*.

And directly beneath the sign, propping it up against the looking-glass, a china saucer, in which Mrs. Brady now slyly laid decoy money: two quarters and two dimes, in four-leaf-clover formation.

Another drawer of the dressing table yielded a bottle of bromo-seltzer, a bottle of aromatic spirits of ammonia, a tin of sodium bicarbonate, and a teaspoon. These were lined up on a shelf above the couch.

Mrs. Brady was now ready for anything. And (from the grim, thin pucker of her mouth) expecting it.

Music came to her ears. Rather, the beat of music, muffled, rhythmic, remote. *Umpa-um, umpa-um, umpa-um-umm*—Mr. "Fiddle" Baer and his band, hard at work on the first fox-trot of the night. It was teasing, foot-tapping music; but the large solemn feet of Mrs. Brady were still. She sat on the couch and opened her newspaper; and for some moments she read uninterruptedly, with special attention to the murders, the divorces, the breaches of promise, the funnies.

Then the door swung inward, admitting a blast of Mr. Fiddle Baer's best, a whiff of perfume, and a girl.

Mrs. Brady put her paper away.

The girl was *petite* and darkly beautiful; wrapped in fur and mounted on tall jeweled heels. She entered humming the rag-time song the orchestra was playing, and while she stood near the dressing table, stripping off her gloves, she continued to hum it softly to herself:

> *"Oh, I know my baby loves me,*
> *I can tell my baby loves me."*

Here the dark little girl got the left glove off, and Mrs. Brady glimpsed a platinum wedding ring.

> *" 'Cause there ain't no maybe*
> *In my baby's*
> *Eyes."*

The right glove came off. The dark little girl sat down in one of the chairs that faced the dressing table. She doffed her wrap, casting it carelessly over the chair back. It had a cloth-of-gold lining, and the name of a Paris house was embroidered in curlicues on the label. Mrs. Brady hovered solicitously near.

The dark little girl, still humming, looked over the articles, "placed here for your convenience," and picked up the scissors. Having cut off a very small hangnail with the air of one performing a perilous major operation, she seized and used the manicure buffer, and after that the eyebrow pencil. Mrs. Brady's mind, hopefully calculating the tip, jumped and jumped again like a taxi-meter.

> *"Oh, I know my baby loves me—"*

The dark little girl applied powder and lipstick belonging to herself. She examined the result searchingly in the mirror and sat back, satisfied. She cast some silver *Klink! Klink!* into Mrs. Brady's saucer, and half rose. Then, remembering something, she settled down again.

The ensuing thirty seconds were spent by her in pulling off her platinum wedding ring, tying it in a corner of a lace handkerchief, and tucking the handkerchief down the bodice of her tight white velvet gown.

"There!" she said.

She swooped up her wrap and trotted toward the door, jeweled heels merrily twinkling.

> *" 'Cause there ain't no maybe—"*

The door fell shut.

Almost instantly it opened again, and another girl came in. A blonde, this. She was pretty in a round-eyed, doll-like way; but Mrs. Brady, regarding her, mentally grabbed the spirits of ammonia bottle. For she looked terribly ill.

The round eyes were dull, the pretty silly little face was drawn. The thin hands, picking at the fastenings of a specious beaded bag, trembled and twitched.

Mrs. Brady cleared her throat. "Can I do something for you, miss?"

Evidently the blonde girl had believed herself alone in the dressing room. She started violently and glanced up, panic in her eyes. Panic, and something else. Something very like murderous hate—but for an instant only, so that Mrs. Brady, whose perceptions were never quick, missed it altogether.

"A glass of water?" suggested Mrs. Brady.

"No," said the girl, "no." She had one hand in the beaded bag now. Mrs. Brady could see it moving, causing the bag to squirm like a live thing, and the fringe to shiver. "Yes!" she cried abruptly. "A glass of water—please—you get it for me."

She dropped on to the couch. Mrs. Brady scurried to the water cooler in the corner, pressed the spigot with a determined thumb. Water trickled out thinly. Mrs. Brady pressed harder, and scowled, and thought, "Something's wrong with this thing. I musn't forget, next time I see Mr. Costello—"

When again she faced her patient, the patient was sitting erect. She was thrusting her clenched hand back into the beaded bag again.

She took only a sip of the water, but it seemed to help her quite miraculously. Almost at once color came to her cheeks, life to her eyes. She grew young again—as young as she was. She smiled up at Mrs. Brady.

"Well!" she exclaimed. "What do you know about that!" She shook her honey-colored head. "I can't imagine what came over me."

"Are you better now?" inquired Mrs. Brady.

"Yes. Oh, yes. I'm better now. You see," said the blonde girl confidentially, "we were at the theater, my boy friend and I, and it was hot and stuffy—I guess that must have been the trouble."

She paused, and the ghost of her recent distress crossed her face. "God! I thought that last act *never* would end!" she said.

While she attended to her hair and complexion, she chattered gayly to Mrs. Brady, chattered on with scarcely a stop for breath, and laughed much. She said, among other things, that she and her "boy friend" had not known one another very long, but that she was "ga-ga" about him. "He is about me, too," she confessed. "He thinks I'm grand."

She fell silent then, and in the looking-glass her eyes were shadowed, haunted. But Mrs. Brady, from where she stood, could not see the looking-glass; and half a minute later the blonde girl laughed and began again. When she went out she seemed to dance out on little winged feet; and Mrs. Brady, sighing, thought it must be nice to be young . . . and happy like that.

The next arrivals were two. A tall, extremely smart young woman in black chiffon entered first, and held the door open for her companion; and the instant the door was shut, she said, as though it had been on the tip of her tongue for hours, "Amy, what under the sun *happened?*"

Amy, who was brown-eyed, brown-bobbed-haired, and patently annoyed about something, crossed to the dressing table and flopped into a chair before she made reply.

"Nothing," she said wearily then.

"That's nonsense!" snorted the other. "Tell me. Was it something she said? She's a tactless ass, of course. Always was."

"No, not anything she said. It was—" Amy bit her lip. "All right! I'll tell you. Before we left your apartment I just happened to notice that Tom had disappeared. So I went to look for him—I wanted to ask him if he'd remembered to tell the maid where we were going—Skippy's subject to croup, you know, and we always leave word. Well, so I went into the kitchen, thinking Tom might be there mixing cocktails—and there he was—and there *she* was!"

The full red mouth of the other young woman pursed itself slightly. Her arched brows lifted. "Well?"

Her matter-of-factness appeared to infuriate Amy. "He was *kissing* her!" she flung out.

"Well?" said the other again. She chuckled softly and patted Amy's shoulder, as if it were the shoulder of a child. "You're surely not going to let *that* spoil your whole evening? Amy *dear!* Kissing may once have been serious and significant—but it isn't nowadays. Nowadays, it's like shaking hands. It means nothing."

But Amy was not consoled. "I hate her!" she cried desperately. "Red-headed *thing!* Calling me 'darling' and 'honey,' and s-sending me handkerchiefs for C-Christmas—and then sneaking off behind closed doors and k-kissing my h-h-husband—"

At this point Amy broke down, but she recovered herself sufficiently to add with venom, "I'd like to slap her!"

"Oh, oh, oh," smiled the tall young woman. "I wouldn't do that!"

Amy wiped her eyes with what might well have been one of the Christmas handkerchiefs, and confronted her friend. "Well, what *would* you do, Vera? If you were I?"

"I'd forget it," said Vera, "and have a good time. I'd kiss somebody myself. You've no idea how much better you'd feel!"

"I don't do—" Amy began indignantly; but as the door behind her opened and a third young woman—red-headed, earringed, exquisite—lilted in, she changed her tone. "Oh, hello!" she called sweetly, beaming at the newcomer via the mirror. "We were wondering what had become of you!"

The red-headed girl, smiling easily back, dropped her cigarette on the floor and crushed it out with a silver-shod toe. "Tom and I were talking to Fiddle Baer," she explained. "He's going to play 'Clap Yo' Hands' next, because it's my favorite. Lend me a comb, will you?"

"There's a comb there," said Vera, indicating Mrs. Brady's business comb.

"But imagine using it!" murmured the red-headed girl. "Amy, darling, haven't you one?"

Amy produced a tiny comb from her rhinestone purse. "Don't forget to bring it when you come," she said, and stood up. "I'm going on out, I want to tell Tom something." She went.

The red-headed young woman and the tall black-chiffon one were alone, except for Mrs. Brady. The red-headed one beaded her incredible lashes. The tall one, the one called Vera, sat watching her. Presently she said, "Sylvia, look here." And Sylvia looked. Anybody, addressed in that tone, would have.

"There is one thing," Vera went on quietly, holding the other's eyes, "that I want understood. And that is '*Hands off!*' Do you hear me?"

"I don't know what you mean."

"You do know what I mean!"

The red-headed girl shrugged her shoulders. "Amy told you she saw us, I suppose."

"Precisely. And," went on Vera, gathering up her possessions and rising, "as I said before, you're to keep away." Her eyes blazed sudden white-hot rage. "Because, as you very well know, he belongs to *me*," she said, and departed, slamming the door.

Between eleven o'clock and one Mrs. Brady was very busy indeed. Never for more than a moment during those two hours was the dressing room empty. Often it was jammed, full to overflowing with curled cropped heads, with ivory arms and shoulders, with silk and lace and chiffon, with legs. The door flapped in and back, in and back. The mirrors caught and held—and lost—a hundred different faces. Powder veiled the dressing table with a thin white dust; cigarette stubs, scarlet at the tips, choked the ash receiver. Dimes and quarters clattered into Mrs. Brady's saucer—and were transferred to Mrs. Brady's purse. The original seventy cents remained. That much, and no more, would Mrs. Brady gamble on the integrity of womankind.

She earned her money. She threaded needles and took stitches. She powdered the backs of necks. She supplied towels for soapy, dripping hands. She removed a speck from a teary blue eye and pounded the heel on a slipper. She curled the straggling ends of a black bob and a gray bob, pinned a velvet flower on a lithe round waist, mixed three doses of bicarbonate of soda, took charge of a shed pink-satin girdle, collected, on hands and knees, several dozen fake pearls that had wept from a broken string.

She served chorus girls and school girls, gay young matrons and gayer young mistresses, a lady who had divorced four husbands, and a lady who had poisoned one, the secret (more or less) sweetheart of a Most Distinguished Name, and the Brains of a bootleg gang. . . .She saw things. She saw a yellow check, with the ink hardly dry. She saw four tiny bruises, such as fingers might make, on an arm. She saw a girl strike another girl, not playfully. She saw a bundle of letters some man wished he had not written, safe and deep in a brocaded handbag.

About midnight the door flew open and at once was pushed shut, and a gray-eyed, lovely child stood backed against it, her palms flattened on the panels at her sides, the draperies of her white chiffon gown settling lightly to rest around her.

There were already five damsels of varying ages in the dressing room. The latest arrival marked their presence with a flick of her eyes and, standing just where she was, she called peremptorily, "Maid!"

Mrs. Brady, standing just where *she* was, said, "Yes, miss?"

"Please come here," said the girl.

Mrs. Brady, as slowly as she dared, did so.

The girl lowered her voice to a tense half-whisper. "Listen! Is there any way I can get out of here except through this door I came in?"

Mrs. Brady stared at her stupidly.

"Any window?" persisted the girl. "Or anything?"

Here they were interrupted by the exodus of two of the damsels-of-varying-ages. Mrs. Brady opened the door for them—and in so doing caught a glimpse of a man who waited in the hall outside, a debonair, old-young man with a girl's furry wrap hung over his arm, and his hat in his hand.

The door clicked. The gray-eyed girl moved out from the wall, against which she had flattened herself—for all the world like one eluding pursuit in a cinema.

"What about that window?" she demanded, pointing.

"That's all the farther it opens," said Mrs. Brady.

"Oh! And it's the only one—isn't it?"

"It is."

"Damn," said the girl. "Then there's *no* way out?"

"No way but the door," said Mrs. Brady testily.

The girl looked at the door. She seemed to look *through* the door, and to despise and to fear what she saw. Then she looked at Mrs. Brady. "Well," she said, "then I s'pose the only thing for me to do is to stay in here."

She stayed. Minutes ticked by. Jazz crooned distantly, stopped, struck up again. Other girls came and went. Still the gray-eyed girl sat on the couch, with her back to the wall and her shapely legs crossed, smoking cigarettes, one from the stub of another.

After a long while she said, "Maid!"

"Yes, miss?"

"Peek out that door, will you, and see if there's anyone standing there."

Mrs. Brady peeked, and reported that there was. There was a gentleman with a little bit of a black mustache standing there. The same gentleman, in fact, who was standing there "just after you came in."

"Oh, Lord," sighed the gray-eyed girl. "Well . . . I can't stay here all *night,* that's one sure thing."

She slid off the couch, and went listlessly to the dressing table. There she occupied herself for a minute or two. Suddenly, without a word, she darted out.

Thirty seconds later Mrs. Brady was elated to find two crumpled one-dollar bills lying in her saucer. Her joy, however, died a premature death. For she made an almost simultaneous second discovery. A saddening one. Above all, a puzzling one.

"Now what for," marveled Mrs. Brady, "did she want to walk off with them *scissors?*"

This at twelve twenty-five.

At twelve thirty a quartette of excited young things burst in, babbling madly. All of them had their evening wraps with them; all talked at once. One of them, a Dresden china girl with a heart-shaped face, was the center of attraction. Around her the rest fluttered like monstrous butterflies; to her they addressed their shrill exclamatory cries.

"Babe," they called her.

Mrs. Brady heard snatches: "Not in this state unless . . ." "Well, you can in Maryland, Jimmy says." "Oh, there must be some place nearer than . . ." "Isn't this marvelous?" "When did it happen, Babe? When did you decide?"

"Just now," the girl with the heart-shaped face sang softly, "when we were dancing."

The babble resumed, "But listen, Babe, what'll your mother and father . . . ?" "Oh, never mind, let's hurry." "Shall we be warm enough with just these thin wraps, do you think; Babe, will you be warm enough? Sure?"

Powder flew and little pocket combs marched through bright marcels. Flushed cheeks were painted pinker still.

"My pearls," said Babe, "are *old*. And my dress and slippers are *new. Now*, let's see—what can I *borrow?*"

A lace handkerchief, a diamond bar pin, a pair of earrings were proffered. She chose the bar pin, and its owner unpinned it proudly, gladly.

"I've got blue garters!" exclaimed a shrill little girl in a silver dress.

"Give me one, then," directed Babe. "I'll trade with you. . . . There! That fixes that."

More babbling, "Hurry! Hurry up!" . . . "Listen, are you *sure* we'll be warm enough? Because we can stop at my house, there's nobody home." "Give me that puff, Babe, I'll powder your back." "And just to think a week ago you'd never even met each other!" "Oh, hurry *up*, let's get *started!*" "I'm ready." "So'm I." "Ready, Babe? You look adorable." "Come on, everybody."

They were gone again, and the dressing room seemed twice as still and vacant as before.

A minute of grace, during which Mrs. Brady wiped the spilled powder away with a damp gray rag. Then the door jumped open again. Two evening gowns appeared and made for the dressing table in a bee line. Slim tubular gowns they were, one green, one palest yellow. Yellow hair went with the green gown, brown hair with the yellow. The green-gowned, yellow-haired girl wore gardenias on her left shoulder, four of them, and a flashing bracelet on each fragile wrist. The other girl looked less prosperous; still, you would rather have looked at her.

Both ignored Mrs. Brady's cosmetic display as utterly as they ignored Mrs. Brady, producing full field equipment of their own.

"Well," said the girl with gardenias, rouging energetically, "how do you like him?"

"Oh-h—all right."

"Meaning 'Not any,' hmm? I suspected as much!" The girl with gardenias turned in her chair and scanned her companion's profile with disapproval. "See here, Marilee," she drawled, "are you going to be a damn fool *all* your life?"

"He's fat," said Marilee dreamily. "Fat, and—greasy, sort of. I mean, greasy in his mind. Don't you know what I mean?"

"I know *one* thing," declared the other. "I know Who He Is! And if I were you, that's all I'd need to know. *Under the circumstances.*"

The last three words, stressed meaningly, affected the girl called Marilee curiously. She grew grave. Her lips and lashes drooped. For some seconds she sat frowning a little, breaking a black-sheathed lipstick in two and fitting it together again.

"She's worse," she said, finally, low.

"Worse?"

Marilee nodded.

"Well," said the girl with gardenias, "there you are. It's the climate. She'll never be anything *but* worse, if she doesn't get away. Out West. Arizona or somewhere."

"I know," murmured Marilee.

The other girl opened a tin of eye shadow. "Of course," she said dryly, "suit yourself. She's not *my* sister."

Marilee said nothing. Quiet she sat, breaking the lipstick, mending it, breaking it.

"Oh, well," she breathed finally, wearily, and straightened up. She propped her elbows on the plate-glass dressing table top and leaned toward the mirror, and with the lipstick she began to make her coral-pink mouth very red and gay and reckless and alluring.

Nightly at one o'clock Vane and Moreno dance for the Club Français. They dance a tango, they dance a waltz; then, by way of encore, they do a Black Bottom, and a trick of their own called the Wheel. They dance for twenty, thirty minutes. And while they dance you do not leave your table—for this is what you came to see. Vane and Moreno. The new New York thrill. The sole justification for the five-dollar couvert extorted by Billy Costello.

From one until half-past, then, was Mrs. Brady's recess. She had been looking forward to it all the evening long. When it began—when the opening chords of the tango music sounded stirringly from the room outside—Mrs. Brady brightened. With a right good will she sped the parting guests.

Alone, she unlocked her cupboard and took out her magazine—the magazine she had bought three hours before. Heaving a great breath of relief and satisfaction, she plumped herself on the couch and fingered the pages.

Immediately she was absorbed, her eyes drinking up printed lines, her lips moving soundlessly.

The magazine was Mrs. Brady's favorite. Its stories were true stories, taken from life (so the editor said); and to Mrs. Brady they were alive, vivid threads in the dull, drab pattern of her night.

FOR STUDY, DISCUSSION, AND WRITING

1. How would you describe the general tone of the story?
2. This is an episodic little story. How many specific episodes does it contain? How many different women, or groups of women, bring their stories into the night club's powder room?
3. Make a statement about the happiness or unhappiness of the women in each of the story's episodes. Speculate about their chances for future happiness.
4. How does the fact that the setting of the story is in the powder room of a night club contribute to the dramatization of the characters of the women in each episode?
5. What is the character of Mrs. Brady? How is her character dramatized?
6. What is ironic about Mrs. Brady's wanting to read her magazine to the exclusion of all that is going on around her?
7. What general observations does "Night Club" make about the Jazz Age?

ERNEST HEMINGWAY
The Killers

The door of Henry's lunch-room opened and two men came in. They sat down at the counter.

"What's yours?" George asked them.

"I don't know," one of the men said. "What do you want to eat, Al?"

"I don't know," said Al. "I don't know what I want to eat."

Outside it was getting dark. The street-light came on outside the window. The two men at the counter read the menu. From the other end of the counter Nick Adams watched them. He had been talking to George when they came in.

"I'll have a roast pork tenderloin with apple sauce and mashed potatoes," the first man said.

"It isn't ready yet."

"What the hell do you put it on the card for?"

"That's the dinner," George explained. "You can get that at six o'clock." George looked at the clock on the wall behind the counter.

"It's five o'clock."

"The clock says twenty minutes past five," the second man said.

"It's twenty minutes fast."

"Oh, to hell with the clock," the first man said. "What have you got to eat?"

"I can give you any kind of sandwiches," George said. "You can have ham and eggs, bacon and eggs, liver and bacon, or a steak."

"Give me chicken croquettes with green peas and cream sauce and mashed potatoes."

"That's the dinner."

"Everything we want's the dinner, eh? That's the way you work it."

"I can give you ham and eggs, bacon and eggs, liver——"

"I'll take ham and eggs," the man called Al said. He wore a derby hat and a black overcoat buttoned across the chest. His face was small and white and he had tight lips. He wore a silk muffler and gloves.

"Give me bacon and eggs," said the other man. He was about the same size as Al. Their faces were different, but they were dressed like twins. Both wore overcoats too tight for them. They sat leaning forward, their elbows on the counter.

"Got anything to drink?" Al asked.

"Silver beer, bevo, ginger-ale," George said.

"I mean you got anything to *drink?*"

"Just those I said."

"This is a hot town," said the other. "What do they call it?"

"Summit."

"Ever hear of it?" Al asked his friend.

"No," said the friend.

"What do you do here nights?" Al asked.

"They eat the dinner," his friend said. "They all come here and eat the big dinner."

"That's right," George said.

"So you think that's right?" Al asked George.

"Sure."

"You're a pretty bright boy, aren't you?"

"Sure," said George.

"Well, you're not," said the other little man. "Is he, Al?"

"He's dumb," said Al. He turned to Nick. "What's your name?"

"Adams."

"Another bright boy," Al said. "Ain't he a bright boy, Max?"

"The town's full of bright boys," Max said.

George put the two platters, one of ham and eggs, the other of bacon and eggs, on the counter. He set down two side-dishes of fried potatoes and closed the wicket into the kitchen.

"Which is yours?" he asked Al.

"Don't you remember?"

"Ham and eggs."

"Just a bright boy," Max said. He leaned forward and took the ham and eggs. Both men ate with their gloves on. George watched them eat.

"What are *you* looking at?" Max looked at George.

"Nothing."

"The hell you were. You were looking at me."

"Maybe the boy meant it for a joke, Max," Al said.

George laughed.

"*You* don't have to laugh," Max said to him. "*You* don't have to laugh at all, see?"

"All right," said George.

"So he thinks it's all right." Max turned to Al. "He thinks it's all right. That's a good one."

"Oh, he's a thinker," Al said. They went on eating.

"What's the bright boy's name down the counter?" Al asked Max.

"Hey, bright boy," Max said to Nick. "You go around on the other side of the counter with your boy friend."

"What's the idea?" Nick asked.

"There isn't any idea."

"You better go around, bright boy," Al said. Nick went around behind the counter.

"What's the idea?" George asked.

"None of your damn business," Al said. "Who's out in the kitchen?"

"The nigger."

"What do you mean the nigger?"

"The nigger that cooks."

"Tell him to come in."

"What's the idea?"

"Tell him to come in."

"Where do you think you are?"

"We know damn well where we are," the man called Max said. "Do we look silly?"

"You talk silly," Al said to him. "What the hell do you argue with this kid for? Listen," he said to George, "tell the nigger to come out here."

"What are you going to do to him?"

"Nothing. Use your head, bright boy. What would we do to a nigger?"

George opened the slit that opened back into the kitchen. "Sam," he called. "Come in here a minute."

The door to the kitchen opened and the nigger came in. "What was it?" he asked. The two men at the counter took a look at him.

"All right, nigger. You stand right there,"Al said.

Sam, the nigger, standing in his apron, looked at the two men sitting at the counter. "Yes, sir," he said. Al got down from his stool.

"I'm going back to the kitchen with the nigger and bright boy," he said. "Go on back to the kitchen, nigger. You go with him, bright boy." The little man walked after Nick and Sam, the cook, back into the kitchen. The door shut after them. The man called Max sat at the counter opposite George. He didn't look at George but looked in the mirror that ran along back of the counter. Henry's had been made over from a saloon into a lunch-counter.

"Well, bright boy," Max said, looking into the mirror, "why don't you say something?"

"What's it all about?"

"Hey, Al," Max called, "bright boy wants to know what it's all about."

"Why don't you tell him?" Al's voice came from the kitchen.

"What do you think it's all about?"

"I don't know."

"What do you think?"

Max looked into the mirror all the time he was talking.

"I wouldn't say."

"Hey, Al, bright boy says he wouldn't say what he thinks it's all about."

"I can hear you, all right," Al said from the kitchen. He had propped open the slit that dishes passed through into the kitchen with a catsup bottle. "Listen, bright boy," he said from the kitchen to George. "Stand a little further along the bar. You move a little to the left, Max." He was like a photographer arranging for a group picture.

"Talk to me, bright boy," Max said. "What do you think's going to happen?"

George did not say anything.

"I'll tell you," Max said. "We're going to kill a Swede. Do you know a big Swede named Ole Andreson?"

"Yes."

"He comes here to eat every night, don't he?"

"Sometimes he comes here."

"He comes here at six o'clock, don't he?"

"If he comes."

"We all know that, bright boy," Max said. "Talk about something else. Ever go to the movies?"

"Once in a while."

"You ought to go to the movies more. The movies are fine for a bright boy like you."

"What are you going to kill Ole Andreson for? What did he ever do to you?"

"He never had a chance to do anything to us. He never even seen us."

"And he's only going to see us once," Al said from the kitchen.

"What are you going to kill him for, then?" George asked.

"We're killing him for a friend. Just to oblige a friend, bright boy."

"Shut up," said Al from the kitchen. "You talk too goddamn much."

"Well, I got to keep bright boy amused. Don't I, bright boy?"

"You talk too damn much," Al said. "The nigger and my bright boy are amused by themselves. I got them tied up like a couple of girl friends in the convent."

"I suppose you were in a convent?"

"You never know."

"You were in a kosher convent. That's where you were."

George looked up at the clock.

"If anybody comes in, you tell them the cook is off, and if they keep after it, you tell them you'll go back and cook yourself. Do you get that, bright boy?"

"All right," George said. "What you going to do with us afterward?"

"That'll depend," Max said. "That's one of those things you never know at the time."

George looked up at the clock. It was a quarter past six. The door from the street opened. A street-car motorman came in.

"Hello, George," he said. "Can I get supper?"

"Sam's gone out," George said. "He'll be back in about half an hour."

"I'd better go up the street," the motorman said. George looked at the clock. It was twenty minutes past six.

"That was nice, bright boy," Max said. "You're a regular little gentleman."

"He knew I'd blow his head off," Al said from the kitchen.

"No," said Max. "It ain't that. Bright boy is nice. He's a nice boy. I like him."

At six-fifty-five George said: "He's not coming."

Two other people had been in the lunch-room. Once George had gone out to the kitchen and made a ham-and-egg sandwich "to go" that a man wanted to take with him. Inside the kitchen he saw Al, his derby hat tipped back, sitting on a stool beside the wicket with the muzzle of a sawed-off shotgun resting on the ledge. Nick and the cook were back to back in the corner, a towel tied in each of their mouths. George had cooked the sandwich, wrapped it up in oiled paper, put it in a bag, brought it in, and the man had paid for it and gone out.

"Bright boy can do everything," Max said. "He can cook and everything. You'd make some girl a nice wife, bright boy."

"Yes?" George said. "Your friend, Ole Andreson, isn't going to come."

"We'll give him ten minutes," Max said.

Max watched the mirror and the clock. The hands of the clock marked seven o'clock, and then five minutes past seven.

"Come on, Al," said Max. "We better go. He's not coming."

"Better give him five minutes," Al said from the kitchen.

In the five minutes a man came in, and George explained that the cook was sick.

"Why the hell don't you get another cook?" the man asked. "Aren't you running a lunch-counter?" He went out.

"Come on, Al," Max said.

"What about the two bright boys and the nigger?"

"They're all right."

"You think so?"

"Sure. We're through with it."

"I don't like it," said Al. "It's sloppy. You talk too much."

"Oh, what the hell," said Max. "We got to keep amused, haven't we?"

"You talk too much, all the same," Al said. He came out from the kitchen. The cut-off barrels of the shotgun made a slight bulge under the waist of his too tight-fitting overcoat. He straightened his coat with his gloved hands.

"So long, bright boy," he said to George. "You got a lot of luck."

"That's the truth," Max said. "You ought to play the races, bright boy."

The two of them went out the door. George watched them, through the window, pass under the arc-light and cross the street. In their tight overcoats and derby hats they looked like a vaudeville team. George went back through the swinging-door into the kitchen and untied Nick and the cook.

"I don't want any more of that," said Sam, the cook. "I don't want any more of that."

Nick stood up. He had never had a towel in his mouth before.

"Say," he said. "What the hell?" He was trying to swagger it off.

"They were going to kill Ole Andreson," George said. "They were going to shoot him when he came in to eat."

"Ole Andreson?"

"Sure."

The cook felt the corners of his mouth with his thumbs.

"They all gone?" he asked.

"Yeah," said George. "They're gone now."

"I don't like it," said the cook. "I don't like any of it at all."

"Listen," George said to Nick. "You better go see Ole Andreson."

"All right."

"You better not have anything to do with it at all," Sam, the cook, said. "You better stay way out of it."

"Don't go if you don't want to," George said.

"Mixing up in this ain't going to get you anywhere," the cook said. "You stay out of it."

"I'll go see him," Nick said to George. "Where does he live?"

The cook turned away.

"Little boys always know what they want to do," he said.

"He lives up at Hirsch's rooming-house," George said to Nick.

"I'll go up there."

Outside the arc-light shone through the bare branches of a tree. Nick walked up the street beside the car-tracks and turned at the next arc-light down a side-street. Three houses up the street was Hirsch's rooming-house. Nick walked up the two steps and pushed the bell. A woman came to the door.

"Is Ole Andreson here?"

"Do you want to see him?"

"Yes, if he's in."

Nick followed the woman up a flight of stairs and back to the end of a corridor. She knocked on the door.

"Who is it?"

"It's somebody to see you, Mr. Andreson," the woman said.

"It's Nick Adams."

"Come in."

Nick opened the door and went into the room. Ole Andreson was lying on the bed with all his clothes on. He had been a heavyweight prizefighter and he was too long for the bed. He lay with his head on two pillows. He did not look at Nick.

"What was it?" he asked.

"I was up at Henry's," Nick said, "and two fellows came in and tied up me and the cook, and they said they were going to kill you."

It sounded silly when he said it. Ole Andreson said nothing.

"They put us out in the kitchen," Nick went on. "They were going to shoot you when you came in to supper."

Ole Andreson looked at the wall and did not say anything.

"George thought I better come and tell you about it."

"There isn't anything I can do about it," Ole Andreson said.

"I'll tell you what they were like."

"I don't want to know what they were like," Ole Andreson said. He looked at the wall. "Thanks for coming to tell me about it."

"That's all right."

Nick looked at the big man lying on the bed.

"Don't you want me to go and see the police?"

"No," Ole Andreson said. "That wouldn't do any good."

"Isn't there something I could do?"

"No. There ain't anything to do."

"Maybe it was just a bluff."

"No. It ain't just a bluff."

Ole Andreson rolled over toward the wall.

"The only thing is," he said, talking toward the wall, "I just can't make up my mind to go out. I been in here all day."

"Couldn't you get out of town?"

"No," Ole Andreson said. "I'm through with all that running around."

He looked at the wall.

"There ain't anything to do now."

"Couldn't you fix it up some way?"

"No. I got in wrong." He talked in the same flat voice. "There ain't anything to do. After a while I'll make up my mind to go out."

"I better go back and see George," Nick said.

"So long," said Ole Andreson. He did not look toward Nick. "Thanks for coming around."

Nick went out. As he shut the door he saw Ole Andreson with all his clothes on, lying on the bed looking at the wall.

"He's been in his room all day," the landlady said down-stairs. "I guess he don't feel well. I said to him: 'Mr. Andreson, you ought to go out and take a walk on a nice fall day like this,' but he didn't feel like it."

"He doesn't want to go out."

"I'm sorry he don't feel well," the woman said. "He's an awfully nice man. He was in the ring, you know."

"I know it."

"You'd never know it except from the way his face is," the woman said. They stood talking just inside the street door. "He's just as gentle."

"Well, good-night, Mrs. Hirsch," Nick said.

"I'm not Mrs. Hirsch," the woman said. "She owns the place. I just look after it for her. I'm Mrs. Bell."

"Well, good-night, Mrs. Bell," Nick said.

"Good-night," the woman said.

Nick walked up the dark street to the corner under the arc-light, and then along the car-tracks to Henry's eating-house. George was inside, back of the counter.

"Did you see Ole?"

"Yes," said Nick. "He's in his room and he won't go out."

The cook opened the door from the kitchen when he heard Nick's voice. "I don't even listen to it," he said and shut the door.

"Did you tell him about it?" George asked.

"Sure. I told him but he knows what it's all about."

"What's he going to do?"

"Nothing."

"They'll kill him."

"I guess they will."

"He must have got mixed up in something in Chicago."

"I guess so," said Nick.

"It's a hell of a thing."

"It's an awful thing," Nick said.

They did not say anything. George reached down for a towel and wiped the counter.

"I wonder what he did?" Nick said.

"Double-crossed somebody. That's what they kill them for."

"I'm going to get out of this town," Nick said.

"Yes," said George. "That's a good thing to do."

"I can't stand to think about him waiting in the room and knowing he's going to get it. It's too damned awful."

"Well," said George, "you better not think about it."

FOR STUDY, DISCUSSION, AND WRITING

1. Why do you suppose Hemingway depicted Max and Al, the two gangsters in the story, so much like stock hoods in an ordinary B-movie?
2. How does the sparse style in which the story is written contribute to its overall tone and mood?
3. From what point of view is the story written? Do we enter the minds of any of the characters?
4. What evidence of Hemingway's belief that life is "all a nothing" does the story provide?
5. Compare and contrast the differing positions taken by Sam, George, and Nick about going to warn Ole Andreson that Max and Al, the killers, are after him.
6. Why do you think Nick Adams, especially after visiting Ole Andreson in Ole's rooming-house, doesn't let the police know about the killers?
7. Thematically, how can the following circumstances be tied together: (1) the lunch-room clock is twenty minutes fast; (2) George confuses the gangsters' orders; (3) although the lunch-room is owned by someone named Henry, George runs the place; and (4) Mrs. Bell manages the rooming-house owned by Mrs. Hirsch?
8. Discuss Mrs. Bell as a foil to Nick Adams.
9. In terms of the so-called Hemingway code, why have Max and Al been sent to kill Ole Andreson? Why doesn't Ole resist?

WILLIAM FAULKNER

That Evening Sun

I

Monday is no different from any other weekday in Jefferson now. The streets are paved now, and the telephone and electric companies are cutting down more and more of the shade trees—the water oaks, the maples and locusts and elms—to make room for iron poles bearing clusters of bloated and ghostly and bloodless grapes, and we have a city laundry which makes the rounds on Monday morning, gathering the bundles of clothes into bright-colored, specially-made motor cars: the soiled wearing of a whole week now flees apparitionlike behind alert and irritable electric horns, with a long diminishing noise of rubber and asphalt like tearing silk, and even the Negro women who still take in white people's washing after the old custom, fetch and deliver it in automobiles.

But fifteen years ago, on Monday morning the quiet, dusty, shady streets would be full of Negro women with, balanced on their steady, turbaned heads, bundles of clothes tied up in sheets, almost as large as cotton bales, carried so without touch of hand between the kitchen door of the white house and the blackened washpot beside a cabin door in Negro Hollow.

Nancy would set her bundle on the top of her head, then upon the bundle in turn she would set the black straw sailor hat which she wore winter and summer. She was tall, with a high, sad face sunken a little where her teeth were missing. Sometimes we would go a part of the way down the lane and across the pasture with her, to watch the balanced bundle and the hat that never bobbed nor wavered, even when she walked down into the ditch and up the other side and stooped through the fence. She would go down on her hands and knees and crawl through the gap, her head rigid, uptilted, the bundle steady as a rock or a balloon, and rise to her feet again and go on.

Sometimes the husbands of the washing women would fetch and deliver the clothes, but Jesus never did that for Nancy, even before father told him to stay away from our house, even when Dilsey was sick and Nancy would come to cook for us.

And then about half the time we'd have to go down the lane to Nancy's cabin and tell her to come on and cook breakfast. We would stop at the ditch, because father told us not to have anything to do with Jesus—he was a short black man, with a razor scar down his face—and we would throw rocks at Nancy's house until she came to the door, leaning her head around it without any clothes on.

"What yawl mean, chunking my house?" Nancy said. "What you little devils mean?"

"Father says for you to come on and get breakfast," Caddy said. "Father says it's over half an hour now, and you've got to come this minute."

"I aint studying no breakfast," Nancy said. "I going to get my sleep out."

"I bet you're drunk," Jason said. "Father says you're drunk. Are you drunk, Nancy?"

"Who says I is?" Nancy said. "I got to get my sleep out. I aint studying no breakfast."

So after a while we quit chunking the cabin and went back home. When she finally came, it was too late for me to go to school. So we thought it was whisky until that day they arrested her again and they were taking her to jail and they passed Mr Stovall. He was the cashier in the bank and a deacon in the Baptist church, and Nancy began to say:

"When you going to pay me, white man? When you going to pay me, white man? It's been three times now since you paid me a cent—" Mr Stovall knocked her down, but she kept on saying, "When you going to pay me, white man? It's been three times now since—" until Mr Stovall kicked her in the mouth with his heel and the marshal caught Mr Stovall back, and Nancy lying in the street, laughing. She turned her head and spat out some blood and teeth and said, "It's been three times now since he paid me a cent."

That was how she lost her teeth, and all that day they told about Nancy and Mr Stovall, and all that night the ones that passed the jail could hear Nancy singing and yelling. They could see her hands holding to the window bars, and a lot of them stopped along the fence, listening to her and to the jailer trying to make her stop. She didn't shut up until almost daylight, when the jailer began to hear a bumping and scraping upstairs and he went up there and found Nancy hanging from the window bar. He said that it was cocaine and not whisky, because no nigger would try to commit suicide unless he was full of cocaine, because a nigger full of cocaine wasn't a nigger any longer.

The jailer cut her down and revived her; then he beat her, whipped her. She had hung herself with her dress. She had fixed it all right, but when they arrested her she didn't have on anything except a dress and so she didn't have anything to tie her hands with and she couldn't make her hands let go of the window ledge. So the jailer heard the noise and ran up there and found Nancy hanging from the window, stark naked, her belly already swelling out a little, like a little balloon.

When Dilsey was sick in her cabin and Nancy was cooking for us, we could see her apron swelling out; that was before father told Jesus to stay away from the house. Jesus was in the kitchen, sitting behind the stove, with his razor scar on his black face like a piece of dirty string. He said it was a watermelon that Nancy had under her dress.

"It never come off of your vine, though," Nancy said.

"Off of what vine?" Caddy said.

"I can cut down the vine it did come off of," Jesus said.

"What makes you want to talk like that before these chillen?" Nancy said. "Whyn't you go on to work? You done et. You want Mr Jason to catch you hanging around his kitchen, talking that way before these chillen?"

"Talking what way?" Caddy said. "What vine?"

"I cant hang around white man's kitchen," Jesus said. "But white man can hang around mine. White man can come in my house, but I cant stop him. When white man want to come in my house, I aint got no house. I cant stop him, but he cant kick me outen it. He cant do that."

Dilsey was still sick in her cabin. Father told Jesus to stay off our place. Dilsey was still sick. It was a long time. We were in the library after supper.

"Isn't Nancy through in the kitchen yet?" mother said. "It seems to me that she has had plenty of time to have finished the dishes."

"Let Quentin go and see," father said. "Go and see if Nancy is through, Quentin. Tell her she can go on home."

I went to the kitchen. Nancy was through. The dishes were put away and the fire was out. Nancy was sitting in a chair, close to the cold stove. She looked at me.

"Mother wants to know if you are through," I said.

"Yes," Nancy said. She looked at me. "I done finished." She looked at me. "What is it?" I said. "What is it?"

"I aint nothing but a nigger," Nancy said. "It aint none of my fault."

She looked at me, sitting in the chair before the cold stove, the sailor hat on her head. I went back to the library. It was the cold stove and all, when you think of a kitchen being warm and busy and cheerful. And with a cold stove and the dishes all put away, and nobody wanting to eat at that hour.

"Is she through?" mother said.

"Yessum," I said.

"What is she doing?" mother said.

"She's not doing anything. She's through."

"I'll go and see," father said.

"Maybe she's waiting for Jesus to come and take her home," Caddy said.

"Jesus is gone," I said. Nancy told us how one morning she woke up and Jesus was gone.

"He quit me," Nancy said. "Done gone to Memphis, I reckon. Dodging them city po-lice for a while, I reckon."

"And a good riddance," father said. "I hope he stays there."

"Nancy's scaired of the dark," Jason said.

"So are you," Caddy said.

"I'm not," Jason said.

"Scairy cat," Caddy said.

"I'm not," Jason said.

"You, Candace!" mother said. Father came back.

"I am going to walk down the lane with Nancy," he said. "She says that Jesus is back."

"Has she seen him?" mother said.

"No. Some Negro sent her word that he was back in town. I wont be long."

"You'll leave me alone, to take Nancy home?" mother said. "Is her safety more precious to you than mine?"

"I wont be long," father said.

"You'll leave these children unprotected, with that Negro about?"

"I'm going too," Caddy said. "Let me go, Father."

"What would he do with them, if he were unfortunate enough to have them?" father said.

"I want to go, too," Jason said.

"Jason!" mother said. She was speaking to father. You could tell that by the way she said the name. Like she believed that all day father had been trying to think of doing the thing she wouldn't like the most, and that she knew all the time that after a while he would think of it. I stayed quiet, because father and

I both knew that mother would want him to make me stay with her if she just thought of it in time. So father didn't look at me. I was the oldest. I was nine and Caddy was seven and Jason was five.

"Nonsense," father said. "We wont be long."

Nancy had her hat on. We came to the lane. "Jesus always been good to me," Nancy said. "Whenever he had two dollars, one of them was mine." We walked in the lane. "If I can just get through the lane," Nancy said, "I be all right then."

The lane was always dark. "This is where Jason got scared on Hallowe'en," Caddy said.

"I didn't," Jason said.

"Cant Aunt Rachel do anything with him?" father said. Aunt Rachel was old. She lived in a cabin beyond Nancy's, by herself. She had white hair and she smoked a pipe in the door, all day long; she didn't work any more. They said she was Jesus' mother. Sometimes she said she was and sometimes she said she wasn't any kin to Jesus.

"Yes, you did," Caddy said. "You were scairder than Frony. You were scairder than T.P. even. Scairder than niggers."

"Cant nobody do nothing with him," Nancy said. "He say I done woke up the devil in him and aint but one thing going to lay it down again."

"Well, he's gone now," father said. "There's nothing for you to be afraid of now. And if you'd just let white men alone."

"Let what white men alone?" Caddy said. "How let them alone?"

"He aint gone nowhere," Nancy said. "I can feel him. I can feel him now, in this lane. He hearing us talk, every word, hid somewhere, waiting. I aint seen him, and I aint going to see him again but once more, with that razor in his mouth. That razor on that string down his back, inside his shirt. And then I aint going to be even surprised."

"I wasn't scaired," Jason said.

"If you'd behave yourself, you'd have kept out of this," father said. "But it's all right now. He's probably in St. Louis now. Probably got another wife by now and forgot all about you."

"If he has, I better not find out about it," Nancy said. "I'd stand there right over them, and every time he wropped her, I'd cut that arm off. I'd cut his head off and I'd slit her belly and I'd shove—"

"Hush," father said.

"Slit whose belly, Nancy?" Caddy said.

"I wasn't scaired," Jason said. "I'd walk right down this lane by myself."

"Yah," Caddy said. "You wouldn't dare to put your foot down in it if we were not here too."

II

Dilsey was still sick, so we took Nancy home every night until mother said, "How much longer is this going on? I to be left alone in this big house while you take home a frightened Negro?"

We fixed a pallet in the kitchen for Nancy. One night we waked up, hearing the sound. It was not singing and it was not crying, coming up the dark stairs. There was a light in mother's room and we heard father going down the hall, down the back stairs, and Caddy and I went into the hall. The floor was cold. Our toes curled away from it while we listened to the sound. It was like singing and it wasn't like singing, like the sounds that Negroes make.

Then it stopped and we heard father going down the back stairs, and we went to the head of the stairs. Then the sound began again, in the stairway, not loud, and we could see Nancy's eyes halfway up the stairs, against the wall. They looked like cat's eyes do, like a big cat against the wall, watching us. When we came down the steps to where she was, she quit making the sound again, and we stood there until father came back up from the kitchen, with his pistol in his hand. He went back down with Nancy and they came back with Nancy's pallet.

We spread the pallet in our room. After the light in mother's room went off, we could see Nancy's eyes again. "Nancy," Caddy whispered, "are you asleep, Nancy?"

Nancy whispered something. It was oh or no, I dont know which. Like nobody had made it, like it came from nowhere and went nowhere, until it was like Nancy was not there at all; that I had looked so hard at her eyes on the stairs that they had got printed on my eyeballs, like the sun does when you have closed your eyes and there is no sun. "Jesus," Nancy whispered. "Jesus."

"Was it Jesus?" Caddy said. "Did he try to come into the kitchen?"

"Jesus," Nancy said. Like this: Jeeeeeeeeeeeeeeeesus, until the sound went out, like a match or a candle does.

"It's the other Jesus she means," I said.

"Can you see us, Nancy?" Caddy whispered. "Can you see our eyes too?"

"I aint nothing but a nigger," Nancy said. "God knows. God knows."

"What did you see down there in the kitchen?" Caddy whispered. "What tried to get in?"

"God knows," Nancy said. We could see her eyes. "God knows."

Dilsey got well. She cooked dinner. "You'd better stay in bed a day or two longer," father said.

"What for?" Dilsey said. "If I had been a day later, this place would be to rack and ruin. Get on out of here now, and let me get my kitchen straight again."

Dilsey cooked supper too. And that night, just before dark, Nancy came into the kitchen.

"How do you know he's back?" Dilsey said. "You aint seen him."

"Jesus is a nigger," Jason said.

"I can feel him," Nancy said. "I can feel him laying yonder in the ditch."

"Tonight?" Dilsey said. "Is he there tonight?"

"Dilsey's a nigger too," Jason said.

"You try to eat something," Dilsey said.

"I dont want nothing," Nancy said.

"I aint a nigger," Jason said.

"Drink some coffee," Dilsey said. She poured a cup of coffee for Nancy. "Do you know he's out there tonight? How come you know it's tonight?"

"I know," Nancy said. "He's there, waiting. I know. I done lived with him too long. I know what he is fixing to do fore he know it himself."

"Drink some coffee," Dilsey said. Nancy held the cup to her mouth and blew into the cup. Her mouth pursed out like a spreading adder's, like a rubber mouth, like she had blown all the color out of her lips with blowing the coffee.

"I aint a nigger," Jason said. "Are you a nigger, Nancy?"

"I hellborn, child," Nancy said. "I wont be nothing soon. I going back where I come from soon."

III

She began to drink the coffee. While she was drinking, holding the cup in both hands, she began to make the sound again. She made the sound into the cup and the coffee sploshed out onto her hands and her dress. Her eyes looked at us and she sat there, her elbows on her knees, holding the cup in both hands, looking at us across the wet cup, making the sound. "Look at Nancy," Jason said. "Nancy cant cook for us now. Dilsey's got well now."

"You hush up," Dilsey said. Nancy held the cup in both hands, looking at us, making the sound, like there were two of them: one looking at us and the other making the sound. "Whyn't you let Mr Jason telefoam the marshal?" Dilsey said. Nancy stopped then, holding the cup in her long brown hands. She tried to drink some coffee again, but it sploshed out of the cup, onto her hands and her dress, and she put the cup down. Jason watched her.

"I cant swallow it," Nancy said. "I swallows but it wont go down me."

"You go down to the cabin," Dilsey said. "Frony will fix you a pallet and I'll be there soon."

"Wont no nigger stop him," Nancy said.

"I aint a nigger," Jason said. "Am I, Dilsey?"

"I reckon not," Dilsey said. She looked at Nancy. "I dont reckon so. What you going to do, then?"

Nancy looked at us. Her eyes went fast, like she was afraid there wasn't time to look, without hardly moving at all. She looked at us, at all three of us at one time. "You member that night I stayed in yawls' room?" she said. She told about how we waked up early the next morning, and played. We had to play quiet, on her pallet, until father woke up and it was time to get breakfast. "Go and ask your maw to let me stay here tonight," Nancy said. "I wont need no pallet. We can play some more."

Caddy asked mother. Jason went too. "I cant have Negroes sleeping in the bedrooms," mother said. Jason cried. He cried until mother said he couldn't have any dessert for three days if he didn't stop. Then Jason said he would stop if Dilsey would make a chocolate cake. Father was there.

"Why dont you do something about it?" mother said. "What do we have officers for?"

"Why is Nancy afraid of Jesus?" Caddy said. "Are you afraid of father, mother?"

"What could the officers do?" father said. "If Nancy hasn't seen him, how could the officers find him?"

"Then why is she afraid?" mother said.

"She says he is there. She says she knows he is there tonight."

"Yet we pay taxes," mother said. "I must wait here alone in this big house while you take a Negro woman home."

"You know that I am not lying outside with a razor," father said.

"I'll stop if Dilsey will make a chocolate cake," Jason said. Mother told us to go out and father said he didn't know if Jason would get a chocolate cake or not, but he knew what Jason was going to get in about a minute. We went back to the kitchen and told Nancy.

"Father said for you to go home and lock the door, and you'll be all right," Caddy said. "All right from what, Nancy? Is Jesus mad at you?" Nancy was holding the coffee cup in her hands again, her elbows on her knees and her hands holding the cup between her knees. She was looking into the cup. "What have you done that made Jesus mad?" Caddy said. Nancy let the cup go. It didn't break on the floor, but the coffee spilled out, and Nancy sat there with her hands still making the shape of the cup. She began to make the sound again, not loud. Not singing and not unsinging. We watched her.

"Here," Dilsey said. "You quit that, now. You get aholt of yourself. You wait here. I going to get Versh to walk home with you." Dilsey went out.

We looked at Nancy. Her shoulders kept shaking, but she quit making the sound. We watched her. "What's Jesus going to do to you?" Caddy said. "He went away."

Nancy looked at us. "We had fun that night I stayed in yawls' room, didn't we?"

"I didn't," Jason said. "I didn't have any fun."

"You were asleep in mother's room," Caddy said. "You were not there."

"Let's go down to my house and have some more fun," Nancy said.

"Mother wont let us," I said. "It's too late now."

"Dont bother her," Nancy said. "We can tell her in the morning. She wont mind."

"She wouldn't let us," I said.

"Dont ask her now," Nancy said. "Dont bother her now."

"She didn't say we couldn't go," Caddy said.

"We didn't ask," I said.

"If you go, I'll tell," Jason said.

"We'll have fun," Nancy said. "They won't mind, just to my house. I been working for yawl a long time. They won't mind."

"I'm not afraid to go," Caddy said. "Jason is the one that's afraid. He'll tell."

"I'm not," Jason said.

"Yes, you are," Caddy said. "You'll tell."

"I won't tell," Jason said. "I'm not afraid."

"Jason ain't afraid to go with me," Nancy said. "Is you, Jason?"

"Jason is going to tell," Caddy said. The lane was dark. We passed the pasture gate. "I bet if something was to jump out from behind that gate, Jason would holler."

"I wouldn't," Jason said. We walked down the lane. Nancy was talking loud.

"What are you talking so loud for, Nancy?" Caddy said.

"Who; me?" Nancy said. "Listen at Quentin and Caddy and Jason saying I'm talking loud."

"You talk like there was five of us here," Caddy said. "You talk like father was here too."

"Who; me talking loud, Mr Jason?" Nancy said.

"Nancy called Jason 'Mister,' " Caddy said.

"Listen how Caddy and Quentin and Jason talk," Nancy said.

"We're not talking loud," Caddy said. "You're the one that's talking like father—"

"Hush," Nancy said; "hush, Mr Jason."

"Nancy called Jason 'Mister' aguh—"

"Hush," Nancy said. She was talking loud when we crossed the ditch and stooped through the fence where she used to stoop through with the clothes on her head. Then we came to her house. We were going fast then. She opened the door. The smell of the house was like the lamp and the smell of Nancy was like the wick, like they were waiting for one another to begin to smell. She lit the lamp and closed the door and put the bar up. Then she quit talking loud, looking at us.

"What're we going to do?" Caddy said.

"What do yawl want to do?" Nancy said.

"You said we would have some fun," Caddy said.

There was something about Nancy's house; something you could smell besides Nancy and the house. Jason smelled it, even. "I don't want to stay here," he said. "I want to go home."

"Go home, then," Caddy said.

"I don't want to go by myself," Jason said.

"We're going to have some fun," Nancy said.

"How?" Caddy said.

Nancy stood by the door. She was looking at us, only it was like she had emptied her eyes, like she had quit using them. "What do you want to do?" she said.

"Tell us a story," Caddy said. "Can you tell a story?"

"Yes," Nancy said.

"Tell it," Caddy said. We looked at Nancy. "You don't know any stories."

"Yes," Nancy said. "Yes, I do."

She came and sat in a chair before the hearth. There was a little fire there.

Nancy built it up, when it was already hot inside. She built a good blaze. She told a story. She talked like her eyes looked, like her eyes watching us and her voice talking to us did not belong to her. Like she was living somewhere else, waiting somewhere else. She was outside the cabin. Her voice was inside and the shape of her, the Nancy that could stoop under a barbed wire fence with a bundle of clothes balanced on her head as though without weight, like a balloon, was there. But that was all. "And so this here queen come walking up to the ditch, where that bad man was hiding. She was walking up to the ditch, and she say, 'If I can just get past this here ditch,' was what she say . . . "

"What ditch?" Caddy said. "A ditch like that one out there? Why did a queen want to go into a ditch?"

"To get to her house," Nancy said. She looked at us. "She had to cross the ditch to get into her house quick and bar the door."

"Why did she want to go home and bar the door?" Caddy said.

IV

Nancy looked at us. She quit talking. She looked at us. Jason's legs stuck straight out of his pants where he sat on Nancy's lap. "I don't think that's a good story," he said. "I want to go home."

"Maybe we had better," Caddy said. She got up from the floor. "I bet they are looking for us right now." She went toward the door.

"No," Nancy said. "Don't open it." She got up quick and passed Caddy. She didn't touch the door, the wooden bar.

"Why not?" Caddy said.

"Come back to the lamp," Nancy said. "We'll have fun. You don't have to go."

"We ought to go," Caddy said. "Unless we have a lot of fun." She and Nancy came back to the fire, the lamp.

"I want to go home," Jason said. "I'm going to tell."

"I know another story," Nancy said. She stood close to the lamp. She looked at Caddy, like when your eyes look up at a stick balanced on your nose. She had to look down to see Caddy, but her eyes looked like that, like when you are balancing a stick.

"I won't listen to it," Jason said. "I'll bang on the floor."

"It's a good one," Nancy said. "It's better than the other one."

"What's it about?" Caddy said. Nancy was standing by the lamp. Her hand was on the lamp, against the light, long and brown.

"Your hand is on that hot globe," Caddy said. "Don't it feel hot to your hand?"

Nancy looked at her hand on the lamp chimney. She took her hand away, slow. She stood there, looking at Caddy, wringing her long hand as though it were tied to her wrist with a string.

"Let's do something else," Caddy said.

"I want to go home," Jason said.

"I got some popcorn," Nancy said. She looked at Caddy and then at Jason and then at me and then at Caddy again. "I got some popcorn."

"I don't like popcorn," Jason said. "I'd rather have candy."

Nancy looked at Jason. "You can hold the popper." She was still wringing her hand; it was long and limp and brown.

"All right," Jason said. "I'll stay a while if I can do that. Caddy can't hold it. I'll want to go home again if Caddy holds the popper."

Nancy built up the fire. "Look at Nancy putting her hands in the fire," Caddy said. "What's the matter with you, Nancy?"

"I got popcorn," Nancy said. "I got some." She took the popper from under the bed. It was broken. Jason began to cry.

"Now we can't have any popcorn," he said.

"We ought to go home, anyway," Caddy said. "Come on, Quentin."

"Wait," Nancy said; "wait. I can fix it. Don't you want to help me fix it?"

"I don't think I want any," Caddy said. "It's too late now."

"You help me, Jason," Nancy said. "Don't you want to help me?"

"No," Jason said. "I want to go home."

"Hush," Nancy said; "hush. Watch. Watch me. I can fix it so Jason can hold it and pop the corn." She got a piece of wire and fixed the popper.

"It won't hold good," Caddy said.

"Yes, it will," Nancy said. "Yawl watch. Yawl help me shell some corn."

The popcorn was under the bed too. We shelled it into the popper and Nancy helped Jason hold the popper over the fire.

"It's not popping," Jason said. "I want to go home."

"You wait," Nancy said. "It'll begin to pop. We'll have fun then." She was sitting close to the fire. The lamp was turned up so high it was beginning to smoke.

"Why don't you turn it down some?" I said.

"It's all right," Nancy said. "I'll clean it. Yawl wait. The popcorn will start in a minute."

"I don't believe it's going to start," Caddy said. "We ought to start home, anyway. They'll be worried."

"No," Nancy said. "It's going to pop. Dilsey will tell um yawl with me. I been working for yawl long time. They won't mind if yawl at my house. You wait, now. It'll start popping any minute now."

Then Jason got some smoke in his eyes and he began to cry. He dropped the popper into the fire. Nancy got a wet rag and wiped Jason's face, but he didn't stop crying.

"Hush," she said. "Hush." But he didn't hush. Caddy took the popper out of the fire.

"It's burned up," she said. "You'll have to get some more popcorn, Nancy."

"Did you put all of it in?" Nancy said.

"Yes," Caddy said. Nancy looked at Caddy. Then she took the popper and opened it and poured the cinders into her apron and began to sort the grains, her hands long and brown, and we watching her.

"Haven't you got any more?" Caddy said.

"Yes," Nancy said; "yes. Look. This here ain't burnt. All we need to do is—"

"I want to go home," Jason said. "I'm going to tell."

"Hush," Caddy said. We all listened. Nancy's head was already turned toward the barred door, her eyes filled with red lamplight. "Somebody is coming," Caddy said.

Then Nancy began to make that sound again, not loud, sitting there above the fire, her long hands dangling between her knees; all of a sudden water began to come out on her face in big drops, running down her face, carrying in each one a little turning ball of firelight like a spark until it dropped off her chin. "She's not crying," I said.

"I ain't crying," Nancy said. Her eyes were closed. "I ain't crying. Who is it?"

"I don't know," Caddy said. She went to the door and looked out. "We've got to go now," she said. "Here comes father."

"I'm going to tell," Jason said. "Yawl made me come."

The water still ran down Nancy's face. She turned in her chair. "Listen. Tell him. Tell him we going to have fun. Tell him I take good care of yawl until in the morning. Tell him to let me come home with yawl and sleep on the floor. Tell him I won't need no pallet. We'll have fun. You member last time how we had so much fun?"

"I didn't have fun," Jason said. "You hurt me. You put smoke in my eyes. I'm going to tell."

V

Father came in. He looked at us. Nancy did not get up.

"Tell him," she said.

"Caddy made us come down here," Jason said. "I didn't want to."

Father came to the fire. Nancy looked up at him. "Can't you go to Aunt Rachel's and stay?" he said. Nancy looked up at father, her hands between her knees. "He's not here," father said. "I would have seen him. There's not a soul in sight."

"He in the ditch," Nancy said. "He waiting in the ditch yonder."

"Nonsense," father said. He looked at Nancy. "Do you know he's there?"

"I got the sign," Nancy said.

"What sign?"

"I got it. It was on the table when I come in. It was a hogbone, with blood meat still on it, laying by the lamp. He's out there. When yawl walk out that door, I gone."

"Gone where, Nancy?" Caddy said.

"I'm not a tattletale," Jason said.

"Nonsense," father said.

"He out there," Nancy said. "He looking through that window this minute, waiting for yawl to go. Then I gone."

"Nonsense," father said. "Lock up your house and we'll take you on to Aunt Rachel's."

" 'Twont do no good," Nancy said. She didn't look at father now, but he looked down at her, at her long, limp, moving hands. "Putting it off wont do no good."

"Then what do you want to do?" father said.

"I don't know," Nancy said. "I can't do nothing. Just put it off. And that don't do no good. I reckon it belong to me. I reckon what I going to get ain't no more than mine."

"Get what?" Caddy said. "What's yours?"

"Nothing," father said. "You all must get to bed."

"Caddy made me come," Jason said.

"Go on to Aunt Rachel's," father said.

"It won't do no good," Nancy said. She sat before the fire, her elbows on her knees, her long hands between her knees. "When even your own kitchen wouldn't do no good. When even if I was sleeping on the floor in the room with your chillen, and the next morning there I am, and blood—"

"Hush," father said. "Lock the door and put out the lamp and go to bed."

"I scared of the dark," Nancy said. "I scared for it to happen in the dark."

"You mean you're going to sit right here with the lamp lighted?" father said. Then Nancy began to make the sound again, sitting before the fire, her long hands between her knees. "Ah, damnation," father said. "Come along, chillen. It's past bedtime."

"When yawl go home, I gone," Nancy said. She talked quieter now, and her face looked quiet, like her hands. "Anyway, I got my coffin money saved up with Mr. Lovelady." Mr. Lovelady was a short, dirty man who collected the Negro insurance, coming around to the cabins or the kitchens every Saturday morning, to collect fifteen cents. He and his wife lived at the hotel. One morning his wife committed suicide. They had a child, a little girl. He and the child went away. After a week or two he came back alone. We would see him going along the lanes and the back streets on Saturday mornings.

"Nonsense," father said. "You'll be the first thing I'll see in the kitchen tomorrow morning."

"You'll see what you'll see, I reckon," Nancy said. "But it will take the Lord to say what that will be."

VI

We left her sitting before the fire.

"Come and put the bar up," father said. But she didn't move. She didn't look at us again, sitting quietly there between the lamp and the fire. From some distance down the lane we could look back and see her through the open door.

"What, Father?" Caddy said. "What's going to happen?"

"Nothing," father said. Jason was on father's back, so Jason was the tallest of all of us. We went down into the ditch. I looked at it, quiet. I couldn't see much where the moonlight and the shadows tangled.

"If Jesus is hid here, he can see us, cant he?" Caddy said.

"He's not there," father said. "He went away a long time ago."

"You made me come," Jason said, high; against the sky it looked like father had two heads, a little one and a big one. "I didn't want to."

We went up out of the ditch. We could still see Nancy's house and the open door, but we couldn't see Nancy now, sitting before the fire with the door open, because she was tired. "I just done got tired," she said. "I just a nigger: It ain't no fault of mine."

But we could hear her, because she began just after we came up out of the ditch, the sound that was not singing and not unsinging. "Who will do our washing now, Father?" I said.

"I'm not a nigger," Jason said, high and close above father's head.

"You're worse," Caddy said, "you are a tattletale. If something was to jump out, you'd be scairder than a nigger."

"I wouldn't," Jason said.

"You'd cry," Caddy said.

"Caddy," father said.

"I wouldn't!" Jason said.

"Scairy cat," Caddy said.

"Candace!" father said.

FOR STUDY, DISCUSSION, AND WRITING

1. From whose point of view is this story told? How does this point of view affect the reader's perception of everything that takes place?
2. Why is Nancy so afraid of Jesus? How is her fear dramatized?
3. Compare and contrast the characters of Jason and Caddy.
4. Discuss what has made Jesus such a dangerous character.
5. What evidence of a racial double standard in Jefferson does the story contain? How has this double standard helped bring about the situation in which Nancy finds herself?
6. How is the father's attitude toward Nancy different from that of anyone else in the story? Does this attitude change during the course of the story?

7. What symbolic value can you assign to the following items: (1) the image of "iron poles bearing clusters of bloated and ghostly and bloodless grapes" at the beginning of the story; (2) the watermelon vine image; (3) the popcorn-popping episode; and (4) the final scene of the story in which Jason rides on his father's back, the child's head higher in the air than his father's head?

8. At the conclusion of the story, Nancy's fate has not been resolved. Why do you think Faulkner decided to leave the story open-ended?

ALBERT MALTZ

The Happiest Man on Earth

Jesse felt ready to weep. He had been sitting in the shanty waiting for Tom to appear, grateful for the chance to rest his injured foot, quietly, joyously anticipating the moment when Tom would say, "Why, of course, Jesse, you can start whenever you're ready!"

For two weeks he had been pushing himself, from Kansas City, Missouri, to Tulsa, Oklahoma, through nights of rain and a week of scorching sun, without sleep or a decent meal, sustained by the vision of that one moment. And then Tom had come into the office. He had come in quickly, holding a sheaf of papers in his hand; he had glanced at Jesse only casually, it was true—but long enough. He had not known him. He had turned away . . . And Tom Brackett was his brother-in-law.

Was it his clothes? Jesse knew he looked terrible. He had tried to spruce up at a drinking fountain in the park, but even that had gone badly; in his excitement he had cut himself shaving, an ugly gash down the side of his cheek. And nothing could get the red gumbo dust out of his suit even though he had slapped himself till both arms were worn out . . . Or was it just that he had changed so much?

True, they hadn't seen each other for five years; but Tom looked five years older, that was all. He was still Tom. God! Was he so different?

Brackett finished his telephone call. He leaned back in his swivel chair and glanced over at Jesse with small, clear, blue eyes that were suspicious and unfriendly. He was a heavy, paunchy man of forty-five, auburn-haired, rather dour-looking; his face was meaty, his features pronounced and forceful, his nose somewhat bulbous and reddish-hued at the tip. He looked like a solid, decent, capable businessman who was commander of the local branch of the

American Legion—which he was. He surveyed Jesse with cold indifference, manifestly unwilling to spend time on him. Even the way he chewed his toothpick seemed contemptuous to Jesse.

"Yes?" Brackett said suddenly. "What do you want?"

His voice was decent enough, Jesse admitted. He had expected it to be worse. He moved up to the wooden counter that partitioned the shanty. He thrust a hand nervously through his tangled hair.

"I guess you don't recognize me, Tom," he said falteringly. "I'm Jesse Fulton."

"Huh?" Brackett said. That was all.

"Yes, I am, and Ella sends you her love."

Brackett rose and walked over to the counter until they were face to face. He surveyed Fulton incredulously, trying to measure the resemblance to his brother-in-law as he remembered him. This man was tall, about thirty. That fitted! He had straight good features and a lank erect body. That was right too. But the face was too gaunt, the body too spiny under the baggy clothes for him to be sure. His brother-in-law had been a solid, strong, young man with muscle and beef to him. It was like looking at a faded, badly taken photograph and trying to recognize the subject: The resemblance was there but the difference was tremendous. He searched the eyes. They at least seemed definitely familiar, gray, with a curiously shy but decent look in them. He had liked that about Fulton.

Jesse stood quiet. Inside he was seething. Brackett was like a man examining a piece of broken-down horseflesh; there was a look of pure pity in his eyes. It made Jesse furious. He knew he wasn't as far gone as all that.

"Yes, I believe you are," Brackett said finally, "but you sure have changed."

"By God, it's five years, ain't it?" Jesse said resentfully. "You only saw me a couple of times anyway." Then, to himself, with his lips locked together, in mingled vehemence and shame, "What if I have changed? Don't everybody? I ain't no corpse."

"You was solid looking," Brackett continued softly, in the same tone of incredulous wonder. "You lost weight, I guess?"

Jesse kept silent. He needed Brackett too much to risk antagonizing him. But it was only by deliberate effort that he could keep from boiling over. The pause lengthened, became painful. Brackett flushed. "Jiminy Christmas, excuse me," he burst out in apology. He jerked the counter up. "Come in. Take a seat. Good God, boy"—he grasped Jesse's hand and shook it—"I am glad to see you; don't think anything else! You just looked so peaked."

"It's all right," Jesse murmured. He sat down, thrusting his hand through his curly, tangled hair.

"Why are you limping?"

"I stepped on a stone; it jagged a hole through my shoe." Jesse pulled his feet back under the chair. He was ashamed of his shoes. They had come from the relief originally, and two weeks on the road had about finished them. All morning, with a kind of delicious, foolish solemnity, he had been vowing to himself that before anything else, before even a suit of clothes, he was going to buy himself a brand-new strong pair of shoes.

Brackett kept his eyes off Jesse's feet. He knew what was bothering the boy and it filled his heart with pity. The whole thing was appalling. He had never seen anyone who looked more down-and-out. His sister had been writing to him every week, but she hadn't told him they were as badly-off as this.

"Well now, listen," Brackett began, "tell me things. How's Ella?"

"Oh, she's pretty good," Jesse replied absently. He had a soft, pleasing, rather shy voice that went with his soft gray eyes. He was worrying over how to get started.

"And the kids?"

"Oh, they're fine . . . Well, you know," Jesse added, becoming more attentive, "the young one has to wear a brace. He can't run around, you know. But he's smart. He draws pictures and he does things, you know."

"Yes," Brackett said. "That's good." He hesitated. There was a moment's silence. Jesse fidgeted in his chair. Now that the time had arrived, he felt awkward. Brackett leaned forward and put his hand on Jesse's knee. "Ella didn't tell me things were so bad for you, Jesse. I might have helped."

"Well, goodness," Jesse returned softly, "you been having your own troubles, ain't you?"

"Yes." Brackett leaned back. His ruddy face became mournful and darkly bitter. "You know I lost my hardware shop?"

"Well sure, of course," Jesse answered, surprised. "You wrote us. That's what I mean."

"I forgot," Brackett said. "I keep on being surprised over it myself. Not that it was worth much," he added bitterly. "It was running downhill for three years. I guess I just wanted it because it was mine." He laughed pointlessly, without mirth. "Well, tell me about yourself," he asked. "What happened to the job you had?"

Jesse burst out abruptly, with agitation, "Let it wait, Tom, I got something on my mind."

"It ain't you and Ella?" Brackett interrupted anxiously.

"Why no!" Jesse sat back. "Why, however did you come to think that? Why Ella and me . . . " He stopped, laughing. "Why, Tom, I'm just crazy about Ella. Why she's just wonderful. She's just my whole life, Tom."

"Excuse me. Forget it." Brackett chuckled uncomfortably, turned away. The naked intensity of the youth's burst of love had upset him. It made him wish savagely that he could do something for them. They were too decent to have had it so hard. Ella was like this boy too, shy and a little soft.

"Tom, listen," Jesse said, "I come here on purpose." He thrust his hand through his hair. "I want you to help me."

"Damn it, boy," Brackett groaned. He had been expecting this. "I can't much. I only get thirty-five a week and I'm damn grateful for it."

"Sure, I know," Jesse emphasized excitedly. He was feeling once again the wild, delicious agitation that had possessed him in the early hours of the morning. "I know you can't help us with money! But we met a man who works for you! He was in our city! He said you could give me a job!"

"Who said?"

"Oh, why didn't you tell me?" Jesse burst out reproachfully. "Why, as soon as I heard of it I started out. For two weeks now I been pushing ahead like crazy."

Brackett groaned aloud. "You come walking from Kansas City in two weeks so I could give you a job?"

"Sure, Tom, of course. What else could I do?"

"God Almighty, there ain't no jobs, Jesse! It's a slack season. And you don't know this oil business. It's special. I got my Legion friends here, but they couldn't do nothing now. Don't you think I'd ask for you as soon as there was a chance?"

Jesse felt stunned. The hope of the last two weeks seemed rolling up into a ball of agony in his stomach. Then, frantically, he cried, "But listen, this man said *you* could hire! He told me! He drives trucks for you! He said you always need men!"

"Oh! . . . You mean my department?" Brackett said in a low voice.

"Yes, Tom. That's it!"

"Oh, no, you don't want to work in my department," Brackett told him in the same low voice. "You don't know what it is."

"Yes, I do," Jesse insisted. "He told me all about it, Tom. You're a dispatcher, ain't you? You send the dynamite trucks out?"

"Who was the man, Jesse?"

"Everett, Everett, I think."

"Egbert? Man about my size?" Brackett asked slowly.

"Yes, Egbert. He wasn't a phony, was he?"

Brackett laughed. For the second time his laughter was curiously without mirth. "No, he wasn't a phony." Then, in a changed voice: "Jiminy, boy, you should have asked me before you trekked all the way down here."

"Oh, I didn't want to," Jesse explained with naive cunning. "I knew you'd say no. He told me it was risky work, Tom. But I don't care."

Brackett locked his fingers together. His solid, meaty face became very hard. "I'm going to say no anyway, Jesse."

Jesse cried out. It had not occurred to him that Brackett would not agree. It had seemed as though reaching Tulsa were the only problem he had to face. "Oh no," he begged, "you can't. Ain't there any jobs, Tom?"

"Sure there's jobs. There's even Egbert's job if you want it."

"He's quit?"

"He's dead!"

"Oh!"

"On the job, Jesse. Last night if you want to know."

"Oh!" . . . Then, "I don't care!"

"Now you listen to me," Brackett said. "I'll tell you a few things that you should have asked before you started out. It ain't dynamite you drive. They don't use anything as safe as dynamite in drilling oil wells. They wish they could, but they can't. It's nitroglycerin! Soup!"

"But I know," Jesse told him reassuringly. "He advised me, Tom. You don't have to think I don't know."

"Shut up a minute," Brackett ordered angrily. "Listen! You just have to look at this soup, see? You just cough loud and it blows! You know how they transport it? In a can that's shaped like this, see, like a fan? That's to give room for compartments, because each compartment has to be lined with rubber. That's the only way you can even think of handling it."

"Listen, Tom . . . "

"Now wait a minute, Jesse. For God's sake just put your mind to this. I know you had your heart set on a job, but you've got to understand. This stuff goes only in special trucks! At night! They got to follow a special route! They can't go through any city! If they lay over, it's got to be in a special garage! Don't you see what that means? Don't that tell you how dangerous it is?"

"I'll drive careful," Jesse said. "I know how to handle a truck. I'll drive slow."

Brackett groaned. "Do you think Egbert didn't drive careful or know how to handle a truck?"

"Tom," said Jesse earnestly, "you can't scare me. I got my mind fixed on only one thing: Egbert said he was getting a dollar a mile. He was making five to six hundred dollars a month for half a month's work, he said. Can I get the same?"

"Sure you can get the same," Brackett told him savagely. "A dollar a mile. It's easy. But why do you think the company has to pay so much? It's easy—until you run over a stone that your headlights didn't pick out, like Egbert did. Or get a blowout! Or get something in your eye so the wheel twists and you jar the truck! Or any other God damn thing that nobody ever knows! We can't ask Egbert what happened to him. There's no truck to give any evidence. There's no corpse. There's nothing! Maybe tomorrow somebody'll find a piece of twisted steel way off in a cornfield. But we never find the driver. Not even a fingernail. All we know is that he don't come in on schedule. Then we wait for the police to call us. You know what happened last night? Something went wrong on a bridge. Maybe Egbert was nervous. Maybe he brushed the side with his fender. Only there's no bridge anymore. No truck. No Egbert. Do you understand now? That's what you get for your God damn dollar a mile!"

There was a moment of silence. Jesse sat twisting his long thin hands. His mouth was sagging open, his face was agonized. Then he shut his eyes and spoke softly. "I don't care about that, Tom. You told me. Now you got to be good to me and give me the job."

Brackett slapped the palm of his hand down on his desk. "No!"

"Listen, Tom," Jesse said softly, "you just don't understand." He opened his eyes. They were filled with tears. They made Brackett turn away. "Just look at me, Tom. Don't that tell you enough? What did you think of me when you first saw me? You thought: 'Why don't that bum go away and stop panhandling?' Didn't you, Tom? Tom, I just can't live like this any more. I got to be able to walk down the street with my head up."

"You're crazy," Brackett muttered. "Every year there's one out of five drivers gets killed. That's the average. What's worth that?"

"Is my life worth anything now? We're just starvin' at home, Tom. They ain't put us back on relief yet."

"Then you should have told me," Brackett exclaimed harshly. "It's your own damn fault. A man has no right to have false pride when his family ain't eating. I'll borrow some money and we'll telegraph it to Ella. Then you go home and get back on relief."

"And then what?"

"And then wait, God damn it! You're no old man. You got no right to throw your life away. Sometime you'll get a job."

"No!" Jesse jumped up. "No. I believed that too. But I don't now," he cried passionately. "I ain't getting a job no more than you're getting your hardware store back. I lost my skill, Tom. Linotyping is skilled work. I'm rusty now. I've been six years on relief. The only work I've had is pick and shovel. When I got that job this spring, I was supposed to be an A-1 man. But I wasn't. And they got new machines now. As soon as the slack started, they let me out."

"So what?" Brackett said harshly. "Ain't there other jobs?"

"How do I know?" Jesse replied. "There ain't been one for six years. I'd even be afraid to take one now. It's been too hard waiting so many weeks to get back on relief."

"Well, you got to have some courage," Brackett shouted. "You've got to keep up hope."

"I got all the courage you want," Jesse retorted vehemently, "but no, I ain't got no hope. The hope has dried up in me in six years waiting. You're the only hope I got."

"You're crazy," Brackett muttered. "I won't do it. For God's sake think of Ella for a minute."

"Don't you know I'm thinking about her?" Jesse asked softly. He plucked at Brackett's sleeve. "That's what decided me, Tom." His voice became muted into a hushed, pained, whisper. "The night Egbert was at our house I looked at Ella like I'd seen her for the first time. She ain't pretty anymore, Tom!" Brackett jerked his head and moved away. Jesse followed him, taking a deep, sobbing breath. "Don't that tell you, Tom? Ella was like a little doll or something, you remember. I couldn't walk down the street without somebody turning to look at her. She ain't twenty-nine yet, Tom, and she ain't pretty no more."

Brackett sat down with his shoulders hunched up wearily. He gripped his hands together and sat leaning forward, staring at the floor.

Jesse stood over him, his gaunt face flushed with emotion, almost unpleasant in its look of pleading and bitter humility. "I ain't done right for Ella, Tom. Ella deserved better. This is the only chance I see in my whole life to do something for her. I've just been a failure."

"Don't talk nonsense," Brackett commented without rancor. "You ain't a failure. No more than me. There's millions of men in the identical situation. It's just the depression, or the recession, or the God damn New Deal, or . . . !" He swore and lapsed into silence.

"Oh no," Jesse corrected him in a knowing, sorrowful tone, "those things maybe excuse other men. But not me. It was up to me to do better. This is my own fault!"

"Oh, beans!" Brackett said. "It's more sun spots than it's you!"

Jesse's face turned an unhealthy mottled red. It looked swollen. "Well I don't care," he cried wildly. "I don't care! You got to give me this! I got to lift my head up. I went through one stretch of hell, but I can't go through another. You want me to keep looking at my little boy's legs and tell myself if I had a job he wouldn't be like that? Every time he walks he says to me, 'I got soft bones from the rickets and you give it to me because you didn't feed me right.' Jesus Christ, Tom, you think I'm going to sit there and watch him like that another six years?"

Brackett leaped to his feet. "So what if you do?" he shouted. "You say you're thinking about Ella. How's she going to like it when you get killed?"

"Maybe I won't," Jesse pleaded. "I've got to have some luck sometime."

"That's what they all think," Brackett replied scornfully. "When you take this job, your luck is a question mark. The only thing certain is that sooner or later you get killed."

"Okay then," Jesse shouted back. "Then I do! But meanwhile I got something, don't I? I can buy a pair of shoes. Look at me! I can buy a suit that don't say 'Relief' by the way it fits. I can smoke cigarettes. I can buy some candy for the kids. I can eat some myself. Yes, by God, I want to eat some candy. I want a glass of beer once a day. I want Ella dressed up. I want her to eat meat three times a week, four times maybe. I want to take my family to the movies."

Brackett sat down. "Oh, shut up," he said wearily.

"No," Jesse told him softly, passionately, "you can't get rid of me. Listen, Tom," he pleaded, "I got it all figured out. On six hundred a month look how much I can save! If I last only three months, look how much it is . . . a thousand dollars . . . more! And maybe I'll last longer. Maybe a couple years. I can fix Ella up for life!"

"You said it," Brackett interposed. "I suppose you think she'll enjoy living when you're on a job like that?"

"I got it all figured out," Jesse answered excitedly. "She don't know, see? I tell her I make only forty. You put the rest in a bank account for her, Tom."

"Oh, shut up," Brackett said. "You think you'll be happy? Every minute, waking and sleeping, you'll be wondering if tomorrow you'll be dead. And the worst days will be your days off, when you're not driving. They have to give you every other day free to get your nerve back. And you lay around the house eating your heart out. That's how happy you'll be."

Jesse laughed. "I'll be happy! Don't you worry, I'll be so happy, I'll be singing. Lord God, Tom, I'm going to feel proud of myself for the first time in seven years!"

"Oh, shut up, shut up," Brackett said.

The little shanty became silent. After a moment Jesse whispered: "You got to, Tom. You got to. You got to."

Again there was silence. Brackett raised both hands to his head, pressing the palms against his temples.

"Tom, Tom . . . " Jesse said.

Brackett sighed. "Oh, God damn it," he said finally, "all right, I'll take you on, God help me." His voice was low, hoarse, infinitely weary. "If you're ready to drive tonight, you can drive tonight."

Jesse didn't answer. He couldn't. Brackett looked up. The tears were running down Jesse's face. He was swallowing and trying to speak, but only making an absurd, gasping noise.

"I'll send a wire to Ella," Brackett said in the same hoarse, weary voice. "I'll tell her you got a job, and you'll send her fare in a couple of days. You'll have some money then—that is, if you last the week out, you jackass!"

Jesse only nodded. His heart felt so close to bursting that he pressed both hands against it, as though to hold it locked within his breast.

"Come back here at six o'clock," Brackett said. "Here's some money. Eat a good meal."

"Thanks," Jesse whispered.

"Wait a minute," Brackett said. "Here's my address." He wrote it on a piece of paper, "Take any car going that way. Ask the conductor where to get off. Take a bath and get some sleep."

"Thanks," Jesse said. "Thanks, Tom."

"Oh, get out of here," Brackett said.

"Tom."

"What?"

"I just . . . " Jesse stopped. Brackett saw his face. The eyes were still glistening with tears, but the gaunt face was shining now with a kind of fierce radiance.

Brackett turned away. "I'm busy," he said.

Jesse went out. The wet film blinded him, but the whole world seemed to have turned golden. He limped slowly, with the blood pounding his temples and a wild, incommunicable joy in his heart. "I'm the happiest man in the world," he whispered to himself. "I'm the happiest man on the whole earth."

Brackett sat watching till finally Jesse turned the corner of the alley and disappeared. Then he hunched himself over with his head in his hands. His heart was beating painfully like something old and clogged. He listened to it as it beat. He sat in desperate tranquillity, gripping his head in his hands.

FOR STUDY, DISCUSSION, AND WRITING

1. What is ironic about the title of the story?

2. In what ways has Tom Brackett been scarred by the Great Depression?

3. Why is Jesse mistaken in thinking that he is a failure as a husband and a father because he has not been able to provide for his family?
4. Despite everything that has happened to him, Jesse retains some degree of personal pride. How is this dramatized in the story?
5. In the end, what persuades Tom Brackett to give Jesse the job? Why does this persuade Brackett?
6. How is this story very much like a one-act play?

JEAN-PAUL SARTRE

The Wall

　　　They pushed us into a large white room and my eyes began to blink because the light hurt them. Then I saw a table and four fellows seated at the table, civilians, looking at some papers. The other prisoners were herded together at one end and we were obliged to cross the entire room to join them. There were several I knew, and others who must have been foreigners. The two in front of me were blond with round heads. They looked alike. I imagine they were French. The smaller one kept pulling at his trousers, out of nervousness.

This lasted about three hours. I was dog-tired and my head was empty. But the room was well-heated, which struck me as rather agreeable; we had not stopped shivering for twenty-four hours. The guards led the prisoners in one after the other in front of the table. Then the four fellows asked them their names and what they did. Most of the time that was all—or perhaps from time to time they would ask such questions as: "Did you help sabotage the munitions?" or, "Where were you on the morning of the ninth and what were you doing?" They didn't even listen to the replies, or at least they didn't seem to. They just remained silent for a moment and looked straight ahead, then they began to write. They asked Tom if it was true he had served in the International Brigade. Tom couldn't say he hadn't because of the papers they had found in his jacket. They didn't ask Juan anything, but after he told them his name, they wrote for a long while.

"It's my brother José who's the anarchist," Juan said. "You know perfectly well he's not here now. I don't belong to any party. I never did take part in politics." They didn't answer.

Then Juan said, "I didn't do anything. And I'm not going to pay for what the others did."

His lips were trembling. A guard told him to stop talking and led him away. It was my turn.

"Your name is Pablo Ibbieta?"

I said yes.

The fellow looked at his papers and said, "Where is Ramon Gris?"

"I don't know."

"You hid him in your house from the sixth to the nineteenth."

"I did not."

They continued to write for a moment and the guards led me away. In the hall, Tom and Juan were waiting between two guards. We started walking. Tom asked one of the guards, "What's the idea?" "How do you mean?" the guard asked. "Was that just the preliminary questioning, or was that the trial?" "That was the trial," the guard said. "So now what? What are they going to do with us?" The guard answered drily, "The verdict will be told you in your cell."

In reality, our cell was one of the cellars of the hospital. It was terribly cold there because it was very drafty. We had been shivering all night long and it had hardly been any better during the day. I had spent the preceding five days in a cellar in the archbishop's palace, a sort of dungeon that must have dated back to the Middle Ages. There were lots of prisoners and not much room, so they housed them just anywhere. But I was not homesick for my dungeon. I hadn't been cold there, but I had been alone, and that gets to be irritating. In the cellar I had company. Juan didn't say a word; he was afraid, and besides, he was too young to have anything to say. But Tom was a good talker and knew Spanish well.

In the cellar there were a bench and four straw mattresses. When they led us back we sat down and waited in silence. After a while Tom said, "Our goose is cooked."

"I think so too," I said. "But I don't believe they'll do anything to the kid."

Tom said, "They haven't got anything on him. He's the brother of a fellow who's fighting, and that's all."

I looked at Juan. He didn't seem to have heard.

Tom continued, "You know what they do in Saragossa? They lay the guys across the road and then they drive over them with trucks. It was a Moroccan deserter who told us that. They say it's just to save ammunition."

I said, "Well, it doesn't save gasoline."

I was irritated with Tom; he shouldn't have said that.

He went on, "There are officers walking up and down the roads with their hands in their pockets, smoking, and they see that it's done right. Do you think they'd put 'em out of their misery? Like hell they do. They just let 'em holler. Sometimes as long as an hour. The Moroccan said the first time he almost puked."

"I don't believe they do that here," I said, "unless they really are short of ammunition."

The daylight came in through four air vents and a round opening that had been cut in the ceiling, to the left, and which opened directly onto the sky. It was through this hole, which was ordinarily closed by means of a trapdoor, that they unloaded coal into the cellar. Directly under the hole, there was a big pile of coal dust; it had been intended for heating the hospital, but at the beginning of the war they had evacuated the patients and the coal had stayed there unused; it even got rained on from time to time, when they forgot to close the trapdoor.

Tom started to shiver. "God damn it," he said, "I'm shivering. There, it is starting again."

He rose and began to do gymnastic exercises. At each movement, his shirt opened and showed his white, hairy chest. He lay down on his back, lifted his legs in the air and began to do the scissors movement. I watched his big buttocks tremble. Tom was tough, but he had too much fat on him. I kept thinking that soon bullets and bayonet points would sink into that mass of tender flesh as though it were a pat of butter.

I wasn't exactly cold, but I couldn't feel my shoulders or my arms. From time to time, I had the impression that something was missing and I began to look around for my jacket. Then I would suddenly remember they hadn't given me a jacket. It was rather awkward. They had taken our clothes to give them to their own soldiers and had left us only our shirts and these cotton trousers the hospital patients wore in mid-summer. After a moment, Tom got up and sat down beside me, breathless.

"Did you get warmed up?"

"Damn it, no. But I'm all out of breath."

Around eight o'clock in the evening, a Major came in with two Falangists.

"What are the names of those three over there?" he asked the guard.

"Steinbock, Ibbieta and Mirbal," said the guard.

The Major put on his glasses and examined his list.

"Steinbock—Steinbock . . . Here it is. You are condemned to death. You'll be shot tomorrow morning."

He looked at his list again.

"The other two, also," he said.

"That's not possible," said Juan. "Not me."

The Major looked at him with surprise. "What's your name?"

"Juan Mirbal."

"Well, your name is here," said the Major, "and you're condemned to death."

"I didn't do anything," said Juan.

The Major shrugged his shoulders and turned toward Tom and me.

"You are both Basque?"

"No, nobody's Basque."

He appeared exasperated.

"I was told there were three Basques. I'm not going to waste my time running after them. I suppose you don't want a priest?"

We didn't even answer.

Then he said, "A Belgian doctor will be around in a little while. He has permission to stay with you all night."

He gave a military salute and left.

"What did I tell you?" Tom said. "We're in for something swell."

"Yes," I said. "It's a damned shame for the kid."

I said that to be fair, but I really didn't like the kid. His face was too refined and it was disfigured by fear and suffering, which had twisted all his features. Three days ago, he was just a kid with a kind of affected manner some people like. But now he looked like an aging fairy, and I thought to myself he would never be young again, even if they let him go. It wouldn't have been a bad thing to show him a little pity, but pity makes me sick, and besides, I couldn't stand him. He hadn't said anything more, but he had turned gray. His face and hands were gray. He sat down again and stared, round-eyed, at the ground. Tom was good-hearted and tried to take him by the arm, but the kid drew himself away violently and made an ugly face. "Leave him alone," I said quietly. "Can't you see he's going to start to bawl?" Tom obeyed regretfully. He would have liked to console the kid; that would have kept him occupied and he wouldn't have been tempted to think about himself. But it got on my nerves. I had never thought about death, for the reason that the question had never come up. But now it had come up, and there was nothing else to do but think about it.

Tom started talking. "Say, did you ever bump anybody off?" he asked me. I didn't answer. He started to explain to me that he had bumped off six fellows since August. He hadn't yet realized what we were in for, and I saw clearly he didn't *want* to realize it. I myself hadn't quite taken it in. I wondered if it hurt very much. I thought about the bullets; I imagined their fiery hail going through my body. All that was beside the real question; but I was calm, we had all night in which to realize it. After a while Tom stopped talking and I looked at him out of the corner of my eye. I saw that he, too, had turned gray and that he looked pretty miserable. I said to myself, "It's starting." It was almost dark, a dull light filtered through the air vents across the coal pile and made a big spot under the sky. Through the hole in the ceiling I could already see a star. The night was going to be clear and cold.

The door opened and two guards entered. They were followed by a blond man in a tan uniform. He greeted us.

"I'm the doctor," he said. "I've been authorized to give you any assistance you may require in these painful circumstances."

He had an agreeable, cultivated voice.

I said to him, "What are you going to do here?"

"Whatever you want me to do. I shall do everything in my power to lighten these few hours."

"Why did you come to us? There are lots of others: the hospital's full of them."

"I was sent here," he answered vaguely. "You'd probably like to smoke, wouldn't you?" he added suddenly. "I've got some cigarettes and even some cigars."

He passed around some English cigarettes and some *puros*, but we refused them. I looked him straight in the eye and he appeared uncomfortable.

"You didn't come here out of compassion," I said to him. "In fact, I know who you are. I saw you with some fascists in the barracks yard the day I was arrested."

I was about to continue, when all at once something happened to me which surprised me: the presence of this doctor had suddenly ceased to interest me. Usually, when I've got hold of a man I don't let go. But somehow the desire to speak had left me. I shrugged my shoulders and turned away. A little later, I looked up and saw he was watching me with an air of curiosity. The guards had sat down on one of the mattresses. Pedro, the tall thin one, was twiddling his thumbs, while the other one shook his head occasionally to keep from falling asleep.

"Do you want some light?" Pedro suddenly asked the doctor. The other fellow nodded, "Yes." I think he was not over-intelligent, but doubtless he was not malicious. As I looked at his big, cold, blue eyes, it seemed to me the worst thing about him was his lack of imagination. Pedro went out and came back with an oil lamp which he set on the corner of the bench. It gave a poor light, but it was better than nothing; the night before we had been left in the dark. For a long while I stared at the circle of light the lamp threw on the ceiling. I was fascinated. Then, suddenly, I came to, the light circle paled, and I felt as if I were being crushed under an enormous weight. It wasn't the thought of death, and it wasn't fear; it was something anonymous. My cheeks were burning hot and my head ached.

I roused myself and looked at my two companions. Tom had his head in his hands and only the fat, white nape of his neck was visible. Juan was by far the worst off; his mouth was wide open and his nostrils were trembling. The doctor came over to him and touched him on the shoulder, as though to comfort him; but his eyes remained cold. Then I saw the Belgian slide his hand furtively down Juan's arm to his wrist. Indifferent, Juan let himself be handled. Then, as though absent-mindedly, the Belgian laid three fingers over his wrist; at the same time, he drew away somewhat and managed to turn his back to me. But I leaned over backward and saw him take out his watch and look at it a moment before relinquishing the boy's wrist. After a moment, he let the inert hand fall and went and leaned against the wall. Then, as if he had suddenly remembered something very important that had to be noted down immediately, he took a notebook from his pocket and wrote a few lines in it. "The son-of-a-bitch," I thought angrily. "He better not come and feel my pulse; I'll give him a punch in his dirty jaw."

He didn't come near me, but I felt he was looking at me. I raised my head and looked back at him. In an impersonal voice, he said, "Don't you think it's frightfully cold here?"

He looked purple with cold.

"I'm not cold," I answered him.

He kept looking at me with a hard expression. Suddenly I understood, and I lifted my hands to my face. I was covered with sweat. Here, in this cellar, in mid-winter, right in a draft, I was sweating. I ran my fingers through my hair, which was stiff with sweat; at the same time, I realized my shirt was damp and sticking to my skin. I had been streaming with perspiration for an hour, at least, and had felt nothing. But this fact hadn't escaped that Belgian swine. He had seen the drops rolling down my face and had said to himself that it showed an almost pathological terror; and he himself had felt normal and proud of it because he was cold. I wanted to get up and go punch his face in, but I had hardly started to make a move before my shame and anger had disappeared. I dropped back onto the bench with indifference.

I was content to rub my neck with my handkerchief because now I felt the sweat dripping from my hair onto the nape of my neck and that was disagreeable. I soon gave up rubbing myself, however, for it didn't do any good; my handkerchief was already wringing wet and I was still sweating. My buttocks, too, were sweating, and my damp trousers stuck to the bench.

Suddenly, Juan said, "You're a doctor, aren't you?"

"Yes," said the Belgian.

"Do people suffer—very long?"

"Oh! When . . . ? No, no," said the Belgian, in a paternal voice, "it's quickly over."

His manner was as reassuring as if he had been answering a paying patient.

"But I . . . Somebody told me—they often have to fire two volleys."

"Sometimes," said the Belgian, raising his head, "it just happens that the first volley doesn't hit any of the vital organs."

"So then they have to reload their guns and aim all over again?" Juan thought for a moment, then added hoarsely, "But that takes time!"

He was terribly afraid of suffering. He couldn't think about anything else, but that went with his age. As for me, I hardly thought about it any more and it certainly was not fear of suffering that made me perspire.

I rose and walked toward the pile of coal dust. Tom gave a start and looked at me with a look of hate. I irritated him because my shoes squeaked. I wondered if my face was as putty-colored as his. Then I noticed that he, too, was sweating. The sky was magnificent; no light at all came into our dark corner and I had only to lift my head to see the Big Bear. But it didn't look the way it had looked before. Two days ago, from my cell in the archbishop's palace, I could see a big patch of sky and each time of day brought back a different memory. In the morning, when the sky was a deep blue, and light, I thought of beaches along the Atlantic; at noon, I could see the sun, and I remembered a bar in Seville where I used to drink manzanilla and eat anchovies and olives; in the afternoon, I was in the shade, and I thought of the deep shadow which covers half of the arena while the other half gleams in the sunlight: it really gave me a pang to see the whole earth reflected in the sky like that. Now, however, no matter how much I looked up in the air, the sky no longer recalled anything. I liked it better that way. I came back and sat down next to Tom. There was a long silence.

Then Tom began to talk in a low voice. He had to keep talking, otherwise he lost his way in his own thoughts. I believe he was talking to me, but he didn't look at me. No doubt he was afraid to look at me, because I was gray and sweating. We were both alike and worse than mirrors for each other. He looked at the Belgian, the only one who was alive.

"Say, do you understand? I don't."

Then I, too, began to talk in a low voice. I was watching the Belgian.

"Understand what? What's the matter?"

"Something's going to happen to us that I don't understand."

There was a strange odor about Tom. It seemed to me that I was more sensitive to odors than ordinarily. With a sneer, I said, "You'll understand, later."

"That's not so sure," he said stubbornly. "I'm willing to be courageous, but at least I ought to know . . . Listen, they're going to take us out into the courtyard. All right. The fellows will be standing in line in front of us. How many of them will there be?"

"Oh, I don't know. Five, or eight. Not more."

"That's enough. Let's say there'll be eight of them. Somebody will shout 'Shoulder arms!' and I'll see all eight rifles aimed at me. I'm sure I'm going to feel like going through the wall. I'll push against the wall as hard as I can with my back, and the wall won't give in. The way it is in a nightmare. . . . I can imagine all that. Ah, if you only knew how well I can imagine it!"

"Skip it!" I said. "I can imagine it too."

"It must hurt like the devil. You know they aim at your eyes and mouth so as to disfigure you," he added maliciously. "I can feel the wounds already. For the last hour I've been having pains in my head and neck. Not real pains—it's worse still. They're the pains I'll feel tomorrow morning. And after that, then what?"

I understood perfectly well what he meant, but I didn't want to seem to understand. As for the pains, I, too, felt them all through my body, like a lot of little gashes. I couldn't get used to them, but I was like him, I didn't think they were very important.

"After that," I said roughly, "you'll be eating daisies."

He started talking to himself, not taking his eyes off the Belgian, who didn't seem to be listening to him. I knew what he had come for, and that what we were thinking didn't interest him. He had come to look at our bodies, our bodies which were dying alive.

"It's like in a nightmare," said Tom. "You want to think of something, you keep having the impression you've got it, that you're going to understand, and then it slips away from you, it eludes you and it's gone again. I say to myself, afterwards, there won't be anything. But I don't really understand what that means. There are moments when I almost do—and then it's gone again. I start to think of the pains, the bullets, the noise of the shooting. I am a materialist, I swear it; and I'm not going crazy, either. But there's something wrong. I see my own corpse. That's not hard, but it's *I* who see it, with *my* eyes. I'll have to get to the point where I think—where I think I won't see anything more. I won't hear anything more, and the world will go on for the others. We're not made to think that way, Pablo. Believe me, I've already stayed awake all night waiting for something. But this is not the same thing. This will grab us from behind, Pablo, and we won't be ready for it."

"Shut up," I said. "Do you want me to call a father confessor?"

He didn't answer. I had already noticed that he had a tendency to prophesy and call me "Pablo" in a kind of pale voice. I didn't like that very much, but it seems all the Irish are like that. I had a vague impression that he smelled of urine. Actually, I didn't like Tom very much, and I didn't see why, just because we were going to die together, I should like him any better. There are certain fellows with whom it would be different—with Ramon Gris, for instance. But between Tom and Juan, I felt alone. In fact, I liked it better that way. With Ramon I might have grown soft. But I felt terribly hard at that moment, and I wanted to stay hard.

Tom kept on muttering, in a kind of absent-minded way. He was certainly talking to keep from thinking. Naturally, I agreed with him, and I could have said everything he was saying. It's not *natural* to die. And since I was going to die, nothing seemed natural any more: neither the coal pile, nor the bench, nor Pedro's dirty old face. Only it was disagreeable for me to think the same things Tom thought. And I knew perfectly well that all night long, within five minutes of each other, we would keep on thinking things at the same time, sweating or shivering at the same time. I looked at him sideways and, for the first time, he seemed strange to me. He had death written on his face. My pride was wounded. For twenty-four hours I had lived side by side with Tom, I had listened to him, I had talked to him, and I knew we had nothing in common. And now we were as alike as twin brothers, simply because we were going to die together. Tom took my hand without looking at me.

"Pablo, I wonder . . . I wonder if it's true that we just cease to exist."

I drew my hand away.

"Look between your feet, you dirty dog."

There was a puddle between his feet and water was dripping from his trousers.

"What's the matter?" he said, frightened.

"You're wetting your pants," I said to him.

"It's not true," he said furiously. "I can't be . . . I don't feel anything."

The Belgian had come closer to him. With an air of false concern, he asked, "Aren't you feeling well?"

Tom didn't answer. The Belgian looked at the puddle without comment.

"I don't know what that is," Tom said savagely, "but I'm not afraid. I swear to you, I'm not afraid."

The Belgian made no answer. Tom rose and went to the corner. He came back, buttoning his fly, and sat down, without a word. The Belgian was taking notes.

We were watching the doctor. Juan was watching him too. All three of us were watching him because he was alive. He had the gestures of a living person, the interests of a living person; he was shivering in this cellar the way living people shiver; he had an obedient, well-fed body. We, on the other hand, didn't feel our bodies any more—not the same way, in any case. I felt like touching my trousers, but I didn't dare to. I looked at the Belgian, well-planted on his two legs, master of his muscles—and able to plan for tomorrow. We were like three shadows deprived of blood; we were watching him and sucking his life like vampires.

Finally he came over to Juan. Was he going to lay his hand on the nape of Juan's neck for some professional reason, or had he obeyed a charitable impulse? If he had acted out of charity, it was the one and only time during the whole night. He fondled Juan's head and the nape of his neck. The kid let him do it, without taking his eyes off him. Then, suddenly, he took hold of the doctor's hand and looked at it in a funny way. He held the Belgian's hand between his own two hands and there was nothing pleasing about them, those two gray paws squeezing that fat red hand. I sensed what was going to happen and Tom must have sensed it, too. But all the Belgian saw was emotion, and he smiled paternally. After a moment, the kid lifted the big red paw to his mouth and started to bite it. The Belgian drew back quickly and stumbled toward the wall. For a second, he looked at us with horror. He must have suddenly understood that we were not men like himself. I began to laugh, and one of the guards started up. The other had fallen asleep with his eyes wide open, showing only the whites.

I felt tired and over-excited at the same time. I didn't want to think any more about what was going to happen at dawn—about death. It didn't make sense, and I never got beyond just words, or emptiness. But whenever I tried to think about something else I saw the barrels of rifles aimed at me. I must have lived through my execution twenty times in succession; one time I thought it was the real thing; I must have dozed off for a moment. They were dragging me toward the wall and I was resisting; I was imploring their pardon. I woke with a start and looked at the Belgian. I was afraid I had cried out in my sleep. But he was smoothing his mustache: he hadn't noticed anything. If I had wanted to, I believe I could have slept for a while. I had been awake for the last forty-eight hours, and I was worn out. But I didn't want to lose two hours of life. They would have had to come and wake me at dawn. I would have followed them, drunk with sleep, and I would have gone off without so much as "Gosh!" I didn't want it that way, I didn't want to die like an animal. I wanted to understand. Besides, I was afraid of having nightmares. I got up and began to walk up and down and, so as to think about something else, I began to think about my past life. Memories crowded in on me, helter-skelter. Some were good and some were bad—at least that was how I had thought of them *before*. There were faces and happenings. I saw the face of a little *novilero* who had gotten himself horned during the *Feria*, in Valencia. I saw the face of one of my uncles, of Ramon Gris. I remembered all kinds of things that had happened: how I had been on strike for three months in 1926, and had almost died of hunger. I recalled a night I had spent on a bench in Granada; I hadn't eaten for three days, I was nearly wild, I didn't want to give up the sponge. I had to smile. With what eagerness I had run after happiness, and women, and liberty! And to what end? I had wanted to liberate Spain, I admired Py Margall, I had belonged to the anarchist movement, I had spoken at public meetings. I took everything as seriously as if I had been immortal.

At that time I had the impression that I had my whole life before me, and I thought to myself, "It's all a god-damned lie." Now it wasn't worth anything because it was finished. I wondered how I had ever been able to go out and have a good time with girls. I wouldn't have lifted my little finger if I had ever imagined that I would die like this. I saw my life before me, finished, closed, like a bag, and yet what was inside was not finished. For a moment I tried to appraise it. I would have liked to say to myself, "It's been a good life." But it couldn't be appraised, it was only an outline. I had spent my time writing checks on eternity, and had understood nothing. Now, I didn't miss anything. There were a lot of things I might have missed: the taste of manzanilla, for instance, or the swims I used to take in summer in a little creek near Cadiz. But death had taken the charm out of everything.

Suddenly the Belgian had a wonderful idea.

"My friends," he said to us, "if you want me to—and providing the military authorities give their consent—I could undertake to deliver a word or some token from you to your loved ones. . . ."

Tom growled, "I haven't got anybody."

I didn't answer. Tom waited for a moment, then he looked at me with curiosity. "Aren't you going to send any message to Concha?"

"No."

I hated that sort of sentimental conspiracy. Of course, it was my fault, since I had mentioned Concha the night before, and I should have kept my mouth shut. I had been with her for a year. Even as late as last night, I would have cut my arm off with a hatchet just to see her again for five minutes. That was why I had mentioned her. I couldn't help it. Now I didn't care any more about seeing her. I hadn't anything more to say to her. I didn't even want to hold her in my arms. I loathed my body because it had turned gray and was sweating— and I wasn't even sure that I didn't loathe hers too. Concha would cry when she heard about my death; for months she would have no more interest in life. But still it was I who was going to die. I thought of her beautiful, loving eyes. When she looked at me something went from her to me. But I thought to myself that it was all over; if she looked at me *now* her gaze would not leave her eyes, it would not reach out to me. I was alone.

Tom too, was alone, but not the same way. He was seated astride his chair and had begun to look at the bench with a sort of smile, with surprise, even. He reached out his hand and touched the wood cautiously, as though he were afraid of breaking something, then he drew his hand back hurriedly, and shivered. I wouldn't have amused myself touching that bench, if I had been Tom, that was just some more Irish play-acting. But somehow it seemed to me too that the different objects had something funny about them. They seemed to have grown paler, less massive than before. I had only to look at the bench, the lamp or the pile of coal dust to feel I was going to die. Naturally, I couldn't think clearly about my death, but I saw it everywhere, even on the different objects, the way they had withdrawn and kept their distance, tactfully, like people talking at the bedside of a dying person. It was *his own death* Tom had just touched on the bench.

In the state I was in, if they had come and told me I could go home quietly, that my life would be saved, it would have left me cold. A few hours, or a few years of waiting are all the same, when you've lost the illusion of being eternal. Nothing mattered to me any more. In a way, I was calm. But it was a horrible kind of calm—because of my body. My body—I saw with its eyes and I heard with its ears, but it was no longer I. It sweat and trembled independently, and I didn't recognize it any longer. I was obliged to touch it and look at it to know what was happening to it, just as if it had been someone else's body. At times I still felt it, I felt a slipping, a sort of headlong plunging, as in a falling airplane, or else I heard my heart beating. But this didn't give me confidence. In fact, everything that came from my body had something damned dubious about it. Most of the time it was silent, it stayed put and I didn't feel anything other than a sort of heaviness, a loathsome presence against me. I had the impression of being bound to an enormous vermin.

The Belgian took out his watch and looked at it.

"It's half-past three," he said.

The son-of-a-bitch! He must have done it on purpose. Tom jumped up. We hadn't yet realized the time was passing. The night surrounded us like a formless, dark mass; I didn't even remember it had started.

Juan started to shout. Wringing his hands, he implored, "I don't want to die! I don't want to die!"

He ran the whole length of the cellar with his arms in the air, then he dropped down onto one of the mattresses, sobbing. Tom looked at him with dismal eyes and didn't even try to console him any more. The fact was, it was no use; the kid made more noise than we did, but he was less affected, really. He was like a sick person who defends himself against his malady with a high fever. When there's not even any fever left, it's much more serious.

He was crying. I could tell he felt sorry for himself; he was thinking about death. For one second, one single second, I too felt like crying, crying out of pity for myself. But just the contrary happened. I took one look at the kid, saw his thin, sobbing shoulders, and I felt I was inhuman. I couldn't feel pity either for these others or for myself. I said to myself, "I want to die decently."

Tom had gotten up and was standing just under the round opening looking out for the first signs of daylight. I was determined, I wanted to die decently, and I only thought about that. But underneath, ever since the doctor had told us the time, I felt time slipping, flowing by, one drop at a time.

It was still dark when I heard Tom's voice.

"Do you hear them?"

"Yes."

People were walking in the courtyard.

"What the hell are they doing? After all, they can't shoot in the dark."

After a moment, we didn't hear anything more. I said to Tom, "There's the daylight."

Pedro got up yawning, and came and blew out the lamp. He turned to the man beside him. "It's hellish cold."

The cellar had grown gray. We could hear shots at a distance.

"It's about to start," I said to Tom. "That must be in the back courtyard."

Tom asked the doctor to give him a cigarette. I didn't want any; I didn't want either cigarettes or alcohol. From that moment on, the shooting didn't stop.

"Can you take it in?" Tom said.

He started to add something, then he stopped and began to watch the door. The door opened and a lieutenant came in with four soldiers. Tom dropped his cigarette.

"Steinbock?"

Tom didn't answer. Pedro pointed him out.

"Juan Mirbal?"

"He's the one on the mattress."

"Stand up," said the Lieutenant.

Juan didn't move. Two soldiers took hold of him by the armpits and stood him up on his feet. But as soon as they let go of him he fell down.

The soldiers hesitated a moment.

"He's not the first one to get sick," said the Lieutenant. "You'll have to carry him, the two of you. We'll arrange things when we get there." He turned to Tom. "All right, come along."

Tom left between two soldiers. Two other soldiers followed, carrying the kid by his arms and legs. He was not unconscious; his eyes were wide open and tears were rolling down his cheeks. When I started to go out, the Lieutenant stopped me.

"Are you Ibbieta?"

"Yes."

"You wait here. They'll come and get you later on."

They left. The Belgian and the two jailers left too, and I was alone. I didn't understand what had happened to me, but I would have liked it better if they had ended it all right away. I heard the volleys at almost regular intervals; at each one, I shuddered. I felt like howling and tearing my hair. But instead, I gritted my teeth and pushed my hands deep into my pockets, because I wanted to stay decent.

An hour later, they came to fetch me and took me up to the first floor in a little room which smelt of cigar smoke and was so hot it seemed to me suffocating. Here there were two officers sitting in comfortable chairs, smoking, with papers spread out on their knees.

"Your name is Ibbieta?"

"Yes."

"Where is Ramon Gris?"

"I don't know."

The man who questioned me was small and stocky. He had hard eyes behind his glasses.

"Come nearer," he said to me.

I went nearer. He rose and took me by the arms, looking at me in a way calculated to make me go through the floor. At the same time he pinched my arms with all his might. He didn't mean to hurt me; it was quite a game; he wanted to dominate me. He also seemed to think it was necessary to blow his fetid breath right into my face. We stood like that for a moment, only I felt more like laughing than anything else. It takes a lot more than that to intimidate a man who's about to die: it didn't work. He pushed me away violently and sat down again.

"It's your life or his," he said. "You'll be allowed to go free if you tell us where he is."

After all, these two bedizened fellows with their riding crops and boots were just men who were going to die one day. A little later than I, perhaps, but not a great deal. And there they were, looking for names among their papers, running after other men in order to put them in prison or do away with them entirely. They had their opinions on the future of Spain and on other subjects. Their petty activities seemed to me to be offensive and ludicrous. I could no longer put myself in their place. I had the impression they were crazy.

The little fat fellow kept looking at me, tapping his boots with his riding crop. All his gestures were calculated to make him appear like a spirited, ferocious animal.

"Well? Do you understand?"

"I don't know where Gris is," I said. "I thought he was in Madrid."

The other officer lifted his pale hand indolently. This indolence was also calculated. I saw through all their little tricks, and I was dumbfounded that men should still exist who took pleasure in that kind of thing.

"You have fifteen minutes to think it over," he said slowly. "Take him to the linen-room, and bring him back here in fifteen minutes. If he continues to refuse, he'll be executed at once."

They knew what they were doing. I had spent the night waiting. After that, they had made me wait another hour in the cellar, while they shot Tom and Juan, and now they locked me in the linen-room. They must have arranged the whole thing the night before. They figured that sooner or later people's nerves wear out and they hoped to get me that way.

They made a big mistake. In the linen-room I sat down on a ladder because I felt very weak, and I began to think things over. Not their proposition, however. Naturally I knew where Gris was. He was hiding in his cousins' house, about two miles outside of the city. I knew, too, that I would not reveal his hiding place, unless they tortured me (but they didn't seem to be considering that). All that was definitely settled and didn't interest me in the least.

Only I would have liked to understand the reasons for my own conduct. I would rather die than betray Gris. Why? I no longer liked Ramon Gris. My friendship for him had died shortly before dawn along with my love for Concha, along with my own desire to live. Of course I still admired him—he was hard. But it was not for that reason that I was willing to die in his place; his life was no more valuable than mine. No life was of any value. A man was going to be stood up against a wall and fired at till he dropped dead. It didn't make any difference whether it was I or Gris or somebody else. I knew perfectly well he was more useful to the Spanish cause than I was, but I didn't give a God damn about Spain or anarchy, either; nothing had any importance now. And yet, there I was. I could save my skin by betraying Gris and I refused to do it. It seemed more ludicrous to me than anything else; it was stubborness.

I thought to myself, "Am I hard-headed!" And I was seized with a strange sort of cheerfulness.

They came to fetch me and took me back to the two officers. A rat darted out under our feet and that amused me. I turned to one of the falangists and said to him, "Did you see that rat?"

He made no reply. He was gloomy, and took himself very seriously. As for me, I felt like laughing, but I restrained myself because I was afraid that if I started, I wouldn't be able to stop. The falangist wore mustaches. I kept after him, "You ought to cut off those mustaches, you fool."

I was amused by the fact that he let hair grow all over his face while he was still alive. He gave me a kind of half-hearted kick, and I shut up.

"Well," said the fat officer, "have you thought things over?"

I looked at them with curiosity, like insects of a very rare species.

"I know where he is," I said. "He's hiding in the cemetery. Either in one of the vaults, or in the gravediggers' shack."

I said that just to make fools of them. I wanted to see them get up and fasten their belts and bustle about giving orders.

They jumped to their feet.

"Fine. Moles, go ask Lieutenant Lopez for fifteen men. And as for you," the little fat fellow said to me, "if you've told the truth, I don't go back on my word. But you'll pay for this, if you're pulling our leg."

They left noisily and I waited in peace, still guarded by the falangists. From time to time I smiled at the thought of the face they were going to make. I felt dull and malicious. I could see them lifting up the gravestones, or opening the doors of the vaults one by one. I saw the whole situation as though I were another person: the prisoner determined to play the hero, the solemn falangists with their mustaches and the men in uniform running around among the graves. It was irresistibly funny.

After half an hour, the little fat fellow came back alone. I thought he had come to give the order to execute me. The others must have stayed in the cemetery.

The officer looked at me. He didn't look at all foolish.

"Take him out in the big courtyard with the others," he said. "When military operations are over, a regular tribunal will decide his case."

I thought I must have misunderstood.

"So they're not—they're not going to shoot me?" I asked.

"Not now, in any case. Afterwards, that doesn't concern me."

I still didn't understand.

"But why?" I said to him.

He shrugged his shoulders without replying, and the soldiers lead me away. In the big courtyard there were a hundred or so prisoners, women, children and a few old men. I started to walk around the grass plot in the middle. I felt absolutely idiotic. At noon we were fed in the dining hall. Two or three fellows spoke to me. I must have known them, but I didn't answer. I didn't even know where I was.

Toward evening, about ten new prisoners were pushed into the courtyard. I recognized Garcia, the baker.

He said to me, "Lucky dog! I didn't expect to find you alive."

"They condemned me to death," I said, "and then they changed their minds. I don't know why."

"I was arrested at two o'clock," Garcia said.

"What for?"

Garcia took no part in politics.

"I don't know," he said. "They arrest everybody who doesn't think the way they do."

He lowered his voice.

"They got Gris."

I began to tremble.

"When?"

"This morning. He acted like a damned fool. He left his cousins' house Tuesday because of a disagreement. There were any number of fellows who would have hidden him, but he didn't want to be indebted to anybody any more. He said, 'I would have hidden at Ibbieta's, but since they've got him, I'll go hide in the cemetery.' "

"In the cemetery?"

"Yes. It was the god-damnedest thing. Naturally they passed by there this morning; that had to happen. They found him in the gravediggers' shack. They opened fire at him and they finished him off."

"In the cemetery!"

Everything went around in circles, and when I came to I was sitting on the ground. I laughed so hard the tears came to my eyes.

FOR STUDY, DISCUSSION, AND WRITING

1. What is the author's tone? What is the story's mood?
2. Discuss the double meaning of the story's wall image.

3. How does Pablo's response to his situation reflect Sartre's existentialist philosophy?

4. Comment on the significance of Tom's remark, "I wonder if it's true that we just cease to exist."

5. What is grimly ironic about the reason the major gives Juan for the three men's being sentenced to death?

6. Describe the prisoners' physical and psychological responses to the news that they have been sentenced to death, noting the differences among them.

7. What is the attitude of the Belgian doctor toward the condemned men? Can you think of any real-life counterparts to this character?

8. As Pablo awaits probable execution, how does he come to regard his relationship with Concha?

9. What is ironic about Pablo's telling his captors that Ramon Gris is hiding in the cemetery?

10. Point out examples of grim humor in the story.

FRANZ KAFKA

A Hunger Artist

During these last decades the interest in professional fasting has markedly diminished. It used to pay very well to stage such great performances under one's own management, but today that is quite impossible. We live in a different world now. At one time the whole town took a lively interest in the hunger artist; from day to day of his fast the excitement mounted; everybody wanted to see him at least once a day; there were people who bought season tickets for the last few days and sat from morning till night in front of his small barred cage; even in the nighttime there were visiting hours, when the whole effect was heightened by torch flares; on fine days the cage was set out in the open air, and then it was the children's special treat to see the hunger artist; for their elders he was often just a joke that happened to be in fashion, but the children stood openmouthed, holding each other's hands for greater security, marveling at him as he sat there pallid in black tights, with his ribs sticking out so prominently, not even on a seat but down among straw on the ground, sometimes giving a courteous nod, answering questions with a constrained smile, or perhaps stretching an arm through the bars so that one might feel how thin it was, and then again withdrawing deep into himself, paying no attention to anyone or anything, not even to the all-important striking of the clock that was the only piece of furniture in his cage, but merely staring into vacancy with half-shut eyes, now and then taking a sip from a tiny glass of water to moisten his lips.

Besides casual onlookers there were also relays of permanent watchers selected by the public, usually butchers, strangely enough, and it was their task to watch the hunger artist day and night, three of them at a time, in case he should have some secret recourse to nourishment. This was nothing but a formality, instituted to reassure the masses, for the initiates knew well enough that during his fast the artist would never in any circumstances, not even under forcible compulsion, swallow the smallest morsel of food; the honor of his profession forbade it. Not every watcher, of course, was capable of understanding this, there were often groups of night watchers who were very lax in carrying out their duties and deliberately huddled together in a retired corner to play cards with great absorption, obviously intending to give the hunger artist the chance of a little refreshment, which they supposed he could draw from some private hoard. Nothing annoyed the artist more than such watchers; they made him miserable; they made his fast seem unendurable; sometimes he mastered his feebleness sufficiently to sing during their watch for as long as he could keep going, to show them how unjust their suspicions were. But that was of little use; they only wondered at his cleverness in being able to fill his mouth even while singing. Much more to his taste were the watchers who sat close up to the bars, who were not content with the dim night lighting of the hall but focused him in the full glare of the electric pocket torch given them by the impresario. The harsh light did not trouble him at all, in any case he could never sleep properly, and he could always drowse a little, whatever the light, at any hour, even when the hall was thronged with noisy onlookers. He was quite happy at the prospect of spending a sleepless night with such watchers; he was ready to exchange jokes with them, to tell them stories out of his nomadic life, anything at all to keep them awake and demonstrate to them again that he had no eatables in his cage and that he was fasting as not one of them could fast. But his happiest moment was when the morning came and an enormous breakfast was brought them, at his expense, on which they flung themselves with the keen appetite of healthy men after a weary night of wakefulness. Of course there were people who argued that this breakfast was an unfair attempt to bribe the watchers, but that was going rather too far, and when they were invited to take on a night's vigil without a breakfast, merely for the sake of the cause, they made themselves scarce, although they stuck stubbornly to their suspicions.

Such suspicions, anyhow, were a necessary accompaniment to the profession of fasting. No one could possibly watch the hunger artist continuously, day and night, and so no one could produce first-hand evidence that the fast had really been rigorous and continuous; only the artist himself could know that, he was therefore bound to be the sole completely satisfied spectator of his own fast. Yet for other reasons he was never satisfied; it was not perhaps mere fasting that had brought him to such skeleton thinness that many people had regretfully to keep away from his exhibitions, because the sight of him was too much for them, perhaps it was dissatisfaction with himself that had worn him down. For he alone knew, what no other initiate knew, how easy it was to fast. It was the easiest thing in the world. He made no secret of this, yet people did not believe him, at the best they set him down as modest, most of them, however, thought he was out for publicity or else was some kind of cheat who found it easy to fast because he had discovered a way of making it easy, and then had the impudence to admit the fact, more or less. He had to put up with all that, and in the course of time had got used to it, but his inner dissatisfaction always rankled, and never yet, after any term of fasting—this must be granted to his credit—had he left the cage of his own free will. The longest period of fasting was fixed by his impresario at forty days, beyond that term he was not allowed to go, not even in great cities, and there was good reason for it, too. Experience had proved that for about forty days the interest of the public could be stimulated by a steadily increasing pressure of advertisement, but after that the town began to lose interest, sympathetic support began notably to fall off; there were of course local variations as between one town and another or one country and another, but as a general rule forty days marked the limit. So on the fortieth day the flower-bedecked cage was opened, enthusiastic spectators filled the hall, a military band played, two doctors entered the cage to measure the results of the fast, which were announced through a megaphone, and finally two young ladies appeared, blissful at having been selected for the honor, to help the hunger artist down the few steps leading to a small table on which was spread a carefully chosen invalid repast. And at this very moment the artist always turned stubborn. True, he would entrust his bony arms to the outstretched helping hands of the ladies bending over him, but stand up he would not. Why stop fasting at this particular moment, after forty days of it? He had held out for a long time, an illimitably long time, why stop now, when he was in his best fasting form, or rather, not yet quite in his best fasting form? Why should he be cheated of the fame he would get for fasting longer, for being not only the record hunger artist of all time, which presumably he was already, but for beating his own record by a performance beyond human imagination, since he felt that there were no limits to his capacity for fasting? His public pretended to admire him so much, why should it have so little patience with him; if he could endure fasting longer, why shouldn't the public endure it? Besides, he was tired, he was comfortable sitting in the straw, and now he was supposed to lift himself to his full height and go down to a meal the very thought of which gave him a nausea that only the presence of the ladies kept him from betraying, and even that with an effort. And he looked up into the eyes of the ladies who were apparently so friendly and in reality so cruel, and shook his head, which felt too heavy on its strengthless neck. But then there happened yet again what always happened. The impresario came forward, without a word—for the band made speech impossible—lifted his arms in the air above the artist, as if inviting Heaven to look down upon its creature here in the straw, this suffering martyr, which indeed he was, although in quite another sense; grasped him around the emaciated waist, with exaggerated caution, so that the frail condition he was in might be appreciated; and committed him to the care of the blenching ladies, not without secretly giving him a shaking so that his legs and body tottered and swayed. The artist now submitted completely; his head lolled on his breast as if it had landed there by chance; his body was hollowed out; his legs in a spasm of self-preservation clung close to each other at the knees, yet scraped on the ground as if it were not really solid ground, as if they were only trying to find solid ground; and the whole weight of his body, a featherweight after all, relapsed onto one of the ladies, who, looking around for help and panting a little—this post of honor was not at all what she had expected it to be—first stretched her neck as far as she could to keep her face at least free from contact with the artist, then finding this impossible, and her more fortunate companion not coming to her aid but merely holding extended in her own trembling hand the little bunch of knucklebones that was the artist's, to the great delight of the spectators burst into tears and had to be replaced by an attendant who had long been stationed in readiness. Then came the food, a little of which the impresario managed to get between the artist's lips, while he sat in a kind of half-fainting trance, to the accompaniment of cheerful patter designed to distract the public's attention from the artist's condition; after that, a toast was drunk to the public, supposedly prompted by a whisper from the artist in the impresario's ear; the band confirmed it with a mighty flourish, the spectators melted away, and no one had any cause to be dissatisfied with the proceedings, no one except the hunger artist himself, he only, as always.

So he lived for many years, with small regular intervals of recuperation, in visible glory, honored by the world, yet in spite of that troubled in spirit, and all the more troubled because no one would take his trouble seriously. What comfort could he possibly need? What more could he possibly wish for? And if some good-natured person, feeling sorry for him, tried to console him by pointing out that his melancholy was probably caused by fasting, it could happen, especially when he had been fasting for some time, that he reacted with an outburst of fury and to the general alarm began to shake the bars of his cage like a wild animal. Yet the impresario had a way of punishing these outbreaks which he rather enjoyed putting into operation. He would apologize publicly for the artist's behavior, which was only to be excused, he admitted, because of the irritability caused by fasting; a condition hardly to be understood by well-fed people; then by natural transition he went on to mention the artist's equally incomprehensible boast that he could fast for much longer than he was doing; he praised the high ambition, the good will, the great self-denial undoubtedly implicit in such a statement; and then quite simply countered it by bringing out photographs, which were also on sale to the public, showing the artist on the fortieth day of a fast lying in bed almost dead from exhaustion. This perversion of the truth, familiar to the artist though it was, always unnerved him afresh and proved too much for him. What was a consequence of the premature ending of his fast was here presented as the cause of it! To fight against this lack of understanding, against a whole world of nonunderstanding, was impossible. Time and again in good faith he stood by the bars listening to the impresario, but as soon as the photographs appeared he always let go and sank with a groan back onto his straw, and the reassured public could once more come close and gaze at him.

A few years later when the witnesses of such scenes called them to mind, they often failed to understand themselves at all. For meanwhile the afore-mentioned change in public interest had set in; it seemed to happen almost overnight; there may have been profound causes for it, but who was going to bother about that; at any rate the pampered hunger artist suddenly found himself deserted one fine day by the amusement-seekers, who went streaming past him to other more-favored attractions. For the last time the impresario hurried him over half Europe to discover whether the old interest might still survive here and there; all in vain; everywhere, as if by secret agreement, a positive revulsion from professional fasting was in evidence. Of course it could not really have sprung up so suddenly as all that, and many premoni-tory symptoms which had not been sufficiently remarked or suppressed dur-ing the rush and glitter of success now came retrospectively to mind, but it was now too late to take any countermeasures. Fasting would surely come into fashion again at some future date, yet that was no comfort for those living in the present. What, then, was the hunger artist to do? He had been applauded by thousands in his time and could hardly come down to showing himself in a street booth at village fairs, and as for adopting another profession, he was not only too old for that but too fanatically devoted to fasting. So he took leave of the impresario, his partner in an unparalleled career, and hired him-self to a large circus; in order to spare his own feelings he avoided reading the conditions of his contract.

A large circus with its enormous traffic in replacing and recruiting men, animals, and apparatus can always find a use for people at any time, even for a hunger artist, provided of course that he does not ask too much, and in this particular case anyhow it was not only the artist who was taken on but his famous and long-known name as well, indeed considering the peculiar nature of his performance, which was not impaired by advancing age, it could not be objected that here was an artist past his prime, no longer at the height of his professional skill, seeking a refuge in some quiet corner of a circus; on the contrary, the hunger artist averred that he could fast as well as ever, which was entirely credible, he even alleged that if he were allowed to fast as he liked, and this was at once promised him without more ado, he could astound the world by establishing a record never yet achieved, a statement that cer-tainly provoked a smile among the other professionals, since it left out of account the change in public opinion, which the hunger artist in his zeal conveniently forgot.

He had not, however, actually lost his sense of the real situation and took it as a matter of course that he and his cage should be stationed, not in the middle of the ring as a main attraction, but outside, near the animal cages, on a site that was after all easily accessible. Large and gaily painted placards made a frame for the cage and announced what was to be seen inside it. When the public came thronging out in the intervals to see the animals, they could hardly avoid passing the hunger artist's cage and stopping there for a moment, perhaps they might even have stayed longer had not those pressing behind them in the narrow gangway, who did not understand why they should be held up on their way toward the excitements of the menagerie, made it impossible for anyone to stand gazing quietly for any length of time. And that was the reason why the hunger artist, who had of course been looking forward to these visiting hours as the main achievement of his life, began instead to shrink from them. At first he could hardly wait for the intervals; it was exhilarating to watch the crowds come streaming his way, until only too soon—not even the most obstinate self-deception, clung to almost consciously, could hold out against the fact—the conviction was borne in upon him that these people, most of them, to judge from their actions, again and again, without exception, were all on their way to the menagerie. And the first sight of them from the distance remained the best. For when they reached his cage he was at once deafened by the storm of shouting and abuse that arose from the two contending factions, which renewed themselves continuously, of those who wanted to stop and stare at him—he soon began to dislike them more than the others—not out of real interest but only out of obstinate self-assertiveness, and those who wanted to go straight on to the animals. When the first great rush was past, the stragglers came along, and these, whom nothing could have prevented from stopping to look at him as long as they had breath, raced past with long strides, hardly even glancing at him, in their haste to get to the menagerie in time. And all too rarely did it happen that he had a stroke of luck, when some father of a family fetched up before him with his children, pointed a finger at the hunger artist, and explained at length what the phenomenon meant, telling stories of earlier years when he himself had watched similar but much more thrilling performances, and the children, still rather uncomprehending, since neither inside nor outside school had they been sufficiently prepared for this lesson—what did they care about fasting?—yet showed by the brightness of their intent eyes that new and better times might be coming. Perhaps, said the hunger artist to himself many a time, things would be a little better if his cage were set not quite so near the menagerie. That made it too easy for people to make their choice, to say nothing of what he suffered from the stench of the menagerie, the animals' restlessness by night, the carrying past of raw lumps of flesh for the beasts of prey, the roaring at feeding times, which depressed him continually. But he did not dare to lodge a complaint with the management; after all, he had the animals to thank for the troops of people who passed his cage, among whom there might always be one here and there to take an interest in him, and who could tell where they might seclude him if he called attention to his existence and thereby to the fact that, strictly speaking, he was only an impediment on the way to the menagerie.

A small impediment, to be sure, one that grew steadily less. People grew familiar with the strange idea that they could be expected, in times like these, to take an interest in a hunger artist, and with this familiarity the verdict went out against him. He might fast as much as he could, and he did so; but nothing could save him now, people passed him by. Just try to explain to anyone the art of fasting! Anyone who has no feeling for it cannot be made to understand it. The fine placards grew dirty and illegible, they were torn down; the little notice board telling the number of fast days achieved, which at first was changed carefully every day, had long stayed at the same figure, for after the first few weeks even this small task seemed pointless to the staff; and so the artist simply fasted on and on, as he had once dreamed of doing, and it was no trouble to him, just as he had always foretold, but no one counted the days, no one, not even the artist himself, knew what records he was already breaking, and his heart grew heavy. And when once in a while some leisurely passer-by stopped, made merry over the old figure on the board, and spoke of swindling, that was in its way the stupidest lie ever invented by indifference and inborn malice, since it was not the hunger artist who was cheating, he was working honestly, but the world was cheating him of his reward.

Many more days went by, however, and that too came to an end. An over-seer's eye fell on the cage one day and he asked the attendants why this perfectly good cage should be left standing there unused with dirty straw inside it; nobody knew, until one man, helped out by the notice board, re-membered about the hunger artist. They poked into the straw with sticks and found him in it. "Are you still fasting?" asked the overseer, "when on earth do you mean to stop?" "Forgive me, everybody," whispered the hunger artist; only the overseer, who had his ear to the bars, understood him. "Of course," said the overseer, and tapped his forehead with a finger to let the attendants know what state the man was in, "we forgive you." "I always wanted you to admire my fasting," said the hunger artist. "We do admire it," said the over-seer, affably. "But you shouldn't admire it," said the hunger artist. "Well then we don't admire it," said the overseer, "but why shouldn't we admire it?" "Because I have to fast, I can't help it," said the hunger artist. "What a fellow you are," said the overseer, "and why can't you help it?" "Because," said the hunger artist, lifting his head a little and speaking, with his lips pursed, as if for a kiss, right into the overseer's ear, so that no syllable might be lost, "because I couldn't find the food I liked. If I had found it, believe me, I should have made no fuss and stuffed myself like you or anyone else." These were his last words, but in his dimming eyes remained the firm though no longer proud persuasion that he was still continuing to fast.
"Well, clear this out now!" said the overseer, and they buried the hunger artist, straw and all. Into the cage they put a young panther. Even the most insensitive felt it refreshing to see this wild creature leaping around the cage that had so long been dreary. The panther was all right. The food he liked was brought him without hesitation by the attendants; he seemed not even to miss his freedom; his noble body, furnished almost to the bursting point with all that it needed, seemed to carry freedom around with it too; somewhere in his jaws it seemed to lurk; and the joy of life streamed with such ardent passion from his throat that for the onlookers it was not easy to stand the shock of it.

But they braced themselves, crowded around the cage, and did not want ever to move away.

Translated by Willa and Edwin Muir

FOR STUDY, DISCUSSION, AND WRITING

1. On the literal level, what events actually take place in the story?
2. Why are we given no names of real places, actual historical events, or real-life persons in the story?
3. Support with specific details from the story the idea that "A Hunger Artist" can be read as an allegory about the plight of the creative artist in modern society or the plight of the religious ascetic in a secular world.
4. Compare and contrast the motivations of the impresario with those of the hunger artist. In what way is the impresario like the impresario of "The Infant Prodigy"?
5. Discuss the possible religious symbolism of the ceremony that accompanies the conclusion of each fast. What point do the reactions of the spectators to this ceremony seem to be making about the condition of the church?
6. What does the panther symbolize? Why have the people come to revere the panther in place of the hunger artist?
7. Compare the qualities of the panther in this story with those of the panther in Balzac's "A Passion in the Desert."
8. The final remarks of the dying hunger artist can be taken as a commentary on the character of creative artists. What point is the hunger artist (Kafka) making?

EUDORA WELTY

A Visit of Charity

It was mid-morning—a very cold, bright day. Holding a potted plant before her, a girl of fourteen jumped off the bus in front of the Old Ladies' Home, on the outskirts of town. She wore a red coat, and her straight yellow hair was hanging down loose from the pointed white cap all the little girls were wearing that year. She stopped for a moment beside one of the prickly dark shrubs with which the city had beautified the Home, and then proceeded slowly toward the building, which was of whitewashed brick and reflected the winter sunlight like a block of ice. As she walked vaguely up the steps she shifted the small pot from hand to hand; then she had to set it down and remove her mittens before she could open the heavy door.

"I'm a Campfire Girl. . . . I have to pay a visit to some old lady," she told the nurse at the desk. This was a woman in a white uniform who looked as if she were cold; she had close-cut hair which stood up on the very top of her head exactly like a sea wave. Marian, the little girl, did not tell her that this visit would give her a minimum of only three points in her score.

"Acquainted with any of our residents?" asked the nurse. She lifted one eyebrow and spoke like a man.

"With any old ladies? No—but—that is, any of them will do," Marian stammered. With her free hand she pushed her hair behind her ears, as she did when it was time to study Science.

The nurse shrugged and rose. "You have a nice *multiflora cineraria* there," she remarked as she walked ahead down the hall of closed doors to pick out an old lady.

There was loose, bulging linoleum on the floor. Marian felt as if she were walking on the waves, but the nurse paid no attention to it. There was a smell in the hall like the interior of a clock. Everything was silent until, behind one of the doors, an old lady of some kind cleared her throat like a sheep bleating. This decided the nurse. Stopping in her tracks, she first extended her arm, bent her elbow, and leaned forward from the hips—all to examine the watch strapped to her wrist; then she gave a loud double-rap on the door.

"There are two in each room," the nurse remarked over her shoulder.

"Two what?" asked Marian without thinking. The sound like a sheep's bleating almost made her turn around and run back.

One old woman was pulling the door open in short, gradual jerks, and when she saw the nurse a strange smile forced her old face dangerously awry. Marian, suddenly propelled by the strong, impatient arm of the nurse, saw next the side-face of another old woman, even older, who was lying flat in bed with a cap on and a counterpane drawn up to her chin.

"Visitor," said the nurse, and after one more shove she was off up the hall.

Marian stood tongue-tied; both hands held the potted plant. The old woman, still with that terrible, square smile (which was a smile of welcome) stamped on her bony face, was waiting. . . . Perhaps she said something. The old woman in bed said nothing at all, and she did not look around.

Suddenly Marian saw a hand, quick as a bird claw, reach up in the air and pluck the white cap off her head. At the same time, another claw to match drew her all the way into the room, and the next moment the door closed behind her.

"My, my, my," said the old lady at her side.

Marian stood enclosed by a bed, a washstand and a chair; the tiny room had altogether too much furniture. Everything smelled wet—even the bare floor.

She held onto the back of the chair, which was wicker and felt soft and damp. Her heart beat more and more slowly, her hands got colder and colder, and she could not hear whether the old women were saying anything or not. She could not see them very clearly. How dark it was! The window shade was down, and the only door was shut. Marian looked at the ceiling. . . . It was like being caught in a robbers' cave, just before one was murdered.

"Did you come to be our little girl for a while?" the first robber asked.

Then something was snatched from Marian's hand—the little potted plant.

"Flowers!" screamed the old woman. She stood holding the pot in an undecided way. "Pretty flowers," she added.

Then the old woman in bed cleared her throat and spoke. "They are not pretty," she said, still without looking around, but very distinctly.

Marian suddenly pitched against the chair and sat down in it.

"Pretty flowers," the first old woman insisted. "Pretty—pretty . . ."

Marian wished she had the little pot back for just a moment—she had forgotten to look at the plant herself before giving it away. What did it look like?

"Stinkweeds," said the other old woman sharply. She had a bunchy white forehead and red eyes like a sheep. Now she turned them toward Marian. The fogginess seemed to rise in her throat again, and she bleated, "Who—are—you?"

To her surprise, Marian could not remember her name. "I'm a Campfire Girl," she said finally.

"Watch out for the germs," said the old woman like a sheep, not addressing anyone.

"One came out last month to see us," said the first old woman.

A sheep or a germ? wondered Marian dreamily, holding onto the chair.

"Did not!" cried the other old woman.

"Did so! Read to us out of the Bible, and we enjoyed it!" screamed the first.

"Who enjoyed it!" said the woman in bed. Her mouth was unexpectedly small and sorrowful, like a pet's.

"We enjoyed it," insisted the other. "You enjoyed it—I enjoyed it."

"We all enjoyed it," said Marian, without realizing that she had said a word.

The first old woman had just finished putting the potted plant high, high on the top of the wardrobe, where it could hardly be seen from below. Marian wondered how she had ever succeeded in placing it there, how she could ever have reached so high.

"You mustn't pay any attention to old Addie," she now said to the little girl. "She's ailing today."

"Will you shut your mouth?" said the woman in bed. "I am not."

"You're a story."

"I can't stay but a minute—really, I can't," said Marian suddenly. She looked down at the wet floor and thought that if she were sick in here they would have to let her go.

With much to-do the first old woman sat down in a rocking chair—still another piece of furniture!—and began to rock. With the fingers of one hand she touched a very dirty cameo pin on her chest. "What do you do at school?" she asked.

"I don't know . . ." said Marian. She tried to think but she could not.

"Oh, but the flowers are beautiful," the old woman whispered. She seemed to rock faster and faster; Marian did not see how anyone could rock so fast.

"Ugly," said the woman in bed.

"If we bring flowers—" Marian began, and then fell silent. She had almost said that if Campfire Girls brought flowers to the Old Ladies' Home, the visit would count one extra point, and if they took a Bible with them on the bus and read it to the old ladies, it counted double. But the old woman had not listened, anyway; she was rocking and watching the other one, who watched back from the bed.

"Poor Addie is ailing. She has to take medicine—see?" she said, pointing a horny finger at a row of bottles on the table, and rocking so high that her black comfort shoes lifted off the floor like a little child's.

"I am no more sick than you are," said the woman in bed.

"Oh, yes you are!"

"I just got more sense than you have, that's all," said the other old woman, nodding her head.

"That's only the contrary way she talks when *you all* come," said the first old lady with sudden intimacy. She stopped the rocker with a neat pat of her feet and leaned toward Marian. Her hand reached over—it felt like a petunia leaf, clinging and just a little sticky.

"Will you hush! Will you hush!" cried the other one.

Marian leaned back rigidly in her chair.

"When I was a little girl like you, I went to school and all," said the old woman in the same intimate, menacing voice. "Not here—another town. . . ."

"Hush!" said the sick woman. "You never went to school. You never came and you never went. You never were anything—only here. You never were born! You don't know anything. Your head is empty, your heart and hands and your old black purse are all empty, even that little old box that you brought with you you brought empty—you showed it to me. And yet you talk, talk, talk, talk, talk all the time until I think I'm losing my mind! Who are you? You're a stranger—a perfect stranger! Don't you know you're a stranger? Is it possible that they have actually done a thing like this to anyone—sent them in a stranger to talk, and rock, and tell away her whole long rigmarole? Do they seriously suppose that I'll be able to keep it up, day in, day out, night in, night out, living in the same room with a terrible old woman—forever?"

Marian saw the old woman's eyes grow bright and turn toward her. This old woman was looking at her with despair and calculation in her face. Her small lips suddenly dropped apart, and exposed a half circle of false teeth with tan gums.

"Come here, I want to tell you something," she whispered. "Come here!"

Marian was trembling, and her heart nearly stopped beating altogether for a moment.

"Now, now, Addie," said the first old woman. "That's not polite. Do you know what's really the matter with old Addie today?" She, too, looked at Marian; one of her eyelids drooped low.

"The matter?" the child repeated stupidly. "What's the matter with her?"

"Why, she's mad because it's her birthday!" said the first old woman, beginning to rock again and giving a little crow as though she had answered her own riddle.

"It is not, it is not!" screamed the old woman in bed. "It is not my birthday, no one knows when that is but myself, and will you please be quiet and say nothing more, or I'll go straight out of my mind!" She turned her eyes toward Marian again, and presently she said in the soft, foggy voice, "When the worst comes to the worst, I ring this bell, and the nurse comes." One of her hands was drawn out from under the patched counterpane—a thin little hand with enormous black freckles. With a finger which would not hold still she pointed to a little bell on the table among the bottles.

"How old are you?" Marian breathed. Now she could see the old woman in bed very closely and plainly, and very abruptly, from all sides, as in dreams. She wondered about her—she wondered for a moment as though there was nothing else in the world to wonder about. It was the first time such a thing had happened to Marian.

"I won't tell!"

The old face on the pillow, where Marian was bending over it, slowly gathered and collapsed. Soft whimpers came out of the small open mouth. It was a sheep that she sounded like—a little lamb. Marian's face drew very close, the yellow hair hung forward.

"She's crying!" She turned a bright, burning face up to the first old woman.

"That's Addie for you," the old woman said spitefully.

Marian jumped up and moved toward the door. For the second time, the claw almost touched her hair, but it was not quick enough. The little girl put her cap on.

"Well, it was a real visit," said the old woman, following Marian through the doorway and all the way out into the hall. Then from behind she suddenly clutched the child with her sharp little fingers. In an affected, high-pitched whine she cried, "Oh, little girl, have you a penny to spare for a poor old woman that's not got anything of her own? We don't have a thing in the world—not a penny for candy—not a thing! Little girl, just a nickel—a penny—"

Marian pulled violently against the old hands for a moment before she was free. Then she ran down the hall, without looking behind her and without looking at the nurse, who was reading *Field & Stream* at her desk. The nurse, after another triple motion to consult her wrist watch, asked automatically the question put to visitors in all institutions: "Won't you stay and have dinner with *us*?"

Marian never replied. She pushed the heavy door open into the cold air and ran down the steps.

Under the prickly shrub she stooped and quickly, without being seen, retrieved a red apple she had hidden there.

Her yellow hair under the white cap, her scarlet coat, her bare knees all flashed in the sunlight as she ran to meet the big bus rocketing through the street.

"Wait for me!" she shouted. As though at an imperial command, the bus ground to a stop.

She jumped on and took a big bite out of the apple.

FOR STUDY, DISCUSSION, AND WRITING

1. What are Marian's motives for visiting the Old Ladies' Home? How does she show her attitude toward the visit?
2. Discuss the possible symbolism of the exterior of the home.
3. Analyze the character of the nurse. How is she like a grown-up Marian?
4. Distinguish between the two old ladies that Marian visits.
5. What is the essential conflict between the two old ladies?
6. What symbolic value can you assign to the red apple in the story?
7. The plant that Marian takes to the old ladies has heart-shaped leaves that are covered with an ash-colored down. Discuss the symbolic value of all this.
8. Does Marian undergo any changes that justify viewing this work as an initiation story?
9. What does this story tell us about modern society's real attitude toward old people?

JESSAMYN WEST

Love, Death, and the Ladies' Drill Team

Emily Cooper, the newest member of the Pocahontas Drill Team, was the first to arrive at the Burnham Building, where the morning practice, called by their drillmaster and team captain, Mrs. Amy Rotunda, was to be held. She stood for a while enjoying the wind—California's warm, dry September wind—before starting up the stairs to Burnham Hall. Burnham Hall was less pretentious than its name, being no more than the drab, unfurnished second floor of the building that housed, on its first floor, Burnham's Hardware, but the only other hall available in the small town of Los Robles was, though its rent was lower, unfortunately located above Sloane & Pierce's Undertaking Parlors.

Emily was halfway up the stairs when she was hailed from the sidewalk below by Mr. Burnham himself, holding a key aloft. "You one of the Pocahontas girls?" he called.

Emily turned about on the stairs and gazed down at the wide-shouldered old man. The wind was lifting his coattails and tossing his white hair about in tufts, like those of the bunch grass she had known as a girl in the Dakotas. She hesitated for a moment before answering. She was a Pocahontas, all right, but "girl" was a different story. She was thirty-six years old, had been married half her life, and had only an hour ago started her youngest off to his first day of school. Then, left without a child in the house for the first time in fifteen years, she had told her passing image in a mirror, "This is the beginning of middle age for you, Emily Cooper." Now "girl."

Mr. Burnham, as if understanding the reason for her hesitation, smiled as she came back down for the key. "My youngest is fifty," he said. Then, perhaps fearing that she might consider such confidences too personal, coming from a stranger, he spoke reassuringly of the weather. "Nice blow we're having—nice touch of wind." He faced about for a second after saying this, to get the full force of the warm, lively agitation, which had everything movable in Los Robles moving.

Actually, this talk of the wind was far more personal to Emily than Mr. Burnham's remark about his children. When he put the key in her hand, she said, "It's wonderful weather. I love the wind." Then she, too, was overtaken by a conviction that there was something unseemly in so much openness with a stranger, and she said a quick thank you and started back up the stairs. As she was unlocking the door, Mr. Burnham called, "Throw open the windows, will you? Modern Woodmen used the hall last night and they're a smoky lot."

Mr. Burnham was right about the Woodmen. Emily felt as if she were stepping into the bowl of a pipe still warm and filled with fumes. There were windows across the entire front of the hall, which faced on Los Robles' Main Street, and she opened them all. Then she pulled a chair up to the middle window and sat down to await the arrival of her teammates. There was not much to be seen on the street below her. Ten o'clock on a Monday morning is not an hour for shoppers, and the children who yesterday would have been out in the wind, shirttails lofted for sails, diving and swooping like birds, but much noisier, were behind closed doors, with shirttails tucked in, and speaking only when nodded to by Teacher. She thought of her own Johnny and hoped he was finding school the wonder he had imagined it. He had left her without a tear, without even a backward look, declaring, with the pleasure of a man who has arrived at a goal long deferred, "Now I am a scholar."

Emily leaned out the window to watch a tumbleweed, blown into town from one of the surrounding barley fields, cross Main at Brown, traveling west swiftly and silently. In the vacant lot across the street, the tall, switch-stemmed dust flowers were bent down almost as low as grass. Beneath the window, the Burnham Hardware sign was swinging, and the awning was bellying and snapping with the sound, she supposed, of a ship under full sail. A few merchants were beginning to go up the street to the Gem for their midmorning cups of coffee. Merchants, the wind revealed, had bodies. Inside their usually unyielding tubes of serge and herringbone, their legs were astonishingly thin. As if in restitution for this exposure, the wind parted their coattails to display their firm and stately bottoms. A black cat passed below, its blackness not even skin-deep, for its hair, wind-blown, exposed a skin as white as that of any butcher-shop rabbit. Emily thrust her hands out across the window sill, feeling through her outspread fingers the full force and warmth of the blowing—as if I were the one true gauge, she thought, the one responsive and harmonious harp.

She was leaning thus, and by now almost half out of the room, when Mrs. Rotunda, the drill captain and coach, and Miss Ruby Graves, the team's star performer, arrived. Emily was new not only to the drill team but to the town of Los Robles, and was still able, she thought, to see people as they really were, unlabeled by a knowledge of their professions or reputations. But "Miss" and "Mrs." are in themselves labels, and Mrs. Rotunda's gray hair, elaborately waved and curled, with a fancy off-center part at the back and sculptured bangs arranged with all the finality of marble, said widow, said woman without a husband, filling in an empty and lonesome life with what, in the old, rich days, she would never have wasted time on. While, somewhat contradictorily, Miss Graves's black hair, long and innocent of the slightest ripple, said spinster, said woman without a husband and reconciled to the idea that her hair, curled or uncurled, was never going to be a matter of moment to any man. But without that "Miss" and "Mrs.," without her knowledge that Amy Rotunda was Fred Rotunda's widow, and Ruby Graves was Milton Graves's unmarried daughter and housekeeper, would she have had all this insight about hair? Emily couldn't say.

It was the same with Opal Tetford and Lacey Philips, who arrived next. Mrs. Tetford's husband was an official in the local Bank of America, while Mrs. Philips's husband owned and operated a big grain ranch out on the edge of town. Knowing this, Emily thought Mrs. Tetford's soft opulence was suited to the protection of vaults and burglar alarms, while Mrs. Philips's rawboned frame was right in its austerity for a background of endless barley fields and rolling, cactus-covered hills.

Mrs. Rotunda said, "I am going to demand that the Woodmen do something about this tobacco smoke. Do they think they're the only ones who use this hall?"

Miss Graves, who prided herself on being unprejudiced about men, though with every reason to justify prejudice, said, "I expect they are chain smokers, Amy. One cigarette after another all evening long."

Mrs. Rotunda, who had no need to conjecture, said, "Well, they could at least use a little Air-Wick afterward." She went to a window and leaned out for a breath of uncontaminated air. The other ladies drew up chairs at the windows. Beneath them, Mr. Sloane, of Sloane & Pierce, passed by on his way to the Gem for his midmorning cup of coffee. Mr. Sloane, like many undertakers, was the picture of rosy durability, an evidence to mourners that though one life had ended, life itself endured.

Mrs. Rotunda withdrew her head from the window and began to pace up and down behind her seated teammates. "No," she declared. "I could never bring myself to do it. Not for a mere two-fifty, anyway."

Emily looked inquiringly at Lacey Philips, who was seated next to her. "The Sloane & Pierce hall rents for two-fifty less than this one," Mrs. Philips explained.

"Save two-fifty at the price of drilling back and forth, quite possibly, over the body of your own dead mother? Not I," said Mrs. Rotunda firmly. "It would take a lot more than two-fifty to reconcile me to that."

Ruby Graves, who, in the manner of maiden ladies, combined extreme idealism on some subjects with extreme matter-of-factness on others, said, "If your mother passed away, Amy, wouldn't they hold the services for her down in Anaheim?"

Mrs. Rotunda replied with patience. "Ruby, I was speaking hypothetically. Mother has owned a plot at Rosemead for I don't know how long, and will, of course, be laid to rest there—not be brought up here to the Sloane & Pierce funeral home to be marched across by Odd Fellows and Knights of Pythias and others for whom such things don't matter. But I only mentioned her as an example. I would have exactly the same scruples about marching over *your* mother."

Ruby turned away from the window. "Mother passed away a year ago Labor Day, Amy," she said in a voice that forgave the forgetfulness.

Mrs. Rotunda put her hands to her head. "Ruby, I could bite my tongue out!" she cried. "My point was—anyone. I'd have too much fellow feeling to be willing to meet above the remains."

Emily said, "I think Sloane & Pierce is a good place for Jehovah's Witnesses to meet, though."

"Do they meet there?" Mrs. Tetford asked. Mrs. Tetford had a reputation for asking questions—trained, they said, by Mr. Tetford, who was a man who liked to supply answers.

Emily nodded.

"Why?" Mrs. Tetford asked.

"I don't know," Emily said.

"I mean why do you think it's a good place for them to meet?"

"Oh. Well, that's one of the things a church is for, isn't it?" Emily asked, and, thinking of her children, seeing them already grown and scattered, and herself and John left alone with their memories, she added, "To remind us that all earthly things pass away?"

Mrs. Rotunda, at the words "pass away," stopped her pacing, and the hall had the silence of a room in which a clock suddenly ceases ticking. The women turned toward her and she extended her arms as if about to ask some extraordinary favor. "Oh, girls!" she cried. "My dear girls! Let's not be morbid. Let's not dwell on the inevitable or we'll have no heart for our practice."

Her life is drilling, Emily thought, smiling. The lodge is her husband and we are her children. She admired Mrs. Rotunda and hoped that, should she ever be left alone, she could be as sensible. Mrs. Rotunda came to the window before which Emily and Lacey sat, and perched between them on the window sill. Gazing down into the street, she shook her head. "Poor girl. Poor, poor girl," she said.

"Imola Ramos?" Emily asked, though there was not, at the moment, anyone else in sight who could possibly be called a girl. Imola was a black-haired, brown-skinned woman of about her own age. Her red-flowered dress, which looked as if it might have started life as a window curtain or a tablecloth, was cut like a Mother Hubbard and belted in closely with what appeared, from the second story of the Burnham Building, to be a piece of gray, frayed clothes-line. It was plain to be seen that she wore no brassière—and not much else, for the wind plastered the big red flowers as close to her thighs as if they were tattooed there.

"Ramos!" Mrs. Rotunda said. "Why, Emily, Imola's name's no more Ramos than yours is. Her name's what it's always been—since she was married, anyway. Fetters. She married LeRoy Fetters so young it's hard to remember that she was born a Butterfield. But it's Fetters now. That Mexican never married her. Couldn't, to do him justice, since LeRoy would never divorce her. And anyway why should he have married her? She was willing to live with him."

"Live with him as man and wife," Ruby explained.

"I never knew they weren't married," Emily said. "I've always heard her called Mrs. Ramos."

Mrs. Rotunda excused this. "You haven't been in Los Robles very long. It takes a little time to catch on to these things."

Imola, who was carrying two shopping bags heavy enough to curve her square shoulders, stepped off the sidewalk and into the vacant lot opposite the Burnham Building. There she set the bags down amidst the blue dust flowers, and while the disturbed cicadas one by one ceased shrilling, she hunted in her purse for her cigarettes. By the time she had her cigarette lighted, the cicadas were once again filling Main Street with their country cries, and Imola, her head on one side, appeared to be listening with pleasure to the sound.

"Why did she leave her husband?" Emily asked.

"That is the mystery," Mrs. Rotunda admitted. "There never was a better man on earth, to my mind, than LeRoy Fetters."

"LeRoy used to wash Imola's hair for her, regular as clockwork, every ten days," Mrs. Philips said.

"Why? I always wondered," Mrs. Tetford asked.

"Pride," Ruby said. "Pure pride in that great mane of black hair."

They were all watching Imola, standing at her ease in the vacant lot, the wind outlining her sturdy body—a woman obviously well and happy.

Disagreeing with Ruby, Mrs. Tetford answered her own question. "In my opinion, LeRoy did it to save the price of a beauty parlor."

Contradicted about motives, Ruby took a new tack. "They say, Mrs. Cooper, that this Mexican manhandles her."

Mrs. Rotunda sniffed. "They say," she said. "I *saw*. Just a week ago today, I saw them having breakfast at the Gem, and Imola had black-and-blue spots the size of quarters on her arms."

Ruby said, "Poor Imola."

"What were *you* doing down at the Gem at breakfast time, Amy?" Mrs. Tetford asked.

"Who said anything about its being breakfast time? As a matter of fact, it was three in the afternoon, and I was having a root-beer float. But those two were having fried eggs and hot cakes, bold as brass, not making the least effort to deceive anyone."

"Why?" Ruby asked. "Why were they having breakfast at that hour?"

"You may well ask, Ruby," said Mrs. Rotunda shortly.

"I feel so sorry for Imola," Mrs. Tetford said.

"They live out near our ranch, you know," Mrs. Philips told them. "They're on the edge of the irrigation ditch, in one of those three-room shacks that the water company furnishes its Mexican workers. Two rooms and a lean-to, really, is what they are. Mattress on the floor, in place of a bed. Old, broken-down, rusty oil stove. Chesterfield with its springs half through the upholstery."

"I wonder how Imola's mother *bears* it," Mrs. Rotunda said.

"Do you ever see them?" Mrs. Tetford asked Mrs. Philips.

"Many's the time. Manuel doesn't seem to have any regular working hours, and in the summertime they do a lot of sporting around together, in and out of the water. And the shoe's on the other foot this time so far's washing is concerned. Imola's the one who does the washing now."

"His hair?" asked Ruby.

"Well, just generally," Mrs. Philips answered.

"A Butterfield washing a Mexican! Sunk that low! It doesn't bear thinking about," Mrs. Tetford said.

"I expect he's pretty dark-skinned?" asked Ruby, who evidently could bear thinking about it.

"They both are," Mrs. Philips explained. "After they finish swimming or washing, whichever it is, they lie around in the sun, sun-tanning. And, like as not, Manuel will play some music for Imola on that instrument of his. That banjo or guitar—I never can tell the two of them apart."

"Fred used to play the clarinet," Mrs. Rotunda said. "He had a natural ear for music and could play anything he'd heard once."

"Is it flat-backed or curved, Lacey?" Mrs. Tetford asked. "This musical instrument?"

"I never did notice."

"Big or little, comparatively speaking?"

"Big," Lacey Philips said.

"It's a guitar, then. I thought it would be. That's the Spanish national instrument."

"He is dressed, I suppose, by the time this music-making starts?" Ruby Graves said.

"Dressed!" Mrs. Philips exclaimed. "Why, Ruby, he sits there strumming out melodies and flinching off flies as innocent of clothes as a newborn babe!"

"And Imola?"

"Naked as a jay bird. Lying in the grass kicking up her heels. Sometimes silent, sometimes singing."

Mrs. Tetford shook her head. "The poor girl."

"Play to her, hit her. I guess Imola runs the full gamut with that man," Ruby speculated.

"Speak of the devil," said Mrs. Philips, motioning with her chin up the street.

Emily, who had been watching Imola as she listened to the talk about her, saw her throw away the stub of her cigarette and wave at the man coming up the street toward her. Ramos was a short, stocky man with a strong, toed-in walk and, when he reached Imola, a quick, white smile. Imola stooped down when he turned in at the vacant lot and brought up out of one of her shopping bags an enormous bunch of purple grapes.

"Isabellas," said Mrs. Philips. "First it's a feast, then it's a fast with them, I guess."

"He's a big, burly fellow," Mrs. Rotunda admitted.

"Naked and singing by the irrigation ditch," Ruby marveled as Imola popped grapes alternately into her own mouth and into that of the Mexican.

"LeRoy Fetters was a registered pharmacist," Mrs. Rotunda told Emily. "A very responsible man. He always took a real interest in whether his prescriptions helped."

"Breakfast at three o'clock," Ruby murmured as the feeding below continued, interspersed with considerable affectionate horseplay. "I wonder what it tastes like at that hour."

"Not a thing in the world to keep you from finding out, is there, Ruby?" Mrs. Rotunda asked.

"I doubt it would be the same alone," Ruby said.

Across the street, the grapes finished, Imola, there in the broad daylight of midmorning and in the middle of Los Robles, first kissed the Mexican full on the mouth, then put a cigarette between his lips and, while he shielded it with his hands, lighted it for him.

The ladies were silent for quite a while after this. Finally, Mrs. Tetford said, "Poor Imola! Where is her pride?"

Imola now lighted a cigarette for herself. Emily, watching the two of them at their ease amid the weeds and dust flowers, the wind carrying their cigarette smoke streaming away from them in transparent plumes, said, to her own surprise, "Pride? Why, Mrs. Tetford, pride doesn't enter in. She loves him."

There was another long silence in the hall. A number of additional members of the drill team had arrived, and Emily felt that her unconsidered word was settling among them like a stone in a pond of still water. But just at the moment when she supposed the last ripple had disappeared, Mrs. Rotunda repeated the word, in a voice that lingered and explored. "Love?" she asked. "Love?"

Is she asking me, Emily thought. But evidently she was not, for before Emily could answer, Mrs. Rotunda had turned her back on the window and was calling the team together. "Girls, girls!" she cried. "Let's not moon! We won't wait for the others. Now, hands on shoulders, and remember, an arm's length apart."

Mrs. Rotunda turned them away from the windows and got them linked together. They reversed by eights, went forward by twos, and formed hollow squares. Emily, still thoughtful, still lingering by the window, saw Imola and the Mexican pick up the shopping bags and proceed, together and equally burdened, down the street. She saw Mr. Sloane return, refreshed, from the Gem to his work. She saw Mr. Burnham out on the edge of the sidewalk, face uplifted as if searching the wind for scents of some lost place or time. She saw how the wind, swooping down off the dry, brown hills, wrapped the soft prints of her drill mates' dresses about their vari-shaped bodies, so that they moved through the elaborate figures of Mrs. Rotunda's planning like women in some picture of past days. And Mrs. Rotunda's brisk commands—"To the rear by twos!" or "The diamond formation!"—were like a little, inconsequential piping, the way the wind, veering, shrills for a second or two through a crack before resuming its own voice, deep and solemn and prophetic.

FOR STUDY, DISCUSSION, AND WRITING

1. Through whose eyes does the reader view the events of the story? What events have contributed to the "crisis" in this person's life?
2. What is ironic about the fact that the drill team is called the *Pocahontas Drill Team?*
3. With the exception of the relationship between Imola and Manuel, how does this story point up sexual isolation between men and women?
4. What is Mrs. Rotunda's idea of a good husband?
5. Contrast Ruby Graves' view of the love affair between Imola Fetters and Manuel Ramos and the view held by Mrs. Rotunda.
6. What does the relationship between Imola and Manuel suggest about the relative importance of pride in a passionate relationship?
7. Why did Imola leave her pharmacist husband? Is it really a "mystery," as Mrs. Rotunda says?

8. Clearly, the wind is an important symbol in this story. What do you think it symbolizes?

9. Point out death images in the story. Why do you think the author relates these images to love?

FLANNERY O'CONNOR

Everything That Rises Must Converge

Her doctor had told Julian's mother that she must lose twenty pounds on account of her blood pressure, so on Wednesday nights Julian had to take her downtown on the bus for a reducing class at the Y. The reducing class was designed for working girls over fifty, who weighed from 165 to 200 pounds. His mother was one of the slimmer ones, but she said ladies did not tell their age or weight. She would not ride the buses by herself at night since they had been integrated, and because the reducing class was one of her few pleasures, necessary for her health, and *free*, she said Julian could at least put himself out to take her, considering all she did for him. Julian did not like to consider all she did for him, but every Wednesday night he braced himself and took her.

She was almost ready to go, standing before the hall mirror, putting on her hat, while he, his hands behind him, appeared pinned to the door frame, waiting like Saint Sebastian for the arrows to begin piercing him. The hat was new and had cost her seven dollars and a half. She kept saying, "Maybe I shouldn't have paid that for it. No, I shouldn't have. I'll take it off and return it tomorrow. I shouldn't have bought it."

Julian raised his eyes to heaven. "Yes, you should have bought it," he said. "Put it on and let's go." It was a hideous hat. A purple velvet flap came down on one side of it and stood up on the other; the rest of it was green and looked like a cushion with the stuffing out. He decided it was less comical than jaunty and pathetic. Everything that gave her pleasure was small and depressed him.

She lifted the hat one more time and set it down slowly on top of her head. Two wings of gray hair protruded on either side of her florid face, but her eyes, sky-blue, were as innocent and untouched by experience as they must have been when she was ten. Were it not that she was a widow who had struggled fiercely to feed and clothe and put him through school and who was supporting him still, "until he got on his feet," she might have been a little girl that he had to take to town.

"It's all right, it's all right," he said. "Let's go." He opened the door himself and started down the walk to get her going. The sky was a dying violet and the houses stood out darkly against it, bulbous liver-colored monstrosities of a uniform ugliness though no two were alike. Since this had been a fashionable neighborhood forty years ago, his mother persisted in thinking they did well to have an apartment in it. Each house had a narrow collar of dirt around it in which sat, usually, a grubby child. Julian walked with his hands in his pockets, his head down and thrust forward and his eyes glazed with the determination to make himself completely numb during the time he would be sacrificed to her pleasure.

The door closed and he turned to find the dumpy figure, surmounted by the atrocious hat, coming toward him. "Well," she said, "you only live once and paying a little more for it, I at least won't meet myself coming and going."

"Some day I'll start making money," Julian said gloomily—he knew he never would—"and you can have one of those jokes whenever you take the fit." But first they would move. He visualized a place where the nearest neighbors would be three miles away on either side.

"I think you're doing fine," she said, drawing on her gloves. "You've only been out of school a year. Rome wasn't built in a day."

She was one of the few members of the Y reducing class who arrived in hat and gloves and who had a son who had been to college. "It takes time," she said, "and the world is in such a mess. This hat looked better on me than any of the others, though when she brought it out I said, 'Take that thing back. I wouldn't have it on my head,' and she said, 'Now wait till you see it on,' and when she put it on me, I said, 'We-ull,' and she said, 'If you ask me, that hat does something for you and you do something for the hat, and besides,' she said, 'with that hat, you won't meet yourself coming and going.' "

Julian thought he could have stood his lot better if she had been selfish, if she had been an old hag who drank and screamed at him. He walked along, saturated in depression, as if in the midst of his martyrdom he had lost his faith. Catching sight of his long, hopeless, irritated face, she stopped suddenly with a grief-stricken look, and pulled back on his arm. "Wait on me," she said. "I'm going back to the house and take this thing off and tomorrow I'm going to return it. I was out of my head. I can pay the gas bill with that seven-fifty."

He caught her arm in a vicious grip. "You are not going to take it back," he said. "I like it."

"Well," she said, "I don't think I ought . . ."

"Shut up and enjoy it," he muttered, more depressed than ever.

"With the world in the mess it's in," she said, "it's a wonder we can enjoy anything. I tell you, the bottom rail is on the top."

Julian sighed.

"Of course," she said, "if you know who you are, you can go anywhere." She said this every time he took her to the reducing class. "Most of them in it are not our kind of people," she said, "but I can be gracious to anybody. I know who I am."

"They don't give a damn for your graciousness," Julian said savagely.

"Knowing who you are is good for one generation only. You haven't the foggiest idea where you stand now or who you are."

She stopped and allowed her eyes to flash at him. "I most certainly do know who I am," she said, "and if you don't know who you are, I'm ashamed of you."

"Oh hell," Julian said.

"Your great-grandfather was a former governor of this state," she said. "Your grandfather was a prosperous landowner. Your grandmother was a Godhigh."

"Will you look around you," he said tensely, "and see where you are now?" and he swept his arm jerkily out to indicate the neighborhood, which the growing darkness at least made less dingy.

"You remain what you are," she said. "Your great-grandfather had a plantation and two hundred slaves."

"There are no more slaves," he said irritably.

"They were better off when they were," she said. He groaned to see that she was off on that topic. She rolled onto it every few days like a train on an open track. He knew every stop, every junction, every swamp along the way, and knew the exact point at which her conclusion would roll majestically into the station: "It's ridiculous. It's simply not realistic. They should rise, yes, but on their own side of the fence."

"Let's skip it," Julian said.

"The ones I feel sorry for," she said, "are the ones that are half white. They're tragic."

"Will you skip it?"

"Suppose we were half white. We would certainly have mixed feelings."

"I have mixed feelings now," he groaned.

"Well let's talk about something pleasant," she said. "I remember going to Grandpa's when I was a little girl. Then the house had double stairways that went up to what was really the second floor—all the cooking was done on the first. I used to like to stay down in the kitchen on account of the way the walls smelled. I would sit with my nose pressed against the plaster and take deep breaths. Actually the place belonged to the Godhighs but your grandfather Chestny paid the mortgage and saved it for them. They were in reduced circumstances," she said, "but reduced or not, they never forgot who they were."

"Doubtless that decayed mansion reminded them," Julian muttered. He never spoke of it without contempt or thought of it without longing. He had seen it once when he was a child before it had been sold. The double stairways had rotted and been torn down. Negroes were living in it. But it remained in his mind as his mother had known it. It appeared in his dreams regularly. He would stand on the wide porch, listening to the rustle of oak leaves, then wander through the high-ceilinged hall into the parlor that opened onto it and gaze at the worn rugs and faded draperies. It occurred to him that it was he, not she, who could have appreciated it. He preferred its threadbare elegance to anything he could name and it was because of it that all the neighborhoods they had lived in had been a torment to him—whereas she had hardly known the difference. She called her insensitivity "being adjustable."

"And I remember the old darky who was my nurse, Caroline. There was no better person in the world. I've always had a great respect for my colored friends," she said. "I'd do anything in the world for them and they'd . . ."

"Will you for God's sake get off that subject?" Julian said. When he got on a bus by himself, he made it a point to sit down beside a Negro, in reparation as it were for his mother's sins.

"You're mighty touchy tonight," she said. "Do you feel all right?"

"Yes I feel all right," he said. "Now lay off."

She pursed her lips. "Well, you certainly are in a vile humor," she observed. "I just won't speak to you at all."

They had reached the bus stop. There was no bus in sight and Julian, his hands still jammed in his pockets and his head thrust forward, scowled down the empty street. The frustration of having to wait on the bus as well as ride on it began to creep up his neck like a hot hand. The presence of his mother was borne in upon him as she gave a pained sigh. He looked at her bleakly. She was holding herself very erect under the preposterous hat, wearing it like a banner of her imaginary dignity. There was in him an evil urge to break her spirit. He suddenly unloosened his tie and pulled it off and put it in his pocket.

She stiffened. "Why must you look like *that* when you take me to town?" she said. "Why must you deliberately embarrass me?"

"If you'll never learn where you are," he said, "you can at least learn where I am."

"You look like a—thug," she said.

"Then I must be one," he murmured.

"I'll just go home," she said. "I will not bother you. If you can't do a little thing like that for me . . ."

Rolling his eyes upward, he put his tie back on. "Restored to my class," he muttered. He thrust his face toward her and hissed, "True culture is in the mind, the *mind*," he said, and tapped his head, "the mind."

"It's in the heart," she said, "and in how you do things and how you do things is because of who you *are*."

"Nobody in the damn bus cares who you are."

"I care who I am," she said icily.

The lighted bus appeared on top of the next hill and as it approached, they moved out into the street to meet it. He put his hand under her elbow and hoisted her up on the creaking step. She entered with a little smile, as if she were going into a drawing room where everyone had been waiting for her. While he put in the tokens, she sat down on one of the broad front seats for three which faced the aisle. A thin woman with protruding teeth and long yellow hair was sitting on the end of it. His mother moved up beside her and left room for Julian beside herself. He sat down and looked at the floor across the aisle where a pair of thin feet in red and white canvas sandals were planted.

His mother immediately began a general conversation meant to attract anyone who felt like talking. "Can it get any hotter?" she said and removed from her purse a folding fan, black with a Japanese scene on it, which she began to flutter before her.

"I reckon it might could," the woman with the protruding teeth said, "but I know for a fact my apartment couldn't get no hotter."

"It must get the afternoon sun," his mother said. She sat forward and looked up and down the bus. It was half filled. Everybody was white. "I see we have the bus to ourselves," she said. Julian cringed.

"For a change," said the woman across the aisle, the owner of the red and white canvas sandals. "I come on one the other day and they were thick as fleas—up front and all through."

"The world is in a mess everywhere," his mother said. "I don't know how we've let it get in this fix."

"What gets my goat is all those boys from good families stealing automobile tires," the woman with the protruding teeth said. "I told my boy, I said you may not be rich but you been raised right and if I ever catch you in any such mess, they can send you on to the reformatory. Be exactly where you belong."

"Training tells," his mother said. "Is your boy in high school?"

"Ninth grade," the woman said.

"My son just finished college last year. He wants to write but he's selling typewriters until he gets started," his mother said.

The woman leaned forward and peered at Julian. He threw her such a malevolent look that she subsided against the seat. On the floor across the aisle there was an abandoned newspaper. He got up and got it and opened it out in front of him. His mother discreetly continued the conversation in a lower tone but the woman across the aisle said in a loud voice, "Well that's nice. Selling typewriters is close to writing. He can go right from one to the other."

"I tell him," his mother said, "that Rome wasn't built in a day."

Behind the newspaper Julian was withdrawing into the inner compartment of his mind where he spent most of his time. This was a kind of mental bubble in which he established himself when he could not bear to be a part of what was going on around him. From it he could see out and judge but in it he was safe from any kind of penetration from without. It was the only place where he felt free of the general idiocy of his fellows. His mother had never entered it but from it he could see her with absolute clarity.

The old lady was clever enough and he thought that if she had started from any of the right premises, more might have been expected of her. She lived according to the laws of her own fantasy world, outside of which he had never seen her set foot. The law of it was to sacrifice herself for him after she had first created the necessity to do so by making a mess of things. If he had permitted her sacrifices, it was only because her lack of foresight had made them necessary. All of her life had been a struggle to act like a Chestny without the Chestny goods, and to give him everything she thought a Chestny ought to have; but since, said she, it was fun to struggle, why complain? And when you had won, as she had won, what fun to look back on the hard times! He could not forgive her that she had enjoyed the struggle and that she thought *she* had won.

What she meant when she said she had won was that she had brought him up successfully and had sent him to college and that he had turned out so well—good looking (her teeth had gone unfilled so that his could be straightened), intelligent (he realized he was too intelligent to be a success), and with a future ahead of him (there was of course no future ahead of him). She excused his gloominess on the grounds that he was still growing up and his radical ideas on his lack of practical experience. She said he didn't yet know a thing about "life," that he hadn't even entered the real world—when already he was as disenchanted with it as a man of fifty.

The further irony of all this was that in spite of her, he had turned out so well. In spite of going to only a third-rate college, he had, on his own initiative, come out with a first-rate education; in spite of growing up dominated by a small mind, he had ended up with a large one; in spite of all her foolish views, he was free of prejudice and unafraid to face facts. Most miraculous of all, instead of being blinded by love for her as she was for him, he had cut himself emotionally free of her and could see her with complete objectivity. He was not dominated by his mother.

The bus stopped with a sudden jerk and shook him from his meditation. A woman from the back lurched forward with little steps and barely escaped falling in his newspaper as she righted herself. She got off and a large Negro got on. Julian kept his paper lowered to watch. It gave him a certain satisfaction to see injustice in daily operation. It confirmed his view that with a few exceptions there was no one worth knowing within a radius of three hundred miles. The Negro was well dressed and carried a briefcase. He looked around and then sat down on the other end of the seat where the woman with the red and white canvas sandals was sitting. He immediately unfolded a newspaper and obscured himself behind it. Julian's mother's elbow at once prodded insistently into his ribs. "Now you see why I won't ride on these buses by myself," she whispered.

The woman with the red and white canvas sandals had risen at the same time the Negro sat down and had gone further back in the bus and taken the seat of the woman who had got off. His mother leaned forward and cast her an approving look.

Julian rose, crossed the aisle, and sat down in the place of the woman with the canvas sandals. From this position, he looked serenely across at his mother. Her face had turned an angry red. He stared at her, making his eyes the eyes of a stranger. He felt his tension suddenly lift as if he had openly declared war on her.

He would have liked to get in conversation with the Negro and to talk with him about art or politics or any subject that would be above the comprehension of those around them, but the man remained entrenched behind his paper. He was either ignoring the change of seating or had never noticed it. There was no way for Julian to convey his sympathy.

His mother kept her eyes fixed reproachfully on his face. The woman with the protruding teeth was looking at him avidly as if he were a type of monster new to her.

"Do you have a light?" he asked the Negro.

Without looking away from his paper, the man reached in his pocket and handed him a packet of matches.

"Thanks," Julian said. For a moment he held the matches foolishly. A NO SMOKING sign looked down upon him from over the door. This alone would not have deterred him; he had no cigarettes. He had quit smoking some months before because he could not afford it. "Sorry," he muttered and handed back the matches. The Negro lowered the paper and gave him an annoyed look. He took the matches and raised the paper again.

His mother continued to gaze at him but she did not take advantage of his momentary discomfort. Her eyes retained their battered look. Her face seemed to be unnaturally red, as if her blood pressure had risen. Julian allowed no glimmer of sympathy to show on his face. Having got the advantage, he wanted desperately to keep it and carry it through. He would have liked to teach her a lesson that would last her a while, but there seemed no way to continue the point. The Negro refused to come out from behind his paper.

Julian folded his arms and looked stolidly before him, facing her but as if he did not see her, as if he had ceased to recognize her existence. He visualized a scene in which, the bus having reached their stop, he would remain in his seat and when she said, "Aren't you going to get off?" he would look at her as at a stranger who had rashly addressed him. The corner they got off on was usually deserted, but it was well lighted and it would not hurt her to walk by herself the four blocks to the Y. He decided to wait until the time came and then decide whether or not he would let her get off by herself. He would have to be at the Y at ten to bring her back, but he could leave her wondering if he was going to show up. There was no reason for her to think she could always depend on him.

He retired again into the high-ceilinged room sparsely settled with large pieces of antique furniture. His soul expanded momentarily but then he became aware of his mother across from him and the vision shriveled. He studied her coldly. Her feet in little pumps dangled like a child's and did not quite reach the floor. She was training on him an exaggerated look of reproach. He felt completely detached from her. At that moment he could with pleasure have slapped her as he would have slapped a particularly obnoxious child in his charge.

He began to imagine various unlikely ways by which he could teach her a lesson. He might make friends with some distinguished Negro professor or lawyer and bring him home to spend the evening. He would be entirely justified but her blood pressure would rise to 300. He could not push her to the extent of making her have a stroke, and moreover, he had never been successful at making any Negro friends. He had tried to strike up an acquaintance on the bus with some of the better types, with ones that looked like professors or ministers or lawyers. One morning he had sat down next to a distinguished-looking dark brown man who had answered his questions with a sonorous solemnity but who had turned out to be an undertaker. Another day he had sat down beside a cigar-smoking Negro with a diamond ring on his finger, but after a few stilted pleasantries, the Negro had rung the buzzer and risen, slipping two lottery tickets into Julian's hand as he climbed over him to leave.

He imagined his mother lying desperately ill and his being able to secure only a Negro doctor for her. He toyed with that idea for a few minutes and then dropped it for a momentary vision of himself participating as a sympathizer in a sit-in demonstration. This was possible but he did not linger with it. Instead, he approached the ultimate horror. He brought home a beautiful suspiciously Negroid woman. Prepare yourself, he said. There is nothing you can do about it. This is the woman I've chosen. She's intelligent, dignified, even good, and she's suffered and she hasn't thought it *fun*. Now persecute us, go ahead and persecute us. Drive her out of here, but remember, you're driving me too. His eyes were narrowed and through the indignation he had generated, he saw his mother across the aisle, purple-faced, shrunken to the dwarf-like proportions of her moral nature, sitting like a mummy beneath the ridiculous banner of her hat.

He was tilted out of his fantasy again as the bus stopped. The door opened with a sucking hiss and out of the dark a large, gaily dressed, sullen-looking colored woman got on with a little boy. The child, who might have been four, had on a short plaid suit and a Tyrolean hat with a blue feather in it. Julian hoped that he would sit down beside him and that the woman would push in beside his mother. He could think of no better arrangement.

As she waited for her tokens, the woman was surveying the seating possibilities—he hoped with the idea of sitting where she was least wanted. There was something familiar-looking about her but Julian could not place what it was. She was a giant of a woman. Her face was set not only to meet opposition but to seek it out. The downward tilt of her large lower lip was like a warning sign: DON'T TAMPER WITH ME. Her bulging figure was encased in a green crepe dress and her feet overflowed in red shoes. She had on a hideous hat. A purple velvet flap came down on one side of it and stood up on the other; the rest of it was green and looked like a cushion with the stuffing out. She carried a mammoth red pocketbook that bulged throughout as if it were stuffed with rocks.

To Julian's disappointment, the little boy climbed up on the empty seat beside his mother. His mother lumped all children, black and white, into the common category, "cute," and she thought little Negroes were on the whole cuter than little white children. She smiled at the little boy as he climbed on the seat.

Meanwhile the woman was bearing down upon the empty seat beside Julian. To his annoyance, she squeezed herself into it. He saw his mother's face change as the woman settled herself next to him and he realized with satisfaction that this was more objectionable to her than it was to him. Her face seemed almost gray and there was a look of dull recognition in her eyes, as if suddenly she had sickened at some awful confrontation. Julian saw that it was because she and the woman had, in a sense, swapped sons. Though his mother would not realize the symbolic significance of this, she would feel it. His amusement showed plainly on his face.

The woman next to him muttered something unintelligible to herself. He was conscious of a kind of bristling next to him, a muted growling like that of an angry cat. He could not see anything but the red pocketbook upright on the bulging green thighs. He visualized the woman as she had stood waiting for her tokens—the ponderous figure, rising from the red shoes upward over the solid hips, the mammoth bosom, the haughty face, to the green and purple hat.

His eyes widened.

The vision of the two hats, identical, broke upon him with the radiance of a brilliant sunrise. His face was suddenly lit with joy. He could not believe that Fate had thrust upon his mother such a lesson. He gave a loud chuckle so that she would look at him and see that he saw. She turned her eyes on him slowly. The blue in them seemed to have turned a bruised purple. For a moment he had an uncomfortable sense of her innocence, but it lasted only a second before principle rescued him. Justice entitled him to laugh. His grin hardened until it said to her as plainly as if he were saying aloud: Your punishment exactly fits your pettiness. This should teach you a permanent lesson.

Her eyes shifted to the woman. She seemed unable to bear looking at him and to find the woman preferable. He became conscious again of the bristling presence at his side. The woman was rumbling like a volcano about to become active. His mother's mouth began to twitch slightly at one corner. With a sinking heart, he saw incipient signs of recovery on her face and realized that this was going to strike her suddenly as funny and was going to be no lesson at all. She kept her eyes on the woman and an amused smile came over her face as if the woman were a monkey that had stolen her hat. The little Negro was looking up at her with large fascinated eyes. He had been trying to attract her attention for some time.

"Carver!" the woman said suddenly. "Come heah!"

When he saw that the spotlight was on him at last, Carver drew his feet up and turned himself toward Julian's mother and giggled.

"Carver!" the woman said. "You heah me? Come heah!"

Carver slid down from the seat but remained squatting with his back against the base of it, his head turned slyly around toward Julian's mother, who was smiling at him. The woman reached a hand across the aisle and snatched him to her. He righted himself and hung backwards on her knees, grinning at Julian's mother. "Isn't he cute?" Julian's mother said to the woman with the protruding teeth.

"I reckon he is," the woman said without conviction.

The Negress yanked him upright but he eased out of her grip and shot across the aisle and scrambled, giggling wildly, onto the seat beside his love.

"I think he likes me," Julian's mother said, and smiled at the woman. It was the smile she used when she was being particularly gracious to an inferior. Julian saw everything lost. The lesson had rolled off her like rain on a roof.

The woman stood up and yanked the little boy off the seat as if she were snatching him from contagion. Julian could feel the rage in her at having no weapon like his mother's smile. She gave the child a sharp slap across his leg. He howled once and then thrust his head into her stomach and kicked his feet against her shins. "Be-have," she said vehemently.

The bus stopped and the Negro who had been reading the newspaper got off. The woman moved over and set the little boy down with a thump between herself and Julian. She held him firmly by the knee. In a moment he put his hands in front of his face and peeped at Julian's mother through his fingers.

"I see yoooooooo!" she said and put her hand in front of her face and peeped at him.

The woman slapped his hand down. "Quit yo' foolishness," she said, "before I knock the living Jesus out of you!"

Julian was thankful that the next stop was theirs. He reached up and pulled the cord. The woman reached up and pulled it at the same time. Oh my God, he thought. He had the terrible intuition that when they got off the bus together, his mother would open her purse and give the little boy a nickel. The gesture would be as natural to her as breathing. The bus stopped and the woman got up and lunged to the front, dragging the child, who wished to stay on, after her. Julian and his mother got up and followed. As they neared the door, Julian tried to relieve her of her pocketbook.

"No," she murmured, "I want to give the little boy a nickel."

"No!" Julian hissed. "No!"

She smiled down at the child and opened her bag. The bus door opened and the woman picked him up by the arm and descended with him, hanging at her hip. Once in the street she set him down and shook him.

Julian's mother had to close her purse while she got down the bus step but as soon as her feet were on the ground, she opened it again and began to rummage inside. "I can't find but a penny," she whispered, "but it looks like a new one."

"Don't do it!" Julian said fiercely between his teeth. There was a streetlight on the corner and she hurried to get under it so that she could better see into her pocketbook. The woman was heading off rapidly down the street with the child still hanging backward on her hand.

"Oh little boy!" Julian's mother called and took a few quick steps and caught up with them just beyond the lamppost. "Here's a bright new penny for you," and she held out the coin, which shone bronze in the dim light.

The huge woman turned and for a moment stood, her shoulders lifted and her face frozen with frustrated rage, and stared at Julian's mother. Then all at once she seemed to explode like a piece of machinery that had been given one ounce of pressure too much. Julian saw the black fist swing out with the red pocketbook. He shut his eyes and cringed as he heard the woman shout, "He don't take nobody's pennies!" When he opened his eyes, the woman was disappearing down the street with the little boy staring wide-eyed over her shoulder. Julian's mother was sitting on the sidewalk.

"I told you not to do that," Julian said angrily. "I told you not to do that!"

He stood over her for a minute, gritting his teeth. Her legs were stretched out in front of her and her hat was on her lap. He squatted down and looked her in the face. It was totally expressionless. "You got exactly what you deserved," he said. "Now get up."

He picked up her pocketbook and put what had fallen out back in it. He picked the hat up off her lap. The penny caught his eye on the sidewalk and he picked that up and let it drop before her eyes into the purse. Then he stood up and leaned over and held his hands out to pull her up. She remained immobile. He sighed. Rising above them on either side were black apartment buildings, marked with irregular rectangles of light. At the end of the block a man came out of a door and walked off in the opposite direction. "All right," he said, "suppose somebody happens by and wants to know why you're sitting on the sidewalk?"

She took the hand and, breathing hard, pulled heavily up on it and then stood for a moment, swaying slightly as if the spots of light in the darkness were circling around her. Her eyes, shadowed and confused, finally settled on his face. He did not try to conceal his irritation. "I hope this teaches you a lesson," he said. She leaned forward and her eyes raked his face. She seemed trying to determine his identity. Then, as if she found nothing familiar about him, she started off with a headlong movement in the wrong direction.

"Aren't you going on to the Y?" he asked.

"Home," she muttered.

"Well, are we walking?"

For answer she kept going. Julian followed along, his hands behind him. He saw no reason to let the lesson she had had go without backing it up with an explanation of its meaning. She might as well be made to understand what had happened to her. "Don't think that was just an uppity Negro woman," he said. "That was the whole colored race which will no longer take your condescending pennies. That was your black double. She can wear the same hat as you, and to be sure," he added gratuitously (because he thought it was funny), "it looked better on her than it did on you. What all this means," he said, "is that the old world is gone. The old manners are obsolete and your graciousness is not worth a damn." He thought bitterly of the house that had been lost for him. "You aren't who you think you are," he said.

She continued to plow ahead, paying no attention to him. Her hair had come undone on one side. She dropped her pocketbook and took no notice. He stooped and picked it up and handed it to her but she did not take it.

"You needn't act as if the world had come to an end," he said, "because it hasn't. From now on you've got to live in a new world and face a few realities for a change. Buck up," he said, "it won't kill you."

She was breathing fast.

"Let's wait on the bus," he said.

"Home," she said thickly.

"I hate to see you behave like this," he said. "Just like a child. I should be able to expect more of you." He decided to stop where he was and make her stop and wait for a bus. "I'm not going any farther," he said, stopping. "We're going on the bus."

She continued to go on as if she had not heard him. He took a few steps and caught her arm and stopped her. He looked into her face and caught his breath. He was looking into a face he had never seen before. "Tell Grandpa to come get me," she said.

He stared, stricken.

"Tell Caroline to come get me," she said.

Stunned, he let her go and she lurched forward again, walking as if one leg were shorter than the other. A tide of darkness seemed to be sweeping her from him. "Mother!" he cried. "Darling, sweetheart, wait!" Crumpling, she fell to the pavement. He dashed forward and fell at her side, crying, "Mamma, Mamma!" He turned her over. Her face was fiercely distorted. One eye, large and staring, moved slightly to the left as if it had become unmoored. The other remained fixed on him, raked his face again, found nothing and closed.

"Wait here, wait here!" he cried and jumped up and began to run for help toward a cluster of lights he saw in the distance ahead of him. "Help, help!" he shouted, but his voice was thin, scarcely a thread of sound. The lights drifted farther away the faster he ran and his feet moved numbly as if they carried him nowhere. The tide of darkness seemed to sweep him back to her, postponing from moment to moment his entry into the world of guilt and sorrow.

FOR STUDY, DISCUSSION, AND WRITING

1. What is Julian's opinion of himself at the beginning of the story?
2. How are the lives of both Julian and his mother tied to the past?

3. Point out specific items or instances that show how Julian is hypocritical.
4. Discuss Julian's mother and the black woman as character foils.
5. In what ways has Julian misjudged his relationship with his mother?
6. What is the symbolic value of the hideous hats worn by Mrs. Chestny and the black woman?
7. Point out instances where the author uses eye descriptions to provide insight into the mental state of her characters.
8. Why does Mrs. Chestny's behavior toward the black child infuriate the child's mother?
9. As a result of his mother's death, do you think Julian has gained any lasting insights into life?

MORDECAI RICHLER

Some Grist for Mervyn's Mill

Mervyn Kaplansky stepped out of the rain on a dreary Saturday afternoon in August to inquire about our back bedroom.

"It's twelve dollars a week," my father said, "payable in advance."

Mervyn set down forty-eight dollars on the table. Astonished, my father retreated a step. "What's the rush-rush? Look around first. Maybe you won't like it here."

"You believe in electricity?"

There were no lights on in the house. "We're not the kind to skimp," my father said. "But we're orthodox here. Today is *shabus*."

"No, no, no. Between people."

"What are you? A wise-guy."

"I do. And as soon as I came in here I felt the right vibrations. Hi, kid." Mervyn grinned breezily at me, but the hand he mussed my hair with was shaking. "I'm going to love it here."

My father watched, disconcerted but too intimidated to protest, as Mervyn sat down on the bed, bouncing a little to try the mattress. "Go get your mother right away," he said to me.

Fortunately, she had just entered the room. I didn't want to miss anything.

"Meet your new roomer," Mervyn said, jumping up.

"Hold your horses." My father hooked his thumbs in his suspenders. "What do you do for a living?" he asked.

"I'm a writer."

"With what firm?"

"No, no, no. For myself. I'm a creative artist."

My father could see at once that my mother was enraptured and so, reconciled to yet another defeat, he said. "Haven't you any . . . things?"

"When Oscar Wilde entered the United States and they asked him if he had anything to declare, he said, 'Only my genius.' "

My father made a sour face.

"My things are at the station, " Mervyn said, swallowing hard. "May I bring them over?"

"Bring."

Mervyn returned an hour or so later with his trunk, several suitcases, and an assortment of oddities that included a piece of driftwood, a wine bottle that had been made into a lamp base, a collection of pebbles, a twelve-inch-high replica of Rodin's *The Thinker*, a bull-fight poster, a Karsh portrait of G.B.S., innumerable notebooks, a ball-point pen with a built-in flashlight, and a framed cheque for fourteen dollars and eighty-five cents from the *Family Herald & Weekly Star*.

"Feel free to borrow any of our books," my mother said.

"Well, thanks. But I try not to read too much now that I'm a wordsmith myself. I'm afraid of being influenced, you see."

Mervyn was a short, fat boy with curly black hair, warm wet eyes, and an engaging smile. I could see his underwear through the triangles of tension that ran from button to button down his shirt. The last button had probably burst off. It was gone. Mervyn, I figured, must have been at least twenty-three years old, but he looked much younger.

"Where did you say you were from?" my father asked.

"I didn't."

Thumbs hooked in his suspenders, rocking on his heels, my father waited.

"Toronto," Mervyn said bitterly. "Toronto the Good. My father's a bigtime insurance agent and my brothers are in ladies' wear. They're in the rat-race. All of them."

"You'll find that in this house," my mother said, "we are not materialists."

Mervyn slept in—or, as he put it, stocked the unconscious—until noon every day. He typed through the afternoon and then, depleted, slept some more, and usually typed again deep into the night. He was the first writer I had ever met and I worshipped him. So did my mother.

"Have you ever noticed his hands," she said, and I thought she was going to lecture me about his chewed-up fingernails, but what she said was, "They're artist's hands. Your grandfather had hands like that." If a neighbour dropped in for tea, my mother would whisper, "We'll have to speak quietly," and, indicating the tap-tap of the typewriter from the back bedroom, she'd add, "in there, Mervyn is creating." My mother prepared special dishes for Mervyn. Soup, she felt, was especially nourishing. Fish was the best brain food. She discouraged chocolates and nuts because of Mervyn's complexion, but she brought him coffee at all hours, and if a day passed with no sound coming from the back room my mother would be extremely upset. Eventually, she'd knock softly on Mervyn's door. "Anything I can get you?" she'd ask.

"It's no use. It just isn't coming today. I go through periods like that, you know."

Mervyn was writing a novel, his first, and it was about the struggles of our people in a hostile society. The novel's title was, to begin with, a secret between Mervyn and my mother. Occasionally, he read excerpts to her. She made only one correction. "I wouldn't say 'whore'," she said. "It isn't nice, is it? Say 'lady of easy virtue.' " The two of them began to go in for literary discussions. "Shakespeare," my mother would say, "Shakespeare knew everything." And Mervyn, nodding, would reply, "But he stole all his plots. He was a plagiarist." My mother told Mervyn about her father, the rabbi, and the books he had written in Yiddish. "At his funeral," she told him, "they had to have six motorcycle policemen to control the crowds." More than once my father came home from work to find the two of them still seated at the kitchen table, and his supper wasn't ready or he had to eat a cold plate. Flushing, stammering apologies, Mervyn would flee to his room. He was, I think, the only man who was ever afraid of my father, and this my father found very heady stuff. He spoke gruffly, even profanely in Mervyn's presence, and called him Moitle behind his back. But, when you come down to it, all my father had against Mervyn was the fact that my mother no longer baked potato kugel. (Starch was bad for Mervyn.) My father began to spend more of his time playing cards at Tansky's Cigar & Soda, and when Mervyn fell behind with the rent, he threatened to take action.

"But you can't trouble him now," my mother said, "when he's in the middle of his novel. He works so hard. He's a genius maybe."

"He's peanuts, or what's he doing here?"

I used to fetch Mervyn cigarettes and headache tablets from the drugstore round the corner. On some days when it wasn't coming, the two of us would play casino and Mervyn, at his breezy best, used to wisecrack a lot. "What would you say," he said, "if I told you I aim to out-Emile Zola?" Once he let me read one of his stories, Was The Champ A Chump?, that had been printed in magazines in Australia and South Africa. I told him that I wanted to be a writer too. "Kid," he said, "a word from the wise. Never become a wordsmith. Digging ditches would be easier."

From the day of his arrival Mervyn had always worked hard, but what with his money running low he was now so determined to get his novel done, that he seldom went out any more. Not even for a stroll. My mother felt this was bad for his digestion. So she arranged a date with Molly Rosen. Molly, who lived only three doors down the street, was the best looker on St. Urbain, and my mother noticed that for weeks now Mervyn always happened to be standing by the window when it was time for Molly to pass on the way home from work. "Now you go out," my mother said, "and enjoy. You're still a youngster. The novel can wait for a day."

"But what does Molly want with me?"

"She's crazy to meet you. For weeks now she's been asking questions."

Mervyn complained that he lacked a clean shirt, he pleaded a headache, but my mother said, "Don't be afraid she won't eat you." All at once Mervyn's tone changed. He tilted his head cockily. "Don't wait up for me," he said.

Mervyn came home early. "What happened?" I asked.

"I got bored."

"*With* Molly?"

"Molly's an insect. Sex is highly over-estimated, you know. It also saps an artist's creative energies."

But when my mother came home from her Talmud Torah meeting and discovered that Mervyn had come home so early she felt that she had been personally affronted. Mrs. Rosen was summoned to tea.

"It's a Saturday night," she said, "she puts on her best dress, and that cheapskate where does he take her? To sit on the mountain. Do you know that she turned down three other boys, including Ready-To-Wear's *only* son, because you made such a *gedille?*"

"With dumb-bells like Ready-To-Wear she can have dates any night of the week. Mervyn's a creative artist."

"On a Saturday night to take a beautiful young thing to sit on the mountain. From those benches you can get piles."

"Don't be disgusting."

"She's got on her dancing shoes and you know what's for him a date? To watch the people go by. He likes to make up stories about them he says. You mean it breaks his heart to part with a dollar."

"To bring up your daughter to be a gold-digger. For shame."

"All right. I wasn't going to blab, but if that's how you feel—modern men and women, he told her, experiment *before* marriage. And right there on the bench he tried dirty filthy things with her. He . . ."

"Don't draw me no pictures. If I know your Molly he didn't have to try so hard."

"How dare you! She went out with him it was a favour for the marble cake recipe. The dirty piker he asked her to marry him he hasn't even got a job. She laughed in his face."

Mervyn denied that he had tried any funny stuff with Molly—he had too much respect for womankind, he said—but after my father heard that he had come home so early he no longer teased Mervyn when he stood by the window to watch Molly pass. He even resisted making wisecracks when Molly's kid brother returned Mervyn's thick letters unopened. Once, he tried to console Mervyn. "With a towel over the face," he said gruffly, "one's the same as another."

Mervyn's cheeks reddened. He coughed. And my father turned away, disgusted.

"Make no mistake," Mervyn said with a sudden jaunty smile. "You're talking to a boy who's been around. We pen-pushers are notorious lechers."

Mervyn soon fell behind with the rent again and my father began to complain.

"You can't trouble him now," my mother said. "He's in agony. It isn't coming today."

"Yeah, sure. The trouble is there's something coming to me."

"Yesterday he read me a chapter from his book. It's so beautiful you could die." My mother told him that F. J. Kugelman, the Montreal correspondent of *The Jewish Daily Forward*, had looked at the book. "He says Mervyn is a very deep writer."

"Kugelman's for the birds. If Mervyn's such a big writer, let him make me out a cheque for the rent. That's my kind of reading, you know."

"Give him one week more. Something will come through for him, I'm sure."

My father waited another week, counting off the days. "E-Day minus three today," he'd say. "Anything come through for the genius?" Nothing, not one lousy dime, came through for Mervyn. In fact he had secretly borrowed from my mother for the postage to send his novel to a publisher in New York. "E-Day minus one today," my father said. And then, irritated because he had yet to be asked what the E stood for, he added, "E for Eviction."

On Friday my mother prepared an enormous potato kugel. But when my father came home, elated, the first thing he said was, "Where's Mervyn?"

"Can't you wait until after supper, even?"

Mervyn stepped softly into the kitchen. "You want me?" he asked.

My father slapped a magazine down on the table. *Liberty*. He opened it at a short story titled *A Doll For The Deacon*. "Mel Kane, Jr.," he said, "isn't that your literary handle?"

"His *nom-de-plume*," my mother said.

"Then the story is yours." My father clapped Mervyn on the back. "Why didn't you tell me you were a writer? I thought you were a . . . well, a fruitcup. You know what I mean. A long-hair."

"Let me see that," my mother said.

Absently, my father handed her the magazine. "You mean to say," he said, "you made all that up out of your own head?"

Mervyn nodded. He grinned. But he could see that my mother was displeased.

"It's a top-notch story," my father said. Smiling, he turned to my mother. "All the time I thought he was a sponger. A poet. He's a writer. Can you beat that?" He laughed, delighted. "Excuse me," he said, and he went to wash his hands.

"Here's your story, Mervyn," my mother said. "I'd rather not read it."

Mervyn lowered his head.

"But you don't understand, Maw. Mervyn has to do that sort of stuff. For the money. He's got to eat too, you know."

My mother reflected briefly. "A little tip, then," she said to Mervyn. "Better he doesn't know why . . . well, you understand."

"Sure I do."

At supper my father said, "Hey, what's your novel called, Mr. Kane?"

"The DIRTY JEWS."

"*Are you crazy?*"

"It's an ironic title," my mother said.

"Wow! It sure is."

"I want to throw the lie back in their ugly faces," Mervyn said.

"Yeah. Yeah, sure." My father invited Mervyn to Tansky's to meet the boys. "In one night there," he said, "you can pick up enough material for a book."

"I don't think Mervyn is interested."

Mervyn, I could see, looked dejected. But he didn't dare antagonize my mother. Remembering something he had once told me, I said, "To a creative writer every experience is welcome."

"Yes, that's true," my mother said. "I hadn't thought of it like that."

So my father, Mervyn and I set off together. My father showed *Liberty* to all of Tansky's regulars. While Mervyn lit one cigarette off another, coughed, smiled foolishly and coughed again, my father introduced him as the up-and-coming writer.

"If he's such a big writer what's he doing on St. Urbain Street?"

My father explained that Mervyn had just finished his first novel. "When that comes out," he said, "this boy will be batting in the major leagues."

The regulars looked Mervyn up and down. His suit was shiny.

"You must understand," Mervyn said, "that, at the best of times, it's difficult for an artist to earn a living. Society is naturally hostile to us."

"So what's so special? I'm a plumber. Society isn't hostile to me, but I've got the same problem. Listen here, it's hard for anybody to earn a living."

"You don't get it," Mervyn said, retreating a step. "*I'm* in rebellion against society."

Tansky moved away, disgusted. "Gorki, there was a writer. This boy. . . ."

Molly's father thrust himself into the group surrounding Mervyn. "You wrote a novel," he asked, "it's true?"

"It's with a big publisher in New York right now," my father said.

"You should remember," Takifman said menacingly, "only to write good things about the Jews."

Shapiro winked at Mervyn. The regulars smiled, some shyly, others hopeful, believing. Mervyn looked back at them solemnly "It is my profound hope," he said, "that in the years to come our people will have every reason to be proud of me."

Segal stood Mervyn for a Pepsi and a sandwich. "Six months from now," he said, "I'll be saying I knew you when. . . ."

Mervyn whirled around on his counter stool. "I'm going to out-Emile Zola," he said. He shook with laughter.

"Do you think there's going to be another war?" Perlman asked.

"Oh, lay off," my father said. "Give the man air. No wisdom outside of office hours, eh, Mervyn?"

Mervyn slapped his knees and laughed some more. Molly's father pulled him aside. "You wrote this story," he said, holding up *Liberty*, "and don't lie because I'll find you out."

"Yeah," Mervyn said, "I'm the grub-streeter who knocked that one off. But it's my novel that I really care about."

"You know who I am? I'm Molly's father. Rosen. Put it there, Mervyn. There's nothing to worry. You leave everything to me."

My mother was still awake when we got home. Alone at the kitchen table. "You were certainly gone a long time," she said to Mervyn.

"Nobody forced him to stay."

"He's too polite," my mother said, slipping her tooled leather bookmark between the pages of *Wuthering Heights*. "He wouldn't tell you when he was bored by such common types."

"Hey," my father said, remembering. "Hey, Mervyn. Can you beat that Takifman for a character?"

Mervyn started to smile, but my mother sighed and he looked away. "It's time I hit the hay," he said.

"Well," my father pulled down his suspenders. "If anyone wants to use the library let him speak now or forever hold his peace."

"*Please, Sam.* You only say things like that to disgust me. I know that."

My father went into Mervyn's room. He smiled a little. Mervyn waited, puzzled. My father rubbed his forehead. He pulled his ear. "Well, I'm not a fool. You should know that. Life does things to you, but . . ."

"It certainly does, Mr. Hersh."

"You won't end up a zero like me. So I'm glad for you. Well, good night."

But my father did not go to bed immediately. Instead, he got out his collection of pipes, neglected all these years, and sat down at the kitchen table to clean and restore them. And, starting the next morning, he began to search out and clip items in the newspapers, human interest stories with a twist, that might be exploited by Mervyn. When he came home from work—early, he had not stopped off at Tansky's—my father did not demand his supper right off but, instead, went directly to Mervyn's room. I could hear the two men talking in low voices. Finally, my mother had to disturb them. Molly was on the phone.

"Mr. Kaplansky. Mervyn. Would you like to take me out on Friday night? I'm free."

Mervyn didn't answer.

"We could watch the people go by. Anything you say, Mervyn."

"Did your father put you up to this?"

"What's the diff? You wanted to go out with me. Well, on Friday, I'm free."

"I'm sorry. I can't do it."

"Don't you like me any more?"

"I sure do. And the attraction is more than merely sexual. But if we go out together it will have to be because you so desire it."

"Mervyn, if you don't take me out on Friday he won't let me out to the dance Saturday night with Solly. Please, Mervyn."

"Sorry. But I must answer in the negative."

Mervyn told my mother about the telephone conversation and immediately she said, "You did right." But a few days later, she became tremendously concerned about Mervyn. He no longer slept in each morning. Instead, he was the first one up in the house, to wait by the window for the postman. After he had passed, however, Mervyn did not settle down to work. He'd wander sluggishly about the house or go out for a walk. Usually, Mervyn ended up at Tansky's. My father would be waiting there.

"You know," Sugarman said, "many amusing things have happened to me in my life. It would make *some* book."

The men wanted to know Mervyn's opinion of Sholem Asch, the red menace, and ungrateful children. They teased him about my father. "To hear him tell it you're a guaranteed genius."

"Well," Mervyn said, winking, blowing on his fingernails and rubbing them against his jacket lapel, "Who knows?"

But Molly's father said, "I read in the *Gazette* this morning where Hemingway was paid a hundred thousand dollars to make a movie from *one* story. A complete book must be worth at least five short stories. Wouldn't you say?"

And Mervyn, coughing, clearing his throat, didn't answer, but walked off quickly. His shirt collar, too highly starched, cut into the back of his hairless, reddening neck. When I caught up with him, he told me, "No wonder so many artists have been driven to suicide. Nobody understands us. We're not in the rat-race."

Molly came by at seven-thirty on Friday night.

"Is there something I can do for you?" my mother asked.

"I'm here to see Mr. Kaplansky. I believe he rents a room here."

"Better to rent out a room than give fourteen ounces to the pound."

"If you are referring to my father's establishment then I'm sorry he can't give credit to everybody."

"We pay cash everywhere. Knock wood."

"I'm sure. Now, may I see Mr. Kaplansky, *if you don't mind?*"

"He's still dining. But I'll inquire."

Molly didn't wait. She pushed past my mother into the kitchen. Her eyes were a little puffy. It looked to me like she had been crying. "Hi," she said. Molly wore her soft black hair in an upsweep. Her mouth was painted very red.

"Siddown," my father said. "Make yourself homely." Nobody laughed. "It's a joke," he said.

"Are you ready, Mervyn?"

Mervyn fiddled with his fork. "I've got work to do tonight," he said.

"I'll put up a pot of coffee for you right away."

Smiling thinly, Molly pulled back her coat, took a deep breath, and sat down. She had to perch on the edge of the chair either because of her skirt or that it hurt her to sit. "About the novel," she said, smiling at Mervyn, "congrats."

"But it hasn't even been accepted by a publisher yet."

"It's good, isn't it?"

"Of course it's good," my mother said.

"Then what's there to worry? Come on," Molly said, rising. "Let's skidaddle."

We all went to the window to watch them go down the street together.

"Look at her how she's grabbing his arm," my mother said. "Isn't it disgusting?"

"You lost by a т.к.о.," my father said.

"*Thanks*," my mother said, and she left the room.

My father blew on his fingers. "Whew," he said. We continued to watch by the window. "I'll bet you she sharpens them on a grindstone every morning to get them so pointy, and he's such a shortie he wouldn't even have to bend over to . . ." My father sat down, lit his pipe, and opened *Liberty* at Mervyn's story. "You know, Mervyn's not *that* special a guy. Maybe it's not as hard as it seems to write a story."

"Digging ditches would be easier," I said.

My father took me to Tansky's for a coke. Drumming his fingers on the counter, he answered questions about Mervyn. "Well, it has to do with this thing . . . The Muse. On some days, with the Muse, he works better. But on other days . . ." My father addressed the regulars with a daring touch of condescension; I had never seen him so assured before. "Well, that depends. But he says Hollywood is very corrupt."

Mervyn came home shortly after midnight.

"I want to give you a word of advice," my mother said. "That girl comes from very common people. You can do better, you know."

My father cracked his knuckles. He didn't look at Mervyn.

"You've got your future career to think of. You must choose a mate who won't be an embarrassment in the better circles."

"Or still better stay a bachelor," my father said.

"Nothing more dreadful can happen to a person," my mother said, "than to marry somebody who doesn't share his interests."

"Play the field a little," my father said, drawing on his pipe.

My mother looked into my father's face and laughed. My father's voice fell to a whisper. "You get married too young," he said, "and you live to regret it."

My mother laughed again. Her eyes were wet.

"I'm not the kind to stand by idly," Mervyn said, "while you insult Miss Rosen's good name."

My father, my mother, looked at Mervyn as if surprised by his presence. Mervyn retreated, startled. "*I mean that*," he said.

"Just who do you think you're talking to?" my mother said. She looked sharply at my father.

"Hey, there," my father said.

"I hope," my mother said, "success isn't giving you a swelled head."

"Success won't change me. I'm steadfast. But you are intruding into my personal affairs. Good night."

My father seemed both dismayed and a little pleased that someone had spoken up to my mother.

"And just what's ailing you?" my mother asked.

"Me? Nothing."

"If you could only see yourself. At your age. A pipe."

"According to the *Digest* it's safer than cigarettes."

"You know absolutely nothing about people. Mervyn would never be rude to me. It's only his artistic temperament coming out."

My father waited until my mother had gone to bed and then he slipped into Mervyn's room. "Hi." He sat down on the edge of Mervyn's bed. "Tell me to mind my own business if you want me to, but . . . well, have you had bad news from New York? The publisher?"

"I'm still waiting to hear from New York."

"Sure," my father said, jumping up. "Sorry. Good night." But he paused briefly at the door. "I've gone out on a limb for you. Please don't let me down."

Molly's father phoned the next morning. "You had a good time Mervyn?"

"Yeah. Yeah, sure."

"Atta boy. That girl she's crazy about you. Like they say she's walking on air."

Molly, they said, had told the other girls in the office at Susy's Smart-Wear that she would probably soon be leaving for, as she put it, tropical climes. Gitel Shalinsky saw her shopping for beach wear on Park Avenue—in November, this—and the rumour was that Mervyn had already accepted a Hollywood offer for his book, a guaranteed best-seller. A couple of days later a package came for Mervyn. It was his novel. There was a printed form enclosed with it. The publishers felt the book was not for them.

"Tough luck," my father said.

"It's nothing," Mervyn said breezily. "Some of the best wordsmiths going have had their novels turned down six-seven times before a publisher takes it. Besides, this outfit wasn't for me in the first place. It's a homosexual company. They only print the pretty-pretty prose boys." Mervyn laughed, he slapped his knees. "I'll send the book off to another publisher today."

My mother made Mervyn his favorite dishes for dinner. "You have real talent," she said to him, "and everything will come to you." Afterwards, Molly came by. Mervyn came home very late this time, but my mother waited up for him all the same.

"I'm invited to eat at the Rosens on Saturday night. Isn't that nice?"

"But I ordered something special from the butcher for us here."

"I'm sorry. I didn't know."

"So now you know. Please yourself, Mervyn. Oh, it's alright. I changed your bed. But you could have told me, you know."

Mervyn locked his hands together to quiet them. "Tell you what, for Christ's sake? There's nothing to tell."

"It's alright, *boyele*," my mother said. "Accidents happen."

Once more my father slipped into Mervyn's room. "It's O.K.," he said, "don't worry about Saturday night. Play around. Work the kinks out. But don't put anything in writing. You might live to regret it."

"I happen to think Molly is a remarkable girl."

"Me too. I'm not as old as you think."

"No, no, no. You don't understand."

My father showed Mervyn some clippings he had saved for him. One news story told of two brothers who had discovered each other by accident after twenty-five years, another was all about a funny day at court. He also gave Mervyn an announcement for the annual y.h.m.a. *Beacon* short story contest. "I've got an idea for you," he said. "Listen, Mervyn, in the movies . . . well, when Humphrey Bogart, for instance, lights up a Chesterfield or asks for a coke you think he doesn't get a nice little envelope from the companies concerned? Sure he does. Well, your problem seems to be money. So why couldn't you do the same thing in books? Like if your hero has to fly somewhere, for instance, why use an unnamed airline? Couldn't he go TWA because it's the safest, the best, and maybe he picks up a cutie-pie on board? Or if your central character is . . . well, a lush, couldn't he always insist on Seagram's because it's the greatest? Get the idea? I could write, say, TWA, Pepsi, Seagram's and Adam's Hats and find out just how much a book plug is worth to them, and you . . . well, what do you think?"

"I could never do that in a book of mine, that's what I think. It would reflect on my integrity. People would begin to talk, see."

But people had already begun to talk. Molly's kid brother told me Mervyn had made a hit at dinner. His father, he said, had told Mervyn he felt, along with the moderns, that in-laws should not live with young couples, not always, but the climate in Montreal was a real killer for his wife, and if it so happened that he ever had a son-in-law in, let's say, California . . . well, it would be nice to visit . . . and Mervyn agreed that families should be close-knit. Not all the talk was favourable, however. The boys on the street were hostile to Mervyn. An outsider, a Torontonian, they felt, was threatening to carry off our Molly.

"There they go," the boys would say as Molly and Mervyn walked hand-in-hand past the pool room, "Beauty and the Beast."

"All these years they've been looking, and looking, and looking, and there he is, the missing link."

Mervyn was openly taunted on the street.

"Hey, big writer. Lard-ass. How many periods in a bottle of ink?"

"Shakespeare, come here. How did you get to look like that, or were you paid for the accident?"

But Mervyn assured me that he wasn't troubled by the boys. "The masses," he said, "have always been hostile to the artist. They've driven plenty of our number to self-slaughter, you know. But I can see through them."

His novel was turned down again.

"It doesn't matter," Mervyn said. "There are better publishers."

"But wouldn't they be experts there," my father asked. "I mean maybe . . ."

"Look at this, will you? This time they sent me a personal letter! You know who this is from? It's from one of the greatest editors in all of America."

"Maybe so," my father said uneasily, "but he doesn't want your book."

"He admires my energy and enthusiasm, doesn't he?"

Once more Mervyn mailed off his novel, but this time he did not resume his watch by the window. Mervyn was no longer the same. I don't mean that his face had broken out worse than ever—it had, it's true, only that was probably because he was eating too many starchy foods again—but suddenly he seemed indifferent to his novel's fate. I gave birth, he said, sent my baby out into the world, and now he's on his own. Another factor was that Mervyn had become, as he put it, pregnant once more (he looks it too, one of Tansky's regulars told me): that is to say, he was at work on a new book. My mother interpreted this as a very good sign and she did her utmost to encourage Mervyn. Though she continued to change his sheets just about every other night, she never complained about it. Why, she even pretended this was nor-mal procedure in our house. But Mervyn seemed perpetually irritated and he avoided the type of literary discussion that had formerly given my mother such deep pleasure. Every night now he went out with Molly and there were times when he did not return until four or five in the morning.

And now, curiously enough, it was my father who waited up for Mervyn, or stole out of bed to join him in the kitchen. He would make coffee and take down his prized bottle of apricot brandy. More than once I was wakened by his laughter. My father told Mervyn stories of his father's house, his boyhood, and the hard times that came after. He told Mervyn how his mother-in-law had been bedridden in our house for seven years, and with pride implicit in his every word—a pride that would have amazed and maybe even flattered my mother—he told Mervyn how my mother had tended to the old lady better than any nurse with umpteen diplomas. "To see her now," I heard my father say, "is like night and day. Before the time of the old lady's stroke she was no sour-puss. Well, that's life." He told Mervyn about the first time he had seen my mother, and how she had written him letters with poems by Shelley, Keats and Byron in them, when all the time he had lived only two streets away. But another time I heard my father say, "When I was a young man, you know, there were days on end when I never went to bed. I was so excited. I used to go out and walk the streets better than snooze. I thought if I slept maybe I'd miss something. Now isn't that crazy?" Mervyn muttered a reply. Usually, he seemed weary and self-absorbed. But my father was irre-pressible. Listening to him, his tender tone with Mervyn and the surprise of his laughter, I felt that I had reason to be envious. My father had never talked like that to me or my sister. But I was so astonished to discover this side of my father, it was all so unexpected, that I soon forgot my jealousy.

One night I heard Mervyn tell my father, "Maybe the novel I sent out is no good. Maybe it's just something I had to work out of my system."

"Are you crazy it's no good? I told everyone you were a big writer."

"It's the apricot brandy talking," Mervyn said breezily. "I was only kidding you."

But Mervyn had his problems. I heard from Molly's kid brother that Mr. Rosen had told him he was ready to retire. "Not that I want to be a burden to anybody," he had said. Molly had begun to take all the movie magazines available at Tansky's. "So that when I meet the stars face to face," she had told Gitel, "I shouldn't put my foot in it, and embarrass Merv."

Mervyn began to pick at his food, and it was not uncommon for him to leap up from the table and rush to the bathroom, holding his hand to his mouth. I discovered for the first time that my mother had bought a rubber sheet for Mervyn's bed. If Mervyn had to pass Tansky's, he no longer stopped to shoot the breeze. Instead, he would hurry past, his head lowered. Once, Segal stopped him. "What's a matter," he said, "you too good for us now?"

Tansky's regulars began to work on my father.

"All of a sudden, your genius there, he's such a b.t.o.," Sugerman said, "that he has no time for us here."

"Let's face it," my father said. "You're zeros. We all are. But my friend Mervyn . . ."

"Don't tell me, Sam. He's full of beans. Baked beans."

My father stopped going to Tansky's altogether. He took to playing solitaire at home.

"What are you doing here?" my mother asked.

"Can't I stay home one night? It's my house too, you know."

"I want the truth, Sam."

"Aw, those guys. You think those cockroaches know what an artist's struggle is?" He hesitated, watching my mother closely. "By them it must be that Mervyn isn't good enough. He's no writer."

"You know," my mother said, "he owes us seven weeks' rent now."

"The first day Mervyn came here," my father said, his eyes half-shut as he held a match to his pipe, "he said there was a kind of electricity between us. Well, I'm not going to let him down over a few bucks."

But something was bothering Mervyn. For that night and the next he did not go out with Molly. He went to the window to watch her pass again and then retreated to his room to do the crossword puzzles.

"Feel like a casino?" I asked.

"I love that girl," Mervyn said. "I adore her."

"I thought everything was o.k., but. I thought you were making time."

"No, no, no. I want to marry her. I told Molly that I'd settle down and get a job if she'd have me."

"Are you crazy? A job? With your talent?"

"That's what she said."

"Aw, let's play casino. It'll take your mind off things."

"She doesn't understand. Nobody does. For me to take a job is not like some ordinary guy taking a job. I'm always studying my own reactions. I want to know how a shipper feels from the inside."

"You mean you'd take a job *as a shipper?*"

"But it's not like I'd really be a shipper. It would look like that from the outside, but I'd really be studying my co-workers all the time. I'm an artist, you know."

"Stop worrying, Mervyn. Tomorrow there'll be a letter begging you for your book."

But the next day nothing came. A week passed. Ten days.

"That's a very good sign," Mervyn said. "It means they are considering my book very carefully."

It got so we all waited around for the postman. Mervyn was aware that my father did not go to Tansky's any more and that my mother's friends had begun to tease her. Except for his endless phone calls to Molly he hardly ever came out of his room. The phone calls were futile. Molly wouldn't speak to him.

One evening my father returned from work, his face flushed. "Son-of-a-bitch," he said, "that Rosen he's a cockroach. You know what he's saying? He wouldn't have in his family a faker or a swindler. He said you were not a writer, Mervyn, but garbage." My father started to laugh. "But I trapped him for a liar. You know what he said? That you were going to take a job as a shipper. Boy, did I ever tell him."

"What did you say?" my mother asked.

"I told him good. Don't you worry. When I lose my temper, you know. . . ."

"Maybe it wouldn't be such a bad idea for Mervyn to take a job. Better than go into debt he could—"

"You shouldn't have bragged about me to your friends so much," Mervyn said to my mother. "I didn't ask it."

"*I'm* a braggard? You take that back. You owe me an apology, I think. After all, *you're* the one who said you were such a big writer."

"My talent is unquestioned. I have stacks of letters from important people and—"

"I'm waiting for an apology, Sam?"

"I have to be fair. I've seen some of the letters, so that's true. But that's not to say Emily Post would approve of Mervyn calling you a—"

"My husband was right the first time. When he said you were a sponger, Mervyn."

"Don't worry," Mervyn said, turning to my father. "You'll get your rent back no matter what. Good night."

I can't swear to it. I may have imagined it. But when I got up to go to the toilet late that night it seemed to me that I heard Mervyn sobbing in his room. Anyway, the next morning the postman rang the bell and Mervyn came back with a package and a letter.

"Not again," my father said.

"No. This happens to be a letter from the most important publisher in the United States. They are going to pay me two thousand five hundred dollars for my book in advance against royalties."

"Hey. Lemme see that."

"Don't you trust me?"

"Of course we do." My mother hugged Mervyn. "All the time I knew you had it in you."

"This calls for a celebration," my father said, going to get the apricot brandy.

My mother went to phone Mrs. Fisher. "Oh, Ida, I just called to say I'll be able to bake for the bazaar after all. No, nothing new here. Oh, I almost forgot. Remember Mervyn you were saying he was nothing but a little twerp? Well, he just got a fantastic offer for his book from a publisher in New York. No, I'm only allowed to say it runs into four figures. Excited? That one. I'm not even sure he'll accept."

My father grabbed the phone to call Tansky's.

"One minute. Hold it. Couldn't we keep quiet about this, and have a private sort of celebration?"

My father got through to the store. "Hello, Sugarman? Everybody come over here. Drinks on the house. Why, of Korsakov. No, wise-guy. She certainly isn't. At her age? It's Mervyn. He's considering a five thousand dollar offer just to sign a contract for his book."

The phone rang an instant after my father had hung up.

"Well, hello Mrs. Rosen," my mother said. "Well, thank you. I'll give him the message. No, no, why should I have anything against you we've been neighbours for years. No. Certainly not. It wasn't *me* you called a piker. Your Molly didn't laugh in my face."

Unnoticed, Mervyn sat down on the sofa. He held his head in his hands.

"There's the doorbell," my father said.

"I think I'll lie down for a minute. Excuse me."

By the time Mervyn came out of his room again many of Tansky's regulars had arrived. "If it had been up to me," my father said, "none of you would be here. But Mervyn's not the type to hold grudges."

Molly's father elbowed his way through the group surrounding Mervyn. "I want you to know," he said, "that I'm proud of you today. There's nobody I'd rather have for a son-in-law."

"You're sort of hurrying things. Aren't you?"

"What? Didn't you propose to her a hundred times she wouldn't have you? And now I'm standing here to tell you alright and you're beginning with the shaking in the pants. This I don't like."

Everybody turned to stare. There was some good natured laughter.

"You wrote her such letters they still bring a blush to my face—"

"But they came back unopened."

Molly's father shrugged and Mervyn's face turned grey as a pencil eraser.

"But you listen here," Rosen said. "For Molly, if you don't mind, it isn't necessary for me to go begging."

"Here she is," somebody said.

The regulars moved in closer.

"Hi," Molly smelled richly of Lily of the Valley. You could see the outlines of her bra through her sweater (both were in Midnight Black, from Susy's Smart-Wear). Her tartan skirt was held together by an enormous gold-plated safety pin. "Hi, doll." She rushed up to Mervyn and kissed him. "Maw just told me." Molly turned to the others, her smile radiant. "Mr. Kaplansky has asked for my hand in matrimony. We are engaged."

"Congratulations!" Rosen clapped Mervyn on the back. "The very best to you both."

There were whoops of approval all around.

"When it comes to choosing a bedroom set you can't go wrong with my son-in-law Lou."

"I hope," Takifman said sternly, "yours will be a kosher home."

"Some of the biggest crooks in town only eat kosher and I don't mind saying that straight to your face, Takifman."

"He's right, you know. And these days the most important thing with young couples is that they should be sexually compatible."

Mervyn, surrounded by the men, looked over their heads for Molly. He spotted her trapped in another circle in the far corner of the room. Molly was eating a banana. She smiled at Mervyn, she winked.

"Don't they make a lovely couple?"

"Twenty years ago they said the same thing about us. Does that answer your question?"

Mervyn was drinking heavily. He looked sick.

"Hey," my father said, his glass spilling over, "tell me, Segal, what goes in hard and stiff and comes out soft and wet?"

"Oh, for Christ's sake," I said. "Chewing gum. It's as old as the hills."

"You watch out," my father said. "You're asking for it."

"You know," Miller said. "I could do with something to eat."

My mother moved silently and tight-lipped among the guests collecting glasses just as soon as they were put down.

"I'll tell you what," Rosen said in a booming voice, "let's all go over to my place for a decent feed and some schnapps."

Our living room emptied more quickly than it had filled.

"Where's your mother?" my father asked, puzzled.

I told him she was in the kitchen and we went to get her. "Come on," my father said, "let's go to the Rosens."

"And who, may I ask, will clean up the mess you and your friends made here?"

"It won't run away."

"You have no pride."

"Oh, please. Don't start. Not today."

"Drunkard."

"Ray Milland, that's me. Hey, what's that coming out of the wall? A bat."

"That poor innocent boy is being railroaded into a marriage he doesn't want and you just stand there."

"Couldn't you enjoy yourself *just once?*"

"You didn't see his face how scared he was? I thought he'd faint."

"Who ever got married he didn't need a little push? Why, I remember when I was a young man—"

"You go, Sam. Do me a favour. Go to the Rosens'."

My father sent me out of the room.

"I'm not," he began, "well, I'm not always happy with you. Not day in and day out. I'm telling you straight."

"When I needed you to speak up for me you couldn't. Today courage comes in bottles. Do me a favour, Sam. Go."

"I wasn't going to go and leave you alone. I was going to stay. But if that's how you feel. . . ."

My father returned to the living room to get his jacket. I jumped up.

"Where are *you* going?" he asked.

"To the party."

"You stay here with your mother you have no consideration."

"God damn it."

"You heard me," But my father paused for a moment at the door. Thumbs hooked in his suspenders, rocking to and fro on his heels, he raised his head so high his chin jutted out incongruously. "I wasn't always your father. I was a young man once."

"So?"

"Did you know," he said, one eye half-shut, "that LIVE spelled backwards is EVIL?"

I woke at three in the morning when I heard a chair crash in the living room; somebody fell, and this was followed by the sound of sobbing. It was Mervyn. Dizzy, wretched and bewildered. He sat on the floor with a glass in his hand. When he saw me coming he raised his glass. "The wordsmith's bottled enemy," he said, grinning.

"When you getting married?"

He laughed. I laughed too.

"I'm not getting married."

"Wha'?"

"Sh."

"But I thought you were crazy about Molly?"

"I was. I am no longer." Mervyn rose, he tottered over to the window.

"Have you ever looked up at the stars," he said, "and felt how small and unimportant we are?"

It hadn't occurred to me before.

"Nothing really matters. In terms of eternity our lives are shorter than a cigarette puff. Hey," he said. "Hey!" He took out his pen with the built-in flashlight and wrote something in his notebook. "For a writer," he said, "everything is grist to the mill. Nothing is humiliating."

"But what about Molly?"

"She's an insect. I told you the first time. All she wanted was my kudos. My fame . . . If you're really going to become a wordsmith remember one thing. The world is full of ridicule while you struggle. But once you've made it the glamour girls will come crawling."

He had begun to cry again. "Want me to sit with you for a while," I said.

"No. Go to bed. Leave me alone."

The next morning at breakfast my parents weren't talking. My mother's eyes were red and swollen and my father was in a forbidding mood. A telegram came for Mervyn.

"It's from New York," he said. "They want me right away. There's an offer for my book from Hollywood and they need me."

"You don't say?"

Mervyn thrust the telegram at my father. "Here," he said. "You read it."

"Take it easy. All I said was . . ." But my father read the telegram all the same. "Son-of-a-bitch," he said. "Hollywood."

We helped Mervyn pack.

"Shall I get Molly?" my father asked.

"No. I'll only be gone for a few days. I want to surprise her."

We all went to the window to wave. Just before he got into the taxi Mervyn looked up at us, he looked for a long while, but he didn't wave, and of course we never saw him again. A few days later a bill came for the telegram. It had been sent from our house. "I'm not surprised," my mother said.

My mother blamed the Rosens for Mervyn's flight, while they held us responsible for what they called their daughter's disgrace. My father put his pipes aside again and naturally he took a terrible ribbing at Tansky's. About a month later, five dollar bills began to arrive from Toronto. They came sporadically until Mervyn had paid up all his back rent. But he never answered any of my father's letters.

FOR STUDY, DISCUSSION, AND WRITING

1. Who tells this story? Who is the narrator?
2. Does the story provide any concrete evidence that Mervyn is really a "creative artist," as he says he is?
3. Early in the story, it is the narrator's mother who is particularly fond of Mervyn. Later on, it is the narrator's father who is proud of Mervyn. What circumstances account for the mother's initial response, and what circumstances account for the later change?

4. Trace the changes in Molly's attitude toward Mervyn. How do you account for these changes?
5. In spite of the fact that Mervyn falsifies the acceptance of his novel by a publisher, does he turn out to be a responsible person?
6. The evening before Mervyn announces that his novel has been accepted for publication, the narrator thinks he hears Mervyn sobbing in his room. What does this suggest about what Mervyn is really going through in his efforts to become an author?
7. In the course of the story, how is Mervyn victimized by the narrator's family?
8. What do you think Mervyn has learned from his experiences in Montreal?
9. A Canadian story, "Some Grist for Mervyn's Mill" seems to contrast the "lyric spirit" of Montreal (French Canada) with the more prosaic disposition of Toronto (English Canada). Point out evidence of this underlying contrast in the story.

GABRIEL GARCÍA MÁRQUEZ

The Handsomest Drowned Man in the World A TALE FOR CHILDREN

The first children who saw the dark and slinky bulge approaching through the sea let themselves think it was an enemy ship. Then they saw it had no flags or masts and they thought it was a whale. But when it washed up on the beach, they removed the clumps of seaweed, the jellyfish tentacles, and the remains of fish and flotsam, and only then did they see that it was a drowned man.

They had been playing with him all afternoon, burying him in the sand and digging him up again, when someone chanced to see them and spread the alarm in the village. The men who carried him to the nearest house noticed that he weighed more than any dead man they had ever known, almost as much as a horse, and they said to each other that maybe he'd been floating too long and the water had got into his bones. When they laid him on the floor they said he'd been taller than all other men because there was barely enough room for him in the house, but they thought that maybe the ability to keep on growing after death was part of the nature of certain drowned men. He had the smell of the sea about him and only his shape gave one to suppose that it was the corpse of a human being, because the skin was covered with a crust of mud and scales.

They did not even have to clean off his face to know that the dead man was a stranger. The village was made up of only twenty-odd wooden houses that had stone courtyards with no flowers and which were spread about on the end of a desertlike cape. There was so little land that mothers always went about with the fear that the wind would carry off their children and the few dead that the years had caused among them had to be thrown off the cliffs. But the sea was calm and bountiful and all the men fit into seven boats. So when they found the drowned man they simply had to look at one another to see that they were all there.

That night they did not go out to work at sea. While the men went to find out if anyone was missing in neighboring villages, the women stayed behind to care for the drowned man. They took the mud off with grass swabs, they removed the underwater stones entangled in his hair, and they scraped the crust off with tools used for scaling fish. As they were doing that they noticed that the vegetation on him came from faraway oceans and deep water and that his clothes were in tatters, as if he had sailed through labyrinths of coral. They noticed too that he bore his death with pride, for he did not have the lonely look of other drowned men who came out of the sea or that haggard, needy look of men who drowned in rivers. But only when they finished cleaning him off did they become aware of the kind of man he was and it left them breathless. Not only was he the tallest, strongest, most virile, and best built man they had ever seen, but even though they were looking at him there was no room for him in their imagination.

They could not find a bed in the village large enough to lay him on nor was there a table solid enough to use for his wake. The tallest men's holiday pants would not fit him, nor the fattest ones' Sunday shirts, nor the shoes of the one with the biggest feet. Fascinated by his huge size and his beauty, the women then decided to make him some pants from a large piece of sail and a shirt from some bridal brabant linen so that he could continue through his death with dignity. As they sewed, sitting in a circle and gazing at the corpse between stitches, it seemed to them that the wind had never been so steady nor the sea so restless as on that night and they supposed that the change had something to do with the dead man. They thought that if that magnificent man had lived in the village, his house would have had the widest doors, the highest ceiling, and the strongest floor, his bedstead would have been made from a midship frame held together by iron bolts, and his wife would have been the happiest woman. They thought that he would have had so much authority that he could have drawn fish out of the sea simply by calling their names and that he would have put so much work into his land that springs would have burst forth from among the rocks so that he would have been able to plant flowers on the cliffs. They secretly compared him to their own men, thinking that for all their lives theirs were incapable of doing what he could do in one night, and they ended up dismissing them deep in their hearts as the weakest, meanest, and most useless creatures on earth. They were wandering through that maze of fantasy when the oldest woman, who as the oldest had looked upon the drowned man with more compassion than passion, sighed:

"He has the face of someone called Esteban."

It was true. Most of them had only to take another look at him to see that he could not have any other name. The more stubborn among them, who were the youngest, still lived for a few hours with the illusion that when they put his clothes on and he lay among the flowers in patent leather shoes his name might be Lautaro. But it was a vain illusion. There had not been enough canvas, the poorly cut and worse sewn pants were too tight, and the hidden strength of his heart popped the buttons on his shirt. After midnight the whistling of the wind died down and the sea fell into its Wednesday drowsiness. The silence put an end to any last doubts: he was Esteban. The women who had dressed him, who had combed his hair, had cut his nails and shaved him were unable to hold back a shudder of pity when they had to resign themselves to his being dragged along the ground. It was then that they understood how unhappy he must have been with that huge body since it bothered him even after death. They could see him in life, condemned to going through doors sideways, cracking his head on crossbeams, remaining on his feet during visits, not knowing what to do with his soft, pink, sea lion hands while the lady of the house looked for her most resistant chair and begged him, frightened to death, sit here, Esteban, please, and he, leaning against the wall, smiling, don't bother, ma'am, I'm fine where I am, his heels raw and his back roasted from having done the same thing so many times whenever he paid a visit, don't bother, ma'am, I'm fine where I am, just to avoid the embarrassment of breaking up the chair, and never knowing perhaps that the ones who said don't go, Esteban, at least wait till the coffee's ready, were the ones who later on would whisper the big boob finally left, how nice, the handsome fool has gone. That was what the women were thinking beside the body a little before dawn. Later, when they covered his face with a handkerchief so that the light would not bother him, he looked so forever dead, so defenseless, so much like their men that the first furrows of tears opened in their hearts. It was one of the younger ones who began the weeping. The others, coming to, went from sighs to wails, and the more they sobbed the more they felt like weeping, because the drowned man was becoming all the more Esteban for them, and so they wept so much, for he was the most destitute, most peaceful, and most obliging man on earth, poor Esteban. So when the men returned with the news that the drowned man was not from the neighboring villages either, the women felt an opening of jubilation in the midst of their tears.

"Praise the Lord," they sighed, "he's ours!"

The men thought the fuss was only womanish frivolity. Fatigued because of the difficult nighttime inquiries, all they wanted was to get rid of the bother of the newcomer once and for all before the sun grew strong on that arid, windless day. They improvised a litter with the remains of foremasts and gaffs, tying it together with rigging so that it would bear the weight of the body until they reached the cliffs. They wanted to tie the anchor from a cargo ship to him so that he would sink easily into the deepest waves, where fish are blind and divers die of nostalgia, and bad currents would not bring him back to shore, as had happened with other bodies. But the more they hurried, the more the women thought of ways to waste time. They walked about like startled hens, pecking with the sea charms on their breasts, some interfering on one side to put a scapular of the good wind on the drowned man, some on the other side to put a wrist compass on him, and after a great deal of *get away from there, woman, stay out of the way, look, you almost made me fall on top of the dead man*, the men began to feel mistrust in their livers and started grumbling about why so many main-altar decorations for a stranger, because no matter how many nails and holy-water jars he had on him, the sharks would chew him all the same, but the women kept piling on their junk relics, running back and forth, stumbling, while they released in sighs what they did not in tears, so that the men finally exploded with *since when has there ever been such a fuss over a drifting corpse, a drowned nobody, a piece of cold Wednesday meat*. One of the women, mortified by so much lack of care, then removed the handkerchief from the dead man's face and the men were left breathless too.

He was Esteban. It was not necessary to repeat it for them to recognize him. If they had been told Sir Walter Raleigh, even they might have been impressed with his gringo accent, the macaw on his shoulder, his cannibal-killing blunderbuss, but there could be only one Esteban in the world and there he was, stretched out like a sperm whale, shoeless, wearing the pants of an undersized child, and with those stony nails that had to be cut with a knife. They only had to take the handkerchief off his face to see that he was ashamed, that it was not his fault that he was so big or so heavy or so handsome, and if he had known that this was going to happen, he would have looked for a more discreet place to drown, in, seriously, I even would have tied the anchor off a galleon around my neck and staggered off a cliff like someone who doesn't like things in order not to be upsetting people now with this Wednesday dead body, as you people say, in order not to be bothering anyone with this filthy piece of cold meat that doesn't have anything to do with me. There was so much truth in his manner that even the most mistrustful men, the ones who felt the bitterness of endless nights at sea fearing that their women would tire of dreaming about them and begin to dream of drowned men, even they and others who were harder still shuddered in the marrow of their bones at Esteban's sincerity.

That was how they came to hold the most splendid funeral they could conceive of for an abandoned drowned man. Some women who had gone to get flowers in the neighboring villages returned with other women who could not believe what they had been told, and those women went back for more flowers when they saw the dead man, and they brought more and more until there were so many flowers and so many people that it was hard to walk about. At the final moment it pained them to return him to the waters as an orphan and they chose a father and mother from among the best people, and aunts and uncles and cousins, so that through him all the inhabitants of the village became kinsmen. Some sailors who heard the weeping from a distance went off course and people heard of one who had himself tied to the mainmast, remembering ancient fables about sirens. While they fought for the privilege of carrying him on their shoulders along the steep escarpment by the cliffs, men and women became aware for the first time of the desolation of their streets, the dryness of their courtyards, the narrowness of their dreams as they faced the splendor and beauty of their drowned man. They let him go without an anchor so that he could come back if he wished and whenever he wished, and they all held their breath for the fraction of centuries the body took to fall into the abyss. They did not need to look at one another to realize that they were no longer all present, that they would never be. But they also knew that everything would be different from then on, that their houses would have wider doors, higher ceilings, and stronger floors so that Esteban's memory could go everywhere without bumping into beams and so that no one in the future would dare whisper the big boob finally died, too bad, the handsome fool has finally died, because they were going to paint their house fronts gay colors to make Esteban's memory eternal and they were going to break their backs digging for springs among the stones and planting flowers on the cliffs so that in future years at dawn the passengers on great liners would awaken, suffocated by the smell of gardens on the high seas, and the captain would have to come down from the bridge in his dress uniform, with his astrolabe, his pole star, and his row of war medals and, pointing to the promontory of roses on the horizon, he would say in fourteen languages, look there, where the wind is so peaceful now that it's gone to sleep beneath the beds, over there, where the sun's so bright that the sunflowers don't know which way to turn, yes, over there, that's Esteban's village.

FOR STUDY, DISCUSSION, AND WRITING

1. What narrative point of view does García Márquez use in this story?
2. Early in the story García Márquez presents a brief description of the village. What does this description suggest about the level of consciousness of the villagers? Are the villagers emerging or regressing?
3. What symbolic significance can be attached to the fact that the drowned man is taller, stronger, and apparently more virile than any of the men in the village?
4. The name "Esteban" is Spanish for "Stephen" and suggests Saint Stephen, who was killed for predicting the end of the world as well as salva-

tion through the Second Coming of Christ. The rejected name "Lautaro" is that of a sixteenth-century Indian who led an unsuccessful revolt against the Spanish colonists. What does the choice of the name "Esteban" for the drowned man suggest about the nature of the changes that will occur in the village?

5. Discuss the significance of the statement that because of Esteban the villagers' houses would have "wider doors, higher ceilings, and stronger floors."

6. Why are the villagers willing to accept the changes that life after Esteban will bring, even though these changes will involve much labor and sweat?

7. What is the thematic point of the story? Does García Márquez offer an optimistic or a pessimistic view of human nature?

JOHN UPDIKE

The Music School

My name is Alfred Schweigen and I exist in time. Last night I heard a young priest tell of a change in his Church's attitude toward the Eucharistic wafer. For generations nuns and priests, but especially (the young man said) nuns, have taught Catholic children that the wafer must be held in the mouth and allowed to melt; that to touch it with the teeth would be (and this was never doctrine, but merely a nuance of instruction) in some manner blasphemous. Now, amid the flowering of fresh and bold ideas with which the Church, like a tundra thawing, responded to that unexpected sun the late Pope John, there has sprung up the thought that Christ did not say *Take and melt this in your mouth* but *Take and eat.* The word is *eat,* and to dissolve the word is to dilute the transubstantiated metaphor of physical nourishment. This demiquaver of theology crystallizes with a beautiful simplicity in the material world; the bakeries supplying the Mass have been instructed to unlearn the science of a dough translucent to the tongue and to prepare a thicker, tougher wafer—a host, in fact, so substantial it *must* be chewed to be swallowed.

This morning I read in the newspaper that an acquaintance of mine had been murdered. The father of five children, he had been sitting at the dinner table with them, a week after Thanksgiving. A single bullet entered the window and pierced his temple; he fell to the floor and died there in minutes, at the feet of his children. My acquaintance with him was slight. He has become the only victim of murder I have known, and for such a role anyone seems drastically miscast, though in the end each life wears its events with a geological inevitability. It is impossible, today, to imagine him alive. He was a computer expert, a soft-voiced, broad-set man from Nebraska, whose intelligence, concerned as it was with matters so arcane to me, had a generous quality of reserve, and gave him, in my apprehension of him, the dignity of an iceberg, which floats so serenely on its hidden mass. We met (I think only twice) in the home of a mutual friend, a professional colleague of his who is my neighbor. We spoke, as people do whose fields of knowledge are miles apart, of matters where all men are ignorant—of politics, children, and, perhaps, religion. I have the impression, at any rate, that he, as is often the case with scientists and Midwesterners, had no use for religion, and I saw in him a typical specimen of the new human species that thrives around scientific centers, in an environment of discussion groups, outdoor exercise, and cheerful husbandry. Like those vanished gentlemen whose sexual energy was exclusively spent in brothels, these men confine their cleverness to their work, which, being in one way or another for the government, is usually secret. With their sufficient incomes, large families, Volkswagen buses, hi-fi phonographs, half-remodelled Victorian homes, and harassed, ironical wives, they seem to have solved, or dismissed, the paradox of being a thinking animal and, devoid of guilt, apparently participate not in this century but in the next. If I remember him with individual clarity, it is because once I intended to write a novel about a computer programmer, and I asked him questions, which he answered agreeably. More agreeably still, he offered to show me around his laboratories any time I cared to make the hour's trip to where they were. I never wrote the novel—the moment in my life it was meant to crystallize dissolved too quickly—and I never took the trip. Indeed, I don't believe I thought of my friend once in the year between our last encounter and this morning, when my wife at breakfast put the paper before me and asked, "Don't we know him?" His pleasant face with its eyes set wide like the eyes of a bear gazed from the front page. I read that he had been murdered.

I do not understand the connection between last night and this morning, though there seems to be one. I am trying to locate it this afternoon, while sitting in a music school, waiting for my daughter to finish her piano lesson. I perceive in the two incidents a common element of nourishment, of eating transfigured by a strange irruption, and there is a parallel movement, a flight immaculately direct and elegant, from an immaterial phenomenon (an exegetical nicety, a maniac hatred) to a material one (a bulky wafer, a bullet in the temple). About the murder I feel certain, from my knowledge of the victim, that his offense was blameless, something for which he could not have felt guilt or shame. When I try to picture it, I see only numbers and Greek letters, and conclude that from my distance I have witnessed an almost unprecedented crime, a crime of unalloyed scientific passion. And there is this to add: the young priest plays a twelve-string guitar, smokes mentholated cigarettes, and seemed unembarrassed to find himself sitting socially in a circle of Protestants and nonbelievers—like my late computer friend, a man of the future.

But let me describe the music school. I love it here. It is the basement of a huge Baptist church. Golden collection plates rest on the table beside me. Girls in their first blush of adolescence, carrying fawn-colored flute cases and pallid folders of music, shuffle by me; their awkwardness is lovely, like the stance of a bather testing the sea. Boys and mothers arrive and leave. From all directions sounds—of pianos, oboes, clarinets—arrive like hints of another world, a world where angels fumble, pause, and begin again. Listening, I remember what learning music is like, how impossibly difficult and complex seem the first fingerings, the first decipherings of that unique language which freights each note with a double meaning of position and duration, a language as finicking as Latin, as laconic as Hebrew, as surprising to the eye as Persian or Chinese. How mysterious appears that calligraphy of parallel spaces, swirling clefs, superscribed ties, subscribed decrescendos, dots and sharps and flats! How great looms the gap between the first gropings of vision and the first stammerings of percussion! Vision, timidly, becomes percussion, percussion becomes music, music becomes emotion, emotion becomes—vision. Few of us have the heart to follow this circle to its end. I took lessons for years, and never learned, and last night, watching the priest's fingers confidently prance on the neck of his guitar, I was envious and incredulous. My daughter is just beginning the piano. These are her first lessons, she is eight, she is eager and hopeful. Silently she sits beside me as we drive the nine miles to the town where the lessons are given; silently she sits beside me, in the dark, as we drive home. Unlike her, she does not beg for a reward of candy or a Coke, as if the lesson itself has been a meal. She only remarks—speaking dully, in a reflex of greed she has outgrown—that the store windows are decorated for Christmas already. I love taking her, I love waiting for her, I love driving her home through the mystery of darkness toward the certainty of supper. I do this taking and driving because today my wife visits her psychiatrist. She visits a psychiatrist because I am unfaithful to her. I do not understand the connection, but there seems to be one.

In the novel I never wrote, I wanted the hero to be a computer programmer because it was the most poetic and romantic occupation I could think of, and my hero had to be extremely romantic and delicate, for he was to die of adultery. Die, I mean, of knowing it was possible; the possibility crushed him. I conceived of him, whose professional life was spent in the sanctum of the night (when, I was told, the computers, too valuable to be unemployed by industry during the day, are free, as it were, to frolic and to be loved), devising idioms whereby problems might be fed to the machines and emerge, under binomial percussion, as the music of truth—I conceived of him as being too fine, translucent, and scrupulous to live in our coarse age. He was to be, if the metaphor is biological, an evolutionary abortion, a mammalian mutation crushed underfoot by dinosaurs, and, if the metaphor is mathematical, a hypothetical ultimate, one digit beyond the last real number. The title of the book was to be "N + 1." Its first sentence went, *As Echo passed overhead, he stroked Maggy Johns' side through her big-flowered dress.* Echo is the artificial star, the first, a marvel; as the couples at a lawn party look upward at it, these two caress one another. She takes his free hand, lifts it to her lips, warmly breathes on, kisses, his knuckles. *His halted body seemed to catch up in itself the immense slow revolution of the earth, and the firm little white star, newly placed in space, calmly made its way through the older points of light, which looked shredded and faint in comparison.* From this hushed moment under the ominous sky of technological miracle, the plot was to develop more or less downhill, into a case of love, guilt, and nervous breakdown, with physiological complications (I had to do some research here) that would kill the hero as quietly as a mistake is erased from a blackboard. There was to be the hero, his wife, his love, and his doctor. In the end the wife married the doctor, and Maggy Johns would calmly continue her way through the comparatively faint . . . Stop me.

My psychiatrist wonders why I need to humiliate myself. It is the habit, I suppose, of confession. In my youth I attended a country church where, every two months, we would all confess; we kneeled on the uncarpeted floor and propped the books containing the service on the seats of the pews. It was a grave, long service, beginning, *Beloved in the Lord! Let us draw near with a true heart and confess our sins unto God, our Father. . . .* There was a kind of accompanying music in the noise of the awkward fat Germanic bodies fitting themselves, scraping and grunting, into the backwards-kneeling position. We read aloud, *But if we thus examine ourselves, we shall find nothing in us but sin and death, from which we can in no wise set ourselves free.* The confession complete, we would stand and be led, pew by pew, to the altar rail, where the young minister, a black-haired man with very small pale hands, would feed us, murmuring, *Take, eat; this is the true body of our Lord and Saviour Jesus Christ, given unto death for your sins.* The altar rail was of varnished wood, and ran around three sides, so that, standing (oddly, we did not kneel here), one could see, one could not help but see, the faces of one's fellow-communicants. We were a weathered, homely congregation, sheepish in our Sunday clothes, and the faces I saw while the wafer was held in my mouth were strained; above their closed lips their eyes held a watery look of pleading to be rescued from the depths of this mystery. And it distinctly seems, in the reaches of this memory so vivid it makes my saliva flow, that it was necessary, if not to chew, at least to touch, to embrace and tentatively shape, the wafer with the teeth.

We left refreshed. *We give thanks to thee, Almighty God, that Thou hast refreshed us through this salutary gift.* The church smelled like this school, glinting with strange whispers and varnished highlights. I am neither musical nor religious. Each moment I live, I must think where to place my fingers, and press them down with no confidence of hearing a chord. My friends are like me. We are all pilgrims, faltering toward divorce. Some get no further than mutual confession, which becomes an addiction, and exhausts them. Some move on, into violent quarrels and physical blows; and succumb to sexual excitement. A few make it to the psychiatrists. A very few get as far as the lawyers. Last evening, as the priest sat in the circle of my friends, a woman entered without knocking; she had come from the lawyers, and her eyes and hair were flung wide with suffering, as if she had come in out of a high wind. She saw our black-garbed guest, was amazed, ashamed perhaps, and took two backward steps. But then, in the hush, she regained her composure and sat down among us. And in this grace note, of the two backward steps and then again the forward movement, a coda seems to be urged.

The world is the host; it must be chewed. I am content here in this school. My daughter emerges from her lesson. Her face is fat and satisfied, refreshed, hopeful; her pleased smile, biting her lower lip, pierces my heart, and I die (I think I am dying) at her feet.

FOR STUDY, DISCUSSION, AND WRITING

1. What specific technique of subjective narration is employed to tell this story?
2. Why does Alfred Schweigen admire the computer programmer and the Catholic priest?
3. How does Schweigen appraise his own character?
4. Relate Schweigen's love of music to his view of what life should be like.
5. Discuss the novel that Schweigen never wrote. How does it relate to his character?
6. Why is Schweigen's wife seeing a psychiatrist? What is ironic about the fact that Schweigen doesn't understand why his wife is seeing a psychiatrist?
7. How does Schweigen feel about his daughter?
8. What is the symbolic significance of the communion wafer, especially in terms of Schweigen's view of life?
9. Discuss the lives of Schweigen and the people who surround him. Are these people happy or unhappy?

JOHN CHEEVER

The Swimmer

It was one of those midsummer Sundays when everyone sits around saying, "I *drank* too much last night." You might have heard it whispered by the parishioners leaving church, heard it from the lips of the priest himself, struggling with his cassock in the *vestiarium*, heard it from the golf links and the tennis courts, heard it from the wildlife preserve where the leader of the Audubon group was suffering from a terrible hangover. "I *drank* too much," said Donald Westerhazy. "We all *drank* too much," said Lucinda Merrill. "It must have been the wine," said Helen Westerhazy. "I *drank* too much of that claret."

This was at the edge of the Westerhazys' pool. The pool, fed by an artesian well with a high iron content, was a pale shade of green. It was a fine day. In the west there was a massive stand of cumulus cloud so like a city seen from a distance—from the bow of an approaching ship—that it might have had a name. Lisbon. Hackensack. The sun was hot. Neddy Merrill sat by the green water, one hand in it, one around a glass of gin. He was a slender man—he seemed to have the especial slenderness of youth—and while he was far from young he had slid down his banister that morning and given the bronze back-side of Aphrodite on the hall table a smack, as he jogged toward the smell of coffee in his dining room. He might have been compared to a summer's day, particularly the last hours of one, and while he lacked a tennis racket or a sail bag the impression was definitely one of youth, sport, and clement weather. He had been swimming and now he was breathing deeply, stertorously as if he could gulp into his lungs the components of that moment, the heat of the sun, the intenseness of his pleasure. It all seemed to flow into his chest. His own house stood in Bullet Park, eight miles to the south, where his four beautiful daughters would have had their lunch and might be playing tennis. Then it occurred to him that by taking a dogleg to the southwest he could reach his home by water.

His life was not confining and the delight he took in this observation could not be explained by its suggestion of escape. He seemed to see, with a cartographer's eye, that string of swimming pools, that quasi-subterranean stream that curved across the county. He had made a discovery, a contribution to modern geography; he would name the stream Lucinda after his wife. He was not a practical joker nor was he a fool but he was determinedly original and had a vague and modest idea of himself as a legendary figure. The day was beautiful and it seemed to him that a long swim might enlarge and celebrate its beauty.

He took off a sweater that was hung over his shoulders and dove in. He had an inexplicable contempt for men who did not hurl themselves into pools. He swam a choppy crawl, breathing either with every stroke or every fourth stroke and counting somewhere well in the back of his mind the one-two one-two of a flutter kick. It was not a serviceable stroke for long distances but the domestication of swimming had saddled the sport with some customs and in his part of the world a crawl was customary. To be embraced and sustained by the light green water was less a pleasure, it seemed, than the resumption of a natural condition, and he would have liked to swim without trunks, but this was not possible, considering his project. He hoisted himself up on the far curb—he never used the ladder—and started across the lawn. When Lucinda asked where he was going he said he was going to swim home.

The only maps and charts he had to go by were remembered or imaginary but these were clear enough. First there were the Grahams, the Hammers, the Lears, the Howlands, and the Crosscups. He would cross Ditmar Street to the Bunkers and come, after a short portage, to the Levys, the Welchers, and the public pool in Lancaster. Then there were the Hallorans, the Sachses, the Biswangers, Shirley Adams, the Gilmartins, and the Clydes. The day was lovely, and that he lived in a world so generously supplied with water seemed like a clemency, a beneficence. His heart was high and he ran across the grass. Making his way home by an uncommon route gave him the feeling that he was a pilgrim, an explorer, a man with a destiny, and he knew that he would find friends all along the way; friends would line the banks of the Lucinda River.

He went through a hedge that separated the Westerhazys' land from the Grahams', walked under some flowering apple trees, passed the shed that housed their pump and filter, and came out at the Grahams' pool. "Why, Neddy," Mrs. Graham said, "what a marvelous surprise. I've been trying to get you on the phone all morning. Here, let me get you a drink." He saw then, like any explorer, that the hospitable customs and traditions of the natives would have to be handled with diplomacy if he was ever going to reach his destination. He did not want to mystify or seem rude to the Grahams nor did he have the time to linger there. He swam the length of their pool and joined them in the sun and was rescued, a few minutes later, by the arrival of two carloads of friends from Connecticut. During the uproarious reunions he was able to slip away. He went down by the front of the Grahams' house, stepped over a thorny hedge, and crossed a vacant lot to the Hammers'. Mrs. Hammer, looking up from her roses, saw him swim by although she wasn't quite sure who it was. The Lears heard him splashing past the open windows of their living room. The Howlands and the Crosscups were away. After leaving the Howlands' he crossed Ditmar Street and started for the Bunkers', where he could hear, even at that distance, the noise of a party.

The water refracted the sound of voices and laughter and seemed to suspend it in midair. The Bunkers' pool was on a rise and he climbed some stairs to a terrace where twenty-five or thirty men and women were drinking. The only person in the water was Rusty Towers, who floated there on a rubber raft. Oh, how bonny and lush were the banks of the Lucinda River! Prosperous men and women gathered by the sapphire-colored waters while caterer's men in white coats passed them cold gin. Overhead a red de Haviland trainer was circling around and around and around in the sky with something like the glee of a child in a swing. Ned felt a passing affection for the scene, a tenderness for the gathering, as if it was something he might touch. In the distance he heard thunder. As soon as Enid Bunker saw him she began to scream: "Oh, look who's here! What a marvelous surprise! When Lucinda said that you couldn't come I thought I'd *die*." She made her way to him through the crowd, and when they had finished kissing she led him to the bar, a progress that was slowed by the fact that he stopped to kiss eight or ten other women and shake the hands of as many men. A smiling bartender he had seen at a hundred parties gave him a gin and tonic and he stood by the bar for a moment, anxious not to get stuck in any conversation that would delay his voyage. When he seemed about to be surrounded he dove in and swam close to the side to avoid colliding with Rusty's raft. At the far end of the pool he bypassed the Tomlinsons with a broad smile and jogged up the garden path. The gravel cut his feet but this was the only unpleasantness. The party was confined to the pool, and as he went toward the house he heard the brilliant, watery sound of voices fade, heard the noise of a radio from the Bunkers' kitchen, where someone was listening to a ball game. Sunday afternoon. He made his way through the parked cars and down the grassy border of their driveway to Alewives Lane. He did not want to be seen on the road in his bathing trunks but there was no traffic and he made the short distance to the Levys' driveway, marked with a PRIVATE PROPERTY sign and a green tube for *The New York Times*. All the doors and windows of the big house were open but there were no signs of life; not even a dog barked. He went around the side of the house to the pool and saw that the Levys had only recently left. Glasses and bottles and dishes of nuts were on a table at the deep end, where there was a bathhouse or gazebo, hung with Japanese lanterns. After swimming the pool he got himself a glass and poured a drink. It was his fourth or fifth drink and he had swum nearly half the length of the Lucinda River. He felt tired, clean, and pleased at that moment to be alone; pleased with everything.

It would storm. The stand of cumulus cloud—that city—had risen and darkened, and while he sat there he heard the percussiveness of thunder again. The de Haviland trainer was still circling overhead and it seemed to Ned that he could almost hear the pilot laugh with pleasure in the afternoon; but when there was another peal of thunder he took off for home. A train whistle blew and he wondered what time it had gotten to be. Four? Five? He thought of the provincial station at that hour, where a waiter, his tuxedo concealed by a raincoat, a dwarf with some flowers wrapped in newspaper, and a woman who had been crying would be waiting for the local. It was suddenly growing dark; it was that moment when the pin-headed birds seem to organize their song into some acute and knowledgeable recognition of the storm's approach. Then there was a fine noise of rushing water from the crown of an oak at his back, as if a spigot there had been turned. Then the noise of fountains came from the crowns of all the tall trees. Why did he love storms, what was the meaning of his excitement when the door sprang open and the rain wind fled rudely up the stairs, why had the simple task of shutting the windows of an old house seemed fitting and urgent, why did the first watery notes of a storm wind have for him the unmistakable sound of good news, cheer, glad tidings? Then there was an explosion, a smell of cordite, and rain lashed the Japanese lanterns that Mrs. Levy had bought in Kyoto the year before last, or was it the year before that?

He stayed in the Levys' gazebo until the storm had passed. The rain had cooled the air and he shivered. The force of the wind had stripped a maple of its red and yellow leaves and scattered them over the grass and the water. Since it was midsummer the tree must be blighted, and yet he felt a peculiar sadness at this sign of autumn. He braced his shoulders, emptied his glass, and started for the Welchers' pool. This meant crossing the Lindleys' riding ring and he was surprised to find it overgrown with grass and all the jumps dismantled. He wondered if the Lindleys had sold their horses or gone away for the summer and put them out to board. He seemed to remember having heard something about the Lindleys and their horses but the memory was unclear. On he went, barefoot through the wet grass, to the Welchers', where he found their pool was dry.

This breach in his chain of water disappointed him absurdly, and he felt like some explorer who seeks a torrential headwater and finds a dead stream. He was disappointed and mystified. It was common enough to go away for the summer but no one ever drained his pool. The Welchers had definitely gone away. The pool furniture was folded, stacked, and covered with a tarpaulin. The bathhouse was locked. All the windows of the house were shut, and when he went around to the driveway in front he saw a FOR SALE sign nailed to a tree. When had he last heard from the Welchers—when, that is, had he and Lucinda last regretted an invitation to dine with them? It seemed only a week or so ago. Was his memory failing or had he so disciplined it in the repression of unpleasant facts that he had damaged his sense of the truth? Then in the distance he heard the sound of a tennis game. This cheered him, cleared away all his apprehensions and let him regard the overcast sky and the cold air with indifference. This was the day that Neddy Merrill swam across the county. That was the day! He started off then for his most difficult portage.

Had you gone for a Sunday afternoon ride that day you might have seen him, close to naked, standing on the shoulders of Route 424, waiting for a chance to cross. You might have wondered if he was the victim of foul play, had his car broken down, or was he merely a fool. Standing barefoot in the deposits of the highway—beer cans, rags, and blowout patches—exposed to all kinds of ridicule, he seemed pitiful. He had known when he started that this was a part of his journey—it had been on his maps—but confronted with the lines of traffic, worming through the summery light, he found himself unprepared. He was laughed at, jeered at, a beer can was thrown at him, and he had no dignity or humor to bring to the situation. He could have gone back, back to the Westerhazys', where Lucinda would still be sitting in the sun. He had signed nothing, vowed nothing, pledged nothing, not even to himself. Why, believing as he did, that all human obduracy was susceptible to common sense, was he unable to turn back? Why was he determined to complete his journey even if it meant putting his life in danger? At what point had this prank, this joke, this piece of horseplay become serious? He could not go back, he could not even recall with any clearness the green water at the Westerhazys', the sense of inhaling the day's components, the friendly and relaxed voices saying that they had *drunk* too much. In the space of an hour, more or less, he had covered a distance that made his return impossible.

An old man, tooling down the highway at fifteen miles an hour, let him get to the middle of the road, where there was a grass divider. Here he was exposed to the ridicule of the northbound traffic, but after ten or fifteen minutes he was able to cross. From here he had only a short walk to the Recreation Center at the edge of the village of Lancaster, where there were some handball courts and a public pool.

The effect of the water on voices, the illusion of brilliance and suspense, was the same here as it had been at the Bunkers' but the sounds here were louder, harsher, and more shrill, and as soon as he entered the crowded enclosure he was confronted with regimentation. "ALL SWIMMERS MUST TAKE A SHOWER BEFORE USING THE POOL. ALL SWIMMERS MUST USE THE FOOTBATH. ALL SWIMMERS MUST WEAR THEIR IDENTIFICATION DISKS." He took a shower, washed his feet in a cloudy and bitter solution, and made his way to the edge of the water. It stank of chlorine and looked to him like a sink. A pair of lifeguards in a pair of towers blew police whistles at what seemed to be regular intervals and abused the swimmers through a public address system. Neddy remembered the sapphire water at the Bunkers' with longing and thought that he might contaminate himself—damage his own prosperousness and charm—by swimming in this murk, but he reminded himself that he was an explorer, a pilgrim, and that this was merely a stagnant bend in the Lucinda River. He dove, scowling with distaste, into the chlorine and had to swim with his head above water to avoid collisions, but even so he was bumped into, splashed, and jostled. When he got to the shallow end both lifeguards were shouting at him: "Hey, you, you without the identification disk, get outa the water." He did, but they had no way of pursuing him and he went through the reek of suntan oil and chlorine out through the hurricane fence and passed the handball courts. By crossing the road he entered the wooded part of the Halloran estate. The woods were not cleared and the footing was treacherous and difficult until he reached the lawn and the clipped beech hedge that encircled their pool.

The Hallorans were friends, an elderly couple of enormous wealth who seemed to bask in the suspicion that they might be Communists. They were zealous reformers but they were not Communists, and yet when they were accused, as they sometimes were, of subversion, it seemed to gratify and excite them. Their beech hedge was yellow and he guessed this had been blighted like the Levys' maple. He called hullo, hullo, to warn the Hallorans of his approach, to palliate his invasion of their privacy. The Hallorans, for reasons that had never been explained to him, did not wear bathing suits. No explanations were in order, really. Their nakedness was a detail in their uncompromising zeal for reform and he stepped politely out of his trunks before he went through the opening in the hedge.

Mrs. Halloran, a stout woman with white hair and a serene face, was reading the *Times*. Mr. Halloran was taking beech leaves out of the water with a scoop. They seemed not surprised or displeased to see him. Their pool was perhaps the oldest in the country, a fieldstone rectangle, fed by a brook. It had no filter or pump and its waters were the opaque gold of the stream.

"I'm swimming across the county," Ned said.

"Why, I didn't know one could," exclaimed Mrs. Halloran.

"Well, I've made it from the Westerhazys'," Ned said. "That must be about four miles."

He left his trunks at the deep end, walked to the shallow end, and swam this stretch. As he was pulling himself out of the water he heard Mrs. Halloran say, "We've been *terribly* sorry to hear about all your misfortunes, Neddy."

"My misfortunes?" Ned asked. "I don't know what you mean."

"Why, we heard that you'd sold the house and that your poor children . . ."

"I don't recall having sold the house," Ned said, "and the girls are at home."

"Yes," Mrs. Halloran sighed. "Yes . . ." Her voice filled the air with an unseasonable melancholy and Ned spoke briskly. "Thank you for the swim."

"Well, have a nice trip," said Mrs. Halloran.

Beyond the hedge he pulled on his trunks and fastened them. They were loose and he wondered if, during the space of an afternoon, he could have lost some weight. He was cold and he was tired and the naked Hallorans and their dark water had depressed him. The swim was too much for his strength but how could he have guessed this, sliding down the banister that morning and sitting in the Westerhazys' sun? His arms were lame. His legs felt rubbery and ached at the joints. The worst of it was the cold in his bones and the feeling that he might never be warm again. Leaves were falling down around him and he smelled wood smoke on the wind. Who would be burning wood at this time of year?

He needed a drink. Whiskey would warm him, pick him up, carry him through the last of his journey, refresh his feeling that it was original and valorous to swim across the county. Channel swimmers took brandy. He needed a stimulant. He crossed the lawn in front of the Hallorans' house and went down a little path to where they had built a house for their only daughter, Helen, and her husband, Eric Sachs. The Sachses' pool was small and he found Helen and her husband there.

"Oh, *Neddy,*" Helen said. "Did you lunch at Mother's?"

"Not *really,*" Ned said. "I *did* stop to see your parents." This seemed to be explanation enough. "I'm terribly sorry to break in on you like this but I've taken a chill and I wonder if you'd give me a drink."

"Why, I'd *love* to," Helen said, "but there hasn't been anything in this house to drink since Eric's operation. That was three years ago."

◄Was he losing his memory, had his gift for concealing painful facts let him forget that he had sold his house, that his children were in trouble, and that his friend had been ill? His eyes slipped from Eric's face to his abdomen, where he saw three pale, sutured scars, two of them at least a foot long. Gone was his navel, and what, Neddy thought, would the roving hand, bed-checking one's gifts at 3 A.M., make of a belly with no navel, no link to birth, this breach in the succession?

"I'm sure you can get a drink at the Biswangers'," Helen said. "They're having an enormous do. You can hear it from here. Listen!"

She raised her head and from across the road, the lawns, the gardens, the woods, the fields, he heard again the brilliant noise of voices over water. "Well, I'll get wet," he said, still feeling that he had no freedom of choice about his means of travel. He dove into the Sachses' cold water and, gasping, close to drowning, made his way from one end of the pool to the other.

"Lucinda and I want *terribly* to see you," he said over his shoulder, his face set toward the Biswangers'. "We're sorry it's been so long and we'll call you *very* soon."

He crossed some fields to the Biswangers' and the sounds of revelry there. They would be honored to give him a drink, they would be happy to give him a drink. The Biswangers invited him and Lucinda for dinner four times a year, six weeks in advance. They were always rebuffed and yet they continued to send out their invitations, unwilling to comprehend the rigid and undemocratic realities of their society. They were the sort of people who discussed the price of things at cocktails, exchanged market tips during dinner, and after dinner told dirty stories to mixed company. They did not belong to Neddy's set—they were not even on Lucinda's Christmas-card list. He went toward their pool with feelings of indifference, charity, and some unease, since it seemed to be getting dark and these were the longest days of the year. The party when he joined it was noisy and large. Grace Biswanger was the kind of hostess who asked the optometrist, the veterinarian, the real-estate dealer, and the dentist. No one was swimming and the twilight, reflected on the water of the pool, had a wintry gleam. There was a bar and he started for this. When Grace Biswanger saw him she came toward him, not affectionately as he had every right to expect, but bellicosely.

"Why, this party has everything," she said loudly, "including a gate crasher."

She could not deal him a social blow—there was no question about this and he did not flinch. "As a gate crasher," he asked politely, "do I rate a drink?"

"Suit yourself," she said. "You don't seem to pay much attention to invitations."

She turned her back on him and joined some guests, and he went to the bar and ordered a whiskey. The bartender served him but he served him rudely. His was a world in which the caterer's men kept the social score, and to be rebuffed by a part-time barkeep meant that he had suffered some loss of social esteem. Or perhaps the man was new and uninformed. Then he heard Grace at his back say: "They went for broke overnight—nothing but income—and he showed up drunk one Sunday and asked us to loan him five thousand dollars. . . ." She was always talking about money. It was worse than eating your peas off a knife. He dove into the pool, swam its length and went away.

The next pool on his list, the last but two, belonged to his old mistress, Shirley Adams. If he had suffered any injuries at the Biswangers' they would be cured here. Love—sexual roughhouse in fact—was the supreme elixir, the pain killer, the brightly colored pill that would put the spring back into his step, the joy of life in his heart. They had had an affair last week, last month, last year. He couldn't remember. It was he who had broken it off, his was the upper hand, and he stepped through the gate of the wall that surrounded her pool with nothing so considered as self-confidence. It seemed in a way to be his pool, as the lover, particularly the illicit lover, enjoys the possessions of his mistress with an authority unknown to holy matrimony. She was there, her hair the color of brass, but her figure, at the edge of the lighted, cerulean water, excited in him no profound memories. It had been, he thought, a light-hearted affair, although she had wept when he broke it off. She seemed confused to see him and he wondered if she was still wounded. Would she, God forbid, weep again?

"What do you want?" she asked.

"I'm swimming across the county."

"Good Christ. Will you ever grow up?"

"What's the matter?"

"If you've come here for money," she said, "I won't give you another cent."

"You could give me a drink."

"I could but I won't. I'm not alone."

"Well, I'm on my way."

He dove in and swam the pool, but when he tried to haul himself up onto the curb he found that the strength in his arms and shoulders had gone, and he paddled to the ladder and climbed out. Looking over his shoulder he saw, in the lighted bathhouse, a young man. Going out onto the dark lawn he smelled chrysanthemums or marigolds—some stubborn autumnal fragrance—on the night air, strong as gas. Looking overhead he saw that the stars had come out, but why should he seem to see Andromeda, Cepheus, and Cassiopeia? What had become of the constellations of midsummer? He began to cry.

It was probably the first time in his adult life that he had ever cried, certainly the first time in his life that he had ever felt so miserable, cold, tired, and bewildered. He could not understand the rudeness of the caterer's barkeep or the rudeness of a mistress who had come to him on her knees and showered his trousers with tears. He had swum too long, he had been immersed too long, and his nose and his throat were sore from the water. What he needed then was a drink, some company, and some clean, dry clothes, and while he could have cut directly across the road to his home he went on to the Gilmartins' pool. Here, for the first time in his life, he did not dive but went down the steps into the icy water and swam a hobbled sidestroke that he might have learned as a youth. He staggered with fatigue on his way to the Clydes' and paddled the length of their pool, stopping again and again with his hand on the curb to rest. He climbed up the ladder and wondered if he had the strength to get home. He had done what he wanted, he had swum the county, but he was so stupefied with exhaustion that his triumph seemed vague. Stooped, holding on to the gateposts for support, he turned up the driveway of his own house.

The place was dark. Was it so late that they had all gone to bed? Had Lucinda stayed at the Westerhazys' for supper? Had the girls joined her there or gone someplace else? Hadn't they agreed, as they usually did on Sunday, to regret all their invitations and stay at home? He tried the garage doors to see what cars were in but the doors were locked and rust came off the handles onto his hands. Going toward the house, he saw that the force of the thunderstorm had knocked one of the rain gutters loose. It hung down over the front door like an umbrella rib, but it could be fixed in the morning. The house was locked, and he thought that the stupid cook or the stupid maid must have locked the place up until he remembered that it had been some time since they had employed a maid or a cook. He shouted, pounded on the door, tried to force it with his shoulder, and then, looking in at the windows, saw that the place was empty.

FOR STUDY, DISCUSSION, AND WRITING

1. Explain what the Lucinda River consists of.
2. Psychologically, what is Neddy Merrill trying to accomplish by "swimming home"?
3. As the story progresses, what reversals in Neddy's life are revealed?
4. What evidence does the story offer that Neddy has blocked out certain memories from his mind? Why do you think he has blocked these things out?
5. What is suggested by the fact that at several points in the story Neddy is confused about the passage of time?
6. How do you account for the fact that Neddy discovers his swimming trunks are too large when he gets out of the pool at the Hallorans'?
7. Comment on the symbolic value of the storm that occurs when Neddy is at the Levys'.
8. What does the circling de Haviland trainer suggest about Neddy Merrill's earlier life?
9. What is suggested about Neddy's character by the reactions of the various people he encounters on his swim, especially Shirley Adams and the Biswangers?
10. Present specific evidence showing that the story is thematically commenting on the emptiness and banality of surburban life.

YUKIO MISHIMA

Three Million Yen

"We're to meet her at nine?" asked Kenzō.
"At nine, she said, in the toy department on the ground floor," replied

Kiyoko. "But it's too noisy to talk there, and I told her about the coffee shop on the third floor instead."

"That was a good idea."

The young husband and wife looked up at the neon pagoda atop the New World Building, which they were approaching from the rear.

It was a cloudy, muggy night, of a sort common in the early-summer rainy season. Neon lights painted the low sky in rich colors. The delicate pagoda, flashing on and off in the softer of neon tones, was very beautiful indeed. It was particularly beautiful when, after all the flashing neon tubes had gone out together, they suddenly flashed on again, so soon that the after-image had scarcely disappeared. To be seen from all over Asakusa, the pagoda had replaced Gourd Pond, now filled in, as the main landmark of the Asakusa night.

To Kenzō and Kiyoko the pagoda seemed to encompass in all its purity some grand, inaccessible dream of life. Leaning against the rail of the parking lot, they looked absently up at it for a time.

Kenzō was in an undershirt, cheap trousers, and wooden clogs. His skin was fair but the lines of the shoulders and chest were powerful, and bushes of black hair showed between the mounds of muscle at the armpits. Kiyoko, in a sleeveless dress, always had her own armpits carefully shaved. Kenzō was very fussy. Because they hurt when the hair began to grow again, she had become almost obsessive about keeping them shaved, and there was a faint flush on the white skin.

She had a round little face, the pretty features as though woven of cloth. It reminded one of some earnest, unsmiling little animal. It was a face which a person trusted immediately, but not one on which to read thoughts. On her arm she had a large pink plastic handbag and Kenzō's pale blue sports shirt. Kenzō liked to be empty-handed.

From her modest coiffure and make-up one sensed the frugality of their life. Her eyes were clear and had no time for other men.

They crossed the dark road in front of the parking lot and went into the New World. The big market on the ground floor was filled with myriad-colored mountains of splendid, gleaming, cheap wares, and salesgirls peeped from crevices in the mountains. Cool fluorescent lighting poured over the scene. Behind a grove of antimony models of the Tokyo Tower was a row of mirrors painted with Tokyo scenes, and in them, as the two passed, were rippling, waving images of the mountain of ties and summer shirts opposite.

"I couldn't stand living in a place with so many mirrors," said Kiyoko. "I'd be embarrassed."

"Nothing to be embarrassed about." Though his manner was gruff, Kenzō was not one to ignore what his wife said, and his answers were generally perceptive. The two had come to the toy department.

"She knows how you love the toy department. That's why she said to meet her here."

Kenzō laughed. He was fond of the trains and automobiles and space missiles, and he always embarrassed Kiyoko, getting an explanation for each one and trying each one out, but never buying. She took his arm and steered him some distance from the counter.

"It's easy to see that you want a boy. Look at the toys you pick."

"I don't care whether it's a boy or a girl. I just wish it would come soon."

"Another two years, that's all."

"Everything according to plan."

They had divided the savings account they were so assiduously building up into several parts, labeled Plan X and Plan Y and Plan Z and the like. Children must come strictly according to plan. However much they might want a child now, it would have to wait until sufficient money for Plan X had accumulated. Seeing the inadvisability, for numerous reasons, of installment buying, they waited until the money for Plan A or Plan B or Plan C had accumulated, and then paid cash for an electric washing machine or refrigerator or a television set. Plan A and Plan B had already been carried out. Plan D required little money, but, since it had as its object a low-priority clothes cupboard, it was always being pushed back. Neither of them was much interested in clothes. What they had they could hang in the closet, and all they really needed was enough to keep them warm in the winter.

They were very cautious when making a large purchase. They collected catalogues and looked at various possibilities and asked the advice of people who had already made the purchase, and, when the time for buying finally came, went off to a wholesaler in Okachimachi.

A child was still more serious. First there had to be a secure livelihood and enough money, more than enough money, to see that the child had surroundings of which a parent need not be ashamed, if not, perhaps, enough to see it all the way to adulthood. Kenzō had already made thorough inquiries with friends who had children, and knew what expenditures for powdered milk could be considered reasonable.

With their own plans so nicely formed, the two had nothing but contempt for the thoughtless, floundering ways of the poor. Children were to be produced according to plan in surroundings ideal for rearing them, and the best days were waiting after a child had arrived. Yet they were sensible enough not to pursue their dreams too far. They kept their eyes on the light immediately before them.

There was nothing that enraged Kenzō more than the view of the young that life in contemporary Japan was without hope. He was not a person given to deep thinking, but he had an almost religious faith that if a man respected nature and was obedient to it, and if he but made an effort for himself, the way would somehow open. The first thing was reverence for nature, founded on connubial affection. The greatest antidote for despair was the faith of a man and woman in each other.

Fortunately, he was in love with Kiyoko. To face the future hopefully, therefore, he had only to follow the conditions laid down by nature. Now and then some other woman made a motion in his direction, but he sensed something unnatural in pleasure for the sake of pleasure. It was better to listen to

Kiyoko complaining about the dreadful price these days of vegetables and fish.

The two had made a round of the market and were back at the toy department.

Kenzō's eyes were riveted to the toy before him, a station for flying saucers. On the sheet-metal base the complicated mechanism was painted as if viewed through a window, and a revolving light flashed on and off inside the control tower. The flying saucer, of deep-blue plastic, worked on the old principle of the flying top. The station was apparently suspended in space, for the background of the metal base was covered with stars and clouds, among the former the familiar rings of Saturn.

The bright stars of the summer night were splendid. The painted metal surface was indescribably cool, and it was as if all the discomfort of the muggy night would go if a person but gave himself up to that sky.

Before Kiyoko could stop him, Kenzō had resolutely snapped a spring at one corner of the station.

The saucer went spinning toward the ceiling.

The salesgirl reached out and gave a little cry.

The saucer described a gentle arc toward the pastry counter across the aisle and settled square on the million yen crackers.

"We're in!" Kenzō ran over to it.

"What do you mean, we're in?" Embarrassed, Kiyoko turned quickly away from the salesgirl and started after him.

"Look, look where it landed. This means good luck. Not a doubt about it."

The oblong crackers were in the shape of decidedly large banknotes, and the baked-in design, again like a banknote, carried the words "One Million Yen." On the printed label of the cellophane wrapper, the figure of a bald shopkeeper took the place of Prince Shotoku, who decorates most banknotes. There were three large crackers in each package.

Over the objections of Kiyoko, who thought fifty yen for three crackers ridiculous, Kenzō bought a package to make doubly sure of the good luck. He immediately broke the wrapping, gave a cracker to Kiyoko, and took one himself. The third went into her handbag.

As his strong teeth bit into the cracker, a sweet, slightly bitter taste flowed into his mouth. Kiyoko took a little mouse-like bite from her own cracker, almost too large for her grasp.

Kenzō brought the flying saucer back to the toy counter. The salesgirl, out of sorts, looked away as she reached to take it.

Kiyoko had high, arched breasts, and, though she was small, her figure was good. When she walked with Kenzō she seemed to be hiding in his shadow. At street crossings he would take her arm firmly, look to the right and the left, and help her across, pleased at the feel of the rich flesh.

Kenzō liked the pliant strength in a woman who, although she could perfectly well do things for herself, always deferred to her husband. Kiyoko had never read a newspaper, but she had an astonishingly accurate knowledge of her surroundings. When she took a comb in her hand or turned over the leaf of a calendar or folded a summer kimono, it was not as if she were engaged in housework, but rather as if, fresh and alert, she were keeping company with the "things" known as comb and calendar and kimono. She soaked in her world of things as she might soak in a bath.

"There's an indoor amusement park on the fourth floor. We can kill time there," said Kenzō. Kiyoko followed silently into a waiting elevator, but when they reached the fourth floor she tugged at his belt.

"It's a waste of money. Everything seems so cheap, but it's all arranged so that you spend more money than you intend to."

"That's no way to talk. This is our good night, and if you tell yourself it's like a first-run movie it doesn't seem so expensive."

"What's the sense in a first-run movie? If you wait a little while you can see it for half as much."

Her earnestness was most engaging. A brown smudge from the cracker clung to her puckered lips.

"Wipe your mouth," said Kenzō. "You're making a mess of yourself."

Kiyoko looked into a mirror on a near-by pillar and removed the smear with the nail of her little finger. She still had two thirds of a cracker in her hand.

They were at the entrance to "Twenty Thousand Leagues Under the Sea." Jagged rocks reached to the ceiling, and the porthole of a submarine on the sea floor served as the ticket window: forty yen for adults, twenty yen for children.

"But forty yen is too high," said Kiyoko, turning away from the mirror. "You aren't any less hungry after you look at all those cardboard fish, and for forty yen you can get a hundred grams of the best kind of real fish."

"Yesterday they wanted forty for a cut of black snapper. Oh, well. When you're chewing on a million yen you don't talk like a beggar."

The brief debate finished, Kenzō bought the tickets.

"You've let that cracker go to your head."

"But it isn't bad at all. Just right when you're hungry."

"You just ate."

At a landing like a railway platform five or six little boxcars, each large enough for two people, stood at intervals along a track. Three or four other couples were waiting, but the two climbed unabashedly into a car. It was in fact a little tight for two, and Kenzō had to put his arm around his wife's shoulders.

The operator was whistling somewhat disdainfully. Kenzō's powerful arm, on which the sweat had dried, was solid against Kiyoko's naked shoulders and back. Naked skin clung to naked skin like the layers of some intricately folded insect's wing. The car began to shake.

"I'm afraid," said Kiyoko, with the expression of one not in the least afraid.

The cars, each some distance from the rest, plunged into a dark tunnel of rock. Immediately inside there was a sharp curve, and the reverberations were deafening.

A huge shark with shining green scales passed, almost brushing their heads, and Kiyoko ducked away. As she clung to her young husband he gave her a kiss. After the shark had passed, the car ground around a curve in pitch darkness again, but his lips landed unerringly on hers, little fish speared in the dark. The little fish jumped and were still.

The darkness made Kiyoko strangely shy. Only the violent shaking and grinding sustained her. As she slipped deep into the tunnel, her husband's arms around her, she felt naked and flushed crimson. The darkness, dense and impenetrable, had a strength that seemed to render clothes useless. She thought of a dark shed she had secretly played in as a child.

Like a flower springing from the darkness, a red beam of light flashed at them, and Kiyoko cried out once more. It was the wide, gaping mouth of a big angler fish on the ocean floor. Around it, coral fought with the poisonous dark green of seaweed.

Kenzō put his cheek to his wife's—she was still clinging to him—and with the fingers of the arm around her shoulders played with her hair. Compared to the motion of the car the motion of the fingers was slow and deliberate. She knew that he was enjoying the show and enjoying her fright at it as well.

"Will it be over soon? I'm afraid." But her voice was drowned out in the roar.

Once again they were in darkness. Though frightened, Kiyoko had her store of courage. Kenzō's arms were around her, and there was no fight and no shame she could not bear. Because hope had never left them, the state of happiness was for the two of them just such a state of tension.

A big, muddy octopus appeared before them. Once again Kiyoko cried out. Kenzō promptly kissed the nape of her neck. The great tentacles of the octopus filled the cave, and a fierce lightning darted from its eyes.

At the next curve a drowned corpse was standing disconsolately in a seaweed forest.

Finally the light at the far end began to show, the car slowed down, and they were liberated from the unpleasant noise. At the bright platform the uniformed attendant waited to catch the forward handle of the car.

"Is that all?" asked Kenzō.

The man said that it was.

Arching her back, Kiyoko climbed to the platform and whispered in Kenzō's ear: "It makes you feel like a fool, paying forty yen for that."

At the door they compared their crackers. Kiyoko had two thirds left, and Kenzō more than half.

"Just as big as when we came in," said Kenzō. "It was so full of thrills that we didn't have time to eat."

"If you think about it that way, it doesn't seem so bad after all."

Kenzō's eyes were already on the gaudy sign by another door. Electric decorations danced around the word "Magicland," and green and red lights flashed on and off in the startled eyes of a cluster of dwarfs, their domino costumes shining in gold and silver dust. A bit shy about suggesting immediately that they go in, Kenzō leaned against the wall and munched away at his cracker.

"Remember how we crossed the parking lot? The light brought out our shadows on the ground, maybe two feet apart, and a funny idea came to me. I thought to myself how it would be if a little boy's shadow bobbed up and we took it by the hand. And just then a shadow really did break away from ours and come between them."

"No!"

"Then I looked around, and it was someone behind us. A couple of drivers were playing catch, and one of them had dropped the ball and run after it."

"One of these days we really will be out walking, three of us."

"And we'll bring it here." Kenzō motioned toward the sign. "And so we ought to go in and have a look at it first."

Kiyoko said nothing this time as he started for the ticket window.

Possibly because it was a bad time of the day, Magicland was not popular. On both sides of the path as they entered there were flashing banks of artificial flowers. A music box was playing.

"When we build our house this is the way we'll have the path."

"But it's in very bad taste," objected Kiyoko.

How would it feel to go into a house of your own? A building fund had not yet appeared in the plans of the two, but in due course it would. Things they scarcely dreamed of would one day appear in the most natural way imaginable. Usually so prudent, they let their dreams run on this evening, perhaps, as Kiyoko said, because the million-yen crackers had gone to their heads.

Great artificial butterflies were taking honey from the artificial flowers. Some were as big as brief cases, and there were yellow and black spots on their translucent red wings. Tiny bulbs flashed on and off in their protuberant eyes. In the light from below, a soft aura as of sunset in a mist bathed the plastic flowers and grasses. It may have been dust rising from the floor.

The first room they came to, following the arrow, was the leaning room. The floor and all the furnishings leaned so that when one entered upright there was a grating, discordant note to the room.

"Not the sort of house I'd want to live in," said Kenzō, bracing himself against a table on which there were yellow wooden tulips. The words were like a command. He was not himself aware of it, but his decisiveness was that of the privileged one whose hope and well-being refuse to admit outsiders. It was not strange that in the hope there was a scorn for the hopes of others and that no one was allowed to lay a finger on the well-being.

Braced against the leaning table, the determined figure in the undershirt made Kiyoko smile. It was a very domestic scene. Kenzō was like an outraged young man who, having built an extra room on his Sunday holidays, had made a mistake somewhere and ended up with the windows and floors all askew.

"You *could* live in a place like this, though," said Kiyoko. Spreading her arms like a mechanical doll, she leaned forward as the room leaned, and her face approached Kenzō's broad left shoulder at the same angle as the wooden tulips.

His brow wrinkled in a serious young frown, Kenzō smiled. He kissed the cheek that leaned toward him and bit roughly into his million-yen cracker.

By the time they had emerged from the wobbly staircases, the shaking passageways, the log bridges from the railings of which monster heads protruded, and numerous other curious places as well, the heat was too much for them. Kenzō finished his own cracker, took what was left of his wife's between his teeth, and set out in search of a cool evening breeze. Beyond a row of rocking horses a door led out to a balcony.

"What time is it?" asked Kiyoko.

"A quarter to nine. Let's go out and cool off till nine."

"I'm thirsty. The cracker was so dry." She fanned at her perspiring white throat with Kenzō's sports shirt.

"In a minute you can have something to drink."

The night breeze was cool on the wide balcony. Kenzō yawned a wide yawn and leaned against the railing beside his wife. Bare young arms caressed the black railing, wet with the night dew.

"It's much cooler than when we came in."

"Don't be silly," said Kenzō. "It's just higher."

Far below, the black machines of the outdoor amusement park seemed to slumber. The bare seats of the merry-go-round, slightly inclined, were exposed to the dew. Between the iron bars of the aerial observation car, suspended chairs swayed gently in the breeze.

The liveliness of the restaurant to the left was in complete contrast. They had a bird's-eye view into all the corners of the wide expanse inside its walls. Everything was there to look at, as if on a stage: the roofs of the separate cottages, the passages joining them, the ponds and brooks in the garden, the stone lanterns, the interiors of the Japanese rooms, some with serving maids whose kimono sleeves were held up by red cords, others with dancing geisha. The strings of lanterns at the eaves were beautiful, and their white lettering was beautiful too.

The wind carried away the noises of the place, and there was something almost mystically beautiful about it, congealed in delicate detail there at the bottom of the murky summer night.

"I'll bet it's expensive." Kiyoko was once more at her favorite romantic topic.

"Naturally. Only a fool would go there."

"I'll bet they say that cucumbers are a great delicacy, and they charge some fantastic price. How much?"

"Two hundred, maybe." Kenzō took his sports shirt and started to put it on.

Buttoning it for him, Kiyoko continued: "They must think their customers are fools. Why, that's ten times what cucumbers are worth. You can get three of the very best for twenty yen."

"Oh? They're getting cheap."

"The price started going down a week or so ago."

It was five to nine. They went out to look for a stairway to the coffee shop on the third floor. Two of the crackers had disappeared. The other was too large for Kiyoko's very large handbag, and protruded from the unfastened clasp.

The old lady, an impatient person, had arrived early and was waiting. The seats from which the loud jazz orchestra could best be seen were all taken, but there were vacant places where the bandstand was out of sight, beside the potted palm probably rented from some gardener. Sitting alone in a summer kimono, the old lady seemed wholly out of place.

She was a small woman not far past middle age, and she had the clean, well-tended face of the plebian lowlands. She spoke briskly with many delicate gestures. She was proud of the fact that she got along so nicely with young people.

"You'll be treating me, of course, so I ordered something expensive while I was waiting." Even as she spoke the tall glass arrived, pieces of fruit atop a parfait.

"Now that was generous of you. All we needed was soda water."

Her outstretched little finger taut, the old lady plunged in with her spoon and skillfully brought out the cream beneath. Meanwhile she was talking along at her usual brisk pace.

"It's nice that this place is so noisy and no one can hear us. Tonight we go to Nakano—I think I mentioned it over the phone. An ordinary private house and—can you imagine it?—the customers are housewives having a class re-union. There's not much that the rich ladies don't know about these days. And I imagine they walk around pretending the idea never entered their heads. Anyway, I told them about you, and they said they had to have you and no one else. They don't want someone who's all beaten up by the years, you know. And I must say that I can't blame them. So I asked a good stiff price and she said it was low and if they were pleased they'd give you a good tip. They haven't any idea what the market rate is, of course. But I want you to do your best, now. I'm sure I don't need to tell you, but if they're pleased we'll get all sorts of rich customers. There aren't many that go as well together as you two do, of course, and I'm not worried, but don't do anything to make me ashamed of you. Well, anyhow, the woman of the house is the wife of some important person or other, and she'll be waiting for us at the coffee shop in front of Nakano station. You know what will happen next. She'll send the taxi through all sorts of back alleys to get us mixed up. I don't imagine she'll blindfold us, but she'll pull us through the back door so we don't have a chance to read the sign on the gate. I won't like it any better than you will, but she has herself to consider, after all. Don't let it bother you. Me? Oh, I'll be doing the usual thing, keeping watch in the hall. I can bluff my way through, I don't care who comes in. Well, maybe we ought to get started. And let me say it again, I want a good performance from you."

It was late in the night, and Kiyoko and Kenzō had left the old lady and were back in Asakusa. They were even more exhausted than usual. Kenzō's wooden clogs dragged along the street. The billboards in the park were a poisonous black under the cloudy sky.

Simultaneously, they looked up at the New World. The neon pagoda was dark.

"What a rotten bunch. I don't think I've ever seen such a rotten, stuck-up bunch," said Kenzō.

Her eyes on the ground, Kiyoko did not answer.

"Well? Did you ever see a worse bunch of affected old women?"

"No. But what can you do? The pay was good."

"Playing around with money they pry from their husbands. Don't get to be that way when you have money."

"Silly." Kiyoko's smiling face was sharply white in the darkness.

"A really nasty bunch." Kenzō spat in a strong white arc. "How much?"

"This." Kiyoko reached artlessly into her handbag and pulled out some bills.

"Five thousand? We've never made that much before. And the old woman took three thousand. Damn! I'd like to tear it up, that's what I'd like to do. That would really feel good."

Kiyoko took the money back in some consternation. Her finger touched the last of the million-yen crackers.

"Tear this up in its place," she said softly.

Kenzō took the cracker, wadded the cellophane wrapper, and threw it to the ground. It crackled sharply on the silent, deserted street. Too large for one hand, he took the cracker in both hands and tried to break it. It was damp and soggy, and the sweet surface stuck to his hands. The more it bent the more it resisted. He was in the end unable to break it.

FOR STUDY, DISCUSSION, AND WRITING

1. Where does this story take place?
2. In what ways are Kenzō and Kiyoko ordinary big-city dwellers?
3. How do Kenzō and Kiyoko make their living?
4. Contrast the way Kenzō and Kiyoko make their living with the nature of their dreams about the future.
5. Identify several ways that Mishima calls attention to the warped and artificial society in which Kenzō and Kiyoko live.
6. What is ironic about Kenzō's faith that if a person respects nature and is obedient to it, success will follow?
7. What is ironic about Kenzō's comment that he would not want to live in

a leaning room like the room in Magicland and Kiyoko's reply, "You *could* live in a room like this, though"?

8. Why do you think the old women who watch the performances of Kenzō and Kiyoko are interested in such shows?

9. What significance can you give to the fact that Kenzō, at the end of the story, is unable to break the one-million-yen cracker?

TONI CADE BAMBARA

The Lesson

Back in the days when everyone was old and stupid or young and foolish and me and Sugar were the only ones just right, this lady moved on our block with nappy hair and proper speech and no makeup. And quite naturally we laughed at her, laughed the way we did at the junk man who went about his business like he was some big-time president and his sorry-ass horse his secretary. And we kinda hated her too, hated the way we did the winos who cluttered up our parks and pissed on our handball walls and stank up our hallways and stairs so you couldn't halfway play hide-and-seek without a goddamn gas mask. Miss Moore was her name. The only woman on the block with no first name. And she was black as hell, cept for her feet, which were fish-white and spooky. And she was always planning these boring-ass things for us to do, us being my cousin, mostly, who lived on the block cause we all moved North the same time and to the same apartment then spread out gradual to breathe. And our parents would yank our heads into some kinda shape and crisp up our clothes so we'd be presentable for travel with Miss Moore, who always looked like she was going to church, though she never did. Which is just one of things the grownups talked about when they talked behind her back like a dog. But when she came calling with some sachet she'd sewed up or some gingerbread she'd made or some book, why then they'd all be too embarrassed to turn her down and we'd get handed over all spruced up. She'd been to college and said it was only right that she should take responsibility for the young ones' education, and she not even related by marriage or blood. So they'd go for it. Specially Aunt Gretchen. She was the main gofer in the family. You got some ole dumb shit foolishness you want somebody to go for, you send for Aunt Gretchen. She been screwed into the go-along for so long, it's a blood-deep natural thing with her. Which is how she got saddled with me and Sugar and Junior in the first place while our mothers were in a la-de-da apartment up the block having a good ole time.

So this one day Miss Moore rounds us all up at the mailbox and it's puredee hot and she's knockin herself out about arithmetic. And school suppose to let up in summer I heard, but she don't never let up. And the starch in my pinafore scratching the shit outta me and I'm really hating this nappy-head bitch and her goddamn college degree. I'd much rather go to the pool or to the show where it's cool. So me and Sugar leaning on the mailbox being surly, which is a Miss Moore word. And Flyboy checking out what everybody brought for lunch. And Fat Butt already wasting his peanut-butter-and-jelly sandwich like the pig he is. And Junebug punchin on Q.T.'s arm for potato chips. And Rosie Giraffe shifting from one hip to the other waiting for some- body to step on her foot or ask her if she from Georgia so she can kick ass, preferably Mercedes'. And Miss Moore asking us do we know what money is, like we a bunch of retards. I mean real money, she say, like it's only poker chips or monopoly papers we lay on the grocer. So right away I'm tired of this and say so. And would much rather snatch Sugar and go to the Sunset and terrorize the West Indian kids and take their hair ribbons and their money too. And Miss Moore files that remark away for next week's lesson on broth- erhood, I can tell. And finally I say we oughta get to the subway cause it's cooler and besides we might meet some cute boys. Sugar done swiped her mama's lipstick, so we ready.

So we heading down the street and she's boring us silly about what things cost and what our parents make and how much goes for rent and how money ain't divided up right in this country. And then she gets to the part about we all poor and live in the slums, which I don't feature. And I'm ready to speak on that, but she steps out in the street and hails two cabs just like that. Then she hustles half the crew in with her and hands me a five-dollar bill and tells me to calculate 10 percent tip for the driver. And we're off. Me and Sugar and Junebug and Flyboy hangin out the window and hollering to everybody, put- ting lipstick on each other cause Flyboy a faggot anyway, and making farts with our sweaty armpits. But I'm mostly trying to figure how to spend this money. But they all fascinated with the meter ticking and Junebug starts laying bets as to how much it'll read when Flyboy can't hold his breath no more. Then Sugar lays bets as to how much it'll be when we get there. So I'm stuck. Don't nobody want to go for my plan, which is to jump out at the next light and run off to the first bar-b-que we can find. Then the driver tells us to get the hell out cause we there already. And the meter reads eighty-five cents. And I'm stalling to figure out the tip and Sugar say give him a dime. And I decide he don't need it bad as I do, so later for him. But then he tries to take off with Junebug foot still in the door so we talk about his mama something ferocious. Then we check out that we on Fifth Avenue and everybody dressed up in stockings. One lady in a fur coat, hot as it is. White folks crazy.

"This is the place," Miss Moore say, presenting it to us in the voice she uses at the museum. "Let's look in the windows before we go in."

"Can we steal?" Sugar asks very serious like she's getting the ground rules squared away before she plays. "I beg your pardon," say Miss Moore, and we fall out. So she leads us around the windows of the toy store and me and

Sugar screamin, "This is mine, that's mine, I gotta have that, that was made for me, I was born for that," till Big Butt drowns us out.

"Hey, I'm goin to buy that there."

"That there? You don't even know what it is, stupid."

"I do so," he say punchin on Rosie Giraffe. "It's a microscope."

"Whatcha gonna do with a microscope, fool?"

"Look at things."

"Like what, Ronald?" ask Miss Moore. And Big Butt ain't got the first notion. So here go Miss Moore gabbing about the thousands of bacteria in a drop of water and the somethinorother in a speck of blood and the million and one living things in the air around us is invisible to the naked eye. And what she say that for? Junebug go to town on that "naked" and we rolling. Then Miss Moore ask what it cost. So we all jam into the window smudgin it up and the price tag say $300. So then she ask how long'd take for Big Butt and Junebug to save up their allowances. "Too long," I say. "Yeh," adds Sugar, "outgrown it by that time." And Miss Moore say no, you never outgrow learning instruments. "Why, even medical students and interns and," blah, blah, blah. And we ready to choke Big Butt for bringing it up in the first damn place.

"This here costs four hundred eighty dollars," say Rosie Giraffe. So we pile up all over her to see what she pointin out. My eyes tell me it's a chunk of glass cracked with something heavy, and different-color inks dripped into the splits, then the whole thing put into a oven or something. But for $480 it don't make sense.

"That's a paperweight made of semi-precious stones fused together under tremendous pressure," she explains slowly, with her hands doing the mining and all the factory work.

"So what's a paperweight?" asks Rosie Giraffe.

"To weigh paper with, dumbbell," say Flyboy, the wise man from the East.

"Not exactly," say Miss Moore, which is what she say when you warm or way off too. "It's to weigh paper down so it won't scatter and make your desk untidy." So right away me and Sugar curtsy to each other and then to Mercedes who is more the tidy type.

"We don't keep paper on top of the desk in my class," say Junebug, figuring Miss Moore crazy or lyin one.

"At home, then," she say. "Don't you have a calendar and a pencil case and a blotter and a letter-opener on your desk at home where you do your homework?" And she know damn well what our homes look like cause she nosys around in them every chance she gets.

"I don't even have a desk," say Junebug. "Do we?"

"No. And I don't get no homework neither," say Big Butt.

"And I don't even have a home," say Flyboy like he do at school to keep the white folks off his back and sorry for him. Send this poor kid to camp posters, is his specialty.

"I do," says Mercedes. "I have a box of stationery on my desk and a picture of my cat. My godmother bought the stationery and the desk. There's a big rose on each sheet and the envelopes smell like roses."

"Who wants to know about your smelly-ass stationery," say Rosie Giraffe fore I can get my two cents in.

"It's important to have a work area all your own so that . . ."

"Will you look at this sailboat, please," say Flyboy, cuttin her off and pointin to the thing like it was his. So once again we tumble all over each other to gaze at this magnificent thing in the toy store which is just big enough to maybe sail two kittens across the pond if you strap them to the posts tight. We all start reciting the price tag like we in assembly. "Handcrafted sailboat of fiberglass at one thousand one hundred ninety-five dollars."

"Unbelievable," I hear myself say and am really stunned. I read it again for myself just in case the group recitation put me in a trance. Same thing. For some reason this pisses me off. We look at Miss Moore and she lookin at us, waiting for I dunno what.

"Who'd pay all that when you can buy a sailboat set for a quarter at Pop's, a tube of glue for a dime, and a ball of string for eight cents? "It must have a motor and a whole lot else besides," I say. "My sailboat cost me about fifty cents."

"But will it take water?" say Mercedes with her smart ass.

"Took mine to Alley Pond Park once," say Flyboy. "String broke. Lost it. Pity."

"Sailed mine in Central Park and it keeled over and sank. Had to ask my father for another dollar."

"And you got the strap," laugh Big Butt. "The jerk didn't even have a string on it. My old man wailed on his behind."

Little Q.T. was staring hard at the sailboat and you could see he wanted it bad. But he too little and somebody'd just take it from him. So what the hell. "This boat for kids, Miss Moore?"

"Parents silly to buy something like that just to get all broke up," say Rosie Giraffe.

"That much money it should last forever," I figure.

"My father'd buy it for me if I wanted it."

"Your father, my ass," say Rosie Giraffe getting a chance to finally push Mercedes.

"Must be rich people shop here," say Q.T.

"You are a very bright boy," say Flyboy. "What was your first clue?" And he rap him on the head with the back of his knuckles, since Q.T. the only one he could get away with. Though Q.T. liable to come up behind you years later and get his licks in when you half expect it.

"What I want to know is," I says to Miss Moore though I never talk to her, I wouldn't give the bitch that satisfaction, "is how much a real boat costs? I figure a thousand'd get you a yacht any day."

"Why don't you check that out," she says, "and report back to the group?" Which really pains my ass. If you gonna mess up a perfectly good swim day least you could do is have some answers. "Let's go in," she say like she got something up her sleeve. Only she don't lead the way. So me and Sugar turn the corner to where the entrance is, but when we get there I kinda hang back. Not that I'm scared, what's there to be afraid of, just a toy store. But I feel funny, shame. But what I got to be shamed about? Got as much right to go in as anybody. But somehow I can't seem to get hold of the door, so I step away for Sugar to lead. But she hangs back too. And I look at her and she looks at me and this is ridiculous. I mean, damn, I have never ever been shy about doing nothing or going nowhere. But then Mercedes steps up and then Rosie Giraffe and Big Butt crowd in behind and shove, and next thing we all stuffed into the doorway with only Mercedes squeezing past us, smoothing out her jumper and walking right down the aisle. Then the rest of us tumble in like a glued-together jigsaw done all wrong. And people lookin at us. And it's like the time me and Sugar crashed into the Catholic church on a dare. But once we got in there and everything so hushed and holy and the candles and the bowin and the handkerchiefs on all the drooping heads, I just couldn't go through with the plan. Which was for me to run up to the altar and do a tap dance while Sugar played the nose flute and messed around in the holy water. And Sugar kept givin me the elbow. Then later teased me so bad I tied her up in the shower and turned it on and locked her in. And she'd be there till this day if Aunt Gretchen hadn't finally figured I was lyin about the boarder takin a shower.

Same thing in the store. We all walkin on tiptoe and hardly touchin the games and puzzles and things. And I watched Miss Moore who is steady watchin us like she waitin for a sign. Like Mama Drewery watches the sky and sniffs the air and takes note of just how much slant is in the bird formation. Then me and Sugar bump smack into each other, so busy gazing at the toys, 'specially the sailboat. But we don't laugh and go into our fat-lady bump-stomach routine. We just stare at that price tag. Then Sugar run a finger over the whole boat. And I'm jealous and want to hit her. Maybe not her, but I sure want to punch somebody in the mouth.

"Watcha bring us here for, Miss Moore?"

"You sound angry, Sylvia. Are you mad about something?" Givin me one of them grins like she tellin a grown-up joke that never turns out to be funny. And she's lookin very closely at me like maybe she plannin to do my portrait from memory. I'm mad, but I won't give her that satisfaction. So I slouch around the store bein very bored and say, "Let's go."

Me and Sugar at the back of the train watchin the tracks whizzin by large then small then gettin gobbled up in the dark. I'm thinkin about this tricky toy I saw in the store. A clown that somersaults on a bar then does chin-ups just cause you yank lightly at his leg. Cost $35. I could see me askin my mother for a $35 birthday clown. "You wanna who that costs what?" she'd say, cocking her head to the side to get a better view of the hole in my head. Thirty-five dollars could buy new bunk beds for Junior and Gretchen's boy.

Thirty-five dollars and the whole household could go visit Granddaddy Nelson in the country. Thirty-five dollars would pay for the rent and the piano bill too. Who are these people that spend that much for performing clowns and $1,000 for toy sailboats? What kinda work they do and how they live and how come we ain't in on it? Where we are is who we are, Miss Moore always pointin out. But it don't necessarily have to be that way, she always adds then waits for somebody to say that poor people have to wake up and demand their share of the pie and don't none of us know what kind of pie she talkin about in the first damn place. But she ain't so smart cause I still got her four dollars from the taxi and she sure ain't gettin it. Messin up my day with this shit. Sugar nudges me in my pocket and winks.

Miss Moore lines us up in front of the mailbox where we started from, seem like years ago, and I got a headache for thinkin so hard. And we lean all over each other so we can hold up under the draggy-ass lecture she always finishes us off with at the end before we thank her for borin us to tears. But she just looks at us like she readin tea leaves. Finally she say, "Well, what did you think of F.A.O. Schwartz?"

Rosie Giraffe mumbles, "White folks crazy."

"I'd like to go there again when I get my birthday money," says Mercedes, and we shove her out the pack so she has to lean on the mailbox by herself.

"I'd like a shower. Tiring day," say Flyboy.

Then Sugar surprises me by sayin, "You know, Miss Moore, I don't think all of us here put together eat in a year what that sailboat costs." And Miss Moore lights up like somebody goosed her. "And?" she say, urging Sugar on. Only I'm standin on her foot so she don't continue.

"Imagine for a minute what kind of society it is in which some people can spend on a toy what it would cost to feed a family of six or seven. What do you think?"

"I think," say Sugar pushing me off her feet like she never done before, cause I whip her ass in a minute, "that this is not much of a democracy if you ask me. Equal chance to pursue happiness means an equal crack at the dough, don't it?" Miss Moore is besides herself and I am disgusted with Sugar's treachery. So I stand on her foot one more time to see if she'll shove me. She shuts up, and Miss Moore looks at me, sorrowfully I'm thinkin. And somethin weird is goin on, I can feel it in my chest.

"Anybody else learn anything today?" lookin dead at me. I walk away and Sugar has to run to catch up and don't even seem to notice when I shrug her arm off my shoulder.

"Well, we got four dollars anyway," she says.

"Uh hunh."

"We could go to Hascombs and get half a chocolate layer and then go to the Sunset and still have plenty money for potato chips and ice-cream sodas."

"Uh hunh."

"Race you to Hascombs," she say.

We start down the block and she gets ahead which is O.K. by me cause I'm goin to the West End and then over to the Drive to think this day through. She can run if she want to and even run faster. But ain't nobody gonna beat me at nuthin.

FOR STUDY, DISCUSSION, AND WRITING

1. What do you think the author is trying to accomplish by having the narrator of the story use the type of language that she does to tell her tale?
2. Discuss whether Miss Moore's project of taking the children to the F. A. O. Schwartz toy store was a good idea. Do you think Miss Moore had any ulterior motives for the outing?
3. What is ironic about the narrator's consistently humorous tone throughout the story?
4. What is the lesson that the children learn from the outing? Is the lesson the same for each child?
5. Although Toni Cade Bambara is the author of this story, you should not confuse her with the story's narrator. Keeping this distinction in mind, what evidence can you find that the narrator is unreliable? Going one step further, can you find other characters in the story who might be identified with Toni Cade Bambara?

RENATA ADLER

Brownstone

The camel, I had noticed, was passing, with great difficulty, through the eye of the needle. The Apollo flight, the four-minute mile, Venus in Scorpio, human records on land and at sea—these had been events of enormous importance. But the camel, practicing in near obscurity for almost two thousand years, was passing through. First the velvety nose, then the rest. Not many were aware. But if the lead camel and then perhaps the entire caravan could make it, the thread, the living thread of camels, would exist, could not be lost. No one could lose the thread. The prospects of the rich would be enhanced. "Ortega tells us that the business of philosophy," the professor was telling his class of indifferent freshmen, "is to crack open metaphors which are dead."

"I shouldn't have come," the Englishman said, waving his drink and breathing so heavily at me that I could feel my bangs shift. "I have a terrible cold."

"He would probably have married her," a voice across the room said, "with the exception that he died."

"Well, I am a personality that prefers not to be annoyed."

"We should all prepare ourselves for this eventuality."

A six-year-old was passing the hors d'oeuvres. The baby, not quite steady on his feet, was hurtling about the room.

"He's following me," the six-year-old said, in despair.

"Then lock yourself in the bathroom, dear," Inez replied.

"He always waits outside the door."

"He loves you, dear."

"Well, I don't like it."

"How I envy you," the minister's wife was saying to a courteous, bearded boy, "reading *Magic Mountain* for the first time."

The homosexual across the hall from me always takes Valium and walks his beagle. I borrow Valium from him from time to time, and when he takes a holiday the dog is left with me. On our floor of this brownstone, we are friends. Our landlord, Roger Somerset, was murdered last July. He was a kind and absent-minded man, and on the night when he was stabbed there was a sort of requiem for him in the heating system. There is a lot of music in this building anyway. The newlyweds on the third floor play Bartók on their stereo. The couple on the second floor play clarinet quintets; their kids play rock. The girl on the fourth floor, who has been pining for two months, plays Judy Collins' "Maid of Constant Sorrow" all day long. We have a kind of orchestra in here. The ground floor is a shop. The owner of the shop speaks of our landlord's murder still. Shaking his head, he says that he suspects "foul play." We all agree with him. We changed our locks. But "foul play" seems a weird expression for the case.

It is all weird. I am not always well. One block away (I often think of this), there was ten months ago an immense crash. Water mains broke. There were small rivers in the streets. In a great skyscraper that was being built, something had failed. The newspapers reported the next day that by some miracle only two people had been "slightly injured" by ten tons of falling steel. The steel fell from the eighteenth floor. The question that preoccupies me now is how, under the circumstances, slight injuries could occur. Perhaps the two people were grazed in passing by. Perhaps some fragments of the sidewalk ricocheted. I knew a deliverer of flowers who, at Sixty-ninth and Lexington, was hit by a flying suicide. Situations simply do not yield to the most likely structures of the mind. A "self-addressed envelope," if you are inclined to brood, raises deep questions of identity. Such an envelope, immutably itself, is always precisely where it belongs. "Self-pity" is just sadness, I think, in the pejorative. But "joking with nurses" fascinates me in the press. Whenever someone has been quite struck down, lost faculties, members of his family, he is said to have "joked with his nurses" quite a lot. What a mine of humor every nurse's life must be.

I have a job, of course. I have had several jobs. I've had our paper's gossip column since last month. It is egalitarian. I look for people who are quite obscure, and report who is breaking up with whom and where they go and what they wear. The person who invented this new form for us is on antidepressants now. He lives in Illinois. He says there are people in southern Illinois who have not yet been covered by the press. I often write about families in Queens. Last week, I went to a dinner party on Park Avenue. After 1 A.M., something called the Alive or Dead Game was being played. Someone would mention an old character from Tammany or Hollywood. "Dead," "Dead," "Dead," everyone would guess. "No, no. Alive. I saw him walking down the street just yesterday," or "Yes. Dead. I read a little obituary notice about him last year." One of the little truths people can subtly enrage or reassure each other with is who—when you have looked away a month, a year—is still around.

The St. Bernard at the pound on Ninety-second Street was named Bonnie and would have cost five dollars. The attendant held her tightly on a leash of rope. "Hello, Bonnie," I said. Bonnie growled. "I wouldn't talk to her if I was you," the attendant said. I leaned forward to pat her ear. Bonnie snarled. "I wouldn't touch her if I was you," the attendant said. I held out my hand under Bonnie's jowls. She strained against the leash, and choked and coughed. "Now cut that out, Bonnie," the attendant said. "Could I just take her for a walk around the block," I said, "before I decide?" "Are you out of your mind?" the attendant said. Aldo patted Bonnie, and we left.

DEAR TENANT:

We have reason to believe that there are impostors posing as Con Ed repairmen and inspectors circulating in this area.

Do not permit any Con Ed man to enter your premises or the building, if possible.

THE PRECINCT

The New York Chinese cabdriver lingered at every corner and at every traffic light, to read his paper. I wondered what the news was. I looked over his shoulder. The illustrations and the type were clear enough: newspaper print, pornographic fiction. I leaned back in my seat. A taxi-driver who happened to be Oriental with a sadomasochistic cast of mind was not my business. I lit a cigarette, looked at my bracelet. I caught the driver's eyes a moment in the rearview mirror. He picked up his paper. "I don't think you ought to read," I said, "while you are driving." Traffic was slow. I saw his mirrored eyes again. He stopped his reading. When we reached my address, I did not tip him. Racism and prudishness, I thought, and reading over people's shoulders.

But there are moments in this place when everything becomes a show of force. He can read what he likes at home. Tipping is still my option. Another newspaper event, in our brownstone. It was a holiday. The superintendent normally hauls the garbage down and sends the paper up, by dumbwaiter, each morning. On holidays, the garbage stays upstairs, the paper on the sidewalk. At 8 A.M., I went downstairs. A ragged man was lying across the little space that separates the inner door, which locks, from the outer door, which doesn't. I am not a news addict. I could have stepped over the sleeping man, picked up my *Times*, and gone upstairs to read it. Instead, I knocked absurdly from inside the door, and said, "Wake up. You'll have to leave now." He got up, lifted the flattened cardboard he had been sleeping on, and walked away, mumbling and reeking. It would have been kinder, certainly, to let the driver read, the wino sleep. One simply cannot bear down so hard on all these choices.

What is the point. That is what must be borne in mind. Sometimes the point is really who wants what. Sometimes the point is what is right or kind. Sometimes the point is a momentum, a fact, a quality, a voice, an intimation, a thing said or unsaid. Sometimes it's who's at fault, or what will happen if you do not move at once. The point changes and goes out. You cannot be forever watching for the point, or you lose the simplest thing: being a major character in your own life. But if you are, for any length of time, custodian of the point—in art, in court, in politics, in lives, in rooms—it turns out there are rear-guard actions everywhere. To see a thing clearly, and when your vision of it dims, or when it goes to someone else, if you have a gentle nature, keep your silence, that is lovely. Otherwise, now and then, a small foray is worthwhile. Just so that being always, complacently, thoroughly wrong does not become the safest position of them all. The point has never quite been entrusted to me.

My cousin, who was born on February 29th, became a veterinarian. Some years ago, when he was twenty-eight (seven, by our childhood birthday count), he was drafted, and sent to Malaysia. He spent most of his military service there, assigned to the zoo. He operated on one tiger, which, in the course of abdominal surgery, began to wake up and wag its tail. The anesthetist grabbed the tail, and injected more sodium pentothal. That tiger survived. But two flamingos, sent by the city of Miami to Kuala Lumpur as a token of good will, could not bear the trip or the climate and, in spite of my cousin's efforts, died. There was also a cobra—the largest anyone in Kuala Lumpur could remember having seen. An old man had brought it, in an immense sack, from somewhere in the countryside. The zoo director called my cousin at once, around dinnertime, to say that an unprecedented cobra had arrived. Something quite drastic, however, seemed wrong with its neck. My cousin, whom I have always admired—for his leap-year birthday, for his pilot's license, for his presence of mind—said that he would certainly examine the cobra in the morning but that the best thing for it after its long journey must be a good night's rest. By morning, the cobra was dead.

My cousin is well. The problem is this. Hardly anyone about whom I deeply care at all resembles anyone else I have ever met, or heard of, or read about in the literature. I know an Israeli general who, in 1967, retook the Mitla Pass but who, since his mandatory retirement from military service at fifty-five, has been trying to repopulate the Ark. He asked me, over breakfast at the Drake, whether I knew any owners of oryxes. Most of the vegetarian species he has collected have already multiplied enough, since he has found and cared for them, to be permitted to run wild. The carnivorous animals, though, must still be kept behind barbed wire—to keep them from stalking the rarer vegetarians. I know a group that studies Proust one Sunday afternoon a month, and an analyst, with that Exeter laugh (embittered mooing noises, and mirthless heaving of the shoulder blades), who has the most remarkable terrorist connections in the Middle East.

The conversation of *The Magic Mountain* and the unrequited love of six-year-olds occurred on Saturday, at brunch. "Bring someone new," Inez had said. "Not queer. Not married, maybe separated. John and I are breaking up." The invitation was not of a kind that I had heard before. Aldo, who lives with me between the times when he prefers to be alone, refused to come. He despises brunch. He detests Inez. I went, instead, with an editor who has been a distant, steady friend but who, ten years ago, when we first came to New York, had once put three condoms on the night table beside the phone. We both had strange ideas then about New York. Aldo is a gentle, orderly, soft-spoken man, slow to conclude. I try to be tidy when he is here, but I have often made his cigarettes, and once his manuscript, into the bed. Our paper's publisher is an intellectual from Baltimore. He has read Wittgenstein; he's always making unimpeachable remarks. Our music critic throws a tantrum every day, in print. Our book reviewer is looking for another job. He found that the packages in which all books are mailed could not, simply could not, be opened without doing considerable damage—through staples, tape, wire, fluttering gray stuff, recalcitrance—to the reviewer's hands. He felt it was a symptom of some kind—one of those cases where incompetence at every stage, across the board, acquired a certain independent force. Nothing to do with books, he thought, worked out at all. We also do the news. For horoscopes, there are the ladies' magazines, which tell you—earnestly—auspicious times to shave your legs. We just cannot compete.

"All babies are natural swimmers," John said, lowering his two-year-old son gently over the side of the rowboat, and smiling. The child thrashed and sank. Aldo dived in and grabbed him. The baby came up coughing, not crying, and looked with pure fear at his father. John looked with dismay at his son. "He would have come up in a minute," John said to Aldo, who was dripping and rowing. "You have to give nature a chance."

My late landlord was from Scarsdale. The Maid of Constant Sorrow is from Texas. Aldo is from St. Louis. Inez's versions vary about where she's from. I grew up in a New England mill town, where, in the early thirties, all the insured factories burned down. It has been difficult to get fire insurance in that region ever since. The owner of a hardware store, whose property adjoined an insured factory at the time, lost everything. Afterward, he walked all day along the railroad track, waiting for a train to run him down. Railroad service has never been very good up there. No trains came. His children own the town these days, for what it's worth. The two cobbled streets where black people always lived have been torn up and turned into a public park since a flood that occurred some years ago. Unprecedented rains came. Retailers had to destroy their sodden products, for fear of contamination. The black section was torn up and seeded over in the town's rezoning project. No one knows where the blacks live now. But there are Negroes in the stores and schools, and on the football team. It is assumed that the park integrated the town. Those black families must be living somewhere. It is a mystery.

At the women's college where I went, we had distinguished faculty in everything, digs at Nuoro and Mycenae. We had a quality of obsession in our studies. For professors who had quarrelled with their wives at breakfast, those years of bright-eyed young women, never getting any older, must have been a trial. The head of the history department once sneezed into his best student's honors thesis. He slammed it shut. It was ultimately published. When I was there, a girl called Cindy Melchior was immensely fat. She wore silk trousers and gilt mules. One day, in the overheated classroom, she laid aside her knitting and lumbered to the window, which she opened. Then she lumbered back. "Do you think," the professor asked, "you are so graceful?" He somehow meant it kindly. Cindy wept. That year, Cindy's brother Melvin phoned me. "I would have called you sooner," he said, "but I had the most terrible eczema." All the service staff on campus in those days were black. Many of them were followers of Father Divine. They took new names in the church. I remember the year when a maid called Serious Heartbreak married a janitor called Universal Dictionary. At a meeting of the faculty last fall, the college president, who is new and male, spoke of raising money. A female professor of Greek was knitting—and working on Linear B, with an abacus before her. In our time, there was a vogue for madrigals. Some of us listened, constantly, to a single record. There was a phrase we could not decipher. A professor of symbolic logic, a French Canadian, had sounds that matched but a meaning that seemed unlikely: Sheep are no angels; come upstairs. A countertenor explained it, after a local concert: She'd for no angel's comfort stay. Correct, but not so likely either.

> Paul: "Two diamonds."
> Inez: "Two hearts."
> Mary: "Three clubs."
> John: "Four kings."
> Inez: "Darling, you know you can't just bid four kings."
> John: "I don't see why. I might have been bluffing."
> Inez: "No, darling. That's poker. This is bridge. And even in poker you can't just bid four kings."
> John: "No. Well, I guess we'd better deal another hand."

The host, for some reason, was taking Instamatic pictures of his guests. It was not clear whether he was doing this in order to be able to show, at some future time, that there had been this gathering in his house. Or whether he thought of pictures in some voodoo sense. Or whether he found it difficult to talk. Or whether he was bored. Two underground celebrities—one of whom had become a sensation by never generating or exhibiting a flicker of interest in anything, the other of whom was known mainly for hanging around the first—were taking pictures too. I was there with an actor I've known for years. He had already been received in an enormous embrace by an Eastern European poet, whose hair was cut too short but who was neither as awkwardly spontaneous nor as drunk as he cared to seem. The party was in honor of the poet, who celebrated the occasion by insulting everyone and being fawned upon, by distinguished and undistinguished writers alike. "This group looks as though someone had torn up a few guest lists and floated the pieces on the air," the actor said. The friend of the underground sensation walked up to us and said hello. Then, in a verbal seizure of some sort, he began muttering obscenities. The actor said a few calming things that didn't work. He finally put his finger on the mutterer's lips. The mutterer bit that finger extremely hard, and walked away. The actor wrapped his finger in a paper napkin, and got himself another drink. We stayed till twelve.

When I worked, for a time, in the infirmary of a branch of an upstate university, it was becoming more difficult with each passing semester, except in the most severe cases, to determine which students had mental or medical problems. At the clinic, young men with straggly beards and stained bluejeans wept alongside girls in jeans and frayed sweaters—all being fitted with contact lenses, over which they then wore granny glasses. There was no demand for prescription granny glasses at all. For the severely depressed, the paranoids, and the hallucinators, our young psychiatrists prescribed "mood elevators," pills that were neither uppers nor downers but which affected the bloodstream in such a way that within three to five weeks many sad outpatients became very cheerful, and several saints and historical figures became again Midwestern graduate students under tolerable stress. On one, not unusual, morning, the clinic had a call from an instructor in political science. "I am in the dean's office," he said. "My health is quite perfect. They want me to have a check-up."

"Oh?" said the doctor on duty. "Perhaps you could come in on Friday."

"The problem is," the voice on the phone said, "I have always thought myself, and been thought by others, a Negro. Now, through research, I have found that my family on both sides have always been white."

"Oh," the doctor on duty said. "Perhaps you could just take a cab and come over."

Within twenty minutes, the political-science instructor appeared at the clinic. He was black. The doctor said nothing, and began a physical examination. By the time his blood pressure was taken, the patient confided that his white ancestors were, in fact, royal. The mood elevators restored him. He and the doctor became close friends besides. A few months later, the instructor took a job with the government in Washington. Two weeks after that, he was calling the clinic again. "I have found new documentation," he said. "All eight of my great-grandparents were pure-blooded Germans—seven from Prussia, one from Alsace. I thought I should tell you, dear friend." The doctor suggested he come for the weekend. By Sunday afternoon, a higher dose of the pill had had its effect. The problem has not since recurred.

The Maid of Constant Sorrow said our landlord's murder marked a turning point in her analysis. "I don't feel guilty. I feel hated," she said. It is true, for a time, we all wanted to feel somehow part—if only because violence offset the ineluctable in our lives. My grandfather said that some people have such extreme insomnia that they look at their watches every hour after midnight, to see how sorry they ought to be feeling for themselves. Aldo says he does not care what my grandfather said. My grandmother refused to concede that any member of the family died of natural causes. An uncle's cancer in middle age occurred because all the suitcases fell off the luggage rack onto him when he was in his teens, and so forth. Death was an acquired characteristic. My grandmother, too, used to put other people's ailments into the diminutive: strokelets were what her friends had. Aldo said he was bored to tearsies by my grandmother's diminutives.

The weather last Friday was terrible. The flight to Martha's Vineyard was "decisional."

"What does 'decisional' mean?" a small boy asked. "It means we might have to land in Hyannis," his mother said. It is hard to understand how anyone learns anything.

Scattered through the two cars of the Brewster-New York train last week were adults with what seemed to be a clandestine understanding. They did not look at each other. They stared out the windows. They read. "Um," sang a lady at our fourth stop on the way to Grand Central. She appeared to be reading the paper. She kept singing her "Um," as one who is getting the pitch. A young man had already been whistling "Frère Jacques" for three stops. When the "Um" lady found her pitch and began to sing the national anthem, he looked at her with rage. The conductor passed through, punching tickets in his usual fashion, not in the aisle but directly over people's laps. Every single passenger was obliged to flick the tiny punched part of the ticket from his lap onto the floor. Conductors have this process as their own little show of force. The whistler and the singer were in a dead heat when we reached the city. The people with the clandestine understanding turned out to be inmates from somewhere upstate, now on leave with their families, who met them in New York.

I don't think much of writers in whom nothing is at risk. It is possible, though, to be too literal-minded about this question. In a magazine, under the heading "$3,000 for First-Person Articles," for example: "An article for this series must be a true, hitherto unpublished narrative of an unusual personal experience. It may be dramatic, inspirational, or humorous, but it must have, in the opinion of the editors, a quality of narrative interest comparable to 'How I Lost My Eye' (June '72) and 'Attacked by a Killer Shark' (April '72). Contributions must be typewritten, preferably *double-spaced* . . ." I particularly like where the stress, the italics, goes.

When the nanny drowned in the swimming pool, the parents reacted sensibly. They had not been there for the event. They had left the nanny at poolside with their youngest child, a girl of five, and the neighbor's twins, a boy and a girl of five, and the neighbor's baby-sitter, an *au pair*, who had become the nanny's dearest friend. When they returned from their morning round of golf, they found a fire truck in the yard, the drowned body of the nanny on the tiles, the three children playing, apparently calmly, under a tree, and two disconsolate firemen trying to deal with the neighbor's baby-sitter, who was hysterical. As an ambulance pulled into the driveway, the mother was already telephoning a doctor; her husband was giving the baby-sitter a glass of water and a sedative. When her hysterics had subsided, the baby-sitter explained what she could. Neither she nor the nanny, it turned out, could really swim. They could both manage a few strokes of the breaststroke, but they had a great fear of water over their heads. All three of what she called the "little ones" were strong and intrepid dog-paddlers. She and the nanny had always confined themselves to admonitions, and their own few stroking motions, from the shallow end. It was on account of these stroking motions that their inability really to swim had never come to anyone's attention or, for that matter, to their own. That morning, the nanny had, unaccountably, stroked a few feet out of her depth, in the direction of her charge. Then, according to the baby-sitter, who may have confused the sequence, things happened very rapidly, in the following order. Nanny's face turned blue. *Then* she swallowed water. Coughing and struggling, she reached her charge and clung to her. They both went under. Long seconds later, the little girl came up, crying and sputtering. In clear view, a few feet beyond the shallow end and beyond the grasp of the baby-sitter, who was trying to maintain her feet and her depth as she held out her hands, the nanny surfaced briefly once more, sank, and drowned.

I once met a polo-playing Argentine existential psychiatrist, who had lived for months in a London commune. He said that on days when the ordinary neurotics in the commune were getting on each other's nerves the few psychopaths and schizophrenics in their midst retired to their rooms and went their version of berserk, alone. On days when the neurotics got along, the psychopaths calmed down, tried to make contact, cooked. It was, he said, as though the sun came out for them. I hope that's true. Although altogether too much of life is mood. Aldo has a married friend who was in love for years with someone, also married. Her husband found out. He insisted that there be no more calls or letters. Aldo's friend called several times, reaching the husband. The girl herself would never answer. In the end, Aldo's friend—in what we regard as not his noblest gesture—sent all the girl's letters, addressed in a packet, to her husband. There was nothing more. I wonder whether the husband read those letters. If he did, I suppose he may have been a writer. In some sense. If not, he was a gentleman. There are also, on the bus, quite often ritual dancers, near-spastics who release the strap and begin a weird sequence of movements, always punctual, always the same. There are some days when everyone I see is lunatic.

I love the laconic. Clearly, I am not of their number. When animated conversations are going on, even with people interrupting one another, I have to curb an impulse to field every remark, by everybody, as though it were addressed to me. I have noticed this impulse in other people. It electrifies the room. It is resolved, sometimes, by conversations in a foreign language. One thinks, it is my turn to try to say something, to make an effort. One polishes a case, a tense, a comment. The subject passes. Just as well. There are, however, people who just sit there, silent. A question is addressed to them. They do not answer. Another question. Silence. It is a position of great power. Talkative people running toward those silences are jarred, time after time, by a straight arm rebuff. A quizzical look, a beautiful face perhaps, but silence. Everyone is exhausted, drinks too much, snarls later at home, wonders about the need for aspirin. It has been that stubborn wall.

I receive communications almost every day from an institution called the Center for Short-Lived Phenomena. Reporting sources all over the world, and an extensive correspondence. Under the title "Type of Event: Biological," I have received postcards about the progress of the Dormouse Invasion of Formentera: "Apart from population density, the dormouse of Formentera had a

peak of reproduction in 1970. All females checked were pregnant, and perhaps this fact could have been the source of the idea of an 'invasion.' " And
the Northwest Atlantic Puffin Decline. I have followed the Tanzanian Army
Worm Outbreak. The San Fernando Earthquake. The Green Pond Fish Kill
("Eighty percent of the numbers involved," the Center's postcard reports,
"were mummichogs.") The Samar Spontaneous Oil Burn. The Hawaiian
Monk Seal Disappearance. And also, the Naini Tal Sudden Sky Brightening.

Those are accounts of things that did not last long, but if you become
famous for a single thing in this country, and just endure, it is certain you will
recur, enlarged. Of the eighteen men who were indicted for conspiracy to
murder Schwerner, Goodman, and Chaney, seven were convicted by a Mississippi jury—a surprising thing. But then a year later, a man was wounded and
a woman killed in a shootout while trying to bomb the house of some Mississippi Jews. It turned out that the informer, the man who had helped the
bombers, and led the F.B.I. to them, was one of the convicted seven—the one,
in fact, who was alleged to have killed two of the three boys who were found
in that Mississippi dam. And what's more, and what's more, the convicted
conspirator, alleged double killer, was paid thirty-six thousand dollars by the
F.B.I. for bringing the bombers in. Yet the wave of anti-Semitic bombings in
Mississippi stopped after the shootout. I don't know what it means. I am in
this brownstone.

Last year, Aldo moved out and went to Los Angeles on a story. I called him
to ask whether I could come. He said, "Are you going to stay this time?" I said
I wasn't sure. I flew out quite early in the morning. On the plane, there was
the most banal, unendurable pickup, lasting the whole flight. A young man
and a young woman—he was Italian, I think; she was German—had just met,
and settled on French as their common language. They asked each other
where they were from, and where they were going. They posed each other
riddles. He took out a pencil and paper and sketched her portrait. She giggled.
He asked her whether she had ever considered a career as a model. She said
she had considered it, but she feared that all men in the field were after the
same thing. He agreed. He began to tell off-color stories. She laughed and
reproached him. It was like that. I wondered whether these things were always, to captive eavesdroppers, so dreary. When I arrived at Aldo's door, he
met me with a smile that seemed surprised, a little sheepish. We talked
awhile. Sometimes he took, sometimes I held, my suitcase. I tried, I thought, a
joke. I asked whether there was already a girl there. He said there was. He met
me in an hour at the corner drugstore for a cup of coffee. We talked. We
returned to the apartment. We had Scotch. That afternoon, quite late, I flew
home. I called him from time to time. He had his telephone removed a few
days later. Now, for a while, he's here again. He's doing a political essay. It
begins, "Some things cannot be said too often, and some can." That's all he's
got so far.

We had people in for drinks one night last week. The cork in the wine bottle broke. Somebody pounded it into the bottle with a chisel and a hammer. We went to a bar. I have never understood the feeling men seem to have for bars they frequent. A single-story drunk told his single story. A fine musician who was with us played Mozart, Chopin, and Beethoven on the piano. It seemed a great, impromptu occasion. Then he said, we thought, "I am now going to play some Yatz." From what he played, it turned out he meant jazz. He played it badly.

We had driven in from another weekend in the country while it was still daylight. Lots of cars had their headlights on. We weren't sure whether it was for or against peace, or just for highway safety. Milly, a secretary in a brokerage office, was married in our ground-floor shop that evening. She cried hysterically. Her mother and several people from her home town and John, whose girl she had been before he married Inez, thought it was from sentiment or shyness, or for some conventional reason. Milly explained it to Aldo later. She and her husband had really married two years before—the week they met, in fact—in a chapel in Las Vegas. They hadn't wanted to tell their parents, or anybody, until he finished college. They had torn up their Las Vegas license. She had been crying out of some legal fear of being married twice, it turned out. Their best man, a Puerto Rican doctor, said his aunt had been mugged in a cemetery in San Juan by a man on horseback. She thought it was her husband, returned from the dead. She had required sedation. We laughed. My friend across the hall, who owns the beagle, looked very sad all evening. He said, abruptly, that he was cracking up, and no one would believe him. There were sirens in the street. Inez said she knew exactly what he meant: she was cracking up also. Her escort, a pale Italian jeweler, said, "I too. I too have it. The most terrible anguishes, anguishes all in the night."

Inez said she knew the most wonderful man for the problem. "He may strike you at first as a phony," she said, "but then, when you're with him, you find yourself naturally screaming. It's such a relief. And he teaches you how you can practice at home." Milly said she was not much of a screamer—had never, in fact, screamed in her life. "High time you did, then," Inez said. Our sportswriter said he had recently met a girl whose problem was stealing all the suede garments of house guests, and another, in her thirties, who cried all the time because she had not been accepted at Smith. We heard many more sirens in the streets. We all went home.

At 4 A.M., the phone rang about fifty times. I did not answer it. Aldo suggested that we remove it. I took three Valium. The whole night was sirens, then silence. The phone rang again. It is still ringing. The paper goes to press tomorrow. It is possible that I know who killed our landlord. So many things point in one direction. But too strong a case, I find, is often lost. It incurs doubts, suspicions. Perhaps I do not know. Perhaps it doesn't matter. I think it does, though. When I wonder what it is that we are doing—in this brownstone, on this block, with this paper—the truth is probably that we are fighting for our lives.

FOR STUDY, DISCUSSION, AND WRITING

1. What is a New York brownstone?
2. Comment on the irony of the types of lives the characters in the story live in light of the fact that New York City is supposed to be the cultural center of America.
3. How does the story dramatize the fact that living in New York City may be hazardous to your health?
4. Discuss the type of personal relationship that the narrator has with Aldo.
5. Point out specific incidents in the story that show people's lack of interest in their employment.
6. To what degree is the narrator-protagonist a dynamic character? Does she undergo any substantial change?
7. Although this story does not have a traditional plot, it does possess a high degree of unity. How is this unity achieved?
8. It is unusual for a current story to include a direct statement of theme. But this one does. What is that statement? Where does it appear?

DONALD BARTHELME

The School

Well, we had all these children out planting trees, see, because we figured that . . . that was part of their education, to see how, you know, the root systems . . . and also the sense of responsibility, taking care of things, being individually responsible. You know what I mean. And the trees all died. They were orange trees. I don't know why they died, they just died. Something wrong with the soil possibly or maybe the stuff we got from the nursery wasn't the best. We complained about it. So we've got thirty kids there, each kid had his or her own little tree to plant, and we've got these thirty dead trees. All these kids looking at these little brown sticks, it was depressing.

It wouldn't have been so bad except that just a couple of weeks before the thing with the trees, the snakes all died. But I think that the snakes—well, the reason that the snakes kicked off was that . . . you remember, the boiler was shut off for four days because of the strike, and that was explicable. It was something you could explain to the kids because of the strike. I mean, none of their parents would let them cross the picket line and they knew there was a strike going on and what it meant. So when things got started up again and we found the snakes they weren't too disturbed.

With the herb gardens it was probably a case of overwatering, and at least now they know not to overwater. The children were very conscientious with the herb gardens and some of them probably . . . you know, slipped them a little extra water when we weren't looking. Or maybe . . . well, I don't like to think about sabotage, although it did occur to us. I mean, it was something that crossed our minds. We were thinking that way probably because before that the gerbils had died, and the white mice had died, and the salamander . . . well, now they know not to carry them around in plastic bags.

Of course we *expected* the tropical fish to die, that was no surprise. Those numbers, you look at them crooked and they're belly-up on the surface. But the lesson plan called for a tropical-fish input at that point, there was nothing we could do, it happens every year, you just have to hurry past it.

We weren't even supposed to have a puppy.

We weren't even supposed to have one, it was just a puppy the Murdoch girl found under a Gristede's truck one day and she was afraid the truck would run over it when the driver had finished making his delivery, so she stuck it in her knapsack and brought it to school with her. So we had this puppy. As soon as I saw the puppy I thought, Oh Christ, I bet it will live for about two weeks and then . . . And that's what it did. It wasn't supposed to be in the classroom at all, there's some kind of regulation about it, but you can't tell them they can't have a puppy when the puppy is already there, right in front of them, running around on the floor and yap yap yapping. They named it Edgar—that is, they named it after me. They had a lot of fun running after it and yelling, "Here, Edgar! Nice Edgar!" Then they'd laugh like hell. They enjoyed the ambiguity. I enjoyed it myself. I don't mind being kidded. They made a little house for it in the supply closet and all that. I don't know what it died of. Distemper, I guess. It probably hadn't had any shots. I got it out of there before the kids got to school. I checked the supply closet each morning, routinely, because I knew what was going to happen. I gave it to the custodian.

And then there was this Korean orphan that the class adopted through the Help the Children program, all the kids brought in a quarter a month, that was the idea. It was an unfortunate thing, the kid's name was Kim and maybe we adopted him too late or something. The cause of death was not stated in the letter we got, they suggested we adopt another child instead and sent us some interesting case histories, but we didn't have the heart. The class took it pretty hard, they began (I think; nobody ever said anything to me directly) to feel that maybe there was something wrong with the school. But I don't think there's anything wrong with the school, particularly, I've seen better and I've seen worse. It was just a run of bad luck. We had an extraordinary number of parents passing away, for instance. There were I think two heart attacks and two suicides, one drowning, and four killed together in a car accident. One stroke. And we had the usual heavy mortality rate among the grandparents, or maybe it was heavier this year, it seemed so. And finally the tragedy.

The tragedy occurred when Matthew Wein and Tony Mavrogordo were playing over where they're excavating for the new federal office building. There were all these big wooden beams stacked, you know, at the edge of the excavation. There's a court case coming out of that, the parents are claiming that the beams were poorly stacked. I don't know what's true and what's not. It's been a strange year.

I forgot to mention Billy Brandt's father, who was knifed fatally when he grappled with a masked intruder in his home.

One day, we had a discussion in class. They asked me, where did they go? The trees, the salamander, the tropical fish, Edgar, the poppas and mommas, Matthew and Tony, where did they go? And I said, I don't know, I don't know. And they said, who knows? and I said, nobody knows. And they said, is death that which gives meaning to life? and I said, no, life is that which gives meaning to life. Then they said, but isn't death, considered as a fundamental datum, the means by which the taken-for-granted mundanity of the everyday may be transcended in the direction of—

I said, yes, maybe.

They said, we don't like it.

I said, that's sound.

They said, it's a bloody shame!

I said, it is.

They said, will you make love now with Helen (our teaching assistant) so that we can see how it is done? We know you like Helen.

I do like Helen but I said that I would not.

We've heard so much about it, they said, but we've never seen it.

I said I would be fired and that it was never, or almost never, done as a demonstration. Helen looked out of the window.

They said, please, please make love with Helen, we require an assertion of value, we are frightened.

I said that they shouldn't be frightened (although I am often frightened) and that there was value everywhere. Helen came and embraced me. I kissed her a few times on the brow. We held each other. The children were excited. Then there was a knock on the door, I opened the door, and the new gerbil walked in. The children cheered wildly.

FOR STUDY, DISCUSSION, AND WRITING

1. Comment on the appropriateness or inappropriateness of the author's tone.
2. From what specific point of view is the story told? How does the point of view dramatize the character of Edgar, the narrator?
3. What do Edgar's language habits and vocabulary suggest about many modern-day schoolteachers?
4. Death seems to embrace almost everything that this school has anything to do with. How does this fact suggest that the story is a metaphorical commentary on contemporary American society?
5. How do you account for Edgar's bland response to all the death and dying in the story?
6. As the deaths continue, the children ask increasingly complicated questions about death and life and end by saying, "It's a bloody shame!" Metaphorically, what are the children doing?
7. What does the arrival of the new gerbil at the story's conclusion suggest? Specifically, why do the children cheer?

MARK STRAND

Mr. and Mrs. Baby

Mr. and Mrs. Baby Wake Up

It is morning in California. The sea, parading its troughs, flashing its foamy crests, keeps heaving itself onto the shore. And the sky sends its delicate, inexhaustible spread of transparence into every atom of air so that the warm dome of promise, of caressing light, can discover the place where the Babys lie buried in the sheeted, blanketed world of slumber. How innocent they are in their easy recumbency. How lucky that the difference between sleep and wakefulness can be so blurred, diminished, and finally erased without pain. The waking of the Babys is a lovely rising from crumpled linen and its odors of cologne into lazy, tentative antemeridian amorousness. Yet in an hour's time how close to sadness they will be in the world of light, its ordeals of fixity, of ornament, of responsibility: Baby Hades.

MARK STRAND, "Mr. and Mrs. Baby," from *The New Yorker*. Reprinted by permission; © 1979 The New Yorker Magazine, Inc.

How Mr. and Mrs. Baby Looked

Mr and Mrs. Baby looked familiar. Bob Baby had the wide but serious mouth of Alan Roscoe when he played in "The Last of the Mohicans," and his blue eyes were like Bing Crosby's in "The Bells of St. Mary's," with the same soft, otherworldly look; yet at times they took on the stern, no-nonsense gaze that was Bing's in "Going My Way." His black hair fell down over his right eye the way Gable's always did. His cheeks had the fallen firmness of Ronald Colman's in "Lost Horizon" or Richard Egan's in "Khyber Patrol." But the marvellous jaw was straight Cooper—the Cooper of "Beau Geste." His nose was Heston's, with the same tip and the same slant of nostril. His walk and his air of purpose were just a cut below Kenneth More's in "The Admirable Crichton"—he always dreamed of going tuxedoed to the beach. His ears were unmistakably Herbert Marshall's, and his eyebrows were perfectly peaked, with just the right amount of hair; in other words, they were Errol Flynn's—the great Flynn of "The Charge of the Light Brigade." His body, alas, was undistinguished, with the same bleached rubescence of Walter Slezak's in all his movies since "Once Upon a Honeymoon."

Babe Baby's face had the transcendental sweetness of Laura La Plante's. But her eyes had the softness, the downward slant of Vilma Banky's in "Son of the Sheik." And yet there was a touch, especially in her left eye, of Dolores Costello. Her cheeks were high but several notches lower than Garbo's, and they had the fullness of Claudette Colbert's, especially when she smiled. Babe had a wholesomeness, too, that was given its imprimatur by her nose. It was not perfectly shaped like Gloria Grahame's, not barren like Betty Hutton's, not swaybacked like Ingrid Bergman's, nor with oversized nostrils like Donna Reed's or Joan Bennett's; it was a nose like the radiant Janet Blair's. It was perky without being prying, it was cute without being cheap, it was noble without being undemocratic. Babe wore her light-brown hair swept back and short, the way Norma Shearer did in "A Free Soul." Her walk was pure assurance, pure Lauren Bacall. And she was as poised, when occasion dictated, as Celeste Holm in "Gentleman's Agreement" or Lilli Palmer in "The Counterfeit Traitor." Best of all, she had the robust aquatic self-possession of Esther Williams in "Pagan Love Song."

Mr. and Mrs. Baby at Breakfast

The ease they felt in each other's presence, though tinged at times with regret, even unhappiness—deep unhappiness, even; irreversible misery, it could be said—allowed them to share some of what was on their minds. And like so many who have spent years together, they could anticipate each other's questions as well as answers. Thus, at breakfast, Bob knew what Babe was thinking when he said, "So you want to know where they came from. And you want to know how they came. They came from Poland and Russia, from France and Germany, from Turkey and the Congo, from Iceland and Italy; they came from China and the Philippines; they came and they came, and

they brought their aunts and cousins, sisters and brothers, mothers and fa-
thers; they brought them by boat, by train, by plane; they walked and they
ran and they came with satchels, trunks, suitcases, boxes; they kept coming in
waves, in droves, in trickles, but they kept coming; they came at night or in
bright day; they came in the wrecking storm, they came in the calm of noon;
they came waving their arms, stamping their feet, speaking Dutch, Rumanian,
Serbian, Czech, Urdu; they came with hats or without—it made no difference
to those hearty people; they wore dark suits and long dresses; many were
overweight, but they came and they came. Some were professors, some were
bricklayers, some were chicken farmers, but they came, and they went to
Arizona and Iowa and Illinois; they came and they went to Nebraska and
Alabama and Maryland; they came and they went to Pennsylvania, Montana,
and Hawaii. They were the Smiths, the Goldbergs, the Rodriguezes, the Babys. Yes, the Babys were part of it, were half of it, were all of it. Everyone was
a Baby and the Babys were everyone."

Babe was silent, then slowly began to laugh in nervous acknowledgment of
the vistas that opened before her, and behind her in case she unexpectedly
turned around. Out of control, her laughter increased in tempo. She shook
and snorted, and even howled, in tribute to what she had heard. Bob, taken
with the unexpected sweep of his speech, could not have been more pleased
by her response.

Mrs. Baby Has an Experience

Babe pulled herself together and went to the beach, some books of poetry
tucked under her arm. She thought more about the future than she did of the
past. And she believed the daily unfolding of events was oblivious of her
needs. What were her needs? And who needed them anyway? She sat on the
sand, read a little, then drifted into thought.

*How did I get here if not below the surface, allowing the deep you-know-what to figure
things out? How did I get here, if not in Bob's blue Mercedes disappearing down into the
canyon, then into this vanishing light? Fix your eyes on the sea and its lunging; lounge, as
you will, in semi-coma, remembering the hand trucks of opportunity, the boatloads of
promise that were exchanged for this distant now, its plungings, its watery walls, its towers
of bubble! Lie back and be stirred by the glitter of sense, as if you were the maker of the
words you heard, heard almost as medleyed sound, a maker of the words you might utter;
for you are the maker of the words you heard, and if there is another maker he is nowhere
near.*

This sudden rush of thoughts scared Babe, scored itself deep into her vision
of self—scarred her, in fact—so she decided to say nothing to Bob of the
mysterious turn her mind had taken.

Mr. Baby Also Has An Experience

There is a time of day when quietness invades the landscape and takes up
residence in all the things one sees. Every leaf, every cloud is suddenly still

and is viewed with unusual clarity, and in that moment it is as if the destiny of each thing were revealed. This awesome ascent into consciousness, into luminous, crystalline recognition was not lost on Mr. Baby, who stood alone on the lawn in front of his house. Brought outside by a restlessness whose source was obscure, he was likewise brought out of himself into a spacious aura of epiphanous light, into an openness of being that took him by surprise. With a knowledge almost too deep for tears, he saw all things ablaze with the glory of their own mortality. He lingered until the world around him suddenly resumed its normal aspect, then he went inside and began to pace on the green living-room rug. He wondered why he was here and not there, why he had chosen the life he had instead of the life he hadn't, why he felt as he did and, sometimes, as he didn't. Thus it was that Bob Baby wrote his first poem and decided to say nothing about it to Babe.

The Babys Skip Lunch

At making do or doing without, the Babys wished to think themselves accomplished. So at lunch, when neither of them took the time to sit down and have a bite, it was done with a grace bordering on the regal. They felt the glory of self-abnegation because they understood too well the degradation of fulfillment. There would be no linen tablecloth today, no silverware, no succession of dishes each with its own bouquet of steam which seemed to ripen in the hazy sunlit air of the dining room. There would be no *tonnarelli alla ciociara*, those thin linguine-like noodles in a sauce of fresh *funghi*, no light, smoky Gavi dei Gavi to wash it down with, or even a *pasticcio con melanzane* so reminiscent of Sicily; no *mozzarella in carrozza*, no beef tongue with green sauce, no grilled zucchini with Sardo cheese, no *pissaladière provençale*, with its hefty aroma of anchovy and onion, no *clafouti* of Bing cherries touched with ginger. There would be no bare table and paper napkins even, no sandwiches, odorless and sterile in small dishes, no gaunt glasses of apple juice, no stopgap noshes of any sort. The dining room would be empty, and the Babys would bask in the image of its foodless clarity and silently applaud the splendor of its austerity, the clean denial of its destiny.

Mr. and Mrs. Baby Have a Good Cry

It was as if the exertion of denial had proved too much, and the ache of emptiness had become more than a meal put aside. They sank into listlessness, each of them slumped in a chair, staring outside, emitting weak, barely audible sighs. The restorative power of consciousness that had worked its magic on them only hours before was now lacking. Each of them felt defeated by a motif that missing lunch was only the most obvious sign of. They were not speaking. It was as if they had forgotten how. They were estranged even from each other. It was this, perhaps, that made them seem now smaller and more frail than ever, and why their sighs gave way to tears and sniffles. They looked at each other pathetically, their eyes seeming to ask: Why, why do we feel this way? The answer came with a volley of sobs and a downpour of tears. The Babys wept without shame.

Mr. and Mrs. Baby Have a Talk

Bob and Babe dried their eyes and looked at each other with an intensity that had been lacking in the moments preceding their cry. And the way each of them sat—Babe with her legs crossed, Bob with his hands clasped behind his head—seemed to suggest that life was good.

"Life *is* good," said Babe. "It's crazy for us to feel the way we did."

"Say," said Bob. "How about we have a bite?"

"Do you think we should?" said Babe. "Don't you think that'd be gilding the lily? I mean, we don't have to eat just to prove life is good."

"I know what you mean," said Bob. Conscious of how much they had been through, he felt mellow. The stillness of the room, its warm, sunlit air contributed to a feeling of having arrived. Everything seemed balanced, complete. It was easy to give in to the benevolence of fate; life was not only good, it was worth waiting for.

"We are such fools," said Babe.

Somewhere up the street a dog barked, and gave up, and barked again. The sound was forlorn and seemed to measure the silence instead of breaking it. Bob didn't mind. He liked the way the afternoon was winding down, the gradual lengthening of shadows everywhere. A small breeze entered the room, barely shaking the sheer muslin curtains. "I know what you mean," he said.

"I'm so happy at this moment I could cry," said Babe, and she jumped up, went quickly to Bob, and kissed him lightly on the cheek. Bob smiled, his hands clasped behind his head.

Mr. and Mrs. Baby Go to a Party

Sometimes on summer evenings, when the light is almost gone, when everything has taken on a heavy, exhausted aspect, there can be felt in the air a restlessness, a furtive rustling, a burgeoning of desire. This evening, while the Babys prepared to go out, the urgency of promised adventure was so palpable that the neighborhood seemed to murmur with pleasure. And when they walked to the party they were almost overcome with the magical intimacy of leaves saturating the air with the odor of green, the sweet seasoning of summer. Furtive above them, above the motionless canopy of maples, was the open gaze of the moon.

Everyone at the party, drifters and flitters, merged willingly into the amiable flow. Round and round they went with round after round of drink, their voices, muted by the low-ceilinged interior, mingling naturally with the barely audible sounds coming from the stereo. There was no change all evening.

Nothing was happening. The Babys stayed only as long as they had to and then walked home.

Mr. and Mrs. Baby Go to Sleep

Now, at day's end, the Babys slip naked into bed, their limbs overcome with weariness, their minds dimming, giving way to the power and grandeur of nothingness, the silent ohs and ahs of oblivion. Oh Babys! Ah Babys! Whither now? Whither later? It's all the same. Among the celestial acts in the theatre of night, in the superdome of the firmament, where distance is a monotonous allegory of diminishment, a shifting of solar dust, a waltzing of matter to the tune of darkness, a grave passage of this and that, what does it mean that you are asleep, adrift in the spectral silt of the unknown? What has the relentless fury of particles to do with you? Pull your covers up to your chins. Sleep tight; another Baby day is on its way.

FOR STUDY, DISCUSSION, AND WRITING

1. Why do you think Mark Strand sets this story in California? Does this geographic setting contribute to the story's overall mood?
2. Why are Mr. and Mrs. Baby described in terms of the physical qualities of various movie stars?
3. What is Mr. Baby saying about the character of modern American people when he answers Mrs. Baby's unasked question about where we all came from?
4. When are Mr. and Mrs. Baby most content?
5. What insights about their condition do Mr. and Mrs. Baby gain as a result of their two experiences?
6. What does the story seem to say about people whose lives are dominated by material goods?
7. Why do Mr. and Mrs. Baby have a good cry? Do you think they gain any lasting insights as a result of their cry?
8. This whole story is based upon a well-known expression. What is the expression? How does the expression relate to the theme and general mood of the story?

Writing Papers About
Short Stories

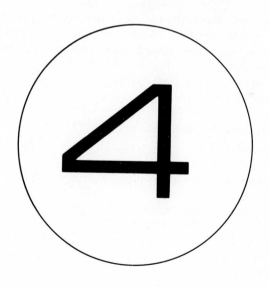

S tudents often approach the task of writing a paper on a literary topic with something less than enthusiasm. This hesitancy stems not from an unwillingness to compose such papers or from an inability to write in general, but rather from confusion about where and how to begin and how to carry the exercise through to a successful conclusion. This section is intended to offer you general and specific tips on writing brief papers that actually say a thing or two about short stories.

When you write about a short story, you do not have to adopt any special, lofty, or high-sounding tone or style. Academese isn't necessary; in fact, such ostentatious language is likely to detract from what you are trying to accomplish. Ordinary expository prose, with clear and precise sentences properly strung together, will do the job. In a similar vein, you should not feel compelled to say something new, original, clever, earth-shaking, or deeply philosophical. After all, the authors of this textbook have said little that has not been said elsewhere by other people. It is unrealistic of you to demand more of yourselves than is required of individuals who have spent their lives studying the various authors and nuances of the short story.

Virtually any paper that you write about a short story will involve some type of analysis. Analysis is a method of exposition that breaks a topic down into its component parts and examines each part by itself for the purpose of providing a better overall understanding. The word "analysis" is derived from the Greek forms *ana*, meaning "throughout," and *lysis*, meaning "a loosening." So, an analysis involves a "loosening into parts." Plot, character, emotion, symbolism, theme, and point of view can all be analyzed.

For convenience, we have divided the types of papers that you are likely to write about short stories into three broad categories: (1) papers that deal with the structural elements of the short story, (2) papers that deal with the outside influences on the short story, and (3) papers that compare and contrast the structural elements of specific stories or the outside influences on specific stories.

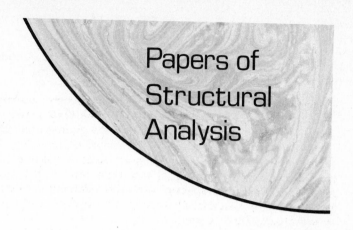

Papers of Structural Analysis

Analysis of Plot

The ability to write a satisfactory plot analysis is fundamental to any other type of writing that you are likely to do about short stories. With rare exceptions, any short story, even the most experimental, consists of a series of actions arranged in some pattern that helps the reader to gain an understanding of the writer's overall purpose. Writing a satisfactory plot summary demonstrates that you have grasped these details and their significance and thus have an intelligent idea of what the writer was driving at when he or she wrote the story.

When we talk about a story's purpose, we do not necessarily mean its theme, because theme is not always an important consideration. For example, Richard Connell's "The Most Dangerous Game" seems less concerned with making a thematic statement than with providing readers a half-hour or so of suspenseful entertainment. In fact, theme hardly enters into the story at all. Similarly, Washington Irving's "The Spectre Bridegroom" seems much less a warning against the dangers of foolish pride than a humorous character study. Of course, it is possible to search out a theme in each of these stories, and indeed in almost any story; but trying to do so, especially through plot analysis, would not only prove difficult but also cause you to overlook the more obvious purposes that the plot serves.

In writing a plot summary, begin by carefully reading the story once or twice to gain an overall impression of the writer's purpose. Keep in mind that purpose can be revealed not only through action but also through such elements as tone, irony, and characterization. Having ascertained what you feel to be the story's primary intent, go through the story again, taking careful notes about happenings that seem important. If the story has a strong, conventional plot line, focus your attention on items such as the precipitating incident, conflict, climax, and denouement, and also jot down any significant events that occur during the period of rising action. In making your notes, do not merely record the happenings themselves, but also indicate why you think they are significant.

At this point, you may find it helpful to draft some sort of summary statement to guide you when you write your paper. The opening sentence of our own write-up on Carson McCullers' "A Tree, A Rock, A Cloud''—'' 'A Tree, A Rock, A Cloud' describes the spiritual odyssey of a man as he comes by gradual stages to realize the nature of ideal love and to experience its power''—served this purpose for us. The remainder of our analysis was intended to support this statement. However, do not feel compelled to include such a statement in your final paper, unless your instructor has asked you to do so.

Any thorough plot analysis must take into account whatever weaknesses come to your attention. In writing about "The Most Dangerous Game," for example, we mentioned as one plot weakness General Zaroff's failure to kill Rainsford at the end of the first or the second day's hunting. If we had intended our write-up to be an exhaustive analysis rather than a suggestive one, we might also have pointed out that Zaroff could not possibly have lived so opulently or maintained such an enormous establishment without a large complement of servants and frequent contact with the mainland. Thus, in real life the outside world would have learned very quickly of Zaroff's activities and put a stop to them.

Perhaps the most objectionable plot weakness, and certainly the most obvious, is the kind that results from an author's use of coincidence or chance to manipulate the lives of characters. Although there is nothing innately wrong with using chance or coincidence to set events in motion, the reader has every right to object when chance or coincidence is used to resolve a dilemma or bring matters to a climax. There is nothing particularly wrong with starting the action of "The Most Dangerous Game" by having Rainsford fall overboard, as unlikely as such an accident might be; but it would strain the credulity of even the most naïve reader to have Zaroff suffer a fatal heart attack just as he is about to shoot Rainsford. On the other hand, if the author's central purpose is to dramatize that chance does indeed play a role in shaping people's lives, then we can't fault the inclusion of chance and coincidence in the action of the story.

Analysis of Character

Because writers often use character as a vehicle for making observations about human nature or the human condition, character analysis can be an excellent means of ascertaining a writer's overall purpose. The first step in writing a character analysis is to zero in on the personality of the individual that you are concerned with. To do this, read the story carefully, answering questions such as these:

1. What does the author tell us about the character's personality, appearance, surroundings, background, and life style?
2. What does the character think or say about himself or herself, the other characters, or the events that take place?
3. Do the character's observations appear to be reasonably correct, or is there good reason for doubting their validity?
4. How do the other characters in the story feel about the one you are investigating, and how accurate do their judgments appear to be?
5. What changes, if any, does the character undergo during the course of the story, and why do these changes occur?

The information gathered by this questioning lends itself to a variety of uses. You may, for example, use it to demonstrate the presence of a particular character trait such as honesty, generosity, or cruelty. You may show that a character is believable or unbelievable, consistent or inconsistent, well or poorly motivated, successful or unsuccessful as an allegorical representation of some segment of society. Or you may note how character is used to make some thematic point.

To a considerable degree, our own analysis of Walter Mitty hinges upon his inner thoughts—his daydreams. We used these daydreams to establish Mitty's weak and impractical nature. If you will recall, Mitty's next-to-last daydream reflects a change in his character, while the final one seems to be making the point that the only heroism possible for great numbers of modern individuals consists in enduring whatever it is that we must endure. Whatever approach you take to your character or characters will determine which information you use and which you ignore.

Analysis of Emotion

Fiction often derives much of its power and appeal from its emotional impact, and its truths strike our minds all the harder because they are conveyed through our feelings. Analyzing a story's emotional element will help you to understand why the story is powerful and appealing as well as what its author may be intending to say.

When you analyze the quality and intensity of the emotions in a story, you must consider the emotions experienced by the characters and those experienced by readers. Keep in mind that most readers derive emotional enjoyment from a story because of their interest in the characters. The reader's emotional satisfaction usually develops from the dramatization of character.

To begin an analysis of emotion, take note of the author's general tone. Do his or her words, including their selection and arrangement, suggest a deliberate attempt to create a particular atmosphere or mood? Consider the following two sets of opening lines. The first is from Dorothy Parker's story "But the One on the Right":

I knew it. I knew if I came to this dinner, I'd draw something like this baby on my left. They've been saving him up for me for weeks. Now, we've simply got to have him—his sister was so sweet to us in London; we can stick him next to Mrs. Parker—she talks enough for two. Oh, I should never have come, never. I'm here against my better judgment, to a decision. That would be a good thing for them to cut on my tombstone: Wherever she went, including here, it was against her better judgment.

The second set is from Edgar Allan Poe's story "The Fall of the House of Usher":

During the whole of a dull, dark, and soundless day in the autumn of the year, when the clouds hung oppressively low in the heavens, I had been passing alone, on horseback, through a singularly dreary tract of country; and at length found myself, as the shades of the evening drew on, within view of the melancholy House of Usher.

The tone of the first excerpt is flippant, urbane, and witty, whereas the tone of the second could hardly be more somber and sinister. In each case, however, the author's emotional tone reflects the emotional experiences of the characters within the story and helps arouse an emotional response within the reader.

Often, by contrast, the writer's tone seems to have little or nothing in common with the emotional state of the story's characters. Such is the situation in Washington Irving's "The Spectre Bridegroom." In this story, Irving says the following about the Baron Von Landshort:

The baron was a dry branch of the great family of Katzenellenbogen, and inherited the relics of the property, and all the pride of his ancestors. Though the warlike disposition of his predecessors had much impaired the family possessions, yet the baron still endeavored to keep up some show of former state. The times were peaceable, and the German nobles, in general, had abandoned their inconvenient old castles, perched like eagles' nests among the mountains, and had built more convenient residences in the valleys: still the baron remained proudly drawn up in his little fortress, cherishing, with hereditary inveteracy, all the old family feuds; so that he was on ill terms with some of his nearest neighbors, on account of disputes that had happened between their great-great-grandfathers.

The tone of the author stands in marked contrast to the general quarrelsomeness of the baron, and this contrast helps heighten the satiric impact of the entire story.

In seeking to make a dramatic impact on their readers, short-story writers often come very near to being poets in their use of rhythm, images, and other poetic devices. This poetic quality is evident throughout "The Fall of the House of Usher." Poe makes use of long, sonorously rhythmical sentences, Latinate words, and alliteration to help create an oppressive sense of dread.

By contrast, notice the very different lyrical quality of the opening lines of Toni Cade Bambara's story "The Lesson":

> Back in the days when everyone was old and stupid or young and foolish and me and Sugar were the only ones just right, this lady moved on our block with nappy hair and proper speech and no makeup. And quite naturally we laughed at her, laughed the way we did at the junk man who went about his business like he was some big-time president and his sorry-ass horse his secretary.

In this instance, staccato rhythms are used to arouse within the reader a sense of the fast-paced urban environment in which the narrator lives and to help create emotional rapport with the narrator's street-wise, unsentimentally honest persona.

Since specific situations also contribute to the reader's overall emotional response to a story, they too should not be overlooked. Few readers can fail to be emotionally affected by the predicament of characters such as Little Chandler in "A Little Cloud," Alfred Schweigen in "The Music School," Charlie in "Flowers for Algernon," Akulína, the jilted peasant girl, in "The Tryst," or the condemned men in "The Wall." We respond to people in such unfortunate circumstances because it is not difficult to imagine ourselves in similar situations.

To be effective, emotion must be in reasonable balance with all other elements of the story. To determine whether an author has exercised reasonable restraint in the portrayal of emotions you might ask yourself these questions:

1. Do the characters seem to overreact?
2. Is the emotional intensity at the point of climax too prolonged?
3. Does the story force a happy ending to pacify the reader?
4. Does the author or narrator seem to tell the reader what emotional responses he or she should have?
5. Does the author try to manipulate the emotions of the reader, as do demagogues, politicians, and some salespeople in real life?

If the answer to one or more of these questions is yes, then the story must be considered as at least a partial failure on the emotional level.

Analysis of Symbolism

Writing a paper that analyzes a story's symbols can prove a little more difficult than doing a plot or character analysis. Almost anything in a story—a character, an action, an object, a setting, a gesture, a situation—may serve a symbolic function. Then, too, symbols are not always easy to detect, and even knowledgeable readers sometimes disagree about whether an item is intended as a symbol or what an item may be intended to symbolize. Nevertheless, the insights you can gain in carrying out such a task can add greatly to your understanding and appreciation of a story. Carrying through an analysis of a story's symbols is not only worthwhile but also often highly satisfying.

Before beginning to search for symbols, it is a good idea to make a broad assessment of the story's purpose, plot, characters, mood, settings, and theme. Once you have done this, reread the story, making careful notes about all items that are mentioned a number of times and the contexts in which they occur. These items may or may not be symbols. If, for instance, the color white is repeatedly mentioned in connection with a naïvely innocent character, you are on strong ground in assuming that you have found a symbol. If, however, the color is randomly associated with an innocent protagonist, an inept white-coated surgeon, a frost-covered car, and the siding on a vacation cottage, you have good cause to doubt that the color has symbolic value.

Instead of repeating one particular symbol, an author may use several different symbols to accomplish a single purpose. To investigate such a possibility, first try to determine the essential quality of whatever you are trying to find symbols for. Then look for things that reflect this quality. In "A Tree of Night," Truman Capote uses a row of fanglike icicles, a decayed railroad coach, and a pair of grotesque traveling companions to help establish a general mood of psychological terror. Each of these symbols is in keeping with the story's mood.

While conducting your search, keep in mind that there are several categories of symbols, and each of them will have a different implication. Of all the categories, cultural symbols—flags, Cadillacs, black cats, four-leaf clovers, and the like—are the easiest to recognize because we are already well acquainted with them and their usual symbolic meaning. As you proceed, ask yourself whether your story's plot, characters, and theme are such that you might expect to find one or more cultural symbols. If, for example, one of the characters is a ruthless businessman, he might drive a long, black Cadillac. If his activities eventually result in financial ruin, that development might be both symbolized and foreshadowed by an accident in which the automobile is demolished.

Assuming that all other elements are appropriate, a story may include one or more Freudian symbols—that is, symbols with sexual implications beyond their literal value. Such symbols may include hard, pointed, penetrating objects (masculine Freudian symbols); soft, yielding, hollow objects (feminine Freudian symbols); or motions that suggest sexual activity. Stories that center on male-female relationships, like the stories by D. H. Lawrence, are likely to be rich in Freudian symbols.

Stories with emotionally or sexually repressed characters are also likely to include a number of Freudian symbols. Truman Capote's "A Tree of Night" includes at least two—Kay's guitar, a feminine Freudian symbol; and the love charm, also a feminine Freudian symbol. In John Steinbeck's "The Chrysanthemums," there is a cluster of items that may be considered broadly Freudian symbols—the "closed" Salinas Valley itself, the pointed stars of Elisa's brief monologue to the tinker, the masculine clothing that Elisa wears when working in the flower garden, the bitter aroma of the chrysanthemums, Elisa's reaching out as if to touch the tinker's trousers, even Elisa's scrubbing herself down with pumice as if trying to rid herself of her long-standing repressions.

Symbols arising from archetypal images are a third category to be taken into account. Such symbols are employed to suggest the fundamental realities of the human condition. A writer may use the waxing and waning of the moon or the ebb and flow of the tides to symbolize the recurring cycle of death and rebirth, sunlight to represent life, or a ring to represent eternity. Symbols of this sort are especially prevalent in stories that are highly thematic or allegorical. In Ralph Ellison's "Flying Home," the sun may be taken as an archetypal image that reflects the human impulse toward self-realization.

Sometimes a symbol may be used ironically, or the symbolic value of an item may change during the course of the story. In preparing your paper, point out any such occurrences that you are able to detect; and don't be afraid to offer your opinion about their significance. Also, do not be afraid to offer your opinion about the general effectiveness of the author's use of symbols. If you think a writer has failed to bring a story off on the symbolic level, or if one particular symbol seems ineffective, say so; and then, in specific terms, explain why you think so.

Analysis of Theme

Determining a story's theme can be rather demanding. Theme results from the working together of everything in the story. If we are to deduce a story's theme, we must consider all the elements that make up the work. Unless we take the time to do this, we run the risk of an incomplete or mistaken interpretation.

One good way to begin a thematic analysis is by seeing whether the author of the story or someone in the story has anything to say about the theme. Although contemporary authors almost never inject personal comments of this sort, the practice was quite common among nineteenth-century writers. Thus, in "The Birthmark," a story that points up the evils of intellectual pride and the obsessive pursuit of ideal beauty, Nathaniel Hawthorne, speaking as himself, makes the thematic point in the story's concluding paragraph:

> Thus ever does the gross Fatality of Earth exult in its invariable triumph over the immortal essence, which, in this dim sphere of half-development, demands the completeness of a higher state. Yet, had Aylmer reached a profounder wisdom, he need not thus have flung away the happiness, which would have woven his mortal life of the self-same texture with the celestial. The momentary circumstance was too strong for him; he failed to look beyond the shadowy scope of Time, and living once for all in Eternity, to find the perfect Future in the present.

Today, any such pronouncements, if they occur at all, will most likely be made by someone in the story rather than by the author. Such is the case in Carson McCullers' "A Tree, A Rock, A Cloud." Here, the conclusion of the old man's story amounts to a thematic statement on the nature of ideal love:

> "For six years now I have gone around by myself and built up my science. And now I am a master. Son, I can love anything. No longer do I have to think about it even. I see a street full of people and a beautiful light comes in me. I watch a bird in the sky. Or I meet a traveler on the road. Everything, Son. And anybody. All strangers and all loved. Do you realize what a science like mine can mean?"

When thematic pronouncements do occur, they are often reinforced by the reactions of one or more of the story's characters. Consider Leo's "Aw shut up! Shut up! Shut up!" as McCullers' old man nears the end of his tale. This outburst shows that the counterman recognizes the truth of what the man has been saying, as does the reaction of the young boy to whom the tale has been told. Without these reactions, the reader might dismiss the old man's words and come to some entirely different, and erroneous, conclusion about the story's theme.

When neither the author nor a character in the story offers a thematic comment, the theme must be deduced from a consideration of the overall pattern of events, setting, symbols, and the like. To see how this might work, let's assume that we have a story in which the protagonist is Mr. Addleman, a pinball addict who for years has tried to better the score he once made on his favorite machine. Each time he is about to accomplish his goal, however, something happens—his elbow is jogged, someone startles him by sneezing, the machine announces "TILT"— and he fails. As the story begins, a light rain is falling and continues to dampen the scene throughout the story. From time to time, a black cat belonging to the proprietor of the pinball gallery appears and rubs itself against the legs of Mr. Addleman's machine. After much labor and frustration, the story ends with a prolonged game in which Mr. Addleman makes exactly the same score that he made many years earlier. Given this collection of information, we are probably on reasonably safe ground in concluding that the story's thematic intent is to show that life is a struggle, unpleasant, fraught with mischance, doomed to end in failure, and that people are crazy to wear themselves out in an effort to make things better.

Now, let's change a few details of the story and see what these changes do to the theme. Instead of a black cat, we now have a cat that is black and white. The rain, instead of continuing without letup, stops midway through the story, and the sun comes out. In the final game, after several near-failures, the protagonist—renamed Mr. Albee—manages not only to beat his original score, but to almost double it, to the unexpected applause of several young toughs in the gallery who have in the past shown only disdain for his efforts.

The new circumstances suggest a different thematic intent. Now the theme seems to say that although life can at times be unpleasant and chancy, any person who tries hard enough can hope to attain at least a measure of success and personal satisfaction.

No analysis of a story's theme should be considered complete unless conflict is taken into account. In fact, conflict is one of the chief means an author has for presenting theme. The conflict may be internal, as is most of the conflict experienced by Claude Fitzsimmons in Irwin Shaw's "The Dry Rock." Or the conflict may pit an individual against society or, as in our two hypothetical examples, against life itself. Finally, the conflict may pit one individual against another. Thus, in John Updike's "A & P," the theme is developed largely through the conflict between Sammy and Lengel.

As you investigate, take time to consider how effectively the theme is carried out. Do all the stylistic and dramatic elements of the story seem to fit together, or do some appear to fly in the face of the meaning the author is apparently trying to convey? If in our story about Mr. Addleman the cat had been white and the rain had turned to sunshine early on, you would probably be justified in concluding that the theme had not been well realized. All this is not meant to suggest that a story must have only one theme. In fact, a story may lend itself to several thematic interpretations. In such stories, though, the various elements must reinforce all the interpretations.

Analysis of Point of View

Point of view—the perspective from which an author presents the events of a story—is intimately linked to the author's dramatic intentions. These intentions can be of many types. For example, one story may seek to shock, another to trace a character's psychological deterioration, and yet a third to contrast two characters' differing conceptions of an event or situation. In addition, dramatic intent may involve how much emotional distance there will be between a reader and the story, as well as the writer's ironic aims. Since each point of view has its own limitations, the author's choice of a suitable one is vital to the successful accomplishment of dramatic intent. Analyzing a story's point of view, then, is an excellent way to determine an author's dramatic aims. Such an analysis can also provide valuable insights into character.

Begin your analysis by determining whether the story was subjective or anonymous narration. Then check to see which particular variation has been employed. With first-person narratives, always check the reliability of the narrator by looking for inconsistencies between what the narrator says are the facts and what the facts are otherwise shown to be. This investigation may reveal that the narrator is simple-minded, a teller of tall tales, a deliberate liar, or a person too emotionally wrought up to see things the way they actually are.

Assuming the narrator is unreliable for one of these reasons, ask yourself why the author has chosen such a character to tell the tale. For example, by using a simple-minded narrator, the author may be ironically contrasting the narrator's perception of a situation with the view of the reader or some other character in the story. Such is the case in much of Daniel Keyes' "Flowers for Algernon." In this particular story, the irony serves to arouse a strong emotional response—in the reader—to Charlie's mental condition.

Whatever a story's point of view may be, try to discover whether one of the characters is serving as a vehicle for the presentation of the author's own views. As you do this, look for a character who seems reliable, who is generally sympathetic, and who displays a mature and reflective cast of mind. In first-person narratives, this character will probably be the "I" who is telling the story. Such is the case in Jean-Paul Sartre's story "The Wall," where the chief character mirrors the author's own existentialist outlook. Once in a while, if the narrator is unsympathetic or unreliable, the writer's views will be conveyed through some other character. Thus, in Ring Lardner's story "Haircut," Doc Stair may be taken as conveying the author's views about how people should behave toward others.

In third-person narratives, the author's views will almost certainly be conveyed by one of the characters whose thoughts are omnisciently revealed to the reader, although it is possible for another character to serve in this capacity. To illustrate the latter situation, the Hallorans, a couple of minor characters in John Cheever's story "The Swimmer," seem to reflect the author's apparent conception of what a sane life, at least in a modern society, should be.

In dramatic third-person narration, also called the "objective point of view," the thoughts of the characters are not given, and there is no "I" telling the story. With stories told from this point of view, we must deduce the author's intentions by carefully noting the specific incidents the author has included. Thus, it is principally the chain of events in John Steinbeck's "The Chrysanthemums" that warns the reader about the dangers of suppressing any person's creative vigor for a long period of time.

The main purpose of analyzing a point of view is to show how a particular narrative viewpoint helps the author to fulfill his or her predetermined intentions. No one point of view will fit every situation. For example, the dramatic monologue is excellent for revealing a single character's state of mind at a particular time, but it is no good at all for tracing the changes in one or more characters over a period of time. Similarly, dual character limited omniscience is unexcelled for showing two individuals' differing conceptions of an event or situation, but it does not lend itself at all well to portraying one person's mature reflections on something that has taken place many years earlier. For authors, choosing a suitable point of view is no haphazard affair; quite the contrary, it requires much careful deliberation.

To see how point of view and dramatic intent work together, let's consider Edgar Allan Poe's "The Fall of the House of Usher." In this story, Poe sought to accomplish two things: to trace his protagonist's gradual descent into madness and to arouse feelings of horror in the reader. Given these purposes, first-person narration was an obvious choice, for it allows a closer examination of the narrator's thoughts and involves the reader more closely in the story than would third-person

narration. But why did Poe choose the technique of narrator as participant rather than another variation of the first-person point of view?

Both the interior monologue and the dramatic monologue are short-
time affairs and therefore unsuitable for following the course of a
gradual change as it occurs. The technique of narrator as observer could
not be used because it would not have allowed the reader direct access
to the protagonist's mind. Diary or epistolary narration might have been
employed, but these after-the-fact techniques would have broken up the
flow of the story and severely weakened the dramatic impact of the
climax. In selecting the narrator-as-participant point of view, Poe clearly
made the best possible choice.

To demonstrate how the story's point of view supports Poe's narrative
intention, we might start by noting that the narrator's reaction as he first
views the Usher mansion—he is plunged into gloom but tries to account
for his feelings—shows that he is impressionable, yet possesses a
strong streak of rationality. Moving on to the first part of the visit, we
might note as further evidence of the narrator's impressionable cast of
mind the unaccountable feelings of dread that he experiences when he
first sees the lady Madeline and views Usher's paintings. To show that
rationality has not yet fled the narrator, we might cite his dismissal of
Usher's theory that inanimate objects possess sentience—the power to
think and feel—and the fact that he likens Usher to a "lost drunkard"
and an "irreclaimable eater of opium."

Having established the narrator's psychological make-up, we might
then turn our attention to the climactic evening of the story and the final
collapse of the narrator's rationality. Here we might point out the narrator's fruitless struggles to "reason off the nervousness that had dominion over me," his rising terror as he gradually becomes convinced that
Madeline has broken out of the burial chamber and is on her way upstairs, and his final hallucinatory glimpse of Usher's dead sister. Poe
also provides other evidence that could be used to trace the narrator's
descent into madness.

Occasionally, especially in more current stories, an author will employ
a shifting point of view. In analyzing this sort of story, be sure to call
attention to the shifts and try to indicate why you think the author used
them. If the shifts seem unwarranted or harmful to the story as a whole,
say so and then give your reasons for holding such a view.

Papers Analyzing Outside Influences

We have discussed several outside influences on the origin, development, and refinement of the modern short story. In the nineteenth-century section we talked about the dramatic increase in newspapers and popular magazines, the rise of intellectual and philosophical movements such as romanticism, realism, positivism, Darwinism, and naturalism, as well as historical events such as the Industrial Revolution, urbanization, and the emergence of capitalism as a strong social force. In the twentieth-century section, we talked about Freudianism, the influence of World War I, Marxism, the rise of totalitarian states, the Jazz Age, the Great Depression of the 1930s, existentialism, the pessimism resulting from the growth of science and technology, and finally the personal alienation growing out of social regimentation on a grand scale. Each of these may be considered outside influences on the short story.

One common way of dealing with outside influences is to show how a story reflects the temper of the time in which it was written. For example, you might analyze the romantic elements in E. T. A. Hoffmann's "The Story of Serapion" or Washington Irving's "The Spectre Bridegroom," the realistic elements in Turgenev's "The Tryst" or Maupassant's "The Piece of String," the specific Freudian symbols in D. H. Lawrence's "The Shades of Spring" or Virginia Woolf's "The String Quartet." You might be interested in showing the ways in which Katharine Brush's "Night Club" mirrors certain aspects of the Jazz Age or Renata Adler's "Brownstone" reflects the alienated existence lived by many modern dwellers of great cities. The possibilities are almost infinite.

How does one organize such a paper? The task is not as difficult as it may seem. First, you define, describe, or detail the outside influence. This will require a little research. Next, you place the author and the story to be discussed squarely within the period or movement of the outside influence. Finally, you point out as many specific elements in the story as you can—or as the length of your paper will allow—that clearly link the work to the outside influences. To simplify matters, let's look at a sample paper:

ULTIMATE URBANIZATION
IN
RENATA ADLER'S "BROWNSTONE"

Urbanization has played a major role in human affairs ever since the first cities grew up several millennia ago. However, it assumed even greater importance in the opening decades of the nineteenth century, when the Industrial Revolution began uprooting great masses of agricultural workers and setting them to labor in the "dark, satanic mills" of Europe and America. Since then, urbanization has proceeded at an ever-accelerating pace, creating vast, sprawling urban centers that dominate the industrialized nations and ushering in an entirely new social and psychological climate. "Brownstone" is a story that explores the tenor of life in contemporary New York City and, by implication, the tenor of life in any other sprawling, almost-out-of-control metropolis.

Several rather negative things clearly emerge in the story. To begin with, urban life holds a considerable element of danger. Walking the streets, people consistently risk being struck by falling girders or even suicides. Impostors disguise themselves as power company employees to gain entrance to apartment buildings. The protagonist's landlord is murdered, and the fact that this crime occurs in a turn-of-the-century brownstone serves as an oblique reminder of the demise of a more genteel pre–urban-sprawl past.

Despite this ever-present element of danger, though, urban people live boring and banal lives. For example, the protagonist writes a gossip column about obscure people, and much of her free time seems to be taken up by parties and her desultory affair with Aldo. Nor is the situation any better with those people around the protagonist: the party-goers squander their time in idle chatter and pointless amusements, her publisher talks in intellectual clichés, and the taxi driver seeks solace in the sexual banality of pornography.

Unpleasantness and mental quirks also mark many of the story's characters. A six-year-old child rejects the overtures of an adoring younger brother, a poet insults the guests at a party given in his honor, Aldo sneers at Inez and the protagonist's grandmother, and the protagonist herself unnecessarily awakens a wino. There is even an unpleasant dog, Bonnie, who snarls at her would-be adopters. Quirkiness takes a variety of forms, ranging from the mild eccentricities of such people as the grandmother and the general who is trying to "repopulate the Ark" to the out-and-out paranoia of the instructor in political science. Institutional madness is represented by the Center for Short-Lived Phenomena and Father Divine's church, with its ridiculously named followers.

Personal commitment of any type seems alien to the protagonist's surroundings. The taxi driver neglects passengers in favor of dirty magazines, the book reviewer looks for another job because he cannot open publishers' packages without hurting his hands, and psychiatrists stuff their patients with "mood elevators" rather than attempting to get at the underlying causes of the patients' difficulties. At no time during the protagonist's liaison with Aldo does she show signs of any real emotional involvement with him. When Aldo refuses to accompany her to Inez's party, she has an ex-lover accompany her. Upon arriving at Aldo's Los Angeles apartment and finding another girl there, she accepts the situation matter-of-factly and returns to New York. Once back, she calls Aldo from time to time, and when he returns she resumes the same old live-in arrangement with him. The whole liaison, like the others in the story, seems to take place in the absence of any close or substantial human feeling.

Throughout the story, the protagonist plays the double role of participant and perceptive commentator; and her meditations betray a severe psychic malaise, a sense of inner anguish that also afflicts several of her friends and leads her to the conclusion: "When I wonder what it is that we are doing, . . . the truth is probably that we are fighting for our lives." As the story ends, sirens sound through the empty streets, offering a symbolic reflection of this inner chaos.

"Brownstone," then, dramatizes to the last detail the notion that our sprawling urban centers have become unfit for human habitation. Given enough time, they destroy both body and soul. And the author, an experienced resident of New York City, writes from a position of authority.

Another effective way to write papers about outside influences is to analyze a story in terms of some specific ism. Papers that take this approach may seek to show that a story's characters and events mirror and make believable all or part of the teachings of some intellectual or philosophical school of thought, such as Marxism, Freudianism, or existentialism. Or such a paper may try to demonstrate that a story offers a case study in sexism, chauvinism, racism, militarism, or whatever.

For example, it is possible to apply a Marxist interpretation to Melville's "Bartleby the Scrivener," beginning with the assumption that John Jacob Astor represents the ruling capitalist class, the lawyer-narrator the bourgeoisie or middle class, and Bartleby and the other copyists in the law office the working proletariat. Similarly, in analyzing Washington Irving's "TheSpectre Bridegroom," one might argue that the entire characterization of Baron Von Landshort's daughter is blatantly sexist. Other possibilities for analysis include applying a Freudian interpretation to Jessamyn West's "Love, Death, and the Ladies' Drill Team" or an existential interpretation to Ernest Hemingway's "The Killers."

When you are dealing with phenomena like sexism, chauvinism, and racism, it is a good idea to begin your analysis by deducing what the author's position on the matter appears to be.

Papers of Comparison and Contrast

W hen we discussed foils—that is, character opposites— we indicated that one of the best ways of pointing up a particular quality in one character is by placing him or her next to someone who lacks that quality. Comparison and contrast, the pointing out of likenesses and differences, serves the same purpose and greatly enhances our perception of the qualities under discussion.

Comparison and contrast is a versatile technique, lending itself equally well to the discussion of structural elements of the short story and outside influences upon the short story. For example, you might compare and contrast the plot elements of Maupassant's "The Piece of String" and Chekhov's "Gooseberries." You might analyze the differences between Nick Adams, George, and Sam in Hemingway's "The Killers" or the similarities of Walter Mitty in Thurber's "The Secret Life of Walter Mitty" and Little Chandler in Joyce's "A Little Cloud." You might talk about the humor of Frank O'Connor's "First Confession," and that of Dorothy Parker's "But the One on the Right," the symbolic correspondences between the trees and the chief characters in Turgenev's "The Tryst," or the thematic similarities in John Updike's "The Music School" and Renata Adler's "Brownstone." You might draw a distinction between the dramatic intentions of two stories told from the same point of view—for example, D. H. Lawrence's "The Shadow in the Rose Garden" and Sherwood Anderson's "Unlighted Lamps." Or you might discuss the romantic elements in E. T. A. Hoffmann's "The Story of Serapion" and Nathaniel Hawthorne's "The Birthmark."

In preparing a paper of comparison and contrast, follow whatever guidelines are appropriate for the matter under discussion. If, for example, you are dealing with emotion, take note of the writer's tone and the emotional state of the characters; look for poetic passages and then ask yourself why the author has resorted to this lyricism; pick out situations that may be intended to evoke emotional responses; and ask yourself whether the story is successful on the emotional level.

There are three different ways to organize papers of comparison and contrast. You can say everything you have to say about one story (or item) and then everything you have to say about the other story or item. A second method of organization brings the individual related points or items as close together as possible. Thus, point 1 of story or item A is compared or contrasted with point 1 of story or item B, and so on. A third method, similar to the first, presents the first story or item in its entirety and then presents the second story or item point by point, making continuous references back to specific corresponding parts of the first story or item.